Janet Charbonneau
651-779-4381

Mental Retardation

Sixth Edition

Mary Beirne-Smith
University of Alabama

Richard F. Ittenbach
Children's Hospital of Philadelphia

James R. Patton
University of Texas

Merrill
Prentice Hall

Upper Saddle River, New Jersey
Columbus, Ohio

Library of Congress Cataloging-in-Publication Data

Beirne-Smith, Mary.
    Mental retardation/Mary Beirne-Smith, Richard F. Ittenbach, James R. Patton.-6th ed.
      p.   cm.
    Includes bibliographical references and index.
    ISBN 0-13-032990-8
    1. Mental retardation.   I. Ittenbach, Richard F. II. Patton, James R. III. Title.
RC570.M386 2002
362.3-dc21   00-051951

Vice President and Publisher: Jeffery W. Johnston
Executive Editor: Ann Davis
Development Editor: Gianna Marsella
Production Editor: Mary M. Irvin
Design Coordinator: Robin G. Chukes
Text Design: Anna Christian
Photo Coordinator: Sandy Lenahan
Cover Design: Thomas Borha
Cover Art: Artville
Production Manager: Laura Messerly
Electronic Text Management: Marilyn Phelps, Melanie Ortega, Karen Bretz
Director of Marketing: Kevin Flanagan
Marketing Manager: Amy June
Marketing Coordinator: Barbara Koontz

This book was set in Schneidler by Prentice Hall, and was printed and bound by R. R. Donnelley & Sons Company. The cover was printed by Lehigh Press.

Photo Credits: Myrleen Ferguson/PhotoEdit: 1; The Ohio Historical Society: 3; Human Policy Press: 11; Edgar A. Doll: 19; Anne Vega/Merrill: 39, 41, 240, 447, 477; Todd Yarrington/Merrill: 61, 149, 372; T. Hubbard/Merrill: 79; Scott Cunningham/Merrill: 82, 98, 151, 197, 235, 249, 277, 311, 313, 316, 403, 427, 437, 469, 482, 499, 503; Stephen Ferry/Liaison Agency, Inc.: 115; Tom Watson/Merrill: 126; Lloyd Lemmerman/Merrill: 135; Doug Martin/Merrill: 155; Steve Allen/The Image Bank: 183; Barbara Schwartz/Merrill: 201, 514; Laura Dwight/Laura Dwight Photography: 218, 388, 420; Dr. Kenneth Salyer, Dallas, TX: 258, 259; Shirley Zeiberg/PH College: 290; Anthony Magnacca/Merrill: 295, 359; Richard Hutchings/PhotoEdit: 342; Brad Feinknopf/Merrill: 435; Jose Carrillo/Merrill: 467.

Prentice-Hall International (UK) Limited, *London*
Prentice-Hall of Australia Pty. Limited, *Sydney*
Prentice-Hall Canada, Inc., *Toronto*
Prentice-Hall Hispanoamericana, S. A., *Mexico*
Prentice-Hall of India Private Limited, *New Delhi*
Prentice-Hall of Japan, Inc., *Tokyo*
Prentice-Hall Singapore Pte. Ltd.
Editora Prentice-Hall do Brasil, Ltda., *Rio de Janeiro*

10 9 8 7 6 5 4 3 2 1
ISBN 0-13-032990-8

Dedicated to the memory of
Ruth Ann Payne
Who contributed to earlier editions of this text
and
Who touched our lives with her spirit, humor,
love, and courage

For the past 200 years, a considerable body of knowledge has been compiled about individuals who are mentally retarded: how they learn, how and what to teach them, and how society treats people who are retarded. The recent move toward inclusion of individuals who are disabled in general education settings is changing the face of education as we know it. Consequently, we are changing the ways in which we serve students who are mentally retarded and the ways in which we train prospective teachers of these students. In addition, recent developments in the field of special education and in the area of mental retardation, such as community technological innovations and medical advances, have made critical the need for informed, educated professionals in this area.

Our purpose in writing the sixth edition of this text is to provide educators and other service providers with timely information about the many facets of mental retardation from a life-cycle perspective. We have tried to digest the literature and add what we have learned from our own experiences. It is exciting to be involved in the area of mental retardation, and we hope that our interest and enthusiasm about individuals who are retarded, their families, their friends, others with whom they come in contact, and the society in which they live come through in this book.

Our challenge was to retain what was valuable from previous editions, add what is current to this edition, and integrate it all into a meaningful whole. Throughout the revision process, we have been mindful of our goal of producing a text that is useful for all professionals who work with individuals who are mentally retarded. As is true in previous editions of this text, we attempt to show relationships between theory and practice; we decode the terminology used in the literature on mental retardation, particularly that associated with causes of retardation; and we relate these terms to the reality of the classroom, the world of work, and the life of the community. In addition, we point out many valuable resources in the field of special education and the area of mental retardation.

FEATURES OF THE SIXTH EDITION

We have retained the features in previous editions for which we received positive feedback from reviewers and users. We begin each chapter with a list of key words and learning objectives. Each key word is defined in the chapter and included in the glossary for easy reference. Each chapter ends with bulleted summary statements. Finally, we have continued to use short features in each chapter to broaden the coverage of topics.

We have organized the text in four parts. In Part I, we concentrate on basic concepts about mental retardation. In this section, we have chapters on historical perspectives, terminology and definition, assessment practices, and individual rights and legal issues. In Part II, we focus on the biology, psychology, and sociology of mental retardation. In this section, we have chapters on biological causes and preventive efforts, psychosocial aspects of mental retardation, and characteristics of individuals with mild mental retardation and individuals with severe mental retardation. In Part III, we look at programming and intervention issues across the lifespan of individuals who are retarded. In this section, we have chapters about infancy and early childhood years, school years, transitional years, and adult years. Finally, in Part IV, we address related issues with chapters on family considerations and a new chapter on assistive technology applications.

Each chapter has been substantially revised, and, where appropriate, we have increased the focus on developmental disabilities and multiculturalism. In addition, we have included a new chapter on assistive technology (Chapter 14).

ACKNOWLEDGMENTS

In revising this text, we were inspired by many individuals. Jim Payne's mentorship and vision for this text motivated us. Our families and friends offered unconditional love and the support we needed to complete the task.

We are indebted to those who contributed their time, energies, and expertise to previous editions: Diane M. Browder, Frances E. Butera, Gary Clark, Lawrence J. Coleman, Jill C. Dardig, Robert M. Davis, Dan Ezell, Keith Hume, Cynthia Jackson, Fay and David Jackson, Eric D. Jones, Allen K. Miller, John A. Nietupski, Jerry Nunnally, Ruth Ann Payne, Greg A. Robinson, Tommy Russell, H. Monroe Snider, Janis Spiers, Carol Thomas, Thomas J. Zirpoli, and Vicki Knight.

We are grateful to our colleagues who contributed to this edition of the text: Mitylene B. Arnold, Shannon H. Kim, Veda Jairrels, Edward Polloway, J. David Smith, and Charlotte Sonnier-York. Their willingness to participate, their expertise, and their excellent work are appreciated.

We are especially grateful to the people who contributed to the research and development of this edition. We could not have completed the revision without the technical and research assistance of Dean Creel, Manuela Dür, Christie Holtman, and Robin Spender. We also wish to express our appreciation to Candace Addison, who spent many hours revising the Instructor's Manual, and Shannon Kim, who devoted innumerable hours to developing our companion website.

We also want to thank the reviewers for their guidance and feedback: Robert Michael, State University of New York, New Paltz; Teresa A. Taber, Georgia State University; Doris Williams, Indiana State University; and Eleanor Boyd Wright, University of North Carolina at Wilmington.

Finally, we wish to express our sincere appreciation to the individuals at Merrill/Prentice Hall who encouraged and supported our efforts. Their patience, understanding, and professionalism are unequaled. We thank Ann Davis, Mary Irvin, Gianna Marsella, Robin Chukes, and Sandy Lenahan.

Discover the Companion Website Accompanying This Book

THE PRENTICE HALL COMPANION WEBSITE: A VIRTUAL LEARNING ENVIRONMENT

Technology is a constantly growing and changing aspect of our field that is creating a need for content and resources. To address this emerging need, Prentice Hall has developed an online learning environment for students and professors alike—Companion Websites—to support our textbooks.

In creating a Companion Website, our goal is to build on and enhance what the textbook already offers. For this reason, the content for each user-friendly website is organized by chapter and provides the professor and student with a variety of meaningful resources.

FOR THE PROFESSOR

Every Companion Website integrates **Syllabus Manager**™, an online syllabus creation and management utility.

- **Syllabus Manager**™ provides you, the instructor, with an easy, step-by-step process to create and revise syllabi, with direct links into Companion Website and other online content without having to learn HTML.
- Students may log on to your syllabus during any study session. All they need to know is the web address for the Companion Website and the password you've assigned to your syllabus.
- After you have created a syllabus using **Syllabus Manager**™, students may enter the syllabus for their course section from any point in the Companion Website.
- Clicking on a date, the student is shown the list of activities for the assignment. The activities for each assignment are linked directly to actual content, saving time for students.
- Adding assignments consists of clicking on the desired due date, then filling in the details of the assignment—name of the assignment, instructions, and whether or not it is a one-time or repeating assignment.
- In addition, links to other activities can be created easily. If the activity is online, a URL can be entered in the space provided, and it will be linked automatically in the final syllabus.
- Your completed syllabus is hosted on our servers, allowing convenient updates from any computer on the Internet. Changes you make to your syllabus are immediately available to your students at their next logon.

FOR THE STUDENT

The Companion Website to accompany *Mental Retardation*, 6th edition, is integrated into the textbook via companion website margin notes, and include these useful features for students:

- **Objectives**—Chapter objectives highlight key concepts and ideas.
- **Self-Test**—Interactive quizzes help students test their knowledge of chapter content. Automatic grading provides immediate feedback: the **Results Reporter** computes a percentage grade after the students submit their self-tests, provides a graphic representation of how many questions were answered correctly and incorrectly, and gives a question-by-question analysis of the quiz. Students are given the option of sending their quiz scores to up to four e-mail addresses (professor, teaching assistant, study partner, etc.).
- **Essay**—Essay questions engage students in higher-level learning and allow them to apply chapter content while honing critical thinking and writing skills. Students may send their essay responses to up to four e-mail addresses (professor, teaching assistant, study partner, etc.).
- **Web Destinations**—Links to www sites relate to chapter content, and are called out in margin notes in the textbook.
- **Glossary**—A complete online glossary helps familiarize students with key vocabulary.
- **Video Case Studies**—Get to know the individuals behind the label. These online video case studies introduce students to six real people representing a variety of age groups and a range of moderate to severe mental retardation. Students can use the 18 video segments to apply what they have learned from the textbook to real life situations. Each of the 14 case studies (one per chapter) involves at least one activity.
- **Read and Respond**—Students have the opportunity to respond to articles about mental retardation and related issues from newspapers around the country. Article responses may be sent to up to four e-mail addresses (professor, teaching assistant, study partner, etc.).
- **Message Board**—A virtual bulletin board provides students a forum on which to post questions or respond to comments from a national audience.
- **Chat**—Chat in real time with anyone who is using the text anywhere in the country. Ideal for discussion and study groups and class projects.

To take advantage of these exciting resources, please visit the *Mental Retardation*, 6th edition, Companion Website at

www.prenhall.com/beirne-smith

Contents

PART II

Biology, Psychology, and Sociology of Mental Retardation   *149*

5   **Biological Sources of Mental Retardation and Efforts for Prevention**   **150**

6 **Psychosocial Aspects of Mental Retardation   196**

7 **Characteristics of Individuals with Milder Forms of Mental Retardation   234**

PART III

Programming and Issues across the Life Span   *311*

9   Infancy and Early Childhood   312

Basic Concepts

CHAPTERS

1 Historical Perspectives

2 Terminology and Definition

3 Assessment of Mental Retardation

4 Individual Rights and Legal Issues

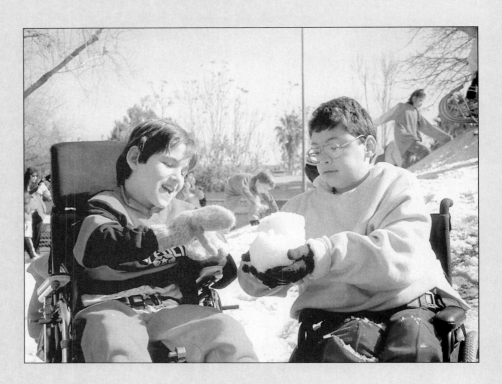

Chapter

1

Historical Perspectives

To review the chapter objectives on-line, go to the companion website at www.prenhall.com/beirne-smith and select Chapter 1, and then choose the Objectives module.

OBJECTIVES

After reading this chapter, the student should be able to

- discuss the underlying dynamics that affect the history of the study of mental retardation
- identify major historical eras associated with certain dominant trends
- discuss the contributions of persons who have had a significant effect on the development of the field
- explain how various sociopolitical events have affected the treatment of people who are mentally retarded
- trace the evolutionary development of contemporary issues

KEY TERMS

eugenics movement

feebleminded

homme sauvage

inclusive environments

mental test

metabolic disturbance

nature–nurture controversy

normalization

pedigree studies

residential facility

right to education

sociopolitical forces

sterilization

The field of mental retardation is rich with history and fascinating to study. Many events and people have influenced the field, and a look at some of them is worthwhile. From a survey of the history of the field, we can gain a better understanding of the factors that have led to the present state of affairs. In many disciplines, however, such study has been sacrificed in recent times in preference to other topics deemed more important. This slighting of history is unfortunate, because professionals in a variety of disciplines associated with mental retardation need to know the contexts that have shaped this field.

While much of the progress made in the field of mental retardation has been due to the unending and dedicated efforts of individuals, strong **sociopolitical forces** have also been at work to influence its development. When studying history, we must appreciate the social climate of a given time. In the past, as in the present, much of what has happened to people with mental retardation has been determined largely by social and political factors. Sociopolitical elements have shaped policy, practice, and treatment of individuals with mental retardation.

Scholars such as Blatt and Sarason have paid much attention to the sociological implications of mental retardation and conclude that mental retardation is very much a social phenomenon. Blatt (1987) states, "Mental retardation is a concept that developed with history. It has changed through time in its nature and in its significance" (p. 9). Sarason (1985) suggests that mental retardation cannot be understood fully unless one examines the society, culture, and history within which it occurs.

In discussing the historical background of mental retardation, we attempt to establish a case for what we call a "recycling phenomenon"—certain issues have resurfaced on different occasions over the course of history. Throughout this chapter, we mention issues that were discussed and debated long ago. You may feel dismayed by the fact that some long-standing issues still remain just that—issues, with "solutions" still forthcoming. The essence of this phenomenon is captured in the following quote:

> Many people also think that the issues facing special education today are completely new. But if you read the historical literature of special education, you will see that today's issues and problems are remarkably similar to those of long ago. Issues, problems, and ideas arise, flower, go to seed, and reappear when the conditions are again right for their growth. (Patton, Blackbourn, & Fad, 1996, p. 305)

This chapter has three primary objectives. First, as already mentioned, we focus on the historical context of mental retardation, giving you a glimpse of both the sociopolitical influences that have determined where we are today and some recurrent themes expressed throughout the short documented history of the field. Second, we present the content of that history—that is, the names, dates, places, and events typically associated with it. Third, we introduce you to the complexities of human services as they relate to programming for people with mental retardation.

For a complete on-line glossary of mental retardation terms, go to the companion website at www.prenhall.com/ beirne-smith and select any chapter, and then choose the Glossary module.

HISTORICAL OVERVIEW

While attitudes toward and treatment of persons who are mentally retarded can actually be traced back to ancient civilizations (including Egypt, Sparta, Rome,

China, and the early Christian world), a documented history relating to mental retardation is rather brief, spanning only about the last 300 years. Accordingly, this chapter focuses on the more recent history with some attention given to earlier times. For the sake of organization, we have divided history into five rather arbitrary time periods, based on an examination of trends in the field of mental retardation (Polloway, Smith, Patton, & Smith, 1996). The reader is encouraged to accept these periods of time for their organizational value, not their exactness. The five eras are as follows:

1. Antiquity: Prior to 1700
2. Emergence and Early Disillusionment of a Field: 1700–1890
3. Facilities-Based Orientation: 1890–1960
4. Services-Based Orientation: 1960–1985
5. Supports-Based Orientation: 1985–Present

Before we proceed through the various periods, we must address terminology. For the most part throughout this chapter, those to whom we refer as mentally retarded will be described in accordance with current systems. While this usage will help us maintain a consistent standard, we would be remiss if we did not mention that, historically, various terms have been used officially to describe these individuals. (These terms are discussed in the next chapter on definitions.) Today, however, many professionals find such terms as *fool, moron, imbecile, idiot,* **feebleminded,** *mental defective,* and *retardate* (among others) to be historically accurate but personally offensive. It should be noted, however, that instances do occur in the chapter where historical terms are used to maintain historical accuracy.

ANTIQUITY: PRIOR TO 1700

Before the 18th century, the concept of mental retardation, regardless of the term used to describe it, was enigmatic to a world that did not have a sophisticated knowledge base with which to understand it. As a result, people around the world held a wide variety of attitudes and perceptions toward people whose mental abilities and adaptive behaviors varied from the norm.

Basically, there was no consensus among Western societies as to who these deviant people were, why they acted the way they did, and how they should be treated. Different societies' responses to these questions ranged from treating these individuals as buffoons and court jesters to perceiving them as demons or as persons capable of receiving divine revelations. As a result, throughout ancient history, different patterns of treatment and interaction developed.

Throughout this early history and continuing until the early 1900s, when we refer to persons with mental limitations, we are speaking specifically of individuals with more severe involvement. Milder forms of retardation as we perceive them today were neither defined nor recognized. During times when physical skills were most important and when few individuals could read or write, most individuals with mild retardation whose social competence was acceptable blended into society without too much difficulty. Not until the early part of the 20th century did mild retardation became a describable condition.

Before 1700, certain developments resulting from the Renaissance of the 15th and 16th centuries created a new social climate that would eventually have direct implications for persons who were mentally retarded. Although the Renaissance was important to the world in many ways, the fact that it "increased man's willingness to look at himself and his environment more openly, naturally, and empirically (i.e., scientifically)" (Maloney & Ward, 1978, pp. 21–22) is particularly noteworthy. The prevailing social forces tended to refocus people's concepts of themselves and the world. The ultimate effects of these changes were reflected in the development of a climate conducive to the philosophy of humanism and the revolutionary fervor of the 18th century.

Before 1700, if any service (using the word loosely) was provided to individuals with special needs, it was protective in nature (i.e., providing housing and sustenance) and often offered in monasteries. Little evidence exists that systematic programs of training or service delivery were available. Although obvious changes were occurring in the world, not much was altering for the 17th-century person with mental retardation.

In America at this time, the family unit was of primary importance, and it assumed much of the responsibility in caring for any exceptional member. This nature of care can be seen in many developing countries throughout the world today. Following European precedents, the colonies enacted laws that "provided for" many individuals who could not care for themselves, by creating almshouses and workhouses. Although looked upon as financial burdens, these individuals, some of whom must have been retarded, were at least taken care of by colonial society.

EMERGENCE AND EARLY DISILLUSIONMENT OF A FIELD: 1700–1890

Arguably the most significant features of the 18th century were the advent of "sensationalism" and the revolutionary changes in both Europe and America. Through the efforts of various philosophers, most notably John Locke (1631–1704) and Jean-Jacques Rousseau (1712–1778), new ideas stressing the importance of the senses in human development began to take hold. These ideas provided new ways of perceiving the nature of the human mind and ultimately influenced educational reform.

As mentioned earlier, Renaissance thinking encouraged a philosophy of humanism, principally concerned with people's worth as human beings and freedom to develop. The idea that all were created equal and had inalienable rights to life, liberty, and the pursuit of happiness was popular. Eventually, these notions came into conflict with the existing philosophies and policies of some established nations, and both Europeans and Americans reacted to these needs for freedom through revolution.

One might wonder what effect these historical events had on people who were mentally retarded. We believe that they had two major implications. First, a new social attitude was established. It held that all "men," even those who had disabilities, had rights. Although this attitude was not always evidenced, it helped lead to a climate that would support efforts to assist these individuals. Second, the times were right for idealistic individuals to put the philosophy of humanism and the ideas of Locke and Rousseau into practice.

The first part of the 19th century can be described as a time of enthusiasm for working with people who had various disabilities, an enthusiasm displayed by a number of devoted individuals. Influenced by the events of the previous century, these pioneers were willing to attempt something that had never been tried before: to help less fortunate people through bona fide treatment programs. Special education and systematic services for individuals with disabilities thus were born in Europe in the early 1800s.

Itard and the Homme Sauvage

The field of special education was dramatically influenced by Jean-Marc Itard (1774–1838). Early in his career, Itard, a medical doctor who initially was concerned with diseases of the ear and the needs of the deaf, became quite interested in a feral child who was found in a wooded area near Aveyron, France, in 1799. Intrigued by this boy, whom he named Victor, Itard felt that he could transform this **homme sauvage** from a state of wildness to one of civilized behavior (Humphrey & Humphrey, 1962).

Believing that Victor's skill deficiencies were fundamentally due to environmental limitations, Itard thought Victor could develop the skills that were absent by training with a systematic program. His program included five major objectives:

1. To render social life more congenial to the boy by making it more like the wild life he had recently kept.
2. To excite his nervous sensibility with varied and energetic stimuli and supply his mind with the raw impression of ideas.
3. To extend the range of his ideas by creating new wants and expanding his relations with the world around him.
4. To lead him to the use of speech by making it necessary that he should imitate.
5. To apply himself to the satisfaction of his growing physical wants, and from this lead to the application of his intelligence to the objects of instruction. (Kanner, 1964, p. 14)

Although Itard worked with Victor for 5 years, he was disappointed because he felt that Victor had not progressed as much as he had planned, particularly in expressive language, and he subsequently terminated the program. From then until Victor's death in 1828, he lived under the care of Madame Guérin, the housekeeper hired to take care of him. Although Itard felt he personally had failed in his efforts with Victor, he nevertheless received accolades from the French Academy of Science in recognition of his work. Itard's importance rests not so much in his success or failure but rather in the precedent that he set by developing and implementing a systematic program of intervention and achieving gains with a child who was considered severely limited. The influence he had on others clearly distinguishes him as one of the most significant pioneers in the field of education using specialized techniques. As Blatt (1987) remarks, "It [Itard's work] was the first of its kind, and all 'firsts' of important movements are especially important" (p. 34).

Seguin's Moral and Physiological Training Methods

One person who was affected by Itard's work was Edouard Seguin (1812–1880). Encouraged by Itard to get involved in the treatment of "idiocy," Seguin was motivated by a strong religious influence to help the less fortunate. Like Itard, Seguin also chose to undertake the education of an *enfant idiot*. After 18 months of intensive work with an "idiot" boy, Seguin could demonstrate that the boy had learned a number of skills. He extended his methods to other children, and in 1837 he established a program for "educating the feebleminded" at the Salpetrière in Paris.

Seguin's methods and educational programs, which were even more systematic than Itard's, stressed physiological and moral education. This methodology, as Seguin developed it, incorporated a general training program that integrated muscular, imitative, nervous, and reflective physiological functions (Seguin, 1846). Elements of the programs developed by Seguin, such as individualized instruction and behavior management, can be found in current practice.

Seguin emigrated to the United States in 1848, principally because of the political unrest in Paris at that time. While he lived in the United States, individuals often sought his advice and expertise on programming in institutional settings. In 1866, he published a book entitled *Idiocy and Its Treatment by Physiological Methods,* which became a major reference work for educating individuals with retardation in the latter part of the 19th century. Seguin also served as the first president of the Association of Medical Officers of American Institutions for Idiotic and Feebleminded Persons. Hervey Wilbur (1880/1976), in his eulogy to Seguin, perhaps best summarized the impact this man had on the field: "He entered upon the work with enthusiasm. There he toiled, till there he grew, little by little, a system—principles and methods—which has been the guide of all later labors in the same direction, the world over" (p. 186).

Guggenbühl and His Abendberg

Another individual who figured significantly during this time in providing services to those who were mentally retarded was Johann Guggenbühl (1816–1863). Guggenbühl has been acknowledged as establishing, in 1841, the first **residential facility** designed to provide comprehensive treatment for individuals who were mentally retarded, with reentry to normal living as the ultimate goal. Called the Abendberg, this facility was located in the mountains of Switzerland.

Well publicized, through the efforts of Guggenbühl himself, the Abendberg drew the attention of many prominent people. The real significance of Guggenbühl's facility rests in its impact on the visitors it attracted, many of whom were interested in establishing similar facilities. As Kanner (1964) notes, "The Abendberg became the destination of pilgrimages made by physicians, philanthropists, and writers from many lands, who promptly published glowing reports when they went back home" (p. 25).

Unfortunately, the glowing reviews and accolades accorded the Abendberg were short-lived, and eventually the facility came under severe criticism. Although forced to close because of mismanagement and the resulting intolerable conditions, in its heyday the Abendberg served as a model of institutional programming that many other facilities in other parts of the world adopted. It also illustrates a program that achieved recognition but was unable to maintain it. Notwithstanding the problems, Guggenbühl created a prototype for institutional care, the effects of which dominated services in the early 20th century and can still be felt today.

American Pioneers: Dix, Howe, and Wilbur

Although the discipline of special education was conceived and born in Europe, the field also prospered from the work of important people and from events that occurred in the United States during the mid-1800s. Three individuals who had much to do with promoting the welfare of and developing services for persons with mental retardation in this country were Dorothea Dix, Samuel Howe, and Hervey Wilbur.

During the early 1840s, Dorothea Dix (1802–1887) zealously campaigned for better treatment of the less fortunate who were housed in asylums, almshouses, poorhouses, and country homes. At that time, no other options were available for such people. Her efforts are reflected in her own words, directed toward the Massachusetts legislature in 1843:

> I come to present the strong claims of suffering humanity. I come to place before the Legislature of Massachusetts the condition of the miserable, the desolate, the outcast. I come as the advocate of helpless, forgotten, insane, and idiotic men and women; of beings sunk to a condition from which the most unconcerned would start with real horror; of beings wretched in our prisons, and more wretched in our almshouses. And I cannot suppose it needful to employ earnest persuasion, or stubborn argument, in order to arrest and fix attention upon a subject only the more strongly pressing in its claims because it is revolting and disgusting in its details. (Dix [1843/1976], p. 5)

Obviously, Dix dramatized what advocacy is all about, and through her efforts she was able to focus much attention on those whom she called "suffering humanity" and for whom there were few advocates. A similar plea could be made today for the large number of homeless people in this country who also lack a strong advocacy base.

Samuel Howe (1801–1876) contributed greatly to providing services for people who were mentally retarded through his efforts to establish public support for their training. In 1848, after visiting Guggenbühl's Abendberg and convincing the Massachusetts legislature to appropriate $2,500 per year for his cause, Howe established the first public setting for training individuals who were mentally retarded. This new program was located in a wing of Boston's Perkins Institution for the Blind, of which Howe was the director. A few months earlier, Hervey Wilbur (1820–1883) had founded the first private setting for treating individuals with mental retardation at his home in Barre, Massachusetts.

From Optimism to Disillusionment

What, then, was the result of the work of pioneers such as Itard, Seguin, Guggenbühl, Howe, Dix, and Wilbur? First, an atmosphere of optimism developed. Many individuals who were mentally retarded, it was thought, could be trained, "cured," and reintegrated into the community as productive citizens. Second, based on this very same hope and enthusiasm, many promises were made, reflected in the lofty goals that were set. Ironically, it was precisely the enthusiasm prevalent at the time that would be partially responsible for the backlash that was to come.

As any student of U.S. history knows quite well, the 1860s were a time of national disharmony, inflamed by years of growing sectional conflict. Prior to the Civil War, America was basically an agrarian society characterized by small farms and towns. After the war, the country began to experience a dramatic change toward urbanization and industrialization. These and other developments had a strong effect on the treatment of persons who were mentally retarded.

This national metamorphosis precipitated many problems, some of which accompanied the increased growth of cities. Correlates of urban life such as crime, poverty, and health issues were later to be associated with retardation. In addition, while industrialization provided vocational opportunities for many people, the skills required were not a good match for many persons with significant limitations.

What happened to the enthusiasm of the mid-1800s? Basically, a critical shift in attitude occurred. This change resulted from consideration of how realistic it was to reintegrate those with retardation into the community. After initially accepting the grandiose claims of many individuals who suggested that those less fortunate could be "cured," critics began to realize that these goals, while laudable, were unrealistic. A pronounced climate of pessimism developed. We know today that those individuals who were considered capable of being cured in the 1800s were indeed capable of skill acquisition, but for most of them, attainment of "normalcy" was not possible. That individuals who were more severely disabled had not changed enough to be able to move back into community settings resulted in a negative perception of this group that pervaded many different areas.

Several problems contributed to this era's disillusionment, but four factors seem to be salient. First, as already mentioned, the population being addressed was not capable of being transformed into totally normal-functioning members of society. Second, community reintegration demands more than merely providing training and placement. If successful reintegration requires community preparation and development, as we think it does, then we should not be surprised that the neglect of this issue in the 1800s led to failure in attempts at reintegration. Sadly, even today, the provision of community services and supports is glaringly inadequate in many cases. Third, after an atmosphere of hope and excitement had been created, many individuals who were retarded were pitied, resulting in two important developments: (a) a dilution of services to individuals who needed systematic, intensive programming and (b) the establishment of more institutions. These developments were to have a tragic effect in the late 1800s. Fourth, the previously mentioned demands of an increasingly more complex society created by postwar urbanization and industrialization worked against those with limited intellectual skills and social competence.

Obviously, these were formidable obstacles to reaching the goals championed by the idealistic pioneers of the early and mid-1800s. While it is easy now to reproach those enthusiasts for creating a no-win situation that ultimately resulted in many regressive developments for those whom they wanted to help, we need to

The idea that institutions are not appropriate for most persons with mental retardation is not new.

understand that these early advocates (however naive) were most sincere in their zeal, hopes, and efforts. Unfortunately, those individuals on whom the great expectations were based were now being perceived as untreatable. It was bad enough that the early enthusiasm had waned, but even more discouraging was the fact that the worst was yet to come.

FACILITIES-BASED ORIENTATION: 1890–1960

As the 19th century came to a close, disillusionment began to take on a more reactionary tone. A change from concern for caring about individuals who had special needs to one for protecting society from them was evident. Institutions originally designed to serve as training facilities from which individuals would leave to return to community settings now began to assume a new custodial role.

During this period of alarm, a number of events caused a dramatic change in social attitudes, weakening most movements favorable to the needs of this group.

Many citizens were now afraid that these people were dangerous to society. Kanner (1964) describes the prevailing perceptions during this time:

> The mental defectives were viewed as a menace to civilization, incorrigible at home, burdens to the school, sexually promiscuous, breeders of feebleminded offspring, victims and spreaders of poverty, degeneracy, crime, and disease. Consequently, there was a cry for the segregation of all mental defectives, with the aim of purifying society, of erecting a solid wall between it and its contaminators. (p. 85)

It did not take long for society to develop ways to control people who were "mentally defective." The principal means for doing this included various forms of segregation, an extreme example of which was **sterilization.** A committee of the American Breeder's Association, formed in 1911, concluded that "segregation for life or at least during the reproductive years must, in the opinion of the committee, be the principal agent used by society in cutting off its supply of defectives" (cited in Kanner, 1964, p. 136). As an added measure of control, institutions strictly segregated men and women to eliminate their chances of producing offspring who would possibly be "feebleminded."

Many contributing factors precipitated repressive events in the late 1800s and early 1900s. Three factors in particular seem to have had a pronounced effect on the creation of this backlash: the eugenics scare, the influx of immigrants to the United States, and the mental test movement.

The Eugenics Scare

Although the thrust of the **eugenics movement** was not felt until the late 1800s and early 1900s, its antecedents can be traced to earlier times. One of the key interests of this movement was to control the number of "feebleminded" persons through selective breeding.

Influenced by the ideas of Charles Darwin, Sir Francis Galton extended Darwin's concept of evolution to humans. In 1869, Galton published *Hereditary Genius,* which espoused the idea that individual traits, most notably genius, were inherited. Galton's work seemed to catalyze the eugenics movement that advocated the genetic control of mental defectives. What Galton established was a theoretical basis for the inheritance of mental defectiveness. Gregor Mendel's discovery of the laws of inheritance in the latter part of the 19th century lent scientific support to Galton's ideas.

Two publications reinforced society's attitude that mental retardation had genetic implications: *The Jukes: A Study of Crime, Pauperism, Disease and Heredity* (Dugdale, 1877) and *The Kallikak Family* (Goddard, 1912). Each of these works traced the genetic relationships of the families under study. Dugdale's original work actually focused on criminality and its correlates, and only later was the added correlate of mental retardation inferred. Goddard's work, however, had as its central theme the notion that feeblemindedness was inherited; elaborate **pedigree studies** (through five generations) were presented as evidence. Goddard's work was very powerful and, along with other related events, fueled the movement to control the menace of feeblemindedness genetically. But many years later, Goddard's research on Martin Kallikak's two distinct family lines was called into question.

✳ Minds Made Feeble

In 1912, Henry Goddard reported the results of his study of the inheritance of feeblemindedness. His book, *The Kallikak Family: A Study on the History of Feeble-Mindedness,* was influential because it underscored the perceived threat of feeblemindedness to society and helped fuel the eugenics movement. The book was very popular, and to this day the Kallikak story is regularly retold in discussions of mental retardation.

The effects of the study are described well by J. David Smith (1985) in *Minds Made Feeble:*

> Goddard's book on the Kallikak family was received with acclaim by the public and by much of the scientific community. . . . Only gradually was criticism forthcoming which questioned the methods used in the study and the implications and conclusions drawn from the data collected. Even in the light of substantive and knowledgeable criticism, however, the essential message of the Kallikak study persisted for years. Even today its influence, in convoluted forms, continues to have a social and political impact. That message is simple, yet powerful. Ignorance, poverty, and social pathology are in the blood—in the seed. It is not the environment in which people are born and develop that makes the critical difference in human lives. People are born either favored or beyond help.

It was this message and the social myth that accompanied it that compelled Smith to investigate and report the complete story of the Kallikak family and of Goddard's study. A few highlights of Smith's findings are presented here:

- Serious questions arise as to whether Deborah Kallikak, the woman with whom

Goddard came into contact and whose ancestors are studied, was actually feebleminded.

- Goddard's professional acquaintance with influential eugenic leaders seems to have had a great influence on his work.

- The methodology used to study the Kallikak family and the skills of those who collected the information are once again questioned.

- The "real" Kallikaks were not as abhorrent as they were described by Goddard. Smith comments, "The truth of their lives was sacrificed to the effort to prove a point. The Kallikak study is fiction draped in the social science of its time."

- The implications of the study proved to be a very potent indictment against the poor, the uneducated, racial minorities, the foreign born, and those classified as mentally retarded or mentally ill, resulting in such social policies as compulsory sterilization, restricted immigration, and institutionalization, which adversely and unfairly affected these groups.

- Through painstaking investigation, Smith determined the real name of the family Goddard studied (Kallikak was a pseudonym). However, he does not reveal the name.

One of Smith's major contributions is his admonition to be aware of the significance and power of social myths: "Social myths are constantly in the making, compelling in their simplicity, and alluring because we want to believe them. Perhaps understanding the Kallikak story will help in recognizing and resisting them."

The details of the social myth perpetuated by Goddard are described in J. D. Smith's (1985) book *Minds Made Feeble.*

Strong evidence that eugenics was being taken seriously can be found in the enactment of sterilization laws during the early 1900s. Indiana holds the dubious distinction of enacting the first such law in 1907. Within 20 years, similar legislation was on the books in 23 states. The constitutionality of these laws was challenged in several states and ultimately upheld by the Supreme Court in the famous case of *Buck v. Bell* (1927). As Smith (1987) highlights, this case "became the precedent for the right of state governments to intervene in the reproductive practices of those citizens deemed defective in some way" (p. 148). The case is noteworthy, not only for the precedent it set but also for two other reasons. First, Carrie Buck, the woman used to test Virginia's compulsory sterilization law, probably was not mentally retarded. Second, the prevailing attitude of the time was clearly expressed in the majority opinion given by Justice Oliver Wendell Holmes:

> We have seen more than once that the public welfare may call upon the best citizens for their lives. It would be strange if it could not call upon those who already sap the strength of the State for these lesser sacrifices, often felt to be much by those concerned, in order to prevent our being swamped with incompetence. It is better for all the world, if instead of waiting to execute degenerate offspring for crime, or to let them starve for their imbecility, society can prevent those who are manifestly unfit from continuing their kind. The principle that sustains compulsory vaccination is broad enough to cover cutting the Fallopian tubes. . . . Three generations of imbeciles are enough. (*Buck v. Bell,* 1927, p. 50)

Immigration

During the second half of the 19th century, the United States experienced a great increase in the number of immigrants, mostly from southern and eastern Europe. As most of these immigrants flocked to the growing urban centers, many problems emerged. Americans of northern and western European origin looked upon these immigrants as inferior; this stance was supported by another study conducted by Goddard (1917), which concluded that many of these foreigners were feebleminded. One outcome of this generalized concern was enactment of the Immigration Restriction Act in 1924. This legislation restricted the flow of Italians, Russians, Hungarians, and Jews into the United States until 1965.

The Testing Movement

A third major trend contributing to the alarmist climate of the early 1900s was the introduction of the **mental test.** In 1905, Alfred Binet and Theodore Simon developed an instrument for use in French schools to screen those students who were not benefiting from the regular classroom experience and might need special services. This intent mirrors the basic tenets of special education that would arise later in the century.

Interestingly, Binet himself was concerned that the instrument that he helped develop might be misused. As Gould (1981) notes, Binet "greatly feared that his practical device . . . could be perverted and used as an indelible label, rather than as a guide for identifying children who needed help" (p. 151). As we know, the mental test has had a lasting effect on the fields of psychology and education. In essence, in the mental scale of intelligence, Binet and Simon created a mechanism for identifying milder forms of retardation that are more noticeable in academic settings. Before this time, those recognizable as mentally retarded were more severely involved, but now, since individuals with less severe mental retardation could be identified, new alarms were being sounded about the magnitude of the problem.

Although Binet and Simon introduced their test in France, before long it was brought to the United States. In 1911, Henry Goddard translated the Binet-Simon scales into English, and in 1916, Lewis Terman of Stanford University refined the mental scales into the instrument known as the Stanford-Binet. (W. Stern, a German psychologist, is given credit for developing the conceptual basis for determining IQ [intelligence quotient].)

Although the first special class for students who were retarded in the United States was established in Providence, Rhode Island, in 1896—predating the testing movement—the development and ultimate translation of the mental scales would have a great effect on education. Separate special classes for these students developed and grew in number. Another event of significance was New Jersey's enactment, in 1911, of legislation mandating education for this type of student. With the beginning of World War I, the military services needed a way to obtain information relatively quickly on large groups of people for use in assigning personnel. Thus, the first group intelligence scales (the alpha and beta tests) were developed and implemented. The results of this testing fed alarmist tendencies by suggesting that mild mental retardation was more widespread than anyone had previously believed. Robert Yerkes's 1921 work on the intellectual capacities of World War I soldiers supported this assumption, further exacerbating negative feelings about retardation.

An alarm had indeed been sounded. Society was frightened by the "menace" of retardation. With the recognition of mental retardation's greater prevalence, its seeming inheritability, and its correlation with crime, poverty, incorrigibility, and disease, it is not difficult to understand how restrictive and segregationist attitudes and practices could develop and dominate. Quite strong by the end of the 1920s, this aura of fear would begin to fade in the ensuing years, but its impact would be long lasting.

Related Sociopolitical Influences

Social attitudes toward individuals with disabilities changed somewhat after World War I. As a part of all warfare, many individuals were wounded and returned to their homes with lasting medical conditions. In 1920, the Vocational Rehabilitation Act (PL 66-236) was enacted to allow civilians to benefit from vocational rehabilitation. Important from the time it was introduced, this legislation has endured as one of the most significant laws created to provide training opportunities and protect the rights of individuals with disabilities. With the end of the war, the need for providing services to wounded veterans had been acknowledged. Now these services were being extended to others who needed them, too.

Lifestyles changed quickly with the stock market crash of 1929 and the Great Depression that followed. The Great Depression was not a pleasant experience; however, some outcomes were beneficial. For example, the Depression caused the average person, who had been unaware of or uninterested in the problems of human need, to appreciate them, for everyone at that time was needy.

Special education as a bona fide professional field took a tremendous step in 1922, when Elizabeth Farrell established the International Council for the Educa-

To learn more about the CEC and other advocacy groups, go to the companion website at www.prenhall.com/ beirne-smith and select Chapter 1, and then choose the Web Destinations module.

tion of Exceptional Children. Prior to this time, the field had had no unifying organizational structure on a national level. Farrell served as the first president of this new organization, now known as the Council for Exceptional Children (CEC), and it became a new institutional force in the field of special education.

Following a period of great concern about the social menace of mental retardation in the early 20th century, some movement toward greater enlightenment was evident, as Maloney and Ward (1978) state:

1. The view of mental retardation as a unitary, recessive, inherited trait began to fade as the science of genetics grew in scope and precision.
2. New clinical studies demonstrated the significance of other, nonhereditary, sources of mental retardation, such as trauma, infection, and endocrine disturbance.
3. The methodological flaws and biased interpretations of the pedigree studies were becoming more and more apparent.
4. Other surveys of institutional populations indicated that over one-half of them had intellectually normal parents, further weakening the singular heredity view and associated calls for eugenic solutions.
5. The older research studies that had linked mental retardation with every conceivable social ill were critically reanalyzed and found wanting.
6. Newer, better controlled, and more objective studies failed to reveal the dramatic links of the previous era. (p. 57)

During the early 1930s, the United States was trying to regain stability both economically and socially. One notable event occurred when President Herbert Hoover convened the first White House Conference on Child Health and Protection in 1930, drawing national attention, albeit briefly, to the needs of individuals with disabilities. Another important trend was the number of classes for special students, which kept increasing.

After the presidential election of 1932, the United States went through many changes. The new president, Franklin D. Roosevelt, influenced this country's attitudes toward the welfare of all its citizens. Roosevelt's New Deal philosophy was responsible for much social change through legislation and the formulation of new programs. One such piece of legislation that affected individuals with special needs was the Social Security Act of 1935. In a nutshell, during the 1930s, two major trends emerged in the treatment of individuals with disabilities: (a) the generation of a new attitude supportive of a public welfare system and (b) the affirmation of responsibility to those in need. Roosevelt's own disability, as a result of polio, was another factor that influenced people's attitudes toward those who were physically different.

With the direct involvement of the United States in World War II, the nation's attention and actions were refocused once again. We can see certain similarities between World War I and World War II vis-à-vis the field of mental retardation. As in World War I, screening of soldiers in the 1940s readjusted the perceived extent of mild retardation. One source that contributed to this changed thinking was a study conducted by Ginzberg and Bray, as described in their book *The Uneducated* (1953). They studied two groups of men being considered for military service. Their primary group consisted of men who were rejected on the basis of mental deficiency; the other group included men who were accepted for service but who experienced major problems in academic skill areas (i.e., literacy).

World War II created increased employment opportunities in war-related industries for individuals who were mentally retarded. When the war was over, the nation as a whole, and many families in particular, felt the realities of disability as wounded soldiers came home. A heightened sensitivity to the needs of disabled veterans thus developed.

As the 1950s began, the field of special education went through changes that would have notable effects in subsequent years. Foremost among these changes was a new national policy concerned with the problems of special groups of people.

In the years following World War II, the United States experienced a period of renewed prosperity. This created a climate in which "the demands of parents, the enthusiasm of professionals, and federal, state and private funding gave new impetus to progress in the area of mental retardation" (Hewett & Forness, 1977). These three forces, augmented by other factors, highlighted this turning point in the history of special education. Although institutional changes were beginning to occur, these events could be classified at best as only a "quiet revolution." Individuals were still being institutionalized at an alarming rate; tragically, many persons who should not have been placed in these settings found themselves there. Furthermore, too many had already suffered sterilization—a personal indignity and a violation of their civil rights. By 1938, compulsory sterilizations had been performed on more than 27,000 people in the United States (Marks, cited in Smith, 1987).

Certainly an important event during this time was the formation in 1950 of the National Association of Parents and Friends of Mentally Retarded Children—later known as the National Association of Retarded Children and now known as the Arc of the United States. This organization, composed mostly of parents of children who were mentally retarded, became an important advocate for these children and source of support for families. Functioning as lobbyist, service provider, and promoter of research, this parent organization had a key effect on the development, expansion, and refinement of services for individuals with mental retardation and their families (Braddock, Hemp, Parish, & Westrich, 1998). Most important, the organization provided a vehicle for its members to express their attitudes, beliefs, concerns, and desires in politically effective and coordinated ways. The eight original purposes of the organization are as follows:

- To promote the general welfare of mentally retarded children of all ages everywhere;
- To further the advancement of all study, ameliorative and preventive research and therapy in the field of mental retardation;
- To develop a better understanding of the problems of mental retardation by the public and cooperate with all public, private and religious agencies, international federal, state, and local departments of education, health and institutions;
- To further the training and education of personnel for work in the field of mental retardation;
- To encourage the formation of parent groups, to advise and aid parents in the solution of their problems; and to coordinate the efforts and activities of these groups;
- To further the implementation of legislation in behalf of the mentally retarded;

- To serve as a clearinghouse for gathering and disseminating information regarding the mentally retarded, and to foster the development of integrated programs in their behalf; and
- To solicit and receive funds for the accomplishment of the above purposes. (National Association of Parents and Friends of Mentally Retarded Children, 1950)

By the early 1950s, the United States was beginning to adopt a national policy committed to the needs of those who were mentally retarded and a policy willing to give financial support to endeavors that addressed these needs. Over the years, social attitudes toward people with retardation had changed from fear and revulsion to tolerance and compassion. Whether sparked by the troubled times of the 1930s and 1940s that the nation as a whole had endured or influenced by purely economic motives during the 1950s, the financial backing required to develop more and better programs was provided. If only for economic reasons, the importance of maximizing the potential of persons who were disabled was beginning to be acknowledged, as was stated by President Dwight D. Eisenhower in a 1954 message to Congress:

> We are spending three times as much in public assistance to care for nonproductive disabled people as it would cost to make them self-sufficient and taxpaying members of their communities. Rehabilitated people as a group pay back in federal income taxes many times the cost of their rehabilitation.

By 1952, 46 of 48 states had enacted legislation for educating students who were identified as mentally retarded. This legislation, however, did not provide programming for all students with mental retardation. Many children in the moderate range and most children in the severe range were still excluded from receiving educational services in public settings. Abeson and Davis (2000) note that in 1949, no state had mandated education for children with IQs below 50.

Not until 1975 and the passage of the Education for All Handicapped Children Act (PL 94-142) was the issue of educating all students with mental retardation formally addressed on a national level. But 1954 is also notable because in that year Congress passed the Cooperative Research Act (PL 83-531), which provided money for research that would focus on mental retardation. In 1958, PL 85-926 was enacted, offering incentives to various organizations (state educational agencies and institutions of higher education) in the form of grants to encourage the preparation of teachers of this group of students. Thus, if we look at federal legislation as an index of national commitment to a cause, then we can see that policy supportive of the needs of people with mental retardation was emerging in the 1950s.

As the decade came to a close, three forces were beginning to shape events. First, a new philosophical view of retardation was forming, as reflected in the 1958 publication of *Mental Subnormality,* published by Masland, Sarason, and Gladwin. These authors stressed that certain social and cultural variables have a strong correlation with mental retardation. The influence of this point of view on the field can be observed in the 1959 definition of mental retardation promoted by the American Association on Mental Deficiency (Heber, 1959). This definition associated intellectual deficits with "impairment in one or more of the following: (1) maturation, (2) learning, and (3) social adjustment" (Heber, 1959, p. 3).

Second, educators and advocates became concerned about the segregation in special classes of students who were mentally retarded. Existing research tended to support the special class setting. Nevertheless, this issue would continue to be debated, resulting in some major changes in the 1970s. In addition, the Supreme Court decision in the *Brown v. Board of Education* (1954) desegregation case also affected thinking and policymaking for individuals with mental retardation.

Third, when the Soviet Union launched *Sputnik* in 1957, the United States responded dramatically; shocked by the event, the country made a commitment to technological development unparalleled in history. The nation's overwhelming desire to grow technologically would focus very sharply on the institution of education. Changes were evidently needed, and many did come about. Both regular and special education were affected by the vigor of the times. The nation was primed for the tumultuous 1960s.

Research and Programmatic Influences

During this period many important developments took place in both social and physical sciences. In 1934, Ivar Asbjörn Fölling, a Norwegian physician, explained the biochemical mechanics related to the **metabolic disturbance** referred to as PKU (phenylketonuria)—a known cause of mental retardation. The importance of this discovery goes beyond this single event:

> This contribution, termed "one of the great discoveries in medical history" by Clemens E. Bonda, at long last made the issue of mental deficiency appear respectable as a legitimate field of research in the biological sciences. Slowly and at first reluctantly, the medical profession began to take an interest. (Kanner, 1964, p. 141)

Edgar A. Doll constructed the Vineland Social Maturity Scale, one of the first attempts to measure what we now call "adaptive behavior."

Two assessment instruments of major importance were developed during this period. In 1935, Edgar Doll published his *Vineland Social Maturity Scale* (VSMS). Use of this scale allowed professionals to gain additional information about a person's "social competence." In 1949, David Wechsler published another intelligence scale, the *Wechsler Intelligence Scale for Children* (WISC). Like the VSMS, this device became very popular. Ever since their publication, these instruments and their subsequent revisions have had a pronounced effect on the identification and classification of many individuals suspected of being mentally retarded.

Another influence on the public perception of mental retardation was a number of studies that seemed to stress the importance of environment as a cause of mental retardation. As the **nature–nurture controversy** was debated, certain studies, most notably those performed by Harold Skeels and his colleagues, questioned the notion that IQ was fixed or constant. Skeels and Dye (1939) inferred that environmental factors have a critical effect on IQ or, if you will, one's classification as mentally retarded.

SERVICES-BASED ORIENTATION: 1960–1985

In the 1960s, a new paradigm was emerging, as described by Polloway et al. (1996):

> On the heels of the facility-based period came a profound shift toward a "services-based paradigm." Through this model, there was an attempt to provide special services to individuals, as a preparation for their subsequent integration into society. Consequently, programs most typically included self-contained special education classes in regular schools, resource or pull-out programs, transitional [sheltered] workshops, related training programs, and the like. . . . In the services model, the assumption was made that appropriate programming for individuals with disabilities would be followed by successful integrated placement. (p. 5)

Sociopolitical Influences

If asked to reflect on the 1960s, one would probably think of the many tragic episodes in a time of rather extreme social change. The violent deaths of national leaders and the widespread opposition and reaction to the Vietnam War are vivid recollections of the 1960s. The early part of this decade was characterized by a generalized enthusiasm, and this mood was quite evident in the area of special education. For many reasons, special education was on center stage during the 1960s.

When President John F. Kennedy assumed office in 1961, he symbolized the energy of our country at that time. Kennedy, who had a sister who was mentally retarded, once again brought national attention to the needs of this group. At the beginning of his administration, he established the President's Panel on Mental Retardation (PPMR), which was to serve as a guide and source for national policy formation. Under the direction of Leonard Mayo, this group published *A Proposed Program for National Action to Combat Mental Retardation* (Mayo, 1962), which set the tone for policy decisions for the next decade. Many of the principal recommendations found in the report relate to the goals of the National Association of Parents and Friends of Mentally Retarded Children and also have a contemporary flavor:

1. Research in the causes of retardation and in methods of care, rehabilitation, and learning.
2. Preventive health measures, including (a) a greatly strengthened program of maternal and infant care directed first at the centers of population where prematurity and the rate of "damaged" children are high; (b) protection against such known hazards to pregnancy as radiation and harmful drugs; and (c) extended diagnostic and screening services.
3. Strengthened educational programs generally and extended and enriched programs of special education in public and private schools closely coordinated with vocational guidance, vocational rehabilitation, and specific training and preparation for employment; education for the adult mentally retarded, and workshops geared to their needs.
4. More comprehensive and improved clinical and social services.
5. Improved methods and facilities for care, with emphasis on the development of a wide range of local community facilities.
6. A new legal, as well as social, concept of the retarded, including protection of their civil rights; life guardianship provisions when needed; an enlightened attitude on the part of the law and the courts; and clarification of the theory of responsibility in criminal acts.
7. Helping overcome the serious problems of manpower as they affect the entire field of science and every type of service through extended programs of recruiting with fellowships; and increased opportunities for graduate students, and those preparing for the professions to observe and learn at first hand about the phenomenon of retardation. Because there will never be a fully adequate supply of personnel in this field and for other cogent reasons, the panel has emphasized the need for more volunteers in health, recreation, and welfare activities, and for a domestic Peace Corps to stimulate voluntary service.
8. Programs of education and information to increase public awareness of the problem of mental retardation. (Mayo, 1962, pp. 14–15)

Other recommendations, not unlike some proposed in the 1990s, included the following:

1. That programs for the retarded, including modern day care, recreation, residential services, and ample educational and vocational opportunities, be comprehensive.
2. That they operate in or close to the communities where the retarded live—that is, that they be community centered.
3. That services be so organized as to provide a central or fixed point for the guidance, assistance, and protection of retarded persons if and when needed, and to assure a sufficient array of continuum of services to meet different types of need.
4. That private agencies as well as public agencies at the local, state, and federal levels continue to provide resources and to increase them for this worthy purpose. While the federal government can assist, the principal responsibility for financing and improving services for the mentally retarded must continue to be borne by states and local communities. (Mayo, 1962, pp. 14–15)

Federal legislation relevant to the field of mental retardation continued to be enacted during the 1960s. In 1963, Congress passed the Mental Retardation Facilities and Mental Health Centers Construction Act, which provided monies for the construction of Mental Retardation Research Centers (MRRCs). These centers conducted organized multidisciplinary research on various complex facets of mental retardation. In 1965, the Elementary and Secondary Education Act (ESEA) (PL 89-10) was passed. Part of this legislation focused attention on the needs of disadvantaged students. In 1966, ESEA was amended, and as a result, the Bureau of Education for the Handicapped (BEH), a subcomponent of the Office of Education (OE), was created.

National policy directed to the needs of the disadvantaged reached its pinnacle with President Lyndon B. Johnson's War on Poverty. With the growing interest in social and cultural determinants of behavior, it is not surprising that much attention was given to environmental causes of retardation. Project Head Start did just that. The concept that early intervention could ameliorate some of the negative effects of unfavorable situations was fashionable and encouraged during the mid-1960s.

If nothing else can be said of the 1960s, certainly we can state that it was a time responsive to personal and civil rights. The civil rights movement was consummated by passage of the Civil Rights Act of 1964; however, this law did not deal directly with people with disabilities. Nevertheless, the achievements and impetus provided by the civil rights movement and the resulting legislation would be realized and extended to people with disabilities in the 1970s through today.

Most notably, the early 1970s were litigious times. A new tactic for ensuring services was beginning to emerge. Previously, courts had been used as a last resort, but now they were used frequently and strategically. Rights afforded the regular citizenry had been denied to many individuals who were mentally retarded, and the courtroom became the forum in which these rights were secured. This policy was supported by parent groups and at least tolerated by a society responsive to human rights infringements, and many issues were brought to the courtroom. Chief among them were rights to education and proper treatment.

The **right to education** issue was sparked in 1971 by a celebrated class action suit, *Pennsylvania Association for Retarded Children* [PARC] *v. Commonwealth of Pennsylvania*. This litigation resulted in an agreement that established the right to free, appropriate public school education for all children who were mentally retarded within the jurisdiction of this federal court district. However, the impact of the court-ordered agreement extended beyond eastern Pennsylvania, as similar suits dealing with the same issue were filed in many other states in the months following the decision.

Although *PARC v. Pennsylvania* was specifically concerned with the exclusion from public education of children whose primary descriptor was retardation, other students with disabilities were soon to enjoy the same right. In that same year, a suit on behalf of all students with special educational needs, regardless of type and severity, was filed in federal district court in Washington, DC. This case, *Mills v. Board of Education of the District of Columbia* (1972), was decided in favor of the plaintiffs, extending the right to education to all children with disabilities.

During this same period, many individuals living in institutions were receiving very little in the way of services beyond custodial care. In 1971, in the case *Wyatt v. Stickney*, the lack of appropriate treatment provided residents at an institution for the mentally retarded in Alabama was contested. Although aspects of this case are still being reviewed, the original decision declared that the residents of Partlow

State School and Hospital were entitled to receive treatment, not just custodial care. The judge enumerated the steps to be taken to comply with this decision.

As can be seen, the courts began to shape certain practices during this time. What may seem strange to the casual observer—yet eminently significant to the special education professional—is the critical and influential roles that judges, lawyers, and expert witnesses played during the litigious early 1970s. To professionals who were often the main service providers to those who were retarded, it seemed that policy was being formed by experts in other fields. Although to a certain extent this is true, knowledgeable parents and special educators were the ones who had realized that rights had not been secured or guaranteed through committee or panel action and that, as a result, legal procedures had become necessary.

The judicial activity of the early 1970s culminated in federal legislation that affected individuals with disabilities. Two pieces of legislation stood unparalleled in history at that time for what they mandated. In 1973, amendments to the Vocational Rehabilitation Act (PL 93-112) were passed. Serving as a bill of rights for people with disabilities, Section 504 of this act ensured that "the handicapped of America should have access to education and jobs, and should not be denied anything that any other citizen is entitled to or already receives" (LaVor, 1977, p. 249). Two years later, the landmark Education for All Handicapped Children Act (EHA) (PL 94-142) was signed into law. The major provisions of this legislation were as follows:

- Every child with a disability between the ages of three and twenty-one is entitled to a free, appropriate public education in the least restrictive environment.
- Due process is ensured to protect the rights of students and their parents.
- Students are entitled to special and related services, which are determined as necessary.
- Every student will have a written Individualized Educational Program (IEP) that parents and school personnel agree upon.
- First priority is given to students previously excluded from educational services and second priority to those whose programs were inappropriate.
- No eligible child is to be rejected from receiving services.

Another federal law that had an impact on persons who were mentally retarded was the Developmental Disabilities Assistance and Bill of Rights Act of 1978 (PL 95-602). This legislation provided a functional way of conceptualizing developmental disabilities as well as funding to assist persons who demonstrate problems in major life function areas.

A major change in the Medicaid program, for which many individuals with mental retardation qualify, occurred in 1981. The optional Home and Community Based Services (HCBS) waiver was created that allowed states to use Medicaid funds for a wider variety of community services. Over time, more states chose to use this option (Abeson & Davis, 2000).

One of the most significant pieces of legislation for persons with mental retardation was passed in 1990: the Americans with Disabilities Act (ADA) (PL 101-336). It has been referred to as the most important action related to civil rights since the Civil Rights Act of 1964 (Hardman, Drew, Egan, & Wolf, 1993). ADA aims to provide civil rights protections for and opportunities to individuals who are disabled. It covers both public and private settings and affects employment, public services, transportation, public accommodations (e.g., restaurants, shopping centers), and telecommunications (e.g., relay services). Even though this legislation is not specifically targeted toward persons with mental retardation, its impact on this group is noteworthy.

Many important court cases took place in the 1980s, three of which are featured here. The case of *Larry P. v. Riles* (1972) was heard in the Ninth Circuit Court of Appeals. This court upheld a lower court ruling prohibiting California schools from using intelligence tests to place black students in classes for students who were mentally retarded. In *Pennhurst State School v. Halderman* (1981), the Supreme Court reversed the Third Circuit Court of Appeals' decision that affirmed the right of the residents of Pennhurst State School and Hospital to adequate habilitation under the Developmentally Disabled Assistance and Bill of Rights Act. The Supreme Court made it clear that this act does not create any substantive rights to adequate treatment. The third litigative action was the first case relating to PL 94-142 heard by the Supreme Court. At issue in this case, *Board of Education of the Hendrick Hudson Central School District v. Rowley* (1982), was whether a female student with a hearing impairment was entitled to interpreter service to provide her with an appropriate education. Although acknowledging the procedural safeguards and need for individual education programs, the Supreme Court determined that states did not have to provide more than a minimal level of the services designated appropriate. As a result of this decision, schools do not have to be concerned with providing optimal educational programs for students with special needs. This has significant implications in terms of programs for students who are retarded.

During the mid-1980s, a dominant theme in general and special education was the growing number of people "at risk" for any number of pejorative outcomes. At the school level, this includes students who are at risk for school failure (potential dropouts, substance abusers, pregnant teenagers). At the adult level, it includes people who are homeless, those who are unemployed or underemployed, and those who are not able to deal successfully with the demands of daily living. Individuals with mental retardation can be found in all these groups.

Trends in Service Delivery

To learn how trends in service delivery have influenced the life of a real person, go to the companion website at *www.prenhall.com/beirne-smith,* select Chapter 1, and then choose the Case Studies module.

With continuing support from state and federal governments, programs and services for individuals who were retarded proliferated almost exponentially. But the spotlight was soon to flicker, if not dim. Lloyd Dunn's 1968 questioning of the efficacy of placing students with mild retardation in special classes symbolized some of the reexamination occurring in the late 1960s and early 1970s.

A new philosophical theme was beginning to take hold. The concept of **normalization,** which originated during the 1950s in Scandinavia, was finding much support in the United States. N. E. Bank-Mikkelsen and Bengt Nirje were eminently responsible for the development and dissemination of this principle in Scandinavia, while Wolf Wolfensberger was instrumental in championing it in the United States.

To a great extent, the emergence of this philosophy was due to a single publication that had a great impact on professionals in the United States. Entitled *Changing Patterns in Residential Services for the Mentally Retarded,* this work included a discussion of the principle of normalization by Nirje (1969), sparking a movement in this country that epitomized the next decade. Nirje defined *normalization* as "making available to the mentally retarded patterns and conditions of everyday life which are as close as possible to the norms and patterns of the mainstream of society" (p. 181).

As more professionals recognized the needs of people with retardation, a new emphasis was placed on community-based services. This trend has continued. To some degree, attention to community issues was a result of parental concern about their now adult children.

During the 1960s, the nature–nurture issue, which had been brewing for many years, seemed to be best answered by those arguing the importance of interaction between heredity and environment. Although supporters of this orientation acknowledged both hereditary and environmental determinants of many types of mild mental retardation, they felt that environmental factors were more influential. In 1969, much attention was drawn to this issue by Arthur Jensen. Jensen (1969) published an article in the *Harvard Educational Review* entitled "How Much Can We Boost IQ and Scholastic Achievement?" He argued that genetic factors are more important than environmental factors in determining IQ (i.e., the high inheritability of intelligence). Where Jensen's article received the most criticism was in his implication that social class and racial variations in intelligence are attributable to genetic differences.

In the changing social climate of the late 1960s, characterized by many forms of reactionary behavior, services to and certain concepts of those with retardation were being challenged. The revolutionary fervor of the 1960s would wane as the 1970s progressed. For exceptional individuals and those working with them, however, the early 1970s was reminiscent of the turbulent prior decade in many ways.

In the entire history of services to persons who are mentally retarded, there had been no period with more visible gains than the early 1970s. Without a doubt, the pioneers of the early 19th century had made great steps in initiating interven-

FIGURE 1.1

Enrollment of Students with Mental Retardation, 1922–1998

Source: Data are from the U.S. Department of the Census and the U.S. Department of Education, Office of Special Education.

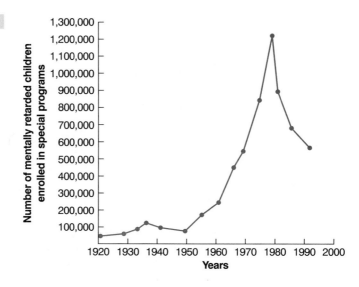

tion; however, events of the 1970s were of similar significance. At long last, it was established that Americans who were mentally retarded had certain personal and civil rights guaranteeing services and protection. As can be seen from Figure 1.1, the number of students receiving special education greatly increased during the 1960s and 1970s. (That this number began decreasing toward the end of the 1970s is discussed later.)

During the late 1960s and 1970s, special education for many students with mental retardation, when it did occur, typically took place in segregated settings. The resource room model, in which students would spend less than half of their school day in a special education setting (i.e., primarily for reading and math instruction), became very popular during this time. However, other academic issues remained, as these students were in general education, usually without any accommodations, during subjects such as science and social studies.

The concept of "mainstreaming" students into general education became fashionable. Although the intent of educating students with mental retardation along with their nondisabled peers was acceptable, this practice was mostly a physical integration without the elements needed for successful inclusion, as is advocated today.

The preparation for the realities of adulthood were often addressed through various vocational training programs. Patton, Polloway, and Smith (2000) describe one common type of program:

> Many students with mild mental retardation participated in work-study programs that were set up in high schools. In this arrangement, the student spent half of the instructional day at a specific job in the community and the other half of the day at school taking classes. In their often-cited book, *A High School Work Study Program for Mentally Subnormal Students,* Kolstoe and Frey (1965) described the job performance skills as well as the academic, personal, and social skills that are essential for meaningful outcomes. (p. 78)

SUPPORTS-BASED ORIENTATION: 1985–PRESENT

Significant changes have occurred in the field of mental retardation in recent years. Polloway and colleagues (1996) suggest that the 1990s were particularly momentous for the field of mental retardation.

> Changes in public attitudes toward persons with disabilities, and the resulting development and provision of services and supports, have been truly phenomenal. Consequently, the 1990s have become an exciting time to be participating in and/or adapting to the changing perspectives on mental retardation and developmental disabilities. One of the most challenging aspects in the field has been the mixed feelings that accompany these changes as we seek to understand new directions and consider their implications. (p. 3)

This supports-based perspective promotes as a basic tenet the notion of maintaining individuals with mental retardation in inclusive settings along with appropriate supports to be used only when needed. Supports might include natural supports, personal supports, various services, and other technical supports.

Sociopolitical Influences

Beginning in the 1980s and continuing into the 1990s, the data indicate that the number of school-age students qualifying for special education as mentally retarded under IDEA has changed dramatically. The total number of students identified as mentally retarded has decreased substantially since the late 1970s (see Figure 1.1). Polloway and Smith (1983) have suggested several factors to account for this decrease: (a) definitional changes and changes in professional thinking, which have encouraged caution and conservatism about identification and misdiagnosis, and (b) the effects of early intervention efforts in preventing some cases of mild retardation.

The impact that the various educational reforms, such as the increasing attention on standards-based education, will have on students with mental retardation is difficult to predict. For instance, the six National Education Goals (see Figure 1.2) put forth in the America 2000 (1991) strategy (which, by the way, were not all reached by 2000) portend positive as well as negative scenarios for students with mental retardation. As an example, the intent of goal 5—for all adults to be literate and have the skills necessary to participate in a global economy and exercise full citizenship—is a worthy one for the country in general. However, for students who may need to concentrate on mastering the skills needed to be successful in

FIGURE 1.2
America 2000: The National Education Goals

By the year 2000:

1. All children in America will start school ready to learn.

2. The high school graduation rate will increase to at least 90 percent.

3. American students will leave grades 4, 8, and 12 having demonstrated competency in challenging subject matter including English, mathematics, science, history, and geography; and every school in America will ensure that all students learn to use their minds well, so they may be prepared for responsible citizenship, further learning, and productive employment in our modern economy.

4. U.S. students will be first in the world in science and mathematics achievement.

5. Every adult American will be literate and will possess the knowledge and skills necessary to compete in a global economy and exercise the rights and responsibilities of citizenship.

6. Every school in America will be free of drugs and violence and will offer a disciplined environment conducive to learning.

their local communities, the part related to competing in a global economy may not hold the same level of importance as it might for others.

Another example of the supports-based, inclusion paradigm is reflected in the 1992 definition of mental retardation approved by the American Association on Mental Retardation (Luckasson et al., 1992a, 1992b). Its emphasis on levels of support across various domains of functioning underscores this supports-based theme. However, as discussed in the next chapter, not all parties have embraced a supports-oriented definition and classification system.

The importance of supports can be found throughout the literature, as the concept is used frequently, in relation to a variety of topics related to individuals with mental retardation: inclusion, transition, living arrangements, employment, and family. At its most fundamental level, the concept of supports is a very common phenomenon, as Patton and Dunn (1998) point out:

> We are all, as Condeluci (1995) noted, interdependent beings. It is very natural to use supports that exist in our everyday environments. We ask co-workers for rides to work when our cars are in the shop. We drop off our children at their grandparents' houses when we need to be away from home. We pay folks to cut our grass, pick up our garbage, dry clean our clothes—we use community services regularly. None of us find anything wrong with it. With this in mind, it is essential that professionals convey to youth with special needs that the use of supports and services is acceptable and useful. (p. 17)

The Individuals with Disabilities Education Act was reauthorized in 1997, although the final regulations were not available until March 1999. While reaffirming the basic tenets of the law passed in 1975, the most recent law has some new twists to it that have implications for students with mental retardation and their families. Some of the key changes include these:

- Students' programs must relate to the general curriculum—the individualized education program (IEP) is the guiding document for assuring that this happens.
- Students with disabilities must be included in general state and district-wide assessments—for some students, provisions can be made for accommodations and, for certain other students, alternative assessments are permissible.
- General education teachers must be included on the IEP team, if the student is participating in the general education environment.
- New procedures have been generated to deal with students who are subject to various disciplinary procedures.
- Parents are clearly identified as a member of the IEP team.

Another area that is very much affected by sociopolitical influences is the institutionalization of individuals with mental retardation. As Braddock, Hemp, and Parish (2000) point out, the number of persons who live out-of-home being served in smaller community settings has increased in recent years. In fact, the number of residents in state institutions continues to drop, as illustrated in Figure 1.3. Of particular note is the fact that seven states have no state-operated institutions (i.e., facilities with 16 or more residents).

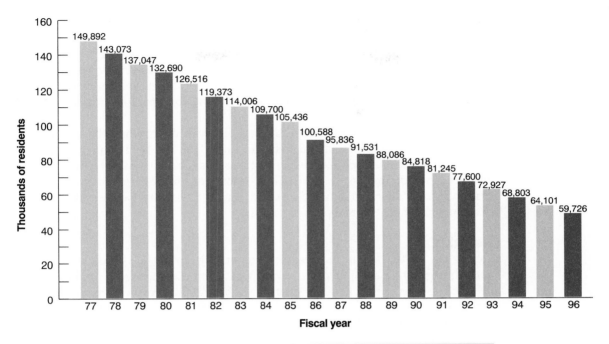

FIGURE 1.3
Residents in State-Operated Institutions

Source: From *The State of the States in Developmental Disabilities* (5th ed., Chap. 2), by D. Braddock, R. Hemp, S. Parish, and J. Westrich, 1998, Washington, DC: American Association on Mental Retardation. Copyright 1998 by David Braddock. Used with permission.

Psychological, Medical, and Health Care Developments

The last 15 years have seen some astonishing developments in the fields of psychology, medicine, and health care. Many of these discoveries of science and research are having a significant impact on persons with mental retardation. Some of the recent developments are described here.

Behavioral Interventions

The application of behavioral analysis techniques to various problematic situations, particularly social ones, is the essence of positive behavioral support. Horner (2000) provides the following explanation of this popular approach to working with behavioral issues: "Positive behavior support involves the assessment and reengineering of environments so people with problem behaviors experience reduction in their problem behaviors and increased social, personal, and professional quality in their lives" (p. 181).

The technology of positive behavioral support has great promise for those individuals whose behaviors interfere with their lives. One of the attractive elements of this methodology, as it applies to children, youth, and adults with mental retardation, is the "committed focus on fixing environments, not people" (Horner, 2000, p. 182).

Genetics

Research of the last several years has brought us to the point where we are now on the brink of knowing the cause of genetically related disorders, many of which are associated with mental retardation. Currently, ongoing research is looking into the genetic abnormalities that cause specific disorders. Other researchers are developing various methodologies such as gene replacement therapy for addressing these issues.

Moser (2000) identifies four technological advances that have been refined in recent years that will continue to have an impact on the field of mental retardation: (a) refined biochemical and enzymatic assays (i.e., diagnostic techniques); (b) advances in neuroimaging (e.g., magnetic resonance imaging); (c) advances in neuroscience (e.g., neuronal activity); and (d) the U.S. Human Genome Project (i.e., development of genetic and physical maps).

Health Care

During the 1990s, health care became a major concern in the United States, and a small but growing amount of attention was given specifically to the health care needs of persons with mental retardation. Cohen (2000) provides a model of health care promotion for individuals with mental retardation that incorporates the notion of support from different entities (see Figure 1.4).

The importance of health care is unassailable, yet its availability to large numbers of folks who desperately need it is still a problem. As Crocker (2000) states, "Access to quality health care remains in our ethos as a natural right (although not

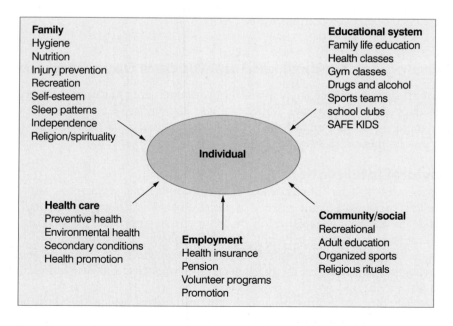

FIGURE 1.4

Model for Individual Health Promotion

Source: From Cohen (2000).

literally an entitlement), yet many individuals are still left out of present coverage, or tumble out of it" (p. 277).

Trends in Service Delivery

The supports-based theme has influenced the delivery of service across the life span. The overall theme is that decisions about service delivery should involve the individual to the greatest extent possible and that appropriate services should be provided in inclusive settings.

A trend that emerged in the latter part of the 1990s is the notion of *empowerment*. The idea of creating situations in which individuals are more active participants in various aspects of their own lives is a logical outgrowth of a supports-based climate. Polloway and colleagues (1996) note that empowerment includes ideas around which professionals within the field of developmental disabilities "finally can rally because it can embrace considerations related to inclusion, curricular needs, and transitions" (p. 8).

An important element of empowerment is *self-determination,* a topic that, although not new, began receiving broad professional attention in the 1990s. Wehmeyer (1993) offers the following explanation of self-determination: "Self-determination refers to the attitudes and abilities necessary to act as the primary causal agent in one's life, and to make choices and decisions regarding one's quality of life free from undue external influence or interference" (p. 16). Individuals who are afforded the freedom of choice and are more involved in making decisions associated with this choice are likely to enjoy a better quality of life. This is due to the fact that they have had a say in the way it should go.

Early Intervention

Infants and toddlers with mental retardation are being provided needed services in their natural environments. One of the most important changes in the nature of services for very young children is placing families at the center of the early intervention system (Guralnick, 2000). A major characteristic of early childhood intervention is the desire to provide families with the supports to assist them in carrying out the key pieces of the individual family service plan (IFSP) in which they can be involved.

The goal of services at the preschool age (i.e., ages 3–5) is to provide an appropriate education in settings with other children who are not disabled. For the most part, this goal has not been achieved, in great part because publicly supported preschool does not exist in the United States. As a result, the options for similar age inclusion are in the private sector. Some inclusion of older preschoolers can occur with kindergarten kids. Nevertheless, the development of effective preschool programs throughout the United States has been remarkable.

Education

Efforts to teach students with mental retardation in **inclusive environments** increased in the 1990s. Although data suggest many students with mental retardation are still receiving the bulk of their education in separate classes (U.S. Department of Education, 1999), efforts to increase the opportunities for inclusion are intensifying, as are wonderful examples of effective inclusionary practices. When inclusion has been successful, the following features are typically present in the classroom: sense of community and social acceptance, appreciation of student diversity, attention to the student's curricular needs, evidence of effective management and instructional practices, and appropriate supports (Smith, Polloway, Patton, & Dowdy, 2001).

Another development that has affected the education of students with mental retardation is the use of technology. Technology has short-term (i.e., assistance with immediate school-related challenges) as well as long-term applications (i.e., useful in a lifelong perspective) for individuals with mental retardation. Technology is changing so fast that we cannot even envision what might be possible 10 years from now.

Adult Issues

At the adult level, the supports-based theme can be easily recognized in a number of current initiatives. One of the most successful models of employment training is *supported employment*—sometimes referred to as *workplace supports*. In this arrangement, a job coach or employment specialist works with the individual on site, providing training and addressing other support needs. The number of individuals who participate in supported employment increased dramatically during the 1990s (Wehman, Revell, & Kregel, 1997).

Even with the substantial increase in the number of people involved in various competitive employment settings, a number of adults are still engaged in sheltered employment settings. The reality is that many more individuals could be working in competitive employment settings, especially in times of low unemployment when workers are desperately needed.

Also on the rise is the creation of housing arrangements where staff is available as necessary to assist individuals with mental retardation (supported living) who live in these settings. For older individuals, specialized approaches have been developed (supported retirement).

FINAL REFLECTIONS

An important concept that applies to all individuals with mental retardation and should guide all research, intervention, and all other aspects of this field is consideration of quality of life. Although professional debate exists as to the validity of this concept and whether it can be measured, the fundamental essence of quality of life can be understood in the context of the eight core quality-of-life dimensions identified by Schalock (1996): emotional well-being, interpersonal relationships, material well-being, personal development, physical well-being, self-determination, social inclusion, and rights. Table 1.1 highlights the comprehensiveness of these dimensions and their relevance to the lives of persons with mental retardation.

To read more about the ethics of withholding treatment and complete a related activity, go to the companion website at www.prenhall.com/ beirne-smith and select Chapter 1, and then choose the Article Response module.

Other issues associated with mental retardation have emerged that are still unresolved. Some of these include a host of ethical issues (e.g., withholding treatment) and the continuing effects of poverty. These and other issues must still be addressed. Cutbacks and restrictions may result from economic problems or policy shifts. If a positive national policy supportive of people with special needs is not carefully maintained, our society will be guilty of social neglect, and people who

TABLE 1.1
Quality-of-Life Indicators

Dimension	Exemplary Indicators	
Emotional well-being	Safety	Freedom from stress
	Spirituality	Self-concept
	Happiness	Contentment
Interpersonal relationships	Intimacy	Interactions
	Affection	Friendships
	Family	Supports
Material well-being	Ownership	Employment
	Financial	Possessions
	Security	Socio-economic status
	Food	Shelter
Personal development	Education	Personal competence
	Skills	Purposeful activity
	Fulfillment	Advancement
Physical well-being	Health	Health care
	Nutrition	Health insurance
	Recreation	Leisure
	Mobility	Activities of daily living
Self-determination	Autonomy	Personal control
	Choices	Self-direction
	Decision	Personal goals/value
Social inclusion	Acceptance	Community activities
	Status	Roles
	Supports	Volunteer activities
	Work environment	Residential environment
Rights	Privacy	Due process
	Voting	Ownership
	Access	Civic responsibilities

Source: From Schalock (2000).

need help will not receive it. Blatt (1987) has poignantly captured the gravity of the situation: "If the business of government isn't charity, and we aren't our brothers' keepers, then some needy people will die before their time, and many needy people will suffer" (p. 83). We must move through this new century with guarded optimism, because what can be done for people needing assistance has been, and will continue to be, grounded in vagaries of the sociopolitical context.

To check your understanding of this chapter, go to the companion website at www.prenhall.com/beirne -smith and select Chapter 1, and then choose the Self-Test module.

Summary

General
- Significant sociopolitical factors have contributed to the evolution of the field of mental retardation.
- Mental retardation is very much a social phenomenon.
- Many contemporary issues are not new.

Antiquity: Prior to 1700

- Before 1700, mental retardation was misunderstood and treated in a variety of mysterious ways.
- Milder forms of mental retardation were not recognizable.
- Custodial care was provided in certain settings.

Emergence and Early Disillusionment of a Field: 1700-1890

- Itard worked with Victor (the Wild Boy).
- Seguin developed instructional methodologies and programs—elements of which are still used today.
- In the United States, key individuals such as Dix, Howe, and Wilbur pioneered care for individuals with special needs.
- Toward the end of the 19th century, important social forces (urbanization and industrialization) were occurring that would have effects on those with cognitive limitations.
- Pessimism about what could be done for persons with mental retardation developed.

Facilities-Based Orientation: 1890-1960

- Institutions became custodial in nature.
- The eugenics movement began, affecting many persons with mental retardation through sterilization, segregation, and limitations on immigration.
- The mental test was developed, and milder forms of retardation were now recognizable.
- A major professional organization for special education teachers was founded.
- Standardized scales for measuring social maturity and intelligence were introduced.
- The largest and most powerful parent organization advocating for people with mental retardation (now called the Arc) was formed.
- Most states enacted legislation for educating some students with mental retardation; many of those with more significant cognitive impairments were still excluded.

Services-Based Orientation: 1960-1985

- President Kennedy established a national agenda for mental retardation.
- The War on Poverty was initiated.
- The principle of normalization began to take hold.
- A series of major court cases began to force important changes.
- The Vocational Rehabilitation Act reauthorization of 1973 became a landmark piece of legislation.
- A free, appropriate public education became available to all students with disabilities with the passage of the Education of All Handicapped Children Act of 1975.
- Community services and placement were championed by advocates.

Supports-Based Orientation: 1985–Present

- The placement of children, youth, and adults into inclusive settings is advocated by parents and professionals.

- The number of residents in institutional settings continues to drop.
- Continued attention on early intervention is promoted.
- The number of students identified by schools as mentally retarded continued to drop, with a slight increase in recent years.
- Employment possibilities are enriched by the implementation of practices such as supported employment.
- The notion of supports is validated and encouraged.
- New medical discoveries (e.g., genome research) offer exciting possibilities.

References

Abeson, A., & Davis, S. (2000). The parent movement in mental retardation. In M. L. Wehmeyer & J. R. Patton (Eds.), *Mental retardation in the 21st century* (pp. 19–34). Austin, TX: PRO-ED.

Blatt, B. (1987). *The conquest of mental retardation*. Austin, TX: PRO-ED.

Braddock, D., Hemp, R., & Parish, S. (2000). Transforming service delivery systems in the states. In M. L. Wehmeyer & J. R. Patton (Eds.), *Mental retardation in the 21st century* (pp. 359–378). Austin, TX: PRO-ED.

Braddock, D., Kemp, R., Parish, S., & Westrich, J. (1998). *The state of the states in developmental disabilities*. Washington, DC: American Association on Mental Retardation.

Buck v. Bell, 274 U.S. 200 (1927).

Cohen, D. E. (2000). Health promotion and disability prevention: The case for personal responsibility and independence. In M. L. Wehmeyer & J. R. Patton (Eds.), *Mental retardation in the 21st century* (pp. 251–264). Austin, TX: PRO-ED.

Condeluci, A. (1995). *Interdependence: The route to community* (2nd ed.). Winter Park, FL: GR.

Crocker, A. C. (2000). Community-based and managed health care. In M. L. Wehmeyer & J. R. Patton (Eds.), *Mental retardation in the 21st century* (pp. 265–279). Austin, TX: PRO-ED.

Dix, D. (1976). Memorial to the legislature of Massachusetts, 1843. (Reprinted in M. Rosen, G. R. Clark, & M. S. Kivitz [Eds.], *The history of mental retardation: Collected papers* [Vol. 1, pp. 3–30]. Baltimore: University Park Press.) (Original work published 1843.)

Doll, E. A. (1935). A genetic scale of maturity. *American Journal of Orthopsychiatry, 5,* 180–188.

Dugdale, R. L. (1877). *The Jukes, a study in crime, pauperism, disease and heredity.* New York: Putnam.

Ginzberg, E., & Bray, D. W. (1953). *The uneducated.* New York: Columbia University Press.

Goddard, H. H. (1912). *The Kallikak family.* New York: Macmillan.

Goddard, H. H. (1917). Mental tests and the immigrant. *Journal of Delinquency, 2,* 243–277.

Gould, S. J. (1981). *The mismeasure of man.* New York: Norton.

Guralnick, M. J. (2000). Early childhood intervention: Evolution of a system. In M. L. Wehmeyer & J. R. Patton (Eds.), *Mental retardation in the 21st century* (pp. 37–58). Austin, TX: PRO-ED.

Hardman, M.L., Drew, C.J., Egan, M.W., & Wolf, B. (1993). *Human exceptionality: Society, School, and Family* (4th ed.). Boston: Allyn & Bacon.

Heber, R. F. (1959). A manual on terminology and classification in mental retardation. *Monograph Supplement to the American Journal of Mental Deficiency, 62.*

Hewett, F. M., & Forness, S. (1977). *Education of exceptional learners* (2nd ed.). Boston: Allyn & Bacon.

Humphrey, G., & Humphrey, M. (Eds. & Trans.). (1962). *Wild boy of Aveyron.* New York: Appleton-Century-Crofts.

Jensen, A. R. (1969). How much can we boost IQ and scholastic achievement? *Harvard Educational Review, 39,* 1–23.

Kanner, L. A. (1964). *A history of the care and study of the mentally retarded.* Springfield, IL: Thomas.

Kolstoe, O. P., & Frey, R. M. (1965). *A high school work study program for the mentally subnormal student.* Carbondale: Southern Illinois University Press.

LaVor, M. L. (1977). Federal legislation for exceptional children: Implications and a view of the field. In R. D. Kneedler & S. G. Tarver (Eds.), *Changing perspectives in special education.* Upper Saddle River, NJ: Merrill/Macmillan.

Luckasson, R., Coulter, D. L., Polloway, E. A., Reiss, S., Schalock, R. L., Snell, M. E., Spitalnik, D. M., & Stark, J. A. (1992a). *Mental retardation: Definition, classification, and systems of support* (9th ed.). Washington, DC: American Association on Mental Retardation.

Luckasson, R., Coulter, D., Polloway, E. A., Reiss, S., Schalock, R., Snell, M., Spitalnik, D., & Stark, J. (1992b). *Mental retardation: Definition, diagnosis, and systems of support.* Washington, DC: American Association on Mental Retardation.

Maloney, M. P., & Ward, M. P. (1978). *Mental retardation and modern society.* New York: Oxford University Press.

Masland, R., Sarason, S., & Gladwin, T. (1958). *Mental subnormality.* New York: Basic Books.

Mayo, L. W. (1962). *A proposed program for national action to combat mental retardation.* Report to the President's Committee on Mental Retardation. Washington, DC: U. S. Government Printing Office.

Moser, H. W. (2000). Genetics and gene therapies. In M. L. Wehmeyer & J. R. Patton (Eds.), *Mental retardation in the 21st century* (pp. 235–250). Austin, TX: PRO-ED.

National Association of Parents and Friends of Retarded Children. (1950). *Constitution and bylaws.* Minneapolis: Author.

Nirje, B. (1969). The normalization principle and its human management implications. In R. B. Krugel & W. Wolfensberger (Eds.), *Changing patterns in residential services for the mentally retarded* (pp. 179–195). Washington, DC: U. S. Government Printing Office.

Patton, J. R., Blackbourn, J. M., & Fad, K. S. (1996). *Exceptional individuals in focus* (6th ed.). Upper Saddle River, NJ: Merrill/Prentice Hall.

Patton, J. R., & Dunn, C. (1998). *Transition from school to young adulthood: Basic concepts and recommended practices.* Austin, TX: PRO-ED.

Polloway, E. A., & Smith, J. D. (1983). Changes in mild mental retardation: Population, programs, and perspectives. *Exceptional Children, 50,* 149–159.

Polloway, E. A., Smith, J. D., Patton, J. R., & Smith, T. E. C. (1996). Historical changes in mental retardation and developmental disabilities. *Education and Training in Mental Retardation and Developmental Disabilities, 31,* 3–12.

Sarason, S. B. (1985). *Psychology and mental retardation: Perspectives in change.* Austin, TX: PRO-ED.

Schalock, R. L. (1996). *Quality of life: Vol. 1. Conceptualization and measurement.* Washington, DC: American Association on Mental Retardation.

Seguin, E. O. (1846). *Traitement moral, hygiene et education des idiots et des autres enfants arrières.* Paris: Baillier.

Skeels, H. M., & Dye, H. B. (1939). A study of the effects of differential stimulation on mentally retarded children. *Convention Proceedings of the American Association on Mental Deficiency, 44,* 114–136.

Smith, J. D. (1985). *Minds made feeble: The myth and legacy of the Kallikaks.* Rockville, MD: Aspen Systems.

Smith, J. D. (1987). *The other voices: Profiles of women in the history of special education.* Seattle, WA: Special Child.

Smith, T. E. C., Polloway, E. A., Patton, J. R., & Dowdy, C. A. (2001). *Teaching students with special needs in inclusive settings* (3rd ed.). Needham Heights, MA: Allyn & Bacon.

U.S. Department of Education. (1999). *Twenty-first annual report to Congress on the implementation of the Individuals with Disabilities Education Act.* Washington, DC: Author.

Wechsler, D. (1949). *Wechsler Intelligence Scale for Children.* San Antonio, TX: Psychological Corporation.

Wehman, P., Revell, W. G., & Kregel, J. (1997). Supported employment: A decade of rapid growth and impact. In P. Wehman, J. Kregel, & M. West (Eds.), *Supported employment research: Expanding competitive employment opportunities for persons with significant disabilities.* Richmond: Virginia Commonwealth University, Rehabilitation Research and Training Center.

Wehmeyer, M. (1993). Self-determination as an educational outcome. *Impact, 6*(4), 16–17, 26.

Wilbur, H. (1976). Eulogy to Edouard Seguin: Remarks made at Seguin's funeral, Clamecy, France, 1880. (Reprinted in M. Rosen, G. R. Clark, & M. S. Kivitz [Eds.], *The history of mental retardation: Collected papers* [Vol. 1, pp. 181–187]. Baltimore: University Park Press.) (Original work published 1880.)

Chapter

2

Terminology and Definition

To review the chapter objectives on-line, go to the companion website at *www.prenhall.com/ beirne-smith* and select Chapter 2, then choose the Objectives module.

OBJECTIVES

After reading this chapter, the student should be able to

- identify several terms used to describe mental retardation
- discuss the concept of disablism and how it relates to mental retardation
- identify key points of the various definitions that have been developed
- highlight the traditional levels of classification and implications of the American Association on Mental Retardation (AAMR) definition
- discuss the issues surrounding the practical implementation of definitions
- list and discuss the factors that influence the prevalence of mental retardation

KEY TERMS

adaptive behavior

clinical judgment

developmental period

disablism

incidence

mental retardation

prevalence

6-hour retarded children

standard deviation

subaverage general intellectual functioning

Mental retardation is a complex condition worthy of close study. Essentially, mental retardation affects the way individuals who have it cope with the various environments in which they find themselves. It is important to note the distinction that has been made between mental retardation as a state and as a trait.

> Mental retardation is not a trait, although it is influenced by certain characteristics or capabilities of the individual. . . . Rather, mental retardation is a state in which functioning is impaired in certain specific ways. This distinction between trait and state is central to understanding. (AAMR, 1992, p. 10)

Mental retardation has been defined and will continue to be defined in various and differing ways, as illustrated in recent times by the proliferation of discussions related to this condition. In addition to the various conceptualizations open to debate, mental retardation entails other meanings as well. On the day-to-day level, "For the individual and the family, mental retardation presents very practical concerns. For the community, state, and nation, it presents educational, social, economic, and political challenges" (Grossman & Tarjan, 1987, p. v).

The definition of mental retardation is explored in depth in this chapter, as we trace the evolution of how various individuals and organizations have perceived the condition. Ways of dealing with mental retardation on an individual basis are addressed throughout the book. Its challenge to society was underscored from a historical perspective in the previous chapter; current sociopolitical implications will be addressed in this chapter.

MENTAL RETARDATION IN CONTEXT

Mental retardation is one type of developmental disability and generally refers to substantial limitations in present levels of functioning. These limitations are manifest in delayed intellectual growth; inappropriate or immature reactions to one's environment; and below-average performance in the academic, psychological, physical, linguistic, and social domains. Such limitations create challenges for individuals to cope with the demands they encounter each day, those that other people of comparable age and social or cultural background would be expected to deal with successfully on an ongoing basis. For example, in school settings, these individuals display patterns of academic and social performance that are below their chronological peers' levels of mastery. Unlike other students who perform below grade level, the principal reason that students with mental retardation do so relates to their problems in reasoning, dealing with abstract concepts, and problem solving. Their school-based difficulties are not *primarily* due to such factors as excessive absences from school or a specific learning disability, although such factors can contribute to their overall school performance.

As mentioned, mental retardation is a type of developmental disability. In recent years, the concept *developmental disability* has often been used to refer to individuals with mental retardation, particularly with adult populations. Although the term *developmental disability* covers a population of individuals other than those with mental retardation, its meaning clearly includes mental retardation. As

For a complete on-line glossary of mental retardation terms, go to the companion website www.prenhall.com/beirne-smith and select any chapter, then choose the Glossary module.

defined in the Developmental Disabilities Assistance and Bill of Rights Act of 1990 (PL 98-527), the term *developmental disability* means a severe, chronic disability of a person 5 years of age or older that

1. is attributable to a mental or physical impairment or combination of mental and physical impairments;
2. is manifested before the person attains age 22;
3. is likely to continue indefinitely;
4. results in substantial functional limitations in three or more of the following areas of major life activity: (a) self-care, (b) receptive and expressive language, (c) learning, (d) mobility, (e) self-direction, (f) capacity for independent living, and (g) economic self-sufficiency;
5. reflects the person's need for a combination and sequence of special, interdisciplinary, or generic care, treatment, or other services that are lifelong or of extended duration and are individually planned and coordinated.

The federal definition accentuates functional limitations in major life activities, suggesting problems associated with a more involved population. Nevertheless, it also applies to persons with milder forms of retardation during some or all of their lives. The implication of chronicity and its potential inappropriateness with very young populations make it different from the most common definitions of mental retardation.

Mental retardation encompasses a heterogeneous group of people with varying needs, presenting features, and life contexts. It is changeable, as some individuals may be asymptomatic at various times of their lives (before formal schooling and often later, as adults). Some professional orientations (AAMR, 1992) suggest that this condition is very much a function of the need for various levels of support. The severity of the condition ranges from mild difficulties in dealing with everyday activities to extreme limitations in basic areas of functioning that make the person dependent on others for basic skilled nursing care.

Stereotypes are all too often easy to make.

Individuals who have few needs for support or who are at the border of retardation create problems of identification and eligibility for intervention/services. Reschly (1988) has stated that as long as the system perceives mental retardation in terms of dichotomy—one is or is not retarded—rather than a continuum, a problem will always persist in classifying individuals at the margins. This point is in great part because of (a) the way we conceptualize and measure intellectual abilities and (b) society's definition of acceptable behavior and toleration of behavior that is different.

Alternative Perspectives

Alternative ways of thinking about mental retardation exist. This section explores select perspectives that have had an impact on the field of mental retardation.

Phenomenological   One perspective is to conceive of mental retardation as solely a social invention, or a reaction to people perceived as different, as some professionals have claimed (Blatt, 1987). Granted, identifiable biological manifestations exist in some individuals who are retarded, but we all have physical differences (e.g., freckles, musculature). Bogdan (1986) describes this orientation:

> The generic term "disabled" and specific disability categories are ways of thinking about and categorizing others. Whether people are thought of as disabled and the criteria used to determine whether someone is disabled has [sic] to do with how the definers think about these things. (p. 347)

Sociological   Mercer (1973a, 1973b) argues that neither a pathological nor a statistical approach to defining mental retardation is adequate for identifying cases of more mild retardation. As an alternative, she offers a social system perspective, which defines mental retardation as "an achieved social status in a social system."

> The status of mental retardate is associated with a role which persons occupying that status are expected to play. A person's career in acquiring the status of playing the role of mental retardate can be described in the same fashion as the career of a person who acquires any other status such as lawyer, bank president or teacher. (Mercer, 1973b)

Mercer's (1973a, 1973b) research findings suggest that individuals are labeled mentally retarded as a function of their performance in social situations. She advocates a more conservative definition of mental retardation, one that would make the measurement of adaptive behavior more practical. According to her view, multiple norm frameworks must be developed to describe adequately children from different sociocultural settings. That is, children must be described (and labeled, if necessary) in relation to their own social and cultural background, without prejudging that background as "deviant" or "deficient." Mercer also recommends that the identification and diagnosis of mental retardation be based on data that include the children's competencies as well as their deficits.

Gold (1980) developed a different sociological conceptualization of mental retardation. His perspective focuses on the ability or failure of society to provide adequate training and education as the measure of retardation rather than on the failure of the individual. Gold's ideas are reflected in the following statement: "The height of a retarded person's level of functioning is determined by the availability of training technology and the amount of resources society is willing to allocate and not by significant limitations in biological potential" (p. 148).

Behavioral   Bijou (1966) took the position that mental retardation should be dealt with from a behavioral perspective. He suggests that:

> [d]evelopmental retardation be treated as observable, objectively defined stimulus–response relationships without recourse to hypothetical mental concepts such as "defective intelligence" and hypothetical biological abnormalities such as "clinically inferred brain injury." From this point of view a retarded individual is one who has a limited repertory of behavior shaped by events that constitute his history. (p. 2)

The behavioral orientation provides one of the most logical bases for considering mental retardation a changeable condition. Without question, this orientation has had, and continues to have, an important impact on the development of educational and therapeutic interventions for individuals with mental retardation.

Multiple Intelligences   Another perspective that has enjoyed much popularity in recent years is the notion of multiple intelligences (Gardner, 2000; Greenspan & Driscoll, 1997). The main message is that professionals' visions of what constitutes intelligent behavior need to expanded beyond the singular focus on conceptual intelligence. This notion is examined more closely later in the chapter.

TERMINOLOGY

People who are mentally retarded over time have been referred to as *dumb, stupid, immature, defective, deficient, subnormal, incompetent,* and *dull.* Terms such as *idiot, imbecile, moron,* and *feebleminded* were commonly used historically to label this population. Although the word *fool* referred to those who were mentally ill, and the word *idiot* was directed toward individuals who were severely retarded, these terms were frequently used interchangeably (Hilliard & Kirman, 1965). Even today, the conditions of mental illness and mental retardation are regularly confused in the media and the popular press. For the sake of distinction, *mental illness,* broadly speaking, is a confused state of thinking involving distorted perceptions of people or one's environment. It may be accompanied by radical changes of mood.

The history of mental retardation is further complicated when we consider that retardation has been confused with physical deformity, cerebral palsy, dwarfism, epilepsy, and deafness. This confusion endures because a combination of these conditions does occur at higher rates in this population.

One of the first steps in understanding a phenomenon is understanding the terms used to describe it, no matter how crude or limited they may be. In the past, *idiot* was used to refer to people of all levels of mental retardation, from mild to profound. It derives from the Greek *idiotes,* meaning a layperson or unskilled worker. The word used to apply to untrained or ignorant people, and it was used in this sense until the 17th century (Penrose, 1966).

According to Kolstoe (1972), the *de praerogative regis* (prerogative of the king [of England]) issued between 1255 and 1290 A.D. defined an idiot as one who "hath no understanding from his nativity" (p. 2). About 200 years later, Sir Anthony Fitzherbert stated that an idiot was "such a person who cannot account or number, nor can tell who his father or mother are, nor how old he is, etc., so as it may appear he has not understanding of reason what shall be his profit or his loss" (Guttmacher & Weihofen, 1952). The key factor in identification as an idiot appears to be lack of understanding.

Idiocy was believed to be inborn and incurable. As mentioned in Chapter 1, one of the first accounts of attempts to cure or at least ameliorate mental retardation was reported by Itard (1801/1962), who worked with a wild boy, Victor. Pinel, a well-known physician of the time, diagnosed Victor as an incurable idiot. Seguin, a student of Itard, followed in his footsteps by attempting to cure individuals with severe limitations; Penrose (1966) reports that "Esquirol referred to Seguin's mission as the removal of the mark of the beast from the forehead of the idiot" (pp. 4–5).

The concept of *idiot* was elusive and confusing, and it covered conditions with little in common with each other; its primary use was to signify severe mental retardation. Although other terms such as *feebleminded* and *mental deficiency* came into use over time, the confusion remained. Attempts to systematize the terminology and definitions of mental retardation have continued to present times.

A different set of terms became popular in school settings. From the 1950s until the early 1980s, most students with mental retardation who were in school were labeled either *educable mentally retarded* (EMR) or *trainable mentally retarded* (TMR). Much of the classic literature on educating children and youth with mental retardation used this terms.

Dunn (1973) proposed the use of the term *general learning disabilities* to refer to individuals with mental retardation. He differentiated this term from *specific learning disabilities*. Given the rise in popularity of the concept of learning disabilities that was occurring this time, Dunn's term never caught on in professional circles.

Today, the most commonly used terms to refer to this condition are *mental retardation* or *developmental disability*. Mental retardation is one type of developmental disability, as noted previously. However, other terms such as *mental deficiency* and *mental subnormality* have also been used. Some professionals like the terms intellectually challenged or mental disability.

The continual search for different terms yields diminishing returns. Any word can come to have a negative connotation. For example, one school district, aware of the detrimental effects of labeling children "mentally retarded," began placing these children in an educational program designed to teach language, arithmetic, and reading directly. A series of commercial programs produced by Science Research Associates, DISTAR (Direct Instructional Systems for Teaching Arithmetic and Reading), was used. Before half the year was over, a group of concerned citizens asked that the program be abandoned because DISTAR was for "dumb" kids, and children not enrolled in DISTAR classes were making fun of the DISTAR children by yelling "DISTAR, DISTAR" at them at recess. It may be impossible to find acceptable terms and useful definitions without proper education and increased understanding of persons who are intellectually disabled.

TABLE 2.1
Socially Devalued Groups and the Common Historical Deviancy Roles into Which They Are Most Apt to Be Cast

People who are devalued due to:	Pity	Charity	Menace	Sick	Sub-human	Ridicule	Dread	Childlike	Holy innocent
Mental disorder	X	X	X	X	X	X	X	X	X
Mental retardation	X	X	X	X	X	X		X	X
Old age	X	X		X	X	X		X	
Alcohol habituation	X	X	X	X		X			
Poverty	X	X	X		X		X		
Racial minority membership			X		X	X	X	X	
Epilepsy	X	X		X			X		
Drug addiction	X	X	X	X					
Criminal offenses			X	X	X		X		
Physical handicap	X	X				X			
Deafness/hearing impairment	X	X							
Blindness/visual impairment	X	X							
Illiteracy	X	X							
Political dissidence			X						

Source: From "An Overview of Social Role Valorization and Some Reflections on Elderly Mentally Retarded Persons" by W. Wolfensberger, 1985. In M. P. Janicki & H. M. Wisniewski (Eds.), *Aging and Developmental Disabilities: Issues and Approaches* (pp. 61–76), Baltimore: Paul H. Brookes. Copyright 1985 by Paul H. Brookes. Reprinted by permission.

DISABLISM AND MENTAL RETARDATION

Many groups of people in our society are not perceived favorably by the community at large. As Wolfensberger (1985) points out, "How a person is perceived affects how that person will be treated" (p. 128). If a certain group of people is perceived negatively, then its members will be treated less than favorably. Wolfensberger has identified groups of people that are devalued in our society, listing the major negative social roles into which these groups are typically cast. His analysis of this devaluation, although over 15 years old, still is applicable today (see Table 2.1).

According to Wolfensberger, only mental disorder (i.e., mental illness) evokes more negative perceptions than mental retardation. It might be proper to mark the "dread" column in Table 2.1 for mental retardation as well, because sufficient examples of this perception exist. For instance, this perception is reflected by the following scenario: parents shielding their children from a group of adults who are mentally retarded seated near them on the bus out of concern that these adults are dangerous. Wolfensberger's analysis has three major implications: (a) persons who are considered retarded will be treated differently, likely badly; (b) this treatment reflects the way society conceptualizes deviancy roles; (c) the perceptions and resultant treatment by others will greatly influence the behavior of people who are retarded.

It is precisely because many individuals with retardation are treated differently from the general population that the concept of disablism is relevant. **Disablism** (changed herein from the former term *handicapism*), similarly to racism, sexism, and ageism, results in mistaken beliefs, prejudices, and pejorative actions on the part of individuals or society in general. Bogdan and Biklen (1977), two profession-als who brought this concept to the public consciousness, define it as "[a] set of assumptions and practices that promote the differential and unequal treatment of people because of apparent or assumed physical, mental, or behavioral differences" (p. 59). This concept applies to a range of people with disabilities, clearly including those who are mentally retarded.

Disablism can be manifested in various ways, most notably through stereotyp-ing, prejudice, and discrimination. Many people view adults with retardation as childlike (stereotyping), which leads to the belief that they are incapable of making decisions for themselves (prejudice), which in turn results in others' making deci-sions for them without their input or knowledge (discrimination). A practical example is the situation in which a person with mental retardation is not allowed to obtain a library card (discrimination) because it is felt (prejudice) that the person is incapable of being responsible for any books that are borrowed (stereotyping).

Many other examples of disablism are possible. A very offensive example is the popular "moron" joke ("Why did the moron . . . ?"). As pointed out earlier, the term *moron* refers to an individual with limited intellectual capacity. These jokes are heard in everyday conversation and can be found in books of "tasteless jokes." Although people with mental retardation are not the only group to suffer from malicious jokes, they certainly are one of the prime targets.

Disablism is also evident in media representations of this group. For instance, the character Zero in the comic strip "Beetle Bailey" might be considered retarded, and he is always portrayed in uncomplimentary ways. Bogdan and Biklen also note that, far too often, newspaper reports associate criminal activity with disability, implying that the disability is somehow responsible for the crime. This perspective certainly has been evident in some media descriptions of people with mental retar-dation. It is important to be aware of instances of disablism and to strive to elimi-nate them. Far too often, blatant examples of disablism go unchallenged.

Note that not all media portrayals of individuals with mental retardation are negative. Some media images are laudable—for example, the documentary *Best Boy,* the characters Benny and Corky on the former television shows *L.A. Law* and *Life Goes On,* and the film *Forest Gump.*

DEFINING MENTAL RETARDATION

Many definitions of mental retardation have been developed, all reflecting the dif-ferent perspectives and perceptions of retardation at a given point in time. Blatt (1987) articulates this notion well:

> Because mental retardation is in the most fundamental and important ways a metaphor (people make of it what they want to, people interpret it in light of their own understandings and prejudices), the definition of "mental retardation" and the terms used to denote the condition represent a hodgepodge of (sometimes irreconcilable) values, words, and ideas. (p. 69)

Whether or not we agree with Blatt's statement, we must deal with the reality that definitions exist and are used to make decisions about persons with retardation.

Central to all definitions of mental retardation is the notion of difficulties in social competence. Historically, this was the prime concern and therefore preeminent criterion. In more recent times, the importance of being able to deal adaptively with the demands of one's environment has been emphasized.

This section has three major foci: (a) a brief examination of some early definitions, (b) a discussion of the series of definitions developed by the AAMR, and (c) a look at some new definitions that have emerged more recently.

Early Definitions

During the first half of the 20th century, two definitions of mental retardation, one developed by Tredgold and the other by Doll, were frequently cited. Tredgold (1937) defined "mental deficiency" as

> a state of incomplete mental development of such a kind and degree that the individual is incapable of adapting himself to the normal environment of his fellows in such a way to maintain existence independently of supervision, control, or external support. (p. 4)

Doll (1941) defined "mental retardation" when he stated:

> We observe that six criteria by statement or implication have been generally considered essential to an adequate definition and concept. These are (1) social incompetence, (2) due to mental subnormality, (3) which has been developmentally arrested, (4) which obtains at maturity, (5) is of constitutional origin, and (6) is essentially incurable. (p. 215)

Both of these definitions stressed the concept of social competence. Arguably, Doll's definition is the most important of the early definitions, as it has continued to influence the defining of the condition. The first four elements of Doll's definition can be found in contemporary definitional perspectives.

The AAMD/AAMR Definitions

In 1919, the American Association for the Study of the Feebleminded, which would later become the American Association on Mental Deficiency (AAMD), and is now known as the American Association on Mental Retardation (AAMR), appointed a Committee on Classification and Uniform Statistics. In 1921, this committee, in collaboration with the National Committee for Mental Hygiene, published the first edition of a manual defining the condition of mental retardation. Subsequent revisions of the manual were printed in 1933, 1941, and 1957.

In 1959, a committee of professionals chaired by Rick Heber developed the fifth AAMD definition of mental retardation. That definition was reprinted with

To access the full text of AAMR's current definition, go to the companion website www.prenhall.com/beirne-smith and select Chapter 2, and then choose the Web Destinations module.

minor changes in 1961. The sixth revision was developed by a committee chaired by Herbert Grossman in 1973. Although the definition was similar to that developed by Heber's committee some years earlier, the interpretation was significantly more conservative. Fewer individuals could be identified as mentally retarded under the Grossman definition than under the Heber definition. It is important to mention that the 1973 AAMD definition was incorporated into the Education for All Children Act (EHA) of 1975 (PL 94-142) as the federal definition of mental retardation.

Grossman's definition was reaffirmed, with minor revisions, in 1977; the next revision was published in 1983. The 1983 version, which, at the time, corresponded to definitions developed by the American Psychiatric Association (1980) and the World Health Organization (1978), described important considerations related to interpretation and clinical judgment used in classifying an individual as mentally retarded. This AAMD definition, like its predecessors, reflected a clinical perspective, relying on measurements and comparisons. Although the definition has been regularly discussed and often criticized within the field, it remained widely accepted and was used by the federal government. The ninth edition of the manual was published in 1992 (AAMR, 1992) and reflected a major paradigmatic shift, emphasizing a more functional definition of mental retardation. Interestingly, this most recent definition has led to a splintering of professionals based on conceptual and practical issues promulgated in the newest AAMR definition.

A review of the development of the AAMR definitions is worthwhile because it highlights the sociopolitical forces that were operative over the years, reflects the evolution of the field, and illustrates changes in thinking about those identified as mentally retarded. All of the AAMD/AAMR definitions presented here contain three major components: subaverage general intellectual functioning, deficits in adaptive behavior, and manifestation during the developmental period. Differences in interpretation of these three elements are notable. A detailed analysis of the more recent AAMD/AAMR definitions follows.

The 1959, 1961 Definitions   Committees of the American Association on Mental Deficiency, chaired by Rick Heber, issued a definition in 1959 that was revised again in 1961. The most notable difference between the two definitions was the introduction of the term *adaptive behavior* in the 1961 definition, replacing the 1959 terms: maturation, learning, and social adjustment. The 1961 Heber definition stated, "Mental retardation refers to subaverage general intellectual functioning which originates during the development period and is associated with impairment in adaptive behavior."

In this 1961 definition, **subaverage general intellectual functioning** refers to performance of at least 1 standard deviation below the mean on a standardized intelligence test. The **standard deviation** is a statistic used to describe the degree to which an individual's score varies from the average or mean score for the population. With this criterion as a guide for diagnosis, it was possible to identify statistically almost 16% of the general population, and perhaps greater proportions of linguistically and culturally diverse groups, as mentally retarded. Figure 2.1 illustrates the concepts of the normal curve, standard deviation, and population mean.

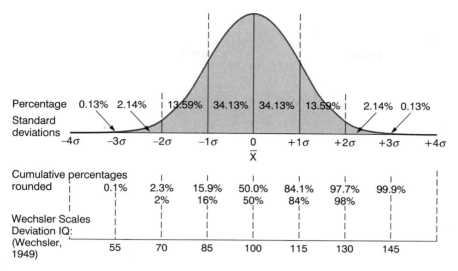

σ = standard deviation
X̄ = population mean—the average score.
The Wechsler Intelligence Scales use a deviation IQ score with a mean of 100 and a standard deviation of 15. In a normal distribution, a person who scores 1σ above the mean receives a Wechsler score of 115. One who scores below 70 on a Wechsler scale (>2σ below the mean) may be classified as mentally retarded if impairments in adaptive behavior are also present.

FIGURE 2.1
The Normal Curve

Source: From "Methods of Expressing Test Scores" (p. 8), 1955, *Test Service Bulletin, 48.* Reprinted by permission.

In the 1961 AAMR manual, the **developmental period** was recognized as variable, but for purposes of definition, it was judged to range from birth through 16 years of age. This period represents the time during which primary growth and development occur.

Adaptive behavior referred to the individual's adaptation to the demands of his or her environment. As suggested, impaired adaptive behavior could be reflected in maturation, learning, or social adjustment. Impaired adaptive behavior was considered in terms of standards and norms of appropriate behavior for the individual's chronological age group. Although deficiency in adaptive behavior was only loosely defined, use of this concept in the Heber definition represented a major departure from the earlier notions of Tredgold (1937) and Doll (1941) of incurability. The AAMR definition recognized that an individual might be deficient in one or more aspects of adaptive behavior at one time in life, but not at another. Favorable changes in social demands and environmental conditions, or in the individual's increased ability to meet natural and social demands, could mean that a person would no longer be called mentally retarded. The Heber (1959, 1961) definition

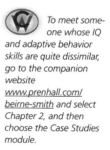

To meet someone whose IQ and adaptive behavior skills are quite dissimilar, go to the companion website *www.prenhall.com/ beirne-smith* and select Chapter 2, and then choose the Case Studies module.

established a very important point: definition reflects an individual's current functioning, not to an ultimate or permanent status.

Events Leading to Further Revisions   Many professionals viewed the 1961 AAMR definition of mental retardation as an improvement over previous definitions, but it was not received without criticism. The concept of adaptive behavior caused considerable debate. Clausen (1972b) argued that the procedures for evaluating adaptive behavior were not adequate for diagnosis. This argument is still waged today, especially in response to the most recent AAMD definition and its suggestion of limitations in adaptive skills areas. Clausen contended that diagnoses of mental retardation should be based solely on the data from psychometric evaluations. He revealed results of an earlier investigation showing that, in spite of the AAMR's inclusion of the concept of adaptive behavior in the definition, diagnoses of mental retardation were frequently made solely on the basis of intelligence test data (Clausen, 1967).

Clausen's proposed psychometric definition was controversial and apparently unpopular, opposed on two basic grounds. First, such a definition could threaten the concept of mental retardation as an alterable or changeable condition. Intelligence test results are quite stable over time; hence, it was possible that important changes in observable behavior would not show on intelligence tests. The second criticism of the psychometric definition was that, on the basis of tests standardized on members of the majority culture, too many children from culturally diverse backgrounds had been misdiagnosed as mentally retarded.

It was generally recognized that the 1961 Heber definition was overinclusive. As pointed out earlier, it was possible to identify statistically almost 16% of the general populations as mentally retarded. Clausen (1972a) suggested that the definition be made more conservative by requiring that an individual IQ score be 2 or more (instead of 1) standard deviations below the mean on an intelligence test. Other professionals recommended that the loose connection between adaptive behavior and intelligence be strengthened. Both positions have been consistently reflected in later revisions of the AAMR definition.

The 1973 AAMD Definition   In 1973, the AAMD committee, now chaired by Grossman, was assigned to review the Manual on Terminology and Classification in Mental Retardation. The definition that emerged stated, "Mental retardation refers to significantly subaverage general intellectual functioning existing concurrently with deficits in adaptive behavior, and manifested during the development period" (Grossman, 1973).

In this version, significantly subaverage intellectual functioning meant performance at least 2 standard deviations below the mean on an intelligence test (i.e., performance comparable to the lower 2.28% of the norm statistically). Adaptive behavior was defined in terms of the degree and efficiency with which the individual meets "the standards of personal independence and social responsibility expected of his age and cultural group" (p. 11). Adaptive behavior was thus considered to be relative to the individual's age and sociocultural group. An expanded set of criteria was provided for the assessment of adaptive behavior.

The 1961 Heber definition included both subaverage intellectual functioning and deficits in adaptive behavior as necessary qualifying conditions for diagnosis.

The relationship between adaptive behavior and intellectual functioning, however, was not clarified sufficiently. Children were consistently labeled mentally retarded on the basis of IQ alone. The two most important distinctions between the 1961 and the 1973 definitions were that (a) subaverage intelligence was defined as 2 standard deviations below the mean, and (b) relationship between adaptive behavior and intelligence was emphasized. Instead of simply requiring intellectual functioning and adaptive behavior to be associated, the committee stated that adaptive behavior deficits and subaverage intellectual functioning had to exist concurrently. In addition, the developmental period was extended from birth to 18 years of age, matching the age when many finish schooling.

In spite of the extension of the developmental period, the 1973 revision was a more conservative definition than those that preceded it. Table 2.2 illustrates this point. According to the 1961 AAMR definition, almost 16% of the general population could have been identified as mentally retarded from a purely psychometric perspective. According to the 1973 definition, less than 3% of the population could be considered mentally retarded from the same perspective. The 1973 revision of the definition resulted in a more than 85% reduction of the number of individuals who could be identified as mentally retarded. This comparison does not indicate the impact of the required connection between adaptive behavior and intelligence, but the two are imperfectly correlated at all levels of performance. Presumably, a number of individuals who might score 2 or more standard deviations below the mean on an intelligence test would not be referred for evaluation if they demonstrated appropriate adaptive skills.

During this time, two significant documents supporting a more conservative, cautious definition of people with mental retardation were published. The first was an article entitled "Special Education for the Mildly Retarded—Is Much of It Justifiable?" by Lloyd Dunn (1968). Dunn, a respected authority in the field of mental retardation and former president of the Council for Exceptional Children, reported that many culturally disadvantaged children were being incorrectly classified as mildly retarded and placed in special classes. The lack of adequate adaptive behavior scales, coupled with the convenient practice of identifying students as mentally retarded on the basis of IQ score alone, fostered the mislabeling of nonretarded children as retarded. Dunn (1968) stated:

> I have loyally supported and promoted special classes for the educable mentally retarded for most of the last 20 years, but with growing disaffection. In my view, much of our past and present practices are morally and educationally wrong. We have been living at the mercy of general educators who have referred our problem children to us. And we have been generally ill prepared and ineffective in educating these children. Let us stop being pressured into continuing and expanding a special education program that we know now to be undesirable for many of the children we are dedicated to serve.
>
> A better education than special class placement is needed for socioculturally deprived children with mild learning problems who have been labeled educable mentally retarded. Over the years, the status of these pupils who come from poverty, broken and inadequate homes, and low status ethnic groups has been a checkered one. (p. 5)

The Six-Hour Retarded Child, published by the President's Committee on Mental Retardation (PCMR, 1970), corroborated Dunn's charge that a significant number

TABLE 2.2

Comparison of Heber, Grossman, and Luckasson et al. AAMR Definitions of Mental Retardation

Term	Heber (1959, 1961)	Grossman (1973)	Grossman (1983)	Luckasson et al. (1992)
General definition	Subaverage general intellectual functioning which originates during the developmental period and is associated with impairment in adaptive behavior.	Significantly subaverage general intellectual functioning existing concurrently with deficits in adaptive behavior and manifested during the developmental period.	Significantly subaverage general intellectual functioning resulting in or associated with concurrent impairments in adaptive behavior and manifested during the developmental period.	Substantial limitations in present functioning. It is characterized by significantly subaverage intellectual functioning, existing concurrently with related limitations in two or more of the following applicable adaptive skill areas: communication, self-care, home living, social skills, community use, self-direction, health and safety, functional academics, leisure, and work. Mental retardation manifests before age 18.
Subaverage	Greater than one standard deviation below the mean.	Significantly subaverage: two or more standard deviations below the mean.	Significantly subaverage: defined as an IQ of 70 or below on standardized measures of intelligence; could be extended upward through IQ 75 or more, depending on the reliability of the intelligence test used.	Similar to Grossman (1983).
Assessment procedure	General intellectual functioning; may be assessed by one or more of the standardized tests developed for that purpose.	Same as Heber.	Same as Heber for intellectual functioning. Adaptive behavior assessed by clinical assessment and standardized scales.	Governed by a series of steps specifying requisite characteristics.
Developmental period	Birth to approximately 16 years.	Birth to 18 years.	Period of time between conception and the 18th birthday.	Similar to Grossman (1983).

of culturally disadvantaged children, especially in urban areas, had been misclassified as mildly retarded and inappropriately placed in special education classes. **Six-hour retarded children** are classified as mentally retarded during the 6 hours they spend in an academic setting but function normally outside school.

Although timely and raising real issues that needed review, the reports by Dunn and the PCMR were emotional, based on systematic observation and a strong philosophical commitment, rather than on rigorous empirical data. Nevertheless, strong face validity existed, and, without question, these two documents had a powerful impact on the field of mental retardation.

TABLE 2.2
(continued)

Term	Heber (1959, 1961)	Grossman (1973)	Grossman (1983)	Luckasson et al. (1992)
Adaptive Behavior	*Impairment in adaptive behavior:* Refers to the effectiveness of the individual to adapt to the natural and social demands of his environment. May be reflected in: 1. Maturation 2. Learning 3. Social adjustment	Defined as effectiveness or degree with which the individual meets the standards of personal independence and social responsibility expected of his age and cultural group. May be reflected in the following areas: *During infancy and early childhood:* 1. Sensory-motor skills development 2. Communication skills 3. Self-help skills 4. Socialization *During childhood and early adolescence:* 5. Application of basic academics in daily life activities 6. Application of appropriate reasoning and judgment in mastery of the environment 7. Social skills *During late adolescence and adult life:* 8. Vocational and social responsibilities and performances	Defined as significant limitations in an individual's effectiveness in meeting the standards of maturation, learning, personal independence, or social responsibility that are expected for his or her age level and cultural group.	Movement from conceptualizing adaptive behavior as a global entity to specification of 10 different adaptive skill areas—as presented in the definition.
Levels of severity	Borderline retardation IQ 68–84 Mild retardation IQ 52–67 Moderate retardation IQ 36–51 Severe retardation IQ 20–35 Profound retardation IQ < 20	——— Mild retardation IQ 52–67 Moderate retardation IQ 36–51 Severe retardation IQ 20–35 Profound retardation IQ < 20	——— Mild retardation IQ 50–55 to approx. 70 Moderate retardation IQ 35–40 to 50–55 Severe retardation IQ 20–25 to 35–40 Profound retardation IQ below 20 or 25 Cannot be determined	Traditional levels abondoned. System advocates use of intensities of needed support that are subclassified into four levels: • intermittent • limited • extensive • pervasive These levels are applied to the adaptive skill areas.

The 1977 AAMD Definition In 1977, the AAMD published its seventh manual on classification and terminology (Grossman, 1977). The wording of the 1977 definition is identical to that of the 1973 version, but the 1977 manual made a few modifications in its interpretation. To begin with, the definition of "significantly subaverage" remained 2 standard deviations below the mean, and the definition of "adaptive behavior" was essentially unchanged. The major change focused on the issue of **clinical judgment**—decision making that is based on the extensive experiences and expertise of an appropriately trained professional. The manual explains in detail the problems of measuring adaptive behavior, yet its importance is highlighted in the following sentence: "For a person to be diagnosed as being mentally retarded, impairments in intellectual functioning must co-exist with deficits in adaptive behavior" (p. 12). The manual goes on to state:

> Individuals with [intelligence] scores slightly above these ceilings [2 standard deviations below the mean] may be diagnosed as mildly retarded during a period when they manifest serious impairments of adaptive behavior. In such cases, the burden is on the examiner to avoid misdiagnosis with its potential stigmatizing effects. (p. 12)

Later, the committee elaborated, stating, "A small minority of persons with IQ's up to 10 points above the guideline ceilings are so impaired in their adaptive behavior that they may be classified as having mild mental retardation" (pp. 19–20).

Although the 1977 definition was worded identically to the 1973 definition, the later manual allowed a diagnosis of mental retardation to be extended to individuals who, according to the previous definition, would not have been so classified.

The 1983 AAMR Definition   In 1983, the AAMR published its eighth manual on classification and terminology. The updated definition read, "Mental retardation refers to significantly subaverage general intellectual functioning resulting in or associated with concurrent impairments in adaptive behavior and manifested during the developmental period" (Grossman, 1983). Clinical judgment remained an important issue—so important, that the appendix cited several short case studies followed by descriptions of the way decisions were reached from the information presented in the cases.

The tone of the manual emphasized that the content was carefully researched and contemplated before publication and that the decisions derived were logical, practical, and consistent with a need to explore a worldwide system of mental retardation. The authors collaborated with representatives of two other major classification systems so that the different systems would be as compatible as possible. The two other systems are the World Health Organization's (1978) system of International Classification of Diseases, Clinical Modification (9th ed.; ICD-9), and the American Psychiatric Association's (1980) *Diagnostic and Statistical Manual of Mental Disorders* (3rd ed.; DSM-III).

The AAMD manual defined *significantly subaverage* as an IQ of 70 or below on a standardized measure of intelligence. Yet this upper limit is intended as a guideline and could be extended to an IQ of 75 or more, provided behavior is impaired and clinically determined to be due to deficits in reasoning and judgment. In this definition, the strict use of standard deviations is discouraged, and the concept of the standard error of measurement inherent in all tests is emphasized.

> Clinicians using the system should be well aware that in determining whether a person is retarded and at what level of intellectual functioning the individual is operating, it is important to understand the concept of standard error of measurement and use it when making a clinical determination of retardation and level of functioning. (AAMR, 1983, p. 7)

No test is perfectly reliable, and some degree of random fluctuation in obtained scores is always expected. The standard error of measurement is an estimate of the degree to which the test scores would be expected to vary because of random error alone. For example, we know that the standard error of measurement on some tests of intelligence is 3 IQ points. If a child received a score of 72 on that test, the examiner should report that the student's true IQ would probably be within the range 69 to 75. The clinician would then decide whether other conditions, such as concurrent deficits in adaptive behavior or cultural difference, were present and associated with the level of performance on the IQ test. According to the 1983 AAMD manual (Grossman, 1983), an individual with an IQ of 75 or higher could be classified as mentally retarded if deficits in adaptive behavior were also present. On the other hand, an IQ of 70 to 67, or perhaps even lower, would not alone provide a sufficient basis for classifying a child from, for example, a minority culture as mentally retarded. The clinician would have to determine to what extent bias affected performance and whether deficits in adaptive behavior were present and associated with the attained level of performance.

You cannot measure something precisely unless you can define it precisely. Intelligence, achievement, and adaptive behavior are ready examples of rather imprecisely defined concepts, as Blatt (1987) emphasized. Therefore, it is naive to treat scores as precise when they are obtained by those measures. The standard error of measurement allows flexibility in interpretation, yet at the same time it provides reasonable structure.

The adaptive behavior component in the 1983 definition remained unchanged, but again, the need for clinical judgment in borderline cases was emphasized. The measurement of adaptive behavior may involve observation, informal interview, or the use of a standardized scale. Adaptive behavior must be compared to norms for the individual's age and cultural group. The manual emphasized throughout that, because of the present state of affairs with adaptive behavior, clinical judgment must be used.

Although the conceptual basis of the developmental period did not change, the range did. The definition stressed that the developmental period begins at conception and extends through age 18.

Even though the 1983 manual was as up-to-date and definitive as possible and was supported by other professional organizations, the committee recognized that, as more data are collected and times change (i.e., as new scientific knowledge and changing social issues arise), the definition of mental retardation will also inevitably change. This is exactly what happened, as a result of the most recent work of the AAMR's Ad Hoc Committee on Terminology and Classification.

The 1992 AAMR Definition   After 4 years of work, the Ad Hoc Committee on Terminology and Classification, chaired by Ruth Luckasson, published the ninth edition of the manual (AAMR, 1992). The new definition signaled many significant changes from its predecessors, as it is much more functional in nature. It stressed the interaction among three major dimensions: a person's capabilities, the environments in which the person functions, and the need for varying levels of support. This interaction and the relationship of these factors to one another are depicted in Figure 2.2.

FIGURE 2.2

General Structure of the
Definition of Mental Retardation

Source: From *Mental Retardation:
Definition, Classification, and Systems
of Supports* (9th ed., p. 10) by the
American Association of Mental
Retardation, 1992, Washington, DC:
American Association on Mental
Retardation. Copyright 1992 by the
American Association on Mental
Retardation. reprinted by permission.

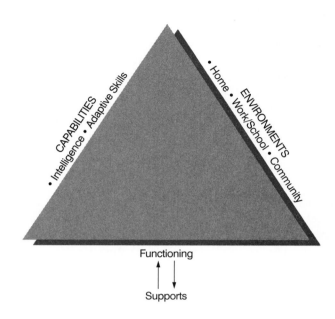

The wording of the most recent definition differed from that of the 1983 version.
Yet, the three major components (intellectual limitations, problems in adaptive areas,
and age of onset) of the previous definitions remain. The 1992 definition reads:

> Mental retardation refers to substantial limitations in present functioning. It is
> characterized by significantly subaverage intellectual functioning, existing concur-
> rently with related limitations in two or more of the following applicable adaptive
> skill areas: communication, self-care, home living, social skills, community use, self-
> direction, health and safety, functional academics, leisure and work. Mental retar-
> dation manifests before age 18. (AAMR, 1992, p. 1)

The following four assumptions are essential to the application of the definition:

1. Valid assessment considers cultural and linguistic diversity, as well as differences in communication and behavioral factors.
2. The existence of limitations in adaptive skills occurs within the context of
   community environments typical of the individual's age peers and is indexed
   to the person's individual needs for supports.
3. Specific adaptive limitations often coexist with strengths in other adaptive
   skills or other personal capabilities.
4. With appropriate supports over a sustained period, the life functioning of the
   person with mental retardation will generally improve. (AAMR, 1992, p. 5)

Although some features of the 1983 definition remain (refer to Table 2.2), significant changes are evident in the 1992 definition. In addition to features already
discussed, the most notable changes follow:

- Specification of adaptive behavior by the identification of 10 adaptive skill
  areas
- A new three-step procedure for diagnosing, classifying, and identifying systems of support (see Figure 2.3).

- A new system for classifying individuals in terms of needed levels of support recommended (discussed in the next section of this chapter) accompanied by the recommendation that reference to the former levels of severity (mild, moderate, severe, and profound) be discontinued
- Development of a profile of needed supports based on four dimensions:
  - Intellectual functioning and adaptive skills
  - Psychological/emotional considerations
  - Physical health/etiology considerations

Dimension I:
Intellectual
Functioning
and Adaptive
Skills
	STEP 1. Diagnosis of mental retardation
	Determines eligibility for supports
	Mental retardation is diagnosed if:
	    1. The individual's intellectual functioning is approximately 70–75 or below.
	    2. There are significant disabilities in two or more adaptive skill areas.
	    3. The age of onset is below 18.

Dimension II:
Psychological/
Emotional
Considerations
 	
Dimension III:
Physical Health/
Etiology
Considerations
 	
Dimension IV:
Environmental
Considerations
	STEP 2. Classification and description
	Identifies strengths and weaknesses and the
	need for supports
	    1. Describe the individual's strengths and weaknesses in reference to psychological/emotional considerations.
	
	    2. Describe the individual's overall physical health and indicate the condition's etiology.
	
	    3. Describe the individual's current environmental placement and the optimal environment that would facilitate his/her continued growth and development.

	STEP 3. Profile and intensities of needed supports
	Identifies needed supports
	Identify the kind and intensities of supports needed for each of the four dimensions.
	    1. Dimension I: Intellectual Functioning and Adaptive Skills
	    2. Dimension II: Psychological/Emotional Considerations
	    3. Dimension III: Physical Health/Etiology Considerations
	    4. Dimension IV: Environmental Considerations

FIGURE 2.3

The Three-Step Process: Diagnosis, Classification, and Systems of Supports

Source: From *Mental Retardation: Definition, Classification, and Systems of Supports* (9th ed., p. 24) by the American Association of Mental Retardation, 1992, Washington, DC: American Association on Mental Retardation. Copyright 1992 by the American Association on Mental Retardation. Reprinted by permission.

- Environmental considerations
- Similarity, in some ways, to other functional definitions of disability (e.g., developmental disabilities)

AAMD/AAMR Systems of Classification
Systems for describing the various levels of mental retardation have been used for decades. The classification scheme that was used widely divided mental retardation into four levels: mild, moderate, severe, and profound.

A constant clamor for changing the classification system has existed for some time. As highlighted earlier, the 1992 AAMR manual suggested a new classification system that abandoned the use of IQ levels. Rather, the ninth edition of the AAMR manual suggests the adoption of a system describing levels of support as a function of the different adaptive skill areas. The four levels of possible needed supports are shown in Figure 2.4. The intent of this system is to explain a person's functional limitations in terms of the degree of support he or she needs to achieve personal growth and development.

Intermittent
Supports on an "as needed basis." Characterized by episodic nature, person not always needing the support(s), or short-term supports needed during life-span transitions (e.g., job loss or an acute medical crisis). Intermittent supports may be high or low intensity when provided.

Limited
An intensity of supports characterized by consistency over time, time-limited but not of an intermittent nature, may require fewer staff members and less cost than more intense levels of support (e.g., time-limited employment training or transitional supports during the school to adult provided period).

Extensive
Supports characterized by regular involvement (e.g., daily) in at least some environments (such as work or home) and not time-limited (e.g., long-term support and long-term home living support).

Pervasive
Supports characterized by their constancy, high intensity; provided across environments; potential life-sustaining nature. Pervasive supports typically involve more staff members and intrusiveness than do extensive or time-limited supports.

FIGURE 2.4
Definition and Examples of Intensities of Supports

Source: From *Mental Retardation: Definition, Classification, and Systems of Supports* (9th ed., p.26) by the American Association of Mental Retardation, 1992, Washington, DC: American Association on Mental Retardation. Copyright 1992 by the American Association on Mental Retardation. reprinted by permission.

CONTEMPORARY DEFINITIONAL PERSPECTIVES

Other definitional efforts, which are alternative to the AAMR definition, have arisen in recent times. In great part, this has occurred because of dissatisfaction with the 1992 AAMR definition and classification guidelines. Smith (1997) points out that various members within the AAMR differed greatly in their opinions of the revised definition. The most critical attacks on the AAMR definition have been waged by Greenspan (1994, 1997), Jacobson and Mulick (1996), and MacMillan and his colleagues (Gresham, MacMillan, & Siperstein, 1995; MacMillan, Gresham, & Siperstein, 1993). Concerns have focused on the following aspects of the definition: the IQ cutoff level, the adaptive skills areas, and the levels of needed supports.

Greenspan (1997) remarks that some important signs are present that indicate displeasure with the 1992 definition. These signs include (a) few state departments adopting the definition, (b) publication of a new manual on mental retardation by the American Psychological Association (Jacobson & Mulick, 1996), and (c) refusal of committees working on revisions of the other definitional manuals to include elements of the AAMR definition. Greenspan goes on to suggest that the publication of the 1992 definition has "served to undermine AAMR's credibility as the 'keeper of the MR definition'" (p. 181)—a distinction that AAMR was arguably able to claim heretofore.

Two alternative definitional perspectives are discussed next. The first is the 1996 definition published by the American Psychological Association (Jacobson & Mulick, 1996). The second definition reflects the most recent thinking of Stephen Greenspan. Interestingly, it is with Greenspan's earlier conceptualizations of social competence that the committee working on the 1992 AAMR definition began their discussions. Both definitional perspectives evolved to a great extent as a result of dissatisfaction with the AAMR definition.

The 1996 American Psychological Association Definition

Spearheaded by Jacobson and Mulick, Division 33 of the American Psychological Association (APA) published its *Manual of Diagnosis and Professional Practice in Mental Retardation* in 1996. The rationale for developing the manual is reflected in its preface: "a comprehensive statement of what MR is, what it means for the individual and society, and how to serve the needs of affected individuals is specifically called for at the present juncture" (p. xiv). APA's definition reads as follows:

> Mental retardation (MR) refers to (a) significant limitations in general intellectual functioning; (b) significant limitations in adaptive functioning, which exist concurrently; and (c) onset of intellectual and adaptive limitations before the age of 22 years. (p. 13)

After inspecting the APA's definition, one realizes that it is essentially a return to the 1983 AAMR definitional constructs with some minor changes. The term *adaptive functioning* is used in place of *adaptive behavior,* and the upper limit of the age of onset has been extended from 18 to 22. The APA manual promotes a classification system that is a return to four ranges of severity: mild, moderate, severe, and profound. As noted in the manual, "Severity is determined by concurrent pres-

TABLE 2.3

Degrees of Mental Retardation

Degree of Mental Retardation	IQ Score Range	IQ Deviation Cutting Point	Extent of Concurrent Adaptive Limitations
Mild	55–70	–2 SD	Two or more domains
Moderate	35–54	–3 SD	Two or more domains
Severe	20–34	–4 SD	All domains
Profound	Below 20	–5 SD	All domains

Note. IQ ranges are approximate due to SE. Limitations in adaptive functioning are relative to expected performance by chronological age and require scores at 22 SD or lower for significance.

Source: From John J. Jacobson and James A. Mulick (Eds.), (1996). *Manual of Diagnosis and Professional Practice in Mental Retardation,* p. 14. Washington, DC: American Psychological Association. Reprinted by permission.

ence of IQ scores within four ranges and adaptive functioning consistent with each range" (Jacobson & Mulick, 1996, p. 14). Table 2.3 depicts the degrees of mental retardation and the relationship of IQ and adaptive functioning.

Professionals with clinical and research interests who liked the 1983 AAMR definition of mental retardation will find solace in the APA's definition. It avoids much of the psychometric dissonance created by the 1992 AAMR definition.

Greenspan's Definition

Initially, some people will find Greenspan's recommendations odious, as they suggest a definitional perspective that attempts to provide a clearer focus on intelligence as the core impairment in mental retardation. However, it is important to recognize that he is proposing a model of intelligence that includes different types of intelligent behavior (i.e., multiple intelligences). Greenspan promotes a tripartite model of intelligence that includes conceptual intelligence (IQ), practical intelligence, and social intelligence as the fundamental components. His conceptualization differs substantially from the multiple intelligence model proposed by Gardner (2000). Fundamentally, he notes that "mental retardation clearly is a cognitive disorder, but cognition can be used for many purposes" (Greenspan, 1997).

Greenspan's proposed definition is as follows:

> Persons who are MR [mentally retarded] are widely perceived to need long-term supports, accommodations or protections due to persistent limitations in social, practical and conceptual intelligence and the resulting inability to meet intellectual demands of a range of settings and roles. These limitations are assumed in most cases to result from abnormalities or events occurring during the development period, and which have permanent effects on brain development and functioning. (p. 186)

This proposed definition of mental retardation contains certain elements of the AAMR orientation (supports, range of settings) while maintaining Greenspan's emphasis on social competence. His classification system includes aspects of the

The definition of mental retardation is a social and political one.

AAMR philosophy and suggests that mental retardation can be divided into three subcategories based on degree of overall disability: limited, extensive, and pervasive. These levels should be based on the need for supports rather than on intellectual dimensions.

TABLE 2.4
Chronology of Definitional Perspectives of Mental Retardation

Author	Definition
Tredgold (1937)	Mental deficiency: "A state of incomplete mental development of such a kind and degree that the individual is incapable of adapting himself to the normal environment of his fellows in such a way to maintain existence independently of supervision, control, or external support."
AAMR (Grossman, 1983)	Mental retardation "refers to significantly subaverage general intellectual functioning resulting in or associated with concurrent impairments in adaptive behavior and manifested during the developmental period."
AAMR (Luckasson et al., 1992)	Mental retardation "refers to substantial limitations in present functioning. It is characterized by significantly subaverage intellectual functioning, existing concurrently with related limitations in two or more of the following applicable adaptive skill areas: *communication, self-care, home living, social skills, community use, self-direction, health and safety, functional academics, leisure and work.* Mental retardation manifests before age 18."
American Psychological Association (Jacobson & Mulick, 1996)	Mental retardation refers to (a) significant limitations in general intellectual functioning; (b) significant limitations in adaptive functioning, which exist concurrently; and (c) onset of intellectual and adaptive limitations before the age of 22 years.

TABLE 2.5
Summary of State Guidelines

State	Term[1]	Definition[2]	IQ Cut-off	Require AB?	Age ceiling	Classification system[3]
Alabama	MR	GV	70	Yes	No	No
Alaska	MR	GA	2 SD	Yes	No	No
Arizona	MR	GA	2 SD	Yes	No	M/M/S/P
Arkansas	MR	GA	No	Yes	No	No
California	MR	GA	No	Yes	No	M/M/S/P
Colorado	SLIC	GA	2 SD	Yes	No	No
Connecticut	MR	GA	2 SD	Yes	No	No
Delaware	MD	GA	70	Yes	No	EMR/TMR/S
District of Columbia	MR	GA	70	Yes	No	M/M/S/P
Florida	MH	GV	2 SD	Yes	No	EMR/TMR/P
Georgia	ID	GV	70	Yes	No	M/M/S/P
Hawaii	MR	GA	2 SD	Yes	No	M/M/S
Idaho	MR	GA	70	Yes	No	No
Illinois	MI	GA	No	Yes	No	M/M/S/P
Indiana	MH	GA	2 SD	Yes	18	M/M/S
Iowa	MD	GV	75	Yes	21	No
Kansas	MR	LV	2 SD	Yes	No	MR/SMD
Kentucky	MD	O	2 SD	Yes	21	M/FMD
Louisiana	MD	GA	70	Yes	No	M/M/S/P
Maine	MR	GA	No	Yes	No	No
Maryland	MR	GV	No	Yes	No	No
Massachusetts	II	O	No	No	No	No
Michigan	MI	O	2 SD	Yes	No	EMR/TMR/S/P
Minnesota	MI	GA	70	Yes	No	M/M/S/P
Mississippi	ED	GA	2 SD	Yes	No	EMR/TMR/S
Missouri	MR	GA	2SD	Yes	18	M/M/S/P

After navigating the maze of actual definitions, and the issues and philosophies associated with them regarding definitions and definitional practices (see Table 2.4), one may be left with solving the problem of determining who is "really" mentally retarded. However, the lesson is not that new definitions are better or more accurate but that the definition of mental retardation is totally a social and political one that rests with the powers that be, and not in the minds of the people who experience intellectual deficits.

OPERATIONALIZING DEFINITIONAL PERSPECTIVES

Previous sections have focused mainly on conceptual issues of definition; now we will look at how definition is put into practice. The relationship between theory and practice in mental retardation is a tenuous one. This section reviews the research that has examined state guidelines in the area of mental retardation, describes some ways that the definition of mental retardation has been operationalized, and presents some of the current issues concerning the roles of intelligence and adaptive behavior in the identification process.

TABLE 2.5
(continued)

State	Term[1]	Definition[2]	IQ Cut-off	Require AB?	Age ceiling	Classification system[3]
Montana	CD	GA	No	Yes	18	No
Nebraska	MH	GA	2 SD	Yes	No	M/M/S/P
Nevada	MR	GA	No	Yes	21	M/M/S/P
New Hampshire	MR	GA	No	Yes	No	No
New Jersey	CI	LA	2 SD	Yes	No	M/S CI
New Mexico	ID	GA	No	Yes	No	No
New York	MR	GA	1.5 SD	Yes	No	No
North Carolina	MD	GA	70	Yes	No	EMR/TMR
North Dakota	MR	GV	70	Yes	18	EMR/TMR
Ohio	DH	GV	80	Yes	No	DH
Oklahoma	MR	GA	2 SD	Yes	18	No
Oregon	MR	GA	2 SD	Yes	No	No
Pennsylvania	MR	GA	80	Yes	No	No
Rhode Island	MR	GA	70	Yes	Yes	M/M/S/P
South Carolina	MD	GV	70	Yes	18	EMR/TMR
South Dakota	MR	GA	70	Yes	18	No
Tennessee	MR	LA	74	Yes	No	No
Texas	MR	GA	2 SD	Yes	No	No
Utah	ID	GA	No	Yes	No	No
Vermont	LI	GA	70	Yes	No	No
Virginia	MR	GA	No	Yes	No	EMR/TMR
Washington	MR	GA	2 SD	Yes	No	No
West Virginia	MI	LA	70–75	Yes	18	M/M/S/P
Wisconsin	CD	GV	70–75	Yes	No	M/M/S/P
Wyoming	MD	GA	No	Yes	No	No

[1]CD = cognitively delayed/cognitive disability, CI = cognitive impairment, DH = developmentally handicapped. ED = educational disability, ID = intellectual disability, II = intellectual impairment, LI = learning impairments, MD = mental disability, MNH = mentally handicapped, MI = mental impairment, MR = mental retardation, SLIC = significantly limited intellectual capacity.

[2]GA = Grossman adapted, GV = Grossman verbatim, LA = Luckasson adapted, LV = Luckasson verbatim, O = other.

[3]EMR = educable mentally retarded, M/FMD = mild and functional metal disability, M/M = mild/moderate, M/SCD = mild and sever cognitive disability, P = profound, S = sever, SMD = severe multiple disabilities, TMR = trainable mentally retarded.

Source: Denning et al. (2000).

State Guidelines

Past studies of various aspects of state departments of education guidelines for defining, identifying, and classifying students with mental retardation (Frankenburg, 1984; Huberty, Koller, & Ten Brink, 1980; Patrick & Reschly, 1982; Utley, Lowitzer, & Baumeister, 1987) have regularly found a great deal of interstate variability. Inconsistency is common in terminology, the adoption of the federal definition of mental retardation (1983 AAMR definition—Grossman, 1983), and (when adopted) the implementation of that definition as originally intended. A sense of

To read about the practical implications of definitions developed at the state level, go to the companion website www.prenhall.com/beirne-smith and select Chapter 2, and then choose the Article Response module.

this interstate variation can be gleaned from the findings of two studies of state guidelines in relation to definition, identification criteria, and classification systems that have been conducted.

The first study, conducted by Utley and colleagues in the latter 1980s, highlighted the reality that little commonality across states existed in terms of implementation. This study includes the following major findings:

- Only 56% of the states used the term *mental retardation*.
- Sixty-one percent of the states cited the AAMR definition.
- Eighty-four percent of the states provided intelligence criteria.
- Only 61% of the states emphasized adaptive behavior.
- Only 10% of the states identified instruments, cutoff points, or deficit areas in adaptive behavior.
- Seventy-four percent used a classification system of some type (only 14% used the AAMR's four-level system).

The second study, conducted in the late 1990s by Denning, Chamberlain, and Polloway (2000), was interested in determining the degree of an impact the 1992 AAMR definition had on practice. These researchers found that once again little commonality existed across states. Furthermore, the most recent AAMR definition has had minimal impact on practice (i.e., changing state guidelines). Table 2.5 provides state-by-state and District of Columbia data.

Two Educational Examples of Operationalization

Two examples of how states have put into practice the conceptual elements of the definition of mental retardation are presented in this section. The first example, from Iowa, illustrates a methodology that incorporates the traditional elements (intellectual functioning, adaptive behavior, and developmental period) associated with definition and educational performance aspects. The second example, from Connecticut, provides a framework that utilizes contemporary conceptualizations of mental retardation.

Iowa Perspective   In 1996 and 1997, Iowa developed technical assistance guidelines for assisting with the identification of students with *mental disabilities,* the term used in this state. The major objective was to operationalize criteria that were based on the definition used in Iowa. The guidelines presented here are the result of a year-long collaborative effort of a study group composed of a variety of participants, including parents, teachers, administrators, support personnel, and other professionals.

For a student to be classified as mentally disabled, the individual must meet all four criteria (Mauer, 1997, p. 192):

1. Intellectual Functioning
   a. The assessment of intellectual functioning must include a variety of information sources, and the determination of mental disability is the responsibility of the entire multidisciplinary team
   b. Full scale IQ score of 75 or less

   2. Adaptive Behavior
      a. Must include direct measures as well as indirect measures that evaluate the individual's performance in comparison to same-age peers from similar cultural backgrounds
      b. Deficits identified in 2 or more adaptive skill areas
   3. Developmental Period
      a. Age 21 and below
      b. Significant discrepancies persist for more than 1 year
   4. Educational Performance
      a. Evaluate the individual's performance in the context of his or her current environment
      b. Deficits identified in all core academic areas (math, reading, language arts, science)
      c. Significant deficit means the individual scores at least one standard deviation below the mean of the national standardization sample
      d. Standardized measures must be further validated by in-school data that documents differences between the individual's performance and the performance of same-age peers from the same cultural background
      e. Assessment of academic performance must also include documentation of resistance to general education interventions

Connecticut Perspective   Connecticut's Department of Education has recently published its *Guidelines for Identifying Children with Intellectual Disability/ Mental Retardation* (State of Connecticut, 2000). What makes the Connecticut situation so unique is that the definition of mental retardation used in the state is based on Greenspan's conceptualization of personal competence.

The guidelines state, "Intellectual disability means significant deficits in conceptual, practical and social intelligence that adversely affect a student's educational performance and are manifested during the developmental period (birth to age 18)." A student must demonstrate deficits in all three components of intellectual competence. Specific eligibility criteria for each of the component intelligences are provided in the guidelines.

The Connecticut initiative is noteworthy because it is highly innovative, and those responsible for gaining approval of this plan should be applauded. Nevertheless, it comes with great challenges, such as getting diagnosticians, school psychologists, and other school-based personnel to accept a different way of doing things. It will also be interesting to see what effect this system has on incidence and prevalence figures, a topic discussed in the last section of this chapter. Professional attention will be focused on the Connecticut experiment over the next few years.

Practice Realities

In many settings across the country, IQ has played and continues to play the dominant role in the decision-making process (Furlong & LeDrew, 1985; Polloway & Smith, 1987). Assessment of adaptive behavior is not being used in the ways that have been suggested.

For a number of plausible reasons, less importance is given to evaluation of adaptive behavior than to IQ. Zigler, Balla, and Hodapp (1984) contention that the concept is "too elusive and ill-defined to be a criterion of mental retardation" (p. 218) is still relevant today. Zucker and Polloway (1987) offer another explanation:

> The concept of adaptive behavior has neither the psychometric history of IQ nor the stability across settings expected by diagnosticians for other scores. Although these concerns may actually represent strengths of adaptive behavior measures, their effect has been to prevent full utility of the measures. (p. 71)

Whatever the reason, adaptive behavior takes a back seat to intellectual functioning in the decision-making process. This reality undermines the value of deter-

FIGURE 2.5

A Scheme of Use of Adaptive Behavior Information in Mental Retardation Classification

Source: From "Incorporating Adaptive Behavior Deficits into Instructional Programs" by D. J. Reschly in *Best Practices in Mental Disabilities* (Vol. 2) edited by J. R. Patton, E. A. Polloway, and L. R. Sargent, 1988, Des Moines, IA: Department of Education. Copyright 1988 by Des Moines, IA, Department of Education. Adapted by permission.

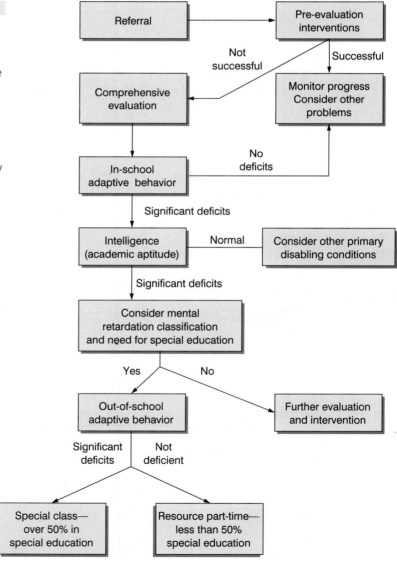

mining typical behavioral regimens and may be a disservice to many students at the margin of eligibility.

What options does this situation leave us? We offer four different ideas. The first is to abandon the use of adaptive behavior as a criterion, as Zigler et al. (1984) suggest. They argue that mental retardation should be defined and assessed solely in terms of intellectual functioning. Greenspan's (1997) conceptualization of mental retardation fits this orientation, as his model stresses intelligence, albeit multiple intelligences. If, however, only conceptual intelligence is being considered, then this is too narrow a view of the terrain. Furthermore, it raises problems when we consider students whose linguistic, cultural, and economic backgrounds are significantly different from those of the majority population.

A second suggestion is that new, innovative assessment systems be developed. These could be based on multiple intelligence conceptualizations or incorporate behaviorally or functionally based measures.

The third view is grounded in the reality that adaptive behavior will continue to be a second-class citizen in the identification process. Instead of being a criterion, it should play a supporting role in (a) justifying eligibility for individuals with IQs above 70, (b) questioning the certification of an individual with an IQ below 70 but with acceptable adaptive behavior skills, and (c) influencing placement and curricular decisions. This may not be the most desirable solution, but it may best reflect reality.

The fourth and last perspective is more stouthearted. It argues that we should continue to strive to develop a system in which in-school and out-of-school aspects of adaptive behavior play a key role. One conceptualization of such an idea has been promoted by Reschly (1988) and is presented in Figure 2.5. The overriding goal is to identify students in need and provide services to them in the most appropriate manner.

INCIDENCE AND PREVALENCE

Prevention and treatment are two of the most pressing issues in the field of mental retardation. To determine causal factors and to deliver services and treatment efficiently, professionals have used estimates of the frequency of mental retardation: incidence and prevalence. Although the words *incidence* and *prevalence* are considered synonymous in some contexts, they have two distinctly different meanings.

Terminology Defined

Incidence refers to the number of new cases identified within a population over a specific period of time. The data for most estimates of incidence are obtained from cases that were clinically identified when individuals entered some form of intervention. Incidence figures are valuable for investigating the causes of a disability and developing prevention programs. For example, researchers have found that maternal age at a child's birth and the incidence of the chromosomal aberration that results in Down syndrome are related. That relationship was determined by comparing the incidence rates of Down syndrome births with populations of mothers from different age ranges. The incidence rate is higher for older mothers.

A Personal View of Retardation

Very seldom do we attempt to consider retardation from the eyes and minds of those whom we so label. This approach, referred to as a phenomenological perspective, provides another vantage point from which to understand retardation.

Katie Tager, 32, resides at a semi-independent living apartment building. She is mildly retarded, but that doesn't stop her from keeping her own apartment, contributing to the community, and being actively involved with other people.

She is putting together two books: *Accepting Me*, a collection of her poems and writings, and *Let Special People Be Free*, a volume of essays, poems, personal stories, and artwork by adults and children with disabilities.

The following poem of Katie's was published in *Arts Access*, a newsletter of the Very Special Arts in Hawaii.

> **Accepting Me**
> accepting me for who
> I am some people find
> it hard to do
> They don't see my disability
> I tell them I am mildly
> retarded but they don't
> believe me
> I tell them some disabilities
> you can see but its
> in my head where it
> happen to me
> I think and do things
> slower than you and
> sometimes its hard for
> me to understand what
> you find easy to know
> I try and learn the
> best I can and accept
> what I am not able to
> do
> Try accepting me you
> will see how much it means to me
> Its not hard to under
> stand and be my friend
> then you'll accept me
> for who I am.

Source: From an item written by John Oh for *Arts Access.*

Although researchers have not determined why chromosomal aberrations are more frequent among older mothers than younger ones, the relationship between maternal age and the incidence of Down syndrome leads to possibilities for prevention.

Prevalence refers to the total number of cases of some condition existing within a population at a particular place or at a particular time. Unlike incidence, prevalence is not concerned with the number of new cases. Therefore, it is not as useful in determining causal relationships. Prevalence statistics are, however, better than incidence statistics for determining need for services. Prevalence rates are frequently represented as percentages.

Prevalence may be conceptualized in two ways: identifiable and true (Grossman, 1983). *Identifiable prevalence* refers to the cases that have come in contact with some system. *True prevalence*, which is a larger figure, assumes that several people who may meet the definitional criteria of mental retardation exist unrecognized by our systems. True prevalence does not include those who once met criteria but no longer do so.

For several reasons, variations in estimates of the incidence and prevalence of mental retardation have been found across studies and populations. Among factors influencing the incidence and prevalence of mental retardation are differences in criteria and methodologies of the researchers and gender, age, community, race, and sociopolitical factors of the group under investigation. We look at each of these factors next.

Factors Associated with Prevalence Rates

Definitional Perspective   The difficulty defining retardation is reflected by the number of reviews on the prevalence of mental retardation that mention the imprecision in definition and general haziness of the concept. For example, in 1959, G. O. Johnson criticized one of the most widely quoted surveys that had been conducted (Census of Referred Suspected Mental Retardation, conducted in Onondaga County, New York, in 1953). He did so because it used a broad definition of mental retardation and, therefore, possibly reported more cases of mental retardation than actually existed according to generally accepted definitions.

It is not unusual for prevalence figures to be estimated without a survey ever being conducted. Hypothetical prevalence statistics can be projected from formal definitions of mental retardation that rely entirely on psychometric data or depend substantially on such data (e.g., earlier AAMR definitions).

If IQ were the only criterion for defining mental retardation, approximately 2.3 percent of the population could be considered mentally retarded. In fact, the United States Office of Education reported in 1971–1972 that 2.3% of the school-age population was mentally retarded (0.8%, moderate or severe; 1.5%, mild). The PCMR estimated that approximately 3% of the population were mentally retarded. However, the validity of the figure of 3% prevalence, which was cited widely in previous times, has been seriously challenged. As early as 1973, prevalence estimates of 1% were being favored (Mercer, 1973a). Most contemporary definitional perspectives of mental retardation suggest a prevalence figure that is below 1%.

Gender   In general, more males than females are identified as mentally retarded at all age levels. Three explanations attempt to account for these gender differences in prevalence. First, biological defects associated with the X chromosome have a greater probability of being manifested by males than by females. Second, it appears that different child-rearing practices and different social demands are associated with gender differences in prevalence. For example, aggressive behavior for males is typically reinforced during child rearing. An aggressive boy who is mentally retarded may not perceive the differences between appropriate and inappropriate situations for being aggressive. Individuals who exhibit behavior problems have greater chances of being identified as retarded than those who do not. Finally, society's demands for self-sufficiency traditionally have been higher for males than females (Robinson & Robinson, 1976); a lower degree of self-sufficiency is a marker for mental retardation, perhaps leading to males being disproportionately classified.

Community Variables   Communities vary in their ability to absorb individuals with limited talents. For example, people are more apt to be identified as mentally retarded in urban communities than in rural ones (MacMillan, 1982). That variation has been subject to different interpretations. First, urban communities are generally perceived as more complex than rural communities. It is commonly believed that the social demands of urban communities are, therefore, more difficult to meet. In the past, individuals with borderline retardation from urban districts were more likely to be identified as mentally retarded, because urban districts tend to have better-developed referral and diagnostic services. Some marginal cases may never be formally diagnosed in rural districts.

Socioeconomic conditions within communities are also related to differences in prevalence rates. Children who are born and reared in less-enriched, lower socioeconomic groups are more likely to be labeled mentally retarded than children from suburban settings. Many attempts have been made to account for the much higher rates of mental retardation among children from lower socioeconomic groups and deprived environments. Interestingly, prevalence figures indicate that, as the severity of retardation increases, cultural and socioeconomic factors become less pronounced. In other words, just as many wealthy families as poor families have children with severe retardation.

Prevalence figures also vary according to a country's level of development. In less developed countries, the situation is paradoxical, as the Committee on Terminology and Classification of the AAMR noted (Grossman, 1983):

> In underdeveloped countries lacking mass immunization programs, proper nutrition, hygiene and sanitation, prenatal care for pregnant women, and other public health services, the incidence of mental retardation and other disorders is high. Under these conditions, whereas incidence may be high, prevalence may be comparatively lower because of excessive infant mortality. (p. 75)

Another relevant fact is that such characteristics as literacy and cognitive ability, which are highly valued in more developed and literate societies, may not be so important in settings that are largely subsistence oriented and have little if any interest or means to identify individuals who might have mental retardation.

Sociopolitical Factors   Evidence suggests that prevalence is influenced significantly by prevailing attitudes, policy, and practices. For instance, since the implementation of PL 94-142, the number of students classified as mentally retarded by school systems throughout the United States has dropped substantially. Polloway and Smith (1983) noticed this trend early on. Analyzing federal data for the period 1976–1981, they found that the number of students between the ages of 3 and 21 served under PL 94-142 and PL 89-313 dropped approximately 13%. An update of these changes (see Figure 2.6) through 1998 indicates that, in general, there has been a significant decrease in the student population. However, in recent years, a slight increase has occurred. It is important to note that not all states and, for that matter, not all local education agencies have experienced the same exact trends. In the aggregate, however, fewer students are identified as mentally retarded, since the federal mandate for special education was implemented in the mid-1970s.

The prevalence rates of students with mild forms of retardation have been most affected by a range of sociopolitical factors, which are highlighted next. This issue has become so acute that the viability of the concept of mild mental retardation has been questioned (MacMillan, Gresham, & Siperstein, 1996). MacMillan et al. argue that mild mental retardation "differs markedly from other cases of mental retardation" (p. 357) and recommend that a new term be used to describe this displaced group of students.

Why this dramatic change? In large part it is because of sociopolitical factors that influenced how we identify and serve students who are decidedly below the norm. One important reason for this change is a more conservative posture on

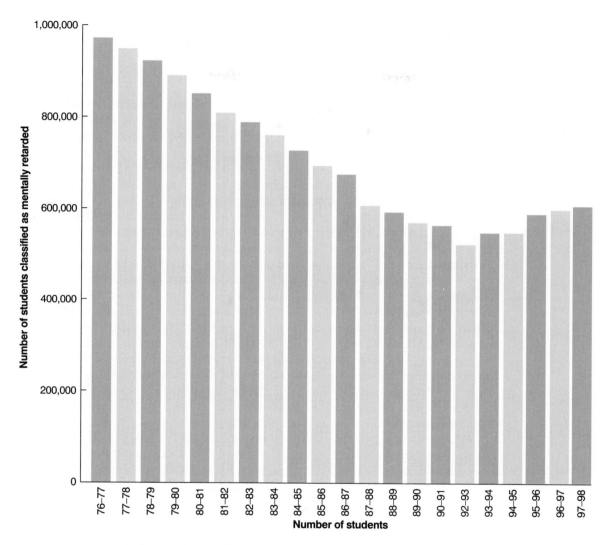

FIGURE 2.6
School-Identified Population (1976–1998)

identifying students as mentally retarded, especially if they are from culturally diverse backgrounds. Professionals in the field are noticeably wary, as they should be, of the misdiagnosis and misplacement of students who are linguistically and culturally diverse. Another reason is that a number of higher-functioning students formerly identified as retarded are now receiving special education services elsewhere. Some students with mild cognitive limitations are now served under the category of learning disabilities—a label that is less stigmatizing than that of mentally retarded. Other factors are also playing a critical role in the changing numbers of students with mental retardation, such as the positive effects of early intervention efforts. Nevertheless, it is important to remember that much of what happens to people who are mentally retarded, including how many of them are so identified, is a function of prevailing social opinion and policy.

FINAL CONSIDERATIONS

The enactment of PL 94-142 and its expanded provisions as amended (1983, 1986, 1990, and 1997) gave official recognition to the importance of developing case registers of individuals with disabilities. That law required local education agencies to conduct and document efforts to identify all children at risk residing within their jurisdiction (i.e., child find). After they have been identified as being at risk, the children must be evaluated to determine whether they are disabled and thus qualify for educational and related services. This task is enormous.

Most policy decisions result either directly or indirectly in allocations of resources to meet goals. Public policy makers include the president, members of federal and state legislatures, county commissioners, school administrators, professional organizations (e.g., Council for Exceptional Children), and special interest groups. Most persons who make or affect policies related to people who are mentally retarded are not professionals in the field. All of them, however, are involved in making decisions about the relative importance of different goals and deciding the appropriate expenditures of resources to meet each goal. Policymakers must identify the most beneficial set of goals and allocate the necessary resources. The prudence and the equity of policy decisions affecting those with mental retardation depend heavily on the decision makers' understanding of the demography of this group.

In 1978, the National Institute of Handicapped Research funded a project to establish a means of providing national estimates of the incidence, prevalence, and other demographic characteristics of Americans with disabilities. The purpose of this effort was to provide an adequate statistical base for policy. Roistacher, Holstrom, Cantril, and Chase (1982) note that by 1978 more than 80 federal agencies (plus many more state and local agencies) were providing services to people with disabilities. Many of the agencies collected incidence, prevalence, and demographic data, but most agencies had different legislative mandates, resulting in different purposes for collecting data. Ultimately, the collected data lacked comparability across agencies. Roistacher et al. state that different definitions and data collection methodologies made aggregation of data impossible. Although definitional and methodological problems can be reduced, these researchers believe that developing an adequate statistical base for policymaking would be beneficial. Furthermore, while knowing that the numbers of people identified as mentally retarded is important, we are only beginning to learn about their demographic and clinical characteristics, attitudes and aspirations, service experiences, and adult outcomes. Collecting such information is important, but data at the national level reflecting a realistic picture of current events are needed if policymakers are to make informed decisions.

To understand the term *mental retardation*, we must begin by establishing a definition. Historically, a variety of attempts has been made to define concisely the condition implied by this term and its precursors. The AAMR definitions of Heber (1959, 1961) and Grossman (1973, 1977, 1983) have reflected the essential dual dimension of the concept of retardation. The most recent AAMR definition (AAMR, 1992) represents a more functional perspective. Nevertheless, professionals continue to question and suggest alternatives, and further evolution is inevitable.

Classification involves delineating specific subgroups of persons who are mentally retarded. This task has given rise to a variety of systems and specific terms. Historically, approaches have categorized persons according to level of severity (e.g., the AAMR system). The current AAMR system now recommends that (a) classification be determined on the basis of levels of support across adaptive skill areas and (b) current systems based on IQ levels be abandoned. Yet, in practice, former systems of classification endure.

Prevalence figures in mental retardation have proven to be difficult to establish; significantly wide ranges have been reported in the literature. Although 3% used to be cited by the government as an estimate of the prevalence of retardation, there is generally no support for this figure today. Most professionals suggest prevalence rates of less than 1%. Additional concerns in prevalence relate to variations based on gender, community environment, and sociopolitical factors.

To check your understanding of this chapter, go to the companion website at www.prenhall.com/ beirne-smith and select Chapter 2, then choose the Self-Test module.

Summary

Mental Retardation in Context
- Mental retardation is a complex condition.
- The condition is characterized by substantial limitations in present levels of functioning.
- Mental retardation encompasses a heterogeneous group of people with varying needs.
- The definition of developmental disabilities overlaps significantly with the AAMR (1992) definition of mental retardation.
- Some professionals suggest that mental retardation be considered a social invention.

Terminology
- Various terms have been used formally to refer to mental retardation.
- Many nonprofessionals confuse the concepts of mental retardation and mental illness.

Disablism and Mental Retardation
- Many groups of people are not perceived favorably in today's society.
- *Disablism* is a term that refers to stereotyping, prejudice, and discrimination based on apparent or assumed physical, mental, or behavioral differences.
- Media portrayals of individuals with mental retardation provide both negative and positive examples.

Defining Mental Retardation
- Early definitions stressed the concept of social competence.
- The definitions developed by the AAMR have typically included three major components: subaverage mental functioning, deficits in adaptive behavior, and occurrence during the developmental period.
- The most recent AAMR (1992) definition represents a more functional perspective to explaining the condition.
- Mental retardation can be classified in a number of ways, with the most common being etiological, intellectual, or behavioral.

- Traditional levels of mental retardation include mild, moderate, severe, and profound.
- The AAMR (1992) system advocates the abandonment of levels based on IQ and recommends that classification be determined on the basis of levels of needed support across adaptive areas.

Contemporary Definitional Perspectives

- Alternative definitions exist, and others will be developed.
- New definitions have emerged—mostly in response to dissatisfaction with the AAMR definition.
- The American Psychological Association developed a definition that was similar to earlier versions of the AAMR definition.
- Greenspan recommends a definition that includes the concept of personal competence and multiple intelligences.

Operationalizing Definitional Perspectives

- The relationship between what is discussed theoretically and what is put into practice can vary greatly.
- Research suggests that no one definition is used consistently in the United States.
- Two models developed by Connecticut and Iowa highlight the ways the definition is being interpreted.
- IQ continues to have more importance in determining whether a student qualifies as being mentally retarded.

Incidence and Prevalence

- The terms *incidence* (i.e., number of new cases) and *prevalence* (i.e., number of existing cases) refer to different types of statistical concepts.
- Prevalence figures have been difficult to determine, with a wide range of figures reported in the literature.
- Most professionals believe prevalence rates to be less than 1%.
- Estimates of incidence and prevalence are influenced by definitional perspectives, gender, community contexts, and sociopolitical factors.

References

American Association on Mental Retardation. (1992). *Mental retardation: Definition, classification, and systems of support* (9th ed.). Washington, DC: Author.

American Psychiatric Association. (1980). *Diagnostic and statistical manual of mental disorders* (3rd ed.). Washington, DC: Author.

Bijou, S. W. (1966). A functional analysis of retarded development. *International Review of Research in Mental Retardation, 1,* 1–19.

Blatt, B. (1987). *The conquest of mental retardation.* Austin, TX: PRO-ED.

Bogdan, R. (1986). The sociology of special education. In R. J. Morris & B. Blatt (Eds.), *Special education: Research and trends* (pp. 344–359). New York: Pergamon.

Bogdan, R., & Biklen, D. (1977). Handicapism. *Social Policy, 7*(5)*,* 59–63.

Clausen, J. A. (1967). Mental deficiency: Development of a concept. *American Journal of Mental Deficiency, 71,* 727–745.

Clausen, J. A. (1972a). The continuing problem of defining mental deficiency. *Journal of Special Education, 6,* 97–106.

Clausen, J. A. (1972b). Quo vadis, AAMD? *Journal of Special Education, 6,* 52–60.

Denning, C. B., Chamberlain, J. A., & Polloway, E. A. (2000). An evaluation of state guidelines for mental retardation: Focus on definition and classification practices. *Education and Training in Mental Retardation and Developmental Disabilities, 35,* 226–232.

Doll, E. A. (1941). The essential of an inclusive concept of mental deficiency. *American Journal of Mental Deficiency, 46,* 214–229.

Dunn, L. M. (1968). Special education for the mildly retarded—Is much of it justifiable? *Exceptional Children, 35,* 5–22.

Dunn, L. M. (Ed.). (1973). *Exceptional children in the schools: Special education in transition* (2nd ed.). New York: Holt, Rinehart, & Winston.

Frankenburg, W. K. (1984). A survey of state guidelines for identification of mental retardation. *Mental Retardation, 22*(1), 17–20.

Furlong, M. J., & LeDrew, L. (1985). IQ = 68 = mildly retarded? Factors influencing multidisciplinary team recommendations on children with FS IQs between 63 and 75. *Psychology in the Schools, 22,* 5–9.

Gardner, H. (2000). *Intelligence reframed: Multiple intelligences for the 21st century.* New York: Basic Books.

Gold, M. W. (1980). An alternative definition of mental retardation. In M. W. Gold (Ed.), *"Did I say that?" Articles and commentary on the Try Another Way System* (pp. 145–150). Champaign, IL: Research Press.

Greenspan, S. (1994). Review of the 1992 AAMR manual. *American Journal of Mental Retardation, 98,* 544–549.

Greenspan, S. (1997). Dead manual walking? Why the 1992 AAMR definition needs redoing. *Education and Training in Mental Retardation and Developmental Disabilities, 32,* 179–190.

Greenspan, S., & Driscoll, J. (1997). The role of intelligence in a broad model of personal competence. In D. P. Flanagan, J. O. Genshaft, & P. L. Harrison (Eds.), *Contemporary intellectual assessment: Theories, tests, and issues* (pp. 131–150). Mahwah, NJ: Erlbaum.

Gresham, F.M., MacMillan, D.L., & Siperstein, G.N. (1995). Critical analysis of the 1992 AAMR definition: Implications for school psychology. *School Psychology Quarterly, 10,* 1–19.

Grossman, H. J. (Ed.). (1973). *Manual on terminology and classification in mental retardation.* Washington, DC: American Association on Mental Retardation.

Grossman, H. J. (Ed.). (1977). *Manual on terminology and classification in mental retardation.* Washington, DC: American Association on Mental Retardation.

Grossman, H. J. (Ed.). (1983). *Classification in mental retardation.* Washington, DC: American Association on Mental Retardation.

Grossman, H. J., & Tarjan, G. (1987). *AMA handbook on mental retardation.* Chicago: American Medical Association, Division of Clinical Science.

Guttmacher, M., & Weihofen, H. (1952). *Psychiatry and the law.* New York: Norton.

Heber, R. E. (1959). A manual on terminology and classification in mental retardation. *Monograph Supplement to the American Journal of Mental Deficiency, 62*.

Heber, R. E. (1961). A manual on terminology and classification in mental retardation (rev. ed.). *Monograph Supplement to the American Journal of Mental Deficiency, 64*.

Hilliard, L. T., & Kirman, B. H. (1965). *Mental deficiency* (2nd ed.). London: Churchill.

Huberty, T. J., Koller, J. R., & Ten Brink, T. D. (1980). Adaptive behavior in the definition of mental retardation. *Exceptional Children, 46,* 256–261.

Itard, J. M. (1962). Wild boy of Aveyron. (G. Humphrey & M. Humphrey, Eds. & Trans.). New York: Appleton-Century-Crofts. (Original work published 1801)

Jacobson, J. W., & Mulick, J. A. (1996). *Manual on diagnosis and professional practice in mental retardation.* Washington, DC: American Psychological Association.

Johnson, G.O. (1959). Here and there in the Onandaga census—Fact or artifact. *Exceptional Children, 25,* 226–231.

Kolstoe, O. P. (1972). *Mental retardation: An educational viewpoint.* New York: Holt, Rinehart, & Winston.

MacMillan, D. L. (1982). *Mental retardation in school and society.* Boston: Little, Brown.

MacMillan, D.L., Gresham, F.M., & Siperstein, G.N. (1993). Conceptual and psychometric concerns over the 1992 AAMR definition of mental retardation. *American Journal of Mental Retardation, 98,* 325–335.

MacMillan, D. L., Gresham, F. M., & Siperstein, G. N. (1996). A challenge to the viability of mild mental retardation as a diagnostic category. *Exceptional Children, 62,* 356–371.

Mercer, J. R. (1973a). *Labeling the mentally retarded.* Berkeley: University of California Press.

Mercer, J. R. (1973b). The myth of 3% prevalence. In G. Tarjan, R. K. Eyman, & C. E. Meyers (Eds.), *Sociobehavioral studies in mental retardation: Monographs of the American Association on Mental Deficiency, 1,* 1–8. Washington, DC: American Association on Mental Deficiency.

Patrick, J. L., & Reschly, D. L. (1982). Relationship of state educational criteria and demographic variables to school-system prevalence of mental retardation. *American Journal of Mental Deficiency, 86,* 351–360.

Penrose, L. S. (1966). *The biology of mental defect* (rev. ed.). Orlando, FL: Grune & Stratton.

Polloway, E. A., & Smith, J. D. (1983). Changes in mild mental retardation: Population, programs, and perspectives. *Exceptional Children, 50,* 149–159.

Polloway, E. A., & Smith, J. D. (1987). Current status of the mild mental retardation construct: Identification, placement, and programs. In M. C. Wang, M. C. Reynolds, & H. J. Wahlberg (Eds.), *The handbook of special education: Research and practice* (pp. 1–22). New York: Pergamon.

President's Committee on Mental Retardation. (1970). *The six-hour retarded child.* Washington, DC: U.S. Government Printing Office.

Reschly, D. (1988). Incorporating adaptive behavior deficits into instructional programs. In G. A. Robinson, J. R. Patton, E. A. Polloway, & L. R. Sargent (Eds.), *Best practices in mental disabilities* (Vol. 2, pp. 53–80). Des Moines: Iowa State Department of Education.

Robinson, N. K., & Robinson, H. B. (1976). *The mentally retarded child* (2nd ed.). New York: McGraw-Hill.

Roistacher, R. C. Holstrom, E. I., Cantrill, A. H. & Chase, J. T. (1982). *Toward a comprehensive data system on the demographic and epidemiological characteristics of the handicapped population: Final report.* Washington, DC: National Institute of Handicapped Research. (ERIC Document Reproduction Service No. ED 182-465)

Smith, J. D. (1997). Mental retardation as an educational construct: Time for a new shared view? *Education and Training in Mental Retardation and Developmental Disabilities, 32,* 167–173.

State of Connecticut. (2000). *Guidelines for identifying children with intellectual disability/mental retardation.* Hartford: State of Connecticut, Department of Education.

Tredgold, A. F. (1937). *A textbook of mental deficiency.* Baltimore: Wood.

Utley, C. A., Lowitzer, A. C., & Baumeister, A. A. (1987). A comparison of the AAMD's definition, eligibility criteria, and classification schemes with state departments of education guidelines. *Education and Training in Mental Retardation, 22,* 35–43.

Wolfensberger, W. (1985). An overview of social role valorization and some reflections on elderly mentally retarded persons. In M. P. Janicki & H. M. Wisniewski (Eds.), *Expanding systems of service delivery for persons with developmental disabilities* (pp. 127–148). Baltimore: Brookes.

World Health Organization. (1978). *International classification on diseases* (9th ed.). Washington, DC: Author.

Zigler, E., Balla, D. A., & Hodapp, R. (1984). On the definition and classification of mental retardation. *American Journal of Mental Deficiency, 89,* 215–230.

Zucker, S. H. & Polloway, E. A. (1987). Issues in identification and assessment in mental retardation. *Education and Training in Mental Retardation, 22,* 69–76.

3

Assessment of Mental Retardation

OBJECTIVES

After reading this chapter, the student should be able to

- discuss different types of theories of intelligence and intellectual development
- identify and describe different instruments used in the practice of intelligence testing today
- discuss different types of theories of adaptive functioning
- identify and describe different instruments used in the practice of adaptive behavior assessment today

To review the chapter objectives on-line, go to the companion website at www.prenhall.com/beirne-smith and select Chapter 3, and then choose the Objectives module.

KEY TERMS

adaptive behavior
American Association on Mental Retardation
assessment
deviation IQ

nature–nurture
Stanford-Binet IV
Wechsler scales

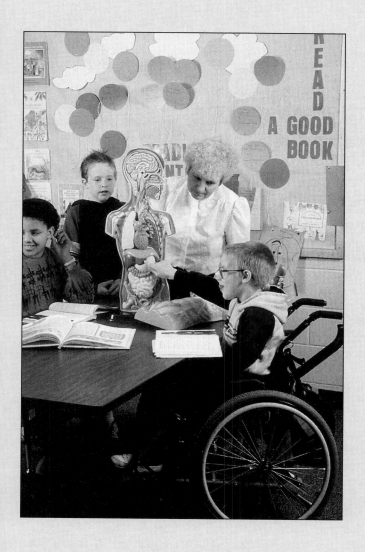

Assessment of mental and special abilities covers a wide range of activities. Though assessment has been defined in different ways by different people, most agree that it is not so much an activity as a process, dynamic and ongoing, and one that changes with the needs of the individual. **Assessment** is the collection of information for educational, psychological, and vocational decision making.

The importance of testing and assessment is not lost on three of education's most prominent professional associations: the American Educational Research Association, the American Psychological Association, and the National Council on Measurement in Education (1999):

> Educational and psychological testing and assessment are among the most important contributions of behavioral science to our society. . . . The proper use of tests can result in wiser decisions about individuals and programs than would be the case without their use and also can provide a route to broader and more equitable access to education and employment. . . . Educational and psychological testing and assessment involve and significantly affect individuals, institutions, and society as a whole. (p. 1)

Educators are required to provide children with individual psychoeducational evaluations prior to placement in special education programs. Policies in most states prescribe that these evaluations include two critical assessment areas: intelligence and adaptive behavior. What follows is an in-depth look at the theories and assessment practices of these two important areas.

For a complete on-line glossary of mental retardation terms, go to the companion website at www.prenhall.com/beirnesmith and select any chapter, and then choose the Glossary module.

THEORIES OF INTELLIGENCE

Theories of intelligence are useful to the extent that they provide educators with an organizing structure for understanding and evaluating how children learn. For teachers and other service providers in the community, the concept of intelligence is most useful when it helps to formulate instructional strategies.

Theories of intelligence can be evaluated from several points of view. For some people, particularly those who work in the field of education, intelligence can be an intricate and well-defined construct; for others, it may be little more than a generally held notion or idea. According to some theorists, it is the efficiency of the process that is important—for example, how much of a given task one can accomplish in a certain period of time. According to others, it may be the relationships among ideas that really matter. For still others, intellectual theories are best understood in the context of their origin (innate or acquired). While nearly all theories of intelligence contain some of these elements, Wechsler's (1958) definition of intelligence offers one of the most cogent explanations: "The aggregate or global capacity of the individual to act purposefully, to think rationally, and to deal effectively with his environment" (p. 7). A brief description of three very general types of theories of intelligence follows.

Traditional *psychometric theories* have their roots in differential psychology, the study of individual and group differences. Psychometric theorists assume that underlying abilities account for most variations in intellectual functioning. The traditional psychometric theorists range from those who believe that a single trait accounts for all mental abilities (e.g., Spearman, 1927; Vernon, 1950) to multifactored theorists who believe that intelligence is best explained by a multitude of traits or factors (Guilford, 1967; Thorndike, 1927; Thurstone, 1938). Most, however, place these models at two ends of a continuum and believe that reality lies somewhere between the two.

Recently, John Carroll (1993) has proposed a three-stratum theory of cognitive abilities that allows for a general ability factor similar to Spearman's *g,* second-level factors referred to as broad ability factors (e.g., crystallized intelligence, fluid intelligence), and 50 or more primary (or narrow) abilities, many of which have been previously identified by Thurstone. Carroll's three-stratum theory synthesizes the factor-analytic work of the past century and offers much promise for new developments in the years ahead.

Information-processing theories, perhaps better than any others, represent the second and most truly interdisciplinary approach to understanding intelligence. With contributions from anthropology, computer science, education, linguistics, and psychology, information-processing theorists focus on the methods by which a person processes information, taking it from sensory stimuli and transferring it to motoric output (Sternberg, 1985).

Among the many theories that emanate from an information-processing model, Sternberg's (1985, 1988) triarchic theory of human intelligence continues to receive some acclaim. The triarchic theory describes a complex and highly integrated system of mental operations that combines such influential elements as the internal world of the individual, the external world of the individual, and one's life experiences. Sternberg (1997) is careful to point out the underlying components and mechanisms in each of the three areas but cautions that while such operations may be found among people of all cultures, the values placed on specific problem-solving strategies and mechanisms may vary. For example, children of one culture may adapt more quickly to the environmental demands of a new community than other children, based on both past experiences and the social worth of the necessary skills. Consequently, what is deemed intelligent in one culture may not be viewed as intelligent in another. What further distinguishes Sternberg's theory from other contemporary theorists is an explanation of how information is processed within each of the three aforementioned areas. That is, he allows for the presence of higher-order problem-solving skills, performance components that allow for the execution of those problem-solving skills, and knowledge acquisition components that allow one to attend, retrieve, and compare the necessary pieces of information.

Another major theory that is receiving a great deal of attention, is Das, Naglieri, and Kirby's (1994) planning, attention, simultaneous, and successive (PASS) processes model. The PASS model of information processing is an extension and validation of Luria's (1980) early theory of human cognitive functioning. Luria first reported and others have since verified the presence of three functional units of information processing. The first functional unit allows a person to become aroused by and attend to environmental stimuli. The second functional unit is responsible for acquiring, holding, and then processing the information, of which there are two main approaches: processing multiple pieces of information all at once in an integrated manner (simultaneous) or processing information in a sequential, temporally organized (successive) manner. The third functional unit, known as the planning unit, provides the individual with the means to analyze cognitive activity, develop a problem-solving strategy, and then evaluate the efficacy of that solution. Das et al. (1994) have suggested that the PASS model offers psychologists and educators a number of options for responding to the special needs of children with disabilities.

The third major category of theories is the most broad, including theories not mentioned in the previous two. Among them is Gardner's (1993) *theory of multiple intelligences*. While reminiscent of the multifactored theories, Gardner's theory allows for multiple definitions of intelligence, including, among others, social and motoric intelligence. Although little in the professional literature validates Gardner's definitions, many educators have embraced it as a new and innovative perspective on intellectual functioning. Whether biological or psychological, developmental or stage-specific, more theories and definitions of intelligence will undoubtedly be developed in the coming years. Gardner's theory may hold promise for people who work with persons with mental retardation. The assumption that all individuals are different, and possess their own unique combination of strengths and weaknesses, is very much in agreement with Gardner's premise that it is possible to be intelligent in specific yet nontraditional ways.

Nature versus Nurture

If teachers view intelligence as fixed and predominantly inherited, then they may view their role as disseminators of information rather than cultivators of learning. This position assigns the responsibility of learning and its opposite, nonlearning, primarily to the person receiving instruction. But if teachers view intelligence as something that can be altered, they may see their job as instrumental in the learning process, thereby allowing them to view a person's learning as an indication of their own effectiveness as teachers.

Teachers must help structure environments in ways that stimulate learning and intellectual growth.

One's beliefs about intelligence and the ways in which individuals learn are very much related to the **nature–nurture controversy,** the question of whether intelligence is innate or acquired. Actually, few authorities claim either the extreme hereditarian or the extreme environmentalist position, believing instead that both factors work together in a sort of duet to influence one's abilities and patterns of responses (Plomin, 1994). The Swiss psychologist Jean Piaget (1952) referred to such a combination of biological and environmental factors as *epigenetic* in nature.

The bulk of this debate concerns the relative proportions of the two ingredients that combine to shape one's intelligence. Researchers generally agree that a person's upbringing affects cognitive development within the constraints of existing biological potential. But how rigid are those constraints? And how powerful are the environmental forces that influence them? Researchers are divided on these issues. Some—such as Bouchard, Lykken, McGue, Segal, and Tellegen (1990); Jensen (1998); and Pedersen, Plomin, Nesselroade, and McClearn (1992)—believe that the hereditary component can be quite strong, perhaps in excess of 70%. That is, 70% or more of the variation in intelligence is attributable to the person's genetic makeup. Others, such as Kamin (1974), believe that one's intelligence has nothing at all to do with genetics.

The actual estimate of heritability depends very much on which relationships are being investigated (e.g., monozygotic twins, dizygotic twins, biological siblings, adoptive siblings) and whether the siblings are raised together or apart and with or without their biological parents. It is not simply a matter of heritability alone, but how the inherited components interact with the environmental components (Mackintosh, 1998). Virtually everyone is familiar with intellectually gifted parents whose children never live up to their "expected" intellectual potential, just as most people are aware of families of very limited social, economic, and intellectual means who have raised children with extraordinary intellectual capabilities. Hence, there is no sure formula for creating the optimum blend between genetic makeup and environmental influence.

The best research to date seems to suggest that the heritability of intelligence is about 50%; however, as with all population estimates, that value is only applicable to the population at large and can vary markedly from individual to individual based on the person's circumstances (Plomin & Petrill, 1997). If heritability is estimated to be around 50%, then the remaining 50% is due to environmental influences, and one can safely say that one's intellectual potential is shaped to a large degree by nonhereditary factors that resonate through all parts of a person's life, into the school, home, and community. Educators and social service delivery personnel must therefore help structure environments in ways that stimulate intellectual growth. In addition, they must accept that changes are both constant and welcome additions where intellectual growth and development are concerned.

Intelligence Quotient

Many find the notion that one's intellectual capacity can be described with a single value unsettling. Although it is still possible to find tests that yield only one score and examiners who define a person's level of academic aptitude in terms of a single value, these tests and examiners are in the minority. The notion of a single IQ score is valid only if a single factor of general ability underlies all problem-solving operations. But, since most people today do not believe in the notion of a lone ability factor, and no major intelligence test is based on a single, underlying dimension, the notion of IQ has indeed changed dramatically since its inception.

Though many of the terms once associated with intelligence and intelligence quotients are no longer accurate, they have remained in the American vocabulary and are worth knowing. The earliest and least sophisticated term for describing a person's level of intellectual functioning is *mental age*. *Mental age* is an estimate of one's intellectual level and is different from chronological age. A 5-year-old who successfully completes tasks typically performed only by children 7 years of age would be considered to have a mental age of 7 years.

Louis Terman first introduced the term *intelligence quotient* (IQ) in 1916 as a better-scoring index than mental age. While no longer used in practice, the IQ is important in a historical sense and is calculated by dividing one's mental age by one's chronological age and multiplying by 100. The disadvantage of a mental age score as compared with a ratio IQ score, such as that proposed by Terman, is that it provides an index of a child's IQ test performance relative to others in a given age group. This technique does not, however, work for adults. Beginning in early adulthood, chronological age increases faster than mental age, making adults in general and older adults in particular appear less apt than they really are.

Today, deviation IQs are used in place of intelligence quotients for all age groups. Although many professionals still refer to these scores as "IQs," they are not IQs, at least not in the same way referred to 75 years ago when the concept was just originating. A **deviation IQ** is nothing more than a subtest raw score converted to a standard score for the examinee's own age group. The standard score for a particular child is derived by subtracting the mean raw score of all children in the respective age group from the raw score of the child and then dividing that value by the raw score standard deviation for all children in that age group. The advantage of a deviation IQ is that a person's relative standing within a particular reference group can be compared with the scores of many others' including those of different ages and ability levels. This is the primary reason that most individually administered, norm-referenced intelligence tests used today have a mean (M) of 100 and a standard deviation (SD) of 15.

ASSESSMENT OF INTELLIGENCE

To find assessment resources, go to the companion website at www.prenhall.com/beirne-smith, select Chapter 3, then choose the Web Destinations module.

Although the testing practices of today differ markedly from those of the time when they were first introduced, the premise has remained very much the same: to distinguish those who are successful at solving problems from those who are not. According to Ittenbach, Esters, and Wainer (1997), the act of assessment is actually a quest in search of an underlying truth. It is a means by which hypotheses are tested and verified using scientifically acceptable methods (Messick, 1988).

While the history of testing is virtually 4,000 years old, the history of modern testing is little more than a century old. Sir Francis Galton (1832–1920) is generally considered to be the founder of formal testing. However, it was actually one of his contemporaries, James McKeen Cattell (1860–1944), who is credited with coining the term *mental tests*. What made Galton and Cattell's influence on the mental testing movement so profound was not their shared interests in eugenics and individual differences so much as their particular blend of skills and abilities. Galton, part scientist and part philosopher, was trying to understand better the inheritance of mental abilities through physical traits, whereas Cattell was interested in differences in physiological functioning through performances on paper-and-pencil tests.

The critical link between the two investigators was mathematician Karl Pearson (1857–1936). According to Ittenbach and Lawhead (1997), "Galton had the ideas, but Karl Pearson had the mathematical acumen to sell it to the world" (p. 31). Cattell then applied the new mathematical operations to test scores of his experimental psychology students at the University of Pennsylvania. From there, the union of statistics and experimental psychology carried forward to all of American psychology.

As a construct, intelligence is a relatively well-accepted and time-honored notion of problem-solving ability. Yet, the definition of intelligence and the way in which it is measured are open to debate. Many have attempted to define intelligence, but few have set out to measure it with any degree of rigor. Those who have tried to measure intelligence have done so with the understanding that they were attempting to explain one of the most complex and elusive components of human functioning. Test developers have been careful to distinguish the construct of intelligence from its assessment—the manner in which information is obtained. Human service providers should be careful to do the same.

The Influence of Alfred Binet

The first effective test of intellectual ability was devised in the early 1900s by French psychologists Alfred Binet, Victor Henri, and Theodore Simon (Schultz & Schultz, 1996). Although Binet had a wide and varied career within the discipline of psychology, it is in the fields of intelligence and psychometrics that he has "had his most concentrated, enduring, and intellectually powerful influence" (Haywood & Paour, 1992, p. 1). In 1904, the French Ministry of Public Instruction appointed Binet to a commission to study the problems of educating children who were not likely to benefit from traditional classroom instruction and who would instead profit from slower-paced educational programs—that is, children with learning problems.

As early as 1895, Binet had already argued in his writings that educational tests were far too narrow in scope and that new tests were needed to understand better the learning process. Thus, Binet and his colleague Theodore Simon devised an instrument to identify children who were considered lacking in mental ability. Their first test, the 30-item Measuring Scale of Intelligence, was published in 1905, then revised in 1908 and revised again in 1911 (as cited in Haywood & Paour, 1992). Their scale was different from others of the day in that it did not just tap sensory experiences but instead allowed for the evaluation of such mental abilities as comprehension, memory, and reasoning, intellectual skills deemed critical for scholastic success. In short, the Binet-Simon scale sampled higher-level, complex processes that the authors believed to be essential elements of intelligence.

Binet and Simon went to great lengths to differentiate between the concepts of natural intelligence and acquired intelligence. They were interested in measuring one's *capacity* to learn rather than simply the amount of knowledge gained. Because reading and writing are learned skills, Binet and Simon's tests of intelligence were constructed to avoid measuring reading and writing. In the initial version of their scale, for example, the child's ability to identify pictured objects, repeat a three-digit series, reproduce geometric figure drawings, define abstract words, and perform similar nonacademic tasks was tested.

Among the many versions of the original Binet-Simon scale used in the United States in the early 20th century, it was actually Terman's Stanford Revision and Extension of the Binet-Simon Scale (1916) that became the template for all subsequent revisions. Terman's version has since been revised in this country three times: in 1937 and 1960 with Maud Merrill and, most recently, in 1986 by Robert Thorndike, Elizabeth Hagen, and Jerome Sattler (1986a). The 1937 and 1960 forms of the Stanford-Binet included such materials as toys and miniature objects (e.g., beads, balls, cars, dolls), which examinees were instructed to manipulate in various ways, and booklets and pictures (animals and household objects, etc.), about which they had to answer questions.

The **Stanford-Binet IV** is an individually administered intelligence test based on a three-level hierarchical model of cognitive abilities. At the top of the model is g, a general reasoning factor. The next level emanates from the work of Horn and Cattell (1966) and divides g into three secondary factors: crystallized abilities, fluid-analytic abilities, and short-term memory. *Crystallized abilities* are cognitive factors an individual needs to acquire and use information necessary to deal with verbal and quantitative concepts, *fluid-analytic abilities* are the cognitive skills needed for solving unfamiliar problems involving nonverbal stimuli, and *short-term memory* is a measure of the individual's ability to retain information until it can be stored for long-term usage. The third level of the model divides crystallized abilities into verbal reasoning and quantitative reasoning, while fluid-analytic abilities are identified by abstract/visual reasoning alone. Short-term memory has no comparable third-level division. Figure 3.1 illustrates the model and the tests that comprise each of these areas.

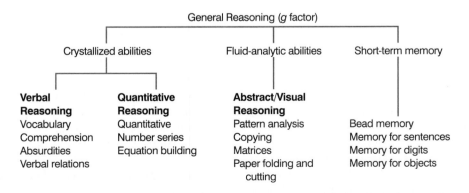

FIGURE 3.1
Stanford-Binet IV Model

In the Stanford-Binet IV, the term *intelligence* has been replaced by the term *cognitive development*. The terms *intelligence, IQ,* and *mental age* are not used in the fourth edition anywhere in the administration or technical manuals (Thorndike et al., 1986b). The term *Standard Age Score* (SAS) serves as a replacement for *IQ.* Five SAS scores are obtainable, one for each of the four areas measured (Verbal Reasoning, Abstract/Visual Reasoning, Quantitative Reasoning, and Short-Term Memory) and the Test Composite. The Composite SAS is a deviation score that is similar, if not identical, to what others consider to be a deviation IQ score. According to Thorndike et al. (1986b), the Stanford-Binet IV has a fourfold purpose:

1. To help differentiate between students who are mentally retarded and those who have specific learning disabilities.
2. To help educators and psychologists understand why a particular student is having difficulty learning in school.
3. To help identify gifted students.
4. To study the development of cognitive skills of individuals from ages 2 to adult. (p. 2)

Each of the items represented in the 15 tests of the Stanford-Binet IV is arranged in levels of increasing difficulty and designated by letter (*A, B, C,* etc.). Each level has two items of approximately equal difficulty. For each test, the examiner must establish a basal age and a ceiling age. The multistage format begins with a Vocabulary test, which is a routing test that determines the entry level for the other tests. No more than 13 tests are given to any subject, and the authors even recommend several abbreviated versions. The raw scores of each test are converted to SASs. For the Composite SAS, $M = 100$ and $SD = 16$, while on the individual-test SASs, $M = 50$ and $SD = 8$.

The Stanford-Binet IV was anxiously anticipated in the hope that it would be a superior instrument, but it has been received with mixed reviews. In its first published form it contained inaccuracies, and replacement manuals did not appear until a year after the test was released for use. Since that time, the Stanford-Binet IV has continued to live up to its name, particularly when examiners need a good measure of general intellectual functioning. Laurent, Swerdlik, and Ryburn (1992) have found the Binet to be particularly effective in discriminating among groups of children with differing intellectual abilities, and a useful predictor of academic achievement.

The Influence of David Wechsler

David Wechsler's (1896–1981) influence on assessment in the schools has been profound. Whereas the Stanford-Binet has served as the standard of intellectual assessment for nearly a century, the Wechsler scales have served as the workhorse. The **Wechsler scales** are a series of three individually administered intelligence tests, modeled after one another, in which a person's intellectual abilities are described using a verbal/motor framework (i.e., Wechsler, 1949, 1955, 1967, 1974, 1981, 1989a, 1991a, 1997). The Wechsler scales have provided the preferred vehicle for the identification and classification of countless school-age children for nearly half a century.

Like Binet, Wechsler was trained as a clinician. Though he worked with adults rather than children, he, too, believed that intelligence was a unitary trait and that it was actually only one part of the broader construct of the human personality. Perhaps the most important feature of the Wechsler scales, and very likely the reason their use in the schools has far exceeded that of the Binet, is that the tests are remarkably similar across the preschool-, elementary-, and secondary-age ranges. As opposed to earlier versions of the Binet in which children of different ages were tested using very different tasks, with the Wechsler scales, children of different ages are exposed to different items but to highly similar tasks, thereby adding an element of consistency to evaluations throughout a child's schooling. Sadly, America's educators will never come to know the instrument that Wechsler had intended to complete his battery of intelligence tests across the life span, the Wechsler Intelligence Scale for the Elderly (WISE), which was under development at the time of his death in 1981 (Kaufman, 1994).

When they first appeared, the Wechsler scales were distinguished by several other innovative features. For example, every Wechsler test is subdivided into smaller scales and subscales. The Wechsler Intelligence Scale for Children–Third Edition, for example, consists of 10 subtests and 3 supplemental ones: 5 verbal subtests with one alternate, and 5 performance (nonverbal) subtests with two alternates. Each subtest theoretically measures a different ability and is treated as a separate entity; combined, all subtests allow the examiner to assess global intellectual capacity. Wechsler (1939) believed that the Binet test of that era did not tap motoric performance, an important facet of intelligence, so he developed a performance scale that complemented the verbal scale in such a way that it offered problem-solving items that required judgment, reasoning, foresight, and planning, but little in the way of verbal ability. Following is a brief description of the three Wechsler tests currently in use today.

Wechsler Preschool and Primary Scale of Intelligence—Revised

The Wechsler Preschool and Primary Scale of Intelligence—Revised (WPPSI-R; Wechsler, 1989a) is a standardized, individually administered test of intelligence intended for use with children 3 years, 0 months through 7 years, 3 months of age. The WPPSI-R is a revision of the original Wechsler Preschool and Primary Scale of Intelligence (WPPSI; Wechsler, 1967). The purpose of the WPPSI-R, as stated in the manual, is to assist with the diagnosis of exceptionalities of young children in educational and private practice settings (Wechsler, 1989b).

The WPPSI-R is divided into two major sections, verbal and performance, both of which yield IQ scores, which in turn combine to yield a full-scale IQ ($M = 100$, $SD = 15$). The WPPSI-R has 12 separate subtests ($M = 10$, $SD = 3$), 10 of which are required, and 2 supplemental subtests. The core test may be administered in 30 to 60 minutes, with the other two subtests requiring an additional 10 minutes. Bonus points are awarded for quick, correct responses.

Although the WPPSI-R remains markedly similar to the parent WPPSI, a number of changes were made to keep pace with new developments in clinical assessment. Only one new subtest has been added, Object Assembly, in which the child is asked to assemble puzzles in a specified time period. New items were created to increase the age range of the test, and more attractive materials were used to encourage the young child's participation.

Wechsler Intelligence Scale for Children—Third Edition

The Wechsler Intelligence Scale for Children—Third Edition (WISC-III; Wechsler, 1991a) is a standardized, individually administered test of intelligence intended for use with children and adolescents aged 6 years, 0 months through 16 years, 11 months. The WISC-III is the third in a series of time-honored and clinically tested instruments (i.e., WISC, WISC-R). Although the publication history of the WISC-III does not yet equal that of its predecessor, the WISC-R (see Kaufman, Harrison, & Ittenbach, 1990), Braden (1995) states that the WISC-III meets the needs of researchers and clinicians alike and offers evolutionary progress toward assessment of cognitive abilities.

The purpose of the WISC-III, as stated in its manual, is to help with educational planning and placement, diagnosis of exceptionality, clinical and neuropsychological assessment, and educational and psychological research (Wechsler,

TABLE 3.1
WISC-III Subtests

Subtest	Underlying abilities
Verbal Scale	
Information	Long-term memory, fund of information, formal education, richness of early learning experiences.
Similarities	Verbal reasoning, analogic thinking, concept formation.
Arithmetic	Concrete reasoning, numerical reasoning, facility with numbers.
Vocabulary	Fund of information, long-term memory, formal education, richness of early learning experiences.
Comprehension	Verbal reasoning, logical reasoning, social reasoning.
Digit Span[*]	Attention, short-term memory, facility with numbers, ability to copy a model.
Performance Scale	
Picture Completion	Attention to detail, visual organization, logical reasoning.
Coding	Short-term memory, visual-motor speed and coordination, facility with numbers, attention.
Picture Arrangement	Attention to detail, visual organization, logical reasoning, social reasoning.
Block Design	Abstract reasoning, visual-motor coordination, ability to copy a model, planning ability.
Object Assembly	Visual organization, visual-motor coordination, logical reasoning.
Symbol Search[*]	Abstract reasoning, ability to mentally copy a model, visual-motor coordination.
Mazes[*]	Planning ability, visual-motor coordination.

Note: [*]denotes optional subtests.

1991b). The three traditional global scales continue to underscore Wechsler's notion of a broad-based measure of intellectual functioning, but with strong verbal and motor components. The same three principal scores ($M = 100$, $SD = 15$) are obtainable: full-scale IQ, verbal IQ, and performance IQ. In addition to the afore-mentioned scores, four new scaled scores may also be computed using the existing subtests: Verbal Comprehension, Perceptual Organization, Freedom from Dis-tractability, and Processing Speed. All four are based on extensive factor-analytic research with the WISC and WISC-R.

Ten subtests are required; the examiner has the option of using 3 additional subtests, all with $M = 10$, $SD = 3$ (see Table 3.1). The entire test may be adminis-tered in 50 to 70 minutes, with the additional three subtests requiring another 15 minutes. Bonus points are awarded for quick, correct responses.

Wechsler Adult Intelligence Scale—Third Edition

The Wechsler Adult Intelligence Scale—Third Edition (WAIS-III; Wechsler, 1997) is a standardized, individually administered test of intelligence intended for use with adults 16 years, 0 months of age and older. The WAIS-III is a revision of the original Wechsler Adult Intelligence Scales (WAIS, WAIS-R). The purpose of the WAIS-III differs somewhat from that of the WPPSI-R and WISC-III in that it, like its fore-runner the WAIS-R, tends to be much more of a clinical rather than a school-based instrument.

Like the WPPSI-R and WISC-III, the WAIS-III provides three composite IQ scores ($M = 100$, $SD = 15$): full-scale IQ, verbal IQ, and performance IQ. Fourteen subtests comprise the WAIS-III ($M = 10$, $SD = 3$), 11 of which are required; total administration time is approximately 90 minutes. As with the other two tests, bonus points are awarded for quick, correct responses.

Other Influential Scales

The Stanford-Binet and Wechsler scales are very popular with school personnel. Despite their historical and clinical importance, however, they are facing increased competition from newer and sometimes theoretically superior instruments. Some of these tests are readily available, inexpensive, and easy to administer and require little in the way of administrator training or time; however, they do not always meet state or local guidelines for use and very often do not provide all the informa-tion needed for an in-depth diagnostic evaluation. See Conoley and Impara (1995) for a review of frequently used measures of intelligence.

Following are brief discussions of two widely used and well-respected instru-ments: the Kaufman Assessment Battery for Children and the Differential Ability Scales. Both instruments offer clinicians and researchers nice alternatives to the Binet and Wechsler scales.

Kaufman Assessment Battery for Children

The Kaufman Assessment Battery for Children (K-ABC; Kaufman & Kaufman, 1983) has gained acceptance as a viable instrument for measuring intellectual func-tioning. It is an individually administered, norm-referenced battery that allows for the measurement of both intelligence and achievement in children 2 years, 6 months to 12 years, 6 months of age. The theoretical basis for this instrument is closely tied to concepts of information processing that have been derived from the work of cognitive psychologists. According to this system, two different processing abilities comprise intellectual functioning: sequential processing ability and simultaneous processing ability. Sequential processing involves using bits of information one after another in a step-by-step, sequential manner. In simultaneous processing, however, one uses bits of information all at once, holistically. Besides the two principal scales used, there are two others, Achievement and Nonverbal. The Nonverbal scale provides another way to assess children with atypical abilities by combining certain subtests that can be administered nonverbally and, equally importantly, requires nonverbal responses.

Differential Ability Scales

The Differential Ability Scales (DAS; Elliott, 1990) is an American descendant of the well-known British Ability Scales. The DAS is a standardized, individually administered test of cognitive functioning intended for use with children 2 years, 6 months to 17 years, 11 months of age. At the top of the hierarchy of possible scores is a General Conceptual Ability score ($M = 100$, $SD = 15$) similar to an IQ score. Composite standard scores for specific ability areas are also available, depending on the age and subtests administered (e.g., Verbal Ability, Nonverbal Reasoning Ability, Spatial Ability). The entire battery consists of 20 subtests (17 cognitive, 3 achievement) and takes about 1 hour to administer. No examinee takes more than 12 subtests.

Independent reviewers report that the instrument was designed "explicitly for use in the schools to identify children with educational problems" (e.g., Sandoval, 1992, p. 89). Of particular note to psychologists and educators testing children are the relatively strong psychometric properties of the DAS and the out-of-level norms (standards for comparison), characteristics that Daniel (1994) believes allow more accurate and readily interpretable standard scores for individuals performing at the lower end of the distribution.

"Culture-Free" Tests

Concern for children from bilingual and minority backgrounds has sparked the development of a number of "culture-free" measures in which there has been an effort to eliminate all cultural factors that might favor one group over another. One such test is the Matrix Analogies Test (Naglieri, 1985), an instrument that is purported to be a much purer measure of nonverbal reasoning ability than other tests. The examinee is shown a matrix of abstract designs with a missing element and is asked to select a design that best completes the picture.

Other tests such as the Leiter International Performance Scale—Revised (Leiter-R; Roid & Miller, 1997), the Universal Nonverbal Intelligence Test (UNIT; Bracken & McCallum, 1998), and the nonverbal scales of many of the Wechsler tests (when administered in the respondent's native language) have also redefined the standards by which culture-fair intellectual assessment is now conducted.

Until the day when the process of evaluating intellectual abilities can be clearly separated from cultural influences at both obvious and subtle levels, there may never be a truly "culture-free" test. The most that can be hoped for in the meantime are tests that minimize the role of language and socially driven expectations and emphasize nonverbal skills and abilities, which many of these tests do quite well.

Criticisms of Intelligence Testing

Considerable controversy surrounds the issue of intelligence testing in the schools. Some critics of intelligence testing find fault with the tests, others with the examiners, and still others with the process. Critics further argue that test scores are subject to various forms of statistical and administrative error and that these scores can vary considerably from one time to another. These points are well taken. Following are brief discussions of some of the import and long-lasting disagreements that continue to plague the practice of intelligence testing.

The concept of intelligence was introduced at a time when the prevailing belief was that intelligence was hereditary and therefore a constant trait. Laypersons and professionals alike generally think of intelligence as a basic, enduring attribute of an individual. But if intelligence is a constant, why do IQ scores fluctuate? When a child receives an IQ score of 95 at age 6, an IQ score of 89 at age 13, and an IQ score of 105 at age 16, does this mean that the child had average intelligence at first but lost intelligence between ages 6 and 13 and became brighter again by 16? Obviously not. The most likely explanation is that the child was influenced by emotional, motivational, or experiential factors.

Examiners also vary with respect to their ability to select and use the best possible instrument for a given person. The basic problem is that, although the word *intelligence* is used to refer to the totality of a person's ability and potential, no finite samples of behavior can possibly demonstrate everything that is worth knowing about that person's capabilities. A major premise of most if not all major intelligence instruments is that a score on an IQ test is not synonymous with intelligence. Other nonintellective factors also play a crucial role in both test performance and daily living (Wechsler, 1991b).

The purpose of today's tests, similar to those of Binet's time, is to predict likelihood for success in traditional academic settings. Although never perfect, the tests are indeed able to signal those for whom academic difficulties may be expected. Despite the defensible rationale for the original and continued development of these instruments, many people treat the tests themselves as if they were the offending party. One must wonder whether such frustration and anger are really directed toward the tests, toward what the tests predict (academic outcomes), or toward the process of implementing educational interventions. Rather than kill the messenger, why not do as Kaufman (1994) has recommended, and *kill the prediction?* "The fact that most children who score very poorly on the WISC-III will also do poorly in school should not be accepted as a statement of destiny" (p. 7). Accurate and in-depth assessment followed by verifiable educational interventions can do much to change a child's likelihood for success in a given academic program.

The second major criticism of intelligence testing pertains to the perception by the public and some members of the profession that IQ tests inadequately cover the broad spectrum of abilities defined as intelligence. Much of this criticism stems from the lack of convergence between the theory and structure of existing tests and the current knowledge base of experimental evidence, particularly as it relates to children with special needs (Das et al., 1994). Authors and publishers of tests are quick to point out that the tests do not measure all components of one's cognitive development but rather a sample of abilities in several key areas. The key areas are most often representative of the author's beliefs about intelligence, given the current state of research in the area. Some tests are designed to cover areas that other tests fail to touch. For example, the WISC-III has a strong fine-motor component, while the Binet does not. On the K-ABC, the fine-motor component is much more subtle, appearing through a combination of other scales. Furthermore, the Stanford-Binet IV has a definable memory scale, while information pertaining to short- and long-term memory must be teased out on the K-ABC and WISC-III. Though very different tasks are used in the respective tests, all fit into a broader framework for understanding the cognitive functioning of people with and without disabilities.

A third major criticism of IQ tests is that they regulate access to educational opportunities and relegate certain students from minority backgrounds to special education programs. School personnel use these tests to help understand why a child is encountering difficulty in traditional academic areas. Whether a child possesses special gifts or special limitations such as mental retardation, each child is entitled to an environment where full academic growth can be realized. IQ tests are not used to change the academic programs of children who are performing well in the classroom; rather, the tests are used by professionals only after the student, parents, teachers, or other service providers have reason to believe that the child is not successful under normal classroom conditions. When used appropriately and within the context of a multidisciplinary team as mandated by the 1997 reauthorization of the Individuals with Disabilities Education Act (IDEA), IQ tests serve only to confirm the presence and nature of learning difficulties observed by others. Simply put, IQ tests are intended to reduce, not increase, the number of children qualifying for special education.

THEORIES OF ADAPTIVE BEHAVIOR

The notion of examining what a person does in typical situations is often much more helpful than what a person *can* do or *might* do under the best of circumstances. Recently, increased attention has been directed toward the adaptive skills of persons with mental retardation. The acquisition of adaptive skills for most people is considered to be a continuous and naturally occurring set of events; for persons with mental retardation, however, the process is anything but continuous and very often plagued with difficulty.

Grossman (1983) has defined **adaptive behavior** as the "degree with which individuals meet the standards of personal independence and social responsibility expected for age and cultural group" (p. 1). More recently, the American Association on Mental Retardation (AAMR; 1992) has emphasized definable skill areas rather than the more abstract term of *adaptive behavior*. Though some people have criticized AAMR's earlier definitions of adaptive behavior as too elusive and ill defined (e.g., Zigler, Balla, & Hodapp, 1984), Kamphaus (1987) has defended the earlier definition as homogenizing, suggesting that it has provided the field with a focus and sense of direction that investigators in other areas have yet to obtain.

Whereas classification of mental retardation requires both an intellective (IQ) and nonintellective (adaptive) component, the formal emphasis on adaptive skills has encouraged a more balanced approach to diagnosis and service delivery where mental retardation is a concern. It is precisely because members of the profession have been willing to pursue a deeper understanding of adaptive behavior that service delivery to persons with mental retardation has vastly improved in recent years. The benefits of an agreed-on definition of adaptive behavior are only now leading to some consensus on its theoretical structure. Theories of adaptation are indeed long-standing but have, for the most part, remained outside the interest of most persons in the field of mental retardation—until recently. Following is a brief discussion of theories of adaptation from biological, psychological, and sociological points of view.

Adaptation has historically been considered a biological phenomenon. The capacity of an organism to adjust to changes in the environment depends largely on two types of responses that allow it to remain at equilibrium with itself (homeostasis) and to function over a normal range of biologically acceptable environments (homeokinesis) (Prosser, 1986). While some such changes occur immediately (e.g., reaction to anxiety and fear, or fever in response to an infection), other changes may take days, weeks, months, or even years to occur (e.g., muscle development in response to maturation). Still others (e.g., a species' collective resistance to a disease or ability to survive in extreme conditions) may take many generations to evolve. Brandon (1990) has defined an organism's adaptedness in terms of biological properties and its capacity to survive in its own environment.

Individuals, alone or in groups, have their own beliefs, attitudes, and desires. Whereas biologists are interested in the adaptive mechanisms of biological systems, psychologists and educators are interested in the richness of the behaviors and their dependence on various environmental conditions (Staddon, 1983). In some areas of functioning, however, both biologists and psychologists have much to say about the responsiveness of people to certain environmental conditions—and responsivity to stress is one such example. According to Hobfall (1998), physiological psychologists have found a high degree of similarity among peoples' responses to single stressors but a high degree of variability among people's tendencies to respond to stressors in general. That is, people tend to have behavioral repertoires that they consider to be successful, specific, and adaptive when confronting stressful or unusual circumstances. For example, Piaget's (1952) early work in organization and adaptation of new information is a key component in our present-day understanding of cognitive development in children. For a child to interpret and adjust to the demands of the external world, new experiences must be understood and modified in the context of preexisting information. Although Piaget limited his work to children, the same principle can be extended across the life span to many different situations and areas of adjustment.

Many adaptive behaviors are less a function of the person than of the organization or social unit to which the person belongs. For example, Lumsden and Wilson (1985) have reported that groups of people, like other animals, generate behavioral patterns that fit the social group to the environment. Even characteristics such as loyalty, morality, and altruism exist in groups of people and other animals because of their survival value to the group. A more obvious example of social adaptation may be found in social systems theory, a sociologically based theory often used to explain the structure and function of organized groups (Gordon, 1991). According to social systems theory, groups that survive over time are those whose development of organizational structures allows them to keep their place of importance in the broader social milieu. Status, roles, norms, and behaviors are as important for the social group as they are for the individuals within the group. Just as "children are born into a world of pre-existing, relatively stable social structures," so are social groups, dictating that they, too, must be "socialized to meet the expectations of the [broader] system" (Mercer, 1978, p. 71).

Adaptive behavior as a valued construct is now receiving the attention that other constructs in psychology and education have known for years. It may be years before the theoretical work of today pays dividends at the service delivery level. Necessarily, much of the research that has been conducted has emphasized the characteristics of the instruments instead of exclusively furthering the development of the construct itself. Among the research that is conceptually based is a growing consensus that adaptive behavior is a multidimensional construct rather than a unidimensional one, with as many as four to six stable factors (e.g., Thompson, McGrew & Bruininks, 1999; Widaman, Reise, & Clatfelter, 1994; Widaman, Stacy, & Borthwick-Duffy, 1993). There is also some evidence that the factor structures themselves may be hierarchical, with one or perhaps two broad factors (i.e., adaptive, maladaptive) having several underlying dimensions (Widaman & McGrew, 1996).

An example of a model that illustrates the hierarchical nature of adaptive behavior rather nicely is Greenspan's (1997) model of personal competence. According to Greenspan, "competent individuals can be defined both in terms of the qualities they bring to various goals and challenges, as well as by their relative degree of success in meeting those goals and challenges" (p. 131). In his model, and consistent with the published literature, are four broad domains of competence: physical competence, affective competence, everyday competence, and academic competence. Greenspan posits a number of lower-order factors that are contained in each of the aforementioned domains, factors that all have relevance for persons with mental retardation as well as for persons of all ability levels. (See Figure 3.2 for a depiction of this model.)

Adaptive behaviors, specifically, are the behavioral skills that are demonstrated in response to environmental demands (Widaman & McGrew, 1996). With the AAMR's shift toward a more functional definition of mental retardation, references to the more vague term of *adaptive behavior* have been replaced by 10 very specific adaptive skill areas: "communication, self-care, home living, social skills, community use, self-direction, health and safety, functional academic, leisure, and work" (AAMR, 1992, p. 1). The change to the more easily definable adaptive skills areas "is not intended as a refutation of the term *adaptive behavior*" (AAMR, 1992, p. 38) but as a response to the limitations of the measurement process itself. It is believed that by emphasizing the 10 skill areas, the potential for agreement on identification and remediation of abilities is enhanced.

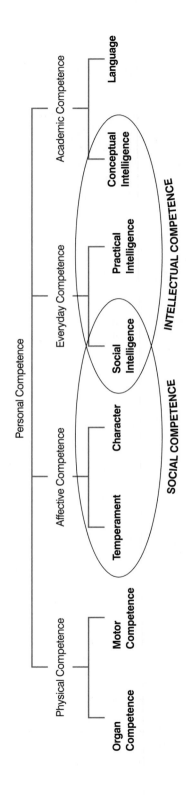

FIGURE 3.2

Greenspan's Model of Personal Competence

Source: From "The Role of Intelligence in a Broad Model of Personal Competence" by S. Greenspan and J. Driscoll in *Contemporary Assessment: Theories, Tests, and Issues* (p. 133) by D. P. Flanagan, J. O. Genshaft, and P. L. Harrison, 1997, New York: Guilford. Copyright 1997 by Guilford. Reprinted by permission.

Adaptive Behavior versus Intelligence

Before intelligence tests were developed, mental retardation was characterized with respect to limitations in social and adaptive functioning (Nihira, 1999). Recent definitions of mental retardation continue to emphasize an individual's ability to function adequately within the individual's principal environment. According to Leland (1978), the ability to cope with the more social demands of one's environment is "the reversible aspect of mental retardation, and it reflects primarily those behaviors which are most likely to be modified through appropriate treatment or training methods" (p. 28).

Adaptive behavior played an increasingly important role in the diagnosis of mental retardation up through the early 1970s, but it wasn't until the 1973 AAMR definition of mental retardation that adaptive behavior joined intelligence as a prominent and complementary component in the diagnosis and classification of mental retardation (see Grossman, 1973). Although the two constructs share much in common, they also stand apart in several substantive ways. First, examiners using measures of adaptive behavior attempt to obtain information about a person's *usual* actions, whereas intelligence tests are designed to obtain information about *maximal* performance. Second, adaptive behavior measures tap a number of different everyday living areas, whereas intelligence tests typically focus on higher-order reasoning abilities. Third, intelligence tests are administered under very controlled conditions, while adaptive behavior information is usually obtained through semistructured interviews with third-party respondents (people who know the person well).

Because of the importance of both adaptive behavior and intelligence, and the notion on the part of many that one may serve as a stand-in for the other, researchers have investigated the relationship between the two constructs. In a comprehensive review of 42 studies documenting the relationship between measures of intelligence and adaptive behavior, Harrison (1987) found a moderate relationship between the two constructs. Others, using more sophisticated statistical techniques, have also found that the two constructs represent separate but related entities (i.e., Ittenbach, Spiegel, McGrew, & Bruininks, 1992; Keith, Fehrman, Harrison, & Pottebaum, 1987; McGrew, Bruininks, & Johnson, 1996).

Thus, research over the past 30 years seems to be confirming what clinicians have suspected for years: that adaptive behavior and intelligence represent distinct but related and complementary constructs. To many clinicians, unfortunately, the importance of the relationship between the two constructs seems to rest on the sometimes useful distinction of optimal (for intelligence) versus daily problem solving (for adaptive behavior). Schalock (1999b) suggests that for service delivery to reach its full potential, practitioners and researchers should consider merging the two constructs within one overarching framework. He offers an overall model of competence with the areas of practical skills, conceptual skills, and social skills as the subdomains of interest. Although his model is similar in many ways to Greenspan's (1997) model of Personal Competence just described, his premise of merging the two components reinforces Greenspan's point that what service providers are interested in and what the field still needs is a systematic means of formally bringing the two components together in a way that fully addresses the needs of persons with mental retardation.

A clear case of the classification and treatment dilemma occurs when children are seen in one setting as mentally retarded (e.g., at school) but appear to function normally in another setting (e.g., with family and friends outside of school). Such is the problem of the well-known "6-hour retarded child" (President's Committee on Mental Retardation, 1970). In late adolescence and adulthood, people are looked upon as mentally retarded when they repeatedly prove incompetent in handling social and vocational responsibilities. Yet social and vocational problems need not grow directly out of ineptitude; it is very common to find adults who were identified as mentally retarded during their school years and who later function quite well in their postschool environments. In fact, most adults with mental retardation, including those with multiple disabilities, adjust very nicely to community living (Conroy, 1996; Larson & Lakin, 1991). (More will be presented on this topic in Chapter 12 on Adult Years.)

ASSESSMENT OF ADAPTIVE BEHAVIOR

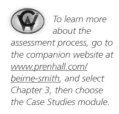

To learn more about the assessment process, go to the companion website at www.prenhall.com/ beirne-smith, and select Chapter 3, then choose the Case Studies module.

The term *adaptive behavior* represents a relatively new name for an old concept (Reschly, 1985). Prior to the Middle Ages, references to one's adaptive skills were informal, and care was provided based on behavioral deviance and physical deformity (Horn & Fuchs, 1987). In light of the long-standing recognition of the relationship between adaptive behavior and mental retardation, assessment of adaptive functioning is much more focused and quantifiable than ever before. Much

Observing children's social and problem-solving skills is an important part of assessing adaptive behavior.

Self-help, personal appearance	**Health care, personal welfare**
Feeding, eating, drinking	Treatment of injuries, health problems
Dressing	Prevention of health problems
Toileting	Personal safety
Grooming, hygiene	Child-care practices
Physical development	**Consumer skills**
Gross motor skills	Money handling
Fine motor skills	Purchasing
	Banking
	Budgeting
Communication	**Domestic skills**
Receptive language	Household cleaning
Expressive language	Property maintenance, repair
	Clothing care
	Kitchen skills
	Household safety
Personal, social skills	**Community orientation**
Play skills	Travel skills
Interaction skills	Utilization of community resources
Group participation	Telephone usage
Social amenities	Community safety
Sexual behavior	
Self-direction, responsibility	
Leisure activities	
Expression of emotions	
Cognitive functioning	**Vocational skills**
Pre-academics	Work habits and attitudes
(e.g., colors)	Job search skills
Reading	Work performance
Writing	Social vocational behavior
Numeric functions	Work safety
Time	
Money	
Measurement	

FIGURE 3.3
Clusters and Specific Adaptive Behavior Areas

Source: From "Adaptive Behavior and Mental Retardation" by R. H. Bruininks, M. L. Thurlow, and C. J. Gilman, 1987, *The Journal of Special Education, 21*(1), p. 74. Copyright 1987 by PRO-ED. Reprinted by permission.

progress has been made in the name of adaptive behavior in the fifty years since Doll's (1947) first Social Maturity Scale, but more work remains.

Although experts in the field appear to have reached relative agreement on the definition of adaptive behavior, and perhaps even on the skills that are believed to comprise it, the actual components of effective adaptive functioning remain much more puzzling. For example, in a content analysis of adaptive behavior measures, Bruininks, Thurlow, and Gilman (1987) found 10 different categories of behaviors composed of 45 different skills (see Figure 3.3). Complicating the measurement process are the realizations that adaptive behavior is a dynamic, ever-changing construct and that it is influenced by such factors as cultural norms, age-related expectations, and a combination of anticipated and idiosyncratic behaviors (Horn & Fuchs, 1987). Whether one is interested in the construct of adaptive behavior or the operationally defined skills that undergird it, attention to tasks that are developmentally appropriate and contextually relevant are important considerations for people whose quests toward personal independence and social responsibility are not to be taken for granted.

Best practice in the assessment of adaptive behaviors requires several key considerations (Harrison & Robinson, 1995). First, the examiner should incorporate adaptive behavior assessment into a broad-based model of assessment and intervention for any child with disabilities. Failure to link the assessment to the probable forms of intervention, at the outset, is to deny the very reason for which the assessment was conducted. Second, the examiner should be able to match the reasons for assessment with the child's *specific* needs so as to answer important questions relevant to both the referral and to the most likely means of intervention. Third, the examiner should use a combination of both norm-referenced and non-norm-referenced measures of performance and adaptive skill functioning when possible. Non-norm-referenced measures such as clinical interviews and observations, sociometric status, and various self-report inventories can provide this valuable function. Finally, the examiner should always include information about adaptive skill functioning in both school and nonschool (e.g., home, work) settings. To use one at the exclusion of the other overlooks an important piece of information relative to everyday living skills.

The Influence of the American Association on Mental Retardation

From the early work of the AAMR's first president, Edouard Seguin, to the contributions of today's leaders, the **American Association on Mental Retardation** (AAMR) has served as the scientific leader in the field of mental retardation. As noted in Chapter 1, Seguin's work on the physiology of mental retardation is well-known. Less well-known are the contributions of Goddard (1907), who challenged Seguin's early work, saying that while individuals who are mentally retarded were limited cognitively, they could still function quite well with adequate preparation and support. The problem, Goddard said, was with the instruction, not with the person; the pace of instruction needed to be slower and conducted with more patience.

Little more than a decade later, the organization's members felt a pressing need to define, diagnose, delineate, and otherwise specify the nature of the "defective delinquent," a term coined by Doll to represent individuals having trouble adapting to society. Meyers, Nihira, and Zetlin (1979) cite Doll's (1947) work as the formal beginning of adaptive behavior assessment. Believing that individual differences occurred in social competence just as in intelligence, Doll (1953) assumed that these differences represented a unitary trait, were developmental in nature, and were essential for an accurate diagnosis of mental retardation.

Reaction to 1992 AAMR Definition of Mental Retardation

The American Association on Mental Retardation's (1992) most recent publisher manual on definition, classification, and systems of supports has generated much discussion. The substance of the definition was discussed in Chapter 2.

Certain members of the American Psychological Association's (APA's) Division 33 (Mental Retardation and Developmental Disabilities) have expressed serious concerns about the latest definition. Some members of this division are so dissatisfied that they have submitted a proposal to develop an alternative manual on definition, tentatively entitled "Manual of Diagnosis and Professional Practice in Mental Retardation," to the APA.

Major criticisms raised by psychologists involve various aspects of the definition, but most of their concerns focus on assessment issues. These concerns include the following:

- The conceptual basis for choosing the 10 adaptive skill areas was arbitrary.
- Certain adaptive skill areas (e.g. leisure skills) are not necessarily part of a diagnosis of mental retardation.
- Technically sound measures do not exist for relating some adaptive skill areas to mental retardation.

- Individually administered, norm-referenced instruments do not exist for certain areas.
- The term *substantial limitations in present functioning* was not defined clearly.
- The criterion of "performance at the 6th percentile or below in at least 2 of 10 areas of life activity" was arbitrarily chosen.
- Great variability across the country in diagnosing mental retardation is likely due to the ambiguities mentioned earlier.
- The role of the psychologist changes to that of psychometrist only.
- The age range for age of onset should be raised to include 21-year-olds.

Counterarguments have been made in reaction to these concerns, and efforts to address some of them are occurring. However, the debate surrounding the new AAMR definition will continue, as other groups attempt to understand the implications of this definition and acknowledge that it differs from other recognized definitions (i.e., those of the World Health Organization and the American Psychiatric Association). Other professional and parent organizations will inevitably generate position statements on this topic.

In 1965, the AAMR initiated a study of the broad dimensions of adaptive behavior. The study produced two adaptive behavior scales, one designed for children 3–12 years of age, and the other for adolescents and adults. The two scales were then combined into one; a second formal scale was then modified and standardized for use in the schools. Two recently revised scales now comprise the family of AAMR Adaptive Behavior Scales, one for residential and community settings and one for school settings. Following is a brief description of each.

AAMR Adaptive Behavior Scale—Residential and Community, Second Edition

The AAMR Adaptive Behavior Scale—Residential and Community, second edition (ABS-RC:2) (Nihira, Leland, & Lambert, 1993a), represents the AAMR's latest revision of a project begun in 1965 to study the broad dimensions of adaptive behavior. The ABS-RC:2 is a norm-referenced, individually administered, comprehensive measure of adaptive and maladaptive behavior intended for use with persons living in residential and community settings. The authors of the ABS-RC:2 report that the scale has a fourfold purpose: to determine strengths and weaknesses in a person's adaptive skills, to identify persons whose adaptive behavior is substantially and significantly different from those of same-age peers, to gauge the progress of persons receiving intervention services, and to serve as a valid measure of adaptive behavior in research studies (Nihira, Leland, & Lambert, 1993b).

Although the ABS-RC:2 has a companion scale, the AAMR Adaptive Behavior Scales—School (ABS-S:2; see the following section), the two scales are completely independent of one another and have their own unique features. The ABS-RC:2 consists of two principal sections: Personal Independence (Part I) and Social Adaptation (Part II). Following is a breakdown of the domains comprising each of the two sections:

Part I	**Part II**
Independent functioning	Social behavior
Physical development	Conformity
Economic activity	Trustworthiness
Language development	Stereotyped/hyperactive behavior
Numbers and time	Sexual behavior
Domestic activity	Self-abusive behavior
Prevocational/vocational activity	Social engagement
Self-direction	Disturbing interpersonal behavior
Responsibility	
Socialization	

Information is obtained through a standardized interview format conducted by an examiner trained in psychodiagnostic methods. Item types vary; some take a Likert-type format with scores ranging from *behavior not present* (0) to *behavior present in highest form* (3), as, for example, when the examiner wishes to know how well a person is able to function when visiting a restaurant. For other items, the examiner may wish to know only whether a behavior is present. Examples of this type of behavior are taking food off others' plates, eating too fast or too slow, or swallowing food without chewing. In each of these cases, the response would be scored as either *yes* (1) or *no* (0).

Five types of profile scores are available through the ABS-RC:2: raw scores, percentiles, domain standard scores, factor quotients, and age equivalents. The ABS-RC:2 was standardized on 4,103 persons from 46 states and is reported in the manual to be representative of all persons with mental retardation nationwide using major demographic variables (Nihira et al., 1993b).

According to the authors, a convenient feature of the ABS-RC:2 is that the scale and the information it provides fit nicely into the three-step model of diagnosis, classification, and support now encouraged for all formal evaluations of persons with mental retardation (see AAMR, 1992). Software is available from the publisher to help with scoring and report writing.

AAMR Adaptive Behavior Scale—School, Second Edition

The AAMR Adaptive Behavior Scale—School, second edition (ABS-S:2) (Lambert, Nihira, & Leland, 1993a), is a norm-referenced, individually administered, comprehensive measure of adaptive and maladaptive behavior intended for use with school-age children. The instrument consists of two parts. Part I is divided into 10 behavior domains important for personal responsibility and independent living (independent functioning, physical development, economic activity, language development, numbers and time, domestic activity, prevocational/vocational activity, self-direction, responsibility, and socialization). Part II assesses social adaptation and maladaptive behavior, and it consists of seven domains (social behavior, conformity, trustworthiness, stereotyped and hyperactive behavior, self-abusive behavior, social engagement, and disturbing interpersonal behavior).

Like its residential and community counterpart, the school version offers a standardized interview format. The standardization sample appears to be relatively strong, with over 1,000 children with and without disabilities from 31 states serving as the normative base. Percentiles, standard scores, and age equivalents are available to the examiner. Five factor scores are also available. Internal consistency estimates for all scores reportedly exceed .80 (Lambert, Nihira, & Leland, 1993b). Software designed to help with scoring and report writing is available from the publisher at an additional cost.

The Influence of Edgar Doll

The Vineland Social Maturity Scale was developed in 1935 by Edgar A. Doll at the Vineland Training School in Vineland, New Jersey. The author's original purpose in constructing the scale was to provide a means of measuring social competence, or "social maturity," to help in the diagnosis of mental deficiency. Recognizing the need for an adaptive behavior component in the classification of persons as mentally subnormal, Doll sought to devise a measure "distinguishing between mental retardation with social incompetence (feeblemindedness) and mental retardation without social incompetence (which is often confused with feeblemindedness)" (Doll, 1965, p. 2). He defined *mental deficiency* as the demonstration of intellectual inadequacy, social inadequacy, and arrested mental development.

The Vineland scales have been revised and renamed the Vineland Adaptive Behavior Scales. There are currently three versions of the scale: interview edition, expanded form (Sparrow, Balla, & Cicchetti, 1984a); interview edition, survey form (Sparrow, Balla, & Cicchetti, 1984b); and classroom edition (Sparrow, Balla, & Cicchetti, 1985). Of these three, the survey form is most similar to the original Vineland scales. The purpose of each of these newer versions is indicated in its title. The first two scales are administered to individuals who know the person being assessed, usually parents or caregivers. The classroom scale is typically completed by the teacher. These scales assess five major domains of adaptive behavior: communication, daily living skills, socialization, motor skills, and maladaptive behavior (assessment of the last domain is optional).

Administration and scoring of the scales follow a structure in which items are organized according to domain. Raw scores are converted to standard scores, percentiles (both national and supplementary, which include norms of different groups of people with disabilities), stanines, age equivalents, and an estimated adaptive level. A sum of all domain standard scores can be converted to an adaptive behavior composite ($M = 100$, $SD = 15$). The Vineland continues to be a popular measure of social competency, and many now place it among the best measures of adaptive behavior.

Other Influential Scales

Contributions to the development of adaptive behavior assessment are not limited to the AAMR and Edgar Doll. Following is a brief discussion of several other instruments that have helped influence the means by which adaptive behavior is measured and explained.

Scales of Independent Behavior—Revised

The Scales of Independent Behavior—Revised (SIB-R; Bruininks, Woodcock, Weatherman, & Hill, 1996a) were developed by Robert Bruininks and his colleagues at the University of Minnesota's Institute on Community Integration. The SIB-R is a norm-referenced, individually administered measure of adaptive and maladaptive behavior "designed to measure functional independence and adaptive functioning in school, home, employment and community settings" (Bruininks, Woodcock, Weatherman, & Hill, 1996b, p. 1). The instrument yields two composite indices, a Broad Independence (adaptive) score and a General Problem Behaviors score. Within the adaptive behavior portion of the instrument are four broad skill areas (Motor Skills, Social Interaction Skills/Communication Skills, Personal Living Skills, Community Living Skills). Within the problem behavior portion are three areas (Internalized Maladaptive Behavior, Asocial Maladaptive Behavior, Externalized Maladaptive Behavior). Each area—or cluster, as it is called in the SIB-R—consists of a number of subscales that allow the examiner to evaluate a person's level of performance in important areas of daily living (see Figure 3.4)

Although the SIB-R is technically part of the Woodcock-Johnson Psychoeducational Battery—Revised (Woodcock & Johnson, 1989), its use does not depend on the rest of the battery and is considered by persons in the field to be a strong and stable instrument in its own right. The advantage of being linked with a broad-based measure of intelligence and achievement such as the Woodcock-Johnson is that it allows for a better understanding of one's adaptive functioning in the context of cognitive and school-related development.

The scoring procedures for the SIB-R are straightforward. When administering adaptive behavior items, the examiner simply asks parents or care providers to rate how well and how often a person performs a given task, ranging from *never* or *rarely* (0), to *very well, always,* or *almost always* (3). For the Problem Behavior scales, the parent or care provider is provided with the description of a series of behaviors and is asked to rate the frequency and severity of occurrence. For example, when asking about disruptive behaviors, the examiner may ask whether the person interferes with the activities of others by "clinging, arguing, picking fights, or screaming." Response options for frequency of occurrence range from *less than once a month* (1) to *one or more times an hour* (5); severity response options range from *not serious* (0) to *extremely serious* (4).

What makes the SIB-R different from other norm-referenced measures of adaptive behavior is its systems-level approach to assessment and intervention. While the SIB-R is part of the Woodcock-Johnson battery, it is also part of a broader adaptive behavior assessment program. For example, the SIB-R is linked to the Checklist of Adaptive Living Skills (Morreau & Bruininks, 1992), a criterion-referenced assessment device that focuses directly on a person's instructional needs and train-

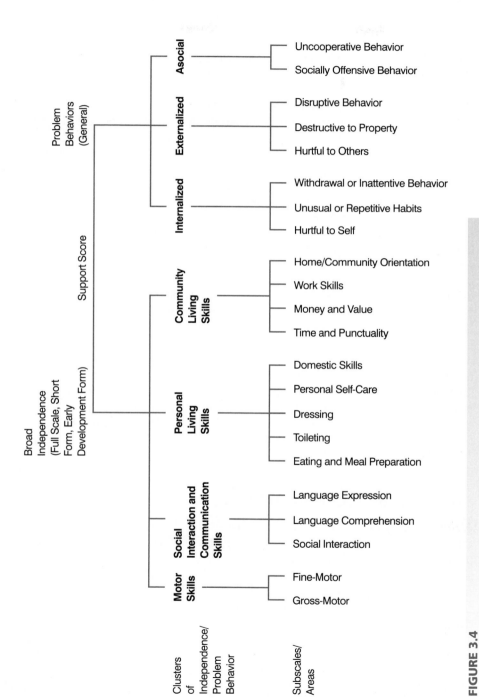

FIGURE 3.4

Structure of the SIB-R

Source: Copyright © 1996 by The Riverside Publishing Company. Reproduced from *Scales of Independent Behavior—Revised Comprehensive Manual* by Robert H. Bruininks, Richard W. Woodcock, Richard F. Weatherman, and Bradley K. Hill with permission of the publisher. All rights reserved.

ing objectives, which are in turn linked to a curriculum-based program containing more than 800 specific and measurable instructional objectives organized into 24 separate life-skill teaching units. According to Cheri Gilman, one of the developers of the Adaptive Living Skills Curriculum (Bruininks, Morreau, Gilman, & Anderson, 1992), even such instructional models as meal planning and preparation, sexuality, home safety, and job search skills are traceable to information obtained with the SIB-R (personal communication, December 16, 1992).

A host of other instruments are also available for use with persons with mental retardation. One such instrument is the Adaptive Behavior Inventory for Children (Mercer & Lewis, 1982). The ABIC is designed to assess adaptive functioning of children from 1 to 5 years of age and measures a child's adaptive functioning through a questionnaire completed by the child's mother or other primary caretaker. The ABIC attempts to minimize cultural bias by offering information about a child's adaptive behavior in the appropriate sociocultural context. The Adaptive Behavior Evaluation Scale: Revised (ABES; McCarney, 1995) obtains information in the 10 adaptive skill areas put forth in the 1992 diagnosis and classification manual. As with the AAMR scales, there are two versions of the ABES, home and school, appropriate for children in grades K–12. The ABES is one of Hawthorne's growing armada of diagnostic instruments that link special needs with service delivery in a practical, user-friendly manner.

Different from the other adaptive scales just mentioned, a new instrument focuses on the needs of adults, specifically. The Independent Living Scales (ILS; Loeb, 1996) consists of five principal scales: memory and orientation, managing money, managing home and transportation, health and safety, and social adjustment. The ILS was designed in such a way as to distinguish among those who can identify and respond to environmental needs, those who can identify problem areas but who need help in addressing them, and, finally, those who are not capable of identifying and meeting even their basic needs. The ILS must be given by a trained examiner and takes approximately 45 minutes to administer.

Criticisms of Adaptive Behavior Assessment

Adaptive behavior has emerged as an important index in the identification of mental retardation. However, its acceptance is not universal, and its definition is still under some debate. Although most professionals and laypersons alike believe that there is a definite nonintellectual component to mental retardation, disagreement remains as to its role and function in the assessment to service sequence.

First, measuring adaptive behavior seems to be much more difficult than simply defining it—and defining it certainly has not been easy. The adaptive behavior tests currently on the market all seem to measure different tasks in different ways. For example, some tests cover tasks considered to be important at home, others at school, and still others in residential facilities. Furthermore, some instruments assess social skills, others assess social intelligence, and still others assess social development. Some measures emphasize domestic skills, whereas others emphasize self-help skills. All represent very important but yet very different types of adaptive capabilities. It is no surprise, then, that researchers and clinicians alike are still struggling to find the true underlying dimensions of the construct known as adaptive behavior. AAMR's new emphasis on adaptive skill areas should help with this diversity.

A second major criticism pertains to the school-age population and the degree to which intellectual factors play a part in the determination of adaptive skills. Some researchers (e.g., Mercer, 1978) see intelligence as an unnecessary part of adaptive functioning, but others (e.g., Reschly, 1985) regard intellectual functioning as a crucial component of adaptive functioning. Problem-solving skills carry over from one environment to the next whether in school, home, play, or otherwise. As evidence continues to mount with respect to subtle but important distinctions between intelligence and adaptive behavior, it is imperative that new frameworks be developed that allow for the integration of both intelligence and adaptive behavior within one over-arching framework. Greenspan's (1997) model of personal competence offers such a framework by dividing personal competence into four key areas across which traditional measures of intelligence and adaptive behavior all play important roles.

A third major criticism of adaptive behavior scales pertains to their use in diverse cultures. Some contend that because they are used with intelligence tests, they are plagued by many of the limitations of intelligence tests from years past. Not so. That is not to say that adaptive behavior measures are perfect when it comes to culture-fairness—they certainly are not. Whether one is actually interested in skills within a single culture or across many cultures, adaptive behavior is, by definition, culture bound. To know what is appropriate for a given age and reference group depends very much on the person's ability to decode and identify subtle and not-so-subtle cultural cues. The issue at hand, then, becomes one of validity and appropriateness rather than simply guilt by (historical) association. In short, what the field needs, according to Craig and Tassé (1999), is culturally competent assessment practices. That means good tests, with good norms, and good evaluators. This, too, will be a challenge for the years ahead.

To read more about the cultural implications of assessment, go to the companion website at www.prenhall.com/beirne-smith, and select Chapter 3, then choose Article Response module.

━━━ **Summary** ━━━━━━━━━━━━━━━━

Theories of Intelligence
- Theories of intelligence may be evaluated along a number of dimensions, such as the source of one's knowledge, the amount of one's knowledge, or the pattern of one's mental processing ability.
- Most people believe that intelligence is epigenetic in nature, a combination of both biological and environmental factors.
- Deviation IQs are considered to be the best index of intellectual ability because they allow an examiner to compare a person's score with others of markedly different ages and ability levels.

Assessment of Intelligence
- The first effective test of intellectual ability was the 30-item Measuring Scale of Intelligence designed by Alfred Binet and Theodore Simon in 1905.
- The Wechsler scales are a series of three individually administered intelligence tests, modeled after one another, in which a person's intellectual abilities are described using a verbal/motor framework.

- Criticisms of intelligence tests take several different forms: some are directed at the tests themselves, others are directed at the examiners who conduct the evaluations, and still others are directed at the assessment process.

Theories of Adaptive Behavior
- *Adaptive behavior* refers to a person's ability to meet age-appropriate standards of independence and personal responsibility.
- Adaptive behavior is considered to be a construct separate from but related to the construct of intelligence.
- The AAMR continues to serve as the scientific leader in the field of mental retardation.

Assessment of Adaptive Behavior
- The first formal measure of adaptive behavior was Doll's (1935) Vineland Social Maturity Scale, developed at the Vineland Training School in Vineland, New Jersey.
- Several different measures of adaptive behavior have been developed over the years, ranging from simple behavioral checklists to in-depth diagnostic interviews.
- When measures of adaptive behavior are criticized, objections are usually directed at such things as the measurement process, the role of intelligence in adaptive functioning, and the culture-bound nature of adaptive behavior skills.

References

American Association on Mental Retardation. (1992). *Mental retardation: Definition, classification, and systems of supports* (9th ed.). Washington, DC: Author.

American Educational Research Association, American Psychological Association, National Council on Measurement in Education. (1999). *Standards for Educational and Psychological Testing*. Washington, DC: American Educational Research Association.

Binet, A., & Simon, T. (1905). Methodes nouvelles pour le diagnostic du niveau intellectuel des anormaux. *Année Psychologique, 11*, 191–244.

Bouchard, T. J., Lykken, D. T., McGue, M., Segal, N. L., & Tellegen, A. (1990). Sources of human psychological differences: The Minnesota study of twins reared apart. *Science, 250*, 223–228.

Bracken, B. A., & McCallum, R. S. (1998). *Universal Nonverbal Intelligence Test*. Chicago: Riverside.

Braden, J. P. (1995). Review of the Wechsler Intelligence Scale for Children—Third Edition. In J. C. Conoley & J. C. Impara (Eds.), *The twelfth mental measurements yearbook* (pp. 1098–1103). Lincoln: University of Nebraska, Burus Institute.

Brandon, R. N. (1990). *Adaptation and environment* (2nd ed.). Princeton, NJ: Princeton University Press.

Bruininks, R. H., Morreau, L. E., Gilman, C. J., & Anderson, J. L. (1992). *Adaptive living skills curriculum*. Chicago, IL: Riverside.

Bruininks, R. H., Thurlow, M. L., & Gilman, C. J. (1987). Adaptive behavior and mental retardation. *The Journal of Special Education, 21*(1), 69–88.

Bruininks, R. H., Woodcock, R. W., Weatherman, R. F., & Hill, B. K. (1996a). *Scales of Independent Behavior—Revised (SIB-R)*. Chicago: Riverside.

Bruininks, R. H., Woodcock, R. W., Weatherman, R. F., & Hill, B. K. (1996b). *Scales of Independent Behavior—Revised (SIB-R): Comprehensive Manual*. Chicago: Riverside.

Carroll, J. B. (1993). *Human cognitive abilities: A survey of factor analytic studies*. New York: Cambridge University Press.

Conoley, J. C., & Impara, J. C. (Eds.). (1995). *The twelfth mental measurements yearbook*. Lincoln: University of Nebraska, Burus Institute.

Conroy, J. W. (1996). The small ICF/MR program: Dimensions of quality and cost. *Mental Retardation, 34*(1), 13–26.

Craig, E. M., & Tassé, M. J. (1999). Cultural and demographic group comparisons of adaptive behavior. In R. L. Schalock (Ed.), *Adaptive behavior and its measurement: Implications for the field of mental retardation* (pp. 419-439). Washington, DC: American Association on Mental Retardation.

Daniel, M. (1994). A review of the Differential Ability Scales. In R. J. Sternberg (Ed.), *Encyclopedia of human intelligence* (pp. 350–354). New York: Macmillan.

Das, J. P., Naglieri, J. A., & Kirby, J. R. (1994). *Assessment of cognitive processes: The PASS theory of intelligence*. Boston: Allyn & Bacon.

Doll, E. A. (1935). A genetic scale of social maturity. *American Journal of Orthopsychiatry, 5*, 180–188.

Doll, E. A. (1947). *Social Maturity Scale*. Circle Pines, MN: American Guidance Service.

Doll, E. A. (1953). *Measurement of social competence: A manual for the Vineland Social Maturity Scale*. Circle Pines, MN: American Guidance Service.

Doll, E. A. (1965). *Vineland Social Maturity Scale: Condensed manual of directions* (1965 ed.). Circle Pines, MN: American Guidance Service.

Elliott, C. D. (1990). *Differential Ability Scales*. San Antonio, TX: Psychological Corporation.

Gardner, H. (1993). *Frames of mind: The theory of multiple intelligences*. New York: Basic Books.

Goddard, H. H. (1907). Psychological work among the feeble-minded. *Journal of Psycho-Asthetics, 12*(1–4), 22.

Gordon, J. R. (1991). *A diagnostic approach to organizational behavior* (3rd ed.). Boston: Allyn & Bacon.

Greenspan, S. (1997). The role of intelligence in a broad model of personal competence. In D. P. Flanagan, J. O. Genshaft, & P. L. Harrison (Eds.), *Contemporary intellectual assessment: Theories, tests, and issues* (p. 133). New York: Guilford.

Grossman, H. J. (Ed.). (1973). *Manual on terminology and classification in mental retardation*. Washington, DC: American Association on Mental Retardation.

Grossman, H. J. (Ed.). (1983). *Manual on terminology and classification in mental retardation*. Washington, DC: American Association on Mental Retardation.

Guilford, J. P. (1967). *The nature of human intelligence*. New York: McGraw-Hill.

Harrison, P. L. (1987). Research with adaptive behavior scales. *Journal of Special Education, 21*(1), 37–68.

Harrison, P. L., & Robinson, B. (1995). Best practices in the assessment of adaptive behavior. In A. Thomas & J. Grimes (Eds.), *Best practices in school psychology—III* (pp. 753–762). Washington, DC: National Association of School Psychologists.

Haywood, H. C., & Paour, J. (1992). Alfred Binet (1857–1922): Multifactored pioneer. *Psychology in Mental Retardation and Developmental Disabilities, 18*, 1–4.

Hobfall, S. E. (1998). *Stress, culture, and community: The psychology and philosophy of stress*. New York: Plenum.

Horn, J. L., & Cattell, R. B. (1966). Refinement of the theory of fluid and crystallized general intelligence. *Journal of Educational Psychology, 57,* 253–270.

Horn, E., & Fuchs, D. (1987). Using adaptive behavior in assessment and intervention: An overview. *Journal of Special Education, 21*(1), 11–26.

Ittenbach, R. F., Esters, I. G., & Wainer, H. (1997). The history of test development. In D. P. Flanagan, J. L. Genshaft, & P. L. Harrison (Eds.), *Contemporary intellectual assessment: Theories, tests, and issues* (pp. 17–31). New York: Guilford.

Ittenbach, R. F., & Lawhead, W. F. (1997). Historical and philosophical foundations of single-case research. In R. D. Franklin, D. B. Allison, & B. S. Gorman (Eds.), *Design and analysis of single-case research* (pp. 13–39). Hillsdale, NJ: Erlbaum.

Ittenbach, R. F., Spiegel, A. N., McGrew, K. S., & Bruininks, R. H. (1992). Confirmatory factor analysis of early childhood ability measures within a model of personal competence. *Journal of School Psychology, 30,* 307–323.

Jensen, A. R. (1998). *The g factor: The science of mental ability*. Westport, CT: Praeger.

Kamin, L. J. (1974). *The science and politics of IQ*. Hillsdale, NJ: Erlbaum.

Kamphaus, R. W. (1987). Conceptual and psychometric issues in the assessment of adaptive behavior. *Journal of Special Education, 21*(1), 27–36.

Kaufman, A. S. (1994). *Intelligent testing with the WISC- III*. New York: Wiley.

Kaufman, A. S., Harrison, P. L., & Ittenbach, R. F. (1990). Intelligence testing in the schools. In T. B. Gutkin & C. R. Reynolds (Eds.), *The handbook of school psychology* (2nd ed.; pp. 289–327). New York: Wiley.

Kaufman, A. S., & Kaufman, N. L. (1983). *Kaufman Assessment Battery for Children (K-ABC)*. Circle Pines, MN: American Guidance Service.

Keith, T. Z., Fehrman, P. G., Harrison, P. L., & Pottebaum, S. M. (1987). The relation between adaptive behavior and intelligence: Testing alternative explanations. *Journal of School Psychology, 24,* 31–43.

Lambert, N., Nihira, K., & Leland, H. (1993a). *AAMR Adaptive Behavior Scale—School* (2nd ed.). Austin, TX: PRO-ED.

Lambert, N., Nihira, K., & Leland, H. (1993b). *AAMR Adaptive Behavior Scale—School (2nd ed.): Technical manual*. Austin, TX: PRO-ED.

Larson, S. A., & Lakin, K. C. (1991). Parent attitudes about residential placement before and after deinstitutionalization: A research synthesis. *Journal of the Association for Persons with Severe Handicaps, 16,* 25–38.

Laurent, J., Swerdlik, M., & Ryburn, M. (1992). Review of validity research on the Stanford-Binet Intelligence Scale: Fourth Edition. *Psychological Assessment, 4*(1), 102–112.

Leland, H. W. (1978). Theoretical considerations of adaptive behavior. In W. A. Coulter & H. W. Morrow (Eds.), *Adaptive behavior: Concepts and measurements* (pp. 21–44). Orlando, FL: Grune & Stratton.

Loeb, P. A. (1996). *Independent Living Scales*. San Antonio, TX: Psychological Corporation.

Lumsden, C. J., & Wilson, E. O. (1985). The relation between biological and cultural evolution. *Journal of Social Biology Structures, 8,* 343–359.

Luria, A. R. (1980). *Higher cortical functions in man* (2nd ed., revised and expanded). B. Haigh, Trans. New York: Basic Books.

Mackintosh, N. J. (1998). *IQ and human intelligence*. New York: Oxford University Press.

McCarney, S. B. (1995). *Adaptive Behavior Evaluation Scale: Revised*. Columbia, MO: Hawthorne Educational Services.

McGrew, K. S., Bruininks, R. H., & Johnson, D. R. (1996). Confirmatory factor analytic investigation of Greenspan's model of personal competence. *American Journal on Mental Retardation, 100*(5), 533–545.

Mercer, J. R. (1978). *System of Multicultural Pluralistic Assessment: Parent interview manual*. San Antonio, TX: Psychological Corporation.

Mercer, J. R., & Lewis, J. F. (1982). *Adaptive Behavior Inventory for Children*. San Antonio, TX: Psychological Corporation.

Messick, S. (1988). The once and future issues of validity: Assessing the meaning and consequences of measurement. In H. Wainer & H. I. Braun (Eds.), *Test validity* (pp. 33–45). Hillsdale, NJ: Erlbaum.

Meyers, R., Nihira, K., & Zetlin, A. (1979). The measurement of adaptive behavior. In N. R. Ellis (Ed.), *Handbook of mental deficiency: Psychological theory and research* (2nd ed., pp. 431–481). Hillsdale, NJ: Erlbaum.

Morreau, E., & Bruininks, R. H. (1992). *Checklist of adaptive living skills*. Chicago: Riverside.

Naglieri, J. A. (1985). *Matrix Analogies Test—Expanded Form*. San Antonio, TX: Psychological Corporation.

Nihira, K. (1999). Adaptive behavior: A historical overview. In R. L. Schalock (Ed.), *Adaptive behavior and its measurement: Implications for the field of mental retardation* (pp. 7–14). Washington, DC: American Association on Mental Retardation.

Nihira, K., Leland, H., & Lambert, N. (1993a). *AAMR Adaptive Behavior Scale— Residential and Community* (2nd ed.). Austin, TX: PRO-ED.

Nihira, K., Leland, H., & Lambert, N. (1993b). *AAMR Adaptive Behavior Scale— Residential and Community (2nd ed.): Technical manual*. Austin, TX: PRO-ED.

Pedersen, N. L., Plomin, R., Nesselroade, J. R., & McClearn, G. E. (1992). A quantitative genetic analysis of cognitive abilities during the second half of the life span. *Psychological Science, 3*, 346–353.

Piaget, J. (1952). *The origins of intelligence in children*. New York: International Universities Press.

Plomin, R. (1994). *Genetics and experience: The interplay between nature and nurture*. Thousand Oaks, CA: Sage.

Plomin, R., & Petrill, S. A. (1997). Genetics and intelligence: What's new? *Intelligence, 24*(1), 53–77.

President's Committee on Mental Retardation. (PCMR). (1970). *The six-hour retarded child*. Washington, DC: U.S. Government Printing Office.

Prosser, C. L. (1986). *Adaptational biology: Molecules to organisms*. New York: Wiley.

Reschly, D. (1985). Best practices: Adaptive behavior. In A. Thomas & J. Grimes (Eds.), *Best practices in school psychology* (pp. 353–368). Kent, OH: National Association of School Psychologists.

Roid, G. H., & Miller, L. J. (1997). *Leiter International Performance Scale—Revised*. Wood Dale, IL: Stoelting.

Sandoval, J. (1992). Using the DAS with multi-cultural populations: Issues of test bias. *Journal of Psychoeducational Assessment, 10*, 8891.

Schalock, R. L. (Ed.). (1999a). *Adaptive behavior and its measurement: Implications for the field of mental retardation*. Washington, DC: American Association on Mental Retardation.

Schalock, R. L. (1999b). The merging of adaptive behavior and intelligence: Implications for the field of mental retardation. In R. L. Schalock (Ed.), *Adaptive behavior and its measurement: Implications for the field of mental retardation* (pp. 43–59). Washington, DC: American Association on Mental Retardation.

Schultz, D. P., & Schultz, S. E. (1996). *A history of modern psychology* (6th ed.). San Diego, CA: Harcourt Brace.

Sparrow, S. S., Balla, D. A., & Cicchetti, D. V. (1984a). *Vineland Adaptive Behavior Scales: Interview edition, expanded form*. Circle Pines, MN: American Guidance Service.

Sparrow, S. S., Balla, D. A., & Cicchetti, D. V. (1984b). *Vineland Adaptive Behavior Scales: Interview edition, survey form*. Circle Pines, MN: American Guidance Service.

Sparrow, S. S., Balla, D. A., & Cicchetti, D. V. (1985). *Vineland Adaptive Behavior Scales: Classroom edition form*. Circle Pines, MN: American Guidance Service.

Spearman, C. E. (1927). *The abilities of man*. New York: Macmillan.

Staddon, J. E. (1983). *Adaptive behavior and learning*. New York: Cambridge University Press.

Sternberg, R. J. (1985). *Beyond IQ: A triarchic theory of intelligence*. New York: Cambridge University Press.

Sternberg, R. J. (1988). *The triarchic mind: A new theory of intelligence*. New York: Viking.

Sternberg, R. J. (1997). The triarchic mind. In D. P. Flanagan, J. Genshaft, & P. L. Harrison (Eds.), *Contemporary intellectual assessment: Theories, tests, and issues* (pp. 92–104). New York: Guilford.

Terman, L. M. (1916). *The measurement of intelligence*. Boston: Houghton Mifflin.

Terman, L. M., & Merrill, M. A. (1937). *Measuring intelligence: A guide to the administration and scoring of the new revised Stanford-Binet tests of intelligence*. Boston: Houghton Mifflin.

Terman, L. M., & Merrill, M. A. (1960). *The Stanford-Binet Intelligence Scale: Manual for the third revision, Form L-M*. Boston: Houghton Mifflin.

Thompson, J. R., McGrew, K. S., & Bruininks, R. H. (1999). Adaptive and maladaptive behavior: Functional and structural characteristics. In R. L. Schalock (Ed.), *Adaptive behavior and its measurement: Implications for the field of mental retardation* (pp. 15–42). Washington, DC: American Association on Mental Retardation.

Thorndike, E. L. (1927). *The measurement of intelligence*. New York: Columbia University, Teacher's College Press.

Thorndike, R. L., Hagen, E. P., & Sattler, J. P. (1986a). *Stanford-Binet Intelligence Scale: Fourth Edition*. Chicago: Riverside.

Thorndike, R. L., Hagen, E. P., & Sattler, J. P. (1986b). *Stanford-Binet Intelligence Scale: Fourth Edition: Guide for Administration and scoring*. Chicago: Riverside.

Thurstone, L. L. (1938). Primary mental abilities. *Psychometric Monographs*, No. 1.

Vernon, P. E. (1950). *The structure of human abilities*. New York: Wiley.

Wechsler, D. (1939). *The measurement of adult intelligence*. Baltimore, MD: Williams & Wilkins.

Wechsler, D. (1949). *Wechsler Intelligence Scale for Children*. San Antonio, TX: Psychological Corporation.

Wechsler, D. (1955). *Wechsler Adult Intelligence Scale*. San Antonio, TX: Psychological Corporation.

Wechsler, D. (1958). *The measurement and appraisal of adult intelligence* (4th ed.). Baltimore, MD: Williams & Wilkins.

Wechsler, D. (1967). *Wechsler Preschool and Primary Scale of Intelligence*. San Antonio, TX: Psychological Corporation.

Wechsler, D. (1974). *Wechsler Intelligence Scale for Children—Revised*. San Antonio, TX: Psychological Corporation.

Wechsler, D. (1981). *Wechsler Adult Intelligence Scale—Revised*. San Antonio, TX: Psychological Corporation.

Wechsler, D. (1989a). *Wechsler Preschool and Primary Scale of Intelligence—Revised*. San Antonio, TX: Psychological Corporation.

Wechsler, D. (1989b). *Wechsler Preschool and Primary Scale of Intelligence—Revised: Manual*. San Antonio, TX: Psychological Corporation.

Wechsler, D. (1991a). *Wechsler Intelligence Scale for Children—Third Edition*. San Antonio, TX: Psychological Corporation.

Wechsler, D. (1991b). *Wechsler Intelligence Scale for Children—Third Edition: Manual*. San Antonio, TX: Psychological Corporation.

Wechsler, D. (1997). *Wechsler Adult Intelligence Scale—Third Edition*. San Antonio, TX: Psychological Corporation.

Widaman, K. F., & McGrew, K. S. (1996). The structure of adaptive behavior. In J. W. Jacobson & J. A. Mulick (Eds.), *Manual of diagnosis and professional practice in mental retardation* (pp. 97–110). Washington, DC: American Psychological Association.

Widaman, K. F., Reise, S. P., & Clatfelter, D. L. (1994). *Assessing the measurement structure of adaptive behavior: Factor analytic versus item response theory approaches.* Paper presented at the Gatlinburg Conference on Research and Theory in Mental Retardation and Developmental Disabilities, Gatlinburg, TN.

Widaman, K. F., Stacy, A. W., & Borthwick-Duffy, S. A. (1993). Construct validity of dimensions of adaptive behavior: A multitrait-multimethod evaluation. *American Journal on Mental Retardation, 98*, 219–234.

Woodcock, R. W., & Johnson, M. B. (1989). *Woodcock-Johnson Psychoeducational Battery—Revised*. Chicago: Riverside.

Zigler, E., Balla, D. A., & Hodapp, R. (1984). On the definition and classification of mental retardation. *American Journal of Mental Deficiency, 89*, 215–230.

Chapter

4

Individual Rights and Legal Issues

 To review the chapter objectives on-line, go to the companion website at www.prenhall.com/ beirne-smith and select Chapter 4, then choose the Objectives module.

Veda Jairrels, Ph.D.
Clark Atlanta University

OBJECTIVES

After reading this chapter, the student should be able to

- understand fundamental concepts and legal bases for establishing the rights of persons who are mentally retarded

- discuss the legal history for establishing educational, institutional, and community rights

- understand the problems that occur when individuals with mental retardation are the victims of crime and are accused of crimes

- identify future trends and issues pertinent to the lives of individuals who are mentally retarded

KEY TERMS

due process	procedural due process
equal protection	quasi-suspect class
habilitation	substantive due process

THE CONTEXT FOR SECURING INDIVIDUALS' RIGHTS

In recent years, the courts and Congress have played major roles in attempting to secure the rights of individuals with disabilities in the areas of education, employment, transportation, public accommodations, and communication. This assistance from the courts, state legislatures, and Congress was not always forthcoming. In the past, individuals suffered discrimination, not only due to the views of society but also as a result of court decisions and legislation, which often reflected those societal views. For example, Yell, Rogers, and Rogers (1998) note that as early as 1893, a state court ruled that children with disabilities could be expelled from school (*Watson v. City of Cambridge,* 1893). Russo, Morse, and Glancy (1998) report that at one time, the majority of states required that certain individuals with disabilities be sterilized.

Brown v. Board of Education (1954) was an event that set the stage for increased educational opportunities and served as a major legal turning point in the lives of people with disabilities (Yell et al., 1998). Russo, Morse, and Glancy (1998) refer to it as the "most significant ruling on education in the history of the United States" (p. 8). In this case, the Supreme Court ruled that the racial segregation concept of separate but equal was unconstitutional. Although this case was filed on behalf of African Americans, Turnbull and Turnbull (2000) state that if

> *disabled* or *students with disabilities* is substituted for *Negro* and *nondisabled* is substituted for *white* wherever those words appear in *Brown*, we can understand why this case is important to the education of students with disabilities and how the Fourteenth Amendment became the constitutional basis for the rights of students with disabilities to be educated. (p. 10)

According to Newcomer and Zirkel (1999), litigation involving special education issues increased tremendously in the past 10 years. Some court decisions were codified in the Individuals with Disabilities Education Act (IDEA) Amendments of 1997 (Walther-Thomas & Brownell, 1998). In this chapter, recent litigation, legislation, major concepts, and future concerns are delineated.

Legal Bases for Establishing Rights

The three levels of government are federal, state, and local. Some powers are shared among these three levels, and other powers are primarily the domain of federal, state, or local government. It is important to note that the federal Constitution and the laws passed by Congress are the supreme law of the land. Turnbull and Turnbull (2000) present a model of the three levels along with their corresponding governing documents (Figure 4.1).

For a complete online glossary of mental retardation terms, go to the companion website at http://www.prenhall.com/ beirne-smith and select any chapter, then choose the Glossary module.

Federal Constitutional Arguments   The Fourteenth Amendment to the Constitution contains two frequently invoked clauses: the **due process** clause ("nor shall any State deprive any person of life, liberty, or property, without due process of law") and the **equal protection** clause ("nor deny to any person within its jurisdiction the equal protection of the laws"). Many of the rights secured and services established for those with retardation have been achieved through litiga-

FIGURE 4.1

A Model of Public Law

Source: From *Free and Appropriate Public Education: The Law and Children with Disabilities,* by H. R. Turnbull III and A. P. Turnbull (6th ed., p. 4). Denver: Love. Copyright 2000 by Love Publishing Company. Reprinted with permission.

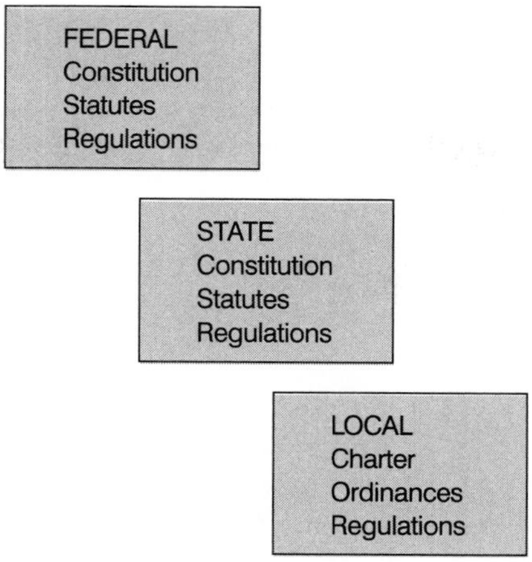

FEDERAL
Constitution
Statutes
Regulations

STATE
Constitution
Statutes
Regulations

LOCAL
Charter
Ordinances
Regulations

tion based on constitutional grounds, particularly on these two principles. Table 4.1 presents the constitutional arguments that have been used most frequently in cases involving persons with mental retardation. This table is only a brief guide to the constitutional basis for litigation; it is not a comprehensive list of all previous, present, or future bases for litigation.

Since the equal protection clause of the Fourteenth Amendment has been the backbone for many rights for persons with mental retardation, we will look at it more closely. There are three types of equal protection analyses (the application of equal protection to a specific claim): (a) "rational basis" analysis, (b) "intermediate" or "middle-tier scrutiny" standard, and (c) "strict scrutiny" analysis. Rothstein (1995) describes these different levels of scrutiny as follows:

> If the individual affected by the practice is a member of a "suspect class" such as a racial minority, or if the right at issue is a "fundamental right" such as a privacy, the practice will be strictly scrutinized (evaluated very carefully). Where the classification is not a specially protected class, or if the right is not an important one, the practice will usually be upheld if there is any rational basis for it. Individuals with disabilities have not been held to be members of a suspect class, but education has been recognized as deserving of "special constitutional treatment," and an intermediate test of heightened scrutiny has been applied. (p. 13)

When the courts apply the rational basis, or traditional analysis, they use a two-pronged test. First, they ask whether the purposes for different treatment sought by the state are legitimate. Second, they investigate whether a "rational" correspondence exists between the purposes of the state action and the classification.

The intermediate scrutiny standard is used when discriminatory practices are claimed against a group of people who share some of the characteristics of a "suspect class." A member of such a group is sometimes referred to as being a member of a **"quasi-suspect" class**. The United States Supreme Court decided in *Cleburne Living Center, Inc. v. City of Cleburne, Texas* (1984) not to grant suspect or quasi-suspect classification status to individuals who are mentally retarded. The Court stressed, however, that "irrational prejudice could not be the basis for unequal treatment" (Rothstein, 1995, p. 63).

TABLE 4.1
Constitutional Arguments Frequently Used in Litigation

Constitutional Argument	Constitutional Basis (Amendment)	Explanation	Example of Application
Equal protection	Fourteenth	No state shall deny to any person within its jurisdiction the equal protection of the laws	Right to education
Due process (substantive)	Fifth (federal) Fourteenth (state)	Protection from unreasonable action	Right to appropriate classification Right to treatment
Due process (procedural)	Fifth (federal) Fourteenth (state)	Guaranteed procedural fairness where the government would deprive one of property or liberty	Placement rights in the criminal justice system
Freedom from cruel and unusual punishment	Eighth	Protection from punishment that is found to be offensive to the ordinary person, that is unfair, or that is grossly excessive for the offense	Right to refuse treatment Right to treatment Rights in prison

The courts apply a strict scrutiny analysis where a practice affects a suspect classification or a fundamental interest. The state must demonstrate a compelling interest for the practice to be upheld.

Federal Statutes and Regulations   Another mechanism for securing the rights of citizens who are mentally retarded that has had and will continue to have significance is federal legislation and its accompanying regulations. As more federal legislation is enacted, reference to it will occur more frequently. This is particularly noteworthy in light of the Supreme Court's reluctance to apply either the intermediate or strict scrutiny standards—standards that make it easier to win equal protection claims (Bateman, 1986).

To date, the United States has enacted a number of major pieces of legislation in this area. A list and accompanying description of some of the more important laws are provided in Table 4.2. These legislative actions establish mandates and provide a legal basis for arguing against unfair treatment.

TABLE 4.2
Major Federal Legislation

Legislation	Year Enacted	Public Law No.	Features
Amendment to Vocational Rehabilitation Act	1973	93-112	* prohibited discrimination against persons with "handicaps" (Section 504 of the Act) * provided a functional definition of "handicap"—mental or physical impairments that limit one or more of a person's major life activities * included persons with conditions that would not be covered by later legislation (e.g., drug-alcohol addition)
Education Amendments of the Elementary and Secondary Education Act 1965	1974	93-380	* provided increased funding to assist states in meeting the right-to-education requirements * required states to develop plans for implementing educational opportunities for all students with disabilities—this included procedural safeguards
Developmental Disabilities Assistance and Bill of Rights Act	1974	94-103	* broadened the term "developmental disabilities" * provided grants to states and university-affiliated programs
Education for All Handicapped Children Act [Individuals with Disabilities Education Act (IDEA)]	1975	94-142	* mandated a free, appropriate education for all students with "handicaps" in the least restrictive environment * provided for nondiscriminatory testing, individualized education programs, procedural safeguards, and parent participation * reauthorized most recently in 1997 as PL 105-17 * now named the Individuals with Disabilities Education Act (IDEA)
Handicapped Children's Protection Act	1986	99-372	* enacted in response to the Supreme court's decision in *Smith v. Robinson* (1984) * allowed courts to award reasonable attorney's fees to parents if the parents complaint is successful
Americans with disabilities Act	1990	101-336	* landmark civil rights legislation—designed to eliminate discrimination * provided civil rights protections to all persons with disabilities, including groups not previously addressed (e.g., HIV) * incorporated a functional definition similar to the Vocational Rehabilitation Act of 1973—limitations in one or more major life activities * stressed equal opportunity, independent living, and economic self-sufficiency * addressed employment, public services (e.g., building, transportation), public accommodations (e.g., restaurants, museums), telecommunications.

Some information used in this table taken from Drew, Logan, and Hardman (1992).

State Constitutions, Statutes, and Regulations   All states have mandates regarding the education of their citizenry in their state constitutions (Underwood & Mead, 1995). The Fourteenth Amendment mandates that states provide their citizens with equal protection. Therefore, state constitutions can also provide a basis for legal action brought on behalf of individuals with disabilities.

Local Charters, Ordinances, and Regulations   These provisions also play an important role in determining the rights of individuals who are mentally retarded. City charters, for instance, typically specify the establishment of various boards (e.g., school boards) and commissions. Ordinances like those that control zoning can be critical in terms of securing housing opportunities for this population. Regulations developed and issued by people in positions of authority, based on policy decisions of various legislative bodies, also affect citizens who are retarded.

The Judicial System   There is a state court system and a federal court system, the latter composed of three levels. First are approximately 100 U.S. District Courts, which are the trial courts and represent the lowest level of authority. Cases from the U.S. District Courts are appealed to one of the 13 Circuit Courts of Appeals. The first 11 Circuit Courts of Appeals handle appeals from designated states and territories, another circuit handles cases from Washington, D.C., and still another circuit hears appeals from the entire nation on certain issues (Yell, 1998). Finally, at the highest level of authority is the Supreme Court.

    State court systems are often organized on a similar three-tier system, but states may vary in the names they assign to each level (Rothstein, 1995). For example in some states, the supreme court is the highest court, but in others, it is the lowest.

TABLE 4.3
Circuit Court of Appeals

Circuit	States and territories in circuits
1	Maine, Massachusetts, New Hampshire, Rhode Island, Puerto Rico
2	Connecticut, New York, Vermont
3	Delaware, New Jersey, Pennsylvania, Virgin Islands
4	Maryland, North Carolina, South Carolina, Virginia, West Virginia
5	Louisiana, Mississippi, Texas
6	Kentucky, Michigan, Ohio, Tennessee
7	Illinois, Indiana, Wisconsin
8	Arkansas, Iowa, Minnesota, Missouri, Nebraska, North Dakota, South Dakota
9	Alaska, Arizona, California, Guam, Hawaii, Idaho, Montana, Nevada, Northern Mariana Island, Oregon, Washington
10	Colorado, Kansas, New Mexico, Oklahoma, Utah, Wyoming
11	Alabama, Florida, Georgia

Source: From www.lawsononline.com.

It is important to know the jurisdiction of a court. For example, the decisions of state courts in Alabama are not binding on state courts in Georgia. A decision by the 11th Circuit Court of Appeals is binding in that circuit only, although the decision may be persuasive authority in another circuit (Yell, 1998). A decision by the U.S. Supreme Court is binding throughout the country. Table 4.3 lists 11 of the Circuit Courts of Appeals and the states and territories that are in them.

LEGAL PRECEDENTS FOR INDIVIDUAL RIGHTS

Access to Education

There is no federal constitutional right to an education. The Supreme Court reiterated this fact in *San Antonio Independent School District v. Rodriguez* (1973) when it stated that education is not a fundamental right guaranteed by the Constitution. The Supreme Court, however, earlier had discussed the importance of education in *Brown*:

> Today, education is perhaps the most important function of state and local governments. Both compulsory school attendance laws and great expenditures for education demonstrate our recognition of the importance of education to our democratic society. It is required in the performance of our most basic public responsibilities, even service in the armed forces. It is the very foundation of good citizenship. Today it is a principal instrument in awakening the child to cultural values, in preparing him or her for later professional training, and in helping the child to adjust normally to his or her environment. In these days, it is doubtful that any child may reasonably be expected to succeed in life if denied the opportunity of an education. Such an opportunity, where the state has undertaken to provide it, is a right which must be made available to all on equal terms.

Turnbull and Turnbull (2000) note that this case challenged the concept of "separateness in education" and that the *"Brown* plaintiffs and children with disabilities had undeniable similarities" (p. 11). Again, it is easy to see how the ruling in *Brown* provided legal arguments that could be used by attorneys for the disabled.

Table 4.4 summarizes some of the early litigation affecting special education. As it shows, the arguments most frequently employed by plaintiffs in right-to-education cases include establishing the importance of education, using equal protection and due process claims, and addressing state and federal statutory provisions. For the most part, if education is provided to the public in general, these plaintiffs have argued, it should be available to all children regardless of level of ability or type of impairment. Another critical factor established in the two major legal cases described later, *Pennsylvania Association for Retarded Children v. Commonwealth of Pennsylvania* and *Mills v. Board of Education of the District of Columbia*, is that all individuals with mental retardation can benefit from education or training. Without the prior establishment of this fact, opponents could have put up substantial opposition to providing educational services to many children and youth who were retarded and who had been excluded from schools. The issue of educability has been discussed professionally (Kauffman & Krouse, 1981; Noonan, Brown, Mulligan, & Rettig, 1982) and has been the focus of litigation (*Timothy W. v. Rochester School District*, 1988).

Keeping children with mental retardation out of school had been a long-standing practice, but in the early 1970s, legal challenges to exclusionary policies were

To learn more about legislation and litigation affecting persons with mental retardation, go to the companion website at www.prenhall.com/beirne-smith and select Chapter 4, then choose the Web Destinations module.

TABLE 4.4
Summary of Early Right-to-Education Litigation

Litigants	Year	Highest Level of Judicial Review	Issues	Implications of Litigations	Arguments Used
Brown v. Board of Education	1954	U.S. Supreme Court	Segregation of students by race Impact of racial segregation on the child's motivation to learn	Segregation by race unanimously declared unconstitutional Established importance of education for advancement Established policy in favor of equal educational opportunity Generalized the purposes of education, not its fundamentality	Equal protection
Pennsylvania Association for Retarded Children (PARC) v. Commonwealth of Pennsylvania	1972	U.S. District Court (PA)	Class action suit—challenging the exclusion of children with mental retardation from free public education Access to education for all citizens with mental retardation Particular learning needs of this population	Consent agreement of both parties Established a right to education for children with mental retardation Established that all children with mental retardation could gain from education and training Demanded appropriate education Demanded preschool services if normal children received such Provided tuition grant assistance Provided due process mechanisms Required the identification of children not already identified Provided for education in the least restrictive setting	Equal protection Due process State statutes
Mills v. Board of Education of District of Columbia	1972	U.S. District Court (DC)	Class action suit—exclusion of all exceptionalities Access to education Use of waiting lists	Extended the logic of *PARC* to all disability groups regardless of the degree of the impairment Gained procedural safeguards Required timetable of implementation Acknowledged alternatives placement	Equal protection Due process District of Columbia Code

TABLE 4.4 (continued)
Summary of Early Right-to-Education Litigation

Case	Year	Court	Issue	Finding	Basis
San Antonio Independent School District v. Rodriguez	1973	U.S. Supreme Court	Claim that a discrimination exists due to being in a poorer school district Challenge to state-financing scheme Assertion that education is a fundamental right	Rejected wealth discrimination claim Left open the fundamentality of some identifiable quantum of education Reaffirmed the importance of education Indicated that denial of education could be used in terms of denial of freedom of speech and right to vote	Discrimination Equal protection
Lebanks v. Spears	1973	U.S. District Court	Challenged Louisiana's failure to provide education/training to a large number of children with mental retardation	Consent agreement Two features not found in *PARC* or *Mills* (1) Education—oriented toward making every child self-sufficient or employable (2) Educational services to adults who were not given services as children Acknowledged additional factors for evaluation in addition to intelligence	Equal protection
Maryland Association for Retarded Children v. Maryland	1974	Circuit Court of Baltimore County	Class action suit on behalf of children with mental retardation and those with physical handicaps being denied free public education	Began to address "appropriateness" issue Required the state to provide the necessary funding	State statutes
In the Interest of H.G., A Child	1974	Supreme Court of North Dakota	Equal educational opportunity	Involved the highest level of judicial review prior to PL 94-142 (1975)	State statutes Equal protection

successful. This litigation paved the way for later federal legislation that would significantly alter the availability of educational services to students with disabilities.

Early in January 1971, the Pennsylvania Association for Retarded Children and the parents of 13 children who were mentally retarded filed a class action suit (*Pennsylvania Association for Retarded Children [PARC] v. Commonwealth of Pennsylvania*) in federal court on behalf of all Pennsylvania residents with mental retardation between the ages of 6 and 21 who were excluded from receiving educational services. At issue was the prevailing policy that denied these school-age children access to public education. Expert testimony stressing the educational benefits (i.e., attainment of self-sufficiency for many, and some level of self-care for others) that all children with mental retardation could gain weighed heavily in this case.

Although settled by means of court-approved consent agreement in October 1971, the PARC case had a profound impact on special education and children and youth with mental retardation. It established a precedent guaranteeing access to publicly supported education for all students who are mentally retarded. Through claims of violations of due process and equal protection rights, the plaintiffs were able to establish that certain Pennsylvania statutes were unconstitutional. Implications of this decision are listed in Table 4.4.

Not long after the consent agreement in PARC was reached, a civil suit (*Mills v. Board of Education of the District of Columbia*) was filed. In this case, the parents and guardians of seven children charged that the board of education was denying these children a publicly supported education. All the plaintiffs in this case qualified as disabled. In August 1972, Judge Waddy ruled in favor of the plaintiffs, in effect declaring that a publicly supported education was the right of all children who were disabled, regardless of the type and severity of their condition. *Mills* actually extended many of the legal guarantees *PARC* had achieved for children who were mentally retarded to children with other disabling conditions. The defendants claimed that funds were insufficient to provide education to all such students. Judge Waddy's reply reflected the attitude of many concerning the exclusionary practices so long in effect:

> The District of Columbia's interest in educating the excluded children clearly must outweigh its interest in preserving its financial resources. If sufficient funds are not available to finance all of the services and programs that are needed and desirable in the system, then the available funds must be expended equitably in such a manner that no child is entirely excluded from a publicly supported education consistent with his needs and ability to benefit therefrom. The inadequacies of the District of Columbia public school system, whether occasioned by insufficient funding or administrative inefficiency, certainly cannot be permitted to bear more heavily on the "exceptional" or handicapped child than on the normal child.

As noted in this decision, limited financial resources are not sufficient reason to exclude students from receiving an appropriate education. But financial resources are limited, and even with IDEA and its recent amendments in effect, financial issues will continue to demand attention.

After *PARC* and *Mills*, right-to-education suits were filed in many other states as well. Soon all students who were mentally retarded were to gain the right to the free, appropriate public education that had previously been denied them, as many of the provisions formulated in the *PARC* consent agreement were later incorporated into the Education for All Handicapped Children Act, now known as the Individuals with Disabilities Education Act (IDEA).

The assumption of a right to education has not gone unchallenged. In 1988, a federal district court in New Hampshire decided in the case of *Timothy W. v. Rochester School District* that, if it seemed that a student could not benefit from special education, the rights guaranteed under IDEA do not apply. This case involved a 13-year-old boy who was profoundly retarded and who had a host of other disabling conditions. He was described as operating at a most basic level and as not having made any progress over a long period of time. The court of appeals reversed the lower court's interpretation of IDEA to allow exclusion from public education in some cases, reaffirming the basic principles underlying the intent of IDEA.

Appropriate Evaluation and Classification

The use of intelligence measures as the primary determinant for identification and placement decisions has long been under scrutiny. The problems associated with intelligence testing have come under fire in a number of legal suits. *Hobson v. Hansen* (1967), *Larry P. v. Riles* (1972), *Diana v. State Board of Education* (1970), and *PASE (Parents in Action on Special Education) v. Hannon* (1980) have specifically considered the use of intelligence tests for this purpose.

In *Hobson v. Hansen* (1967), the practice of denying to poor school-age children educational services equal to those of the more affluent was determined to be unconstitutional. The court found that students were being "tracked" into ability groups on the basis of instruments that seemed to be biased against African American students and those from lower socioeconomic groups. Schools in the District of Columbia were no longer permitted to use IQ measures to place children in tracks, and a close review of classification practices was ordered. This case is important to those interested in mental retardation because it addressed the consequences of being labeled mentally retarded.

In *Larry P. v. Riles* (1972, 1974, 1979, 1984), the courts held that IQ tests could not be used as the primary determinant in placing African American students in classes for the educable mentally retarded. Initially, intelligence tests could not be used to identify African American students as mentally retarded; in 1986 an expanded injunction was issued that banned the use of these instruments with African American students for any assessment purpose (Taylor, 1990). MacMillan and Balow (1991) note that, as a repercussion of *Larry P.*, the three largest school districts in California decided to ban the use of intelligence tests with all students, regardless of race, for special education purposes.

In 1988, however, a group of African American parents filed a complaint alleging that the 1986 order, which prevented their children from voluntarily taking IQ tests for purposes of placement in special education classes, violated their due process and equal protection rights. The court found that the plaintiffs' due process rights had been violated, ordering that the 1986 modification be vacated (*Larry P. v. Riles*, 1992).

Just as *Larry P.* specifically concerned the problems of African American children who were being misclassified, other cases brought in California have focused on the problems of other ethnic groups in placement decisions. In *Diana v. State Board of Education* (1970), the injured party, representing Spanish-speaking children, argued that many such students had been placed in classes for students with mild retardation on the basis of individual intelligence tests that were considered culturally biased. The children involved in this lawsuit spoke primarily Spanish but were given intelligence tests in English. Although *Diana* was settled out of court, it resulted in clear changes in the methods and procedures used for identifying and placing students in special classes.

It would be misleading to suggest that these were the only lawsuits involving appropriate classification and placement or that all litigation has been decided in the same way. In a class action suit filed in an Illinois federal district court (*PASE [Parents in Action on Special Education] v. Hannon*, 1980), the use of intelligence tests to place minority students in special classes designed for children with mild retardation again came into question. This time, however, the court ruled differently, declaring the tests nondiscriminatory and this practice valid when additional measures are also employed. The court closely examined specific intelligence tests for possible racial bias. So few items were found suspect that the court decided that these measures should be considered culturally neutral. The court went on to underscore the importance of clinical judgment in the interpretation of IQ results and the decision-making process.

The diametrically opposed findings in *PASE* and *Larry P.* have added more confusion to an already controversial area. The misuse of IQ measures continues to undergo professional scrutiny, as concern for misdiagnosis and misplacement

The inclusion of students with mental retardation was achieved on the basis of equal protection arguments.

remains a top priority in the referral and placement process. As Taylor (1990) suggests, the issue of nondiscriminatory evaluation has not been put to rest.

In *W.B. v. Matula* (1995), another case relevant to the issue of identification and evaluation, a school district had failed to identify and provide an appropriate education to a student. W.B., the parent of the student, sued, and the 3rd U.S. Circuit Court of Appeals held that the plaintiff was not precluded from seeking monetary damages. Some attorneys who specialize in the area of special education law believe that this is a major ruling for those seeking damages (Bleemer, 1995).

Free Appropriate Education

Once an appropriate education was mandated by IDEA, it was inevitable that the term *appropriate education* would need to be defined. The issue is discussed routinely at individualized education program (IEP) meetings, but it was never formally addressed until 1982. Then the U.S. Supreme Court ruled in *Board of Education of the Hendrick Hudson Central School District v. Rowley*—the first case argued on the basis of PL 94-142 to reach this highest level of judicial review.

To learn more about accessing a free appropriate education, go to the companion website at www.prenhall.com/beirnesmith and select Chapter 4, then choose the Case Studies module.

Although the plaintiff named in this particular litigation, Amy Rowley, was a student with a hearing impairment, the case has significant implications for students who are mentally retarded. This is because the Court specified criteria for a "free appropriate public education" in the majority opinion written by Justice Rehnquist:

> According to the definitions contained in the Act, a "free appropriate public education" consists of educational instruction specially designed to meet the unique needs of the handicapped child, supported by such services as are necessary to permit the child "to benefit" from the instruction. Almost as a checklist for adequacy under the Act, the definition also requires that such instruction and services be provided at public expense and under public supervision, meet the State's educational standards, approximate the grade levels used in the State's regular education, and comport with the child's IEP. Thus, if personalized instruction is being provided with sufficient supportive services to permit the child to benefit from the instruction, and the other items on the definitional checklist are satisfied, the child is receiving a "free appropriate public education" as defined by the Act.

A number of important issues in interpreting IDEA arose in this case, and they have had and will continue to have bearing on litigation. First, the Court discussed the importance of a "basic floor of opportunity" for students, which means that all students should have reasonable opportunity for learning. The Court stressed that the act intends students to obtain special instruction and related services that are individually developed to provide educational benefit to students with disabilities. Unfortunately, the term *educational benefit* suffers from the same ambiguity that *appropriate education* does.

The issue that has received the most attention involves the "level of education" to be provided to students. What type of services should be provided, and to what extent must they be offered? In *Rowley*, the U.S. Supreme Court reversed the Second Circuit Court of Appeals' ruling that Amy Rowley was entitled to an interpreter. The Court's interpretation of congressional intent in enacting PL 94-142 suggested that programs do not have to develop students to their maximum potential. The Court noted that language addressing this particular issue was "noticeably absent" in the federal statute.

The *Rowley* decision initially sent shock waves through the field of special education, as many thought that students with disabilities would suffer from school systems' taking narrow interpretations of this case. Special education professionals feared that schools would have too easy a time demonstrating that students were getting "educational benefit" in programs that were not providing needed supportive services (DuBow & Greer, 1984). Blatt's (1987) concern was that schools would (a) have more freedom to decide what is acceptable for students with special needs, (b) no longer be motivated to provide optimal programs, and (c) meet a "far lesser" standard. This scenario, fortunately, has not materialized.

Federal regulations published in 1999 address the issue of children placed in private schools when the parents believe their children are not receiving a free appropriate public education (FAPE). If a hearing officer determines that the school district had not made FAPE available to the student and that the private school placement is appropriate, then the parents can be reimbursed. These regulations also state that the appropriateness of a placement does not depend on whether the placement meets state standards (C.F.R. §300.403[c]). There are several limitations on reimbursement. For example, to be eligible for reimbursement, the parents must have informed the IEP team that they were rejecting the placement of the school district and that they intended to place their child in a private school at the expense of the school district (C.F.R. §300.403[d][1][i]).

Appropriate Placement

Placing students who are mentally retarded in educational settings that are appropriate to their needs is becoming a major issue in the field. Debate goes on between those who want to maintain the guarantees of a continuum of service delivery options as specified in IDEA and those who advocate full inclusion in general education settings as the only option. The discussion about this issue will continue.

Turnbull and Turnbull (2000) assert that the 1997 amendments of IDEA strengthened the provisions of least restrictive environment (LRE). Although several cases have dealt with this issue, for brevity, two significant cases are discussed in this section.

In *Daniel R. R. v. State Board of Education* (1989), the Fifth Circuit Court of Appeals developed a two-faceted test to determine whether a placement is appropriate and consistent with the concept of LRE. The *Daniel* test requires attention to the following components while considering other factors related to the student and school: Can a student be educated satisfactorily in the general education classroom, with the use of supplementary aids and services? Has the school placed the student in the least restrictive setting to the maximum extent appropriate?

In *Sacramento City Board of Education v. Holland* (1994), the court fashioned a four-prong test that considered the academic benefits to the student, the nonacademic benefits, the student's effect on the general education teacher and students, and the costs of having the student with a disability in the general education classroom (DeMitchell & Kerns, 1997).

General education consists of the general classroom, extracurricular activities, and nonacademic activities (20 U.S.C. §1414[d][1][A][iii]). A critical provision of the 1997 amendments is that the IEP must explain the extent that a student will not participate in these environments (20 U.S.C. §1414[d][1][A][iv]). Turnbull and Turnbull (2000) state that this provision, coupled with the stipulations of the amendments regarding discipline and financial considerations, codified the results of *Daniel R.R. v. State Board of Education* (1989) and *Sacramento City Board of Education v. Holland* (1994).

Related Services

Under IDEA, students are entitled to related services, if needed, particularly if they allow a student to benefit from a free appropriate public education. It has not always been clear, however, whether certain services qualify as "related services," especially those that are more medically oriented and that many children with more severe forms of retardation need.

In *Irving Independent School District v. Tatro* (1984), the U.S. Supreme Court ruled that a student with spina bifida was entitled to clean intermittent catheterization (CIC) services (a procedure that empties the bladder). The Court used a two-prong test to determine whether a service is a related service: (a) Is the requested service a supportive service necessary for the child to benefit from special education? Then, (b) is the requested service excluded as a medical service? If a service is a medical service, then it does not qualify as a related service. The Court decided that this supportive service (i.e., CIC) could be performed by a school nurse and therefore was not an excludable medical service. According to *Tatro*, only services that had to be performed by a physician were medical services that could be excluded as a related service.

Even with the ruling of the Supreme Court, lower courts differed in their interpretation of the second prong of the *Tatro* test. Some stated that a multifactor test considering such factors as cost could determine whether a service could be considered as an excludable medical service. In *Cedar Rapids Community School District v. Garret F.* (1999), the Supreme Court rejected this viewpoint, stating that there was no legal authority for use of a multifactor test to determine whether a service could be classified as a medical service and therefore be excluded as a related service. The Supreme Court agreed with the Circuit Court of Appeals, which stated that *Tatro* "established a bright-line test: the services of a physician (other than for diagnostic and evaluation purposes) are subject to the medical services exclusion, but services that can be provided in the school setting by a nurse or qualified layperson are not" (*Cedar Rapids Community School District v. Garret F.* 1997, p. 825).

Although many would argue that the decision in *Tatro* was quite clear, the *Garret F.* decision reiterated the test unequivocally. At this point, there would appear to be little room for controversy on this issue.

Other litigation further delineated what is considered to be a related service under IDEA. Transportation to and from a placement that has been designated as appropriate for providing special services is considered a related service, as found in two cases involving individuals with mental retardation: *Hurry v. Jones* (1984) and *Alamo Heights School District v. State Board of Education* (1986).

The issue of whether psychotherapy is a related service has major implications for schools, as such a ruling might require expensive services (e.g., out-of-state residential placement) that public schools do not provide. Various litigation has produced differing outcomes. Several cases, including *T.G. v. Board of Education of Piscataway* (1983) and *Max M. v. Thompson* (1984), have contested this issue and found psychotherapy to be a related service. Other litigation, *McKenzie v. Jefferson* (1983), has found that the residential component of placement in a residential facility is medical, not educational, in nature and does not have to be paid for by a school district.

Extended School Year

An important case regarding the extended school year (ESY) was *Armstrong v. Kline* (1979). This case was originally filed in federal district court in Pennsylvania and later appealed to the Third Circuit Court of Appeals. The foremost issue in this litigation was that significant gaps (e.g., summer breaks) in the educational programs of certain students caused losses in skill development (regression) that required an unreasonable amount of time to make up (recoupment) and therefore entitled students to an extended school year. The decisions of both courts found the defendant's policy of limiting educational services to a maximum of 180 days inflexible, thus preventing students from receiving an appropriate education.

According to the 1997 amendments to IDEA, the school district must provide an extended school year if the IEP team determines that an extended school year is necessary to provide a child, regardless of the disability, with FAPE. The school district may not unilaterally limit the length, type, or amount of services.

Expulsion

As mentioned earlier, the 1997 amendments codified the results of court cases, such as *Honig v. Doe* (1988) and *J.B. v. Independent School District* (1995). Therefore, school districts may have already implemented many of the provisions of the amendments. The following list summarizes some of those amendments:

1. There can never be a complete cessation of educational services (FAPE) for a student with a disability (C.F.R. 34 §300.121[a]).
2. School personnel may unilaterally suspend students with disabilities for a total of 10 days or less (C.F.R. 34 §300.520).
3. If a suspension or a change of placement is greater than 10 days, a manifestation hearing must be conducted. The purpose is to determine whether the misbehavior is a manifestation of the disability. If the misbehavior is not a manifestation of the disability, then the student can be disciplined the same as students without disabilities but a complete cessation of FAPE cannot occur (C.F.R. §300.523).
4. School personnel may unilaterally place a student who brings a weapon or illegal drugs to school in an interim alternative educational setting for 45 days (34 C.F.R. §300.520[a][2]).

5. Even if a student is not currently receiving special education services, the student may be eligible for the procedural rights of IDEA if the school district had knowledge that the student had a disability (C.F.R. §300.527).

The issue of the continuation of educational services is controversial. According to Engelhard (1999), the House and Senate have proposed juvenile justice bills that would allow school officials to terminate educational services to students with disabilities who bring weapons to school. In response to this proposed legislation that would terminate services, the Council for Exceptional Children and other organizations issued a policy statement which advocated for the continuation of educational services for extremely disruptive students. Because these groups recognize the importance of safety issues, the policy directive stated that this continuation of services could occur in alternative programs.

INSTITUTIONAL RIGHTS

In this section we introduce the legal maneuverings that have become the backdrop for many changes in institutional settings. Much of this section is devoted to a fundamental right that had been denied many of those confined to institutions for too long: the right to treatment.

The terms *treatment* and *habilitation* are often used interchangeably, although some professionals do make a distinction. Both imply the delivery of some type of service, and they have been at the center of much discussion concerning those living in large, segregated residential facilities. Baer (1981) interprets the various courts' definitions of **habilitation** to mean "behavior change in the direction of those skills that cumulatively allow community living" (p. 91). Although this definition is very general, it does give a sense of purpose. Lakin and Bruininks (1985), analyzing the view of habilitation promoted in *Youngberg v. Romeo* (1982), remark that the U.S. Supreme Court defines *habilitation* as something that ensures "safety and freedom from undue restraint." The usefulness of this perspective is questionable.

The treatment issue revolves around the notion that if individuals are placed, often involuntarily, in restrictive institutional settings, then constitutionally they are entitled to services. Many landmark cases have looked at this issue; a few are presented here. Most notable among them are *Wyatt v. Stickney* (1972), *New York Association for Retarded Children v. Rockefeller* (1973), *O'Connor v. Donaldson* (1974), *Halderman v. Pennhurst* (1977), and *Youngberg v. Romeo* (1982).

Wyatt v. Stickney

The legal impetus for reform was dramatized in the litigation of a landmark case, *Wyatt v. Stickney*, in 1972. This case had a direct impact on the adequacy of services in residential facilities for individuals with mental retardation. The plaintiffs in this class action suit built their case on the grounds that the residents of the Partlow State School (located in Tuscaloosa, Alabama) were being denied their right to treatment. Although this was a class action suit, it was originally filed by the legal guardian of Ricky Wyatt against the Alabama Department of Mental

Hygiene in 1970. Specifically, in *Wyatt*, Ricky Wyatt (named plaintiff) represented all residents in the state of Alabama who were involuntarily confined in the state's hospitals.

The decision of Judge Johnson of the District Court for the Middle District of Alabama, North Division, declared that the constitutional rights of those residents were being violated under the Fourteenth Amendment. This state's failure to provide proper treatment in its residential facilities moved the court to draw up a precedent-setting 22-page appendix that defined minimum treatment standards for the state school to adopt. The order and the decree of the *Wyatt* decision were comprehensive in their coverage of residents' right to treatment and habilitation, records and review, physical environment, medication, and admissions policies. Minimum treatment standards include the following:

1. Individuals who were borderline or mildly retarded shall not be placed in residential institutions.
2. Admission to a residential institution shall be granted following the determination that the client-environment match is the least restrictive habilitative setting.
3. Institutions must attempt to move residents in the following manner:
   a. To a less structured living environment
   b. From larger to smaller facilities
   c. From larger to smaller living units
   d. From group to individual residence
   e. From segregated to integrated community living
   f. From dependent to independent living

To summarize the importance of *Wyatt*, let us look at what it achieved. First, the case focused exclusively on individuals with mental retardation residing in institutions. Second, the court issued a set of minimum standards and monitoring procedures for residential facilities that would serve as a model to other states. Third, the case recognized the constitutional rights of these residents.

The Fifth Circuit Court of Appeals later essentially upheld the earlier decision of the Alabama federal court, reemphasizing that residents have a constitutional right to treatment. Furthermore, this decision allowed the federal court to set standards and monitor their implementation.

In 1986, a consent agreement was approved in federal district court in Alabama, providing a settlement to this litigation, which had been initiated 14 years earlier. Over the course of time, the original *Wyatt* case had been reopened periodically to review the status of the implementation of what the court had ordered in Judge Johnson's original decision (*Wyatt v. Hardin*, 1975; *Wyatt v. Ireland*, 1979). The 1986 agreement was conciliatory; both plaintiffs and defendants made compromises. But as Marchetti (1987) describes it, "It appeared that all parties to the litigation and the federal court were seeking a justifiable reason for returning the mental health system back to the state's 'control,' while protecting the rights of the class members" (p. 249). Marchetti provides an excellent chronology of the *Wyatt* litigation, a concise description of the consent decree, and an interesting discussion of the implications of this action.

New York Association for Retarded Children v. Rockefeller

Another case presented here because of the attention it received is *New York Association for Retarded Children v. Rockefeller* (1973). This case is commonly referred to as "the Willowbrook case," since the institution under scrutiny was the Willowbrook State School.

This case, like *Wyatt*, originated after complaints were voiced concerning reductions in staff. It focused on three major issues: overcrowding, understaffing, and the absence of community alternatives to institutionalization. Even though conditions did improve, the court's rulings were not as comprehensive and powerful as they had been in *Wyatt*. What may be most important about the Willowbrook case is the national attention it received. It made more people aware of the deplorable conditions and the lack of programming that existed in many such settings.

O'Connor v. Donaldson

Another suit that had an impact on institutionalized people, decided by the Fifth Circuit Court of Appeals, was *O'Connor v. Donaldson* (1974). The plaintiff, Donaldson, had been committed to an institution in 1957 by his father. It was determined that the defendants were aware at the time of Donaldson's placement that he was neither reckless nor dangerous to himself or others. Once he was institutionalized, Donaldson received neither adequate treatment nor therapy. The decision by the court awarded the plaintiff $38,000 in compensatory and punitive damages, which were to be paid personally by the defendants. In this particular case, the defendants were held personally liable. Subsequently the case was sent to the court of appeals, where the original decision was upheld. *O'Connor v. Donaldson* is significant in that it established the illegality of involuntarily institutionalizing a person who is not dangerous and who is able to function without institutional care.

Halderman v. Pennhurst

The first case concerning individuals who were retarded and residing in institutions to reach the U.S. Supreme Court was *Halderman v. Pennhurst* (1977). This case is fascinating because, in addition to the issues related to correcting unsatisfactory conditions at a large state-run facility (located in southeastern Pennsylvania), it ultimately sought to deinstitutionalize all residents, thereby closing down large, segregated facilities.

In the original action, begun in 1974, Terri Lee Halderman, a 20-year-old resident of Pennhurst, filed suit on behalf of herself and all present and future residents of the facility, alleging that subhuman conditions and the lack of habilitative programming at Pennhurst violated their statutory and constitutional rights.

In the first phase of the nonjury trial, begun in 1977, the court spent 32 days hearing testimony to establish the truth of Halderman's allegations. By the end of this exposition, any illusions of Pennhurst State School and Hospital as a facility for the "care and training" of persons with mental retardation were erased. These excerpts from the opinion of presiding Judge Raymond Broderick suggest the quality of "care and training" afforded to residents there:

> Pennhurst is almost totally impersonal. Its residents have no privacy—they sleep in large, overcrowded wards, spend their waking hours together in large day rooms and eat in a large group setting. . . .
>
> All residents on Unit 7 go to bed between 8:00 and 8:30 P.M., are awakened and taken to the toilet at 12:00–12:30 A.M., and returned to sleep until 5:30 A.M. when they are awakened for the day, which begins with being toileted and then having to wait for a 7:00 A.M. breakfast. . . .
>
> The physical environment at Pennhurst is hazardous to the residents, both physically and psychologically. There is often excrement and urine on ward floors, and the living areas do not meet minimal professional standards for cleanliness. Outbreaks of pinworms and infectious disease are common. . . .
>
> Obnoxious odors and excessive noise permeate the atmosphere. Such conditions are not conducive to habilitation. Moreover, the noise level in the day rooms is often so high that many residents simply stop speaking. . . .
>
> Residents' records commonly contain a notation that they would benefit from specific types of programming. However, such programming has, for the most part, been unavailable. The average resident receives only 1½ hours of programming per weekday and no programming on weekends. No one, except those in school, gets more than 3½ to 4 hours per day. If one factors out those programs which are not considered beneficial, the average drops to about 15 minutes per day. . . .
>
> On the whole, the staff at Pennhurst appears to be dedicated and trying hard to cope with the inadequacies of the institution. Nearly every witness who testified concerning Pennhurst stated that it was grossly understaffed to adequately habilitate the residents.

The Broderick court held that confinement at Pennhurst clearly deprives residents of their right to nondiscriminatory habilitation, minimally adequate care, due process, equal protection, freedom from harm, and treatment by least restrictive means. Broderick ordered the eventual closing of Pennhurst and the establishment of suitable community settings to which residents could transfer. Moreover, he ordered that an individualized program plan (IPP) be developed for each remaining resident and that monitoring procedures be established for the duration of the facility's operation.

Pennhurst officials and their various codefendants appealed this decision in 1979 to the Third Circuit Court of Appeals. The appeals court affirmed the right of every individual with mental retardation to receive habilitative care in the least restrictive setting possible as well as his or her private right of action to enforce this right. Although the appeals court did not mandate Pennhurst's termination, it upheld 38 of the 41 paragraphs of Judge Broderick's order, along with his belief that persons with retardation would benefit most from community placement. The Third Circuit Court of Appeals based its judgment on statutory grounds—the 1974 Developmental Disabilities Assistance and Bill of Rights Act. The court stated that this legislation created substantive rights to habilitative services for individuals who were retarded.

In 1981, the U.S. Supreme Court reversed the appeals court decision. The high court recognized the inadequate conditions at Pennhurst but did not feel that the congressional intent of the Developmental Disabilities Act created rights and required adequate treatment. McCarthy (1983) summarizes the Court's position: "The Supreme Court declared that the Act was not intended to create new substantive rights; it was designed to encourage, but not to mandate, better services for the developmentally disabled" (p. 519). McCarthy goes on to suggest that the Supreme Court position seems to be that it will strictly interpret funding legislation and will not demand that states provide services not explicitly stated in the laws.

In January 1984, out-of-court negotiations began between the parties involved in this case. By fall of that year, a settlement had been reached in which the state agreed to close Pennhurst, thus ending 10 years of litigation. Although this famous case did not achieve all the outcomes desired by the plaintiffs, Pennhurst will remain a byword in the movement to close institutions.

Youngberg v. Romeo

In *Youngberg v. Romeo* (1982), the U.S. Supreme Court ruled that individuals with severe retardation who were involuntarily confined to any state facility had a constitutional right to habilitative services to ensure their safety and freedom from undue restraint—a decidedly restrictive view of habilitation. The Court reasoned that this right is based on the **substantive due process** provisions of the Fourteenth Amendment.

As Turnbull (1982) has indicated, the case affects professionals in significant ways. It spotlights the roles of professionals and professional differences of opinion by acknowledging that there are various models of treatment and a lack of

General education includes extra curricular and non academic activities, along with general classroom education.

consensus about which is best. The Court also recognized that professionals in the field of mental retardation are in much better positions than judges or juries to make decisions about treatment. Lakin and Bruininks (1985) note that the Supreme Court seems to have established a more limited role for federal courts in decisions of this type.

Olmstead v. L.C.

A recent case concerning institutions is *Olmstead v. L.C.* (1999). The Supreme Court decided that states should place individuals in community settings instead of institutions when the professionals deem that this setting is the most appropriate. The individual's wishes about where he or she lives must be considered, and the placement change must represent a reasonable accommodation for the states.

According to Hayden (1998), there were 71 court cases from 1971 to 1997 involving persons with mental retardation who were institutionalized. Hayden also notes that cases in later years alleged some of the same violations that were litigated in earlier years. By 1998, 128 of the 346 state-operated institutions for individuals with mental retardation had closed, with 11 others scheduled to cease operation by 2000.

COMMUNITY RIGHTS

Much of the litigation directed at securing reasonable treatment in institutional settings (e.g., *Wyatt*) also suggested that efforts be undertaken to establish living conditions in community settings for as many individuals as possible. In line with the goal of providing living conditions as close to normal as possible, advocates have championed the notion of community placement. The resultant community movement has taken hold, and many more individuals with mental retardation are pursuing their lives in more inclusive ways.

The right to live in community settings has not come without a struggle in many localities. This outcome has been most obvious in community opposition to the establishment of group homes. Henderson and Vitello (1988) state that three kinds of barriers can interfere with the community living movement: (a) local zoning ordinances, (b) state legislation that requires advance notification and in some cases permission from neighbors, and (c) restrictive covenants (e.g., people in a neighborhood are able to enforce a specific covenant to preserve the neighborhood's character). Of the three situations, the first has received the most attention.

The case of *Cleburne Living Center, Inc. v. City of Cleburne, Texas* (1984) illustrates the problems that arise when a community opposes a group home. The principal obstacle in this case, as well as others like it, is the attempt to establish a group home in a "single-family residence" zone. In the past, group homes were commonly located in less desirable areas that were industrially or commercially zoned—areas for which permits were easier to obtain.

In this case, the Cleburne Living Center, Inc., was notified that a special-use permit would have to be approved before it could establish a group home for adults with mental retardation. The city council denied this permit on the basis that such a "hospital for the feebleminded" violated a local zoning ordinance. A suit was filed in federal district court claiming that the constitutional rights of these adults were being violated. The federal court upheld the city's decision to deny the request. On appeal, the Fifth Circuit Court of Appeals reversed the district court's ruling, citing that the ordinance was unconstitutional. This case was eventually appealed to the U.S. Supreme Court, which also found the zoning ordinance to be a violation of the plaintiff's **equal protection** rights.

Adults with mental retardation living in community settings should be entitled to the same rights as other citizens. Gardner and Chapman (1985) have developed a list of rights that persons living in community-based residential programs should enjoy (presented in Table 4.5). This list is not exhaustive, but it does give a sense of the rights we take for granted that have not always been available to people with retardation. To this list could be added other more controversial rights such as the right to marry, the right to be parents, and the right to raise children. An overriding right for all is the right to associate with others.

ISSUES THAT SPAN A LIFETIME

Unfortunately, individuals with mental retardation are subject to the same ills and problems that affect the rest of society. The withholding of medical treatment, acts of sexual abuse, and domestic violence can impact the lives of the mentally retarded. They can also be the victims of crime or become criminal defendants. These problems have implications not only for the legal system but for educators as well.

TABLE 4.5
Rights of Persons in Community-Based Residential Programs

Right to services in the least restrictive environment
Right to normalized living conditions
Right to dignity and respect
Right to freedom from discomfort and deprivation
Right to appropriate clinical, medical, and therapeutic services
Right to vote
Right to religious worship
Right to private communication
Right to free association
Right to physical exercise
Right to seasonal, clean, neat clothing
Right to manage personal funds
Right to bed, dresser, and storage area
Right to privacy
Right to access to public media
Right to adequate nutrition
Freedom from unnecessary medication and mechanical, chemical, or physical restraints
Freedom from involuntary servitude
Right to equal protection and due process

Source: From *Staff Development in Mental Retardation Services: A Practical Handbook* by J. F. Gardner and M. S. Chapman, 1985, Baltimore: Paul H. Brookes. Copyright 1985 by Paul H. Brookes. Reprinted by permission.

Withholding Treatment

Individuals who are mentally retarded and who need transplants are often denied. Doctors and transplant center officials claim that they are not discriminating against individuals who are mentally retarded. They consider, however, how well the individuals will be able to take care of themselves and consequently their transplanted organs. They maintain that they are trying to give transplants to the individuals who will benefit the most. The result is that individuals who are mentally retarded are often not given transplants.

Hardie (2000) has chronicled the story of Julie, 27, a young woman with Down syndrome, who needs a heart-lung transplant. Hardie maintains that only one person with Down syndrome has ever received a heart-lung transplant, although there may be thousands of people with Down syndrome who need them. Perhaps Julie's mother said it best when she stated, "Doctors take an oath to doctor everybody. Don't [*sic*] that mean anything?" (p. H1)

Sexual Abuse

From childhood to adulthood, sexual abuse can be a concern for individuals who are retarded. When one considers the characteristics of individuals with disabilities, especially those who are mentally retarded, that make them vulnerable, it is understandable that sexual offenders might select them as suitable targets. Indeed, according to Hume (1999), children with disabilities are abused (sexually and in other ways) at higher rates than children without disabilities. Generally, child sexual offenders look for children whom they consider to be susceptible to their advances. In explaining how victims are selected, one offender stated, "I would probably pick the one who appeared more needy, the child hanging back from others and feeling picked on." Another offender offered that he would "look for the kid who is easy to manipulate" (p. 8).

Reaching adulthood does not make those who are mentally retarded safe from sexual abuse. Sobsey (1997) reports that physical and sexual abuse rates are 4 to 10 times higher for adults with disabilities than those adults without disabilities. Sorensen (1997) relates that five women who are mentally retarded were raped by the owner of the home facility where they lived. Perhaps many of these crimes are not reported (Sobsey, 1997), and therefore it may not be possible to know the full extent of the problem.

Domestic Violence

If women without disabilities can become victims of domestic violence, then there is no reason to believe that women who are mentally retarded are somehow protected from this problem. Although literature focusing on women who are mentally retarded and the victims of domestic violence is limited, Carlson (1997) has explored this topic and contends that factors such as dependency, low self-esteem, and learned helplessness can increase the potential for domestic violence. Such women may not have contact with their families, which can help ensure continued exposure to violence.

Carlson (1997) relates the story of Nancy, a mildly mentally retarded woman who lived independently in an apartment that was supervised by an agency that assisted individuals with developmental disabilities. Nancy finally admitted that she was being beaten by her boyfriend, William. Although Nancy wanted to end the relationship, she had been afraid to speak with the supervising agency about her problems. A representative from a domestic violence services organization and a case worker from the supervising agency developed an intervention plan. They spoke with Nancy's landlord and with the police to inform them of the situation. They also obtained a restraining order against William, and the police agreed to notify and warn William not to harass Nancy. They taught Nancy several steps to take if William attempted to contact her.

If women who are not retarded have difficulty extricating themselves from abusive situations, then there is no reason to believe that women who are mentally retarded will not also have difficulty removing abusive people from their lives. These individuals may need assistance in developing solutions and navigating the legal system.

Crime Victims

Sorensen (1997) contends that crimes are committed against individuals with disabilities at higher rates than individuals without disabilities. Moreover, Sobsey (1997) states that when these crimes are reported, law enforcement officials are hesitant to investigate and prosecute because they believe that the cases cannot be won. Sorensen asserts that even with the higher crime rates, prosecutors often have few caseloads that include individuals with disabilities. In the case of the five women who were raped (mentioned in the preceding paragraphs), initially, the local district attorney refused to prosecute.

Another tragic incident occurred when a man who was mentally retarded was poisoned and died after the owner of the home in which he lived collected and served him wild mushrooms (Sorensen, 1997). She served the mushrooms in an effort to save money on the grocery bill. The man had previously complained that he was not getting enough to eat. The woman was not charged with a crime. In other words, some prosecutors discriminate and do not provide individuals who are disabled with equal protection under the law.

When those who commit crimes against individuals who are disabled are prosecuted, they receive more lenient sentences as compared to sentences for crimes committed against those without disabilities (Petersilia, 1998). Sobsey (1997) found evidence of lighter sentences throughout the world. He relates the case of a mother in France who killed her autistic daughter; she received probation. Even in death, there may be no justice for individuals with disabilities.

Criminal Defendants

From the apprehension of the suspect to the execution of the convicted, the legal system is fraught with inequities for those who are mentally retarded (Petersilia, 1998). At each stage, individuals who are mentally retarded are at a decided disadvantage.

At the apprehension stage, one police officer summed up the problem by stating that the mentally retarded are "the last to leave the scene, the first to get arrested, and the first to confess" (Petersilia, 1998 p. 5). It does not help that many police officers have not been trained to recognize and deal with individuals who are disabled. Laski and Keefe (1997) give an example of a man with autism who liked to walk back and forth in front of his home. Two police officers noticed him in front of his house and decided that he was a "peeping Tom." In the confrontation that ensued, the officers threw him on the ground, which resulted in the man sustaining a physical injury.

Many factors can complicate matters for individuals who are mentally retarded at the interrogation stage. Some individuals may wish to hide their disability (Edwards & Reynolds, 1997). They may not want police officers to know that they do not understand the questions and consequently may avoid answering them (Keyes, 1997). In one study, Everington and Fulero (1999) found that individuals with mental retardation were less likely to understand their Miranda rights. They also concluded that individuals with mental retardation were "more likely to respond to leading questions and to coercion" (p. 218). Individuals who are mentally retarded may also confess to crimes that they did not commit, in an effort to please authority figures (Petersilia, 1998). Therefore, people who are mentally retarded may be wrongly convicted of a crime.

Beyond the issue of those who are wrongly convicted, what should happen to individuals who are mentally retarded and guilty of a crime punishable by death? Keyes, Edwards, and Perske (1997) list some of the characteristics of individuals who are mentally retarded as being impulsiveness and possessing a lack of cause-and-effect reasoning, poor judgment, and, of course, lower intelligence. Keyes et al. state that because of these characteristics, individuals who are mentally retarded lack the culpability necessary for imposition of the death penalty. They also calculated that 30 individuals with mental retardation were executed in the United States from 1976 to 1996. (The box on p. 141 presents the Council for Exceptional Children's position statement on this topic.)

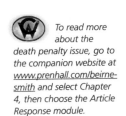

To read more about the death penalty issue, go to the companion website at www.prenhall.com/beirne-smith and select Chapter 4, then choose the Article Response module.

Implications

There may be common solutions to the aforementioned issues of the withholding of medical treatment, sexual abuse, domestic violence, and the problems inherent in the criminal justice system. These solutions may involve developing self-advocacy skills, advocacy by other organizations, and more training for doctors, educators, and law enforcement officials.

Students with disabilities should be taught how to advocate for themselves if they are being abused or accused of a crime. If they are accused of a crime, this self-advocacy may consist of merely teaching them to say, "I need to see a lawyer." One youth, Henry, who is mentally retarded, attended a special training program where he was taught this statement (Houchins, 1997). Henry had witnessed two boys trying to burglarize a newspaper stand. A police officer drove up, and the offenders accused Henry of the crime. When the officer questioned Henry, he would only respond, "I need a lawyer." Henry also gave the officer a card that instructed him to

Capital Punishment and Individuals with Mental Retardation

It has been estimated that as many as one in eight persons on death row across the United States has mental retardation. Although a number of professional organizations have protested, most defendants with mental retardation are currently without meaningful protection from execution. In 1989, the Supreme Court in the *Penry* case ruled that the Constitution does not prohibit the execution of a person because of mental retardation even though that person does not meet the requirements of culpability. Without full comprehension of the law and its processes, there is a substantial chance that a person with mental retardation will be convicted and sentenced to death.

Deterrence and retribution have been advanced as two rationales for the death penalty. The deterrence theory of capital punishment holds that execution will not only prevent the punished from killing again, but will also indirectly deter others. This is predicated on the assumption that the actor will weigh choices and possible consequences. In this regard, the individual must be cognizant of the crimes for which the death penalty is imposed and believe execution is a probably consequence of conviction. For the individual with mental retardation, the goal of deterrence is problematic. The individual is unlikely to have premeditated his crime, may have acted on impulse and lacks the ability to think strategically while considering the future. If the fact that the commission of a certain act may forfeit life cannot be understood, the death penalty as a deterrent loses meaning.

Retribution also is problematic for the individual with mental retardation. Retribution requires that the punishment fit the crime and seeks to meet society's concern for vengeance and faith in the criminal justice system. By definition, the imposition of the death penalty should be used only to accommodate retribution when lesser punishment will not. Additionally, the criminal must be sufficiently culpable to warrant this most severe penalty. The mental and behavioral capacities of the person with mental retardation are likely to preclude the level of culpability necessary to inflict the death penalty since they are challenged in their abilities to discriminate, communicate, control impulsivity, and recall. While these individuals may

recognize an act as right or wrong, they often may not possess a full understanding of this concept and may not link prior action to later punishment. Many persons with mental retardation cannot comprehend such critical legal concepts as "right," "waver," "elements of the offense charged," and Miranda warnings.

The Supreme Court has required for two decades that capital punishment be imposed only when it's served a valid deterrent or retributive purpose that a lesser sentence could not. Moreover, the Court has recognized that questions raised concerning the legitimate use of the death penalty in individual cases are essentially questions of personal responsibility, personal characteristics, and moral guilt. In the case of persons with mental retardation the prudent course is to assume these individuals as a class cannot attain the level of culpability necessary to satisfy the deterrent and retributive goals of capital punishment.

The use of the death penalty for a person with mental retardation is improper and inhumane. Such action serves no legitimate societal interest. It can never satisfy society's demand that punishment must fit both the crime and the criminal's culpability. The individual and social harm of imposing the death penalty on a person who cannot satisfy a reasonable and societal standard of culpability is great.

Recognizing this fact, the Board of Directors of CEC-MR resolves that capital punishment of persons with mental retardation is cruel and inappropriate, is a tragic flaw in the legal system of the United States as it currently addresses the issues of justice for persons with mental retardation, and should not be imposed.

This statement was originally drafted by Dana Cooper, JD, and Kathleen Marshall, Ph.D. (University of South Carolina).

Source: From *MRDD Position Statement: Capital Punishment and Individuals with Mental Retardation* (Approved at the Board of Director's Meeting, October 3, 1992) by Division on Mental Retardation and Developmental Disabilities of the Council for Exceptional Children, 1992, Reston, VA: Council for Exceptional Children. Copyright 1992 by the Council for Exceptional Children. Reprinted by permission.

A Criminal with a Conscience

Mike FitzPatrick, 48, is a man with autism who lives in Syracuse, New York. He works as a janitor, shops for himself, and drives a car.

One day while on vacation in 1999, FitzPatrick stopped at a bank in Clifton Springs, New York. Unbeknownst to FitzPatrick, a bank in the town had been robbed earlier that month. Because of his behavior in the bank, he was suspected of being a bank robber. Police later questioned FitzPatrick, and he confessed to robbing the bank. He was arrested and charged with the crime.

FitzPatrick's parents knew that he was innocent. His mother explained that he confessed because he tries to please people. She stated that he thought by confessing, the police would allow him to go home.

Fortunately for FitzPatrick, the real bank robber, David Harrington, 30, is a man with a conscience, in at least some respects. Harrington became distraught upon hearing that FitzPatrick, a man with a disability, had been charged with the robbery. He then confessed and gave information that only the real robber could have known.

Although this story had a happy ending, it is easy to imagine other outcomes. Without Harrington's admission of guilt, FitzPatrick could have been sentenced to 25 years in prison. "Liberty and justice for all" should not depend on the conscience of a criminal.

Source: From "A Simple Man: Autistic Man Wrongly Accused of Robbery," 1999, by J. Siceloff. Available: www.more.abcnews.go.com/onair/2020/2020_991213_autistic_feature.html

call Henry's mother or the mental health retardation hotline. Subsequently Henry testified against the two boys, and they were convicted.

Self-advocacy skills may not be an option for everyone who is mentally retarded. If possible, these individuals should be taught how to access the services of organizations that can help protect them. Individuals like Julie (described earlier), however, will need other parties to help save their lives. Parents, social workers, teachers, and other concerned individuals must be aware of organizations, both public and private, that can help. For example, the Association of Retarded Citizens (ARC) provides assistance to individuals accused of crimes. It also develops sentencing alternatives for convicted offenders with disabilities (Reynolds & Berkobien, 1997).

Possible solutions also hold implications for doctors, teachers, and law enforcement officials. Doctors may stereotype individuals with Down syndrome, viewing them as a monolithic group unable to care for themselves. Doctors may need more information about the services and support systems currently provided to individuals with disabilities. Teachers must specifically train students with disabilities how to deal with issues of abuse and inform them of their rights in the criminal justice system. Many law enforcement officials also need additional training, and some police departments have developed training programs (Fulton, 1997). The National Judicial College developed a curriculum to assist judges when they are dealing with individuals who are mentally retarded. Another organization that provides training is the Disability Rights Education and Defense Fund, Inc. This organization was founded in 1979 to protect and advance the civil rights of people with disabilities.

PERSISTING PROBLEMS

We address two potential problems in this section: noncompliance with IDEA, and improvement in the lives of people who were school-age prior to the passage of PL 94-142.

According to the National Council on Disability (NCD), there may be a problem with the enforcement of IDEA ("Back to School," 2000). The NCD concludes that "every state was out of compliance with IDEA requirements to some degree; in the sampling of states studied, noncompliance persisted over many years" (p. 1). They base their conclusions on a review of Department of Education records from 1994 to 1998. The NCD also states that the Department of Education was not effectively using its enforcement authority to ensure compliance.

These are serious allegations. Current noncompliance with IDEA could have a detrimental effect on individuals with disabilities for many years into the future.

In contrast, members of the Council for Exceptional Children (CEC) counter that the report of the NCD did not accurately portray state compliance with IDEA, stating that some state noncompliance involved minor procedural violations. They agree, however, that efforts must be made to provide all students with their rights under IDEA ("Report Gives Unbalanced Impression," 2000).

Also troubling is the situation of those adults who grew up during a time in which FAPE was not provided (Kaye, 1997) and as a result may not be living their lives to their fullest potential. They may have deficiencies in such areas as functional academics, vocational training, and independent living. Kaye contends that more should be done to retrain these individuals.

The ramifications of a lack of FAPE in the past, coupled with possible state noncompliance with IDEA today, should be closely examined. These are both issues that could impact negatively those with disabilities. The NCD is urging Congress to ensure full implementation with IDEA. Congress, policymakers, educators, and parents should also question whether enough has been done to retrain individuals who were denied FAPE.

FINAL THOUGHTS

The fields of science and technology may hold much promise for individuals who are mentally retarded. Biotechnology may have an effect on the reduction of mental retardation in future years (Baker, 1997). Advances have been made in gene therapy, genetic engineering, fetal surgery, human genome research, and biomedical research that could have an impact on individuals with disabilities. Baker asserts that 21st-century "medical technology may remove certain genetic markers or diminish any residual impact to the extent that only subtle physical or behavioral remnants will suggest that an individual needs support" (p. 378).

Computer technology may also be beneficial. The uses of computers for individuals who are mentally retarded may be limited only by our imagination. Scientists have already developed wearable computers, and experts in the field are stating that man and machine will become one through this technology (Bookman, 2000b). Other scientists are attempting to combine living brain cells with electronics to create a bionic brain (Bookman, 2000a).

All of these areas may potentially involve the courts and legislation. Many legal and ethical questions may need to be answered. Will there be limitations, legal or ethical, on the uses of technology? Who will decide the answers to these questions? How much input will individuals with disabilities and their advocates have in formulating policy? Although these advancements hold much promise, there may also be room for abuse. Society will have the challenge of ensuring that technology will be used to help and not harm individuals with disabilities.

To check your understanding of this chapter, go to the companion website at www.prenhall.com/beirne-smith and select Chapter 4, then choose the Self-Test module.

Summary

The Context for Securing Individuals' Rights

- *Brown v. Board of Education* (1954) was a significant ruling that provided legal precedents for individuals with disabilities.
- Certain legal terms such as *equal protection* and *due process* must be understood.
- Persons with mental retardation historically have been vulnerable to purposely unequal treatment.
- Mechanisms for securing rights are found at the federal, state, and local levels.

Legal Precedents for Individual Rights

- Individuals with disabilities are afforded certain rights regarding access to education, evaluation, classification, appropriate education, placement, related services, the extended school year, and expulsion.
- A noteworthy history of litigation exists that has tried to secure the right to treatment or habilitation for those confined to institutional settings.

Issues That Span a Lifetime

- Individuals who are mentally retarded may be denied certain medical services because of their disability.
- Issues relevant to crime, such as sexual abuse and domestic violence, can affect individuals who are mentally retarded.

Persisting Problems

- Congress and other officials must ensure compliance with IDEA.
- The training needs of individuals with disabilities who grew up prior to the provision of FAPE may need to be reevaluated.

Final Thoughts

- Technology may hold great promise as well as challenge for improving the lives of the mentally retarded.

References

Alamo Heights Independent School District v. State Board of Education, 790 F.2d 1153 (1986).

Armstrong v. Kline, 476 F.Supp. 583 (1979).

Back to school on civil rights: Advancing the federal commitment to leave no child behind. (2000, January/February). *LDA Newsbriefs, 35,* 1, 24.

Baer, D. (1981). The nature of intervention research. In R. Schiefelbusch & D. Bricker (Eds.), *Early language: Acquisition and intervention* (pp. 559–573). Baltimore, MD: University Park Press.

Baker, P. C. (1997). Presidential address 1997: Benchmarks for the next millennium. *Mental Retardation, 35,* 373–380.

Bateman, B. (1986). Equal protection for the handicapped. *Special Education Today,* p. 14.

Blatt, B. (1987). The conquest of mental retardation. Austin, TX: PRO-ED.

Bleemer, R. (1995). Court allows special education damages trial. *New Jersey Law Journal, 142*(9), 6.

Board of Education of the Hendrick Hudson Central School District v. Rowley, 458 U.S. 176 (1982).

Bookman, J. (2000a, April 2). Building a computer from brain cells. *Atlanta Journal-Constitution,* p. A14.

Bookman, J. (2000b, March 26). Wearable computers: We'll strap them on just like wristwatches. *Atlanta Journal-Constitution,* pp. A1, A14.

Brown v. Board of Education of Topeka, Kansas, 347 U.S. 483 (1954).

Carlson, B. E. (1997). Mental retardation and domestic violence: An ecological approach to intervention. *Social Work, 42*(1), 79–89.

Cedar Rapids Community School District v. Garret F. 106 F.3d 822 (8th Cir. 1997).

Cedar Rapids Community School District v. Garret F. 119 S.Ct. 992 (1999).

Cleburne Living Center Inc. v. City of Cleburne, Texas, 735 F.2d 832 (5th Cir. 1984).

Daniel R. R. v. State Board of Education, 874 F.2d 1036 (5th Cir. 1989).

DeMitchell, T., & Kerns, G. K. (1997). Where to educate Rachel Holland? Does least restrictive environment mean no restrictions? *The Clearing House 70,* 161–166.

Diana v. State Board of Education, C-70-37 R.F.P. (N.D. California), January 7, 1970, and June 18, 1972.

Drew, C. J., Logan, D. R., & Hardman, M. L. (1992). *Mental retardation: A life cycle approach* (5th ed.). Upper Saddle River, NJ: Merrill/Prentice Hall.

DuBow, S., & Greer, S. (1984). Special Education law since *Rowley. Clearinghouse Review , 17,* 1001–1007.

Edwards, W. J., & Reynolds, L. A. (1997). Defending and advocating on behalf of individuals with "mild" mental retardation in the criminal justice system. *Impact 10*(2), 12–13. (ERIC Document Reproduction Service no. ED 411 627)

Engelhard, J. B. (1999, Fall). Children and youth action network. *DLD Times, 17,* 6.

Everington, C., & Fulero, S. (1999). Competence to confess: Measuring understanding and suggestibility of defendants with mental retardation. *Mental Retardation, 37,* 212–220.

Fulton, F. (1997). Challenging stereotypes and ignorance: The San Francisco Police Department. *Impact 10*(2), 18. (ERIC Document Reproduction Service no. ED 411 627)

Gardner, J. F., & Chapman, M. S. (1985). *Staff development in mental retardation services: A practical handbook.* Baltimore, MD: Brookes.

Halderman v. Pennhurst State School and Hospital, 446 F.Supp. 1295 (E.D. Pa. 1977), *aff'd* in part, remand in part. Nos. 84-1490, 78-1564, 78-1602 (3rd Cir. December 13, 1979).

Hardie, A. (2000, April 9). *Atlanta Journal-Constitution*, pp. H1, H8.

Hayden, M. F. (1998). Civil rights litigation for institutionalized persons with mental retardation: A summary. *Mental Retardation, 36,* 75–83.

Henderson, R. A., & Vitello, S. J. (1988). Litigation related to community integration. In L. W. Heal, J. I. Haney, & A. R. Novak Amado (Eds.), *Integration of developmentally disabled individuals into the community* (2nd ed., pp. 272–282). Baltimore, MD: Brookes.

Hobsen v. Hansen, 269 F.Supp. 401 (D.D.C. 1967, *aff'd* sub norm).

Honig v. Doe, 108 S.Ct. 592 (1988).

Houchins, J. (1997). Breaking the cycle: "Justice now!" *Impact, 10*(2), 10. (ERIC Document Reproduction Service No. 411 627)

Hume, R. (1999, November/December). Learning disabilities and child sexual abuse. *LDA Newsbriefs, 34,* 8–9, 15, 18.

Hurry v. Jones, 734 F.2d 829 (1st Cir. 1984).

Irving Independent School District v. Tatro, 104 S.Ct. 3371 (1984).

J.B. v. Independent School District, 21 IDELR 1157 (D. Minn. 1995).

Kauffman, J. M., & Krouse, J. (1981). The cult of educability: Searching for the substance of things hoped for, the evidence of things not see. *Analysis & Intervention in Developmental Disabilities, 1,* 53–60.

Kaye, S. H. (1997). Disability watch: The status of people with disabilities in the United States. (ERIC Document Reproduction Service No. ED 417 540)

Keyes, D. W. (1997). The expert witness: Issues of competence, criminal justice, mental retardation. *Impact, 10*(2), 14–16. (ERIC Document Reproduction Service No. 411 627)

Keyes, D., Edwards, W., & Perske, R. (1997). People with mental retardation are dying, legally. *Mental Retardation, 35*(1), 59–63.

Lakin, K. C., & Bruininks, R. H. (1985). Challenges to advocates of social integration of developmentally disabled persons. In K. C. Lakin & R. H. Bruininks (Eds.), *Strategies for achieving community integration of developmentally disabled citizens* (pp. 313–330). Baltimore, MD: Brookes.

Larry P. v. Riles, 343 F.Supp. 1306 (N.D. Cal. 1972), *aff'd* 502 F.2d 963 (9th Cir. 1974), 495 F.Supp. 926 (N.D. Cal. 1979) *aff'd,* 793 F.2d 969 (9th Cir. 1984).

Larry P. v. Riles, No. C-71-2270 RFP, 1992 Lexis 13677 (N.D. Cal. 1992).

Laski, F., & Keefe, K. (1997). The ADA in the justice system. *Impact, 10*(2), 2–3. (ERIC Document Reproduction Service No. 411 627)

MacMillan, D. L., & Balow, I. H. (1991). Impact of *Larry P.* on education programs and assessment practices in California. *Diagnostique, 17,* 57–69.

Marchetti, A. G. (1987). *Wyatt v. Stickney:* A consent decree. *Research in Developmental Disabilities,* 8, 249–259.

Max M. v. Thompson, 566 F.Supp. 1330, 592 F.Supp. 1437, 592 F. Supp. 1450 (N.D. IL. 1984).

McCarthy, M. M. (1983). The *Pennhurst* and *Rowley* decisions: Issues and implications. *Exceptional Children,* 49, 517–522.

McKenzie v. Jefferson, 566 F.Supp 43 (D.D.C 1983).

Mills v. Board of Education of District of Columbia, 348 F.Supp. 866 (D.D.C. 1972).

Newcomer, J. R., & Zirkel, P. A. (1999). An analysis of judicial outcomes of special education cases. *Exceptional Children, 65,* 469-480.

New York Association for Retarded Children v. Rockefeller, 357 F.Supp. 752 (E.D. N.Y. 1973). Final consent judgment entered, Civil Nos. 72C 356, 72C 357 (E.D. N.Y. entered May 5, 1975).

Noonan, M. J., Brown, F., Mulligan, M., & Rettig, M. A. (1982). Educability of severely handicapped persons: Both sides of the issue. *Journal of the Association for Persons with Severe Handicaps, 7,* 3–12.

O'Connor v. Donaldson, 493 F.2d 507 (5th Cir. 1974), vacated and remanded on the issues of immunity, 95 S. Ct. 258b (1975).

Olmstead v. L.C. 526 U.S. 1037 (1999).

PASE (Parents in Action on Special Education) v. Hannon, 506 F.Supp. 831. (N.D. Ill. 1980).

Pennsylvania Association for Retarded Children (PARC) v. Commonwealth of Pennsylvania, 334 F.Supp. 1257 (E.D. Pa. 1971), 343 F.Supp. 279 (E.D. Pa. 1972).

Petersilia, J. (1998, January). *Persons with developmental disabilities in the criminal justice system: Victims, defendants, and inmates.* Statement prepared for the California Senate Public Disabilities in the Criminal Justice System." Available: mrrc.bio.uci.edu

Report gives unbalanced impression of special education practices. (2000, March). *CEC Today, 6,* 1, 9, 15.

Reynolds, L. A., & Berkobien, R. (1997). The ARC: Tackling criminal justice issues at national, state, and local levels. *Impact, 10*(2), 8–9. (ERIC Document Reproduction Service No. ED 411 627)

Rothstein, L. F. (1995). *Special education law.* New York: Longman.

Russo, C. J., Morse, T. E., & Glancy, M. C. (1998). Special education: A legal history and overview. *School Business Affairs, 64*(8), 8–12.

Sacramento City Unified School District Board of Education v. Rachel H., 14 F.3d 1398 (9th Cir. 1994).

San Antonio Independent School District v. Rodriguez, 411 U.S. 1 (1973).

Sobsey, D. (1997). Equal protection of the law for crime victims with developmental disabilities. *Impact, 10*(2), 6–7. (ERIC Document Reproduction No. ED 411 627)

Sorenson, D. D. (1997). The invisible victims. *Impact, 10*(2), 1, 26. (ERIC Document Reproduction No. ED 411 627)

Taylor, R. L. (1990). The Larry P. Decision a decade later: Problems and future directions. *Mental Retardation,* iii–v.

T.G. v. Board of Education of Piscataway, 576 F.Supp. 420 (D.N.J. 1983).

Timothy W. v. Rochester School District, 875 F.2d 954 (1st Cir. 1988).

Turnbull, A. P. (1982). Preschool mainstreaming: A policy and implementation analysis. *Education, Evaluation and Policy Analysis, 4* (3), 281–291.

Turnbull, H. R., III, & Turnbull, A. P. (2000). *Free appropriate public education* (6th ed.). Denver: Love.

Underwood, J. K., & Mead, J. F. (1995). *Legal aspects of special education and pupil services.* Boston: Allyn & Bacon.

Walther-Thomas, C., & Brownell, M. T. (1998). An interview with Dr. Mitchell Yell: Changes in IDEA regarding suspension and expulsion. *Intervention in School and Clinic, 34*(1), 46–49.

Watson v. City of Cambridge, 32 N.E. 864 (Mass. 1893).

W.B. v. Matula, 67 F.3rd 484 (3rd. Cir. 1995).

Wyatt v. Hardin, Civil Action No. 3195-N (M.D. Ala. 1975).

Wyatt v. Ireland, Civil Action No. 3195-N (M.D. Ala. 1979).

Wyatt v. Stickney, 344 F.Supp. 387, 344 F.Supp. 373 (M.D. Ala. 1972), 334 F.Supp. 1341, 325 F.Supp. 781 (M.D. Ala. 1971), 772 *aff'd* sub nom. *Wyatt v. Aderholt,* 503 F.2d, 1305 (5th Cir. 1974).

Yell, M. L. (1998). *The law and special education.* Upper Saddle River, NJ: Prentice Hall.

Yell, M. L., Rogers, D., & Rogers, E. L. (1998). The legal history of special education: What a long strange trip it's been! *Remedial & Special Education, 19,* 219–228.

Youngberg v. Romeo, 102 S.Ct. 2452 (1982).

Part Two

Biology, Psychology, and Sociology of Mental Retardation

CHAPTERS

Chapter

5

Biological Sources of Mental Retardation and Efforts for Prevention[1]

 To review the chapter objectives on-line, go to the companion website at www.prenhall.com/ beirne-smith and select Chapter 5, then choose the Objectives module.

Edward A. Polloway, Ed.D.
Lynchburg College in Virginia

J. David Smith, Ed.D.
Longwood College

OBJECTIVES

After reading this chapter, the student should be able to

- discuss the basic principles of genetics
- identify and discuss the major biological causes of mental retardation
- suggest various ways that mental retardation can be prevented
- identify selected ethical issues facing the field

[1]The authors acknowledge the assistance of Phyllis Lane and Jolie Chamberlain in the development of this chapter.

KEY TERMS

amniocentesis

autosomes

chromosomes

deletion

dominant inheritance

Down syndrome

fragile X syndrome

genes

genetics

heterozygous

homozygous

Human Genome Project

hydrocephalus

hypoxia

innate

karyotypes

meiosis

microcephaly

mosaicism

myelomeningocele

nondisjunction

phenylketonuria (PKU)

polygenetic inheritance

Prader-Willi syndrome (PWS)

recessive inheritance

teratogens

translocation

The task of sorting out the many causes of mental retardation is a formidable one. From the primitive beginnings of the study of retardation in the earliest part of recorded history to the more advanced efforts in the 21st century, the search for causation has been complex and challenging. The goal of this chapter is to provide a foundation for understanding the complexities in the causes of mental retardation.

Causes of retardation and related developmental disabilities have traditionally been divided into two categories: biological (or physiological) and environmental (or psychological and sociological). Such a taxonomic grouping of causes might be thought to create an apparently clear dichotomy of specific causes into either biological or environmental cases. However, most often, factors from both these domains are relevant in individual cases of mental retardation.

Although hundreds of specific factors have been identified as causative agents of mental retardation, the number of cases of retardation with unknown causes is still as large as those that are known and specifiable; that is, in only about 50% of cases of retardation can a cause be specified. A key problem is that causes are often undetermined for the large category of people diagnosed as having mild mental retardation.

Known and specifiable biological causes are often classified as pathological, organic, or clinical. Although such causes may result in cases at all levels of retardation, most attention in the past was drawn to their etiological roles in cases associated with more severe disabilities. Pathological factors can be identified in from 60% to 75% of cases where an individual's IQ falls below 50 (McLaren & Bryson, 1987). But the traditional association of a single, organic cause with severe retardation is too simplistic; many individuals with mild retardation may also be affected because of such etiological factors. The other traditional assumption—that mild retardation is the result of multiple, unspecifiable environmental events—has given way to the fact that this is only a "broad brush" distinction (Moser, 2000) and thus that from 25% to 40% of all cases of mild retardation may have a specific identifiable cause (McLaren & Bryson, 1987).

Clearly these data are influenced significantly by state prevalence rates in that states with high rates of retardation (e.g., Alabama: 2.85%) are likely thus to have a lower percentage associated with identified biological causes than would a state with a lower prevalence (e.g., California: 0.45%). Regardless of these data, it is nevertheless important to recognize that many individuals with mild disabilities are also frequently affected by genetic and other biological causes and that psychological and social influences are equally important in cases of severe disability. Finally, as we enter this new millennium, there is increasing confidence that the cause of virtually all cases of mental retardation may be identifiable (Moser, 2000).

Given this confounding complexity, why should educators, psychologists, and other behavioral scientists spend time studying the causation of mental retardation? Kolstoe (1972), in his classic work, notes that familiarity with etiological factors in mental retardation facilitates multidisciplinary communication, is an essential element of professionalism, and is important in enabling professionals to make accurate information available to parents. Furthermore, in certain situations, etiological information from educators and child care professionals can contribute to a more accurate diagnosis. The role of teachers, for example, may include monitoring the effects of ongoing or progressive disorders that may hinder daily performance, preventing future occurrences through parent counseling, or facilitating immediate change (e.g., intervention in a case of child abuse).

Finally, information is beginning to accumulate on the fact that research may identify educational and psychological intervention strategies that may be etiology-specific. Therefore, an understanding of causation may ultimately lead to alternative approaches to curriculum and instruction (e.g., Powell, Haughton, & Douglas, 1997; Hodapp, 1997). Hodapp suggests that the field of mental retardation has generated both a no-specificity view of relationship between etiology and behavior (i.e., specific genetic disorders have no specific effects on behavior) as well as a total-specificity position (i.e., genetic disorders associated with a distinctive behavioral pattern in almost every case of a disorder). He recommends a compromise that is beneficial to consider in this chapter. In this "partial-specificity view,"

> a few different genetic disorders show an identical behavior among those affected, and this behavior differs from the behavior of individuals with other types of mental retardation. Thus, it is not as if all genetic disorders have identical effects on behavior nor that each genetic disorder has unique effects. Instead a few disorders show similar effects, which are, in turn, not shared by mixed etiological groups. (p. 70)

While a general awareness of causative factors is necessary for any professional in the field of mental retardation, the mechanisms of specific causes may require multidisciplinary involvement. Input from various disciplines (e.g., biology, medicine, epidemiology, social work, psychology, psychiatry) often is essential to determine whether a cause can be specified or is even relevant to treatment and/or education. That many etiologies cannot be currently identified also serves as a stimulus for continuing research.

Finally, while considering information on causation, it is important that the reader not lose sight of the fact that behind these data are persons affected by the various causative agents. As Blatt (1987) cautions, "Treatises that deal with etiological conditions rarely recognize the human being [in] the superficially unattractive trappings of the condition" (p. 128). Readers must not overlook the fact that we are talking about real people who happen to have a given condition.

This discussion of causes begins with attention to terminology and then focuses on genetics, other biological causes, and environmental influences. It concludes with attention to the prevention of mental retardation and related ethical issues.

TERMINOLOGY

As noted earlier, the task of understanding the causes of mental retardation and developmental disabilities is challenging, and translating specific terms for known causes into useful information can be particularly difficult. This section offers ways to understand some of the labels ascribed to representative syndromes associated with retardation.

The terminology used to identify various syndromes comes primarily from three sources: (a) conventional wisdom or practices related to a specific historical era, (b) names of persons who initially identified or described the condition, and (c) biomedical terms describing the cause or the resultant disabilities.

Several examples illustrate historical names for syndromes. Perhaps best known is the term *mongolism,* which was coined by J. Langdon Down in 1866, two decades after Seguin's identification of the condition (Menolascino & Egger, 1978). For 100 years, this term, which was assigned simply because of Down's inaccurate observation that one frequent characteristic of the syndrome was facial similarity to Asians, prevailed in medical and psychological circles. Jordan (1976) has suggested that the term's popularity can be traced to Rudyard Kipling's 19th-century idea of the "white man's burden." This concept assumed the genetic inferiority, including mental inferiority, of non-Caucasian races. Realization that the syndrome is found in all racial groups (including persons from Mongolia) eventually aided in the necessary withdrawal of the racist term from the vocabulary of most professionals, although its use occasionally persists in the general public and in some popular media.

TABLE 5.1
Biomedical Terminology

Stems and Affixes	Meaning	Example(s)
ab-, abs-	from, away	abnormal, abscess
amnio-	pertaining to embryonic sac	amniocentesis
anomalo-	irregular	chromosomal anomaly
auto-	self, same	autism, autosomes
-cele, -coele	sac, cavity	meningocele
-cephalo-	head, brain	hydrocephalus
-encephalo-	head, brain	encephalitis
endo-	inner, inside	endogenous
ex-, extra-	outside, away from	exogenous
fibro-	connective tissues	neurofibromatosis
galacto-	milk	galactosemia
glyco-, gluco-	sweet, sugar	glycogen, hyperglycemia
hydro-	water	hydrocephalus
hyper-	over, more than usual	hyperkinetic
hypo-	under, less than usual, lowered	hypothyroidism
-lepsy	seizure	epilepsy, narcolepsy
lipo-	fat	lipids
macro-, mega-	large	macrocephaly, acromegaly
meningo-	central nervous system membranes	meningitis
micro-	small	microcephaly
myelo-	marrow, spinal cord	myelomeningocele
neuro-	nerve	neurofibromatosis
-osis	condition of	toxoplasmosis
-plasia	cellular growth	skeletal dysplasia
-plasma	blood	toxoplasmosis
-plegia	paralysis	monoplegia, paraplegia
-semia	sign, symptom	galactosemia
-somy, -some, soma-	body	chromosome, trisomy
toxo-	poisonous	toxemia
-trophy	nutrition, nourishment	atrophy, dystrophy

Source: From *Introduction to Military Medicine and Surgery,* Study Guide 6, 1975, Fort Sam Houston, TX: Academy of Health Sciences, U.S. Army.

Ultrasound, or sonography, has led to our understanding of the prenatal environment.

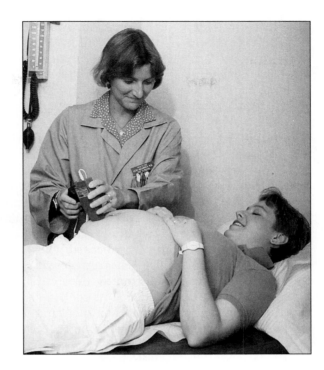

A second, more direct way to identify a clinical syndrome is to attach to it the name of the researcher who contributed in a major way to its understanding. For instance, professionals now identify as Down syndrome the chromosomal condition disorder that J. Langdon Down described in some detail. Other relatively well-known syndromes so named include Tay-Sachs, after the British and American physicians who described the characteristics of the condition in the late 1880s, and Lesch-Nyhan syndrome, named for two of the three researchers who first identified this disorder in 1964.

The third source of syndrome labels is biomedical terminology. Although some of these terms are frequently used by laypersons, their meanings often seem obscure, in spite of their grounding in common terminology forms. Thus, many of the labels convey primary features of the disorder, either causal or characteristic. Table 5.1 lists some of the more common terms used to identify clinical disorders. For each entry, the specific derivatives are noted, along with their common meaning and examples of their use.

Although labels are only an attempt to refer to complex medical, biological, or behavioral phenomena, simply being familiar with the derivatives can be of assistance in understanding the nature of these disorders and terms related to them. Several specific terms illustrate the system. For example, *toxoplasmosis* indicates a condition (*-osis*) of poisonous (*toxo-*) blood (*-plasm*). Although the clinical definition of toxoplasmosis is much more specific, the word, when analyzed, gives a fair suggestion of what the condition is about. Another example is *hydrocephalus*. The term refers to a disorder resulting from a blockage of cerebrospinal fluid, but breaking the word down into "water" (*hydro-*) and "head" or "brain" (*cephalo-*) provides a

For a complete on-line glossary of mental retardation terms, go to the companion website http://www.prenhall.com/ beirne-smith and select any chapter, then choose the Glossary module.

descriptive picture of the condition. A third example is the disorder called **myelomeningocele**. As the term suggests, this condition is characterized by a saclike mass (*-cele*) on the spinal cord (*myelo-*) containing membrane tissue of the central nervous system (*-meningo-*).

GENETIC DISORDERS

Genetics is the study of heredity and its variations. As such, its scope is enormous and its complexities great. Advances in genetics over the past 60 years rival those in any area of science. The contributions of geneticists to understanding the causes of developmental disabilities are particularly noteworthy. In the last 10 years, this knowledge base has mushroomed due to research on gene mapping and DNA sequencing under the auspices of the **Human Genome Project**.

An understanding of heredity begins with the study of genes. **Genes** are the basic biological units carrying inherited physical, mental, or personality traits. Between 50,000 and 100,000 genes are present in each human cell. Genes occupy specific positions on **chromosomes**, the threadlike or rodlike bodies that contain genetic information and material. As the Human Genome Project has progressed, the careful mapping of gene sites on the chromosomes has reached a point where the full human map will apparently soon be revealed, resulting in the identification of about 80,000 genes (Hall, 2000).

Chromosomes vary widely in size and shape, but for human cells, the normal pattern is consistent. Each cell contains 23 pairs of chromosomes. The embryo initially receives one member of each pair from each parent. There are two types of chromosomes: autosomes and sex chromosomes. **Autosomes** are matching pairs and constitute 44 of the 46 chromosomes within the usual human complement (i.e., 22 of the 23 pairs). Sex chromosomes make up the other pair. The letters *X* is used to represent the female sex chromosome and *Y* to represent the male sex chromosome. While the X chromosome contains a substantial amount of genetic information, the Y functions primarily as a determinant of male gender. At conception, an X chromosome is contributed by the mother, while either an X or a Y is contributed by the father. The XX combination creates a female, and the XY a male.

The precise and rather fragile roles of genes and chromosomes as building blocks of development are dramatically represented in mental retardation research. The most prevalent general groups of biological causes of retardation are genetic transmission of traits (i.e., genetic disorders) and chromosomal abnormalities. But even in these seemingly clear-cut cases of genetic transmission, it is important to keep in mind that development is still shaped significantly by environmental influences.

GENETIC TRANSMISSION

Many traits are transmitted from one generation to the next according to the makeup of a specific gene pair. We thus can trace many specific characteristics to the presence or absence of a single gene. Transmission can occur through autosomal dominant or recessive inheritance and through sex-linked inheritance. In **dominant inheritance**, an individual gene can assume "control" over, or mask, its partner and will operate whether the two elements of an individual gene pair are similar or dissimilar to each other. **Recessive inheritance** refers to genes that cannot control their partners. In a sense they "recede" when paired with a dissimilar mate and become influential only when matched with another recessive gene. Pairs of genes carrying the same trait are called **homozygous**; pairs carrying different traits are **heterozygous.** Homozygous pairs are necessary for the case of recessive inheritance, whereas either homozygous or heterozygous pairs can lead to instances of dominant inheritance.

The dynamics of dominant and recessive inheritance are illustrated in Figure 5.1. Capital letters typically are used to indicate dominant traits; lowercase letters commonly denote recessive traits. In the typical case of dominant inheritance (Example A), only one parent would have the specific dominant trait in question, which is transmitted, theoretically, to two of their four children. In the common case of recessive inheritance (Example B), probability suggests that at each conception, chances are one in four that the child will be homozygous and will manifest the recessive trait (hh), two in four that he or she will be a heterozygous carrier for the succeeding generation (Hh, hH), and one in four that he or she will be homozygous, for the dominant gene, therefore lacking the recessive gene altogether (HH).

Dominant Transmission

Dominant inheritance determines a variety of common traits, including brown eyes and prematurely white hair. Several rare physical disorders are carried as dominant traits. Frequently these disorders are structural; that is, they occur with visible signs. General examples include Marfan's syndrome (which manifests itself through tall stature, loose joints of the limbs, and heart disorders) and achrondoplasia (dwarfism). Relevant to our focus in this chapter, neurofibromatosis and tuberous sclerosis are examples of dominant gene disorders that may involve mental retardation.

Neurofibromatosis (NF) is also known as von Recklinghausen's disease, named for the man who first described the disorder in 1882. The gene for neurofibromatosis has been identified as occupying a site on chromosome 17 (Rasmussen & Fried-

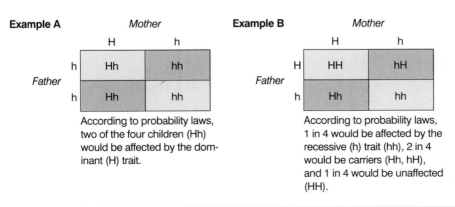

FIGURE 5.1
Dominant and Recessive Inheritance

man, 1999). It affects about 1 in 3,000 newborns (Polloway & Rucker, 1997; Rasmussen & Friedman, 1999), with about 50% of the cases being inherited and the remainder caused by genetic *mutations* occurring spontaneously. It is identifiable by light brown patches (called café-au-lait) on the skin and/or by multiple, soft, fibrous swellings or tumors (neurofibromas) that grow on nerves or appear elsewhere on the body and can result in severe physical deformities (Clayman, 1989). It has been speculated that neurofibromatosis was the affliction from which both John Merrick (the "Elephant Man") and Quasimodo (the Hunchback of Notre Dame) suffered (Blatt, 1987), but there is limited agreement on this association. Surgical procedures for tumors may be recommended (i.e., when the growths cause complications or have a major effect on comfort or appearance), although the tumors may recur.

Neurofibromatosis varies greatly in how it is expressed (i.e., variable expressivity) from case to case. The café-au-lait patches are primarily a cosmetic concern, but the locations of the tumors will have an effect on mental development, which may be severe if they occur on the brain. Otherwise, the individual may be in the normal range of intelligence. The majority of children with NF, however, are likely to have academic problems, with an estimated 30%–60% having learning disabilities (Brewer, Moore, & Hiscock, 1997; Nativio & Belz, 1990; Rasmussen & Friedman, 1999). A continuing concern is for the psychological development of individuals who see themselves as deformed and question whether they should have children.

Tuberous sclerosis (TS) is another skin disease carried by a dominant gene. The two words derive from the Latin and Greek for "rootlike" and "hardening," respectively. Its tumors are similar to potatoes in density and destroy the cells in the organs where they are found (Menolascino & Egger, 1978). As with neurofibromatosis, the changes resulting from tuberous sclerosis are primarily structural rather than biochemical, a common finding in autosomal disorders. The degree of expressivity of the gene can result in great variation in characteristics of the people who have the disease. In the mild form, no retardation or serious health problems occur; in the severe variety, tumors can result in dysfunction of a number of organs (e.g., brain, lungs, kidneys), followed by mental deterioration, epilepsy, and early death. Most individuals with TS experience some cognitive difficulties (Harrison, O'Callaghan, Hancock, Osborne, & Bolton, 1999).

Recessive Transmission

Recessive inheritance is commonly associated with blue eyes and a variety of other physical traits, but it also involves disorders capable of producing severe disabilities and serious health impairments. General health-related examples include sickle-cell anemia and cystic fibrosis, while examples in the field of mental retardation include phenylketonuria, Tay-Sachs disease, and galactosemia. Because transmission of recessive traits is a function of the union of two carriers (see Figure 5.1), controlling these disorders entails using genetic screening measures to identify unknowing carriers.

Recessive transmission is often associated with those disorders that can be traced to dysfunction in the body's mechanisms for the processing of food—so-called inborn errors of metabolism. In particular, imbalances related to fats, carbohydrates, and amino acids have been well established as causative agents of retardation and related disabilities. However, their rarity is such that they result in a limited number of cases of mental retardation. Collectively they occur in approximately 1 in 4,000 births (Hall, 2000).

Tay-Sachs Disease   Metabolic disorders resulting from an increase in lipids, or fats, in the body's tissues are frequently progressive, degenerative diseases. The developmental profile is typically that of a normal progression until onset of the disorder, from which point the condition rapidly worsens. *Tay-Sachs disease,* for example, is inherited as an autosomal recessive trait. It is disproportionately prevalent among persons of Ashkenazic Jewish background, although recent findings have shown that it occurs more frequently among the general population than originally thought. Infants with Tay-Sachs disease appear normal at birth. The disease is typically manifested late in the child's 1st year, followed by a course of severe retardation, convulsions, blindness, paralysis, and death by the age of 4. There is no cure for Tay-Sachs disease, and it remains one of the most challenging causes of disabilities.

Galactosemia   An example of a carbohydrate disorder is *galactosemia,* a recessive condition characterized by the inability to metabolize galactose, a form of sugar found in milk, into glucose (Widerstrom, Mowder, & Sandall, 1991). The physiological changes occurring in galactosemia again are biochemical rather than structural, a feature common in recessive disorders. Manifestations of the syndrome may include retardation, liver and kidney dysfunction, and cataracts. Following identification of the disorder, the removal of dairy products from the child's diet has proved successful in interrupting the progress of deterioration. Koch and colleagues (1988) report on longitudinal research indicating that early treatment generally leads to unimpaired intellectual development. The IQs of children treated early (prior to 4 months of age) were reported to be within the normal range.

Phenylketonuria   Diet control can also mediate the effects of genetic transmission of the amino acid disorder **phenylketonuria (PKU),** the most common of the genetic disorders and the most publicized success story in the preventive literature. PKU is caused by an autosomal recessive gene and, if left untreated, is frequently associated with aggressiveness, hyperactivity, and retardation. However, since it was first described by Ivar Asbjörn Folling in 1934, PKU has been virtually eliminated as a causative factor in severe retardation, despite its incidence of 1 in every 12,000 to 15,000 births. PKU has played a significant role in the field because it was the first inborn metabolic anomaly proven to cause retardation. Its discovery led to both increased research into etiology and a pronounced change in the aura of hopelessness that once surrounded mental retardation. Figure 5.2 illustrates the historical discovery process for PKU, and the box "Robert Guthrie and the PKU Story" provides an overview of the key work of Robert Guthrie in this field.

As noted in Figure 5.2, the treatment regimen for PKU is related to restrictions in intake of phenylalanine, common in high-protein foods. Thus, the diet is predicated on the need for the substitution of other foods and synthetic proteins. With the elimination of phenylalanine from the diet, the deleterious effect could thus be significantly reduced.

Levitas (1998) summarizes the nature of the legendary treatment for PKU:

> Persons on this diet may not partake of the most common and widely enjoyed fast foods and barbecued staples in the American diet, making participation in family and community events difficult. . . . The diet can be heavy in carbohydrate snack substitutes, making it almost the opposite of what most people think of as a "diet"; new caregivers, and even casual contacts in the person's life, must be educated about the basis for the components of the diet, which must be strictly adhered to. The caregivers must be reminded to avoid all "diet foods" sweetened with Aspartame, which is a potent source of phenylalanine. The caregivers must learn to tolerate the liquid tyrosine supplement, which smells and tastes extremely "fishy."

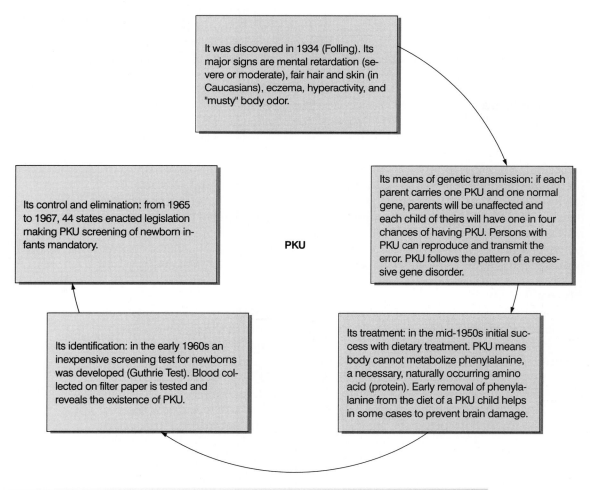

FIGURE 5.2

Phenylketonuria (PKU)

Source: From *Mental Retardation: The Known and the Unknown* (p. 25), by President's Committee on Mental Retardation, 1976, Washington, DC: U.S. Government Printing Office.

✳ Robert Guthrie and the PKU Story

Advances in the field of mental retardation and developmental disabilities have come in a variety of ways. Certainly key societal commitments have included support for research as well as for enabling legislation for educational programs and litigations to confirm basic human rights. However, behind most of these achievements often are individuals who have made a significant difference. As discussed in Koch's (1997) biography of Robert Guthrie, it is clear that he was one. Schroeder (1999) writes in his review of this book that it

> captures the science, the drama, the serendipity, and the chance events that resulted in the development over the last 50 years of screening tests for phenylketonuria (PKU) and of mass screening methods for metabolic errors in general as a major tool for the prevention of mental retardation. How did it happen that hundreds of millions of newborn infants around the world have been screened for a variety of metabolic disorders largely due to the efforts of one

man? That is a story worth tracing. One needs to observe Bob Guthrie's contributions as a scientist and as a human being. . . .

Three major contributions to newborn screening programs earn Bob Guthrie a place in the history of research in mental retardation: (a) he showed the blood specimens of three tiny spots on filter paper were safe and useful screening methods; (b) he developed the bacterial inhibition assay for phenylalanine in the blood spot, the first method of diagnosing PKU using blood; and (c) he advocated for mass screenings of newborns and children all over the world. This was a revolutionary concept which required proselytizing in wide sectors of the medical and public health communities. His devising of inexpensive analytic methods was the key to their acceptance. That was the breakthrough from a public health standpoint.

> Fortunately, the liquid can be flavored with fruit juices, vanilla, [and] honey and can be frozen into a "slushy" with flavorings. (p. 113)

The early results of diet treatment for PKU were most encouraging. Johnson, Koch, Peterson, and Friedman (1978) reported that a group of 148 treated PKU children did not significantly differ from the general population in the prevalence of congenital anomalies or major neurological defects. Intellectual development near or within the normal range thus was considered achievable. Children treated very early—before they were a month old—had significantly higher IQs than those whose treatment began in the 2nd month (Koch et al., 1988); continued adherence to the diet had positive results as well, while diet cessation in individuals continues to show a decrement in IQ (Levitas, 1998).

Two major problems remained, however. First, the diet prescribed for children with PKU can be unappealing and hard to follow, and it may be difficult to balance protein restrictions against the protein needs of developing children. For years, the special diet was generally discontinued by approximately school age, but this practice caused concern. For example, Matthews, Barabas, Cusack, and Ferrari (1986) reported decreases in social quotients for individuals for whom the diet was discontinued at age 5½ years. In children who maintained their diets to the age of 10, Fishler, Azen, Henderson, Friedman, and Koch (1987) found higher school achievement, intellectual level, language, and perceptual skills. Clarke, Gates, Hogan, Barrett, and MacDonald (1987) conclude:

The bulk of evidence appears . . . to indicate that older children allowed access to unrestricted diets do experience some deterioration in intelligence, that this is associated with specific neuropsychological deficits that are not attributable simply to their intellectual handicap, and that this deficit is at least partly reversible by a return to dietary . . . restriction. . . . [A]lthough the data would support efforts to maintain older children with PKU on . . . restricted diets for as long as possible, the meager short-term clinical benefits, along with the well-known difficulty of re-introducing the therapeutic diet in older children . . . suggest that long-term return to dietary treatment is unlikely to succeed except in unusually highly motivated patients. (p. 260)

Research continues on the issue of treatment discontinuation in adolescents and adults with PKU; this research is likely to eventually yield definitive directions for future treatment (Griffiths, Smith, & Harvie, 1997). Most recently, Levitas (1998) reviewed research in the area and gave a compelling case for a life-long phenylalanine-free diet treatment for persons with PKU. Acceptance of this recommendation would have an obvious effect on a second issue (discussed next) that emerged with the study of PKU.

The second issue concerns women who were treated in childhood for PKU. As adults, these women's metabolic imbalances can harm their unborn children. In this instance, the problem is not a genetic one but rather an increased risk to the fetus during pregnancy due to the mother's elevated level of inappropriately processed phenylalanine. Consequences can include retardation, heart disease, and microcephaly (Schultz, 1983); therefore, women should reinstate their restricted diet during pregnancy. Evidence of this concern can be noted by consumers in common product warnings—for example on diet sodas or some low-fat foods (e.g., yogurt)—that these items contain phenylalanine. Unless pregnancy is avoided, Koch et al. (1988) indicate that the effects of maternal PKU could offset the preventive benefits of screening programs and dietary treatment interventions.

Sex-Linked Inheritance

A third type of genetic transmission is through sex-linked (or X-linked) inheritance. This name derives from a variety of recessive traits carried on the X chromosome. Females have two X chromosomes, and a specific gene carrying a disorder can be dominated by its mate. But males (XY) will be affected by a single recessive gene carried on the X chromosome, because there is no second X chromosome whose genes could potentially dominate the pathology-producing recessive trait. Instead, males have a Y chromosome, which does not carry genes that will counterbalance the X-linked gene. A female can be affected only if her father is affected and her mother is a carrier. Thus, the problem of sex-linked inheritance is particularly significant for males (see Figure 5.2).

In the general population, X-linked recessive traits of concern include color blindness, hemophilia, and Duchenne-type muscular dystrophy, and a variety of other conditions that may be as much as ten times more common in males than in females. The unique nature of sex-linked recessive inheritance is perhaps best illustrated by the presence of the disorder of hemophilia within the royal families of Europe. In a story often told, many of the ancestors of Queen Victoria of England, a carrier for hemophilia, either carried the disease or, in the case of some males, experienced the impact of this disorder. Most notably, the son of the last czar of Russia, Nicholas II, had hemophilia, which ultimately became a contributor to the downfall of the Romanov dynasty (see Massie, 1967, for an ancestral outline reflecting the recurrence of hemophilia).

Lesch-Nyhan Syndrome   In the field of mental retardation, the most common example of sex-linked recessive inheritance is *Lesch-Nyhan syndrome*. The disorder, first identified in 1964 (Lesch & Nyhan, 1964), is inherited as an X-linked recessive and thus is much more common among males. According to Nyhan (1976), it is the second most common metabolic disorder (after PKU). The most striking manifestation of Lesch-Nyhan syndrome is an apparently uncontrollable urge to cause injury to oneself and, to a lesser extent, to others.

Typically, children with Lesch-Nyhan syndrome will begin displaying extreme self-injurious behavior (SIB) when acquiring teeth. They may bite ferociously and, in their frenzy, rip and tear tissue (Libby, Polloway, & Smith, 1983; Nyhan, Johnson, Kauffman, & Jones, 1980). Aside from SIB, they may hit, pinch, and bite others; use obscene language; spit; and engage in a variety of disruptive actions because of their inability to control their impulses (Hoefnagel, Andrew, Mireault, & Berndt, 1965). When unrestrained, they may scream as if terrified of the pain they might inflict on themselves, while when restrained they seem more calm.

Both biomedical and educational interventions have been attempted with children who have Lesch-Nyhan syndrome. Drug treatment to alter metabolism has proven efficacious on a short-term basis. Continued work on biochemical processes in the brain also offer great promise. Educational interventions with children with Lesch-Nyhan historically have included a variety of attempts at behavioral change, with variant levels of success (Anderson, Dancis, & Alpert, 1978; Bull & LaVecchio, 1978).

Fragile X Syndrome   A disorder that was first noted in 1943 but began to receive significant attention after its formal discovery in 1979 is **fragile X syndrome**. After Down syndrome, this syndrome is the most common clinical type of retardation. It is also the most common hereditary cause of retardation (Lachiewicz, Harrison, Spiridigliozzi, Callanan, & Livermore, 1988). The actual mechanism for genetic transmission is far too complex for discussion herein, so it is sufficient to say that it is linked to the X chromosome, although different from the recessive transmission pattern discussed above.

In a traditional karyotype of fragile X syndrome, the fragile site appears as a pinched or restricted location on the lower arm of the X chromosome (Barker, 1990). However, more recently, the region containing the gene for fragile X has been isolated. The gene seems to occur in about 1 in 1,500 males and about 1 in 1,000 females in the general population (Clayman, 1989), although much lower prevalence rates have been cited (Maes, Fryns, Ghesquiere, & Borghgraef, 2000). Diagnosis can be made prenatally, although most often it is made clinically during early childhood after observation of developmental delays and/or the appearance of large ears (Buyse, 1990). Maes et al. (2000) provide a screening checklist for use with persons suspected of having the syndrome.

According to Barker (1990), common physical characteristics of fragile X include prominent jaws, macro-orchidism (large testes), long and thin faces, long and soft ears and hands, prominent foreheads, and enlarged heads. The syndrome has been associated in males with severe retardation, although reports of its occurrence in individuals with various levels of retardation (and also with normal intelligence) suggest the need for caution and careful consideration of environmental experience (Rogers & Simensen, 1987). Maes et al. (2000) report on a sample of persons with fragile X who were retarded. For children, the statistics were 6.59%, profound; 29.9%, severe; 48.1%, moderate; and 15.6%, mild. For adults, the figures were 14%, profound; 71%, severe; and 21%, moderate. The nature of the sample, however, limits its generalizability to the overall population. Behavioral manifestations may include attentional difficulties, repetitive behaviors, and gaze avoidance, while speech and language patterns may include echolalia, perseverative use of given utterances, and palilalia (i.e., repeating statements at increasing rates of speed and loudness) (Bellinger, Rucker, & Polloway, 1997). Although males with fragile X are typically thought to be infertile, instances exist where this has not been the case.

Women who have the fragile X chromosome are frequently clinically viewed as carriers and may not be identified because of low expressivity (Barker, 1990); however, an estimated one-third may also be partially affected and may have mild disabilities (Rogers & Simensen, 1987). A pattern of varied strengths and weaknesses is particularly apparent in girls who have fragile X. Although not frequently mentally retarded, such girls are often learning disabled (Neely, 1991).

A consistent relationship between fragile X and autism has been reported in the literature, with males with fragile X having a 5%–46% prevalence of autism or autistic-like behaviors. On the other hand, children with autism are found to have the fragile X pattern in about 15% of cases. While males with fragile X often exhibit autistic-type behaviors, they are usually less significant than the behaviors seen in persons who are clinically diagnosed as autistic. However, the similarity in behavior patterns does lead to difficulty in making a diagnosis of typical autistic-like behaviors versus clinical autism (Bellinger et al., 1997; Cantu, Stone, Wing, Langee, & Williams, 1990).

Polygenic Inheritance

To learn more about the Human Genome Project and some specific causes of mental retardation, go to the companion website at *www.prenhall.com/ beirne-smith* and select Chapter 5, then choose the Web Destinations module.

The preceding discussion has focused on single-gene anomalies, reflecting the mechanism by which one gene controls one trait (or a given condition). Many traits, however, do not fit simple rules but are transmitted through **polygenetic inheritance**. Polygenic or multigenic inheritance has particular importance for potential contributions to the etiology of the so-called psychosocial causes of retardation (see Chapter 6). Unlike the one-gene/one-trait pattern of numerous disorders associated with retardation (e.g., PKU), in polygenic inheritance, the interaction of multiple genes and networks influences individual intellectual functioning. Since the complexity of this phenomenon makes precise evaluation difficult in single cases, researchers depend on statistical data from population samples in seeking to understand polygenetic inheritance. That is, "genetic predictions . . . have to be based on empirical data from population statistics. Simple genetic models just do not apply" (Scarr & Carter-Saltzman, 1982, p. 804). The concept of heritability and the database on inheritance (i.e., twin studies) are discussed in the next chapter.

CHROMOSOMAL DEVIATIONS

A second major source of biological causes of disabilities are chromosomal anomalies. Although these disorders are rare in the general population, their numbers are significant among those cases of developmental disabilities in which cause can be specified.

The intensive research on chromosomes that began in the late 1950s and early 1960s provided an increasingly detailed portrait of both typical and atypical chromosomal patterns. These patterns are clarified through the use of **karyotypes**. The process of karyotyping includes taking a picture of the chromosomes in a human cell, enlarging it, cutting out the pictures of individual chromosomes, and then arranging the chromosomes by pairs from the largest (numbered as pair 1) to the smallest (pair 22), followed by the sex chromosomes (XX or XY).

Approximately 10% of pregnancies begin with some chromosomal imbalance, but most of these abort spontaneously during the first 3 months of pregnancy. A small number of these pregnancies proceed to full term, and the children born illustrate the potential effects of irregularities in the arrangement or alignment of autosomes or sex chromosomes. Chromosomal errors can be identified in approximately 1 in 200 live births.

While genetic disorders are classified as hereditary, chromosomal problems are often more accurately termed **innate**, since an abnormal chromosome arrangement is present at conception but is not the product of hereditary exchange. Disorders of this type usually result from abnormalities occurring during the stage of cell division called **meiosis**. During meiosis, individual reproductive cells divide and then pair up to form the genetic foundation of the embryo. The normal process includes 23 chromosomes from each parent, which are paired to form the new organism's complement of 46 chromosomes. Figure 5.3 illustrates the karyotypes for a male and a female with normal chromosomal patterns.

Several specific abnormalities that occur during the process of chromosomal arrangement and alignment result in either too much or too little chromosomal material being present. In **nondisjunction**, a given parental pair of chromosomes fails to split at conception, causing the formation of a group of three chromosomes (a *trisomy*) in lieu of the normal pair. A trisomy on chromosome 21 is the most common cause of Down syndrome; trisomies on 18 and 13 are also described in the literature. In **translocation**, a fragment of chromosomal material is located across from or exchanged with another chromosomal pair. For example, a translocation that results in Down syndrome occurs when a fragment broken off from chromosome pair 21 attaches to a chromosome from group 15. In **deletion**, a portion of the original genetic material is absent from a specific chromosome pair. Finally, **mosaicism** is an uneven pattern of dissimilar cells (such as of 46 or 47 chromosomes).

Before the 1950s, causes of the disorders now classified under chromosomal anomalies were unknown. Seminal research published by Lejeune and his colleagues (Lejeune, Gautier, & Turpin, 1959) and other cytogeneticists then led to a much clearer understanding of the nature of chromosomal abnormalities. As men-

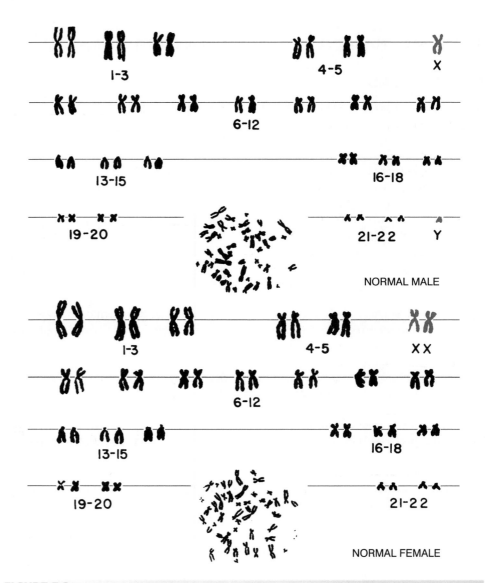

FIGURE 5.3

Normal Chromosonal Karyotypes

Source: From *Handbook of Mental Retardation Syndromes* (pp. 33–34), by C. H. Carter, 1975, Springfield, IL: Charles C. Thomas. Reprinted by permission of Charles C. Thomas, Publisher.

tioned earlier, aberrations in the number or arrangement of chromosomes are likely to damage the developing organism. Down syndrome and cri-du-chat syndrome are examples of autosomal disorders; Klinefelter and Turner syndromes come from sex chromosome abnormalities. As a generalization, disorders in autosomes are more often associated with mental retardation, whereas anomalies associated with sex chromosomes are more commonly associated with learning disabilities (Bender, Puck, Salbenblatt, & Robinson, 1986; Smith, Dowdy, Polloway, & Blalock, 1997).

Down Syndrome

Down syndrome is the best-known, most prevalent, and most frequently researched biologically caused condition associated with mental retardation and developmental disabilities. For many laypersons, the concept of a person with mental retardation has historically been virtually synonymous with a Down syndrome individual. A reasonable estimate of the prevalence of the syndrome is about 1 in 1,000 births (Cate & Ball, 1999) and roughly 5%–6% of all persons identified as mentally retarded.

Study of the disorder has revealed three separate chromosomal causes. The first and most common, trisomy 21, is due to the failure of one pair of parental chromosomes to separate at conception, resulting in the child's having 47 chromosomes. This abnormality has historically been found more often in children born to older mothers, and researchers have suggested a variety of reasons.

Specific factors that have been suspected of causing trisomy 21 include medication and drugs; exposure to radiation, chemicals, or hepatitis viruses; and the possible absence of a mechanism in the mother to abort the fetus spontaneously. It is important to realize that, although risk is related to age and increases to approximately 1 in 30 at 45 years old, age itself is a correlate and not the cause. There has also been an assumption of linkage of paternal, rather than maternal, age with Down syndrome in an estimated 20%–25% of cases of trisomy 21 (Abroms & Bennett, 1980). With the increased public awareness of the correlation between age and risk of occurrence, many older parents undergo prenatal screening for Down syndrome and may then consider abortion. This fact, plus the reality that births to parents over 40 are relatively rare, results in the large majority of births of children with Down syndrome actually being to younger parents.

A second form of Down syndrome is caused by a translocation transmitted hereditarily by carriers. Although this translocation is usually to chromosome pairs 13 or 15, the extra material comes from pair 21 and forms, in a sense, a partial trisomy. Mosaicism, the uneven division that creates cells varying in chromosome numbers (some 47 and some 46), is the third and rarest form of the condition.

Down syndrome is frequently associated with a variety of specific physical traits, including the following:

- Short stature
- Flat, broad face with small ears and nose
- Short, broad hands with incurving fingers
- Upward slanting of the eyes with folds of skins (epicanthic folds) at the inside corner of the eye
- Small mouth and short roof, which may cause the tongue to protrude and contribute to articulation problems
- Single crease across the palm
- Reduced muscle tone (hypotonia) and hyperflexibility of joints
- Heart defects (in about one-third of instances)
- Increased susceptibility to upper respiratory infections
- Incomplete or delayed sexual development

These traits vary greatly from one individual to another. Thus, no overgeneralizations should be made according to the defining characteristics that must or may be associated with Down syndrome. Most significant is the association of the condition with a moderate or severe forms of retardation (discussed further later). Many of the behavioral characteristics traditionally associated with Down syndrome have not been documented in research or require some further explication. For example, the stereotype of the child with Down syndrome who is cheerful, affectionate, rhythmic, and unusually dexterous has not been empirically established. Furthermore, while children with Down syndrome may exhibit more frequent and intense, repetitive behaviors, Evans and Gray (2000) report that they did not differ from young children (matched on MA) who were nondisabled in terms of the numbers of compulsive behaviors in which they engaged.

A relatively recent change in the syndrome picture concerns life expectancy. In 1929, expectancy for individuals with Down syndrome was only 9 years; by 1990, that average had increased to over 50 years (Eyman, Call & White, 1991). As age increases, association of the syndrome with Alzheimer's disease also increased. Individuals with Down syndrome apparently run a much greater risk of developing Alzheimer's disease (Stark, Menolascino, & Goldsbury, 1988; Zigman, Schupf, Lubin, & Silverman, 1987). The association is not unexpected, given the identified locus for Alzheimer's on chromosome pair 21. Epstein (1988) has pointed out that the loss of intellectual functioning associated with advanced age will be seen even more often in individuals with Down syndrome now that life expectancies have increased.

Most significant have been the data collected on the intellectual functioning of children with Down syndrome. Traditionally, the syndrome had been assumed to result most often in moderate retardation, with rare cases reaching a ceiling IQ of 70. Occasional anecdotal reports of ability and special talents, such as in the classic diary of Nigel Hunt (1967), were considered more interesting and unusual than typical.

The first comprehensive study that altered views on this issue was reported by Rynders, Spiker, and Horrobin (1978). Their review of 15 studies provided data on the intelligence test scores of children with Down syndrome that indicated a significant range in level of functioning and refuted the alleged ceiling IQ of 70.

Optimistic data on the abilities of children with Down syndrome then continued to accumulate. Early intervention seems to be the key to the future. Rynders and Horrobin (1990) provide further support in subsequent research supporting higher expectations for academic achievement in students with Down syndrome. They caution that IQs frequently diminish over time and, therefore, achievement levels should be stressed in assessing level of functioning and designing educational programs.

Individual case histories add further fuel to the excitement building around Down syndrome. For example, an illustration of the range of effects of the mosaic form of Down syndrome was offered by Turkington (1987), who described the life of a 35-year-old woman with Down syndrome who had completed an associate arts degree in early childhood education and hoped to become certified as a teacher. The success of the 1990s television show *Life Goes On* was due in large part to the character portrayed by Chris Burke, a teenager with Down syndrome.

In addition to the encouraging data on intellectual development, efforts in plastic surgery should be mentioned. Such efforts, most notably in Israel and related to the work of Reuven Feuerstein and his colleagues, have demonstrated that the physical stigmata of Down syndrome can be reduced. May (1988) provides a good discussion of the rationales, benefits, and cautions of plastic surgery for people with Down syndrome. According to research reported by May and Turnbull (1992), the majority (88%) of plastic surgeons were familiar with the procedures, and 24% had performed it. Reasons given for the surgery included (in rank order) to normalize appearance, to improve speech and eating abilities, to improve breathing, and as a response to parental request.

Two overriding points must be made clear. First, individuals with Down syndrome are primarily and foremost people who have needs, desires, and rights similar to those of other people. Second, the effects of intensive interventions with young children who have Down syndrome have only been evaluated since the late 1970s; thus, historical descriptions of the syndrome are no longer accurate. For example, as reported in the popular press, Charles de Gaulle had a child with Down syndrome. At the time of her early death in 1948, he reflected the sentiments of parents of an earlier historical era when he comforted his wife by saying of their deceased daughter, "Come . . . now she is like everybody else." The perspective for this quote in the new millennium would rather much more clearly focus on the similarity and equality of people with Down syndrome *in life*.

Prader-Willi Syndrome

Another condition that has been linked to an autosomal abnormality is **Prader-Willi syndrome (PWS)**. Specifically, it is most often related to a partial deletion of chromosome 15. Most cases of Prader-Willi syndrome appear to be caused by deletion of a portion of the long arm of the paternal chromosome. Approximately 70% of all persons with PWS have this paternal deletion. For a significant portion of the remaining 30%, the condition appears to be the result of maternal uniparental disomy of the 15th chromosome; that is, both chromosomes are contributed by the mother with none from the father (Holm et al., 1993; Scott et al., 1997).

The most significant characteristics of PWS are insatiable appetite (and hence obesity) and small features and stature, and the condition has also been associated with mild retardation and learning disabilities. The biological mechanism underlying the syndrome brings about a preoccupation with eating that has prompted observers to suggest that, for a Prader-Willi child, "life is one endless meal." In fact, recent research points to the fact that individuals with Prader-Willi syndrome were more likely than a comparison group of individuals (including those both retarded but not Prader-Willi and nonretarded) to endorse eating food that was contaminated as well as to eat highly unusual combinations of edible and inedible foods (e.g., cake with grass) (Dykens, 2000).

The characteristics associated with Prader-Willi syndrome generally become evident in two stages: an infantile hypotonic phase and a childhood/adulthood obesity phase (Donaldson et al., 1994). Initially, a major paradox is their failure-to-thrive condition, given that failure to thrive subsequently turns into excessive eating and obesity as the child increases in age. In addition, babies with Prader-Willi generally experience hypotonia; thus, the term "floppy baby" has frequently been used to describe them during infancy. Between the ages of 1 and 3 years, the characteristics of the second phase of the syndrome begin to become apparent. This

To learn more about Prader-Willi syndrome, go to the companion website at *www.prenhall.com/beirne-smith* and select Chapter 5, then choose the Case Studies module.

phase may include hyperphagia (i.e., an insatiable appetite) and constant preoccupation with food with uncontrollable eating often leading to life-threatening obesity. Also noted during this phase are delayed psychomotor development, signs of cognitive impairment, and delayed and/or abnormal pubertal development (Scott et al., 1997, p. 4).

As persons with Prader-Willi syndrome develop, a pattern of significant behavioral difficulties often emerges including temper tantrums, impulsivity, aggression, and stubbornness (Dyckens, Cassidy, & King, 1999). In addition, some research indicates that individuals with Prader-Willi syndrome are more likely to engage in self-injurious behavior, with skin picking being the most prevalent form being reported (Symons, Butler, Sanders, Feurer, & Thompson, 1999).

Goldman (1988) notes that the association of Prader-Willi syndrome with obesity has led to the assumption that the expected life span for individuals with the disorder is limited, at least in part because of the physical complications of being grossly overweight. In contrast, her research indicates that older individuals with the syndrome do exist but may be unidentified. Since the disorder was first described only in 1956, obviously some older persons could have escaped detection. Goldman describes two adult women for whom the desire to overeat continued with no evidence of their understanding the need to manage intake. They obtained food through their own devices. "Even when the environment is believed to be controlled, these persons evidently engage in some variety of successful covert foraging" (p. 101).

Additional information on the mechanics of the disorder and the effectiveness of various treatment options continues to be available as research develops. Intervention strategies that involve early intervention, exercise, monitoring of caloric intake, education about appropriate food choices, environmental controls, and specialized transition planning are indicated (Scott et al., 1997).

Other Sex Chromosomal Anomalies

Abnormalities in the sex chromosomes have also been found to affect development adversely. Two such conditions are discussed next; their karyotypes are shown in Figure 5.4.

Klinefelter syndrome (now more commonly referred to as *XXY males*) is a condition initially described in 1942 by Dr. Harry Klinefelter, in which males receive an extra X chromosome so that they have an XXY arrangement. The clinical pattern includes frequent social retardation, sterility and underdevelopment of the male sex organs, and the acquisition of female secondary sex characteristics. The syndrome may be associated with mild levels of intellectual retardation. Because some children of the XXY pattern may not develop the formal syndrome, the term *Klinefelter syndrome* has now more often been replaced by describing individuals with the extra X chromosome as XXY males (Bach, 1997).

Deficits increase with the number of X chromosomes (XXXY, XXXXY). Incidence is relatively high: 1 in 500 to 1,000 male births. Although no specific cure exists, physical aspects of the condition can be alleviated through surgery and testosterone treatment. XXY males can have problems with auditory perception, receptive and expressive language, and a general deficit in processing linguistic

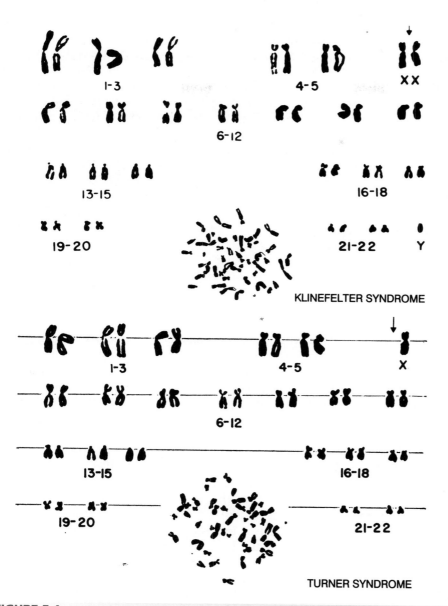

FIGURE 5.4

Sex Chromosonal Abnormalities

Source: From *Handbook of Mental Retardation Syndromes* (pp. 39, 45), by C. H. Carter, 1975, Springfield, IL: Charles C. Thomas. Reprinted by permission of Charles C. Thomas, Publisher.

information (Bender, Fry, Pennington, Puck, Salonblatt, & Robinson, 1983), as well as being prone to difficulties in the formation of positive social relationships, depression, and significant mood changes (Bock, 1997). Although often discussed in relation to mental retardation, XXY in males is more commonly associated with learning disabilities (which is consistent with the earlier note that autosomal anomalies are more often associated with mental retardation, whereas sex chromosomal disorders are more often associated with learning disabilities).

A sex chromosomal disorder in females, *Turner syndrome,* results from an absence of one of the X chromosomes (XO). It is the only syndrome with a true monosomy (i.e., one chromosome) and thus the only one in which individuals with the syndrome show fewer than 46 chromosomes. Its rarity (1 in 2,500 female births; Rovet, 1993) is underscored by the fact that over 95% of fetuses conceived with the XO pattern are spontaneously aborted.

Although Turner syndrome is not usually a cause of mental retardation, it is worthy of mention because it is often associated with learning disabilities. Some data indicate that the pattern of females with XO syndrome includes lower performance scale and full-scale IQ scores (but not lower verbal scores) and with somewhat lower educational and occupational attainments than their peers. Common problems are in spatial relations and hence mathematical abilities, memory, attention, and social competence (Downey et al., 1991; Rovet, 1993). As with Klinefelter syndrome, Turner syndrome produces deviations from normal development, with lack of secondary sex characteristics, sterility, and short stature as common features.

CRANIAL MALFORMATIONS

Several conditions associated with retardation manifest themselves as cranial malformations. The most dramatic is *anencephaly*—literally, the absence of major portions of the brain. Although anencephaly, for obvious reasons, is not associated with any treatments, it has been the subject of exciting research. A major type of neural tube defect (i.e., a defect occurring in the brain or spinal cord), it has been associated with the federal requirements (1998) that food manufacturers of grain products must add the nutrient folic acid to their products because of the positive effects of folic acid on the appropriate development of the neural tube (American Association of Mental Retardation, 1996). This change in the dietary complement of folic acid has proved to have a significant reductive effect on this disorder as well as on spina bifida (i.e., a hole in the tube that surrounds the spinal cord that may or may not be related to mental retardation).

Two other cranial malformations are indirectly associated with mental retardation. Children who have **microcephaly** are characterized by a small, conical skull, a curved spine that typically leads to a stooping posture, and severe retardation. In rare cases, the condition can be transmitted genetically, probably as an autosomal recessive trait, but it is more commonly a secondary consequence of such conditions as congenital rubella or fetal alcohol syndrome (discussed later), or it may be the result of environmental exposure (e.g., radiation). Individuals affected by microcephaly have been characterized as imitative, good-natured, and lively. There is no known cure.

Hydrocephalus consists of at least six types of problems associated with interference in the flow of cerebrospinal fluid within the skull. The most common type of blockage results in progressive enlargement of the cranium and subsequent brain damage. Physical manifestations of this condition differ widely; however, an enlarged skull is not present in all cases. Hydrocephalus may result from polygenic inheritance or as a secondary effect of maternal infections or intoxications. The effects of this condition can be reduced in many infants by draining off the fluid, using shunts to decrease the cranial pressure. (*Shunts* are valves or tubes surgically inserted under the child's skin to pump the fluid away from the brain and maintain proper flow.) The results of shunt treatment have been very encouraging in preventing head enlargement, the symptom most often associated with an increase in the probability of retardation.

Wolraich (1983) indicates that proper treatment of hyrdocephalus can ensure the survival of affected children, although significant disabilities remain a possibility. Milder cases may escape detection, with no ill effects noted. For example, some observers think that Einstein may have had a mild, nonprogressive case of hydrocephalus (Beck, 1972).

OTHER CONGENITAL FACTORS

In addition to cranial malformations, other congenital factors include a variety of conditions that may be associated with harmful factors called **teratogens.** These can significantly affect prenatal (and, in some cases, postnatal) development. The first widespread public exposure to the awesome power of teratogenic agents came from the thalidomide tragedy of the 1960s. Intended as a relaxant during pregnancy, this drug caused severe physical deformities (e.g., missing and/or shortened limbs) in many fetuses. This discussion focuses on some of the specific forces that have been identified as having teratogenic effects.

Maternal Disorders

The brain is especially susceptible to damage through maternal disease during the first 3 months of pregnancy. Infection of the mother by rubella (i.e., German measles) early in pregnancy has been found to result in fetal defects in up to 50% of cases. This is particularly significant because rubella has historically been a disease of epidemic occurrence. Recently developed immunization procedures help to limit its incidence, but trends in the 1990s indicate increases in the disease. In addition to retardation, *congenital rubella* can result in heart disease, blindness, and deafness. It has been one of the primary causes of severe multiple disabilities among children.

Congenital syphilis (as well as other venereal diseases) is another maternal disease that can damage the central nervous system and result in severe effects in developing fetuses. Perhaps the most alarming feature of this disorder has been its increasing prevalence in late 1900s after it had nearly been eradicated. This may be due in part to antibiotic-resistant strains of the disease. Research has also addressed the possible effects of maternal acquired immune deficiency syndrome (AIDS) as an agent of congenital disabilities.

One other significant possible cause of retardation that may function as an insult to the fetus is *blood-group incompatibility* between mother and unborn child. Most commonly, the condition occurs as a result of the Rh factor, a protein on the surface of red blood cells. Rh-positive blood cells contain this protein; Rh-negative cells do not. When an Rh-positive male and an Rh-negative female conceive an Rh-positive child, neither mother nor fetus is adversely affected. At birth, however, the mother's immune system will react to the fetus's Rh-positive blood by forming antibodies to the Rh factor. These antibodies remain in the mother's system and will enter the bloodstream of the next Rh-positive baby conceived, attacking its central nervous system and possibly resulting in retardation, epilepsy, and cerebral palsy. Treatment of this immune response focuses on preventing the destructive antibodies from forming. One technique is to vaccinate the mother with Rh immunoglobulin serum midway through each suspected Rh-positive pregnancy and within 72 hours of its termination (whether by birth, miscarriage, or abortion). This serum destroys the Rh-positive cells that pass from the infant's to the mother's bloodstream, inhibiting the development of antibodies that would otherwise attack the next fetus carried. This procedure does not alter the mother's immune response mechanism but can remove the stimuli that engage it.

Substance Exposure

A great deal of research has addressed the effects of drugs and industrial chemicals on the fetus. Particular attention has been given to nicotine, caffeine, lysergic acid (LSD), and other related drugs. The results of exposure to these substances are clear, and we should assume that pregnant women should also avoid any other powerful chemical substance.

The first significant breakthrough of understanding in this domain was with alcohol consumption. Problems associated with alcohol have been generally acknowledged for years. For example, Haggard and Jellinek (1942) noted that "infants born to alcoholic mothers sometimes had a starved, shriveled and imperfect look" (p. 165). But despite this long-standing suspicion of teratogenic effects, only since the 1970s has the nature of fetal alcohol syndrome (FAS) been documented. Jones, Smith, Ulleland, and Streissguth (1973) coined the term *fetal alcohol syndrome* after studies of eight unrelated offspring born to chronically alcoholic mothers showed a recognizable pattern of major and minor malformations, growth deficiencies, and developmental disabilities.

The best estimates of FAS occurrence are between 1 and 3 cases per 1,000 births (Ackerman, 1998; Warren & Bast, 1988). Other studies have also reinforced this approximate rate of occurrence, placing the figure at 1 in 650 births (Webb, Hochberg, & Sher, 1988). At this rate, FAS is clearly among leading known causes of mental retardation, along with Down syndrome (Abel & Sokol, 1986). Although the precise prevalence is not clear, conservative estimates stand at 5,000 children born with FAS each year (Stark, Menolascino, & Goldsbury, 1988).

In FAS, the mother's heavy alcohol consumption has direct toxic effects on the fetus. Exact levels of consumption that cause FAS are not known, but those mothers who are alcoholic, who have several drinks per day, or who engage in binge drinking run a confirmed, significant risk of damaging their unborn children. Risk rates are particularly high during the first trimester of pregnancy. Research continues on the risks of light or moderate drinking. An important area of study has been *fetal alcohol effects* (FAE), a more subtle disorder associated with learning and attentional problems. Given the risk of FAE, a common recommendation is for total abstinence from alcohol drinking during pregnancy.

The characteristics of FAS can be separated into three primary features: central nervous system dysfunction (e.g., mild-to-moderate retardation), craniofacial malformations (e.g., cleft palate, microcephaly), and prenatal and postnatal growth development (e.g., low birth weight). A diagnosis of FAS is warranted when a child has a cluster of disorders within these three areas (Griesbach & Polloway, 1991).

While fetal alcohol syndrome has frequently been associated with lower levels of functioning and hence mental retardation, also growing is evidence of difficulties associated with the retention, abstract thinking, and mathematics. Kerns, Don, Mateer, and Streissguth (1997) report on a group of adolescents and young adults identified as having FAS and not being mentally retarded. They confirm the presence of learning-related challenges in this population. As they note, "cognitive impairments of this nature and degree might account, in part, to the widespread reports and observations of functional difficulties that individuals with FAS manifest in school, home, and community" (p. 691). Implications for educators are discussed further by Ackerman (1998) and for families and communities by Streissguth (1997).

In recent years, attention has broadened to other drugs, most notably cocaine. The number of children exposed to drugs prenatally has climbed exponentially in some cities in the United States, with estimates in the late 1980s indicating that 10% to 11% of all births were thought to be to drug-exposed mothers (Stoddard, 1992). However, significant problems persist in determining the actual number.

The concerns that have been raised by this increase in substance abuse among pregnant women has often generated more heat than light in the media. Vincent, Poulsen, Cole, Woodruff, and Griffith (1991) make two key points about the knowledge base:

1. The media have painted a dire picture of infants who were exposed to alcohol and other drugs in utero. This picture is not fully supported by research or clinical experience with these children: We do not know the [exact] incidence of prenatal exposure to alcohol and other drugs, nor do we [clearly] know the long-term effects of such exposure.
2. Many women who abuse alcohol and other drugs during pregnancy also experience other psychological, social, and medical events that can affect the health of their children. Thus, the risks of substance exposure are often compounded by other difficulties, such as inadequate housing, medical care, child care, and nutrition, that place these children at risk for developmental delays. (pp. 1-2)

These cautions are useful in considering directions for the future and in planning intervention strategies. It is with these in mind that the following possible characteristics are noted for children who are at risk due to prenatal exposure to drugs. Poulsen (1991, cited by Vincent et al., 1991) indicates that problem areas could include

- exhibition of behavioral extremes,
- being easily overstimulated,
- low tolerance for changes,
- constant testing of limits set by adults,
- difficulty in reading social cues,
- difficulty in establishing and maintaining relationships with peers,

- language delays,
- sporadic mastery of skills,
- inconsistent problem-solving strategies,
- auditory processing and word retrieval difficulties,
- decreased capacity to initiate and organize play, and
- decrease in focused attention and concentration.

PREMATURITY AND PERINATAL CONCERNS

The advances in technology supporting premature and low-birth-weight children as well as for addressing perinatal concerns have dramatically changed the prognosis for these neonates over the last 30 years. For example, McNab and Blackman (1998) have summarized recent research on mortality rates and indicate that from 1985 to 1995, the mortality rates in the United States for infants with birth weights of 500 to 749 grams (approximately 1–1.5 pounds) decreased 31%, while mortality for those 750 to 1,499 grams (1.5–3.5 pounds) decreased by 53%. They noted that consequently 47% of infants weighing 1 to 1.5 pounds survived the first year, while 80% of those between 750 and 999 grams did as well. For infants over

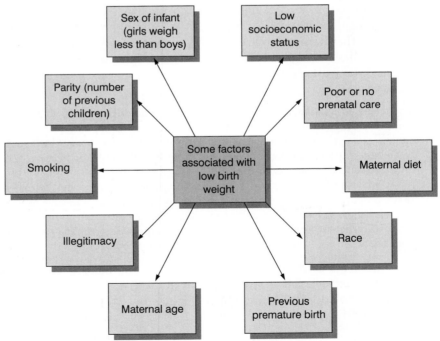

Prematurity: Gestation time of less than 37 weeks.
Low Birth Weight: Weight at birth equal to or less than 2,500 grams.

FIGURE 5.5
Low Birth Weight and Prematurity

Source: From *Mental Retardation: The Known and the Unknown* (p. 31), by President's Committee on Mental Retardation, 1976, Washington, DC: U.S. Government Printing Office.

1,000 grams, the survival rate was more than 90%. Clearly, medical science has significantly and positively affected the prognosis for these babies.

In addition to the complexity of causes of prematurity and low birth weight (see Figure 5.5), determining the effects of prematurity continues to be a difficult task. Full-term infants are born between 37 and 41 weeks, and normal birth weight is above 5.5 pounds (Widerstrom et al., 1991). Extremely short pregnancies (less than 28 weeks) or very low birth weights (below 1,500 grams, or 3.5 pounds) frequently present problems. For less substantial deviations from the norm in term or weight, the results are not so clear. Data indicate that the relationship among prematurity, birth weight, and mental retardation is most significant for very low birth weight.

In addition to low IQ, prematurity has also been linked to increased occurrence of cerebral palsy, attentional deficits, and other neurological and medical complications. The technological efforts exhibited in neonatal intensive care units (NICUs) represent the most effective response to the challenges presented by these special infants by providing a medically responsive facility that coincidentally offers the neonate a psychologically supportive environment. Widerstrom et al. (1991, p. 114) cite the recommendations of Bennett (1986) for NICU practical guidelines:

* Recognize the unusual physiological stresses being endured by the premature infant.
* Modify the environment to decrease overstimulation (specifically screen out grossly bombarding and unnecessary sensory stimuli such as handling during periods of quiet sleep).
* Introduce diurnal rhythms to promote behavioral organization. Gradually facilitate reciprocal visual, auditory, tactile, vestibular-kinesthetic, and social feedback during alert periods.
* Immediately terminate or alter approaches that produce avoidance responses.
* Educate and assist parents in reading, anticipating, and appropriately responding to their own infant's cues and signals, thus fostering and reinforcing parents' feelings of competence.

Oxygen deprivation, referred to as **hypoxia** or anoxia, can result from such birth difficulties as knotted umbilical cord, extremely short or long labor, or breech birth. Anoxia has long been associated with pronounced deficiencies in the affected infant, including lower IQ scores (Graham, Ernhart, Thurston, & Craft, 1962; McLaren & Bryson, 1987). The deficiencies it produces may vary greatly and are often unstable, so it is difficult to give an accurate prognosis for a child who experiences anoxia. Other problems at birth that can be traumatic include the delivery itself and the specific anesthetic procedures used.

McNab and Blackman (1998) provide an important summary of the current challenges facing infants with birth complications and their families when they note:

Despite the ability of neonatologists to provide life-saving measures for very sick babies, allowing them to be discharged from the hospital, significant obstacles often face many of these infants and their families once they are home. Ongoing health problems in these children can hamper or delay the normal course of motor, cognitive, language, and social development. Community early intervention professionals such as educators, social workers, and physical, occupational and speech therapists can improve these children's' long-term outcomes by being knowledgeable about these health problems and devising creative family-centered early intervention strategies. (p. 198)

POSTNATAL BIOLOGICAL CONCERNS

A variety of postnatal traumatic events leading to disabilities can occur throughout early childhood. McLaren and Bryson (1987) have estimated that the prevalence of mild retardation stemming from trauma and neglect is as high as 15%. *Head injuries* account for the greater part of such cases. It has been estimated that 1 in 30 newborns will experience a serious brain injury before the teen years are completed (Allison, 1992). Eighty-nine percent of injuries are caused by falls, bicycle and motor vehicle accidents, and sports-related activities. The highest risk years are between 15 and 25, with boys being twice as likely to be affected as girls, and with motor vehicle accidents being the most common cause of injury (Pipitone, 1992; Vernon-Levett, 1991). The relationship of auto accidents to brain injury has spurred the passage by all states of mandatory child-restraint laws.

Child abuse is a special concern, particularly because of the relationship between children's disability and their abuse. Child abuse can result from and aggravate primary disabilities. Zantal-Weiner (1987) notes in her review that children with disabilities are less able to defend themselves from abuse, have greater difficulty determining appropriate and inappropriate contact and telling anyone of the abuse once it has occurred, are more dependent on those who abuse them, are less likely to report abuse, and are seen as less credible when they do report it. In addition to striking, other negative so-called disciplinary actions like violent shaking can potentially play a role in brain hemorrhage and retardation. Signs of a "shaken baby" include vomiting, seizures, blood pooling in the eyes, apnea (spells of interrupted breathing), irritability, sleeping difficulties, and drowsiness; outcomes may include hypertension, cerebral palsy, subcranial or subdural hemorrhages, coma, and death.

Lead poisoning, which may lead to encephalitis, is permanently and progressively damaging to the central nervous system because of lead's role as a neurotoxicant. It can cause seizures, cerebral palsy, and retardation. Other effects of lead poisoning include gastrointestinal disturbances (e.g., anorexia, vomiting) and central nervous system manifestations (e.g., convulsions, drowsiness, irritability). Although commercial paints no longer contain lead, poisoning is still a factor in residences where a child has access to old, peeling paint. Conscious urban renewal is reducing the scope of this problem through repainting with unleaded paints. In older homes, lead paint can also enter the body through inhalation of dust or fumes, such as during renovation work (Marino et al., 1990) or from the soil around the houses. The existence of high lead levels remains most serious in inner-city areas where abatement efforts have not been fully implemented. Elevated lead blood levels can also be caused by water from lead water pipes, by prolonged breathing of polluted air, as in towns with lead smelters and heavy traffic congestion, and by the young child's mouthing and eating objects containing lead (see Table 5.2). There may be no such thing as a safe level for heavy metals in the body (Stark et al., 1988); research continues on the potential effects on cognition in children who are exposed to low levels of lead contamination (Minder, Das-Smaal, & Orlebeke, 1998). The box on page 180 provides more information about the effects of lead and other neurotoxicants on development.

Nutritional deficiencies are also worth noting here, although these are obviously both prenatal and postnatal concerns. Developmental deficiencies can occur when either the mother or child has an inadequate diet. Malnutrition during gesta-

TABLE 5.2
Increased Risks for Lead Poisoning

- Residence built before 1978
- Residence with chipped, cracked, or peeling paint
- Residence with lead pipes or lead-soldered copper pipes
- Residence near waste sites and lead industry
- Lead present in water above 500 ppm
- Leaded ceramics and leaded crystal, especially those imported from Mexico, Italy and China
- Residence adjacent to major highways built before 1986
- Family members who work in industry using lead (battery plants, electronics, stained glass, and mining)
- Hobbies using lead (ammunition, molding, and fishing weights)
- Food from cans soldered with lead
- History of eating nonfood substances (e.g., paint chips, pencils, crayons, ashes, and dirt)
- History of poor nutrition, especially low iron, calcium, or vitamin C
- Playing with old or imported lead toys and old keys
- Elevated lead level, above 10 micrograms per deciliter

Source: Adapted from Lynchburg College Symposium (1997).

tion or the first 6 months of life hinders the development of brain cells and can lead to as much as a 40% deficit in their number. Resnick (1988) states that the first two trimesters may be most critical to the prevention of such lacks, although he also indicated that maternal nutrition before pregnancy may be even more important. Since later brain growth is in weight rather than in number of cells, the effects of early malnutrition have long been viewed as irreversible (see the classic research by Cravioto, DeLicardie, & Birch, 1966). However, it has also long been recognized that it is difficult to assess the true detrimental effect of poor nutrition because it tends to accompany other unfavorable circumstances—inadequate housing, substandard living conditions, poor hygiene, and poor prenatal care, as well as diets high in calories but low in important nutrients.

PREVENTION

The purpose of this section is to survey the tools, techniques, and procedures that assist in the process of <u>preventing retardation</u>. Progress has been particularly significant during the last 40 years. Inspired by a government commitment to prevent the occurrence of 50% of all cases of retardation by the end of the century (President's Committee on Mental Retardation, 1976b), researchers have tackled virtually all causes of retardation. In every known case, a specific preventive measure has been identified.

Kids at Risk: Chemicals in the Environment

For more than 40 years, the family shared the big house and two trailers a mile from [a] chemical plant . . . In time, the 18 of them learned to put up with the rotten-cabbage odor that wafted through town. The plant, after all, is what stood between many residents and poverty. Besides, there were family troubles: Jeanette Champion, 44, is nearly blind and has what she calls a "thinking problem." Her 45-year-old brother, David Russell, can't read or write. Her 18-year-old daughter, Misty Pate, has suffered seizures and bouts of rage. Misty's 15-year-old cousin, Shane Russell, reads at a second-grade level.

The . . . plant has made industrial and pharmaceutical chemicals since the 1930s. But for decades it also saturated the area with polychlorinated biphenyls. PCBs have long been linked to cancer. More recently, however, researchers have discovered evidence tying the compounds to lack of coordination, diminished IQ, and poor memory among children. So when the extent of the PCB contamination . . . became clear a few years ago, a hazy picture came into focus. Perhaps the multigenerational problems of some families were not the result of poverty or bad genes. Perhaps they were caused by the chemicals in the ground. . . .

Children are particularly vulnerable to toxic chemicals. Normal brain development begins in the uterus and continues through adolescence. It requires a series of complex processes to occur in a carefully timed sequence: Cells proliferate and move to the correct spot, synapses form, neural circuits are refined, and neurotransmitters and their receptors grow. Neurotoxicants may slow, accelerate, or otherwise modify any of these processes. Says Philip Landrigan of New York's Mt. Sinai School of Medicine: "You end up with gaps in the wiring."

The idea that substances in the environment can harm the human brain is not new. In ancient Rome, miners were felled by what the medical literature of the time called "lead colic." The Mad Hatter in Lewis Carroll's *Alice's Adventures in Wonderland* comes from the 19th-century expression "mad as a hatter," a reference to mercury's effects on felt-hat makers. Over the past 70 years, adults and children around the world have been poisoned—and, in some cases, killed—by mercury in fish, PCBs in rice oil, a fungicide in seed grain, and a rat-killing agent in tortillas. After hearings in 1985, the House Committee on Science and Technology reported that there were 850 known neurotoxicants, any of which "may result in devastating neurological or psychiatric disorders that impair the quality of life, cripple and potentially reduce the highest intellect to a vegetative state." The report prompted virtually no action.

Today, however, the federal government is under increasing pressure from pediatricians, academics, and its own scientists, all clamoring for more testing of neurotoxicants. Agency officials are focusing on [lead] pesticides, mercury, and PCBs.

Source: From "Kids at Risk" by S. Kaplan and J. Morris, June 19, 2000, *U.S. News Online.* Available: www.USNews.com/usnews/issue/000619/poison.htm

Graham and Scott (1988) have developed a comprehensive model for conceptualizing prevention (Figure 5.6). They distinguish three levels of prevention: (a) primary—risk conditions can be eliminated so that a condition never comes into existence, (b) secondary preventive efforts reduce or eliminate the effects of an existing risk factor, and (c) tertiary intervention assists a child who has a disability. Furthermore, Crocker (1992) has identified the specific activities associated with a comprehensive prevention program (Table 5.3). These considerations are implicit in the discussions that follow.

Preconception

Preventive measures taken before conception can avert hereditary, innate, congenital, and other constitutional disorders. One basic tool is genetic counseling, an

FIGURE 5.6

The Developmental Continuum of Risk

Source: From "The Impact of Definitions of Higher Risk on Services to Infants and Toddlers" (p. 25), by M. Graham and K. G. Scott, 1988, *Topics in Early Childhood Special Education, 8*(3). Adapted by permission.

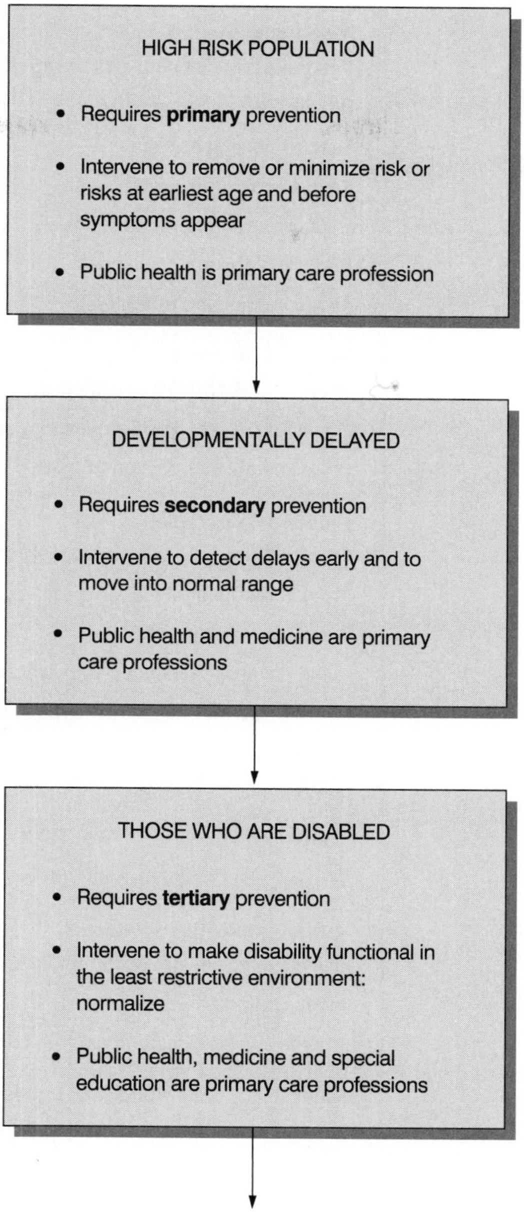

HIGH RISK POPULATION

- Requires **primary** prevention

- Intervene to remove or minimize risk or risks at earliest age and before symptoms appear

- Public health is primary care profession

DEVELOPMENTALLY DELAYED

- Requires **secondary** prevention

- Intervene to detect delays early and to move into normal range

- Public health and medicine are primary care professions

THOSE WHO ARE DISABLED

- Requires **tertiary** prevention

- Intervene to make disability functional in the least restrictive environment: normalize

- Public health, medicine and special education are primary care professions

attempt to determine risks of occurrence or recurrence of specific genetic or chromosomal disorders. The tools of the genetic counselor include the family history and personal screening. Study of the persons' genetic and general medical history is particularly concerned with evidence of spontaneous abortions or stillbirths, relatives' age at death and causes of death, and the existence of any intrafamily marriages that might bear on the presence of specific genetic disorders. Screening is primarily for carriers of recessive trait disorders. Blood samples can be analyzed rather easily and inexpensively. Based on an understanding of the mathematical probabili-

TABLE 5.3

Elements of a Comprehensive
Prevention Program

Prenatal strategies

Ensure family planning and timing of pregnancies

Provide genetic counseling

Test for genetic carriers

Provide adequate prenatal care and diagnostics

Reduce teenage pregnancy rates

Reduce births out of wedlock

Avoid alcohol and other teratogenic substances during pregnancy

Perinatal strategies

Screen newborns for disorders

Screen newborns for diseases (e.g., HIV)

Provide early intervention for at-risk infants (e.g., those born prematurely)

Preschool strategies

Enroll children in early intervention programs

Provide parental education and support

Avoid lead in environment

Avoid hazards associated with brain injury

Reduce occurrences of child abuse and neglect

Use safety restraints in vehicles

Immunize for diseases

Provide proper medical care and treatment

Plan for appropriate transition to school

School preventive strategies

Provide effective instruction and relevant curriculum

Involve parents in education

Provide a family life curriculum to future parents

Federal and state policy strategies

Commit to a reduction in poverty

Reduce the prevalence of homelessness

Provide public information about prevention

Support comprehensive prevention programs

Develop and provide universal health-care programs

ties associated with recessive, dominant, or sex-linked inheritance, prospective parents can make an informed decision about the risks of having a child who may be developmentally disabled.

Other specific means of prevention are also available during this period. Immunization for maternal rubella can prevent women from contracting this disease

Prenatal precautions, including good nutrition, fetal monitoring, and protection from disease, can help avert congenital problems.

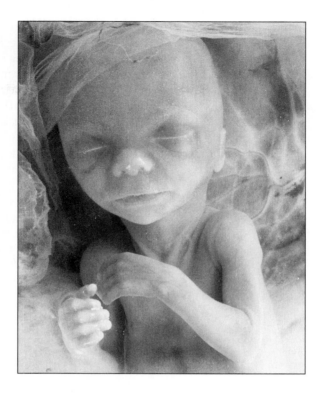

during pregnancy. Blood tests can identify the presence of venereal diseases. Adequate maternal nutrition can lay a sound metabolic foundation for later childbearing. Family planning in terms of size, appropriate spacing, and age of parents can also affect a variety of specific causal agents.

During Gestation

Two general approaches to prevention during pregnancy are prenatal care and analysis for possible genetic disorders. Numerous prenatal precautions can be taken to avert congenital problems. Adequate nutrition, fetal monitoring, and protection from disease are certainly the grounding of prenatal care. Avoidance of teratogenic substances resulting from both exposure (e.g., radiation) and personal consumption (e.g., alcohol and drugs) also relate specifically to this period.

Analysis of the fetus for the possible presence of genetic or chromosomal disorders is a key component of genetic counseling. This analysis may include amniocentesis, chorionic villi sampling (CVS), fetoscopy, fetal biopsy, and ultrasound. Usually performed during the 14th to 16th week of pregnancy, **amniocentesis** involves drawing amniotic (embryonic sac) fluid for biochemical analysis of fetal cells (see Figure 5.7). In the majority of cases where amniocentesis is used, its primary purpose has been the detection of such chromosomal errors as Down syndrome.

Generally, the technique is safe. However, the patient should be informed of certain considerations, including the risk of about 0.5% or less of a miscarriage, the possibility of an unsuccessful culture of fetal cells, and the possibility of disorders

To read more about amniocentesis, go to the companion website at www.prenhall.com/beirne-smith and select Chapter 5, then choose the Arrticle Response module.

remaining undiagnosed by the procedure. More recently, the procedure has been used earlier in gestation, but the risks are slightly increased.

A more recent technique for prenatal diagnosis is CVS, which can also provide information on chromosomal and biochemical anomalies. In CVS, chorionic tissue (fluffy material that forms the placenta) is withdrawn. The test can be performed after approximately 9 weeks of gestation, with initial results (chromosomal analysis) within 2 days and a full culture 2 weeks after sampling. The most significant advantage of the process is that it allows an earlier analysis of fetal status. It has been estimated that CVS is associated with a risk rate for miscarriage and other complications only slightly higher than that for amniocentesis (about 1% or less).

These two analytical techniques have three purposes. Most encouraging, of course, is that negative tests assuage parental fears or anxieties. Second, the result can confirm suspicions of disorders and give the parents a chance to determine what to expect. They also may alert the physician to the need for careful monitoring prenatally, perinatally, and postnatally. Finally, the information can be used as a basis for decisions about abortion. The use of these techniques along with elective

FIGURE 5.7
Amniocentesis

Source: From *Fetal Monitoring and Fetal Assessment in High-Risk Pregnancy* by S. M. Tucker, 1978, St. Louis: C. V. Mosby. Copyright 1978 by C. V. Mosby. Reprinted by permission.

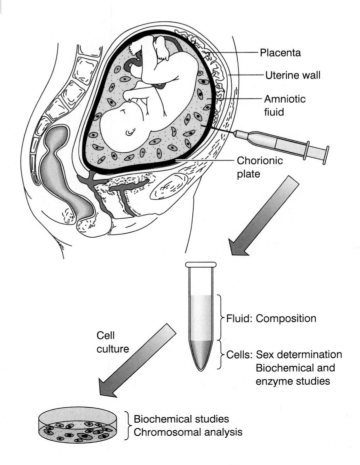

Use of the Triple Test

In recent years, the process of diagnosing Down syndrome prior to birth has been advanced through a blood sampling procedure during the second trimester of pregnancy. A multiple marker test, the triple test screening procedure, provides an initial determination of whether a pregnancy is at high risk and then provides a basis for consequent testing such as through the use of amniocentesis. Because Down syndrome is the most prevalent medical chromosomal disorder associated with mental retardation, the triple test is often used in conjunction with questions about this syndrome although it can be used for other chromosomal disorders as well.

The triple test is a set of three screening mechanisms:

- Maternal serum alpha-feto protein (AFP)
- Unconjugated estriol
- Human chorionic conadotropin

Each of these three analyses are derived from blood samples and considered in conjunction with related information (i.e., age and weight of the mother, ethnic group, gestational age of the fetus and the number of fetuses). Once the results are obtained from the three tests, a statistical formula calculates the risk for Down syndrome.

The triple test has been advocated for certain apparent reasons: it is cheaper to perform, it is faster (results available in 1–3 days versus 2 weeks for amniocentesis), and there is no risk to the fetus. While the accuracy rates of the test remain under review, it provides an initial direction for determining whether further diagnostics should be performed. Cate and Ball (1999) indicate an overall detection rate of 56%, with a 7% false positive rate.

Source: From "The Triple Test" (pp. 34–35), by K. Apolloni, 1998, *Advance for Speech-Language Pathologists & Audiologists, 10.*

abortion has significantly reduced the occurrence of a number of specific disorders, although obviously it has also generated much controversy. (See also the box "Use of the Triple Test" for an alternative approach to screening, especially for Down syndrome.)

Pueschel (1991) stresses that genetic counseling never results in value-free messages to parents. Professionals should not advocate a particular action but must transmit factual data and present alternatives. In the case of a genetic disorder, he notes that this could include terminating the pregnancy or allowing it to continue to term and, in the latter case, either caring for the child or seeking adoption.

One other technique that has contributed to an understanding of the prenatal environment is *ultrasound,* or *sonography.* This technique can be used for possible determination of hydrocephalus, some central nervous system disorders, and limb anomalies. The technique is also used to determine the location for amniocentesis, to assist in delivery, and as a common adjunct to fetal therapy, which seeks to correct conditions existing in utero.

At Delivery

Prevention at delivery is based on anticipating possible problems. Pregnancies deserving of special attention include those involving very young or older mothers, the mother's low socioeconomic status, inconsistent prenatal care, closely spaced pregnancies, drug exposure during pregnancy, and a history of previous children with genetic disorders.

Several specific measures are associated with the perinatal period. The most common is the Apgar test of vital signs (Apgar, 1953), an evaluation routinely given in American hospitals at 1 and 5 minutes after the birth of a child. The physician rates each of the following factors on a scale of 0 to 2: heart rate, respiratory effort, muscle tone, skin color, and reflex response. An Apgar score of 8 to 10 suggests the newborn is healthy and responsive; scores of 5 to 7 and 0 to 4 indicate moderate and severe depression, respectively. Initially, screening using such a scale can assist in preliminary decision making about children who may be at risk for specific disorders, and a more comprehensive assessment then follows. Intensive intervention can begin almost immediately for premature and other infants identified as having a particular difficulty.

Computer-assisted obstetric measures aid in the close monitoring of both mother and child, and another helpful measure during the first 3 days after birth is injection of Rh immunoglobulin serum, as described earlier (see the section entitled "Maternal Disease"). If a child is born to a mother who did not have the necessary series of injections in the course of a previous pregnancy, a complete transfusion of the newborn's blood can prevent the destruction of its blood cells by the mother's antibodies.

Early Childhood

Several types of intervention are important during early childhood. Proper nutrition is critical throughout development, but particularly so during the first 6 months. Dietary restrictions for specific metabolic disorders should be maintained until no longer required. Avoidance of hazards in the child's environment can prevent brain injury, and avoidance of exposure to substances such as lead and mercury are mandatory to proper development.

Perspective

The preceding discussion has highlighted a variety of preventive measures that target the various causes of retardation discussed earlier. For biological causes, the advances of the last 40 years have been breathtaking. In terms of psychosocial causes, the successes that have been achieved are tempered by the obvious need for greater commitment. Whether society is willing to devote the necessary resources to breaking the poverty cycle and altering the effects of psychosocial causes, with the goal of reducing the prevalence of retardation, is still an unanswered question. Governmental commitment, especially at the federal level, is very important.

It is clear that, regardless of whether or not a child already has a disability, growing up in restricting conditions interferes with a child's opportunity to develop and mature as well as his or her more privileged peers. The negative consequences of an unstimulating environment must be diminished through the most promising intervention strategies. As Baroff (1974) wrote more than 25 years ago, "Equality of opportunity is a ghastly charade if individuals are so stunted by early experiences" that they do not take advantage of opportunities for treatment that are available (p. 116). By facilitating children's cognitive, academic, social, and emotional development, we increase the chances of having a future population of healthy, self-sufficient, mature adults. Intervention strategies with a preventive aim must work to identify children at risk and establish strategies designed to facilitate the development of each one of them.

ETHICAL ISSUES

Human Genome Project

Remarkable developments in molecular biology and genetic engineering are reported daily in the popular press. Further advances in scientific knowledge and medical technology will almost certainly change the course of the human experience. The eradication of what are considered diseases, disorders, and defects may become a reality before the end of the new century. A critical question in the advance of medicine, however, may be how diseases, disorders, and defects are defined. Is mental retardation, in this context, a disease, a defect, or a human difference? Is mental retardation a condition to be prevented in all circumstances, or is it part of the spectrum of human variation? Depending on the answer, what does this say about the status of people with this condition in a society that values human equality? What does it say about their fundamental value as people?

The danger that people with mental retardation will be further devalued as genetic intervention techniques increase is illustrated by recent remarks by James Watson. Winner of the Nobel Prize and codiscoverer of DNA, Watson was also the first director of the Human Genome Project. In his capacity as leader of the effort to map and sequence the genetic makeup of human beings, Watson also advocated careful consideration of the ethical, legal, and social implications of the project. Yet, in an article entitled "Looking Forward," Watson questioned the value of people with severe disabilities when he spoke of the decisions faced by "prospective parents when they learn that their prospective child carries a gene that would block its opportunity for a meaningful life" (Watson, 1993, p. 314). In the same article he speaks of parents who do not undergo genetic testing. "So we must also face up to the ethical and practical dilemma, facing these individuals who could have undergone genetic diagnosis, but who for one reason or another declined the opportunity and later gave birth to children who must face up to lives of hopeless inequality" (p. 315). More recently Watson spoke to the German Congress of Molecular Medicine and condemned the eugenic philosophy that resulted in the atrocities of the Nazi era. Then, in a seeming contradiction, he advocated what might be termed "parental eugenics." He asserted that the "truly relevant question for most families is whether an obvious good will come from having a child with a major handicap." From this perspective, Watson said, "seeing the bright side of being handicapped is like praising the virtues of extreme poverty" (Lee, 1998, p. 16). As it becomes potentially possible to identify virtually all persons at risk for having a child affected by a genetic disorder (Moser, 2000), the excitement over prevention prospects must be sobered by the ethical aspects of this knowledge. It is therefore critical to consider carefully the actions that can be taken before and after birth, once a specific disability, or risk of a disability, has been identified.

Our earlier discussion of amniocentesis focused on its use to detect specific genetic disorders, especially Down syndrome. Public encouragement to screen for the disorder led to an increase in the number of abortions of fetuses found to be affected. But, as Smith (1981) noted 20 years ago, "The ease with which the abortion of Down syndrome fetuses is accepted as the best alternative, even by people who otherwise oppose abortion, may be related to the conventional wisdom or popular misunderstanding of the level of mental retardation or other disabilities associated with this condition" (p. 9).

Smith questioned whether children with Down syndrome had become defined as an out-group, something less than human, through the process of *pseudospeciation*—that is, placing certain human beings in a separate "species" on the basis of group characteristics such as race or disability.

The question of selective abortion of individuals with disabilities concerns more than just Down syndrome. Lehr and Brown (1984) summarize the arguments in favor of the practice as including the possible need for intensive medical surgery, the potentially negative effects on the family (e.g., financial difficulty of caring for the child), and the drain of valuable resources from society. Included in the reasons against the practice are opposition to abortion in general, presumed devaluation of the humanness of persons who are disabled, and possible spillover effects into services for young children (if the fetus does not have the right to life, why should the child be entitled to support?).

Another major ethical concern is the question of the right to life after birth of children who are disabled. Newspaper accounts of the cases of Baby Doe in Indiana; Baby Jane Dow in New York: Phillip Becker, a California teenager with Down syndrome; and Baby Gabriel in Canada sensitized the public to issues that for years had been quietly debated in professional circles. In most cases, the argument is whether a child's disability should be a primary factor in the decision to provide maximum medical care. In addition to the important legal questions involved, philosophical issues are also significant in this arena.

Orelove and Sobsey (1984) summarize the debates surrounding ethics and moral values as reflecting several positions in reference to individuals with severe disabilities. These positions include the following:

* Treat all nondying newborns, with focus only on medical indications for treatment.
* Terminate the lives of selected nonpersons, with the justification that nontreatment is appropriate if an infant is defective and thus not counted as a person.
* Withhold treatment according to parental discretion, on the assumption that care could be withheld as an act of mercy to the infant and for relief to the suffering parents.
* Withhold treatment according to quality of life, with decisions based on the potential for so-called meaningful life.
* Withhold treatment judged not in the child's best interests, under the presumption that the treatment would maintain a burden of existence for the infant. (pp. 341-343)

An additional ethical issue is that of "do not resuscitate orders" for persons with special needs. Given the complexity of the medical needs of some individuals, this area promises to be of great concern in the future. Smith's (1995) discussion of John Lovelace, an adult with mental retardation who was deinstitutionalized, provides a vivid discussion of this issue.

A Position Statement on the Right of Children with Mental Retardation to Life-Sustaining Medical Care and Treatment

The Board of Directors of the Division on Mental Retardation of the Council for Exceptional Children resolves that the fact that a person is born with mental retardation or acquires mental retardation during development is not a justifiable reason, in and of itself, for terminating the life of that person. Mental retardation alone is not a nullification of quality or worth in an individual's life and should not be used as a rationale for the termination of life through direct means nor the withholding of nourishment or life sustaining procedures.

Background

The issue of pediatric euthanasia is complex and troubling to professionals in the field of mental retardation. A most basic question posed by this dilemma is that of who is to make the decision to deny treatment or nourishment to a child who has mental retardation. Most often involved in this decision are parents, physicians, and, in most cases which become public, the courts. Arguments have been made for and against the role of each of these parties in making such a decision.

Support for parents as decision makers derives from the concept that children are the property of their parents and that they have the final voice in any crucial matter concerning their offspring. Critics of this view believe that parents are often emotionally distraught and lack adequate information on which to base their decision when faced with such a dilemma. Their decision may be unduly influenced by fears concerning raising the child or of institutional placement.

Physicians often feel that they are in the best position to make an objective decision. It has been observed, however, that they often are motivated by their perception of what will prevent suffering in the family. It is argued that physicians should not be the decision makers because their duty is to preserve life, not to judge which lives deserve preservation.

Parents of newborns and physicians have rarely had the opportunity to experience living or working with individuals having mental retardation across the course of their lives. As special educators serving children with disabilities from infancy through adulthood, the Board of Directors of CEC-MR observes that mental retardation alone does not necessarily cause a life of pain, suffering or absence of life quality for the affected persons, and that it should not imply a justification for the termination of life. Research and experience with persons having mental retardation demonstrate that all people can learn, all can participate (at least partially) in the wide range of human experiences and most become productive citizens and are valued human beings by persons who truly know them. It is with these factors in mind that CEC-MR takes a public position on this issue.

Source: From *CEC-MR Position Statement on the Right of Children with Mental Retardation to Life Sustaining Medical Care and Treatment* by J. D. Smith, September 1988, CEC-Report, p. 2. Copyright 1988 by the Council for Exceptional Children. Reprinted by permission.

The increased attention to ethical issues demands the scrutiny and advocacy of professional educators. In fact, as Smith (1989a) notes, special educators may often be better informed than physicians concerning the possibilities and potentialities for the lives of children with disabilities. They are in a unique position to act as advocates. In this vein, the Division on Mental Retardation of the Council for Exceptional Children (CEC-MR) has promulgated a position statement (Smith, 1988b) that supports the right to life for persons with mental retardation and encourages professional advocacy (see the box).

We conclude with this single statement: Professionals in the field of mental retardation must carefully evaluate their positions on these issues and be prepared to express and defend them.

FINAL THOUGHTS

Hundreds of specific factors have been identified as causes of mental retardation and developmental disabilities. Nevertheless, in the vast majority of individual cases, a specific cause cannot be identified.

To understand etiology, we must first understand the principles of genetics, since a large percentage of biological causes stem from recessive, dominant, and sex-linked inheritance and from chromosomal abnormalities. Other causes include prenatal infections and intoxications, brain injury, malnutrition, cranial malformations, disorders related to pregnancy, and environmental influence.

Prevention of retardation requires an intensive program that begins before conception and continues throughout the developmental period. Every specifiable cause of retardation has a preventive measure of one type or another.

Advances in medial technology have created ethical problems that society must face. Each person must accept the responsibility of becoming informed on these issues and developing her or his own position.

To check your understanding of this chapter, go to the companion website at http://www.prenhall.com/beirne-smith and select Chapter 5, then choose the Self-Test module.

Summary

Introduction

- The cause of mental retardation is often a complex issue.
- Professionals in the field of mental retardation need to have a general awareness of causes.
- Terminology used to describe various etiologies comes from three sources: conventional wisdom, names of specific people, and biomedical vocabulary.

Genetic and Chromosomal Deviations

- Genetics is the study of heredity with a particular focus on genes.
- Mental retardation can result from problems with genetic material on either autosomes or sex chromosomes.
- Karyotypes are the resultant charting of chromosomes.
- The most recognizable condition associated with chromosomal anomalies is Down syndrome.

Other Etiological Domains

- Cranial malformations involve conditions such as hydrocephaly.
- Many different toxic substances can significantly affect prenatal and postnatal development.
- Prematurity and other perinatal factors are related to a number of birth defects, including limited intellectual capacity.
- Events such as head injuries and child abuse can also contribute to mental retardation.

Prevention

- Prevention of retardation requires an intensive program that begins before conception and continues throughout the developmental period.
- Every specifiable cause of retardation has a preventive measure of one type or another.

Ethical Issues
- Advances in medical technology have created ethical problems that society must face.

References

Abel, E. L., & Sokol, R. J. (1986). Fetal alcohol is now a leading cause of mental retardation. *The Lancet, 2*(8517), 1222.

Abroms, K. K., & Bennett, J. W. (1980). Current genetic and demographic findings in Down's Syndrome: How are they represented in college textbooks on exceptionality? *Mental Retardation, 18,* 101–107.

Ackerman, M. E. (1998). *Fetal alcohol syndrome: Implications for educators.* (ERIC Document Reproduction Service No. ED 426 560)

Allison, M. (1992). The effects of neurologic injury on the maturing brain. *Headlines, 3*(5), 2–10.

American Association of Mental Retardation. (1996, Summer). Folic acid additive to grain ordered by FDA. *AAMR News and Notes, 10,* p. 8.

Anderson, L., Dancis, J., & Alpert, M. (1978). Behavioral contingencies and self-mutilation in Lesch-Nyhan disease. *Journal of Consulting and Clinical Psychology, 46,* 529–536.

Apgar, V. (1953). A proposal for a new method of evaluation of the newborn infant. *Current Researches in Anesthesia and Analgesia, 32,* 260–264.

Apolloni, K. (1998). The triple test. *Advance for Speech-Language Pathologists & Audiologists, 10,* 34–35.

Barker, M. (1990, April). *Clinical overview of the Fragile X syndrome.* Paper presented at the 68th annual meeting of the Council for Exceptional Children, Toronto, Canada.

Baroff, G. S. (1974). *Mental retardation: Nature, cause and management.* New York: Wiley.

Beck, J. (1972). Spina bifida and hydrocephalus. In V. Apgar & J. Beck (Eds.), *Is my baby alright? A guide to birth defects* (pp. 288–298, 400–414). New York: Simon & Schuster.

Bellinger, D. M., Rucker, H., & Polloway, E. A. (1997). Fragile X syndrome in males: Programmatic, behavioral and educational implications. *ERIC Document Reproduction Service* (information not available at time of publication).

Bender, B., Fry, E., Pennington, B., Puck, M., Salonblatt, J., & Robinson, S. (1983). Speech and language development in 41 children with sex chromosomes anomalies. *Pediatrics, 71,* 262–266.

Bender, B. G., Puck, M. H., Salbenblatt, J. A., & Robinson, A. (1986). Cognitive development of children with sex chromosome abnormalities. In S. D. Smith (Ed.). *Genetics and learning disabilities* (pp. 175–201). San Diego: College-Hill Press.

Bennett, W. J. (1986). *What works: Research about teaching and learning.* Washington, DC: U.S. Government Printing Office.

Blatt, B. (1987). *The conquest of mental retardation.* Austin, TX: PRO-ED.

Buyse, M. L., (1990). *Birth defects encyclopedia.* Dover, MA: Center for Birth Defects Information Services.

Cantu, E. S., Stone, J. W., Wing, A. A., Langee, H. R., & Williams, C. A. (1990). Cytogenetic survey for autistic Fragile X carriers in a mental retardation center. *American Journal of Mental Retardation, 94,* 442–447.

Cate, S., & Ball, S. (1999). Multiple marker screening for Down syndrome: Whom should we screen? *Journal of the American Board of Family Practice, 12,* 367–374.

Clarke, J. T., Gates, R. D., Hogan, S. E., Barrett, M., & MacDonald, G. W. (1987). Neuropsychological studies on adolescents with phenylketonuria returned to phenylalanine-restricted diets. *American Journal of Mental Retardation, 92,* 255–262.

Clayman, C. B. (Ed.). (1989). *The AMA encyclopedia of medicine.* New York: Random House.

Cravioto, J., DeLicardie, E. R., & Birch, H. G. (1966). Nutrition, growth, and neurointegrative development: An experimental and ecological study. *Pediatrics, 38* (Suppl. 2), 319.

Crocker, A. C. (1992). Data collection for the evaluation of mental retardation prevention activities: The fateful 43. *Mental Retardation, 30,* 303–317.

Donaldson, M. D. C., Chu, C. E., Cooke, A., Wilson, A., Greene, S. A., Stephenson, J. B. P. (1994). The Prader-Willi syndrome. *Archives of Disease in Childhood, 70,* 58–63.

Downey, J. Elkin, E. J., Ehrhardt, A. A., Meyer-Bahlburg, H. F., Bell, J. J., & Morishima, A. (1991). Cognitive ability and everyday functioning in women with Turner syndrome. *Journal of Learning Disabilities, 24,* 32–39.

Dykens, E. M. (2000). Contaminated and unusual food combinations: What do people with Prader-Willi syndrome choose? *Mental Retardation, 138,* 163–171.

Dykens, E. M., Cassidy, S. D., & King, B. H. (1999). Maladaptive behavior differences in Prader-Willi syndrome due to maternal deletion versus maternal uniparental disomy. *American Journal on Mental Retardation, 104,* 67–77.

Epstein, C. J. (1988). New approaches to the study of Down syndrome. In F. J. Menolascino & J. A. Stark (Eds.), *Preventive and curative intervention in mental retardation* (pp. 35–6). Baltimore: Brookes.

Evans, D. W., & Gray, F. L. (2000). Compulsive-like behavior in individuals with Down syndrome: Its relation to mental age level, adaptive and maladaptive behavior. *Child Development, 71,* 288–300.

Eyman, R. F., Call, T. E., & White, J. F. (1991). Life expectancy of persons with Down syndrome. *American Journal of Mental Retardation, 95,* 603–612.

Fishler, K., Azen, C. G., Henderson, R. Friedman, E. G., & Koch, R. (1987). Psychoeducational findings among children treated for phenylketonuria. *American Journal of Mental Retardation, 92,* 65–73.

Goldman, J. J. (1988). Prader-Willi syndrome in two institutionalized older adults. *Mental Retardation, 26,* 97–102.

Graham, F. K., Ernhart, C. B., Thurston, D., & Craft, M. (1962). Development three years after perinatal anoxia and other potentially damaging experiences. *Psychological Monographs, 76*(Whole No. 522).

Graham, M., & Scott, K. G. (1988). The impact of definitions of higher risks on services to infants and toddlers. *Topics in Early Childhood Special Education, 8,* 23–28.

Griesbach, L. S., & Polloway, E. A. (1991). *Fetal alcohol syndrome.* (ERIC Document Reproduction Service No. 326 035).

Griffiths, P., Smith, C., & Harvie, A. (1997). Transitory hyperphenylalanineaemia in children with continuously treated phenylketonuria. *American Journal on Mental Retardation, 102,* 27–36.

Haggard, H. W., & Jellinek, E. M. (1942). Alcohol explained. Garden City, NY: Doubleday.

Hall, J. G. (2000). Molecular and clinical genetics for the practicing pediatrician. *Advances in Children's Health 2000: Pediatric Academic Societies and the American Academy of Pediatrics Year 2000 Joint Meeting.* N.p.: Pediatric Academic Societies and the American Academy of Pediatrics.

Harrison, J. E., O'Callaghan, F. J., Hancock, E., Osborne, J. P., & Bolton, P. F. (1999). Cognitive deficits in normally intelligent patients with tuberous sclerosis. *American Journal of Medical Genetics, 88,* 642–646.

Hodapp, R. M. (1997). Direct and indirect behavioral effects of different genetic disorders of mental retardation. *American Journal on Mental Retardation, 102,* 67–79.

Hoefnagel, D., Andrew, E. D., Mireault, N. G., & Berndt, W. O. (1965). Hereditary choreoathetosis, self-mutilation, and hyperuricemia in young males. *New England Journal of Medicine, 273,* 130–135.

Holm, V. A., Cassidy, S. B., Butler, M. G., Hanchett, J. M., Greenswag, L. R. Whitman, B. Y., & Greenberg, F. (1993). Prader-Willi syndrome: Consensus diagnostic criteria. *Pediatrics, 182,* 398–402.

Hunt, N. (1967). *Nigel Hunt: The diary of a mongoloid youth.* New York: Garrett.

Johnson, C. F., Koch, R., Peterson, R. M., & Friedman, E. G. (1978). Congenital and neurological abnormalities in infants with phenylketonuria. *American Journal of Mental Deficiency, 82,* 375–379.

Jones, K. L., Smith, D. W., Ulleland, C. N., & Streissguth, A. P. (1973). Patterns of malformation in offspring of chronic alcoholic mothers. *The Lancet, 1*(1267), 1271.

Jordan, T. E. (1976). *The mentally retarded* (4th ed.). Upper Saddle River, NJ: Merrill/Prentice Hall.

Kerns, K. A., Don, A., Mateer, C. A., & Streissguth, A. (1997). Cognitive deficits in nonretarded adults with fetal alcohol syndrome. *Journal of Learning Disabilities, 30,* 685–693.

Koch, J. H. (1997). *Robert Guthrie—The PKU story: Crusade against mental retardation.* N. p.: Hope.

Koch, R., Friedman, E. C., Azen, C., Wenz, E., Parton, P., Ledue, X., & Fishler, K. (1988). Inborn errors of metabolism and the prevention of mental retardation. In F. J. Menolascino & J. A. Stark (Eds.), *Preventive and curative intervention in mental retardation* (pp. 61–90). Baltimore: Brookes.

Kolstoe, O. P. (1972). *Mental retardation: An educational viewpoint.* New York: Holt, Rinehart, & Winston.

Lachiewicz, A., Harrison, C., Spiridigliozzi, G. A., Callanan, N. P., & Livermore, J. (1988). What is the Fragile X syndrome? *North Carolina Medical Journal, 49,* 203–208.

Lee, T. (1998, March/April). You probably won't like James Watson's ideas about us. *Ragged Edge,* p. 16.

Lehr, D. M., & Brown, F. (1984). Perspectives on the severely handicapped. In E. L. Meyden (Ed.), *Mental retardation: Topics of today and issues of tomorrow* (pp. 41–65). Reston, VA: Council of Exceptional Children.

Lejeune, J., Gautier, M., & Turpin, r. (1959). Etudes des chromosomes somatiques de neuf enfants mongoliers. *Academie de Science, 248,* 1721–1722.

Lesch, M., & Nyhan, W. L. (964). A familial disorder of uric acid metabolism and central nervous system function. *American Journal of Medicine, 36,* 561–570.

Levitas, A. (1998). MR syndromes: Phenylketonuria (PKU) and the hyperphenylalanineisma II. *Mental Health Aspects of Developmental Disabilities, 1,* 113–118.

Libby, J. D., Polloway, E. A., & Smith, J. D. (1983). Lesch-Nyhan syndrome: A review. *Education and Training of the Mentally Retarded, 18,* 226–231.

Maes, B., Fryns, J. P., Ghesquiere, Q., & Borghgraef, M. (2000). Phenotypic checklist to screen for fragile X syndrome in people with mental retardation. *Mental Retardation, 38,* 207–215.

Marino, P. E., Landrigan, P. J., Graef, J., Nussbaum, A., Bayan, G., Boch, K., & Boch, S. (1990). A case report of lead poisoning during renovation of a Victorian farmhouse. *American Journal of Public Health, 80,* 1183.

Massie, R. K. (1967). *Nicholas and Alexandra.* New York: Atheneum.

Matthews, W. S., Barabas, G., Cusack, E., & Ferrari, M. (1986). Social quotients of children with phenylketonuria before and after discontinuation of dietary therapy. *American Journal of Mental Deficiency, 91,* 92–94.

May, D. C. (1988). Plastic surgery for children with Down syndrome: Normalization or extremism? *Mental Retardation, 26,* 17–19.

May, D. C., & Turnbull, N. (1992). Plastic surgeons' opinions of facial surgery for individuals with Down syndrome. *Mental Retardation, 30,* 29–33.

McLaren, J., & Bryson, S. E. (1987). Review of recent epidemiological studies of mental retardation: Prevalence, associated disorders, and etiology. *American Journal of Mental Retardation, 92,* 243–254.

McNab, T. C., & Blackman, J. A. (1998). When medical complications of the critically ill newborn: Review for early intervention professionals. *Topics in Early Childhood Special Education, 18,* 197–205.

Menolascino, F. J., & Egger, M. L. (1978). *Medical dimensions of mental retardation.* Lincoln: University of Nebraska Press.

Minder, B., Das-Smaal, E. A., & Orlebeke, J. F. (1998). Cognition in children does not suffer from very low lead exposure. *Journal of Learning Disabilities, 31,* 495–502.

Moser, H. W. (2000). Genetics and gene therapies. In M. L. Wehmeyer & J. R. Patton (Eds.), *Mental retardation in the 21st century* (pp. 235-250). Austin, TX: PRO-ED.

Nativio, D. G., & Belz, C. (1990). Childhood neurofibromatosis. *Pediatric Nursing, 16,* 575–580.

Neely, C. W. (1991). Family bonds: A mother's story about Fragile X syndrome. *LDA/Newsbriefs, 24*(4), 3, 6, 8.

Nyhan, W. L. (1976). Behavior in the Lesch-Nyhan syndrome. *Journal of Autism & Childhood Schizophrenia, 6,* 235–252.

Nyhan, W. L., Johnson, H. G., Kaufman, I. A., & Jones, K. (1980). Serotonergic approaches to the modification of behavior in the Lesch-Nyhan syndrome. *Applied Behavior in Mental Retardation, 1,* 25–40.

Orelove, F. P., & Sobsey, R. (1987). *Multiple disabilities: A transdisciplinary approach.* Baltimore: Brookes.

Pipitone, P. (1992). Acquired pediatric brain damage: Diverse causes. *Headlines, 3*(5), 5.

Polloway, E. A., & Rucker, H. (1997). Etiology: Biological and environmental considerations. In T. E. C. Smith, C. A. Dowdy, E. A. Polloway, & G. E. Blalock (Eds.), *Children and adults with learning disabilities* (pp. 160–187). Boston: Allyn & Bacon.

Powell, L., Houghton, S., & Douglas, J. (1997). Comparison of etiology-specific cognitive functioning profiles for individuals with fragile X and individuals with Down syndrome. *Journal of Special Education, 31,* 362–376.

President's Committee on Mental Retardation (PCMR). (1976b). *Mental retardation: The known and the unknown.* Washington, DC: U.S. Government Printing Office.

Pueschel, S. M. (1991). Ethical considerations relating to prenatal diagnosis of fetuses with Down syndrome. *Mental Retardation, 29,* 185–190.

Rasmussen, S. A., & Friedman, J. M. (1999). NF1 gene and neurofibromatosis type 1. *American Journal of Epidemiology, 151,* 33–40.

Resnick, O. (1988). Nutrition, neurotransmitter regulation and developmental pharmacology. In F. J. Menolascino & J. A. Stark (Eds.), *Preventive and curative intervention in mental retardation* (pp. 161–176). Baltimore: Brookes.

Rovet, J. (1993). The psychoeducational characteristics of children with Turner syndrome and adolescents with insulin-dependent diabetes mellitus. *Journal of Learning Disabilities, 26,* 333–341.

Rogers, R. C., & Simensen, R. J. (1987). Fragile X syndrome: A common etiology of mental retardation. *American Journal of Mental Deficiency, 91,* 445–449.

Rynders, J. E., & Horrobin, J. M. (1990). Always trainable? Never educable? Updating educational expectations concerning children with Down syndrome. *American Journal of Mental Retardation, 95,* 77–83.

Rynders, J. E., Spiker, D., & Horrobin, J. M. (1978). Underestimating the educability of Down syndrome children: Examination of methodological problems in recent literature. *American Journal of Mental Deficiency, 82,* 440–448.

Scarr, S., & Carter-Saltzman, L. (1982). Genetics and intelligence. In R. J. Sternberg (Ed.). *Handbook of human intelligence* (pp. 798–896. Cambridge, UK: Cambridge University Press.

Schroeder, S. R. (1999). A review of "Robert Guthrie: The PKU Story" by J. H. Koch. *American Journal of Mental Retardation, 104,* 392–393.

Schultz, F. R. (1983). Phenylketonuria and other metabolic diseases. In J. A. Blackman (Ed.). *Medical aspects of developmental disabilities in children birth to three* (pp. 197–201). Iowa City: University of Iowa Press.

Smith, J. D. (1981). Down's syndrome, amniocentesis and abortion: Prevention or elimination? *Mental Retardation, 19,* 8–11.

Smith, J. D. (1988b, September). CEC-MR position statement on the right of children with mental retardation to life sustaining medical care and treatment. *CEC-Report,* p. 2.

Smith, J. D. (1989). On the right of children with mental retardation to life sustaining medical care and treatment: A position statement. *Education and Training in Mental Retardation, 24,* 3–6.

Smith, J. D. (1995). *Pieces of purgatory: Mental retardation in and out of institutions.* Pacific Grove, CA: Brooks-Cole.

Stark, J. A., Menolascino, F. J., & Goldsbury, T. L. (1988). An updated search for the prevention of mental retardation. In F. J. Menolascino & J. A. Stark (Eds.), *Preventive and curative intervention in mental retardation* (pp. 3–25). Baltimore: Brookes.

Stoddard, K. (1992). The changing role of teachers: Refocus on the family. *LD Forum, 17*(1), 15–17.

Streissguth, A. (1997). *Fetal alcohol syndrome: A guide to families and communities.* Baltimore: Brookes.

Symons, F. J., Butler, M. G., Sanders, Feurer, I. D., & Thompson, T. (1999). Self-injurious behavior in Prader-Willi syndrome: Behavioral forms and body location. *American Journal on Mental Retardation, 104,* 260–269.

Turkington, C. (1987). Special talents. *Psychology Today, 20,* 42–46.

Vincent, L. J., Poulsen, M. K., Cole, C. K., Woodruff, G., & Griffith, D. R. (1991). *Born substance abused, educationally vulnerable.* Reston, VA: Council for Exceptional Children.

Warren, K. R., & Bast, R. J. (1988). Alcohol-related birth defects: An update. *Public Health Reports, 103,* 68–642.

Watson, J. (1993). Looking forward. *Gene, 135,* 309–315.

Webb, S., Hochberg, M. S., & Sher, M. R. (1988). Fetal alcohol syndrome: Report of a case. *Journal of American Dental Association, 116,* 196–198.

Widerstrom, A. H., Mowder, B. A., & Sandall, S. R. (1991). *At-risk and handicapped newborns and infants.* Upper Saddle River, NJ: Prentice Hall.

Wolraich, M. L. (1983). Hydrocephalus. In J. A. Blackman (Ed.), *Medical aspects of developmental disabilities in children birth to three* (pp. 137–141). Iowa City: University of Iowa Press.

Zantal-Weiner, K. (1987). *Child abuse and handicapped children.* Reston, VA: ERIC Clearinghouse on Handicapped and Gifted Children.

Zigman, W. S., Schupf, N., Lubin, R. A., & Silverman, W. P. (1987). Premature regression of adults with Down syndrome. *American Journal of Mental Retardation, 92,* 161–168.

Chapter

6

Psychosocial Aspects of Mental Retardation

 To review the chapter objectives on-line, go to the companion website at www.prenhall.com/ beirne-smith and select Chapter 6, then choose the Objectives module.

Shannon H. Kim, Ph.D.
University of Mississippi

Richard F. Ittenbach, Ph.D.
The Children's Hospital of Philadelphia

OBJECTIVES

After reading this chapter, the student should be able to

- discuss the relationship among mental retardation and behavioral, psychological, and other types of developmental disorders
- explain ways in which environmental influences may impact the psychosocial functioning of persons with mental retardation
- describe methods of intervention designed to improve the psychosocial functioning of persons with mental retardation

KEY TERMS

applied behavior analysis (ABA)
behavioral risk factors
developmental disabilities
dual diagnosis
learned helplessness

parenting style
psychopharmacology
psychosocial
transition shock

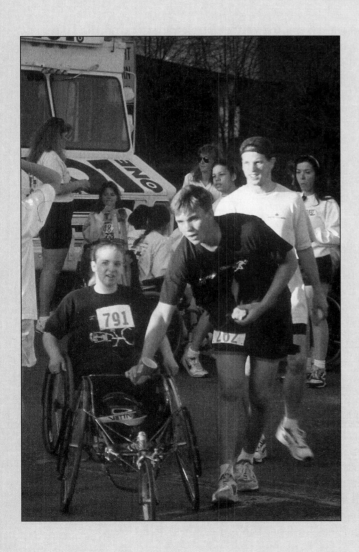

For a complete on-line glossary of mental retardation terms, go to the companion website www.prenhall.com/ beirne-smith and select any chapter, then choose the Glossary module.

The term *psychosocial* began to appear in the English language around the turn of the 20th century. It serves as a simple descriptor of the interaction between psychological and social attributes. However, there is nothing simple about this interaction. Current scientific information indicates that the reasons people think, feel, act, and interact in the ways they do are complex and multifaceted. In this chapter, we will examine aspects of the person that affect psychological and social well-being, as well as some environmental influences that may influence psychosocial functioning. Finally, we will describe some methods of intervention commonly used to enhance the psychosocial functioning of persons with mental retardation.

INDIVIDUAL ASPECTS

The label "mental retardation" refers to a very diverse group of people and does not provide much information about a person's psychosocial functioning. With or without mental retardation, people vary in terms of personality, behavior, and social acceptance. In this section, we will discuss some of the aspects of individuals that impact psychosocial functioning, paying attention to how these attributes are particularly important for persons with mental retardation.

Personality

Several different theories of personality development exist, but many can be compiled into two categories: type theories and trait theories. Additional work has been published investigating the particular personality correlates of mental retardation. Overall, little research of this type exists, although anecdotal generalizations about personality persist and seem to be accepted by a wide audience.

Type Theories   Theories of personality type group people into various categories. For example, the theory developed by Carl Jung and incorporated into the Myers-Briggs Type Indicator (Myers & McCaulley, 1985) describes people in terms of four didactic categories: introversion-extraversion, intuition-sensing, thinking-feeling, and judging-perceiving.

Briefly explained, introverted people prefer the world of ideas, whereas extraverted people prefer the world of people. Intuitive people enjoy abstract thought and possibilities; sensing people prefer working with known facts. Thinking people make decisions based on logic, while feeling people base decisions on relationships. Finally, judging people prefer structure and plans; perceiving people prefer a more spontaneous life.

It is not uncommon to encounter descriptions of persons with mental retardation that could be attributed to personality types. This is especially true when one considers the intuitive-sensing and the thinking-feeling dichotomies. Abstract thought is often difficult for people with mental retardation, and the desire to please others is frequently observed. However, empirical investigation of personality type in this population is absent from the professional literature.

Trait Theories

Trait theories conceptualize personality as a series of elements existing on a continuum as opposed to the either-or orientation of the type theories. Many different trait theories have been proposed, but most research supports a five-factor model known as the "Big Five." Costa and McRae (1986) describe the Big Five traits as degrees of (a) neuroticism (worry, insecurity); (b) extraversion (sociability, affection); (c) openness (independence, imagination, desire for variety); (d) agreeableness (trust, cooperation); and (e) conscientiousness (organization, carefulness, self-discipline).

As with the theories of personality type, little information is available concerning the influence of mental retardation on the expression of personality traits. However, certain traits are repeatedly described as psychosocial risk factors. High levels of agreeableness are often blamed when people are unduly influenced to engage in dangerous or unhealthy activities. The insecurity associated with the neuroticism trait could also be attributed to such commonly referenced characteristics as learned helplessness and external locus of control.

However one conceptualizes the components of personality, it is clear that individual differences will have an impact on psychosocial well-being. For example, most of the research conducted on the personality of persons with mental retardation has focused on disorders and psychopathology rather than more normative patterns of individual differences. The reason for this trend in the research may well be the rather restrictive nature of the American Psychiatric Association's (1994) taxonomy of mental health disorders itself. However, evaluation formats are also implicated. Relatively lengthy self-report questionnaires are generally used, and many people with mental retardation may have difficulty completing the forms.

Zigler's Personality Variables

One response to the lack of personality research has been provided by Ed Zigler. Zigler has hypothesized that people with mental retardation possess the same personality structures as the general population, but they experience social consequences that lead to a tendency toward certain traits. He has identified five personality features commonly observed in mental retardation: low expectancy of success, fear of failure, need for social reinforcement, outer-directedness, and overdependency (Zigler, 1999).

It is hypothesized that low expectancy of success and fear of failure form two components of the phenomenon known as learned helplessness. **Learned helplessness** refers to decreased levels of response that occur when one feels that negative outcomes are uncontrollable—in other words, that it doesn't matter what one does; a negative outcome will result. Thus, motivation to try greatly decreases. An increased rate of learned helplessness is said to exist among persons with mental retardation. This is a logical and widely accepted assumption, but little research exists to verify this characterization (Weisz, 1999).

Zigler's other three personality variables refer to a person's tendency to rely on instruction or approval from others in judging the merits of his or her own actions. The need for social reinforcement and tendencies toward outer-directedness and overdependency are thought to occur in response to repeated failure and from a value system that ranks attention from others more highly than individual achievement (Bybee & Zigler, 1999).

Psychiatric Disorders

Mental health disorders can undeniably have detrimental effects on a person's life. People with mental retardation who also have a psychiatric disorder are said to have a **dual diagnosis**. For many years, it was believed that people with mental retardation did not have mental health concerns. Professionals regarded symptoms of mental illness to be related to the primary disability (Reiss, McKinney, & Napolitan, 1990). However, many prevalence studies have since been conducted, indicating that this population is actually at an *increased* risk for psychiatric disorders (Lovell & Reiss, 1993). There is also an increased risk for symptoms of distress not quite meeting criteria for psychiatric diagnosis (Reiss, 1994; Schacter, Pless, & Bruck, 1991).

Internalizing Disorders   Mood and anxiety disorders are often referred to as *internalizing disorders* because they result in emotional angst or despondency that exist entirely within the person. Investigators have found rates of mood disorders between 3% and 15% among persons with mental retardation, as compared with rates of 2% to 5% in the general population (Lovell & Reiss, 1993; Reber & Borcherding, 1997; Reiss, 1994).

Internalizing disorders such as major depression and generalized anxiety disorder can magnify the negative feelings associated with many stressors people with mental retardation face on a daily basis. Sadness, irritability, lethargy, or overactivity may all be observed in persons with such diagnoses. Negative feelings can be self-perpetuating, as rejection by others can lead to the development of feelings of social inadequacy and low self-esteem, which in turn lead to further rejections (Baroff, 1991).

Identifying symptoms of internalizing disorders in persons with mental retardation can be a complicated process. Generally speaking, mental health practitioners base diagnoses on three forms of information: the patient's self-report of symptoms, clinical observations, and standardized assessment instruments. Traditional diagnostic procedures rely heavily on a person's ability to report symptoms, and many people with mental retardation do not have communication skills that are adequate for this purpose. Additionally, it can be difficult to diagnose disorders through observation because atypical symptoms may be exhibited. This seems especially true when considering people with more severe forms of mental retardation (Lovell & Reiss, 1993). Finally, conventional assessment instruments are generally not designed for use with this population. Specialized instruments have been developed but thus far have not been considered especially useful by practitioners (Rush & Frances, 2000).

Thought Disorders   Psychotic disorders such as schizophrenia and dementia disorders such as Alzheimer's disease are classified as thought disorders because the primary feature is disturbed forms of thinking. Psychotic disorders are characterized by hallucinations and delusions, while the symptoms of dementia disorders include confusion and impaired memory.

Psychotic disorders are generally estimated to occur in about 3% of persons with mental retardation, as opposed to the 1% rate for the population at large

Communication is one of the most important skills addressed in special education settings.

(Reid, 1993). Alzheimer's-type dementia is thought to have a direct biological link with the most common biological cause of mental retardation, Down syndrome, and some investigators believe that all persons with Down syndrome will eventually be affected by Alzheimer's disease, given a long enough life (Visser et al., 1997).

Disorders that affect thoughts and perception can be particularly problematic for persons with mental retardation, not only with regard to daily functioning but also with obtaining treatment. This is particularly true for people with limited communication abilities; it is difficult to determine whether a person is having hallucinations if he or she does not speak. We will discuss other treatment issues later in this chapter.

Conduct Disorders   Mental retardation is often associated with the expression of aberrant behaviors. Although these behaviors often result from skill deficits, they may also be related to a psychiatric disorder, such as conduct disorder. Estimates of conduct disorder have ranged from 12% to 45%, as compared with 3% to 4% of the general population (Lovell & Reiss, 1993).

Psychological disabilities such as conduct disorder render it more difficult for persons to participate meaningfully in community settings. It has been shown that people with dual diagnoses who exhibit challenging behaviors are at risk for involuntary admission to psychiatric hospitals (Khan et al., 1993; Morgan & Lowin, 1989) and to public residential facilities (Hill & Bruininks, 1984; Parsons, May, & Menolascino, 1984; Szymanski, 1994). Even if the person is not placed in an inpatient setting, the presence of significant emotional or behavioral problems often leads caregivers to place precautionary limitations on the activities in which a person is allowed to participate (Hill & Bruininks, 1984).

Whether or not a conduct disorder exists, challenging behaviors are more likely to occur in response to life stressors. People with mental retardation are often faced with obstacles that limit their ability to accomplish personal goals. If extreme behaviors such as aggression, self-injury, and tantrums occur in response to this frustration, a vicious cycle may begin in which relationships with significant others are stressed, and more difficulties attaining personal goals are experienced.

Developmental Disabilities

As you have no doubt come to understand by now, it is not unusual for mental retardation to be accompanied by other types of conditions and disorders. Disorders occurring in childhood and imposing limitations on independence are commonly referred to as **developmental disabilities**. When mental retardation occurs with other developmental disabilities, additional psychosocial effects are felt. An understanding of the other condition is necessary to increase the person's quality of life. Many disorders, including mental retardation, can be classified as developmental disabilities. We will discuss only a few of the more common: cerebral palsy, epilepsy, and autistic disorders.

Cerebral Palsy

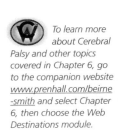

To learn more about Cerebral Palsy and other topics covered in Chapter 6, go to the companion website www.prenhall.com/beirne-smith and select Chapter 6, then choose the Web Destinations module.

Cerebral palsy is a broad term used to define a variety of conditions affecting a person's ability to move and maintain posture or balance. These disorders result from problems with the brain's ability to control the muscles. There are several different types of cerebral palsy and even more ways of classifying symptoms. Classification labels usually describe muscle tone, location of the brain injury, and location of the movement problems.

Descriptors of muscle tone are necessary because all people with cerebral palsy have abnormal muscle tone, whether it is increased, decreased, or a combination of the two. Increased muscle tone is described as "high tone," "hypertonia," or "spasticity." When muscle tone is increased, the muscles feel stiff and movements are jerky or awkward. Decreased muscle tone is referred to as "low tone," "hypotonia," or "floppiness." Muscles are relaxed to the point that it is difficult for the person to support his or own weight to sit upright, hold the head up, or speak clearly. People who have a combination of increased and decreased muscle tone are said to have a "fluctuating" or "variable" tone. In such cases, the person may have low muscle tone when at rest but high tone when engaged in activity.

Classification schemes based on the location of brain injury are divided into three types: spastic, choreoathetoid, and mixed-type. *Spastic* cerebral palsy, the most common type, is caused by damage to the part of the brain that controls voluntary movement. Symptoms include high muscle tone, jerky movements or contracted limbs. *Choreoathetoid* cerebral palsy is caused by damage to the areas of the brain that make movements appear smooth and uninterrupted. Symptoms include involuntary, purposeless movements and low muscle tone. *Mixed-type* cerebral palsy occurs when the brain is damaged in both areas; a combination of symptoms will result.

Cerebral palsy does not always affect all areas of the body equally, so a classification scheme also exists to identify the region of the person's body that is affected. The terms used are *monoplegia, diplegia, hemiplegia, quadriplegia,* and *double hemiplegia. Monoplegia* suggests only one limb on one side of the body is affected.

TABLE 6.1

Psychosocial Development Issues in Cerebral Palsy

Stage and approximate age	Developmental task	Obstacles	Interventions
Trust vs. mistrust (birth to 18 months)	To form a loving and trusting relationship with the primary caregiver	This stage is usually resolved through touch and cuddling. Some children with cerebral palsy may find usual positions and touches uncomfortable	Physical or occupational therapists can assist parents in learning how to hold or touch their child in a manner that would be comfortable for her or him
Autonomy vs. shame (18 months to 3 years)	To learn to control one's experiences through walking, grasping, and controlling the bowels	Adequate muscular control may not be available to accomplish these tasks	Physical or occupational therapy can improve skills; some surgical interventions can increase mobility; adaptive equipment can help increase independence
Initiative vs. guilt (3 to 6 years)	To assert oneself and take initiative	For some children with cerebral palsy, verbal expression can be difficult	Speech-language interventions can help the person learn to communicate more effectively
Industry vs. inferiority (6 to 12 years)	To successfully master problems and learning demands in competitive settings	Cognitive skills may be behind same-age peers, or the person may not possess adequate speech or motor skills to express knowledge	Educational interventions that are individually designed may allow the person to see his or her progress
Identity vs. role confusion (adolescence)	To achieve a social identity	Due to the disability, peers may not perceive persons with cerebral palsy in the way they would like to be perceived	Provide exposure to community settings and provide peer training
Intimacy vs. isolation (young adulthood)	To form intimate relationships	People with limited mobility may not be taken seriously as potential life partners	Provide exposure to community settings in which the person can meet people with similar interests that transcend disability
Generativity vs. stagnation (middle adulthood)	To contribute to the next generation through parenting or mentoring	Reliance on care providers may decrease the person's ability to care for others	Emphasize the importance of the emotional support the person can provide to others
Ego integrity vs. despair (late adulthood)	To feel that one has lived an acceptable, fulfilling life	If one has had dreams that one's body would not allow one to fulfill, dissatisfaction may result	Person-centered planning should occur throughout the lifespan

Diplegia means the legs are affected. *Hemiplegia* refers to cerebral palsy affecting one side of the body, with the arm more affected than the leg, trunk, or face. *Quadriplegia* suggests difficulties in the whole body, with the legs and feet more affected than arms and hands. The whole body is also affected in *double hemiplegia,* but the legs and arms are the most affected areas (Gersh, 1998).

Among persons with mental retardation, about 5% to 20% are estimated also to have cerebral palsy (Batshaw & Shapiro, 1997). Among persons with cerebral palsy, estimates of mental retardation range from one quarter to two-thirds (Blacklin, 1991; Pellegrino, 1997). Estimates of mental retardation among persons with cerebral palsy have decreased in recent years, as early intervention and innovations in assessment have led to more precise estimates of intelligence among people who have motor and speech impairments (Blacklin, 1991). In general, the more severe the cerebral palsy, the higher the chances for mental retardation, and vice versa (Batshaw & Shapiro, 1997).

Psychosocial implications of cerebral palsy relate to how the person feels about him- or herself and how others perceive the person. The psychosocial developmental tasks described by Erikson (1980) may be more difficult for children with cerebral palsy. Table 6.1 on page 203 points out some additional obstacles these children face at each stage. To assure better adjustment, it is important that the independence of children with cerebral palsy be encouraged.

Epilepsy   The term *epilepsy* refers to a medical condition in which a person experiences recurrent seizures that cannot be explained by external causes such as injury, illness, or drugs. This is an umbrella term that includes many types of seizures and seizure disorders. About 10% of all persons with mental retardation are also diagnosed with epilepsy; the rate increases as the severity of the mental retardation increases. Seizures can take many forms. Some types affect consciousness; others do not. Some involve spastic jerking; others simply involve staring. Some are easy to identify; others are more difficult. Seizures are classified into one of two broad categories: *partial* seizures affect only part of the brain; *generalized* seizures affect the whole brain. Table 6.2 describes some of the different types of seizures (Freeman, Vining, & Pillas, 1997).

Epilepsy can have many psychosocial consequences. To begin with, the seizures themselves can be accompanied by behavioral changes. It is not unusual for a seizure to be preceded by emotional changes, which may include fear or irritability. This experience is often referred to as an *aura.* During the aura, some persons feel that something bad is about to happen. Others are aware that a seizure is about to occur.

Most forms of epilepsy are well controlled with medication. However, the medications sometimes have cognitive, behavioral, or emotional side effects. Phenobarbitol, especially, is associated with these effects, and for this reason it is no longer considered a first-choice treatment. Other medications may have side effects that are less debilitating but interfere with psychosocial functioning in their own way. For example, some medications can cause persons to tire easily. Others have cosmetic side effects such as gum swelling, weight gain, and increased body hair (Freeman et al., 1997). Such effects may lead to embarrassment and lower self-esteem.

TABLE 6.2
Seizure Classification

International classification	Consciousness	Motor symptoms	Other symptoms
Partial seizures			
Simple partial	Not impaired	May involve jerking in any area of the body; may stay in one part of the body or spread to other parts	May involve sensory experiences such as tingling or burning; may trigger autonomic symptoms such as rapid heart beat or flushing; may stimulate emotions or memories
Complex partial	Impaired	Complex, automatic movements such as picking at clothes or wandering around the room	May or may not begin with a simple partial seizure
Generalized seizures			
Absence	Impaired	Usually none, but atypical absence symptoms can include jerking or automatic movements	Staring that is often confused with daydreaming
Myoclonic	Not impaired	Single jerking movement of a muscle group or the whole body	Myoclonic jerks sometimes occur in a series in infants; this form of epilepsy is known as "infantile spasms"
Atonic	Not impaired	Sudden loss of muscle tone or posture resulting in the muscle group (or whole body) going limp	
Tonic-clonic	Impaired	Stiffening that leads to the person falling on the ground followed by rhythmic rapid jerking	The person may drool or have difficulty breathing, and the bladder may empty After the seizure, the person will be unresponsive for a period of time then may be sleepy or confused

Other ways in which epilepsy may interfere with psychosocial development relate to confidence and fear. The experience of having a seizure can be frightening and embarrassing. For some people, seizures may be a personal nuisance largely unnoticed by others. For others, particularly those who have generalized seizures, the episode may attract much attention. Sometimes seizures are accompanied by loss of bladder control as well as muscular rigidity and jerking. As you can imagine, embarrassment after a seizure or fear that one will occur in public are commonly felt.

While experiencing a seizure in public may cause an array of emotions in the person with epilepsy, witnessing a seizure may also arouse uncomfortable feelings on the part of friends and strangers alike. Additionally, for persons who experience absence seizures, their symptoms may be misinterpreted as daydreaming or inattentiveness. Particularly for school-age children, this may lead to reprimands or other behavioral consequences. To prevent negative reactions from inhibiting the person with epilepsy, it is important that friends, family, teachers, employers, and others interacting with the person be educated about seizures and epilepsy.

Autistic Disorders   *Autistic disorder* is a type of developmental disability that occurs with and without mental retardation. Like epilepsy and cerebral palsy, the term itself is an umbrella term describing a spectrum of disorders that share some common features. Those features are usually referred to as a triad of impairments in the social, communication, and imagination-behavioral areas of development.

Subsumed within the category of autistic disorders are autism, pervasive developmental disorder, Asperger's syndrome, and childhood disintegrative disorder. To merit a diagnosis of *autism,* a person must demonstrate significant impairments in all three areas of the triad, with onset before age 3. *Pervasive developmental disorder* may be diagnosed if the person exhibits many symptoms of autism, but not enough to warrant that diagnosis. *Childhood disintegrative disorder* is indicated if the autistic symptoms do not occur until after age 3. Finally, *Asperger's syndrome* may be diagnosed if the person exhibits the social and behavioral characteristics but does not have all of the language difficulties required for a diagnosis of autism (American Psychiatric Association, 1994).

Current prevalence estimates indicate that autism occurs in approximately 7 to 17 out of every 10,000 children, with rates of Asperger's syndrome significantly higher and pervasive developmental disorder and childhood disintegrative disorder much lower. However, among persons with mental retardation, autistic disorders are estimated to occur in about 10% to 30%, with prevalence rates increasing with the severity of mental retardation. Asperger's syndrome is usually not associated with mental retardation (Gillberg, 1999).

By definition, people with autistic disorders have impaired psychosocial functioning. The first realm of the triad involves difficulties with social interaction. For some, this may mean the person shows little interest in the activities of others, instead preferring the stimulation of their own inner world. Others may be more interactive, but still these relationships rarely have a reciprocal nature. That is, although the person may learn some important social phrases such as, "How are you?" they do not fully engage in an interactive, empathetic relationship.

Psychosocial problems may be perpetuated by the impairments in the other realms of the triad as well. People who have problems expressing themselves are bound to become frustrated when dealing with other people. Many people with autism are completely nonverbal. Others may use words in a nonfunctional manner. For example, *echolalia,* or the repeating of words previously heard, is not uncommon. In this case, language is used more for self-stimulation than for communication. Still others use language in a more functional manner but do not have a firm grasp on the rules of language usage. For example, a person might not understand the difference in the statements "I want ice cream" and "I don't want ice cream." In such conversations, both parties are likely to become frustrated. Finally, some people with autistic disorders use language functionally (i.e., for requesting or refusing) but do not seem to understand the social dynamics of language. The use of language to express feelings, dreams, and concern for others may elude the person, further inhibiting the development of social relationships. An inability to use language to express emotions effectively can also lead to the use of challenging behaviors such as aggression or avoidance, which also place the person at risk for social rejection.

Aggressive-type behaviors are not exhibited by all persons with autism, but all do exhibit some behaviors that may be perceived as odd. It is not unusual for people with autism to be preoccupied with specific objects and to spend a lot of time interacting with those things. Obsessive and compulsive behaviors may also be exhibited (e.g., being unable to concentrate if a cabinet door is ajar; feeling compelled to leave through the same door used to enter; being more interested in lining toys up than in playing with them). Movement is also important to some persons, and they may be observed bouncing, rocking, swinging, or hugging at unusual times or places.

ENVIRONMENTAL ASPECTS

Psychosocial forces underlie virtually all facets of daily living. These forces, like the people in whom they reside, represent a fusion of biological, psychological, and sociological factors. As such, people are forever trying to balance the needs, wishes, and desires of forces that often conflict with one another. This section will briefly discuss many of the key environmental factors affecting the psychosocial adjustment of people with mental retardation.

Family Environments

For most people, the family of origin constitutes the single greatest influence in a person's life. Not only is the family the primary reference point for most children, but it is through the family that children come to know and understand the social world around them. The enduring influence lasts a lifetime and, in many cases, may even carry forward to successive generations.

Early Development   The first few years of a child's life are crucial to successful development at later ages. Early childhood is a time in which attachments are made, skills are learned, and behavioral repertoires are established. Because families act as the bridge between the community and the individual, early childhood is also the time at which families lay out their expectations for appropriate and inappropriate social conduct.

In a now famous study of early childhood development, Skeels and Dye (1939) investigated the reversibility of the effects of nonstimulating orphanage environments on children. The purpose of the study was to offer 13 children (average IQ = 64) living in an orphanage the care, nurturance, and stimulation of a child raised by loving, attentive, natural parents. This was done through the use of trained adolescent care providers. Of the 13 children in the experimental group, all but 2 were considered by state law to be unsuitable for adoption at the outset of the study, because of mental retardation. For the control group, only 2 of the 12 children were classified as having mental retardation and, thus, unsuitable for adoption.

In 1965, more than 25 years after the original study had begun, Skeels (1966) again located the subjects. His follow-up study reported that 11 of the 13 children had married, and all but one of the marriages were still intact. The adults' mean level of education was 12th grade; four had completed one or more years of college. All were either self-supporting or functioning as homemakers. Their occupations ranged from professional work and business to domestic service (the two who had not been adopted), and their income was consistent with state and national averages.

Conversely, the control subjects showed an initial drop in mean IQ of 26 points and as a result were generally not eligible for adoption. When Skeels located them in 1965, he found that these 11 subjects (one had died) had a mean educational level of third to fourth grade. Four of the subjects in the control group were institutionalized, unemployed, and costing the state approximately $200 per month each. Findings such as these led Skeels (1966) to conclude that practitioners and policymakers now had conclusive evidence in favor of the importance of early intervention and its ability to overcome the limitations of environmental deprivation.

Skeels and Dye's conclusions have been both endorsed and challenged over the years. Most early childhood proponents believe in the importance of enrichment and early intervention but differ as to the extent of its value. Although it is true that many effects of early deprivation can be overcome with programmed intervention, some sociocultural variables seem highly resistant to change and present the developing person with some rather insurmountable barriers. A discussion of some of these factors follows.

Demographics   Growing up in an orphanage such as that just described represents only one of many different risk factors for mental retardation. Growing up without parents is tragic and brings with it a number of potential problems; however, it does not, by any means, guarantee that a person will develop mental retardation. In fact, mental retardation, like other forms of developmental disability, seems to occur without regard for cultural and demographic boundaries.

Although mental retardation seems to know no boundaries, it is observed in disproportionately high numbers in the more vulnerable segments of the population such as the poor, the disenfranchised, and ethnic minorities. The reason for this phenomenon stems from mental retardation's strong social and cultural components. That is, if certain sociocultural forces are strong enough, the symptoms of social and/or cultural mental retardation can mimic those of biologically based mental retardation, as in the case of children deprived of appropriate enrichment and stimulatory experiences.

In a recent study using the 1994/1995 National Health Interview Survey data of more than 46,000 U.S. households, Larson et al. (2000) found striking differences in the prevalence rates of mental retardation across key demographic categories such as age, race, and economic status. For example, people whose earned income placed them below the poverty line were three times more likely to have mental retardation than those who did not live in poverty. In addition, people who were black were two to three times more likely to have mental retardation than people who were not black. Not surprisingly, the prevalence rates of children and adolescents are not only consistent with each other but four to five times greater than that of adults.

For people with mental retardation and developmental disabilities, specifically, striking patterns of prevalence also emerged. For example, males outnumber females three to two, one-third of all young adults with mental retardation have less than an eighth grade education (12% with no formal education at all), and

TABLE 6.3

Percentage of People Living in
Poverty by Age and Race

Variable	People with MR/DD (%)	People without MR/DD (%)
All People	32.3	12.9
Age group		
0 through 5 years	32.8	21.8
6 through 17 years	33.4	17.7
18+ years	31.7	10.7
Racial group		
Black	56.1	29.5
White	26.7	10.3
Other	33.2	17.0

Source: From "Prevalence of Mental Retardation and/or
Developmental Disabilities: The [1994/1995] NHIS-D" by S. A.
Larson, K. C. Lakin, L. Anderson, N. Kwak, J. H. Lee, and D.
Anderson, *MR/DD Data Brief, 1*(2), Minneapolis: University of
Minnesota, Institute on Community Integration, Research
and Training Center on Community Living.

nearly one-third of all children with mental retardation live in a single-parent household. Sadly, over half of all people with mental retardation who are black live in poverty (56%). For whites with mental retardation, the risk of living in poverty is 2½ times greater than that of the general population (see Table 6.3).

Distinguishing among influential factors can be very difficult. For example, people with lower levels of education tend to earn less money than those with higher levels of education. There are disproportionately higher numbers of single-parent families living below the poverty line, the parents of which generally have lower levels of education and lower levels of annual earned income. In addition, ethnic minorities and women tend to have less education, earn less money, and have relatively greater numbers of single-parent households than others (U.S. Department of Commerce, 1999). Such a pattern usually translates to more risk factors for mental retardation.

But demographics alone do not put a person at risk for a diagnosis of mental retardation. A more likely risk factor is an inability to access community services, services that are disproportionately distributed away from those who need them most (Robinson & Rathbone, 1999). People who meet multiple criteria of vulnerability do not always have the same access to essential services as others. In addition, society still holds those who are culturally different at a decided disadvantage when it comes to full community inclusion. People from culturally different populations learn a different set of social rules than those who are not culturally different. Hence, the general approach to life, participation in society, and means of coping with adversity when it arises often require a different perspective in a culturally different society.

Parenting Style   The role of the parent or primary care provider cannot be understated. Childhood is a time of "positive feelings toward oneself, others, and the larger world. . . . children who are nurtured, encouraged, and accepted by adults and peers will be emotionally well adjusted. Children who are abused, neglected or rejected can suffer social and mental health difficulties" (Trawick-Smith, 2000, p. 292).

The social and emotional challenges of caring for a family member with mental retardation poses particular difficulty to parents, due in large part to the importance and deeply held emotions associated with caring for someone with a pervasive and lifelong developmental disorder. Not only must the family struggle with meeting the service-related needs of their loved ones, but they must also struggle with their own feelings about the disability, their role in the disability, and what they can do to protect their loved one from further burden.

Consider for a minute the demands placed on a single minority mother with a minimum-wage job that is both physically and mentally demanding, who has little in the way of a formal education, few if any predictable social services and supports, and her own feelings of remorse about how best to care for her child with a disability. Add to that the permanent and unyielding nature of the disability and a child with moderate support needs, poor language skills, and moderate amounts of aberrant behavior (see Gray, 1998). The result is precious little time for anything other than the absolute essentials of caretaking—for oneself, the loved one with mental retardation, or other family members.

All parents have a particular style of caring for the family irrespective of temporary stressors. Most often, it is predicated on the temperaments of the individual parents. For example, some parents tend to respond to upsetting situations *faster* than others, as in the case of acceptance, anger, forgiveness, and so forth. Furthermore, some parents experience their emotions much more *strongly* than others, as with joy, love, and sorrow. These temperamental preferences then carry over to one's **parenting style** and can be observed in such areas as discipline and expectations for success. In the first case, discipline, some parents are quick to judge their children's actions, whereas others are not. Of those who are quick to reach judgment, some are consistently harsh in their reactions while others are much more lenient and save the harshness for serious or repeated violations. In the second case, expectations for success, some parents quickly and consistently adopt high or low expectations for their children, while others adapt their expectations to the circumstances at hand. How firmly they adhere to a position depends on the strength of the particular conviction. Identifying one's dispositional tendencies and striving to reach a balance is the key to a healthy family lifestyle (McHugh & Slavney, 1998).

Caring for a family member with mental retardation is difficult under any set of circumstances. In an era of increased single-parent households, longer work weeks, smaller family support systems, and increased demands at the school and community levels, challenges exist that were not known decades ago. Even the best and most psychologically healthy parents can be pushed to their limits in the face of multiple stressors. Yet through it all, persons with mental retardation continue to survive and thrive due to loving, caring, and the absolute commitment of their parents.

Unrelenting Love

For most parents, looking in on their sleeping children at day's end offers a time to reflect on their life together as a family and the unfolding life of the young child. Presented here is a passage taken from Gene Stallings's (1997) book *Another Season*, in which that special time is interrupted with the reality of an unrelenting disability, mental retardation. Through it all, however, this young NFL head coach found comfort and strength from his son, his disability, and their time together at the end of each day.

　　Once again, I found myself going into Johnny's room in the middle of *every night* [italics added] to make sure that he was breathing. In the dark, I'd sit on a chair next to his bed and watch him lying there, all buttoned up in his red pajamas, his mouth wide open, trying hard to suck in air while making strange noises, his chest heaving up and down, and I'd think to myself how I wouldn't want to do very much if I had to gasp for my breath the way Johnny did. It seemed just like yesterday that he was that little boy whose days were so precarious. He had struggled for his breath for twenty-six years, yet somehow his body had adjusted. But now as I sat there and looked at him, I wondered how much longer he could possibly go on like this. I put my ear to his chest so that I would hear his heartbeat, just as I had done throughout his childhood, and I thought how much I'd like to have my son's courage and determination, particularly during this junction in my life.

Source: From *Another Season: A Coach's Story of Raising an Exceptional Son*, by G. Stallings and S. Cook, 1997. Boston: Little, Brown.

Living Environments

Finding a safe, stable, and loving home environment constitutes one of the most important decisions of a lifetime. Many persons with mental retardation have precisely that, but many do not. For those who do not, the search for an optimal home environment can be a long and difficult one.

Residential Settings　　Most people will readily admit that children growing up in a large urban setting will have different experiences than children growing up in a small rural setting. Furthermore, children growing up with many brothers and sisters or many extended relatives living in a single household will learn to approach life differently than will those who grow up as an only child. In each of these scenarios, the rules of socialization and daily living are indeed different.

　　Many years ago, families of people with mental retardation had relatively few residential living options available to them. Parents could care for their child in their own home, just as they would their other children, or they could have the state assume responsibility by placing the child in an institution (or public residential facility). Parents were frequently asked to make this decision shortly after the birth of their child, and very frequently, the physicians, nurses, or significant others would encourage placement in an institution. Families today have many more options than the two just mentioned and, in addition, are far less likely to be encouraged by health service providers to shift their care to a large facility. The major reason for this shift is an increasing recognition that *where* a person lives generally determines *how* a person lives.

TABLE 6.4

Percentages of Previous and Sub-sequent Residential Placements for Persons Living in Large State Facilities in 1985 and 1998

Source: Anderson, L., Lakin, K.C., Prouty, R.W., and Polister, B. 1999. Characteristics and Movement of Residents of Large State Facilities. In R. W. Prouty & K.C. Lakin (Eds.). *Residential Services for Persons with Developmental Disabilities: Status and Trends through 1998.* (pp. 55, 57). Minneapolis: University of Minnesota, Institute on Community Integration, Research and Training Center on Community Living.

Residential Setting	Previous place of Residence[a]		Subsequent place of Residence[b]	
	1985	1998	1985	1998
Natural family home	39.2	20.9	17.1	10.8
Foster home	3.5	2.3	7.1	6.3
Group home				
15 or fewer persons	5.6	14.4	40.4	50.9
16 to 63 persons	3.5	3.8	7.4	3.7
Large facility				
Nonstate (64+ persons)	1.8	2.1	3.8	0.7
State (64+ persons)	20.6	25.3	10.1	6.1
Boarding home	0.5	0.5	3.2	3.1
Nursing facility	1.6	1.7	4.1	2.6
Semi/independent living	1.0	1.9	1.4	9.2
Mental health facility	13.6	12.0	1.4	1.5
Correctional facility	2.3	10.3	0.2	0.0
Unknown/other	6.7	5.9	3.7	5.0

Note*: 1998 statistics are based upon: [a]1,511 new admissions and [b]2,953 discharges.

To read about some issues related to the expansion of community group homes, go to the companion website at www.prenhall.com/beirne-smith and select Chapter 6, then choose the Article Response module.

The vast majority of people with mental retardation now live in a natural family home—that is, their own home or that of a family member (Fujiura, 1998; Larson et al., 2000). Those who do not live in a natural family home, which is approximately 10% to 20% of all persons with mental retardation, live in a dynamic and exceptionally fluid residential service system. Table 6.4 lists many of the different residential placement options now elected by families of persons with mental retardation and the rates with which the alternative placements have either been accepted or rejected in favor of the institution for years 1985 and 1998.

The most obvious pattern observed in Table 6.4 is the sheer number of placement options. In addition, a much smaller percentage of people left their natural family home for an institution in 1998 than in 1985 (20.9% vs. 39.2%), due in large part to the changing philosophy about institutional placements and the number of placement options available. Parents who cannot care for a child at home can now opt for a smaller community-based facility before seeking placement in an institution. Interestingly, 1 in 4 people is now entering institutions from other institutions, primarily because of the large number of facility closures. With respect to people exiting institutions, one-half went into small group homes (50.9%) in 1998, up from 40.4% in 1985. Furthermore, 9.2% of all discharges were to independent or semi-independent living settings in 1998 as compared with only 1.4% in 1985. Both of these patterns reflect the trends toward smaller, community-based settings (Anderson, Lakin, Prouty, & Polister, 1999).

With the emphasis on smaller settings in recent years, why are some people still opting for larger settings at all, and what are the implications for one's level of psychosocial adjustment? The most obvious and frequently elicited answer is that the person's needs often extend beyond what the family or personnel of a small group home can realistically offer. For example, Blacher and colleagues (Blacher & Baker, 1992; Bromley & Blacher, 1992) have identified a number of psychosocial variables that cause a family to seek an institutional placement, such as the complexity of the disability, number and type of daily stressors experienced by the family, number of parents in the home, level of parental education, and proximity of the out-of-home facility.

While the family's level of psychosocial adjustment would certainly extend to the person with mental retardation, other considerations exist beyond those of the family. More important perhaps are the psychosocial factors at work in the person with mental retardation. The demands of living in a congregate care facility, of any size, are just different from the demands of living in one's own home. As such, people must either be comfortable with it or adapt to a lifestyle of living with others with whom they would probably not otherwise choose to live. One's identity, independence, esteem, and general sense of worth as a person often hinge on the comfort level with the living environment and with those with whom they live.

Relocation Issues　　Given the rather fluid nature of the residential service system today, one might wonder whether the ever-changing landscape of living options is a cause or a consequence of the service delivery system. There are problems with the service delivery system and with the transition process, certainly, but they are not always (or exclusively) a reflection of the system itself, the willingness of the people in the system to help others, or the people who are changing residences. For example, people who are uprooted from familiar settings and moved into new surroundings sometimes have real difficulty adjusting even under the best of circumstance. Yet, people with mental retardation, by definition, generally have difficulty with adjustment and adaptability. Hence, movement from one setting to another, no matter how well intentioned or how well planned, often brings with it a number of unexpected challenges.

When problems arise that stem from the person's emotional response to change, patience and empathic counseling from staff members at both ends of the transition continuum are the most appropriate avenues of intervention. The person transitioning to the new setting should be reassured that feelings of anxiety and separation are normal and probably only temporary and that expectations of success will heavily influence the new community member's transition. The person who has been thoroughly prepared for the move will naturally have higher expectations for success than someone who is less well prepared.

Coffman and Harris (1980) have identified a set of symptoms that they call **transition shock**, a condition analogous to the adjustment problems of people who have recently gotten divorced, returned from war, been released from prison, or relocated to new countries. A number of common characteristics exist among these disenfranchised groups:

Cue problems.   Responding inappropriately to cues that were relevant in the old environment but not in the new one (e.g., bells signaling mealtime in institutions), or failing to respond to cues peculiar to the new environment

Value discrepancies.   Personal traits developed by rigid institutional routines that are not likely to be valued in the new community settings (e.g., dependence, deference to others, and an inability to make decisions)

Emergence over time.   Problems associated with transition shock often do not occur immediately but rather incubate for a period of time.

Persons unfamiliar with developmental disabilities may tend to forget that people with mental retardation experience the full range of emotions. In addition, they may fail to recognize that transition shock is an emotional reaction and that feelings of despondency, loneliness, anxiety, and hostility are no less proper for those with mental retardation than they are for persons without mental retardation.

Heller (1984) reviewed the literature on relocation difficulties and notes the following general trends: no significant increase in mortality rates, some decreases in constructive behaviors, increases in physical/medical problems, and increases in social withdrawal. Heller points out that one's reactions will likely vary according to the characteristics of the person, degree of disruption, availability of support systems, and quality of the sending and receiving environments. Another critical factor in relocation research is the timing of the move. It seems that the impact of the move is most keenly felt during the first few weeks of the transition, thereby making it prudent to evaluate the person's adjustment initially and not simply defer evaluation until later in the transition process.

Lifestyle Considerations

Virtually all of the issues faced by persons with mental retardation seem to include, in one way or another, psychosocial factors. The more psychologically healthy and socially integrated a person is, the fewer the barriers and the greater the opportunities for meaningful experiences. Consequently, activities designed to promote one's health and well-being in all areas of daily living generally translate to a higher quality of life overall.

The link between quality of life and general level of health is a close one (Cohen, 2000). As indicated previously, people with mental retardation do indeed experience health problems in disproportionately greater numbers than those without mental retardation. Although many problems and life events are beyond anyone's control, particularly for people with multiple disabilities, many secondary disabilities can be moderated or improved substantially by simple changes in lifestyle.

The repetitive, willful actions that contribute to the development of related or secondary conditions are often referred to as **behavioral risk factors**. Cohen (2000) believes that behavioral risk factors can be divided into four distinct categories: nutrition, hygiene, exercise, and adherence to a medical regimen. Well known among service providers are the primary needs of persons with mental retardation (e.g., cognition, adaptive behavior, social functioning). Less well known are the secondary needs of persons with mental retardation, those that stem from lifestyle preferences and actions. A brief discussion of such factors follows.

Good eating habits, more than anything else, offers a number of immediate benefits to people of all ages and ability levels. The most obvious benefit is decreased likelihood for obesity, a phenomenon that may affect as many as 25% of all adults with mental retardation. A substantially lower metabolic rate than that found in persons without mental retardation is increasingly being implicated (Allison et al., 1998). The risk is certainly not limited to persons with disabilities but is a by-product of contemporary American life, one that includes a plethora of fast foods, snack foods, and an entertainment-based video lifestyle. For the person with limited social and recreational opportunities, the battle against sound nutrition can be a lifelong one. The benefits, however, can be offset with lowered risks of autoimmune disorders, cancer, heart disease, hypertension, and other conditions, all of which can make the primary disability much more difficult to accommodate.

A second but equally important area of focus for persons with mental retardation is personal hygiene, which is not as immediately obvious as nutrition, perhaps, but every bit as critical. As an essential life-skill area, habits of hygiene are often important determinants of independent living status. That is, those who can wash, bathe, brush their teeth and hair, and have appropriate toileting skills are generally able to have some degree of autonomy and independent living. More important, however, is the need for sound hygiene with respect to general level of health. If any one of the aforementioned areas is overlooked for more than a few days, the results can range anywhere from alienation from others to major illness. Even subtle omissions of daily routine and responsibility can result in increased vulnerability to other, more disabling conditions.

Many have written about the importance of exercise to a healthy lifestyle. Similar to the benefits of good nutrition mentioned earlier, vigorous exercise conducted on a regular basis can also reduce the risks of other complicating factors such as strokes, heart attacks, obesity, and other disabling conditions. Whereas athletics and physical exercise are often presented to people with disabilities as opportunities for leisure, socialization, and mainstreaming, they are less often presented as an opportunity for enhanced physical health and well-being. Those who exercise regularly are likely to maintain a healthy, active lifestyle longer in life and be less vulnerable to both primary and secondary disabilities.

Lack of compliance with an established medical regimen represents another prominent risk factor. Different from issues surrounding nutrition, hygiene, and exercise in which daily care is usually at the discretion of the person, failure to comply with an established medical regimen usually places the person at an immediate and elevated risk of deleterious consequences. For the person with mental retardation, medical care may not be discretionary and often is essential for daily living. This is yet another important determinant for independent or semi-independent living. Those who can manage an established medical regimen, either alone or with the help of a care provider, can usually do fairly well in an independent (or semi-independent) living situation. Those who cannot usually require an assisted living arrangement. In this regard, people with mental retardation are no different from anyone else.

A fifth area of behavioral risk is that associated with substance use and abuse. Though not formally identified by Cohen (2000) as a separate risk factor, service providers express growing concern that as people with mental retardation move into more normative and less protective settings, the risk of substance use and abuse increases.

The available data on drugs of abuse by persons with mental retardation are scant. However, Christian and Poling (1997) have reviewed the published literature and conclude that people with mental retardation are experimenting with drugs of abuse, but in seemingly smaller proportions than those without mental retardation. They further suggest that while people with mental retardation seem to be at no greater risk of addictive behaviors by virtue of their disability, those who are currently taking other prescriptive medications for related disorders are at greater risk for more serious complications due to the use and abuse of the controlled substances. Other consequences are also noteworthy: decreased levels of independence, increased difficulties with cognition and social adjustment, and delayed acquisition of important new social and problem-solving skills (Watson, Franklin, Ingram, & Ellenberg, 1998).

So how do the lifestyle issues presented here relate to one's level of mental retardation? The answer is a complex one and may well be more indirect than direct. Neglecting one's health status, whether it is related to nutrition, hygiene, exercise, adherence to a medical regimen, substance abuse, or some other important factor, can yield many negative consequences, from increased levels of acting out to complete social withdrawal (see Kennedy & Thompson, 2000). If untreated for any length of time, the secondary problems can begin to manifest themselves as primary health-related concerns and, as a result, threaten one's quality of life well beyond what should otherwise have been the case. Anything that increases a person's vulnerability to other, more debilitating conditions also has a negative effect on the person's general level of adjustment and functioning status, individually as well as socially. Therefore, not only does mental retardation itself have strong psychosocial correlates, but by association, anything that complicates the mental retardation process also does.

INTERVENTIONS

Identification of problem areas will be meaningless unless a treatment can be devised that results in a better life for the person. Professionals in such diverse fields as education, social work, psychology, speech therapy, physical therapy, and occupational therapy work to ensure that no diagnosis is meaningless. In this section, we will discuss some of the more helpful types of psychosocial interventions developed or implemented by professionals in each of these fields. However, the importance of structuring interventions to meet an individual's specific needs cannot be overemphasized.

A good intervention is one that begins with an assessment of the person's needs. The outcome of the assessment should be a precise definition of the problem or problems. For example, a child may be referred for help because of difficulty making friends. This is a good place to begin, but more information is needed before an intervention can be applied with any chance of success. Does the child

Decision process: Whether to use simple technology

Learner: _____   Date: _____
Domain: _____   Team: _____
Environment: _____   _____
Goal: _____   _____
_____   _____
                                     _____
                                     _____

Functional OBJECTIVES	Learner's current ABILITIES	BARRIERS which prevent or limit learner from achieving the objective	INTERVENTIONS or SOLUTIONS

FIGURE 6.1
Decision-Making Matrix

Source: From *Selection and Use of Simple Technology in Home, School, Work, and Community Settings* (p. 18), by J. Levin and L. Scherfenberg, 1990, Minneapolis, MN: AbleNet.

have trouble making friends because of behaviors that others reject, because of a general lack of communication skills, or because of an inability to initiate contact with others? There are a multitude of possible reasons. Though this process may seem obvious, it is often overlooked or improperly executed. Figure 6.1 presents a chart that can be useful for precisely defining problems and developing appropriate interventions. The chart is designed to assess technological needs, but it could be adapted to use with a variety of interventions.

Educational Interventions

Many types of psychosocial intervention can be implemented in educational settings. Classroom education is often based on a functional skills curriculum designed to teach the person to live in an integrated society. Because educational interventions are thoroughly covered in other sections of this book, we will take a look at only three types that directly relate to psychosocial functioning: life skills training, social skills training, and peer training.

Assessment of a student's preferences in a variety of areas, including play, should be a part of any successful intervention.

Life Skills   Many of the psychosocial issues described earlier in this chapter relate to deficits in knowledge that typically occur in persons with mental retardation. These knowledge deficits are the subject of many educational endeavors and are usually contained within a student's transition plan. Problems associated with basic life skills such as how to perform basic hygiene and homemaking tasks, navigate oneself around town, follow the rules in games, and manage money can cause many problems with others as well as with one's own self-concept.

Any successful intervention must begin with a thorough assessment of the skills the person has already attained. Although standardized measures are commercially available, curriculum-based assessment procedures are generally held to be the most helpful. This procedure allows the teacher to assess a child's competencies, then develop goals and objectives based on that assessment. With clear learning objectives, the teacher can continually assess progress and modify the teaching as necessary.

Perhaps the key to success in teaching life skills is to ensure the motivation of the learner. One determinant of student motivation is the amount of input one has over the learning objectives. Students are more likely to dedicate themselves to attaining goals that are personally meaningful. Therefore, initial assessment should include a method of gaining information from the student about preferences in a variety of different areas. For example, what are some favorite things to do (read, learn, play)? What does the child want to do after graduation? What are the things that seem to stand in the way of completing important and meaningful goals?

As with vocational instruction, life skills instruction should be provided in natural environments to be maximally effective. Generalization of skills learned to new environments can be difficult for people with mental retardation. Therefore, it will be easier to learn banking skills in a bank, transportation skills at the bus stop, basketball rules on the court, and so forth. Cronin and Patton (1993) provide an excellent guide for integrating life skills into the classroom setting.

Social Skills   If educational training is truly to prepare a person for life in the community, social skills training must be an integrated part of the curriculum. Deficits in social skills can lead to many types of undesirable outcomes, not the least of which is social isolation. People with mental retardation sometimes exhibit behaviors that seem immature or out of place. Difficulties understanding that behaviors acceptable in one setting are not acceptable in another are also frequently observed. Social skills training can be useful in such cases.

Like other types of skills training, social skills are best learned if multiple opportunities for practice are provided. Social skills training should consist of two parts. The first part consists of teaching rules and societal norms. Many tools exist for assessing and teaching social skills (see Riches, 1997). Most formats consist of group instruction, complete with discussion, repetition of the rule, rehearsal, and role play. The instruction should always be supplemented by application in real-world settings.

The second part of social skills training is not as simple to teach. Much interpersonal behavior is dependent on one's ability to assess the intentions and feelings of others. This can be difficult for persons with mental retardation. Consider the case of Charlie, the lead character in the book *Flowers for Algernon* by Daniel Keyes (1966). Every day Charlie goes to work in a bakery with people he considers his best friends. Charlie is very helpful and respectful toward his friends. When they ask him to do something, he sets aside his own needs and does what they ask of him. However, Charlie does not realize they are making fun of him and taking advantage of him. He believes that because they talk to him and smile at him and call him "buddy," they must be his friends.

Often we become so involved with teaching people with mental retardation to behave in ways that are not offensive that we forget to teach them that people without mental retardation can also be offensive. A person with social skills should not only be able to behave nicely, they should also know when others are not being nice to them. Admittedly, this is a difficult task. Members of the self-advocacy and self-determination movements have begun work in this area. It involves helping people with mental retardation to define precisely what they want out of life and to stand up for their dreams. It also involves teaching them how to assess problems in their own lives: how those problems developed, who led them into the problems, and who can be depended on for help when problems arise (Gaylord, Abery, Dahl, & Chelberg, 1993/1994).

Peer Training   No intervention will help people with mental retardation to meld into society unless society is willing to accept them. In educational settings, this is being accomplished by exposing students to children with disabilities of all types through inclusive educational practice. However, simply situating children next to their peers is often not enough. Peer training is sometimes warranted.

Peer training can be conducted in many ways and for many purposes. The *Yes I Can!* curriculum (Abery, Schoeller, Simunds, Gaylord, & Fahnestock, 1997) is one example of an educational program designed to facilitate the social inclusion of junior and senior high school students with disabilities. The program provides two forms of peer training. In the first phase, the students without disabilities are educated about the needs and challenges of students with disabilities. In the second phase, the peers are trained to facilitate social inclusion. Each of these types of interventions has been shown to benefit the person with mental retardation. Many studies also indicate such endeavors have benefits for the peers (McLaughlin, Warren, & Schofield, 1996).

Many authors have commented on the attitudinal barriers faced when people without disabilities have no experience with persons who have mental retardation. On the one hand, fear, embarrassment, or avoidance may occur. On the other hand, a reliance on stereotyped beliefs may lead to interactions based on pity or overprotection (Abery et al., 1997). Education and information can assist persons without disabilities in learning to relate to people with disabilities on a personal level.

The other role of peer training is to enable students to facilitate the social inclusion of persons with disabilities. In the *Yes I Can!* curriculum, students with disabilities are paired with a student facilitator (who may or may not also have disabilities). The facilitator provides companionship and serves as a bridge between the student with disabilities and the rest of the school. The facilitator has the duty to identify barriers and opportunities for the formation of friendships.

Family Interventions

Service providers are increasingly seeking a family-centered approach to intervention. This trend has grown out of the recognition that disability does not occur in a vacuum. The family members are affected collectively and individually, and their responses can be therapeutic or counterproductive. Some research also indicates that positive outcomes are had by all when a family member learns how to help the person with a disability. In this section, we will discuss three types of family intervention that are commonly encountered: early intervention, parent training, and person-centered planning.

To learn more about early intervention, go to the companion website at www.prenhall.com/beirne -smith and select Chapter 6, then choose the Case Studies module.

Early Intervention   Early intervention has been shown to be useful for alleviating an array of problems, including challenging behavior, communication skills, and motor development. The term is generally used to describe therapy and/or training provided to children and families of children aged 5 or younger. The sessions may be conducted in the family home or in a clinic, depending on the individual's needs and the array of services available in the community.

Early intervention services generally begin with a comprehensive developmental assessment of the child's skills. This assessment may include information about the child's medical history, vision, hearing, problem solving, attention span, cognitive abilities, receptive and expressive language, fine- and gross-motor skills, and so

Peer Connections

Peer Connections is the name of a class designed to facilitate social inclusion at Eden Prairie High School in Eden Prairie, Minnesota. Joy Keachie, a teacher at Eden Prairie High School, describes the outcome of the class for one of her students:

> Chris is a young man with Down syndrome who functions in the mild to moderate range of mental impairment. Although he had many inclusion opportunities, he was still having some difficulties in the social skills area. He would "switch" from age appropriate behavior to acting very immature when he was feeling uncomfortable or when he had an "audience." He would run from adults when he knew he had done something wrong or was upset with someone, and would hide in hallways or under desks, tables, and sewing machines before and during class. He seemed to enjoy his role as the "clown" and the attention he was receiving, negative as it was.
>
> The changes in Chris during his two years in Peer Connections have been dramatic! He became friends with a young man who was a senior and in the Peer Connections class. The Peer Connections teachers asked T.J. to help Chris understand that his behavior wasn't really getting him what he wanted. When T.J. would ask him to "get it together," Chris was usually able to comply. In addition to being peer partners in class, T.J. made time for Chris outside of class with such activities as watching Chris' adaptive rec team play soccer, taking him out to get something to eat, playing video games, having dinner with Chris' family, and talking on the phone. When Chris began his person-centered social inclusion planning process, he wanted T.J. to be a part of his team. By being a good friend and role model for Chris, T.J. was able to help Chris learn appropriate behaviors both in and out of school. By the end of the second quarter, Chris was no longer hiding in or out of the classroom. His inappropriate behaviors almost disappeared and he became a leader in the classroom and in the Y's Act drama group after school.
>
> In his junior year, Chris became a facilitator in the Peer Connections class. He showed amazing maturity in class and other settings in the school working with the students who are younger or have more severe disabilities than his. One of the other students from his group chose him to be on her person-centered planning team and he has been one of the most helpful people on her team. Chris has not only developed his own social skills and self-esteem, he is reaching out to others with and without disabilities and building a network of friends.

Source: Excerpted and adapted from "Pals, Parties, and Proms" by J. Keachie, 1997, *Impact, 3*(10), 19.

forth. Ecological assessments of the child's home environment may also be conducted. These assessments focus on the amount of support the primary caregiver can provide as well as the availability of other caregivers to assist. The purpose of this assessment is to identify areas in which the family may need assistance or additional information or training (Jarrett, 1991).

Early intervention usually combines direct training of the child with instruction of the primary caregiver(s) as to how to continue training at home. As in other areas of special education, specific goals with observable behavioral objectives are written to assess progress. Early intervention as a process has been found to be effective in alleviating or preventing many types of developmental obstacles. However, as indicated previously, early intervention is not always successful. Ramey and Ramey (1992) have provided some excellent guidelines for increasing the likelihood that early intervention programs will be successful. Six elements are identified: exploration, mentoring, celebration, rehearsal, protection, and language. Briefly explained, children are encouraged to be curious about their surroundings. An environment of acceptance, encouragement, and positive regard is fostered, with meaningful reinforcement provided by those who matter most to the child. Teaching consists not only of direct instruction but also adult mentorship and repetition. All of this is provided in a setting in which language is paramount. Children are surrounded by both written and spoken forms, and they are constantly encouraged to use language themselves.

Parent Training   Parent training is often provided as a part of early intervention services, but it may also be provided across the life span to assist parents in caring for their children. Parent training often begins before the child is even born. Topics during gestation generally focus on matters that pertain to the child's physical health and well-being, ranging from the mother's nutrition, to diaper changes, to environmental enrichment activities.

Once parents notice that their children are developing in an atypical manner, a different set of needs arises. The usefulness of diagnoses has been debated for years, but many parents describe feelings of worry and stress before they obtain a diagnosis. Once the diagnosis is obtained, the stressful wondering is often replaced by sadness or even grief. Parent training at this juncture is focused on acceptance, resolving guilt and negative thoughts, and/or alleviating depressive or anxious feelings. Several interventions have been shown to be helpful, especially cognitive-behavioral therapy (Floyd, Singer, Powers, & Costigan, 1996).

TABLE 6.5
Outcomes of Parent Training

1. Social validity: Do parents find the goals and the methods of the program worthwhile?
2. Enrollment: Do parents enroll in the program?
3. Completion: Do parents maintain good attendance?
4. Participation: Do parents become engaged in the program and carry out homework?
5. Consumer satisfaction: Do parents express satisfaction with the program?
6. Proficiency: Do parents learn what the program aims to teach?
7. Child gains: Do children show demonstrable gains?
8. Generalization of child gains: Do child gains generalize across settings? To nontargeted behaviors?
9. Maintenance of child gains: Do child gains last?
10. Maintenance of teaching: Do parents continue to put what they learned into practice at home months or years later?
11. Family benefits: Are there beneficial changes in the parents' well-being or in the family system?
12. Advocacy: Do parents become better advocates for their child's education?

Source: From *Parent Training and Developmental Disabilities* (p. 12) by B. L. Baker, 1989, Washington, DC: American Association on Mental Retardation. Copyright 1989 by the American Association on Mental Retardation. Reprinted with permission.

Obtaining a diagnosis of mental retardation is useless unless the question "Now what?" can be answered. Parent training can often be a partial answer to that question. There is no single formula for successful parent training. Like all other interventions described here, success depends on individual needs. Often parents simply need information about finances, service providers, advocacy, and other areas. This type of "parent training" can often be provided in a single session.

Other types of parent training focus on helping the parents help the child through direct instruction. The focus may be on teaching the child to acquire skills, or it may be on reducing problem behaviors. Like early intervention, the training may occur in the home or in a training center. Time-limited programs may focus on specific problems identified through individual assessment procedures (Baker, 1996). The success or failure of any parent training program is judged from outcomes. Some suggested outcomes are listed in Table 6.5.

A discussion of family interventions would not be complete without including person-centered planning. Many different definitions of person-centered planning can be found in the professional literature, but in its essence the term refers to a process of creating and developing goals for the future. Person-centered planning should be contrasted with service-centered planning. Service-centered plans list the services and supports available and attempt to determine whether a given individual needs them. Person-centered plans ask "What do you want?" and then identify the supports that are needed to get there.

Person-centered planning involves input from the people who care most about the individual of interest. In some cases, these people will speak for the individual, in whole or in part. Everyone involved in the person-centered planning process is there to propose solutions whereby the person can achieve important goals. Questions asked include not only "What do you want?" but "Where are you now?" "What are the obstacles to what you want?" and "How can those obstacles be overcome?"

Person-centered planning is described here as a psychosocial intervention because it has a special function as a method of encouraging self-determination. It was developed out of a concern that well-meaning service providers were inhibiting people in the name of protection. In keeping people safe, service providers have been guilty of taking away the rights of people and their families to take risks to attain their own life goals. Many of the psychosocial problems described earlier in this chapter relate directly to having external controls on their lives. Person-centered planning is meant to alleviate such problems (Abery & McBride, 1998).

Mental Health Interventions

Persons with mental retardation who have psychiatric or behavioral disorders present psychosocial challenges of a pressing nature. Much has been written, and many intervention techniques have been developed. In this section, we will discuss three approaches to treatment that have demonstrated efficacy: applied behavior analysis, psychotherapy, and psychopharmacology.

Applied Behavior Analysis   **Applied behavior analysis (ABA)** is the scientific study of environmental events that change behavior to solve human

problems. Diagnostic categories are irrelevant in ABA, because it focuses on specific, observable behaviors. When implemented correctly and consistently, it has been shown to be highly effective in solving a wide array of behavioral issues. The ABA approach generally consists of three stages: assessment, training, and maintenance. The assessment phase of ABA begins with a precise definition of the problem (or target) behavior. For example, "hyperactivity" would be more precisely defined in terms of the individual's behavior (e.g., leaving his or her seat; changing tasks within 5 minutes; running around the room). Once the behavior has been defined in measurable, observable terms, the functional assessment can begin.

Functional assessment is a procedure used to determine the purpose of a given behavior. Does the person leave his or her seat to escape tasks or to get the attention of the teacher or peers? The outcome of the functional assessment is very important, because the treatment will be based on these results. Misidentifying the function can lead to counterproductive treatments. Time-out is a good example. If a child is engaging in out-of-seat behavior because of a need for attention, then time-out is a good solution. But, if the child is engaging in out-of-seat behavior to escape a difficult learning task, then the intended isolation of time out may actually be preferable to staying with the more onerous learning task. In this particular case, time-out may not be a good solution at all because it achieves the child's objective of getting out of the learning the material (Carr & Wilder, 1997).

Once the function of a behavior has been identified, many behavioral treatments have been described and may be applied. Most treatments can be categorized into one of three types: noncontingent reinforcement, extinction, and differential reinforcement (Iwata, 2000). *Noncontingent reinforcement* involves allowing the person free access to the intended goal (the reinforcer), thereby making the inappropriate behavior unnecessary. *Extinction* involves blocking a person's access to the reinforcer when inappropriate behavior is demonstrated. *Differential reinforcement* involves blocking the person's access to the reinforcer when the misbehavior occurs but allowing him or her to access the reinforcer with a more appropriate behavior. These interventions require consistency in application across time, settings, and people.

After the person has learned the appropriate behavior and/or stopped exhibiting the inappropriate behavior, training should not just cease; a behavioral maintenance plan should be developed. During the training phase, the reinforcement schedule is usually continuous. That is, the person is given the reinforcer every time the desired behavior is observed, and the reinforcer is blocked every time the inappropriate behavior is observed. This method encourages the person to learn quickly. However, imagine what would happen if you learned your teacher would take away a difficult task every time you raised your hand. Most of us would raise our hands constantly.

To keep the person from resorting back to some inappropriate behavior, yet encourage his ability to function in "the real world," maintenance therapy focuses on decreasing the person's expectancy of always getting what is wanted. This is done by gradually increasing the amount of time the person must wait for reinforcement after displaying the appropriate behavior, while continuing to block reinforcement when the inappropriate behavior is displayed. However, timing is everything. This process will not be successful if conducted too soon or too quickly.

Cognitive-Behavioral Therapy   Several authors have noted that, although the behavioral orientation has dominated psychological services provided to persons with mental retardation, other formats may also be helpful. Cognitive-behavioral therapy, play therapy, and group therapy have all been described as having a place in the treatment of people with dual diagnoses (see Dosen & Petry, 1993; Jordan & Powell, 1996; Matson, 1982). However, little research is available to document the usefulness of such treatments with persons who have mental retardation. Cognitive-behavioral therapy (CBT) is the only one of these approaches recommended for use in AAMR's treatment guidelines (Rush & Frances, 2000).

CBT involves a combination of behavioral techniques with thought restructuring. Thought restructuring is conducted when a person's thoughts about a particular event create stress. Examples include negative ideas about one's own abilities and expectations of disastrous results. Some commonly used approaches to CBT include relaxation training, self-instruction, and visualization exercises.

CBT has been found somewhat useful in treating mood and anxiety disorders in persons with mild to moderate levels of mental retardation. This is one of its major uses among the general population, as well (Nathan, Gorman, & Salkind, 1999). When using CBT, or any other type of psychotherapy, therapists must adapt their sessions to the client's needs. Techniques must often be simplified, and repeated trials are necessary. The therapist should use clear, simple, concrete language, paying special attention to the person's ability to participate in activities that require skills such as reading and writing. It appears that individual success in psychotherapy is more related to the abilities of the therapist than to the abilities of the client (Hurley, Pfadt, Tomasulo, & Gardner, 1996).

Psychopharmacology   The final form of psychiatric treatment to be covered in this chapter is **psychopharmacology**, or the use of medications to treat psychiatric disorders. Psychopharmacology has a long and complicated history in the treatment of people with mental retardation. In less illustrious times, it was not unusual to find people with mental retardation continuously sedated so that problem behaviors could not occur. To prevent such misuses from occurring, strict regulations and treatment guidelines have been developed. Psychopharmacological interventions should be used to treat specific psychiatric or behavioral disorders, effectiveness should be documented, and the person should be monitored for side effects.

Psychopharmacology can be helpful in the treatment of many types of psychiatric disorders, whether a person has mental retardation or not (Nathan, Gorman, & Salkind, 1999). Stimulant medications such as Ritalin and Cylert can be useful in treating attention deficit–hyperactivity disorder; antidepressant medications such as Prozac and Zoloft can be helpful in treating eating disorders, sleep disorders, depressive disorders, and anxiety disorders. Antianxiety medications such as Valium and Ativan can be useful in treating sleep and anxiety disorders, and antipsychotic medications such as Risperdal and Zyprexa can be useful in treating bipolar disorder and schizophrenia. However, if misused, any and all of these medications can have negative effects.

The selection of appropriate psychopharmacological agents for persons with mental retardation is even more complicated than for the general population because it is sometimes difficult to ascertain whether behaviors seen are symptoms of a psychiatric disorder or simple developmental issues. Furthermore, as discussed earlier in this chapter, sometimes persons with mental retardation exhibit atypical signs of psychiatric disorders. To streamline the use of psychopharmacological agents, a consensus panel published best-practice guidelines, which list appropriate uses for specific agents as well as recommendations in dosage and duration of treatment (Reiss & Aman, 1998).

As with all medications, psychopharmacological agents have side effects, ranging from annoying to paralyzing to life-threatening. Some effects occur only temporarily, while others can last even after the medication is stopped. Therefore, it is very important that persons with mental retardation and their caregivers be provided with information about possible side effects before beginning treatment. This allows them to make an informed decision about beginning treatment and to monitor their well-being once treatment has begun.

Specialized Therapies

People who have speech and/or motor difficulties are likely to come into contact with a variety of professional therapists, including physical therapists, occupational therapists, and speech therapists. These therapies may be provided in home settings, center or clinical settings, or school settings. In this section, we will look at each of these types of specialized therapies in turn.

Physical Therapy   Physical therapy interventions are designed to treat problems related to gross-motor skills. Physical therapy is most often provided to infants or children who have nervous system impairments that impede their ability to acquire movements in the normal developmental sequence or to people who have lost movement abilities due to injury.

Physical therapists cannot begin treatment until a thorough assessment has been performed. Standardized tests are available that compare the child's motor development with the development of same-age peers. The therapist also observes the child in various positions and situations in order to observe both fine and gross motor movements. From this assessment, an individualized treatment plan will be developed, complete with goals and objectives to measure progress.

The treatment process usually consists of exercises to increase mobility conducted in therapy sessions. In working with children, therapy includes the use of a variety of toys and sensory stimuli that are both therapeutic and interesting for the child. To further encourage progress, the therapist will often assign homework between sessions or a home follow-up plan after the sessions have finished. Finally, the therapist may recommend specialized equipment such as braces, splints, shoe inserts, walkers, wheelchairs, or special seating to assist in mobility or posture.

The most direct outcome of physical therapy is increased mobility, but many indirect social consequences also ensue. With increased mobility comes greater functional independence. As the child becomes more independent and capable of a wider range of activities, opportunities for social interaction and integration increase, and from that comes opportunities for enhanced self-worth, self-esteem, and self-satisfaction.

Family stress may also be reduced when the child begins to mobilize with greater independence. Additionally, timely physical therapy services may prevent more invasive medical procedures later in life (Foltz, DeGangi, & Lewis, 1998; Kurtz & Harryman, 1997).

Occupational Therapy   Occupational therapy has much in common with physical therapy, in that it is concerned with movement and increasing functional independence. The difference is one of scope. Occupational therapy generally focuses on the development of fine motor skills and sensory processing. Table 6.6 lists some typical skills occupational therapists can help develop.

Like physical therapists, occupational therapists will begin with a thorough assessment. Standardized tests are administered in the areas of fine motor, perceptual, and oral-motor development. During the observational portion of the assessment, the therapist will observe the child's responses to various stimuli involving touch and movement. The primary caretaker may also be interviewed with regard to the child's self-care skills (Foltz et al., 1998).

The occupational therapist can be helpful in achieving a variety of goals, so there are several different approaches to treatment. Neurodevelopmental treatment

TABLE 6.6
Skills Developed through
Occupational Therapy

Skill areas	Example behaviors
Movement quality	Keeping head up Trunk and shoulder positioning
Basic hand skills	Holding Manipulating
Complex hand skills	Cutting Writing
Hand-eye coordination	Throwing Catching
Weight bearing	Crawling Reaching
Self-care skills	Dressing Grooming
Oral-motor skills	Chewing Swallowing
Perceptual skills	Puzzle completion Letter recognition
Sensory processing skills	Touching Acknowledging movements
Sensory integration	Balancing Planning movements
Nonverbal communication	Gesturing Responding

Source: Adapted from Foltz, DeGangi, and Lewis (1998).

(NDT) and sensory integration (SI) are two of the most commonly used approaches. NDT is based on the idea that motor skills evolve in a developmental sequence, and children must master early movements before they can move on to more controlled fine-motor skills. Therapy, therefore, consists of providing experiences that prevent abnormal movements while encouraging normal patterns of motion.

Sensory integration therapy is based on the idea of a normal developmental process by which people learn to process information received through the senses. When this process of development is interrupted, the child may have problems responding to new situations, developing more complex motor skills, mastering conceptual thinking, and regulating behavior. Treatment involves providing specific sensory experiences, such as manipulating items of different textures, balancing on balls, and navigating obstacle courses. By improving a person's ability to understand and interpret environmental stimuli, it is thought that various aspects of psychosocial functioning will improve (Kranowitz, 1998). However, few outcome data are currently available to assess results outside the therapy session.

Speech and Language Therapy   Speech and language therapy is designed to address and increase a person's ability to communicate effectively. Among persons with mental retardation, the speech language pathologist (SLP) can serve a variety of functions, from improving articulation to teaching forms of non-verbal communication.

Like the other therapists discussed in this chapter, the SLP begins with an assessment. This assessment will begin with a hearing evaluation conducted by an audiologist to rule out any hearing problems. After obtaining a thorough developmental history, the SLP will assess oral-motor skills and language skills. Oral-motor skills relate to the child's ability to physically produce speech. Breathing, jaw movement, lip usage, swallowing, saliva production, babbling, sound production, and sound quality are all assessed as oral-motor skills. In the language assessment, standardized assessment instruments are generally used. Expressive and receptive language are examined, as well as vocabulary, auditory processing, and pragmatic use of language (Foltz et al., 1998).

The assessment will indicate which of a variety of forms of treatment are most likely to be beneficial. Persons who have oral-motor skill deficiencies may be treated with direct therapy provided by the therapist. Sessions may be conducted in school or clinical settings, and the frequency will depend on the intensity of the child's needs. The therapist may also teach primary caregivers methods of massage or stimulation that will encourage skill development.

For children with language disorders, intervention methods will focus on the functional use of any of a variety of modes of communication. Children who use words ineffectively may be given direct instruction in problem areas, with opportunities for practice in natural settings. Children who use words infrequently may be encouraged to increase word production through behavioral teaching strategies. Still other children may be physically incapable of using speech, and may require training in some form of augmentative techniques, such as sign language or computer-assisted technology.

To check your understanding of this chapter, go to the companion website at http://www.prenhall.com/beirne-smith and select Chapter 6, then choose the Self-Test module.

Summary

Individual Aspects

- Persons with mental retardation have a wide range of personality character-istics, each of which may influence psychosocial functioning.
- Research indicates that persons with mental retardation may be at increased risk for certain types of psychiatric disorders.
- Persons who have additional developmental disabilities, such as epilepsy, cerebral palsy, or autism, may need additional supports to bolster their psychosocial functioning.

Environmental Aspects

- The family of origin has much influence on the psychosocial adjustment of a child with mental retardation.
- Most people with mental retardation today live in natural family homes and attend neighborhood schools.
- Lifestyle considerations such as alcohol and drug use, nutrition, exercise, and medical compliance are just as pressing for persons who have mental retardation as for the general population.

Interventions

- Many skills essential for social and emotional well-being can easily be incorporated into the educational curriculum.
- Families can be involved in many aspects of the intervention process, from assessment to education to implementation of specific intervention procedures.
- Among mental health interventions, research indicates that applied behavior analysis, cognitive-behavioral therapy, and psychopharmacology are the most useful approaches for use with persons who have mental retardation in addition to a mental health disorder.
- Specialized therapies such as physical therapy, occupational therapy, and speech and language therapy may have large, although often indirect, effects on psychosocial functioning.

References

Abery, B., & McBride, M. (1998). Look—and understand—before you leap. *Impact,* *11*(2), 2–3, 26.

Abery, B., Schoeller, K., Simunds, E., Gaylord, V., & Fahnestock, M. (1997). *Yes I can social inclusion.* Minneapolis: University of Minnesota, Institute on Community Integration, Research and Training Center on Community Living.

Allison, D. B., Packer-Munter, W., Pietrobelli, A., Alfonso, V. C., & Faith, M. S. (1998). Obesity and developmental disabilities: Pathogenesis and treatment. *Journal of Developmental and Physical Disabilities, 10*(3) 215–255.

American Psychiatric Association. (1994). *Diagnostic and statistical manual of mental disorders* (4th ed.). Washington, DC: Author.

Anderson, L., Lakin, K. C., Prouty, R. W., & Polister, B. (1999). Characteristics and movement of residents of large state facilities. In R. W. Prouty & K. C. Lakin (Eds.), *Residential services for persons with developmental disabilities: Status and trends through 1998* (pp. 55, 57). Minneapolis: University of Minnesota, Institute on Community Integration, Research and Training Center on Community Living.

Baker, B. L. (1996). Parent training. In J. W. Jacobson & J. A. Mulick (Eds.), *Manual of diagnosis and professional practice in mental retardation* (pp. 289–300). Washington, DC: American Psychiatric Association.

Baroff, G. S. (1991). *Developmental disabilities: Psychosocial aspects*. Austin, TX: Pro-ed.

Batshaw, M. L., & Shapiro, B. K. (1997). Mental retardation. In M. L. Batshaw (Ed.), *Children with disabilities* (4th ed., pp. 335–360). Baltimore: Brookes.

Blacher, J., & Baker, B.L. (1992). Toward meaningful family involvement in out-of-home placement settings. *Mental Retardation, 30,* 35–43.

Blacklin, J. S. (1991). Your child's development. In E. Geralis (Ed.), *Children with cerebral palsy: A parent's guide* (pp. 175–208). Bethesda, MD: Woodbine House.

Bromley, B. E., & Blacher, J. (1992). Parental reasons for out-of-home placement of children with severe handicaps. *Mental Retardation, 29,* 275–280.

Bybee, J., & Zigler, E. (1999). Outerdirectedness in individuals with and without mental retardation: A review. In E. Zigler & D. Bennett-Gates (Eds.), *Personality development in individuals with mental retardation* (pp. 165–205). Cambridge: Cambridge University Press.

Carr, J. E., & Wilder, D. A. (1997). *Functional assessment and intervention: An introduction to the assessment and intervention of problem behavior*. Reno, NV: High Tide.

Christian, L., & Poling, A. (1997). Drug abuse in persons with mental retardation: A review. *American Journal on Mental Retardation, 102*(2), 126–136.

Coffman, T. L., & Harris, M. C. (1980). Transition shock and adjustments of mentally retarded persons. *Mental Retardation, 18*(3), 28–32.

Cohen, D. E. (2000). Health promotion and disability prevention: The case for personal responsibility and independence. In M. L. Wehmeyer & J. R. Patton (Eds.), *Mental retardation in the 21st century* (pp. 251–264). Austin, TX: PRO-ED.

Costa, P. T., Jr., & McRae, R. R. (1986). Personality stability and its implications for clinical psychology. *Clinical Psychology Review, 6,* 406–423.

Cronin, M. E., & Patton, J. R. (1993). *Life skills instruction for all students with special needs: A practical guide for integrating real-life content into the curriculum*. Austin, TX: Pro-ed.

Dosen, A., & Petry, D. (1993). Treatment of depression in persons with mental retardation. In R. J. Fletcher & A. Dosen (Eds.), *Mental health aspects of mental retardation: Progress in assessment and treatment* (pp. 242–261). New York: Lexington.

Erikson, E. (1980). *Identity and the life cycle* (2nd ed.). New York: Norton.

Floyd, F. J., Singer, G. H. S., Powers, L. E., & Costigan, C. L. (1996). Families coping with mental retardation: Assessment and therapy. In J. W. Jacobson & J. A. Mulick (Eds.), *Manual of diagnosis and professional practice in mental retardation* (pp. 277–288). Washington, DC: American Psychiatric Association.

Foltz, L. C., DeGangi, G., & Lewis, D. (1998). Physical therapy, occupational therapy, and speech and language therapy. In E. Geralis (Ed.), *Children with cerebral palsy: A parent's guide* (pp. 251–252). Bethesda, MD: Woodbine House.

Freeman, J. M., Vining, E. P. G., & Pillas, D. J. (1997). *Seizures and epilepsy in childhood: A guide for parents* (2nd ed.). Baltimore: Johns Hopkins University Press.

Fujiura, G. T. (1998). Demography of family households. *American Journal of Mental Retardation, 103*(3), 225–235.

Gaylord, V., Abery, B., Dahl, L. A., & Chelberg, G. (1993/1994). *Impact: Feature Issue on Self-determination, 6*(4).

Gersh, E. S. (1998). What is cerebral palsy? In E. Geralis (Ed.), *Children with cerebral palsy: A parent's guide* (pp. 1-32). Bethesda, MD: Woodbine House.

Gillberg, C. (1999). Autism and spectrum disorders. In N. Bouras (Ed.), *Psychiatric and behavioural disorders in developmental disabilities and mental retardation.* Cambridge: Cambridge University Press.

Gray, D. E. (1998). *Autism and the family: Problems, prospects, and coping with the disorder.* Springfield, IL: Thomas.

Grossman, D. C. (1999). *Great issues for medicine in the twenty-first century: Ethical and social issues arising out of advances in the biomedical sciences.* New York: New York Academy of Sciences.

Heller, T. (1984). Issues in adjustment of mentally retarded individuals to residential relocation. In N. R. Ellis & N. W. Bray (Eds.), *International review of research in mental retardation* (Vol. 12, pp. 123–147). Orlando, FL: Academic Press.

Hill, B. K., & Bruininks, R. H. (1984). Maladaptive behaviors of mentally retarded individuals in residential facilities. *American Journal on Mental Deficiency, 88*(4), 380–387.

Hurley, A. D., Pfadt, A., Tomasulo, D., & Gardner, W. I. (1996). In J. W. Jacobson & J. A. Mulick (Eds.), *Manual of diagnosis and professional practice in mental retardation* (pp. 371–391). Washington, DC: American Psychiatric Association.

Iwata, B. A. (2000). *Functional analysis methodology for assessment and treatment of severe behavior disorders.* Unpublished manuscript, University of Florida at Gainesville.

Jarrett, M. H. (1991). Early intervention and special education. In E. Geralis (Ed.), *Children with cerebral palsy: A parent's guide* (pp. 261–296). Bethesda, MD: Woodbine House.

Jordan, R., & Powell, S. (1996). Encouraging flexibility in adults with autism. In H. Morgan (Ed.), *Adults with autism: A guide to theory and practice* (pp. 74–88). Cambridge: Cambridge University Press.

Kennedy, C. H., & Thompson, T. (2000). Health conditions contributing to problem behavior among people with mental retardation and developmental disabilities. In M. L. Wehmeyer and J. R. Patton (Eds.), *Mental retardation in the 21st century* (pp. 211–231). Austin, TX: Pro-ed.

Keyes, D. (1966). *Flowers for Algernon.* New York: Harcourt-Brace.

Khan, A. M., Cumella, S., Krishnan, V., Iqbal, M., Corbett, J., & Clarke, D. (1993). New long-stay patients at a mental handicap hospital. *Mental Handicap Research, 6*(2), 165–173.

Kranowitz, C. S. (1998). *The out-of-sync child: Recognizing and coping with sensory integration dysfunction.* New York: Berkeley.

Kurtz, L. A., & Harryman, S. E. (1997). Rehabilitation interventions: Physical therapy and occupational therapy. In M. L. Batshaw (Ed.), *Children with disabilities* (4th ed., pp. 709-726). Baltimore: Brookes.

Larson, S. A., Lakin, K. C., Anderson L., Kwak, N., Lee, J. H., & Anderson, D. (2000). Prevalence of mental retardation and/or developmental disabilities: Analysis of the 1994/1995 NHIS-D. *MR/DD Data Brief, 1*(2). Minneapolis: University of Minnesota, Institute on Community Integration, Research and Training Center on Community Living.

Levin, J., & Scherfenberg, L. (1990). *Selection and use of simple technology in home, school, work, and community settings*. Minneapolis, MN: AbleNet.

Lovell, R. W., & Reiss, A. L. (1993). Dual diagnoses: Psychiatric disorders in developmental disabilities. *Pediatric Clinics of North America, 40*(3), 579–592.

Matson, J. L. (1982). The treatment of behavioral characteristics of depression in the mentally retarded. *Behavior Therapy, 13*, 209–218.

McHugh, P. R., & Slavney, P. R. (1998). *The perspectives of psychiatry* (2nd ed.). Baltimore, MD: Johns Hopkins University Press.

McLaughlin, M. J., Warren, S. H., & Schofield, P. F. (1996). Creating inclusive schools: What does the research say? *Impact, 9*(2), 4–5.

Morgan, C. J., & Lowin, A. (1989). *A study of dually diagnosed psychiatric inpatients: Adults with developmental disabilities who were also psychiatric inpatients at state or community hospitals*. Olympia, WA: Washington State Department of Social and Health Services.

Myers, I. B., & McCaulley, M. H. (1985). *Manual: A guide to the development and use of the Myers-Briggs Type Indicator*. Palo Alto, CA: Consulting Psychologists Press.

Nathan, P. E., Gorman, J. M., & Salkind, N. J. (Eds.). (1999). *Treating mental disorders: A guide to what works*. New York: Oxford University Press.

Parsons, J. A., May, J. G., & Menolascino, F. J. (1984). The nature and incidence of mental illness in mentally retarded individuals. In F. J. Menolascino & J. A. Stark (Eds.), *Handbook of mental illness in the mentally retarded* (pp. 3–43). New York: Plenum.

Pellegrino, L. (1997). Cerebral palsy. In M. L. Batshaw (Ed.), *Children with disabilities* (4th ed., pp. 499–528). Baltimore: Brookes.

Ramey, C. T., & Ramey, S. L.(1992). Effective early intervention. *Mental Retardation, 30*(6), 337-345.

Reber, M., & Borcherding, B. G. (1997). Dual diagnosis: Mental retardation and psychiatric disorders. In M. L. Batshaw (Ed.), *Children with disabilities* (4th ed., pp. 405–424). Baltimore: Brookes.

Reid, A. (1993). Schizophrenic and paranoid syndromes in persons with mental retardation: Assessment and diagnosis. In R. J. Fletcher & A. Dosen (Eds.), *Mental health aspects of mental retardation: Progress in assessment and treatment* (pp. 98–110). New York: Lexington.

Reiss, S. (1994). Psychopathology in mental retardation. In N. Bouras (Ed.), *Mental health in mental retardation: Recent advances and practices* (pp. 67–78). Cambridge: Cambridge University Press.

Reiss, S., & Aman, M. G. (Eds.). (1998). *Psychotropic medications and developmental disabilities: The international consensus handbook*. Columbus: Ohio State University, Nisonger Center for Mental Retardation and Developmental Disabilities.

Reiss, S., McKinney, B. E., & Napolitan, J. T. (1990). Three new mental retardation service models: Implications for behavior modification. In J. L Matson (Ed.),

Handbook of behavior modification with the mentally retarded (2nd ed., pp. 51–70). New York: Plenum.

Riches, V. (1997). *Everyday social interaction: A program for people with disabilities* (2nd ed.). Baltimore: Brookes.

Rimmer, J. H. (2000). *Achieving a beneficial fitness: A program and a philosophy in mental retardation*. Washington, DC: American Association on Mental Retardation.

Robinson, E. G., & Rathbone, G. N. (1999). Impact of race, poverty, and ethnicity on services for persons with mental disabilities: Call for cultural competence. *Mental Retardation, 37*(4), 333–338.

Rush, A. J., & Frances, A. (Eds.).(2000). Treatment of psychiatric and behavioral problems in mental retardation. *American Journal on Mental Retardation, 105*(3).

Schacter, D. C., Pless, I. B., & Bruck, M. (1991). The prevalence and correlates of behaviour problems in learning disabled children. *Canadian Journal of Psychiatry, 36*, 323–331.

Skeels, H. M. (1966). Adult status of children with contrasting early life experiences. *Monographs of the Society for Research in Child Development, 31*.

Skeels, H. M., & Dye, H. B. (1939). A study of the effects of differential stimulation on mentally retarded children. *Convention Proceedings of the American Association on Mental Deficiency, 44*, 114–136.

Szymanski, L. S. (1994). Mental retardation and mental health: Concepts, aetiology, and incidence. In N. Bouras (Ed.), *Mental health in mental retardation: Recent advances and practices* (pp. 19–33). Cambridge: Cambridge University Press.

Trawick-Smith, J. (2000). *Early childhood development* (2nd ed.). Upper Saddle River, NJ: Merrill/Prentice Hall.

U.S. Department of Commerce. (1999). *Statistical abstract of the United States* (119th ed.). Washington, DC: U.S. Government Printing Office.

Visser, F. E., Aldenkamp, A. P., Van Huffelen, A. C., Kuilman, M., Overweg, J., & Van Wijk, J. (1997). Prospective study of the prevalence of Alzheimer-type dementia in institutionalized individuals with Down syndrome. *American Journal on Mental Retardation, 101*(4), 400–412.

Watson, A. L., Franklin, M. E., Ingram, M. A., & Ellenberg, L. B. (1998). Alcohol and other drug abuse among persons with disabilities. *Journal of Applied Rehabilitation Counseling, 29*(2), 22–29.

Weisz, J. R. (1999). Cognitive performance and learned helplessness in mentally retarded persons. In E. Zigler & D. Bennett-Gates (Eds.), *Personality development in individuals with mental retardation* (pp. 17–46). Cambridge: Cambridge University Press.

Zigler, E. (1999). The individual with mental retardation as a whole person. In E. Zigler & D. Bennett-Gates (Eds.), *Personality development in individuals with mental retardation* (pp. 1–16). Cambridge: Cambridge University Press.

Chapter

7

Characteristics of Individuals with Milder Forms of Mental Retardation

To review the chapter objectives on-line, go to the companion website at www.prenhall.com/ beirne-smith and select Chapter 7, then choose the Objectives module.

OBJECTIVES

After reading this chapter, the student should be able to

- discuss the general descriptors and caveats that apply to this group
- identify the demographic characteristics that describe this group
- discuss those characteristics that affect performance in school and community: motivation, sociobehavioral, learning, speech and language, and physical and health characteristics
- provide a description of educational placement, services received, and graduation rates

KEY TERMS

educable mental retardation (EMR)
grouping
learned helplessness

locus of control
mediation
trainable mental retardation (TMR)

The best way to gain an understanding of individuals who are mildly mentally retarded is to spend time with those so labeled. We recognize, however, that many students enrolled in an introductory course in mental retardation may not have this opportunity. With this in mind, we designed this chapter to give the reader an understanding of the characteristics of this group.

CHARACTERISTICS OF MILDER RETARDATION

To learn more about mild mental retardation, go to the companion website at www.prenhall.com/beirne-smith and select Chapter 7, then choose the Case Studies module.

By definition, individuals who are mentally retarded are distinguished from people who are not retarded on the basis of intellectual functioning and adaptive skills. Significantly subaverage intellectual functioning has traditionally been described along a continuum of mild, moderate, severe, and profound, according to the degree to which a person's measured general intelligence deviates from the normal range. The term *adaptive behavior* historically has been used to convey the nature of one's personal independence and social responsibility.

In both of these domains, the amount or degree of deficit is of prime importance. According to the manual on definition offered by the American Association on Mental Retardation (AAMR, 1992), importance is given to the interaction of (a) the individual's capabilities, (b) the various personal and social environments that one encounters on a daily or regular basis, and (c) the individual's actual functional performance. Based on this interaction, persons who are mentally retarded will display different needs and require varying levels of assistance across adaptive skills areas.

In this chapter, we examine the characteristics and needs of individuals who require little or no support systems in most adaptive skills areas. In the next chapter, we take a closer look at individuals who require more intensive levels of support.

The characteristic behaviors discussed in this section are frequently observed among people who have various levels of retardation at different stages of life. As previously mentioned, many factors influence individual functioning and behavior. Some of these variables are organic involvement, such disabling conditions as sensory or orthopedic impairments, problems relating to health, the nature of environmental demands, the family's concern and resources, the availability of services (both medical and educational), and the age at which the retardation was diagnosed and intervention was begun.

Individuals who are mildly retarded demonstrate adaptive behavior and intellectual functioning at the upper end of the retardation continuum. According to the most recent AAMR definition (1992), the assessed intellectual functioning of individuals who are retarded is an IQ standard score of approximately 70 to 75 or below, with concurrent deficits in adaptive skill areas.

Evidence suggests that the number of individuals who are mildly mentally retarded varies greatly from one locality to another. According to the *Twenty-first Annual Report to Congress on the Implementation of the Individuals with Disabilities Education Act* (U.S. Department of Education, 1999), the percentage of children who are mentally retarded, ages 6 to 17, served under IDEA Part B during the 1997–98 school year, ranged from a high of 2.77 in Alabama to lows of 0.30 in New Jersey and 0.20 in America Samoa. Although the number of school-age children with dis-

TABLE 7.1

Number of Children Ages 6 to 21 Served under IDEA, Part B, by Disability during the 1997–98 School Year

State	All disabilities	Specific learning disabilities	Speech or language impairments	Mental retardation	Emotional disturbance
Alabama	91,025	39.379	16,812	22,621	5,618
Alaska	16,005	9,586	3,357	755	827
Arizona	75,240	44,163	11,634	6.480	5,071
Arkansas	48,870	21,841	8,332	12,224	400
California	547,309	329,881	117,880	31,118	19,840
Colorado	65,734	33,764	11,521	3,220	8,497
Connecticut	69,532	34,930	12,201	4,101	8,752
Delaware	14,559	9,191	1,572	1,908	718
District of Columbia	7,292	4,210	366	1,184	1,079
Florida	307,149	147,557	72,270	36,935	35,608
Georgia	133,347	42,225	28,819	28,583	22,340
Hawaii	16,930	8,292	2,539	2,499	2,048
Idaho	22,824	13,566	3,550	2,709	627
Illinois	250,193	126,222	54,079	26,067	29,722
Indiana	129,584	55,129	35,370	21,216	9,857
Iowa	63,820	30,834	6,998	14,095	8,873
Kansas	50,027	21,560	11,128	5,697	4,766
Kentucky	71,242	21,954	18,515	18,120	5,285
Louisiana	84,690	37,715	16,751	12,927	5,914
Maine	30,086	13,100	7,067	1,211	4,258
Maryland	99,438	45,130	26,619	6,301	7,668
Massachusetts	148,364	90,785	22,676	14,435	12,733
Michigan	181,578	86,543	37,392	21,401	17,562
Minnesota	92,966	39,456	15,605	10,316	17,568
Mississippi	57,598	29,399	17,615	7,260	375
Missouri	119,545	64,154	24,620	12,747	9,540
Montana	17,016	9,574	3,396	1,165	1,105
Nebraska	37,691	15,965	9,181	5,944	2,873
Nevada	28,414	18,263	4,688	1,672	1,549
New Hampshire	24,676	12,530	5,169	983	2,148
New Jersey	189,219	105,557	47,457	4,631	12,499
New Mexico	45,349	27,368	8,544	2,142	3,454
New York	373,002	210,348	51,271	16,703	45,149

abilities served under IDEA has increased by 29.42% since 1988–89, there have been only moderate increases in the number of children categorized as mentally retarded. While the number of children with learning disabilities, ages 6 to 21, increased by 38.13%, for example, the number of children with mental retardation, ages 6 to 21, increased by only 4.64% (U.S. Department of Education, 1999) (see Tables 7.1 and 7.2).

Those who have studied the categorization of students who are mentally retarded (MacMillan & Borthwick, 1980; Polloway & Smith, 1983) have suggested that a "new" group of students is being identified as mildly mentally retarded and

TABLE 7.1 (continued)
Number of Children Ages 6 to 21 Served under IDEA, Part B, by Disability during the 1997–98 School Year

State	All disabilities	Specific learning disabilities	Speech or language impairments	Mental retardation	Emotional disturbance
North Carolina	142,628	61,465	27,277	27,466	9,710
North Dakota	11,738	5,692	3,212	1,250	808
Ohio	208,954	79,852	43,845	49,767	12,950
Oklahoma	71,735	39,555	14,109	9,598	3,278
Oregon	61,346	32,446	13,993	3,956	3,880
Pennsylvania	202,665	106,908	38,590	27,496	18,702
Puerto Rico	45,466	21,567	5,033	13,467	818
Rhode Island	24,971	14,843	4,515	1,132	2,222
South Carolina	84,223	37,011	19,172	17,428	5,701
South Dakota	13,245	6,747	3,233	1,478	517
Tennessee	119,077	58,481	25,353	16,099	3,457
Texas	443,341	265,049	67,693	24,688	35,480
Utah	49,326	28,737	8,480	3,411	4,470
Vermont	11,000	4,522	1,769	1,328	1,710
Virginia	134,902	66,423	24,595	14,434	12,206
Washington	98,535	46,861	16,374	7,587	5,126
West Virginia	43,482	19,613	10,744	8,565	2,082
Wisconsin	100,027	46,651	17,261	12,917	16,006
Wyoming	11,508	5,903	2,832	674	917
American Samoa	394	303	17	35	3
Guam	1,808	1,380	150	102	11
Northern Marianas	330	202	9	39	6
Palau	96	75	4	6	2
Virgin Islands	1,833	739	281	589	54
Bur. of Indian Affairs	8,348	4,850	1,646	526	755
U.S. and outlying areas	5,401,292	2,756,046	1,067,181	603,408	455,194
50 states, D.C. & P.R.	5,388,483	2,748,497	1,065,074	602,111	454,363

Please see data notes for an explanation of individual state differences.

Developmental delay is applicable only to children 3 through 9.

Data based on the December 1, 1997 count, updated as of September 1, 1998.

Source: From U.S. Department of Education, Office of Special Education Programs, Data Analysis System (DANS).

that people now classified in this group are lower functioning than those called "mildly mentally retarded" in previous decades. For this reason, it is not advisable to compare research results of ten or more years ago with more recent findings, as the subjects are likely to differ in many important independent variables. Similarly, many conclusions made about the "traditional" group may not hold for this "new" group of students.

While the slower rate at which children who are retarded develop motor, social, and language skills may differ noticeably from their peers, milder forms of retardation have not often been suspected until the children enter school. Frequently, a combination of difficulty with academic subjects and behavioral problems generates concern. Learning problems sometimes appear to be specific to one subject, such as reading, but more often they are recognized across subjects.

Children who do not have the verbal and communication skills of their age mates may withdraw from interpersonal relationships or seek attention in inappropriate ways. Inappropriate social behavior can result from any number of factors. These children may misbehave because they cannot clearly distinguish between acceptable and unacceptable standards of behavior. Problem behavior can also result from the frustrations of scholastic failure or as an attempt to gain acceptance from other children, who might encourage deviant behavior.

Some individuals who are retarded also have significant psychiatric disorders, resulting in a dual diagnosis. Reber (1992) remarks that a higher prevalence of these problems occurs with children who are mentally retarded than with those who are not retarded. We present a more detailed discussion of this topic later in the chapter.

TABLE 7.2

Percentage Change in the Number of Children with Disabilities Served by Disability and Age Group, 1988–89 through 1997-98

Disability	Age groups			
	6–11	12–17	18–21	6–21
Specific learning disabilities	30.96	44.12	36.81	38.13
Speech/language impairments	10.44	13.06	-20.23	10.54
Mental retardation	11.16	5.65	17.01	4.64
Emotional disturbance	14.39	26.54	23.16	21.97
Multiple disabilities	23.2	35.48	17.57	26.93
Hearing impairments	18.67	30.08	-.23	21.98
Orthopedic impairments	45.63	49.29	.80	43.03
Other health impairments	308.46	286.01	69.25	279.87
Visual impairments	13.92	19.06	11.67	16.07
Autism[*]	206.52	149.79	67.29	172.86
Deaf-blindness	-12.67	29.33	-31.99	-2.07
Traumatic brain injury[*]	200.27	227.93	120.36	200.86
All disabilities	24.31	37.58	15.85	29.42
Number of children with disabilities 1988–89	2,185,507	1,754,729	233,276	4,173,512
Number of children with disabilities 1997–98	2,716,854	2,414,187	270,251	5,401,292

[*]Reporting of autism and traumatic brain injury was first required for 1992–93. The percentage change for these two categories reflects changes in the 6 years since 1992–93.

Note: Developmental delay is not reflected in this table because1997–98 was the first year states could use this category.

Source: From U.S. Department of Education, Office of Special Education Programs, Data Analysis System (DANS).

Although by definition, individuals who are retarded are different, they have the same needs as individuals who are not retarded.

A number of terms have been used to describe individuals who have been identified formally as mentally retarded and subsequently provided with special education and related services. Even though the use of traditional labels for levels of retardation (mild, moderate, severe, and profound) is discouraged in the latest AAMR manual on definition, classification, and systems of supports, it is likely that many existing terms will continue to be used. This will happen because many states and provinces have established certain terminology, and it will take some time for this to change, even given the desire to do so.

For a complete on-line glossary of mental retardation terms, go to the companion website www.prenhall.com/beirne-smith and select any chapter, then choose the Glossary module.

Two terms that have a long history of usage in school settings are **educable mental retardation (EMR)** and **trainable mental retardation (TMR).** Lately, these terms have fallen into disfavor with most professionals in the field; however, they are still used in certain locations. The term *EMR* referred to students whose abilities were adequate for them to profit from an academically oriented curriculum; *TMR* referred to students whose programs emphasized the "training" of basic functional skills (e.g., self-help skills). The underlying thinking associated with these terms and the programmatic decisions based on them have changed dramatically in recent years. As a result, their usage has declined drastically as well.

Although some data support the contention that individuals who are mildly retarded display more secondary problems than the population as a whole (Barlow & Durand, 1995; Borthwick-Duffy, & Eyman, 1990), the vast majority of these individuals can lead satisfying and productive lives. Adults who are mildly mentally retarded are capable of securing and maintaining employment and becoming economically self-sufficient. However, adult outcome data (e.g., the large amount of unemployment and underemployment) provide a chilling realization that much work must still be done. With increased knowledge about how individuals who are retarded learn, and with more effective methodology for improving their performance, we should be able to provide even better programs, sensitive to both current and future needs.

DEMOGRAPHIC CHARACTERISTICS

Information about the characteristics and background of a given population enables us better to understand, prepare for, and serve the needs of that group. For two reasons, the following discussion focuses primarily on the demographics of individuals who are mildly mentally retarded. First, this segment of the population appears to have changed the most in the past few years. Second, individuals who need more intensive systems of support are generally not overrepresented in any given socioeconomic or racial group; they are fairly evenly distributed throughout the general population.

Gender

More boys than girls are labeled "mentally retarded." In Dunn's (1973) review of the literature on persons who are mildly retarded and his subsequent description of that population, he states that students labeled EMR were more likely to be male. This apparently still holds true, if figures in recent studies characterizing individuals who are mildly retarded are indicative of the population as a whole (Epstein, Polloway, Patton, & Foley, 1989; Larson, Lakin, Anderson, Kwak, Lee, & Anderson, 2000; Polloway, Epstein, Patton, Cullinan, & Luebke, 1986; Wagner, Newman, & Shaver, 1989).

Reasons given for a preponderance of males include greater role expectations placed on males; aggressive behavior more often exhibited by males, leading to referral and subsequent labeling; and a higher probability of such biological factors as gender-linked influences affecting male children. A possibility also exists that gender bias in the diagnostic/classification process may affect disproportionately the number of males categorized as mentally retarded (U.S. Department of Education, 1996).

Ethnicity

Reviewers of demographic data historically have reported a disproportionate number of racial and ethnic minority children being labeled as mildly mentally retarded (Doll, 1962; Dunn, 1973; Epstein et al., 1989; Manni, Winikur, & Keller, 1980; Polloway et al., 1986). During the 1960s, 1970s, and 1980s, the racial imbalance in the makeup of EMR classes became the focus of much litigation, which in part led to changes in the procedures for identifying and labeling children as mentally retarded. But even with definitional changes and more stringent identification procedures, the same trend continues in evidence today.

According to recent studies (Larson et al., 2000; Oswald, Coutinho, Best, & Singh, 1999), the percentage of African American students placed in special education programs is high relative to the percentage of these students in the general school population. In some disability categories and in some states, Hispanic students are over- and underrepresented relative to their proportion of the total school population. The disproportionate representation of African American students in special education programs, in part, may be attributed to relatively low income and the disabilities associated with poverty; such school-related factors as ambiguity and subjectivity in the assessment, referral, and placement processes; and variability in counting, analyzing, and reporting procedures. When all these variables are accounted for, however, a disproportionate representation of African American students still remains in programs for students who are mentally retarded.

Socioeconomic and Family Patterns

Information available on secondary school–level youth who are disabled (U.S. Department of Commerce, 1999) indicates that these youth, when compared to the general population of youth, are more likely to

- live in single-parent families,
- come from families characterized by lower socioeconomic status, and
- live in a family that has a lower household income.

The implication drawn from this information is that these factors may affect the educational performance, physical and health status, and adult outcomes of these youth. It is also important to recognize that these findings are related to all youth with disabilities—not just those who are mentally retarded.

Environmental deprivation as a variable in the etiology of mental retardation is recognized by the AAMR in its inclusion of "psychosocial disadvantage" as an etiological classification. The description associated with this category implies that individuals experience impoverished environmental conditions involving poor housing, inadequate nutrition, and inadequate medical care. In at least one study describing this population (Epstein et al., 1989), factors sometimes associated with low socioeconomic status, such as a preponderance of single-parent homes, children raised by people other than their natural parents, and family involvement with one or more community agencies for support services, have been substantiated as contributing elements.

The higher prevalence of milder forms of mental retardation among low-income families has been acknowledged for some time (Westling, 1986). This disproportionate representation, however, appears to be almost entirely limited to those needing less intensive systems of supports. Socioeconomic conditions do not appear to affect the prevalence of those with more extensive and intensive needs (MacMillan & Reschly, 1998).

MOTIVATIONAL AND SOCIOBEHAVIORAL CHARACTERISTICS

Children who are mentally retarded have the same basic physiological, social, and emotional needs as children who are not. Because of their experiences in dealing with environments in which they are less able to display appropriate adaptive skills, however, they often develop patterns of behavior that serve further to distinguish them from those who are not retarded. For example, members of this group show a higher prevalence of emotional and behavioral problems (Barlow & Durand, 1995; Fraser & Rao, 1991, Lovell & Reiss, 1993). The motivational and behavioral characteristics presented in this section are generalizations supported by studies of groups of people who are retarded. Because individuals are unique, and there is at least as much variability among those who are retarded as among persons who are not retarded, the following generalizations will not fit every individual.

Motivational

Many early investigations came from research in the field of social learning theory and concentrated on distinctions between individuals who were mildly retarded and those who were not retarded. This discussion, however, has relevance for those with slightly more intensive needs as well.

External Locus of Control   Locus of control refers to how one perceives the consequences of one's behavior. Individuals who operate primarily from an internal locus of control see events—both positive and negative—as results of their own actions. Those who see positive and negative events as primarily controlled by such outside forces as fate, chance, or other people have an external locus of control.

Young children tend to be externally oriented, perceiving many circumstances and events in their lives as being beyond their control. As children mature, however, they become more aware of the influence of their own actions. As a result, they gradually shift to a more internal locus of control, although this is not as true of students with mild disabilities. Students who are mildly retarded tend to remain more externally oriented than do their peers who are not disabled and thus demonstrate less adaptive capabilities as adolescents and adults (Wehmeyer, 1994). External control, therefore, is considered a more debilitating orientation, as it keeps individuals from accepting responsibility for their own successes and failures and from developing self-reliance and self-regulatory behaviors. Wehmeyer, Palmer, Agran, Mithaug, and Martin (2000) have stated that skill in self-determination, the ability to act instead of being acted upon, is critical for students to achieve positive adult outcomes.

Learned helplessness is another term sometimes used to reflect the belief that failure will crown even the most extraordinary efforts (Stipek, 1993). Seligman (1975), who originated the concept of learned helplessness, notes that the phenomenon occurs when individuals perceive that events cannot be controlled by their actions. In school settings, for example, learners believe that regardless of the quality or quantity of their response, the outcome will be negative.

Expectancy of Failure   *Expectancy* refers to the reinforcement that is anticipated as a result of a given behavior. Rotter (1954) postulated two types of expectancies. The first is the expectation of a particular type of reinforcement, such as a tangible reward or social approval. The second involves expectations generalized from the results of past experiences with particular types of problem-solving activities. In other words, new situations are approached with either the expectation of success or the expectation of failure, based on what the individual has experienced in the past.

Studies by Cromwell (1963), Cummins and Das (1980), and Schloss, Alper, and Jayne (1994) involving subjects who were retarded found them to have a high expectancy of failure. Zigler (1973) and Balla and Zigler (1979) note that an individual who has accumulated experiences of failure sets lower aspirations and goals in an effort to avoid additional disappointment. Heber (1964) points out that this fear of failure may become circular: The expectation of lack of success lowers the amount of effort put into a task, performance of the task is thus below what might be anticipated from the individual's capabilities, and the expected failure becomes a reality.

Those working with individuals who demonstrate the debilitating attitude of expecting to fail must create situations that encourage and reward effort. It is important for these individuals to experience success and to recognize it when it occurs. However, it is equally important to teach them how to deal with failure and how to persevere.

Outerdirectedness   Another result of attempts to avoid failure is a style of problem-solving called *outerdirectedness.* Instead of being self-reliant in problem solving, the outerdirected individual relies on situational or external cues for guidance (Bybee & Zigler, 1992).

While this type of behavior is certainly not limited to those who are retarded, Zigler (1999) suggests that it prevails among this group because they have learned to distrust their own abilities, again because of the frequency with which they have failed in the past. Efficient problem solving necessarily involves using both external cues and one's own cognitive resources. The use of external cues may be an appropriate adaptation to one's limitations (Bybee & Zigler, 1992). However, relying too heavily on external cues could result in a dependence on them, even for a task well within one's own capabilities (Balla & Zigler, 1979).

In the three motivational orientations discussed (locus of control, expectancy for failure, and outerdirectedness), one recurring factor is the detrimental effect of repeated failures. Perhaps the most important implication for those working in the field, then, is the necessity of providing children who are retarded with tasks at which they can succeed. This holds true for both social and academic settings. Allowing the child to be successful is an invaluable motivational tool. Yet all children, disabled and otherwise, need to learn to deal with failure as well. A sensitive teacher can shape classroom experiences in such a way that the child gains enough self-confidence through repeated successes to be able to rebound from an occasional inevitable failure. Parents and teachers need to be sensitive to their own expectations for the child, so that they do not inadvertently reinforce the child's negative expectations. They must take care to avoid conveying the idea that they think the child is not competent to handle simple tasks. Rather, parents and teachers should require all children to assume the responsibilities that are within their grasp, make it clear to them exactly what is expected of them, and allow them the opportunities to try.

Other ways to increase the chances of success are setting specific, realistic goals, providing immediate feedback for specific behavior, and rewarding accomplishments. If the child has repeatedly failed at a certain task, the situation should

Positive Supports

A Definition of Positive Supports

Positive supports are actions and beliefs that reflect respectful interpersonal relationships, choice, communication, inclusive communities, and self-determination to assist a person to become a more independent, contributing member of the community. They encompass a variety of strategies that are considered unconditionally for a person who may be exhibiting behaviors that challenge family members, educational staff, service providers, and/or the community. People also require positive supports during other times in their lives. A committed group of diverse people collaborate to identify, develop, and secure the needed supports, while acknowledging a person's individuality. Positive supports recognize people's rights to make informed choices, take risks, and contribute in the decision-making process.

Foundations of Positive Supports

- Community
- Being heard
- Individualized supports
- Ongoing support
- Enhanced quality of life

Core Elements of Positive Support

- Active member of an inclusive community
- Person-centered planning
- Communication
- Choice
- Friendship
- Collaborative team
- Control resides with person
- Support during crises
- Teaching/building competencies

Positive Supports Questions to Ask

Is the support you provide to individuals with disabilities positive in its approach? Take a moment to answer the questions below to find out.

1. Does the person have the opportunity to make informed choices that impact his/her life (e.g., real life choices such as who, or what agency will provide support, hiring and firing staff, where to live/work, and what/how much to eat)?

2. Does the person have a way to communicate his/her needs and wants throughout the entire day?
3. Does the person have reciprocal relationships in his/her life? (While paid staff at times develop reciprocal relationships with a person, these paid relationships should not be the only ones a person has.)
4. Is the person an active member of the community, participating in events of his/her choice on an individual basis? (This does not include activities designed exclusively for individuals with disabilities.)
5. Is person-centered planning used to identify supports based upon the person's dreams, goals, strengths, and needs ensuring that the supports are unique to him/her?
6. Do supporters reevaluate what is needed when identified supports do not appear beneficial?
7. Do supporters listen to and acknowledge the concerns and requests that a person may have no matter how he/she makes that request (e.g., talking, use of behavior)?
8. Do supporters acknowledge that their own values, behavior, and needs may influence their interactions with and the behavior of others?
9. Do supporters respect the person's right to take risks after he/she has obtained relevant information and the support needed to evaluate the information?
10. Does the person advocate for him- herself to determine his/her own life?
11. Are identified supports flexible to meet the everchanging needs a person may have?
12. Do we recognize and accept the diversity of the people we work with and support?

Source: From "Positive Supports" and "Positive Supports Questions to Ask," 1996, *Centerpoint, 1*(2), pp. 3-4. Copyright 1996 by the Center for Community Inclusion, University of Maine at Orono. Reprinted by permission.

be restructured to present a novel approach that makes success possible. Finally, although it is desirable to help children who are retarded become more inner-directed and self-reliant, their tendency to rely heavily on external cues should be used to advantage. Teachers and parents should provide appropriate behavior models for children.

Self-Regulatory Behaviors

Ultimately, we would like all individuals to exert control over their lives. For them to do so, it is essential that they develop self-regulation of many behaviors across different settings and maintain the behaviors over time. Despite the desirability of developing self-regulation in persons with mental retardation, Whitman (1990) warns that they are likely to be delayed in acquiring this skill. This admonition is based on the fact that self-regulation is a linguistically guided process, and this group displays linguistic limitations. Nevertheless, the goal of developing self-regulatory behaviors is warranted and attainable. A strong rationale for achieving self-regulation with persons who are mentally retarded is offered by Whitman (1990):

> By exercising self-control, persons with retardation can increase the probability that they will act effectively without external direction, maintain what they have learned, and generalize learned responses to situations where training contingencies have not been applied. Moreover, by self-regulation of their behavior, they are more likely to be able to live in more normalized settings where close supervision is not possible. Finally, because independent action is valued by our society, individuals with retardation who become more autonomous are also more likely to be reacted to more positively by others, which in turn will increase their feeling of self-efficacy. (p. 348)

Sociobehavioral

Children and adolescents who are more severely mentally retarded historically have been described as displaying more social and behavioral problems than their peers who are not disabled (Lovell & Reiss, 1993). According to Guralnick and Weinhouse (1984), in play settings, for example, young children who are severely developmentally delayed interact less frequently with their peers and engage more frequently in solitary or unoccupied activities. Similarly, in work settings, adults who are more severely retarded demonstrate difficulty in accepting criticism, resolving conflicts, following instructions, and engaging in conversation (Sherman, Sheldon, Harchik, Edwards, & Quinn, 1992). Studies focusing on students who are mildly retarded confirm similar problems in this population as well (Epstein, Cullinan, & Polloway, 1986; Polloway et al., 1985; Russell & Forness, 1985). Some of the specific problem areas include disruptiveness, attention deficits, low self-esteem (Polloway et al., 1985), overactivity (Polloway et al., 1986), distractibility and other attention-related problems (Epstein et al., 1989), and difficulty in interpersonal cognitive problem solving (Healey & Masterpasqua, 1992).

Individuals whose needs for supports are minimal often have difficulty in establishing and maintaining interpersonal relationships. They may, for example, have trouble developing close personal friends, as evidence has indicated that they are more often rejected than accepted by their peers (Polloway et al., 1986). This frequency of rejection is associated with the degree of inappropriateness of behavior they display. Furthermore, inappropriate behavior and peer rejection may be apparent as early as preschool. Kopp, Baker, and Brown (1992), for example, found that preschoolers who were developmentally delayed demonstrated less positive affect and more disruptive and regressive behaviors that interrupted play than did their peers who were not developmentally delayed. Findings from such studies as these have important implications for the social acceptance and subsequent friendship formation of these students.

Some educators have implied that the lower the intellectual level, the more pronounced the behavioral deviations. This suggests that individuals with greater needs for supports would exhibit more behavioral problems than those with fewer needs for supports. There does appear to be a higher incidence of behavioral and psychiatric disorders in individuals referred to as moderately retarded (Lovell & Reiss, 1993). A wide range of behaviors may be evidenced in such individuals, including distractibility, hyperactivity, mood disturbances, and stereotypical behaviors. Health-related problems as well as the effects of medication may affect attention and concentration, leading both to a slower, more limited acquisition of social skills and to an increase in inappropriate behaviors.

A growing area of concern focuses on the mental health needs of individuals who are retarded. The extent of the problem is evidenced in data reported by

TABLE 7.3
Psychiatric Conditions That Accompany Dual Diagnosis

Psychiatric disorders

Bipolar disorders (e.g., mania and depression)

Schizophrenia

Major depression with psychotic features

Obsessive-compulsive disorders

Delirium and dementia

Attention deficit hyperactivity disorder

Anxiety disorders

Psychoactive substance use disorders

Genetic syndromes associated with mental retardation and abnormal behavior

Fragile X syndrome

Rett syndrome

Prader-Willi syndrome

Lesch-Nyhan syndrome

Source: Reber (1992).

Borthwick-Duffy and Eyman (1990) showing that approximately 10% of the clients served by the state of California have been dually diagnosed (i.e., given both a mental retardation and a psychiatric diagnosis). There are numerous patterns of behavior that might result in a dual diagnosis. Table 7.3 provides some examples of psychiatric disorders that some individuals with milder forms of mental retardation might display, based on a discussion by Reber (1992).

Because being able to meet more normal behavioral expectations is often a consideration in the decision to integrate special students into general education programs, social skill problems may contribute to more restrictive placements. Also, a great many variables influence the learning process. Better social, motivational, and behavioral adjustment is likely to relate to better academic functioning. Another major consideration is that successful adult adjustment requires competence in many social and behavioral areas (Cronin & Patton, 1993). Curricular attention to this area would enable a more successful integration into community life.

Further implications extend into higher education, where professionals are trained to work with exceptional students. In the area of mental retardation, teachers need to prepare themselves for a diversity of social and behavioral problems and receive training in appropriate intervention and management techniques for dealing with them (Epstein et al., 1986). Training is also needed in ways to incorporate social skills into the curriculum and in methods and materials by which such skills may be taught.

LEARNING CHARACTERISTICS

We may think of learning as the process whereby practice or experience produces a change in behavior that is not due to maturation, growth, or aging. The definition implies (a) that the changed behavior is relatively permanent, as distinguished from responses to, for example, drugs or fatigue; and (b) that the learner is involved and participating, not just changing because of physical growth or deterioration.

Learning is a hypothetical construct and, as such, cannot be measured directly. How much or how little learning has actually taken place can be inferred only from performance. If a student points to the object that the teacher has just named or spells a word correctly, we assume that learning has taken place. If the student performs the task incorrectly or does not attempt the task at all, we assume that learning has not occurred. Since learning can be measured only indirectly, we must be cautious in interpreting performance levels as direct indicators of learning. A great many factors influence whether and how a pupil responds in any given situation.

We have implied that physical maturity can result in behavioral changes. The development of such motor skills as walking appears not to be influenced by training or experience until the child has the necessary physical maturity. Delayed development, however, is a characteristic of people who are retarded, and the degree of delay is generally related to the severity of the retardation and the presence of other inhibiting conditions. People who expect a person with disabilities to acquire skills at the normal rate may end up frustrated and may fail in their attempts to teach new skills. Training and practice will not supplant the maturation process, but studies of infant stimulation provide enough encouragement to justify training and practice to enhance development.

*The degree of delayed develop-
ment is generally related to the
severity of the retardation and
the presence of other inhibiting
conditions.*

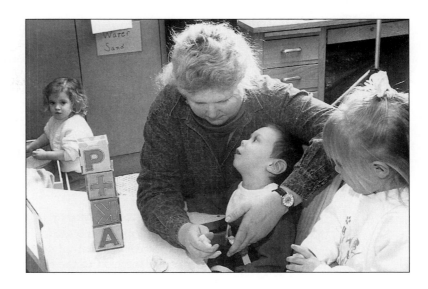

Cognitive Development

Quantitative versus Qualitative Perspectives   Use of the concept of
mental age (MA) to express the level of cognitive functioning of a given individual
has given rise to differing orientations from which to view the cognitive development of persons who are retarded. For example, cognitive development may be
viewed as quantitative and comparable among individuals of similar MA, regardless
of chronological age. This perspective, the developmental position, assumes that
cognitive development, at least for the youngster who is mildly retarded, is similar
to that of a younger child who is not retarded. According to Kail (1992), Tomporowski and Tinsley (1994), and Zigler (1999), such children progress through the
same developmental levels in the same sequence as do children who are not
retarded, although at a slower rate and lower level of ultimate functioning.

Proponents of this point of view believe that children who are retarded fail
because they are presented with tasks beyond their current ability level. Educational programs based on a developmental model would, therefore, use traditional
teaching strategies but be geared primarily to the individual's MA. The developmental view of cognitive growth can be thought of as a series of steps or stages in
which new tasks are presented only when the child reaches the level of mental ability appropriate to that task.

Proponents of the difference position, however, view the cognitive development of persons who are retarded as being qualitatively different from that of
those who are not retarded. Ellis and Dulaney (1991) contend that there are differences in the ways in which this group processes information and that the main
task of research is to describe these areas of difference. The implications for teaching are that unique teaching methods and materials are needed to overcome or
lessen the effects of the deficiency.

Research favoring one orientation over the other is plentiful. Firm conclusions, however, are difficult to reach because of the many variables that affect cognitive development (e.g., etiology of the retardation, motivational differences, problems associated with matching individuals based on MA). Regardless of one's position on this issue, the research in this area adds to our larger understanding of the learning process of individuals who are retarded.

Since much of the developmentally oriented research is based on Piaget's theory of carefully sequenced stages of development, we briefly present this theory along with its application for learners who are retarded. In this section, we describe some learning processes where distinctions between learners who are retarded and learners who are not have been noted.

Cognitive-Developmental Theory   The original tenets of cognitive-developmental theory were formulated by Jean Piaget, based on observations of his own ("normal") children. He viewed mental development as a result of the continuous interaction with and adaptation to the environment, or the child's perception of it. According to Piaget (1969), each child progresses through stages of development in which various cognitive skills are acquired. The main stages of development, along with approximate age norms, are

1. Sensorimotor stage—birth to 2 years
2. Preoperational stage—2 to 7 years
3. Concrete operations—7 to 11 years
4. Formal, or abstract, operations—11 years and older

The sensorimotor stage is characterized by sensory experiences and motor activity. As young children become more aware of the surrounding environment, they begin to distinguish between themselves and other persons and objects. The second stage, preoperational, involves more than purely physical operations. Children begin to use symbols for the people and objects around them, assimilate customs, and acquire new experiences by imitating the actions of others. During the concrete operations stage, children develop further abilities to order and classify objects. Although mental operations are more highly developed, children are usually limited to solving problems with which they have had direct or concrete experience. The ability to perform abstract thinking and reason by hypothesis is said to develop around the age of 11 or 12 and characterizes the formal operations, or abstract, stage.

Piagetian theory has been related to children who are mentally retarded by Inhelder (1968) and Woodward (1963, 1979), who view the child who is retarded as progressing through the same stages of cognitive development as peers who are not retarded, with the major differences being in rate and highest level achieved. The age at which a child who is retarded will reach each stage will be later, and the more severe the retardation, the slower the progression through the stages. In addition, individuals who are mentally retarded may not achieve all stages of development. According to Inhelder, children who are mildly mentally retarded may reach the concrete operations level, but individuals who have been called moderately retarded will go no further than the preoperational stage. Those who are severely or profoundly retarded will remain at the sensorimotor level.

According to Piagetian theory, mental development progresses as a result of children's interactions with their surroundings. The educator's role, therefore, is that of a provider of materials and opportunities appropriate to children's stage of development, with which they can interact. Teachers of students who are retarded need to be aware of the developmental sequences to determine a child's readiness for a particular task and to consider the slow rate and the expected optimal level of functioning when planning curricula for children with varying levels of retardation.

Processes Involved in Learning

Individuals who are mentally retarded, by definition, perform below average on tests of intelligence and are slow and inefficient learners. Whether one subscribes to the developmental or difference model of the cognitive functioning of people who are retarded, the practical issue of providing an optimum learning environment remains. Toward this end, a vast amount of research has been conducted in the area of learning and applied to individuals who are retarded. Most researchers have concentrated their efforts on one aspect of learning, such as attention or memory. In generalizing the findings to educational programming, however, we must emphasize that implications from various theories relating to separate aspects of learning should be used in combination to offer learners who are retarded the best opportunities for realizing their potential.

To learn more about teaching and learning processes, go to the companion website at www.prenhall.com/beirne-smith and select Chapter 7, then choose the Article Response module.

The major processes that are discussed in this section include attention variables, mediational strategies, memory, and transfer/generalization. Table 7.4 summarizes the major features of each of these along with select references that are associated with each process. The discussion that follows details some of the seminal research in these areas.

Attention Variables   In any learning situation, attention to the task at hand is critical for successful learning. Zeaman and House (1963) did much of the early work in the area of attention. Their experiments involved two-choice visual discrimination tasks in which subjects were rewarded for choosing the dimension (color, shape, size) that the investigator had previously selected as the correct choice. Responses were recorded and translated into learning curves or graphs illustrating the percentage of correct responses upon each trial. Analysis of the curves revealed that learning the discrimination tasks had two stages. In the first, subjects responded correctly about 50% of the time, or at about chance level. During the second stage, however, correct responses increased dramatically, resulting in a sharp rise on the learning curve. Zeaman and House have suggested that the first stage is an attention phase, where the subject randomly attends to various aspects of the task. Once the subject has focused on the key features of the task, or selectively attends to the critical stimuli, the second phase begins (see Figure 7.1).

Zeaman and House (1963) compared the learning curves obtained from performances of children who were or were not retarded whose MAs varied. They found the two stages in the curves of all groups, as well as the sharp rise in performance at the beginning of the second stage. The difference between the groups was the number of trials composing the first stage. Children with lower MAs required more

TABLE 7.4

Learning-Related Characteristics

Characteristic	Description	Reference
Attention Variables	• Difficulty in the three major components of attention: attention span (length of time on task), focus (inhibition of distracting stimuli), and selective attention (discrimination of important stimulus characteristics). • Key concern is to train students to be aware of the importance of attention and to learn how to actively monitor its occurrence.	Alabiso (1977) Zeaman and House (1963, 1979) Connis (1979) Howell, Rueda, and Rutherford (1983) Kneedler and Hallahan (1981)
Mediational Strategies	• Less likely than normal learners to employ effective techniques for organizing information for later recall. • Typical techniques of mature learners include verbal rehearsal and repetition, labeling, classification, association, and imagery. • Research indicates that students who are retarded have difficulty producing mediational strategies. • Tend to be "inactive learners"	Spitz (1966) Bray (1979) Robinson and Robinson (1976) Strichart and Gottlieb (1983)
Memory	• Difficulty in the area of short-term memory (STM) but retain information over the long term. • Long-term memory (LTM) is usually similar to that of persons who are not disabled. • Certain STM problems involving nonsensical tasks have been associated with deficits in the spontaneous use of mediational strategies. • As noted above, strategy production is difficult for students with mild retardation, but improvements in recall can be achieved when they are shown how to proceed in an organized, well-planned fashion.	Belmont (1966) R.C. Cohen (1982) Baumeister and Brooks (1981) Borkowski and Cavanaugh (1979)
Transfer/Generalization	• Tend to show deficiencies in the ability to apply knowledge or skills to new tasks, problems, or stimulus situations. • Such difficulties relate to the inability to form learning sets. • In particular, they may fail to use previous experience to formulate rules that will help solve future problems of a similar nature.	Stephens (1972) Stevenson (1972) Robinson and Robinson (1976)

Source: Reprinted with permission of Merrill, an imprint of Prentice Hall, from *Exceptional Children and Youth,* 6th ed., by Norris G. Haring, Linda McCormick, and Thomas G. Haring. Copyright © 1994 by Prentice Hall.

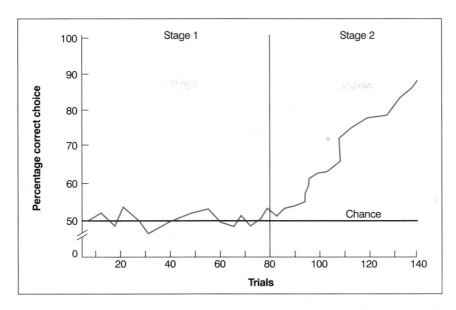

FIGURE 7.1

Typical Learning Curve Generated by Persons with Retardation on discrimination Task in Zeaman House (1963) Study

trials in the attention phase than did children with higher MAs. Zeaman and House therefore concluded that subjects who were retarded needed more time to learn to attend to the relevant dimensions of the stimuli.

In updating their theory, Zeaman and House (1979) also note a relationship between MA and the number of dimensions that a subject could attend to simultaneously. Learners who were retarded could not attend to as many dimensions simultaneously as could those who were not retarded. In addition, some learners who were retarded seemed to prefer some dimensions over others, which also may have affected their response. This is particularly relevant if, as Brooks and McCauley (1984) maintain, such learners have less attention to allocate, and "attentional allocation is a problem in general for mentally retarded people that may extend to all domains of information processing" (p. 482).

The initial research by Zeaman and House continues to generate investigations, but from it we can draw implications for teaching students who are retarded. For example, teachers should (a) present initial stimuli that vary in only a few dimensions, (b) direct the child's attention to these critical dimensions, (c) initially remove extraneous stimuli that may distract the child from attending to the task at hand, (d) reward the child for attending to the task, and (e) increase the difficulty of the task over time.

Mediational Strategies   After attending to a specific stimulus, an individual must organize and store it so that it can be recalled when needed. Spitz (1966) refers to this process as "input organization" and has conducted research to determine the functioning in this area of persons who are mentally retarded.

Spitz's (1966) research led him to theorize that the input step in the learning process was more difficult for subjects who were retarded than for other subjects, because of a deficiency in their ability to organize the input stimuli for storage and recall. This finding has generated a great deal of research into strategies that teachers may use to enhance a student's ability to categorize incoming data. Two such methods are grouping and mediation.

Spitz (1973, 1979) sees **grouping,** or clustering material prior to its presentation, as more beneficial to the learner who is retarded than presenting material in random order. Restructuring the perceptual field for individuals who characteristically have difficulty at this stage of the learning process should facilitate memory and recall. Grouping is perhaps the simplest method of organizing information. Material may be grouped spatially, in different visual arrangements; temporally, with a pause or time lapse between items; perceptually, with certain items enclosed in a shape or configuration; or categorically, by content or commonality of items.

Stephens (1966) has further broken down the categories of grouping by content into physical similarity (e.g., items of the same color), function (e.g., articles of clothing), concepts (e.g., plants, animals), and sequential equivalence (e.g., subjects and objects as used in grammatical arrangements). Work by Stephens (1972) in presenting stimuli according to types of grouping indicates that the most basic type of grouping is that of physical similarity. As a child increases in MA, more advanced grouping strategies are used. This same progression was reported for subjects who were not retarded as well as for subjects who were mildly retarded.

A mediator is something that goes between or connects. In verbal learning, **mediation** refers to the process by which an individual connects a stimulus and a response. One approach to the study of verbal learning, *paired associate learning,* focuses on verbal mediation as a means of learning responses to stimulus words or elements. In this technique, the subject is generally presented with pairs of words. Then only the first word in each pair is repeated, and the subject tries to recall the second. Verbalizing the connection between the two stimulus words seems to enhance performance. In studies reviewed by Meyers and MacMillan (1976), researchers noted marked improvements in tasks of this type, even by subjects who were retarded, when the subjects were instructed in mediation strategies or provided with such mediators as sentences relating the stimulus to the response. The meaningfulness of the material and the use of stimulus words or objects familiar to the subject (Estes, 1970) also facilitated learning in paired associate tasks.

Several implications for teaching can be drawn from this research. First, materials presented to learners who are retarded should be familiar or have some relevance for them. Second, information should be grouped or organized into meaningful parts. Finally, such learners should be instructed in mediational strategies.

Memory   Memory, the ability to retrieve information that has been stored, is one of the most heavily researched components of the learning process. As one would expect, individuals who are retarded tend to perform less well on tasks of memory than do their age- or grade-level peers. Moreover, the more severely retarded the individual, the greater the deficit in memory displayed.

Researchers have hypothesized that the root of memory problems in individuals who are retarded may be related to a lack of selective attention (Westling & Fox,

2000); inefficient or nonexistent rehearsal strategies (Brooks & McCauley, 1984); delay in developing learning sets (Merrill, 1990); or an inability to generalize learned skills to new settings, with different people, or in different ways (Stevens, 1972). Polloway and Patton (1997) state that an inability to generalize skills hampers the ability of individuals who are retarded to be more independent and reduces their need for external supports.

Early researchers of memory processes usually made a distinction between short-term memory (STM) and long-term memory (LTM). Information recalled after a period of days or months or longer is usually referred to as being in LTM, whereas data stored from a few seconds to a few hours are in STM. Most early researchers contended that once learned, information is retained over the long term about as well by those who are retarded as by those who are not (Belmont, 1966; Ellis, 1963). In the area of STM, however, early researchers concluded that learners who are retarded appeared to have considerable difficulty (Borkowski, Peck, & Damberg, 1983; Ellis, 1963). Swanson and Cooney (1991) hypothesize that the memory function in learners with mild disabilities is developmentally delayed. Merrill (1990) found that learners with mental retardation required more time than their age-mates to reach levels of automaticity and fluency in memory processes and thus were less able to handle large chunks of cognitive information at one time.

Smith, Polloway, Patton, and Dowdy (1998) recommend stressing meaningful content and using specific strategy instruction to teach students to proceed in an organized, planned manner. Belmont and Butterfield (1971) and Brown, Campione, and Murphy (1974) report success in efforts to improve STM performance among these learners, by direct teaching or by rehearsal or practice procedures, although the effects of the training appeared to be specific to the training task at hand and not readily transferable to other situations (Belmont & Butterfield, 1977).

The major rehearsal strategies noted by Mercer and Snell (1977) in their review of studies of STM were verbal rehearsal and image rehearsal. Verbal rehearsal relates to the concept of self-instruction and refers to labeling aspects of a task and verbalizing these labels aloud or silently while the task is being performed. In image rehearsal, a form of visualization, the individual is taught to associate aspects of a task with pictures of events that will help to recall them.

Drew, Hardman, and Hart (1996) and Dunn (1973) criticize the early research on memory problems in individuals who were retarded as plagued with methodological problems that made interpretation difficult, and they note that currently, researchers of memory processes had moved toward an information processing model. Sternburg (1997) notes that information-processing researchers investigate how individuals acquire, process, and use sensory stimuli.

Executive control and *metacognition* are components of an information processing model. These two terms apply to the process one consciously goes through to determine the need for a strategy, analyze a problem, anticipate outcomes of various actions, select a strategy to solve the problem, and monitor progress toward the solution (Raymond, 2000). Researchers have noted that learners who are retarded generally do not spontaneously employ executive control processes (Brown, 1974; Merrill, 1990; Sternberg & Spear, 1985), but that they can be taught to use them effectively (Borkowski et al., 1983; Sternberg, 1997). Other teaching techniques to facilitate recall include (a) organizing material into meaningful segments, (b) using reinforcement and incentives for remembering, (c) modeling use of appropriate strategies, (d) using spaced and repeated practice, (e) reminding and encouraging the learner to use rehearsal strategies, and (f) using reconstructive elaborations.

Observational Learning

Modeling, imitation, and *learning through observation* are the terms most often associated with *observational learning,* which refers to learning from demonstrations by others. Much of the research in this area has been done by Bandura (1986) and his associates. It substantiates the important role that observational learning plays in acquiring social behaviors, gender roles, language, and religious and political practices. In addition, modeling and imitation are involved in the development of new behaviors and the modification of existing ones, and they may result in the learning of inappropriate as well as appropriate responses.

Certain characteristics of individuals who are retarded give support to the use of this tool to teach new behaviors. The tendency of these learners to be outerdirected or look to others for cues or guidance in problem solving (Turnure & Zigler, 1964), and their suggestibility (Zigler, 1999), indicate that modeling can be effectively used for acquiring or changing behavior. Suggestions for using observational learning as a teaching tool include (a) being aware that any behavior may serve as a model, (b) using prompts or cues to direct students' attention, (c) calling attention to students exhibiting desirable behavior, (d) ignoring undesirable behavior so that others do not model it in an attempt to gain attention, and (e) rewarding imitation of appropriate behavior.

SPEECH AND LANGUAGE CHARACTERISTICS

To learn more about speech and language characteristics, go to the companion website at www.prenhall.com/beirne-smith and select Chapter 7, then choose the Web Destinations module.

Speech and language problems occur with greater frequency among individuals identified as mentally retarded than among those not so identified (Bernstein & Tiegerman, 1993; Warren & Abbeduto, 1992). This is not unexpected, since cognitive ability and language development are closely related. The speech problems most often seen are difficulties in articulation, voice, and stuttering (Hardman, Drew, & Egan, 1996). Common articulation errors include the substitution, omission, addition, or distortion of sounds, which make speech less intelligible. Language disorders that commonly accompany mental retardation include delayed language development and a restricted or limited active vocabulary (Spradlin, 1968). Language is so important to independent functioning that prospective parents, parents of high-risk children, and day care personnel should be trained in various means of encouraging language development.

As corroboration of the evidence that students who are mildly retarded display lower overall functioning than those classified similarly before the passage of PL 94-142, we see an increasing occurrence of secondary handicapping conditions (MacMillan, 1989; MacMillan & Borthwick, 1980). For example, Epstein et al. (1989) gathered information from the individualized education programs (IEPs) of 107 children identified as mildly retarded and receiving special education in northern Illinois. Speech and language problems were the most frequent secondary disability; well over half the students were eligible for and receiving speech and language therapy. Language deficits may be related to such factors as absence of or limited adequate speech and language models and less encouragement to use language. A disproportionate number of students who are mildly retarded are also members of cultural or ethnic minorities (U.S. Department of Commerce, 1999), which may also play a role in the language deficiencies found in this population.

Recent research on the language abilities of individuals who are retarded offers some interesting findings. Abbeduto and Nuccio (1991) studied the receptive language abilities of this group and found that students who were retarded focused on the formal, sequential aspects of spoken language rather than on its semantic, conceptual aspects. Individuals who were not retarded demonstrated the latter abilities. In a study on the use of repair behaviors (i.e., the speaker's effort to make an utterance understood when a listener indicates a problem in understanding), Scudder and Tremain (1992) found that students who were retarded displayed appropriate repair behaviors. However, as situations became more demanding, students who were retarded did not reuse effective strategies and became more frustrated.

Among those whose needs are more pronounced, speech and language disorders are even more common, because of not only their decreased intellectual development but also the increased possibility of concomitant disabling conditions. The motor dysfunction accompanying cerebral palsy, for example, can seriously impede the ability to produce intelligible speech. A higher prevalence of hearing impairment also exists in this population, and poor hearing affects articulation and may contribute to a further delay in the acquisition of language. Many students, especially those with Down syndrome, have frequent bouts of middle-ear infections during their childhood years (Pueschel, 1997). The conductive hearing loss these infections can cause also delays language and creates speech problems (Balkany, Downs, Jafek, & Krajicek, 1979).

One of the features typically found in the child with Down syndrome is a protruding tongue. Tongue reduction surgery, often in combination with facial surgery, has become increasingly common as a means of diminishing some of the more obvious characteristics. The usefulness of such surgery in improving speech, however, is dubious. Lemperle and Rada (1980) report more intelligible speech for a majority of 63 children with Down syndrome after undergoing surgery, although no formal speech evaluations were conducted. In other studies, Olbrisch (1982) and Lemperle (1985) sent questionnaires to families of children who had received tongue reduction surgery and reported that 88% and 68%, respectively, of the parents perceived speech improvement. Parsons, Iacone, and Rozner (1987) took formal speech assessment measures before surgery, 4 weeks after surgery, and again 6 months after surgery with 27 children with Down syndrome. The number of articulation errors did not differ significantly across time, although the parents were almost unanimous in perceiving speech improvement.

PHYSICAL HEALTH CHARACTERISTICS

In general, the physical health characteristics and needs of persons who are mildly retarded do not differ dramatically from those of other individuals. More pro-

✳ Changing the Look of Mental Retardation

Plastic surgeons can straighten the slanted eyes, build up the cheekbones, and minimize the protruding tongue commonly found in children with Down syndrome. But should they? Plastic surgery remains the most controversial treatment offered Down syndrome children.

The 1½- to 2½-hour operation is fairly straightforward. Surgeons can build up the bridge of the nose, cheekbone, and chin with bone grafts or synthetics, change the slant of the eyes and cut fat from the lower eyelids. There are usually no facial scars because the work is done through the mouth or by cutting skin flaps behind the hairline. The tongue, which appears too large and protrudes from an unusually small mouth, is reduced by about one-fifth.

Advocates of surgery believe that children with Down syndrome are rejected partly because of their physical features, and that improving their appearance may result in greater social acceptance. Critics respond that there is little hard evidence that surgery has these effects. In fact, it has to be admitted that even the most gifted plastic surgeons can't make a child with down syndrome look entirely normal. After surgery, the gait, neck, and body proportions are still unusual. Even the face remains clearly different. "I've yet to see a child after the operation," says Diane Crutcher of the National Down Syndrome Congress "who doesn't look like a child with Down syndrome." Moreover, say some critics, the surgery is itself a kind of rejection, a message that the children are not acceptable as themselves.

Before and after: Advocates of surgery say it reduces the stigma often associated with Down syndrome. Critics say it sends the message that the children are unacceptable in appearance as they are.

Photos courtesy of Dr. Kenneth Salyer, Dallas, TX

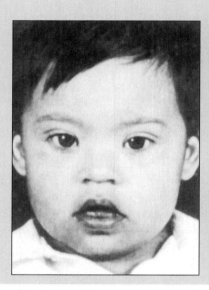 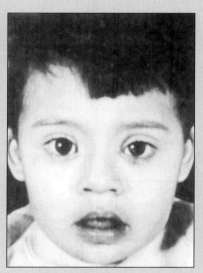

nounced physical and health concerns, however, tend to co-occur in individuals who are more severely retarded. The following discussion highlights selected conditions of retardation as well as general health considerations that have specific implications for this population.

Selected Conditions

We begin with motor development, which even in those who are mildly retarded may be delayed and markedly less accomplished than in the child who is not

It is society's preoccupation with "good looks" that should change, these critics argue, not the faces of children with Down syndrome.

Even those who advocate the operation admit that not every child with Down syndrome is a good candidate for surgery, and both parents and child must go through an intensive screening process before their surgeon lifts a scalpel. "The surgery should be performed only in children whose quality of life can be improved by the procedures," cautions Garry S. Brody, clinical professor of plastic surgery at the University of Southern California. Surgery is immediately ruled out if the child is profoundly retarded or has life-threatening physical problems. In addition, parents must be realistic about what the surgery will and won't do. "If you think the child is going to roll out of the operating room with 20 more IQ points," says Crutcher, "you're going to be disappointed."

While controversial, plastic surgery remains an option for those willing to try every avenue. The American Society of Plastic and Reconstructive Surgeons operates a toll-free number (800/635-0635) for information on reconstructive and cosmetic surgery for Down syndrome, and offers a referral list of board certified plastic surgeons qualified to perform the operation.

Source: From "Special Talents" by C. Turkington, 1987, *Psychology Today*, September, p. 45. Reprinted with permission from Psychology Today Magazine, copyright © 1987 (Sussex Publishers, Inc.).

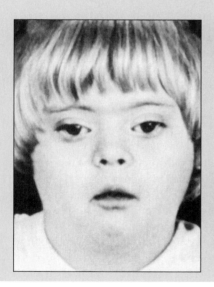 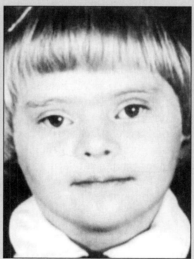

retarded. Motor deficits include problems of balance, locomotion, and manipulative dexterity (Bruininks, 1974). The growth rate may be slower, and these individuals are generally shorter and lighter than children who are not retarded (Bruininks, 1974; Mosier, Grossman, & Dingman, 1965). Reschly, Robinson, Volmer, and Wilson (1988) demonstrated that, as the severity of retardation increases, so do problems in motor skills areas; this relationship is depicted in Table 7.5.

Sensory defects are also more common among individuals who are retarded, with visual and auditory problems frequently noted (Barlow, 1978). Color blindness appears to be more prevalent among individuals who are moderately retarded than among those who are more mildly retarded or normal (O'Connor, 1975). Early

TABLE 7.5

Analysis of Motor Skills across IQ Levels

IQ	N	$\overline{X}$[a]	s.d.	Total with Weaknesses[b]	
				N	%
<50	39	2.10	1.07	29	74
50–54	33	2.18	1.10	23	70
55–59	35	2.46	1.07	17	49
60–64	52	2.48	0.96	25	48
65–69	59	2.53	0.95	24	41
70–74	121	3.08	0.91	26	21
75–79	155	2.95	0.88	40	26
80–84	118	2.97	0.85	30	25

[a]Mean scores were derived from a Likert rating scale that used the anchor points of 1 = Significant Weakness, 2 = Weakness, 4 = Strength, and 5 = Significant Strength.

[b]Total was formed by the sum of the Significant Weakness and Weakness ratings.

Source: From *Iowa Mental Disabilities Research Project: Final Report and Executive Summary* by D. Reschly, G. Robinson, L. Volmer, and L. Wilson, 1988, Des Moines: State of Iowa, Department of Education. Copyright 1988 by State of Iowa, Department of Education. Reprinted by permission.

screening for sensory defects is essential, as specific correctional devices or types of intervention may be indicated. In fact, early identification of any health problems may be critical to the child's total development. Although the retardation itself may obscure problems or impede efforts to diagnose them, early intervention and treatment may lessen the effects of the disability and influence the rate and level of development the child may attain.

Down Syndrome   A child who is retarded may be classified as a clinical type. To be regarded as a specific clinical type, an individual must show certain facial, body, and disorder characteristics relating to a particular syndrome associated with mental retardation. There are a number of these syndromes, but the one most frequently associated with mental retardation is Down syndrome.

Besides their distinct physical appearance, children with Down syndrome frequently have specific health-related problems. Many have structural defects of the heart that may threaten their survival, although surgical procedures can be successful in correcting the defect. Lung abnormalities are also frequent in children with Down syndrome, resulting in susceptibility to upper respiratory infections. The incidence of leukemia is higher than in the normal population. Other common health problems of Down syndrome are eye and ear infections, obesity, skin problems (primarily due to their characteristically rough and dry skin), problems of the teeth and gums, and hearing impairments (Pueschel, 1997).

Individuals who work with children with Down syndrome should be alert to signs of infection, particularly ear and upper respiratory infections, so that early medical treatment can prevent more serious problems. Physical education and exercise programs should also be provided, although the type and amount of activity required of a particular child should be planned with the guidance of medical personnel.

Cerebral Palsy   Not all children with cerebral palsy are mentally retarded (Pellegrino, 1997); however, a child who does have this condition presents a number of health-related problems. Cerebral palsy is a neuromuscular disability that may result from damage to the brain at birth or during the first 4 years of life. While the condition may include any number of intellectual, sensory, and behavioral disorders, the motor disability presents several potential problems. Because of fluctuating muscle tone, hypertonicity, or hypotonicity, children with cerebral palsy may exhibit atypical posture and movements that limit their participation in learning activities. Limbs that are not exercised may lose their usefulness altogether. Children with cerebral palsy, therefore, usually require professional assistance in handling and positioning. Some children may be in movement or exercise programs that need to be repeated at certain intervals during the day. According to Rainforth and York (1991), the goals of positioning assistance include stabilizing the body, maintaining proper body alignment, and increasing participation in learning activities. Professionals working with a child who wears a brace or cast should be alert to such signs of circulation problems as swelling, coldness, change of color, and evidence of infection, as well as other skin problems.

Individuals working with youngsters who have both retardation and cerebral palsy must be aware of a number of other problems that sometimes accompany the disorder. Speech difficulties complicated by lack of muscle control are common and often require speech therapy or other special educational measures. Visual and auditory problems are also seen more frequently in the child with cerebral palsy, and corrective measures to improve vision or hearing may be warranted. Difficulties with chewing and swallowing may present real hazards if the child is given such foods as hard candy, popcorn, and chewing gum. Teachers should consult the parents for specific instructions about eating and drinking. As with other disabilities, upper respiratory infections are common, and early symptoms should be reported, since the consequences of such infections may be severe.

Seizure Disorders   Seizures are another health problem often associated with cerebral palsy, but they are also characteristic of other conditions that may accompany mental retardation (Freeman, Vining, & Pillas 1997). Because convulsive disorders are significantly more common among those who are retarded than among those who are not, teachers working with these individuals should be trained to respond appropriately and be aware of the possible side effects of seizure control medication (Epstein et al., 1989).

Seizures vary from momentary disturbances, which may go unnoticed (absence, or petit mal), to episodes involving jerking of the muscles and loss of consciousness (tonic-clonic seizure, or grand mal). Some children experience an aura of sensation just before a seizure begins and may be able to give some indication that it is imminent. In some children, the likelihood of a seizure is increased by external factors, such as flickering lights or loud sounds, or the child's physical condition, such as being highly excited, ill, or fatigued. By being aware of these cues, teachers can be alert to circumstances that might precede or precipitate seizures.

Once a seizure occurs, it should not be interrupted. The major concern is to keep the child from injuring him- or herself. During a tonic-clonic (grand mal) seizure, the child should be eased to the floor, furniture and other objects pushed away, and, if possible, restrictive clothing loosened and the child turned on his or her side to aid breathing. Someone should remain with the child until the seizure ends and then allow the child to rest.

Substance Abuse   Until recently, little was written on this topic as it pertains to individuals who are retarded, and the common perception was that this group was less likely to have problems than those without retardation (Ferrara, 1992). Although some studies support this perception (Christian & Poling, 1997; Delaney & Poling, 1990), reason for concern persists. Other sources suggest that problems associated with substance abuse, when it does occur, may arise more quickly and at lower levels of drug use for this group (Resource Center on Substance Abuse and Prevention and Disabilities, 1992). This finding is extremely disturbing, given the fact that more individuals who are retarded live in communities where this threat is widespread.

General Health Considerations

Nutrition   Proper kinds and amounts of food are necessary for the general well-being of all children. Poor diet not only arrests biological development and diminishes resistance to disease and illness but is also a negative factor in social adjustment and academic learning (Cohen, 2000). Inadequate or unbalanced diets may be a result of insufficient food, poor supervision of meals and snacks, or lack of understanding of the importance of proper nutrition and how to provide it.

Illness and Disease   As might be expected, children who are retarded are more susceptible to disease and illness than are children who are not. Poor nutrition and lack of adequate health care (including immunizations) appear to be major factors in promoting problems among children from lower socioeconomic classes. Children who are mildly retarded often have additional disabling conditions or health problems that account for their relatively poor health. The frequency of heart and lung disorders among Down syndrome children is just one example.

Several specific problems are commonly noted among children who are retarded. Colds and upper respiratory infections are more frequent and often last longer than in other children. The seriousness of the symptoms can be compounded by the presence of other disorders such as cardiac conditions.

The incidence of dental problems is also relatively high among children who are retarded. Dental problems are often due to poor nutrition, failure to brush teeth regularly, or absence of routine dental checkups.

Accidents and Injury   Children who are developmentally delayed, as indicated, can be poorly coordinated and awkward. Add to this the poor judgment and impaired reasoning that may come with subaverage intellectual ability, and a higher than average accident rate can be predicted. Conditions accompanying the retardation—limited vision, muscle weakness, motor disabilities, and seizures—may also contribute to increased injuries. This group can also suffer physical injury due to abuse (Zirpoli, 1986).

Physical Activity   A certain amount of exercise and activity is necessary to the total well-being of any individual. For the child who is mentally retarded, a planned program of physical activity is essential for a number of reasons. Individuals who are mildly retarded may not differ appreciably in physical and motor skills from those who are not retarded, and sports and other physical activities may provide an opportunity for expression and achievements as well as an outlet for tension. Gains in physical strength and motor coordination as well as feelings of accomplishment often enhance social and personal adjustment.

For those individuals who deviate more markedly from their nondisabled peers both mentally and physically, planned physical education and recreation programs offer enjoyment and a productive use of leisure time as well as the typical benefits associated with physical activity. Adaptive equipment and materials enable individuals with certain conditions to participate in a wide variety of games and activities.

While opportunities for physical education and recreation historically have been neglected with respect to people who are mentally retarded (Chinn, Drew, & Logan, 1979), the outlook for the future is far more encouraging (Beasley, 1982; Halle, Silverman, & Regan, 1983). Provisions of the Individuals with Disabilities Education Act include not only physical education but also recreation and leisure education as related services that must be extended to all students. Community agencies and citizens' groups are becoming more actively involved in providing opportunities for recreation. The Special Olympics program remains a viable source of physical activity as well. Programs offered by colleges and universities designed to train professionals in techniques for working with students with disabilities in the area of physical education and recreation are increasing in number and scope.

EDUCATIONAL CHARACTERISTICS

In this section we examine various facets of the educational programs of students with mild to moderate retardation. Specifically, we focus on placement options, curricular and service issues, and performance characteristics.

The diagnosis of milder forms of retardation and any subsequent delivery of special services typically take place after a student has encountered difficulty with the academic, social, or behavioral requirements of general education. As evidence accumulates that this population is less able and has more accompanying disabilities than similarly labeled students of a decade ago (MacMillan, 1989), we can expect earlier diagnosis. Support for this is evidenced by the results of a study by Polloway et al. (1986) of the IEPs of 234 public school students who were identified as EMR. The average age at the time of placement for the younger students in the study (ages 6 to 11) was 5.5 years, as opposed to 7.5 years for the older students (ages 12 to 18). In addition, the U.S. Department of Education (1999) reports an increase of 19% in the number of infants and toddlers receiving early intervention services by December 1, 1997. The earlier diagnoses imply that special education and related services are being provided earlier in the school careers of children who are mildly retarded than was the case in the past.

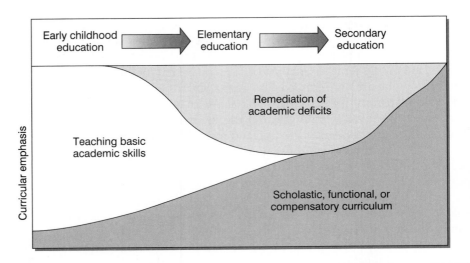

FIGURE 7.2
Curricular Emphasis across Levels of Schooling

Source: Adapted from Michael L. Hardman, Clifford J. Drew, M. Winston Egan, and Barbara Wolf, *Human Exceptionality: Society, School, and Family,* 4th ed. Copyright © 1993 by Allyn and Bacon. Reprinted by permission.

Some students who are mildly retarded have been placed in general education for the majority of the school day, with a smaller proportion of time being spent in a special education setting. Data from the U.S. Department of Education (1999), however, continue to paint a picture of limited inclusion in general education classes. Whereas students who are learning disabled or emotionally disturbed are spread across general education classrooms, resource rooms, and separate special education classrooms, students who are retarded are most often placed in separate special education classrooms. Predictably, students who are mildly retarded are more often served in general education classes than are students who are moderately or severely retarded. At the junior and senior high levels, students who are mildly retarded may be assigned to resource sections of academic subjects. Special educators usually teach these classes, focusing on the academic goals specified in the IEPs. Other periods in the school day may be spent in such classes as health, physical education, athletics, vocational classes, or any one of a number of elective subjects if these are considered appropriate for the individual student. Additional research, however, is necessary to confirm that limited integration of pupils who are mildly retarded into general education programs is a trend.

Retardation and its accompanying problems are recognized earlier in a child with more limited intellectual abilities and adaptive functioning. The more exaggerated developmental delays in motor and language skills and/or physical and health problems are usually responsible for early contacts with medical personnel and community agencies (Westling & Fox, 2000). With early identification comes a greater chance for eligibility for services now available for preschool-age children as well as for infants and toddlers.

Programmatic Realities

Preparing students to deal successfully with the demands of adulthood and to live as independently as possible should be the primary goals of any program. The particular demands of adulthood for which one needs to be prepared will vary somewhat depending on probable subsequent environments. Moreover, the nature of the program will also be influenced by the individual's level of schooling (i.e., elementary vs. secondary). The emphasis of curriculum will change as a function of school level and needs of the individual. Figure 7.2 illustrates a two-dimensional (curricular approach and level of schooling) model for deciding the nature of instructional programs. Fundamentally, programs must develop a student's competence in the following areas: employment or further education, home and family, leisure pursuits, community involvement, physical and emotional health, personal responsibility, and interpersonal relationships (Cronin & Patton, 1993)

Interestingly enough, however, while the literature favors a broad-based curriculum, recent studies of IEP goals for students who are mildly retarded indicate a strong emphasis on academic goals (Epstein et al., 1989; McBride & Forgnone, 1985). In light of the more recent descriptions of this population, it is not surprising that professionals in the field are calling for a more comprehensive approach to the education of these students, one that includes life skills preparation (Brolin, 1995; Cronin & Patton, 1993), social skills training (Gresham, 1982; Polloway et al., 1986), and vocational training (Brolin & Brolin, 1979; Edgar, 1987; Jaquish & Stella, 1986).

Related services are provided to students who have been identified as disabled to enable them to benefit fully from their educational program. It is likely that many individuals may have secondary impairments and will need additional related services. In the study by Epstein et al. (1989), the majority of the IEPs for students with mild retardation listed some type of secondary problem. Nearly 90% of the students had speech and language disorders; and sensory disorders (particularly visual impairment), convulsive disorders, and emotional and behavioral disorders were more common than in the general population. This study is consistent with other research (MacMillan, 1982; MacMillan & Borthwick, 1980) that characterizes many individuals who are mildly retarded as displaying multiple disabilities and therefore being in need of more related services and support personnel.

School programs for those who need more supports deviate markedly from the general school program in the past. Programs are designed to reflect both the developmental age (level of ability) and the chronological age of the student in selecting goals leading to self-sufficiency (Brown, Nietupski, & Hamre-Nietupski, 1976). The curriculum for this group typically includes self-help, basic readiness, independent living, communication, socialization, recreation, leisure skills, and cognitive development (Geiger, Brownsmith, & Forgnone, 1978; Snell & Renzaglia, 1986). Researchers advocate the use of age-appropriate materials to teach functional skills that relate to the present or anticipated environmental needs (Brown, Branston, Hamre-Nietupski, Pumpian, Certo, & Gruenewald, 1979).

As the inclusion movement grows, we anticipate that more students whose needs for supports are greater will be provided services in general education settings. Much work needs to be done to accomplish this goal. For this goal to become a reality, changes to current systems are required. Furthermore, changes must be made within the personnel preparation programs of both general and special educators to create the conditions that foster effective inclusive environments.

Academic Achievement

Students who are retarded are likely to show deficits in all academic areas. The majority of students who are mildly retarded read at levels lower than expected for their MA, and of the various aspects of reading, comprehension appears to be the most difficult for them (Carter, 1975; Dunn, 1973). In mathematics, the majority of students can learn the basic computations; however, mathematical reasoning and appropriate application of concepts to problem-solving tasks are more difficult for this group. Functional arithmetic skills involving money, time, and measurement, because they are important for community living, are an integral part of the curriculum (Westling, 1986).

The school exit rate for students who are mentally retarded has remained fairly stable over the past 5 years. According to the U.S. Department of Education (1999), results of research studies on students with disabilities leaving school indicate that students who received vocational training during their secondary school years have achieved positive long-term results in terms of greater success at independent living, higher rates of employment, and greater community participation.

To check your understanding of this chapter, go to the companion website at www.prenhall.com/beirne-smith and select Chapter 7, then choose the Self-Test module.

Summary

General

- Not every person who is mentally retarded may display all the characteristics discussed in this chapter.
- This chapter focuses on individuals who require few or no supports systems in most adaptive skills areas.
- Those considered mentally retarded are part of a heterogeneous group.
- Individuals who are mildly retarded have been referred to as educable or trainable in the past.

Demographic Characteristics

- More males than females are identified.
- Historically there has been a disproportionate number of racially different and ethnic minority children being labeled as mildly mentally retarded.
- Some data support the description that many youth who are mentally retarded live in single-parent families and come from families characterized by lower socioeconomic status.

Motivational and Sociobehavioral Characteristics

- Motivational characteristics include external locus of control, expectancy for failure, outerdirectedness, and more limited self-regulatory behaviors.
- Social and behavioral problems are more likely, with some students displaying psychiatric problems as well.

Learning Characteristics

- By definition, this group has problems in cognitive areas; however, there is some difference of opinion whether cognitive development is qualitatively or quantitatively different from that of children who are not retarded.
- Various processes (attention, mediation strategies, memory, generalization) associated with learning can be problematic for this group.

Speech and Language Characteristics

- Speech and language problems occur with great frequency among this population.
- Delayed language development is expected.

Physical Health Characteristics

- Motor development may be delayed.
- Sensory deficits are more common among persons who are mentally retarded.
- Individuals with Down syndrome have a number of physical features common to this condition.
- Cerebral palsy and seizure disorders occur more frequently in persons who are retarded.
- The data on the extent of substance abuse in this group are equivocal at this time.

Educational Characteristics

- Students who are mentally retarded enjoy limited inclusion in general education settings.
- Studies of IEP goals indicate a predominance of academic goals.
- Many students qualify for related services.
- The school exit rate for students who are retarded has remained fairly stable over the past 5 years.

References

Abbeduto, L., & Nuccio, J. B. (1991). Relation between receptive language and cognitive maturity in persons with mental retardation. *American Journal on Mental Retardation, 96,* 143–149.

American Association on Mental Retardation. (1992). *Mental retardation: Definition, classification, and systems of supports* (9th ed.). Washington, DC: Author.

Balkany, T. J., Downs, M. P., Jafek, B. W., & Krajicek, H. J. (1979). Hearing loss in Down's syndrome: A treatable handicap more common than generally recognized. *Clinical Pediatrics, 18,* 116–118.

Balla, D. A., & Zigler, E. (1979). Personality development in retarded persons. In N. R. Ellis (Ed.), *Handbook of mental deficiency: Psychological theory and research* (2nd ed., pp. 154–168). Hillsdale, NJ: Erlbaum.

Bandura, A. (1986). *Social foundations of thought and action: A social cognitive theory.* Upper Saddle River, NJ: Merrill/Prentice Hall.

Barlow, C. F. (1978). *Mental retardation and related disorders.* Philadelphia: Davis.

Barlow, D. H., & Durand, V. M. (1995). *Abnormal psychology: An integrated approach.* Pacific Grove, CA: Brooks/Cole.

Beasley, C. R. (1982). Effects of jogging program on cardiovascular fitness and work performance of mentally retarded adults. *American Journal of Mental Deficiency, 86,* 609–613.

Belmont, J. M. (1996). Long term memory in mental retardation. *International Review of Research in Mental Retardation, 1,* 219–255.

Belmont, J. M., & Butterfield, E. C. (1971). Learning strategies as determinants of memory deficiencies. *Cognitive Psychology, 2,* 411–420.

Belmont, J. M., & Butterfield, E. C. (1977). The instructional approach to developmental cognitive research. In R. V. Kail & J. W. Hasen (Eds.), *Perspectives on the development of memory and cognition* (pp. 437–481). Hillsdale, NJ: Erlbaum.

Bernstein, D. K., & Tiegerman, E. (1993). *Language and communication disorders in children.* Upper Saddle River, NJ: Merrill/Prentice Hall.

Borkowski, J. G., Peck, V. A., & Damberg, P. R. (1983). Attention, memory and cognition. In J. L. Matson & J. A. Mulick (Eds.), *Handbook of mental retardation* (pp. 479–497). New York: Pergamon.

Borthwick-Duffy, S. A., & Eyman, R. K. (1990). Who are the dually diagnosed? *American Journal on Mental Retardation, 94,* 586–595.

Bower, A. C. (1978) Learning. In J. P. Das & D. Baine (Eds.), *Mental retardation for special educators* (pp. 48–81). Springfield, IL: Thomas.

Brady, P. M., Manni, J. L., & Winikur, D. W. (1983). Implications of ethnic disproportion in programs for the educable mentally retarded. *Journal of Special Education, 17,* 295–302.

Brolin, D. E. (1997). *Life-centered career education: A competency based approach* (5th ed.) Reston, VA: Council for Exceptional Children.

Brolin, J. C., & Brolin, D. E. (1979). Vocational education for special students. In D. Cullinan & M. Epstein (Eds.), *Special education for adolescents: Issues and perspectives.* Upper Saddle River, NJ: Merrill/Prentice Hall.

Brooks, P. H., & McCauley, C. (1984). Cognitive research in mental retardation. *American Journal of Mental Deficiency, 88,* 479–486.

Brown, A. L. (1974). The role of strategic behavior in retardate memory. *International Journal of Research in Mental Retardation, 7,* 55–111.

Brown, A. L., Campione, J. C., & Murphy, M. D. (1974). Keeping track of changing variables: Long-term retention of a trained rehearsal strategy by retarded adolescents. *American Journal of Mental Deficiency, 78,* 453–466.

Brown, L. F., Branston, M. B., Hamre-Nietupski, S. M., Pumpian, I., Certo, N., & Gruenewald, L. (1979). A strategy for developing chronological-age-appropriate and functional curricular content for severely handicapped adolescents and young adults. *Journal of Special Education, 13,* 81–90.

Brown, L. F., Nietupski, J., & Hamre-Nietupski, S. (1976). The criterion of ultimate functioning and public school services for severely handicapped students. In M. A. Thomas (Ed.), *Hey don't forget about me: Education's investment in the severely, profoundly, and multiply handicapped* (pp. 2–15). Reston, VA: Council for Exceptional Children.

Bruininks, R. H. (1974). Physical and motor development of retarded persons. *International Review of Research in Mental Retardation, 7,* 209–261.

Bybee, J., & Zigler, E. (1992). Is outerdirectedness employed in a harmful or beneficial manner by students with and without mental retardation? *American Journal on Mental Retardation, 96,* 512–521.

Carter, J. L. (1975). Intelligence and reading achievement of EMR in three educational settings. *Mental Retardation, 13(5),* 26–27.

Chinn, P. C., Drew, C. J., & Logan, D. R. (1979). *Mental retardation: A life cycle approach* (2nd ed.). St Louis: Mosby.

Christian, L., & Poling, A. (1997). Drug abuse in persons with mental retardation: A review. *American Journal on Mental Retardation, 102*(2), 126–136.

Cohen, D. E. (2000). Health promotion and disability prevention: The case for personal responsibility and independence. In M. L. Wehmyer & J. R. Patton (Eds.), *Mental retardation in the 21st century* (pp. 251–264). Austin, TX: PRO-ED.

Cromwell, R. L. (1963). A social learning approach to mental retardation. In N. R. Ellis (Ed.), *Handbook of mental deficiency: Psychological theory and research* (pp. 41–91). New York: McGraw-Hill.

Cronin, M. E., & Patton, J. R. (1993). *Life skills instructions for all students with special needs: A practical guide for integrating real life content into the curriculum.* Austin, TX: PRO-ED.

Cummins, J. P., & Das, J. P. (1980). Cognitive processing, academic achievement, and WISC-R performance in EMR children. *Journal of Consulting and Clinical Psychology, 46,* 777–779.

Delaney, D., & Poling, A. (1990). Drug abuse among mentally retarded people: An overlooked problem? *Journal of Alcohol and Drug Education, 35,* 48–54.

Doll, E. A. (1962). Historical survey of research and management of mental retardation in the United States. In E. P. Trapp & P. Hinestein (Eds.), *Readings on the exceptional child* (pp. 21–68). New York: Appleton-Century-Crofts.

Dunn, L. M. (1973). Children with mild general learning disabilities. In L. M. Dunn (Ed.), *Exceptional children in the schools: Special education in transition* (2nd ed., pp. 126–133). New York: Holt, Rinehert, & Winston.

Drew, C. J., Hardman, M. L., & Hart, A. W. (1996). *Designing and conducting research in education and social science.* Needham Heights, MA: Allyn & Bacon.

Edgar, E. (1987). Secondary programs in education: Are many of them justifiable? *Exceptional Children, 53,* 555–561.

Ellis, N. R. (1963). The stimulus trace and behavioral inadequacy. In N. R. Ellis (Ed.), *Handbook of mental deficiency* (pp. 134–158). New York: McGraw-Hill.

Ellis, N. R. (1969). A behavioral research strategy in mental retardation: Defense and critique. *American Journal of Mental Deficiency, 73,* 557–566.

Ellis, N. R. (1970). Memory process in retardates and normals. *International Review of Research in Mental Retardation, 4,* 1–32.

Ellis, N. R., & Dulaney, C. L. (1991). Further evidence for the cognitive inertia of persons with mental retardation. *American Journal on Mental Retardation, 95,* 613–621.

Epstein, M. H., Cullinan, D., & Polloway, E. A. (1986). Patterns of maladjustment among mentally retarded children and youth. *American Journal of Mental Deficiency, 91,* 127–134.

Epstein, M. H., Polloway, E. A., Patton, J. R., & Foley, R. (1989). Mild retardation: Student characteristics and services. *Education and Training of the Mentally Retarded, 24,* 7–16.

Estes, W. K. (1970). *Learning theory and mental development.* New York: Academic Press.

Ferrara, M. L. (1992). *Substance abuse treatment program for persons with mental retardation.* Austin: Texas Commission on Alcohol and Drug Abuse.

Fraser, W. I., & Rao, J. M. (1991). Recent studies of mentally handicapped young people's behavior. *Journal of Child Psychology and Psychiatry, 32,* 79–108.

Freeman, J. M., Vining, E. P. G., & Pillas, D. J. (1997). *Seizures and epilepsy in childhood: A guide for parents* (2nd ed.). Baltimore: Johns Hopkins University Press.

Geiger, W., Brownsmith, K., & Forgnone, C. (1978). Differential importance of skills for TMR students perceived by teachers. *Education and Training of the Mentally Retarded, 13,* 259–264.

Gresham, F. M. (1982). Misguided mainstreaming: The case for social skills training with handicapped children. *Exceptional Children, 48,* 422–433.

Guralnick, M. J., & Weinhouse, E. (1984). Peer-related social interactions of developmentally delayed young children: Their development and characteristics. *Developmental Psychology, 20,* 815–827.

Halle, J. W., Silverman, N. A., & Regan, L. (1983). The effects of a data-based exercise program on physical fitness of retarded children. *Education and Training of the Mentally Retarded, 18(3),* 221–225.

Hardman, M. L., Drew, C. J., & Egan, M. W. (1996). *Human exceptionality: Society, school, and family* (5th ed.). Boston: Allyn & Bacon.

Healey, K. N., & Masterpasqua, F. (1992). Interpersonal cognitive problem-solving among children with mild mental retardation. *American Journal on Mental Retardation, 96,* 367–372.

Heber, R. F. (1964). Personality. In H. A. Stevens & R. F. Heber (Eds.), *Mental retardation: A review of research* (pp. 143–174). Chicago: University of Chicago Press.

Inhelder, B. (1968). *The diagnosis of reasoning in the mentally retarded.* New York: Day.

Jaquish, C., & Stella, M. A. (1986). Helping special needs students move from elementary to secondary school. *Counterpoint, 7(1),* 1.

Kail, R. (1992). General information processing by persons with mental retardation. *American Journal on Mental Retardation, 97,* 333–341.

Kopp, C. B., Baker, B. L., & Brown, K. W. (1992). Social skills and their correlates: Preschoolers with developmental disabilities. *American Journal on Mental Retardation, 96,* 357–366.

Larson, S. A., Lakin, K. C., Anderson, L., Kwak, N., Lee, J. H., & Anderson, D. (2000). Prevalence of mental retardation and/or developmental disabilities: Analysis of the 1994/1995 NHIS-D. *MR/DD Data Brief, 1(2).* Minneapolis: University of Minnesota, Institute on Community Integration, Research and Training Center on Community Living.

Lemperle, G. (1985). Plastic surgery. In D. Lane & B. Stratford (Eds.), *Current approaches to Down's syndrome* (pp. 131–145). New York: Holt, Rinehart, & Winston.

Lemperle, G., & Rada, D. (1980). Facial plastic surgery in children with Down's syndrome. *Plastic and Reconstructive Surgery, 66,* 337–342.

Lovell, R. W., & Reiss, A. L. (1993). Dual diagnosis: Psychiatric disorders in developmental disabilities. *Pediatric Clinics of North America, 40,* 579–592.

MacMillan, D. L. (1982). *Mental retardation in school and society* (2nd ed.). Boston: Little, Brown.

MacMillan, D. L. (1989). "New" EMRs. In G. A. Robinson, J. R. Patton, E. A. Polloway, & L. R. Sargent (Eds.), *Best practices in mental retardation* (pp. 1–20). Reston, VA: Council for Exceptional Children, Division on Mental Retardation and Developmental Disabilities.

MacMillan, D. L., & Borthwick, S. (1980). The new educable mentally retarded population: Can they be mainstreamed? *Mental Retardation, 18,* 155–158.

MacMillan, D. L., & Reschly, D. J. (1998). Overrepresentation of minority students: The case for greater specificity or reconsideration of the variables examined. *Journal of Special Education, 32,* 15–24.

Manni, J. L., Winikur, D. W., & Keller, M. (1980). *The status of minority group representation special education programs in the state of New Jersey.* Trenton: New Jersey State Department of education. (ERIC Document Reproduction Service No. ED 203 575)

McBride, J. W., & Forgnone, C. (1985). Emphasis of instruction provided LD, EH, and EMR students in categorized and cross-categorical programming. *Journal of Research (Development in Education, 18(4),* 50–54.

Mercer, C. D., & Snell, M. E. (1977). *Learning theory research in mental retardation: Implications for teaching.* Upper Saddle River, NJ: Merrill/Prentice Hall.

Merrill, E. C. (1990). Attentional resource allocation and mental retardation. In N. W. Bray (Ed.), *International review of research in mental retardation: Vol. 16* (pp. 51–88). San Diego, CA: Academic Press.

Meyers, C. E., & MacMillan, D. L. (1976). Utilization of learning principles in retardation. In R. Koch & J. Dobson (Eds.), *The mentally retarded child and his family: A multidisciplinary handbook* (2nd ed., pp. 323–348). New York: Brunner/Mazel.

Mosier, H. D., Grossman, H. J., & Dingman, H. F. (1965). Physical growth in mental defectiveness. *Pediatrics, 36,* 465-519.

O'Connor, N. (1975). Imbecility and color blindness. *American Journal of Mental Deficiency, 62,* 83-87.

Olbrisch, R. R. (1982). Plastic surgical management of children with Down's syndrome: Indications and results. *British Journal of Plastic Surgery, 35,* 195-200.

Oswald, D. P., Coutinho, M. J., Best, A. M., & Singh, N. N. (1999). Ethnic representation in special education: The influence of school-related economic and demographic variables. *Journal of Special Education, 32,* 194–206.

Parsons, C. L., Iacone, T. A., & Rozner, L. (1987). Effect of tongue reduction on articulation in children with Down's syndrome. *American Journal of Mental Deficiency, 91,* 328–332.

Payne, J. S., Polloway, E. A., Smith, J. E., & Payne, R. A. (1981). *Strategies for teaching the mentally retarded* (2nd ed.). Upper Saddle River, NJ: Merrill/Prentice Hall.

Pellegrino, L. (1997). Cerebral palsy. In M. L. Batshaw (Ed.), *Children with disabilities* (4th ed., pp. 499-528). Baltimore: Brookes.

Piaget, J. (1969). *The theory of stages in cognitive development.* New York: McGraw-Hill.

Polloway, E. A., Epstein, M. H., & Cullinan, D. (1985). Prevalence of behavior problems among mentally retarded students. *Education and Training of the Mentally Retarded, 20,* 3–13.

Polloway, E. A., Epstein, M. H., Patton, J. R., Cullinan, D., & Luebke, J. (1986). Demographic, social, and behavioral characteristics of students with educable mental retardation. *Education and Training of the Mentally Retarded, 21,* 27–34.

Polloway, E. A., & Patton, J. R. (1997). *Strategies for teaching learners with special needs* (5th ed.). Upper Saddle River, NJ: Merrill/Prentice Hall.

Polloway, E. A., & Smith, J. D. (1983). Changes in mild mental retardation: Population, programs, and perspectives. *Exceptional Children, 50,* 149–159.

Pueschel, S. M. (1997). *Down syndrome: The ARC's Q&A on Down syndrome.* Available: http://thearc.org/faqs/mimrqa.html (1997, February 5).

Rainforth, B., & York, J. (1991). Handling and positioning. In F. Orelove & D. Sobsey (Eds.), *Educating children with multiple disabilities: A transdisciplinary approach* (pp. 79–118). Baltimore: Brookes.

Raymond, E. B. (2000). *Learners with mild disabilities: A characteristic approach.* Boston: Allyn & Bacon.

Reber, M. (1992). Dual diagnosis: Psychiatric disorders and mental retardation. In M. Batshaw & Y. M. Perret (Eds.), *Children with disabilities: A medical primer* (3rd ed., pp. 421–440). Baltimore: Brookes.

Reschly, D., Robinson, G., Volmer, L., & Wilson, L. (1988). *Iowa mental disabilities research report: Final report and executive summary.* Des Moines: Iowa State Department of Education.

Resource Center on Substance Abuse and Prevention and Disabilities. (1992). *Mental retardation: A look at alcohol and other drug abuse prevention.* Washington, DC: U.S. Department of Health and Human Services, Office for Substance Abuse Prevention.

Rotter, J. B. (1954). *Social learning and clinical psychology.* Upper Saddle River, NJ: Merrill-Prentice Hall.

Russel, A.T., & Forness, S.R. (1985). Behavioral disturbance in mentally retarded children in TMR and EMR classrooms. *American Journal of Mental Deficiency, 89,* 338–344.

Schloss, P. J., Alper, S., & Jayne, D. (1994). Self-determination for persons with disabilities: Choice, risk, and dignity. *Exceptional Children, 60,* 215–225.

Scudder, R. R., & Tremain, D. H. (1992). Repair behaviors of children with and without mental retardation. *Mental Retardation, 30,* 277–282.

Seligman, M. E. (1975). *Helplessness: On depression, development, and death.* San Francisco: Freeman.

Sherman, J. A., Sheldon, J. B., Harchik, A. E., Edwards, K., & Quinn, J. M. (1992). Social evaluations of behaviors comprising three social skills and a comparison of the performance of people with and without mental retardation. *American Journal on Mental Retardation, 96,* 419–431.

Smith, T. E. C., Polloway, E. A., Patton, J. R., & Dowdy, C. A. (1998). *Teaching students with special needs in inclusive settings* (2nd ed.). Boston: Allyn & Bacon.

Snell, M. E., & Renzaglia, A. M. (1986). Moderate, severe and profound handicaps. In N. G. Haring & L. McCormick (Eds.), *Exceptional children and youth* (4th ed., pp. 271–310). Upper Saddle River, NJ: Merrill/Prentice Hall.

Spitz, H. H. (1966). The role of input organization in the learning and memory of mental retardates. *International Review of Research in Mental Retardation, 2,* 29–56.

Spitz, H. H. (1973). Consolidating facts into the schematized learning and memory of mental retardates. *International Review of Research in Mental Retardation, 6,* 149–168.

Spitz, H. H. (1979). Beyond field theory in the study of mental deficiency. In N. R. Ellis (Ed.), *Handbook of mental deficiency: Psychological theory and research* (2nd ed., pp. 121–141). Hillsdale, NJ: Erlbaum.

Spradlin, J. E. (1968). Environmental factors and the language development of retarded children. In S. Rosenberg & J. H. Koplin (Eds.), *Developments in applied psycholinguistic research* (pp. 261–290). New York: Macmillan.

Stephens, W. E. (1966). Category usage of normal and subnormal children on three types of categories. *American Journal of Mental Deficiency, 71,* 266–273.

Stephens, W. E. (1972). Equivalence formation by retarded and nonretarded children at different mental ages. *American Journal of Mental Deficiency, 77,* 311–313.

Sternberg, R. J. (1997). The triarchic theory of intelligence. In D. P. Flanagan, J. Genshaft, & P. L. Harrison (Eds.), *Contemporary intellectual assessment: Theories, tests, and issues* (pp. 92–104). New York: Guilford.

Sternberg, R. J., & Spear, L. C. (1985). A triarchic theory of mental retardation. *International Review of Research in Mental Retardation, 13,* 301–326.

Stipek, D. J.(1993). *Motivation to learn: From theory to practice* (2nd ed.). Boston: Allyn & Bacon.

Swanson, H. L., & Cooney, J. B. (1991). Learning disabilities and memory. In B. Y. L. Wong (Ed.), *Learning about learning disabilities* (pp. 103–127). San Diego, CA: Academic Press.

Tomporowski, P. D., & Tinsley, V. (1994). Effects of target probability and memory demands on the vigilance of adults with and without mental retardation. *American Journal on Mental Retardation, 96,* 525–530.

Turnure, J., & Zigler, E. (1964). Outer-directedness in the problem solving of normal and retarded children. *Journal of Abnormal and Social Psychology, 69,* 427–436.

U.S. Department of Commerce. (1999). *Statistical abstract of the United States* (119th ed.). Washington, DC: Author.

U.S. Department of Education. (1996). *Eighteenth annual report to Congress on the implementation of the Individuals with Disabilities Education Act.* Washington, DC: Office of Special Education Programs, U.S. Department of Education.

U.S. Department of Education. (1999). *Twenty-first annual report to Congress on the implementation of the Individual with Disabilities Education Act.* Washington, DC: Office of Special Education Programs, U.S. Department of Education.

Wagner, M., Newman, L., & Shaver, D. (1989). *The National Longitudinal Transition Study of Special Education Students: Report on procedures for the first wave of data collection (1978).* Menlo Park, CA: SRI International.

Warren, S. F., & Abbeduto, L. (1992). The relation of communication and language development to mental retardation. *American Journal on Mental Retardation, 97,* 125-130.

Wehmeyer, M. L. (1994). Perceptions of self-determination and psychological empowerment of adolescents with mental retardation. *Education and Training in Mental Retardation, 29,* 9-21.

Wehmeyer, M. L., Palmer, S. B., Agran, M., Mithaug, D. E., & Martin, J. E. (2000). Promoting causal agency: The self-determined learning model of instruction. *Exceptional Children, 66,* 439-453.

Westling, D. L. (1986). *Introduction to mental retardation.* Upper Saddle River, NJ: Merrill-Prentice Hall.

Westling, D. L., & Fox, L. (2000). *Teaching students with severe disabilities.* Upper Saddle River, NJ: Merrill/Prentice Hall.

Whitman, T. L. (1990). Self-regulation and mental retardation. *American Journal on Mental Retardation, 94,* 347-362.

Woodward, W. M. (1963). The application of Piaget's theory to research in mental deficiency. In N. R. Ellis (Ed.), *Handbook of mental deficiency* (pp. 297-324). New York: McGraw-Hill.

Woodward, W. M. (1979). Piaget's theory and the study of mental retardation. In N. R. Ellis (Ed.), *Handbook of mental deficiency: Psychological theory and research* (2nd ed., pp. 169-195). Hillsdale, NJ: Erlbaum.

Zeaman, D., & House, B. J. (1963). The role of attention in retardate discrimination learning. In N. R. Ellis (Ed.), *Handbook of mental deficiency: Psychological theory and research* (pp. 159-223). Hillsdale, NJ: Erlbaum.

Zeaman, D., & House, B. J. (1979). A review of attention theory. In N. R. Ellis (Ed.), *Handbook of mental deficiency: Psychological theory and research* (2nd ed., pp. 63-120). Hillsdale, NJ: Erlbaum.

Zigler, E. (1969). Development verses difference theories of mental retardation and problems of motivation. *American Journal of Mental Deficiency, 73,* 536-556.

Zigler, E. (1973). The retarded child as a whole person. In D. K. Routh (Ed.), *The experimental psychology of mental retardation* (pp. 231-322). Chicago: Aldine.

Zigler, E. (1999). The individual with mental retardation as a whole person. In E. Zigler & D. Bennett-Gates (Eds.), *Personality development in individuals with mental retardation* (pp. 1-16). Cambridge: Cambridge University Press.

Zirpoli, T. (1986). Child abuse and children with handicaps. *Remedial and Special Education, 7*(2), 39-48.

Chapter

8

Characteristics of Persons with Severe Mental Retardation

 To review the chapter objectives on-line, go to the companion website at www.prenhall.com/beirne-smith and select Chapter 8, and then choose the Objectives module.

Shannon H. Kim, Ph.D.
University of Mississippi

Mitylene B. Arnold, Ph.D.
University of Mississippi

OBJECTIVES

After reading this chapter, the student should be able to

- discuss ways in which severe mental retardation is defined and identify some common behavioral, communication, physical, and emotional characteristics

- describe appropriate curricula and methods of instruction for persons with severe mental retardation, and explain the philosophical model on which these ideas are based

- identify and describe suitable outcomes for persons with severe mental retardation

- discuss the various types of supports accessed by persons with severe mental retardation

KEY TERMS

behavior analysis

community-referenced instruction

ecological model

extensive supports

functional assessment

natural supports

person-centered planning

pervasive supports

I n the previous chapter, you were introduced to the group of people who comprise the majority of individuals with mental retardation. But what about the rest? Who are they? What are they like? As the definition of mental retardation has changed throughout the years, so has society's perceptions of the group known as persons with severe mental retardation. They are quite possibly our most vulnerable population. Easily observed to be different, they encounter prejudice and fear throughout their lives. Despite such legislative efforts as the Individuals with Disabilities Education Act of 1997 (IDEA) and the Americans with Disabilities Act of 1990 (ADA), they are still very often excluded from school and community activities. This chapter will consider some common characteristics of this traditionally underserved segment of the population. An expanded focus on educational practices, outcome goals, and support functions will follow.

CHARACTERISTICS OF SEVERE MENTAL RETARDATION

Generally speaking, individuals who require more extensive supports than those described in the previous chapter are referred to as persons with severe mental retardation. The "severe" label encompasses the groups specifically designated as having moderate, severe, and profound levels of mental retardation. This section will discuss the current definitions of severe mental retardation, demographic information, functional characteristics, and environmental influences.

Today's Definitions

The definition of mental retardation offered by the latest American Association on Mental Retardation manual (AAMR; American Association on Mental Retardation, 1992) discontinued the use of the distinguishing terms *mild, moderate, severe,* and *profound*. For the purposes of this chapter, persons with severe forms of mental retardation are those who require extensive and/or pervasive supports to function with maximal success. More extensive support needs are differentiated from more limited support needs in frequency, duration, and urgency. We will return to the discussion of supports later in this chapter. Specifically, **extensive supports** are provided regularly, in at least some environments, and on a long-term basis. **Pervasive supports** are provided on a constant basis, across all environments, and are of a potentially life-sustaining nature (AAMR, 1992). Supports may be provided to assist with basic and/or complex tasks of daily life, with management of emotional or psychological concerns, or with physical health needs.

Though the AAMR definition has been considered the definitive one in the field of mental retardation, the *Diagnostic and Statistical Manual of Mental Disorders: Fourth Edition* (DSM-IV; American Psychiatric Association, 1994) has been the generally accepted authority for diagnosing psychological disorders. The DSM-IV is used primarily by professionals in the fields of psychology and psychiatry, and it still adheres to the levels of severity used in Grossman's (1983) AAMR definition for diagnostic purposes. The manual gives in-depth descriptions of the various levels of mental retardation. For example, people with moderate retardation are described as profiting from vocational services and training in social skills. People

For a complete on-line glossary of mental retardation terms, go to the companion website at *http://www.prenhall.com/ beirne-smith* and select any chapter, and then choose the Glossary module.

with severe mental retardation are presented as usually able to learn sight words and function well in the community. People with profound mental retardation are described as needing the most intensive supports with respect to self-help, vocational, and communication skills.

The definitions provided by AAMR and the DSM-IV are designed for diagnostic purposes, and specialized knowledge is required to apply them to individual cases. The sociopolitical climate of the past 30 years has generated a number of special interest groups and service providers to ensure that persons with mental retardation and other disabilities are afforded the opportunities that all citizens of the United States have come to expect. Such organizations are not generally responsible for diagnosing disabilities but do need to expressly define the populations they are designed to serve. The Association for Persons with Severe Handicaps (TASH), the advocacy leader for persons with severe disabilities, offers a more person-centered perspective through the following definition:

> … individuals of all ages who require extensive ongoing support in more than one major life activity in order to participate in integrated community settings and to enjoy a quality of life that is available to citizens with fewer or no disabilities. Support may be required for life activities such as mobility, communication, self-care, and learning, and necessary for independent living, employment and self-sufficiency. (Lindley, 1990, p. 1)

These definitions present an image of individuals who need varying but intensive levels of support to participate in society. Definitions that define supports needed for participation in the community facilitate the processes of needs assessment, goal setting, and quality-of-life evaluation. Definitions are important for accessing the service delivery system, but due to the highly individualistic, complex nature of these individuals, the specification of each individual's educational goals and support needs provides the most meaningful information.

Current Demographics

Chapter 2 introduced the idea that the definitions of mental retardation reflect the times in which they are drafted; that "people make of it what they want to, people interpret it in light of their own understandings and prejudices" (Blatt, 1987, p. 69). People with more severe forms of mental retardation have often suffered in the face of such perceptions. Miscalculation of their potential is documented throughout history. One must only look to such descriptions as provided by Goddard in 1920:

> Yet they are the persons who make for us our social problems. The emphasis here is on the word *"incapable."* This is the thing that we have heretofore ignored. We have known that these people *did not* compete successfully and that they *did not* manage their affairs with ordinary prudence, but we have not recognized that they were fundamentally *incapable* of so doing. (p. 5)

Unfortunately, the winds of change were slow to come. Nearly a half-century later, the same sentiment is reflected by another author: "The profoundly retarded individual is considered, on the basis of current knowledge and practices, incapable of profiting from any type of training or education" (Stevens, 1964, p. 4).

FIGURE 8.1
Percentages of Population with Mental Retardation

Data taken from APA (1994, p. 41).

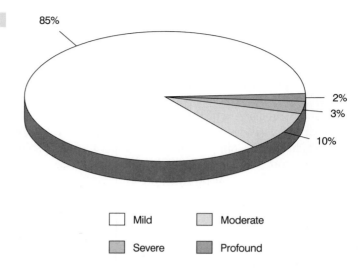

Why is the road to understanding the needs, capabilities, and *humanity* of these individuals so long? One reason may well be that it is difficult to understand that which we do not see. Besides the fact that individuals with severe forms of mental retardation have known little community integration until recent times, our understanding is hampered by their status as a relatively rare segment of the population. As depicted in Figure 8.1, of the approximately 1% to 3% of the total population who have mental retardation, only about 15% experience the need for extensive supports. Specifically, about 10% are within the moderate range, with 3% in the severe range, and only about 2% in the profound range (APA; American Psychiatric Association, 1994).

Severe forms of mental retardation are generally recognized earlier in life than are the milder cases. More pronounced developmental delays and additional related medical conditions make this earlier diagnosis possible. Unlike the milder forms of mental retardation, environmental deprivation is not usually an associated factor. Although certain prenatal factors such as premature births are more common in impoverished areas, the prevalence of the condition is relatively stable across all socioeconomic classes (APA, 1994).

Functional Characteristics

Although one's IQ score no longer dictates any specific range of mental retardation in the most recent AAMR definition, one would generally expect that as IQ decreases, the intensity of needed supports increases. This is often a valid assumption, but it does not hold true in every case. For example, an individual who has an IQ below 50 may function with limited or intermittent supports, just as an individual with an IQ above 55 may need extensive or pervasive supports. Though IQ is an integral part of the definition of mental retardation, it is generally not the most useful source of information about a person's needs and abilities.

❋ "Oh, What a Beautiful Mourning"

The poem printed here was written by Marc Gold, a respected leader in the area of vocational training and a strong champion for the rights of people with mental retardation. This poem, read at the end of a speech that Gold gave in 1973, has been cited often since then and is used in the opening sound track of the film *Try Another Way*. Embedded in the poem is commentary about expectations, perceptions, testing, opportunities, and capabilities. The message of this poem is as relevant today as it was in 1973 or when its author reflected back on it (Gold, 1980).

An End to the Concept of Mental Retardation

Oh, What a Beautiful Mourning
If you could only know me for who I am
Instead of for who I am not,
There would be so much more to see

'cause there's so much more that I've got.
So long as you see me as mentally retarded,
Which supposedly means something, I guess,
There is nothing that you or I could ever do
To make me a human success.
Someday you'll know that tests aren't built
To let me stand next to you.
By the way you test me, all they can do
Is make me look bad through and through.
And someday soon I'll get my chance,
When some of you finally adapt.
You'll be delighted to know that though I'm MR,
I'm not all handicapped.

Source: From "An End to the Concept of Mental Retardation: Oh, What a Beautiful Mourning" (pp. 143–144), by M. W. Gold in *Did I Say That? Articles and Commentary on the Try Another Way System*, 1982, Champaign, IL: Research Press. Reprinted with permission.

A more salient information source for identifying an individual who requires extensive supports is adaptive skill assessment. The American Association on Mental Retardation (1992) has provided 10 areas of adaptive skill used to generate a profile of a person's strengths and weaknesses. Some of these skill areas, such as communication, home living, and self-care, have been the focus of education in treatment plans for years. Others, such as social and leisure skills, are being brought to the fore as more persons with greater degrees of disability move into the community.

Although the range of skills and abilities possessed by individuals varies considerably, a few broad statements may be made about the functional characteristics of this group as a whole. People with severe mental retardation frequently have more than one disability, and they often have physical characteristics that draw attention. They learn new skills slowly and have difficulty applying knowledge gained in one context to another. They often have limited communication skills and sometimes exhibit problem behaviors. However, one must not overlook positive attributes. Although progress may be slow, people with severe mental retardation do learn, and they can form relationships based on love, fun, and common interests (Heward, 1996).

Environmental Considerations

A diagnosis of mental retardation reflects the characteristics of an individual relative to society as a whole. The constructs of intelligence, adaptive behavior, psychological well-being, emotional stability, and even physical health exist as continua with no precise dividing line between the haves and the have-nots. It stands to reason that persons who lack a sense of comfort and familiarity with the society in which they live, or who lack the tools necessary for success in that environment, are likely to demonstrate skill deficits and aberrant behaviors. An American taking an intelligence test designed for an unfamiliar society could easily score in the below-average range. She may have difficulty with skills deemed very simple, her natural emotional reactions may be seen as abnormal, and her physical dexterity and skills could be interpreted to be underdeveloped. She could easily be considered to have "extensive support needs." However, the longer she lives in the new society, the more comfortable people around her try to make her, and the more they teach her about their culture, the more independent she will become and the less support she will require.

We cannot expect persons with severe mental retardation to develop higher-level skills unless they are involved with the community to which they are expected to conform. As with all human beings, the relationship between persons with severe mental retardation and the community is a reciprocal one. The more society is willing to invest in providing supports, the higher the likelihood that the individual will learn to function without them. This is not to say that we can "cure" mental retardation. However, we can and should expect that "with appropriate supports over a sustained period of time, the life functioning of individuals with mental retardation will generally improve" (AAMR, 1992, p. 109). Studies of skill acquisition of persons with severe mental retardation who have increased interactions with the community verify this expectation. Kennedy and Itkonen (1994) indicate social gains under such conditions. Several authors, including Snell (1993) and Wilcox and Bellamy (1982), have noted, for example, that students with more severe mental retardation who participate in a community-based curriculum find and retain jobs at a greater rate than do those who participate in self-contained educational programs.

On the topic of increased interactions between persons who have disabilities and those who do not, questions about the impact on society at large naturally arise. Research has indicated that authority figures and nondisabled peers develop helpful, accepting, positive attitudes toward persons with severe mental retardation after inclusive experiences (Strully & Strully, 1989). Block and Rizzo (1995) discuss the development of facilitative attitudes of nondisabled peers and authority figures after inclusive experiences. Over time, reports of positive outcomes for both the person with mental retardation and the non-disabled peers have become more frequent (see Gaylord, Abery, & Schoeller, 1997). So, it would seem that community involvement with persons who have extensive support needs can be a positive experience for all.

BEHAVIORAL CHARACTERISTICS

Over the years, much time and attention have been dedicated to assisting persons with mental retardation to develop a repertoire of productive and socially adaptive behaviors. The ability to demonstrate appropriate behavior while inhibiting challenging behavior impacts many areas of a person's life (Hill & Bruininks, 1984; Larson, 1991; Reichle & Light, 1992). In addition to covering common behavioral issues, this section will describe the science of behavior analysis and the types of interventions commonly used to teach adaptive behaviors and reduce challenging behaviors.

Behavioral Issues

As described earlier, persons with extensive support needs are likely to have difficulty acquiring new skills, applying the skills they've already learned to new situations, and communicating their wants, needs, thoughts, and feelings (Heward, 1996). However, these skills are helpful in functioning successfully in the social world. For this reason, persons with severe mental retardation are likely to concentrate a great deal of time on learning such adaptive skills (see Wehman & Kregel, 1997).

Compounding the problems associated with slower development of adaptive behaviors are the risks of developing challenging behaviors. People with severe mental retardation sometimes develop difficult behaviors such as aggression and self-injury, as well as self-stimulatory behaviors such as persistent rocking and hand flapping. However, the presence of severe mental retardation should not be taken as the sole explanation for challenging behavior. Research has indicated that such behaviors are neither inevitable nor incorrigible in this population. Instead, they are strongly related to training and environmental circumstances (Luiselli & Cameron, 1998).

Although adaptive and challenging behaviors are generally thought to be separate constructs (Bruininks & McGrew, 1987), they are not unrelated. Challenging behaviors are often eliminated by teaching adaptive behaviors such as communication, choice making, and social skills (Horner & Carr, 1997; Reichle & Wacker, 1993; Van Houten & Axelrod, 1993). Additionally, both types of behavior have been shown to improve in enriched, accepting environments (Koegel, Koegel, & Dunlap, 1996).

Behavior Analysis

The idea that behavior and environment are related is nothing new. The work of psychologist B. F. Skinner (1953) first explained the relationship. Skinner termed the relationship operant, because the person voluntarily "operates" on the environment to get what he wants. The science of **behavior analysis**, or the study of environmental events that change behavior, arose from Skinner's work. Behavior analysis was a logical tool for use with persons with severe mental retardation, because unlike other forms of psychological intervention, it does not require the person to report internal events such as thoughts and feelings that may be driving behavior. With behavior analysis, the psychologist is able to identify the events in the environment that are maintaining a behavior and manipulate them to encourage the development of new behaviors (Miller, 1997).

The usefulness of behavior analysis with persons who have severe forms of mental retardation was further increased by the integration of functional assessment techniques. **Functional assessment** is a process of identifying the purpose, or function, of a given behavior to teach a more adaptive method of addressing that need. Although categorizations of behavioral function vary, the four functions presented by Iwata et al. (1994a, 1994b) are commonly cited: social attention, escape from demand, access to tangible items such as food or toys, and self-stimulation or sensory reinforcement.

Functional assessment has become a widely accepted first step in developing behavior modification plans. The usefulness of the process is underscored by provisions of IDEA (1997), which require that a functional assessment be conducted if a student with a disability is placed in an alternative educational setting for more than 10 days due to behavior. A functional assessment may involve direct observations of the student by a person trained in behavioral psychology, environmental manipulations in which the student's responses to various consequences are observed, or structured interviews with the student, his parents, or teachers (O'Neill, Horner, Albin, Storey, & Sprague, 1990).

To learn more about functional assessment and other topics discussed in Chapter 8, go to the companion website at www.prenhall.com/ beirne-smith and select Chapter 8, then choose the Web Destinations module.

Behavioral Interventions

Once a functional assessment has been completed, appropriate interventions may be developed. Many options are available for reducing challenging behaviors and increasing desired behaviors. Commonly, these interventions are based on the principles of reinforcement. That is, desired behaviors are reinforced, or followed by a pleasant consequence, while the desired consequence is withheld following challenging behaviors. For example, if a functional assessment indicates that Amy grabs people to get attention, attention would be withheld when she grabbed. To prevent her from developing new challenging behaviors, an appropriate method of gaining attention should be taught (Carr & Durand, 1985; Horner & Carr, 1997). For example, Amy could be given immediate attention for raising her hand, calling her teacher's name, or presenting a picture symbol.

Other forms of intervention are available that do not require direct training of the individual. Generally, such interventions involve making modifications to the person's environment (Horner & Carr, 1997). For example, if a functional assessment indicates that Bob only hits himself when he hears loud music, it makes sense to simply eliminate loud music from his environment. Similarly, behaviors identified as self-stimulatory may be addressed by giving the person access to alternative activities that provide the same sensory response (e.g., scheduling access to a trampoline for a person who jumps up and down). For people who engage in problem behaviors to access tangible items, providing noncontingent access to those items often eliminates the need for the person to engage in the behavior (Vollmer, Iwata, Zarcone, Smith, & Mazaleski, 1993).

A final note regarding problem behavior relates to the idea of life quality. People who live active, balanced lives have higher degrees of psychological and emotional health (Baroff, 1991). Simple adjustments regarding the exercise of personal choice or increased involvement with peers have often been shown to be successful "treatments" for problem behavior in this population (e.g., Horner, 1980; Koegel et al., 1996). When conducting behavioral assessments, it is important to consider such factors as personal choice making, involvement in reciprocal relationships, and active engagement in fun and meaningful activities.

COMMUNICATION CHARACTERISTICS

In our world, words are the building blocks of understanding. The ability to produce and interpret language is vital for successful living in society. The importance of language is demonstrated by its inclusion as a construct for measurement in adaptive behavior and cognitive assessment instruments (e.g., *Scales of Independent Behavior— Revised* [Bruininks, Woodcock, Weatherman, & Hill, 1996]; *Stanford–Binet Intelligence Scale—Fourth Edition* [Thorndike, Hagen, & Sattler, 1986]; *Vineland Adaptive Behavior Scales* [Sparrow, Balla, & Cicchetti, 1984a, 1984b, 1985; *Wechsler Intelligence Scale for Children—Third Edition* [Wechsler, 1991]). For people with severe mental retardation, communication skills are often jeopardized by difficulties with speech and language. This section will describe speech and language development, assessment and treatment of communication problems, and considerations for teaching communication skills.

Speech and Language Development

The development of speech and language is a complicated and fascinating process that is only partially understood. The human brain seems biologically predestined to code and decode language. The development of language has an impact on other cognitive processes such as memory and problem solving. Under normal circumstances, language learning and speech production are dynamic processes that begin at birth. Crying, reaching, and imitating are all precursors that indicate language readiness (Salkind, 1994).

For persons with severe mental retardation, language development is usually delayed or interrupted. The rate of speech/language disorder among this group is estimated at 90% (National Institute of Neurological Disorders and Stroke, 1988). Although the problems are often grouped together, speech and language disorders are distinct phenomena that may occur together or separately. Speech problems occur when sounds are absent or distorted to the extent that the speaker cannot be easily understood. Language disorders may occur in two forms: receptive and expressive. Receptive problems are indicated when a person cannot understand, or decode, the rules of language. Expressive problems occur when the person cannot use the rules of language well enough to share their experiences (Paul-Brown & Diggs, 1993).

Investigations of the speech and language skills of persons with severe mental retardation have indicated a wide array of skill level, ranging from direct behaviors that reveal the person's wants and needs to gesturing to verbal fluency (Mar & Sall, 1999). Regardless of the mode of communication, people with more severe forms of mental retardation are likely to take a practical approach to communication. That is, communication attempts are more likely to occur when the person wants to access an object or request assistance. More social functions, such as commenting on surroundings or asking about the well-being of others, are less frequently observed (McLean, Brady, McLean, & Behrens, 1999; McLean & Snyder-McLean, 1991).

Assessment and Interventions

Most people with severe mental retardation will participate in a speech/language assessment at some point in life. Such assessments are usually part of the comprehensive evaluation procedures that are required for many types of services (Kubiszyn & Borich, 1996). Assessments may consist of teacher/family interviews, physical examinations, standardized tests, and/or direct observations by speech-language pathologists. Hearing evaluations are routinely administered, as well (Paul-Brown & Diggs, 1993).

Assessment results are used to design and implement interventions. For persons who use words to communicate but experience difficulties with producing specific sounds, a speech therapist may provide direct training through prompting and imitation exercises. Several computer programs have become available that may increase motivation or provide additional practice opportunities (Paul-Brown & Diggs, 1993). For many people with severe mental retardation, however, the production of understandable speech is not possible. Interventions for those people must focus on assisting the person to communicate despite all obstacles (Kaiser, 1993a).

Among nonverbal communication methods, Soto, Belfiore, Schlosser, and Haynes (1993) indicate that gesturing and manual signing are the most commonly used. Again, a wide array of skill level is present among persons using manual language. Rudimentary forms of sign language include pointing and forming gestures that mimic the behavior desired (e.g., pointing to a favored toy to indicate a desire to play with it; imitating the motion of bringing food to the mouth to indicate a desire to eat). People with more advanced communication skills may learn less obvious signs from organized sign languages, such as clapping the hands together to indicate "school" or crossing the arms at the wrists to indicate "work."

Still other persons with severe mental retardation may benefit from some type of augmentative communication device. Augmentative communication may take many forms, including pointing to or presenting pictures of desired objects or activities. In a more sophisticated version, pictures are arranged on an electronic board and a synthesized voice is activated when the person touches the picture (Soto et al., 1993). Although all types of communication interventions can work, the rate of skill acquisition and the extent to which skills are maintained and generalized to new situations depend on the instructional strategies used (Romski & Sevcik, 1993).

Instructional Strategies

The first step in ensuring a person benefits from communication training is to choose the most appropriate mode or modes of intervention. Factors to consider include visual discrimination skills, motor skills, ability to keep up with a device, skills of the conversational partners, setting appropriateness, and preferences of the individual (Soto et al., 1993).

Once the communication mode has been selected, the teaching method must be considered. Research indicates that communication skills are learned more quickly and are retained for longer periods of time when naturalistic approaches are used (Kaiser, Yoder, & Keetz, 1992). Naturalistic approaches have the following characteristics: teaching occurs during everyday activities at home, at school, and in the community; the environment is arranged to encourage communication; the student's interests are incorporated as motivators to communicate; and natural consequences are provided (Halle, Alpert, & Anderson, 1984).

The importance of naturalistic instruction cannot be overemphasized. To maximize the student's potential for learning a new sign or picture, instructors begin by teaching words that represent favorite objects or activities. This will ensure that the reinforcement will be powerful and repeat trials will be welcome. Use of the new word should be incorporated into real-life situations, throughout the day, and across all settings. The favored items are placed in the environment so that they may be seen, but not accessed without communicating. All attempts to communicate are met with encouragement and corrective feedback (Kaiser, 1993b).

Perhaps the most important element of naturalistic language training is the use of natural consequences. In other words, when the student forms a sign or points to a picture, the item or activity requested should be immediately presented. Social praise is often paired with the object (Romski & Sevcik, 1993). While the addition of praise may be advantageous for some, teachers should be aware that the praise may be confusing for other learners. That is, the child may have difficulty learning whether the picture or sign represents the object or the teacher's attention (Bondy & Frost, 1994).

PHYSICAL AND EMOTIONAL HEALTH CHARACTERISTICS

For people with the most pervasive support needs, life is often complicated by the existence of concomitant conditions. Sometimes health and physical concerns are paramount, and the intensity of needed supports is much greater. For others, psychiatric or emotional issues may add to the level of support required. This section will provide an introductory discussion of medical conditions, sensory and motor conditions, and psychiatric disorders that may coexist with severe mental retardation.

Medical Conditions

Medical conditions offer challenges for any person, regardless of talents or abilities. For people with severe mental retardation, however, these challenges are often compounded by the inability to successfully communicate pain or discomfort. Additionally, persons with extensive and pervasive support needs represent such a small segment of the population that their complex, specialized needs may not be especially well understood by community health-care providers. Health considerations for this group are twofold: congenital conditions and acquired conditions. The term *congenital* refers to conditions present from birth. Many of the disorders that result in mental retardation also cause physical and health problems, such as tumors, seizures, and organ failure. For such persons, medical concerns are usually chronic and sometimes intense.

Even those persons who do not have chronic congenital conditions may encounter significant difficulties when they develop medical conditions. Illnesses that are fairly easily conquered in mainstream America may have more dire effects in persons with severe mental retardation. Again, communication problems are often to blame. The inability to self-report feeling ill can result in benign illnesses progressing to more serious conditions before they are discovered. Even when the illness is known, other obstacles to overcome may include obtaining adequate nutrition, exercise, and hydration.

Sensory and Motor Disorders

People with severe mental retardation encounter the full range of sensory disorders. Oftentimes, the disorder that leads to mental retardation also results in blindness, hearing impairment, deafness, or deaf/blindness. The impact of such disorders can be strong. Methods for teaching persons with sensory disorders must be integrated with methods for teaching people with mental retardation to maximize the person's chances for successful living.

The range of motor abilities for persons with severe mental retardation ranges from very athletic to virtually immobile. Whereas some persons may be able to climb mountains, others may be unable to chew their food. Even the healthiest of individuals may have physical limitations that warrant extensive supports. For example, a person born without a right hand may require a prosthetic device, specially constructed tools and utensils, and extended time allowances for tasks requiring the use of two hands.

Psychiatric Disorders

To learn more about severe mental retardation, go to the companion website at www.prenhall.com/beirne-smith and select Chapter 8, then choose the Case Studies module.

The issue of dual diagnosis, as discussed in Chapter 7, has implications for individuals with severe mental retardation as well as those with milder forms of mental retardation. Mental illness has been estimated to occur about 5% to 15% more often among persons with mental retardation residing outside institutions than among the general population (Parsons, May, & Menolascino, 1984). These rates increase if individuals living in institutions are also considered (Spreat, Telles, Conroy, Feinstein, & Columbatto, 1987). Impulse control disorders, anxiety disorders, and mood disorders are cited as having a high rate of diagnosis in the severe to profound ranges (King, DeAntonio, McCracken, & Forness, 1994).

Diagnosing psychological disorders may be problematic in that the symptoms can be misinterpreted or altogether unnoticed for persons with severe or profound mental retardation. For example, a study by Meins (1995) indicated that depressive symptoms are more likely to mimic acting-out behavior (e.g., psychomotor agitation and irritable mood) than typical sadness. Issues such as these have led to the questioning of the applicability of the DSM-IV definitions of psychiatric disorders to individuals with severe and profound mental retardation. However, the DSM-IV is the definitive diagnostic source for such disorders, and its classification system is recommended for use by AAMR (1992). The manual advises that information should be garnished from several sources in order to guard against misdiagnosis. Behavioral observations, interviews with the individual and his or her significant others, medical examinations, and psychometric evaluations are some examples of valuable sources of information for the diagnostic process. Table 8.1 lists some commonly used standardized instruments for psychiatric diagnoses.

EDUCATIONAL CONCERNS

Little historical information about the education of persons with severe mental retardation is known. Education of such persons simply was not a subject of great concern in centuries past. The contributions of 19th-century reformists (e.g.,

TABLE 8.1

Psychiatric Assessment Tools for Persons with Severe Disabilities

Assessment Tool	Purpose
Aberrant Behavior Checklist (ABC) (Aman–1986)	For persons with mental retardation in residential settings; may indicate areas for further exploration
The Maladaptive Behavior Rating Subscale of the AAMD Adaptive Behavior Scale—Revised (American Association on Mental Deficiency, 1974)	A component of adaptive behavior assessment that may indicate areas for further exploration
The Psychopathology Instrument for Mentally Retarded Adults (PIMRA) (Matson, 1988)	Diagnostic screening instrument for persons with mental retardation; although the PIMRA is largely a self-report measure, there is an informant interview as well
The Reiss Screen for Maladaptive Behavior (Reiss 1987)	Diagnostic screening instrument for persons aged 12 and up who have mild, moderate, or severe mental retardation

Eduoard Seguin, Samuel G. Howe) laid the groundwork for subsequent models of instruction for persons with mental retardation (Safford & Safford, 1996). McDonnell, McDonnell, Hardman, and McCune (1991) provide an excellent description of the three major educational models used since 1900: institutional, developmental, and ecological. This section will discuss each of these models as well as curriculum development and teaching strategy.

Institutional Model

During the early 1900s, it was commonly believed that persons with severe mental retardation were incapable of learning. Institutions were built to separate and protect such people from society and to protect society from them. Unfortunately, persons with disabilities were even held responsible for an array of societal problems including crime, immorality, venereal disease, and prostitution (Wolfensberger, 1972).

During this period, the institutional model defined the provision of educational services to persons with severe mental retardation. This model was based on the belief that persons with severe disabilities were "sick," unable to learn, and a menace to society (McDonnell et al., 1991). Institutions were structured on a medical model of service delivery. Services were based on a diagnosis of the individual's pathology and a treatment plan to return to a "healthy" state. This philosophy offered little hope for persons with the most extensive needs. Many professionals believed that to try to teach basic skills to individuals with severe mental retardation was unkind since there was no hope of mastery (McDonnell & Hardman, 1995). As early as the 1940s, empirical evidence began to show that institutions limited the development of their residents (Kaplan, 1943).

Regardless of what model is used, early intervention is important.

Developmental Model

America's behind-the-scenes look at institutional life triggered social, judicial, and legislative mandates for change. One consequence was a shift to a developmental model of education, a model that encompassed the principle of normalization—the idea that persons with severe disabilities should live *as much as possible* like their peers without disabilities (Nirje, 1969; Wolfensberger, 1972). The developmental model conceives of persons with disabilities as those who can benefit from training and educational instruction. This model is based on two primary assumptions: (a) persons with severe disabilities learn in the same way as their peers without disabilities, but they require more time to master skills; and (b) persons with disabilities have the right to participate in the normal routines of life and to establish a lifestyle comparable to that of their peers without disabilities.

Although the developmental model of education was a remarkable improvement over its predecessor, it was founded on two faulty premises. First, the notion of being developmentally similar was based on the statistical concept of "mental age." Individuals who scored below 30 on an intelligence test were considered to have a "mental age" similar to that of a very young child. Practitioners assumed that a person with a "mental age" of 2 should play with 2-year-old toys until they had reached the "developmental" age of 3. Second, the principle of normalization led to environments that were "worklike," "homelike," and "classroomlike." Far from including persons with severe mental retardation in meaningful educational experiences, the developmental model forced persons with disabilities to "prepare" to enter school and to "get ready" for more time in the classroom and cafeteria. The achievement of predetermined developmental goals and objectives would indicate a person was ready to move to a less restrictive environment. The ultimate goal was for the student to move through the channels to full-time regular class placement. Figure 8.2 visually represents this continuum of services (Taylor, 1988).

The developmental model was unsuccessful because persons with severe mental retardation do not follow a slowed-down version of normal learning. The characteristics of the individual's disability prevented the achievement of developmental milestones and accordingly diminished his or her chances of moving to less restrictive environments. Research in the early 1980s documented that significant numbers of adults with severe disabilities were unemployed (Wehman, Kregel, & Seyfarth, 1985), had little interaction with peers without disabilities (Harris & Associates, 1986), had no friends outside their residential programs (Bercovici, 1983), and had little independence or autonomy in making lifestyle choices (Scheerenberger & Felsenthal, 1977). Again, research indicated the need to move to a more effective educational model to ensure that persons with severe mental retardation could become fully participating members of society.

Ecological Model

More recently, best practices in educational services have been based on the **ecological model**. This model includes the beliefs that people with disabilities have a right to participate in educational, economic, and social aspects of the community and that educational programs should be designed to enable persons with severe

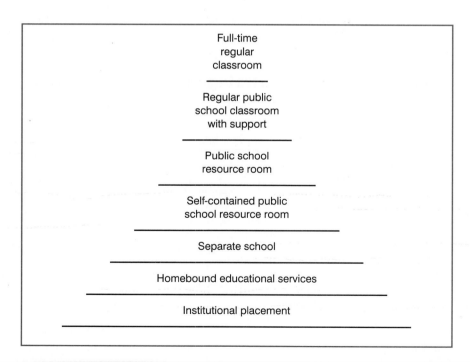

FIGURE 8.2

Continuum of Educational Services: Hierarchy of Environmental Restrictiveness Information

Adapted from Taylor (1988, p. 43).

disabilities to select supports that will enable them to participate fully in a broad range of school and community activities.

Based on a philosophy of "place then train," the ecological model enables persons with severe mental retardation to learn in the environment in which the particular skills will be used, rather than learning the skill in a segregated setting and attempting to generalize it to a second setting.

Educational programming is highly individualized and built on a three-phase process to maximize the fit between the individual and the environment (Schalock, 1986). First, the specific demands of the activity and the environment are evaluated in relation to each person's behavioral abilities. Second, an assessment of the barriers preventing the person's achievement in the particular setting is conducted. Third is the development of supports designed to overcome the barriers to success. With this method, some individuals may achieve total independence, whereas others will be involved in partial participation, depending on the levels of support each needs and receives (see Snell, 1993).

Proponents of the ecological model have paved the way for innovations in supported living, employment, and education. These developments have led to new avenues of inclusion for persons with severe mental retardation. Programs based on the ecological model identify life options that meet personalized needs, then assist the student to attain those goals through very specific supports. Rusch, Chadsey-Rusch, and Johnson (1991) provide research data suggesting that the ecological model provides more positive outcomes for individuals with severe disabilities than those in the developmental model.

Curriculum and Teaching Strategies

Educational programming for persons with severe mental retardation has made great strides in the last 20 years. Teaching methods relate directly to traditional learning theory and the methods of applied behavior analysis. Systematic instruction of students with severe mental retardation has provided empirical data to illustrate that learning actually occurs (Snell, 1993). Optimal educational programs are generally **community referenced**, or related to actual incidents that naturally occur in the environment. Instructional time is too valuable to waste learning unnecessary skills. The most useful learning activities are both functional and age appropriate. For example, a 17-year-old will probably derive more benefit from learning to recognize words and symbols that warn of danger than from learning the alphabet song.

Because education is designed to enhance the student's ability to function successfully in a world inhabited largely by people without disabilities, it is important that instruction be delivered in integrated settings. Consider the difference between a person from Iowa who took a class in Spanish as a high school sophomore and a person from Iowa who spent his sophomore year as an exchange student in Spain. Although it is possible to learn about another culture without experiencing it firsthand, opportunities for learning are greatly enhanced through direct experience. Brown et al. (1989) list four reasons that all school-age children should be educated in the same settings. First, students without disabilities who are edu-

Travel Training for Persons with Cognitive or Physical Disabilities

Traveling independently on public transportation is one occasion when a person with a cognitive impairment must perform with absolutely no assistance. Training a person with a cognitive impairment to use public transportation requires a comprehensive and individualized instructional program. Before a person with a cognitive disability can safely use public transportation, she or he must demonstrate 100% consistency in many functional skill areas, beyond simply learning the travel route to and from a destination.

Before travel training begins, a travel trainer determines a student's strengths and weaknesses, assesses how much support the student can expect from her or his parents or guardians, and reviews the travel route to determine the feasibility of traveling to a specific destination. Travel training begins only when the student is ready to learn the travel route and has support from parents or guardians. It's notable that a student with a cognitive disability does not necessarily have to know how to read a clock, make change, or understand survival signs to succeed in a travel training program, though these skills certainly are assets.

A comprehensive travel training program for people with a cognitive disability should consist of the following:

Phase 1: Detailed instruction in specific travel routes, fare costs, boarding and deboarding sites, and the demonstration of pedestrian skills necessary for this travel route, as well as constant practice in life skills such as appropriate interaction with community workers and with strangers, use of public telephone, and appropriate behavior in public places.

Phase 2: Direct observation of the student by the travel trainer to verify that the student has learned all necessary travel skills taught in Phase 1.

Phase 3: Instruction in emergency procedures. Emergencies can include boarding the wrong transit vehicle, missing a stop, or losing one's fare or transfer pass.

Phase 4: Assessment of the student's interactive skills with strangers. Travel training programs may use plainclothes police officers or travel trainers whom the student has not met to approach the traveling student and try to extract personal information from him or her. Students pass this assessment procedure if they do not impart personal information to or leave with a stranger.

Phase 5: Indirect observation of the student. As the student walks to and from the transit stop and rides the transit vehicle independently, her or his performance is assessed at a distance by a travel trainer, who follows in a car. The student is aware that she or he is being observed.

Phase 6: Covert observation and assessment. The student is not aware that she or he is being observed.

Phase 7: Follow-up observations. Periodically, a student who successfully completes a travel training program should be covertly observed to verify that she or he is still practicing safe travel skills.

While different travel training programs may vary the order in which they teach travel skills, the teaching methods of travel training programs should be the same. The average length of a quality travel training program is fifteen sessions, though training time will vary according to the complexity of the travel route and the nature of the student's disability.

Once a person with a cognitive impairment begins to travel independently along one travel route, typically, she or he learns other travel routes with relative ease. Sometimes intense instruction is required to travel to a new destination, especially if reaching the new destination requires new or more advanced pedestrian skills or different modes of transportation.

Source: From "Travel Training for Persons with Cognitive or Physical Disabilities: An Overview" (pp. 7–9), by P. J. Voorhees, 1996, *NICHCY Transition Summary, 9.*

cated alongside students with disabilities are more likely to function as responsible adults in a pluralistic society. Second, integrated schools provide more meaningful instructional environments. Third, families have greater access to activities in neighborhood schools. Finally, integrated schools offer more opportunities to develop a wide range of social relationships. If a child associates exclusively with persons who have severe disabilities, chances are very good that he or she will assume at least some of the maladaptive behaviors they display. Likewise, the child has a better chance of acquiring more adaptive behaviors if they are displayed by classmates without disabilities on a daily basis.

Integrated learning settings are as important for adults as they are for children. If anyone has ever tried to tell you how to ride a bicycle, then you understand that it is not always easy to apply information you've learned *about* a skill to actually *performing* that skill. When teaching a person who has pronounced difficulties learning new information, it is very important to give the person every advantage. For adults, this means that job skills are better taught on the job, and domestic skills are better taught in the person's home.

What should these persons be taught? The determination of curriculum is overwhelmingly important for learners with severe mental retardation. Skills are typically found in the domains of self-help, domestic, leisure, communication, vocational, community, and social/friendship. Recently, self-determination skills have been added to best-practice curricula. The need to teach self-determination was first documented in the literature related to employment. Although persons with significant levels of mental retardation were able to complete requisite job skills, they were frequently dependent on their job coaches to "cue" them to begin and end tasks. As similar studies were completed, they presented a picture of individuals who were taught to "wait until told" rather than to self-initiate activities. Additionally. educators have become more familiar with the "locus of control" literature from psychology and thus have begun to incorporate student directed learning within the functional curriculum. Choice and autonomy are considered integral to a best practice approach to education.

APPROPRIATE OUTCOMES

Researchers and practitioners who work with persons who have mental retardation are constantly working to improve their own efforts (see Schalock, 1999). In the not-so-distant past, efficacy of services, programs, interventions, and supports was measured by observable changes in the individual's behavior. In recent years, however, leaders in the field have pointed out many other variables that should be considered (Campo, Sharpton, Thompson, & Sexton, 1997). In the field of education, the importance of variables that prepare the student for community life have been emphasized (e.g., Cronin & Patton, 1993). The deinstitutionalization movement spawned interest in quality-of-life outcomes (e.g., Schalock, 1996). Those persons interested in impacting service provision and supports planning put forth the ideas of personal outcomes (see Blake, Prouty, & Lakin, 1995). Although the specific domains of these approaches sometimes overlap, each operates under a slightly different philosophy. This section will provide an overview of each approach.

Educational Outcomes

John Dewey (1966) told us that good schools should work to develop good citizens. With this philosophy in mind, leaders in the field of special education took on the responsibility of ensuring that students with severe mental retardation left school with the skills required to live successfully in society. To measure success, educators would have to define specific outcomes of interest. Although conceptualizations differ, most proposed outcomes could fall into one of three categories: independence, productivity, and community integration.

Independence is a broad construct that encompasses many aspects, most notably self-reliance and self-determination. *Self-reliance* refers to a person's ability to take care of him- or herself. Skills that reflect self-reliance range from feeding oneself to living in a home alone. Educational programs offer many opportunities to encourage self-reliance. As described earlier, *self-determination* refers to a person's ability to set and navigate his or her own life course. Skills that educators may help to develop include making choices, communicating preferences, setting achievable goals, and self-advocating (Wehmeyer, 1993).

In U.S. society, independence is largely tied to productivity, which is generally defined as holding a job and being economically self-sustaining. Therefore, the most desirable outcome for all individuals, including those with severe mental retardation, is competitive employment. For this to occur, education and training must focus on vocational instruction and on-the-job skill development. Research

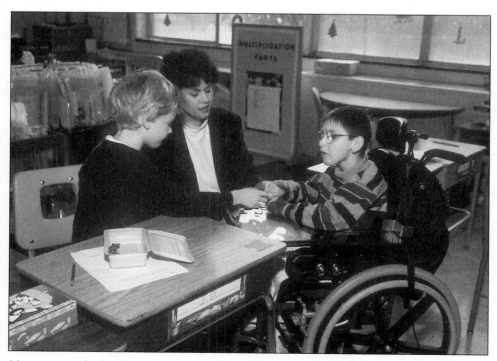

Most proposed educational outcomes will be in the categories of independence, productivity, or community integration.

generated during the past 20 years demonstrates that competitive employment is a viable outcome for persons with severe mental retardation (Hill, Wehman, Kregel, Banks, & Metzler, 1987). Rusch, Enchelmaier, and Kohler (1994) have identified the following as outcome components for successful school-to-work transition: development of individual transition plans; demonstration of improved work opportunities; job placement in competitive, integrated settings; and documentation of progress in employment-related skills.

Without social integration, the value of living a productive and independent life is questionable. Common activities that the majority of the population can take for granted are sometimes difficult for a person with severe mental retardation to access. Barriers may include lack of knowledge of such resources (Schleien, Ray, & Green, 1996), deficits in social skills (Gaylord-Ross & Chadsey-Rusch, 1991), and social self-consciousness (Zetlin & Turner, 1985). Elective participation in religious activities is an example of a commonly overlooked element of true community membership. Riordan and Vasa (1991) indicate that clergy were aware of few persons with disabilities in their congregations, so provisions for their education and participation in rites of passage have been infrequent. Peer groups are important sources of social support for all people—persons with severe mental retardation are no different. We all share the need for human interaction. Educational settings provide a wonderful opportunity for teaching the person to overcome such barriers and for teaching nondisabled peers to prevent many of those barriers from being constructed.

To learn more about barriers to community resources, go to the companion website at www.prenhall.com/beirne-smith and select Chapter 8, then choose the Article Response module.

Quality-of-Life Outcomes

Although the deinstitutionalization movement grew from the idea that institutional living prevented persons from living fulfilling lives, early studies of the effects of moving out of an institution were largely confined to behavioral outcomes (see Larson & Lakin, 1989). As other gains were realized, the term *quality of life* began to be explored (e.g., Schalock, Keith, Hoffman, & Karan, 1989). Many endeavors to define and delineate the term precisely have been undertaken, and far too many aspects have been proposed to cover here. However, certain terms tend to reappear, including *self-determination, productivity, community involvement, interpersonal relationships,* and *personal satisfaction.* As the first three concepts were covered in the educational outcomes sections, the discussion now turns to interpersonal relationships and personal satisfaction.

The recognition that meaningful personal relationships should be included as a desired outcome for persons with extensive support needs arose when physical inclusion practices resulted in continued feelings of rejection and isolation (Bercovici, 1983). Although it is important that persons with severe mental retardation see and be seen by their nondisabled peers, other interventions are sometimes necessary to ensure true social involvement. Possibilities include teaching the person with mental retardation where and how to find others with common interests and educating nondisabled peers about the person behind the disability (Schoeller, 1997).

The concept of personal satisfaction is a much broader construct than the outcomes discussed thus far. This is because personal satisfaction is a function of all of the other outcomes, plus other factors that may or may not be known. Personal satisfaction reflects the person's general sense of happiness. Assessment of a person's happiness or satisfaction can be difficult. Multiple measures are often necessary, providing an opportunity for the person to share experiences at their own level and on a wide array of topics (Dudley, Calhoun, Ahlgrim-Delzell, & Conroy, 1998).

Personal Outcomes

Although the concept of quality of life represents a laudable leap in philosophy, one seemingly valid complaint has been lodged again and again: there is no such thing. That is, there is no universal construct because each person judges his or her own quality of life based on different criteria. Whereas one person may value independence above all else, another person may value relationships with significant others (Hatton, 1998).

The strategies of **person-centered planning** arose parallel to the interest in quality of life. Although the two constructs are based on a philosophy that people with mental retardation are entitled to live well-rounded lives, some differences do exist. Whereas the interest in quality of life has largely been based on a desire to define and analyze its components, proponents of person-centered planning adhere to the notion that outcomes are diverse and individualized. In other words, the person should be enabled to express his or her own goals, and outcome assessment should be based on the movement made toward attaining those goals (Gaylord et al., 1998).

Person-centered planning begins by asking the person what he or she wants life to be like. People who care about the individual are invited to join the process; their role is especially important when planning with a person who has severe mental retardation. They are sometimes called on to speak for the person or to translate the person's attempts to communicate. Other persons involved in the planning process include service providers and educators who are able to identify resources for attaining goals. For each goal that is set, a diagram for the future is made. Diagrams include the steps necessary for getting from where the person is to where he or she wants to be, as well as the supports and resources to be accessed along the way. Outcomes are clear, individualized, and easily measured (Pearpoint & Forest, 1998).

SUPPORTS

The concept of supports has appeared throughout this chapter. By now you have probably gathered that a support is a resource that enhances a person's ability to live, learn, and work with greater independence. Persons with severe mental retardation will vary in the number and intensity of supports needed. Some may be able to function successfully with less extensive supports in one or more areas but will very likely need increased levels of individually designed supports in the majority of areas. The American Association on Mental Retardation (1992) sought to explicitly define different kinds of supports and the functions they serve. Table 8.2 lists some of these supports, and they will be referred to throughout this section as we discuss the planning and implementation of supports.

TABLE 8.2
Support Function and Representative Activities

Support Function[a]	Representative Activities		
Befriending	Advocating	Evaluating	Befriending
	Car pooling	Communicating	Associating
	Supervising	Training	Collecting data
	Instructing	Giving feedback	Socializing
Financial planning	Working with SSI-Medicaid	Assisting with money management	Budgeting
	Advocating for benefits	Protection and legal assistance	Income assistance and planning/considerations
Employee assistance	Counseling	Supervisory training	Crisis intervention/assistance
	Procuring/using assistive technology devices	Job performance enhancement	Job/task accommodation and redesigning job/work duties
Behavioral support	Functional analysis	Manipulation of ecological and setting events	Building environment with effective consequences and minimizing the use of punishers
	Multicomponent instruction	Teaching adaptive behavior	
	Emphasis on antecedent manipulation		
In-home living assistance	Personal maintenance/care	Communication devices	Respite care
	Transfer and mobility	Behavioral support	Attendant care
	Dressing and clothing care	Eating & food management	Homehealth aides
	Architectural modifications	Housekeeping	Homemaker services and med alert devices
Community access and use	Carpooling/rides program	Recreation/leisure involvement	Community use opportunities and interacting with generic agencies
	Transportation training	Community awareness opportunities	
		Vehicle modification	
Health assistance	Medical appointments	Emergency procedures	Hazard awareness
	Medical interventions	Mobility (assistive devices)	Safety training
	Supervision	Counseling appointments	Physical therapy and related activities and
	Med Alert devices	Medication taking	Counseling interventions

[a] The support functions and activities may need to be modified slightly to accommodate individuals of different ages.

Source: From AAMR (1992, p. 104).

Supports Planning

For persons with severe mental retardation to achieve maximal independence, the necessary supports must be accessible in all domains of life. Coordinating the various supports needed in different environments can be an exceptionally difficult task. Input should be sought not only from professionals involved in such areas as education, psychology, and medicine but also from family members and the person with severe mental retardation. The involvement of family members is valuable not only for their ideas but because they can assist others in understanding the many ways their loved one expresses any preferences, needs, and opinions. AAMR's (1992) position is that "the intensities of supports can be determined at least in part by the person with mental retardation" (p. 105). Every person can justifiably expect to be treated with respect and dignity; this includes participation in his or her own life planning. According to the Americans with Disabilities Act of 1990:

> individuals with disabilities are a discrete and insular minority who have been faced with restrictions and limitations, subjected to a history of purposeful unequal treatment, and relegated to a position of political powerlessness in our society, based on characteristics that are beyond the control of such individuals and resulting from stereotypic assumptions not truly indicative of the individual ability of such individuals to participate in, and contribute to, society; the Nation's proper goals regarding individuals with disabilities are to assure equality of opportunity, full participation, independent living, and economic self-sufficiency for such individuals. (U.S.C. 12101, Sec. 2.a.7, 2.a.8)

Beyond legality, the principles of motivation and goal attainment demonstrate the importance of including the person with mental retardation in the assessment and decision-making process. There is value inherent in the person's input; namely, who would have better insight into what is needed or wanted? Research shows that people who participate in planning their course of action have a greater likelihood of follow-through than those whose course is planned for them (Berkman & Meyer, 1988; Egan, 1994). Additionally, if the overarching goal of support is to promote independence through choice and self-advocacy, would it not be hypocritical to disallow the person's participation in the planning process?

Natural Supports

Many support activities can be performed by the person who uses the support or by significant others. Support activities that are provided without the aid of technology or service agencies are termed **natural supports**. If the individual implements the activity independently, it is considered to be a personal support. This should not be confused with skills learned through education and treatment. Boggs (cited in AAMR, 1992) explains this difference as follows:

> Capacity or competence, if developed or restored through training or treatment, belongs to the individual and may in fact reduce disability . . . personal support services facilitate function while present but do not reduce the intrinsic disability. This fact should not be obscured as long as the individual can/will once more experience the consequences of his functional disability if he . . . loses the personal support. (p. 107)

Personal resources make excellent supports for independent thinking and self-determination. They can be useful as schedule reminders, trouble-shooters, or aids in navigating multistep tasks. For example, a person may have a guide for grocery shopping that facilitates memory and decision making and eliminates the need for reading skills. Persons with severe mental retardation may use personal supports to control intense emotional reactions or to monitor his or her physical well-being for signs of threat to safety or health. For example, a person with a lifelong health concern, such as Lesch-Nyhan syndrome (characterized by intense compulsions to self-mutilate) might provide personal support by self-restraining when the compulsion arises. Though supports such as these are implemented entirely by the person, they serve to compensate for specific skill deficits. Grocery guides do not enhance the memory of the person using them—they replace the need for memory. Likewise, the person with Lesch-Nyhan will still feel a compulsion to self-mutilate. Self-restraint is a way that the individual can provide him- or herself with support until the compulsion passes.

Many forms of support enlist the participation of other people. Employees, friends, and volunteers may provide support in areas such as transportation, accessing community stores and facilities, handling household repairs, and completing daily living tasks (Heyne, Storley, Rone, Levine, & Denelle, 1996). The involvement of others is likely to be necessary for any individual with more extensive support needs, but it may be of primary or of tertiary importance. Pervasive support resources are likely to be more intrusive, involving more people than limited or even extensive supports. It may be necessary for others to assist these individuals with tasks basic to survival. Examples include providing medical care, preparing meals the person can swallow and digest, assisting with personal hygiene needs, monitoring his or her health and safety, and representing the person's interests to others outside the home.

Other people can function as support resources in an extensive, but not pervasive manner, as well. The possibilities for involving others exist in every activity listed in Table 8.2. Support may be given overtly, such as providing job training, assisting with money management, intervening in crisis situations, or actively teaching skills. Alternatively, more subtle ways of providing support also exist in such forms as interacting socially, offering advice, providing information, and making introductions. None of us, whether we have a severe disability or not, can get along in the world without receiving support from others.

When others are providing assistance to an individual with severe mental retardation, it must be remembered that a *support* becomes a *hindrance* the moment it is no longer necessary. Supports should enhance each person's sense of confidence, self-esteem, and independence (Abery, 1994). The implementation of appropriate supports is expected to facilitate advancement and decrease the intensity, frequency, or duration of that support need. Individuals whose supports are faded or withdrawn should provide feedback about their success without the support, and service providers and significant others should continue to monitor the person's needs for such support (AAMR, 1992).

Supplementary Supports

We can observe that several support functions and activities can be accessed through service delivery if they cannot be obtained in the person's natural environment (see Table 8.2). Of particular relevance to persons with severe mental retardation are such activities as advocating, supervising, financial management, offering in-home assistance, accessing transportation, and providing health assistance. Persons with extensive or pervasive support needs are less apt to become totally independent in these areas than individuals with less intensive needs. Over the years, family members may not be able to provide as much support. Also, the intensity of required involvement may be so great that primary care givers need relief or even specialized help (Smith, Majeski, & McClenny, 1996). For example, a person who has a psychological disorder such as schizophrenia could require a psychiatrist's services. Family members of a person who cannot assist with mobility may find they are no longer able to provide the physical assistance necessary to meet his or her needs safely. Consequently, it is very important to have outside services available.

Sometimes the greatest service support is information about other resources or about legislation that protects and promotes the welfare of persons with disabilities. The U.S. Department of Education Office of Special Education and Rehabilitative Services funds Parent Information Centers in each state to address parental concerns. Similarly, within the Department of Health and Human Services, the Administration on Developmental Disabilities and the Administration on Children and Families maintain family preservation/family support initiatives. These initiatives provide funding vouchers to families whose relatives are deemed "institution-eligible" and living at home. The provisions make access to such services as behavioral training, respite care, social work, psychological, and nutritional services financially feasible.

As helpful as all of the supports provided by significant others and service agencies can be, sometimes persons with extensive support needs wish to further their independence by, in essence, eliminating the intermediary. For example, a student who has a speech impairment may have friends who are able to interpret for unfamiliar listeners. This is one example of a natural support provided by others. However, occasions may arise when the student really wants to express herself without the assistance of her friends. Persons living today have a very distinct advantage over previous generations in this area—technology. As our scientific knowledge base continues to grow at an astounding rate, opportunities are presented to meet the needs of persons with severe mental retardation. In fact, Meyer, Eichinger, and Park-Lee (1987) found technological supports to be among the highest-rated items in their analysis of quality indicators in educational services for students with severe disabilities.

In addition to devices available to provide a voice to the expressions of persons with speech impairments, persons with multiple severe disabilities are being presented with opportunities to communicate in ways that require no voice and no hands. Computerized technology is another commonly seen technological support in place for those with extensive and pervasive needs. We can expect even more inventive, independence-promoting concepts to be unveiled as time goes by.

The movement toward greater community involvement and independent living arrangements has also furthered the cause of technological support development. By mandating equal access to community facilities, public transportation, and job opportunities, the ADA has forced human ingenuity (Bleyer, 1992). This new legislation includes everything from architectural accommodations to job task reconceptualization (Johnson & Lewis, 1994). Individuals need homes that they can navigate—lower counters for persons who use wheelchairs, safety measures in bathrooms for persons with less developed grip, muscle tone, or seizure disorders. Safety precautions are not limited to the bathroom, either. Also available are stoves and irons that turn themselves off, water temperature regulators, and telephone security systems that automatically call for help if the person does not "check in" as scheduled.

Although none of these types of supports are intrinsically tied to persons with severe mental retardation, their existence makes it more feasible for persons with such extensive needs to live independently than has ever been thought before. While some supports, such as hearing aids, have been addressing needs for many years, the newer developments are instilling hope in a wide range of individuals. Bellamy (1990) reminds us, however, that extensive architectural and state-of-the-art technological supports will not be useful if they are not cost-effective. In the same spirit as their initiatives to ensure access to services, the Department of Health and Human Services now makes funding available to persons with disabilities for such architectural essentials as widening doorways, building ramps, and making bathrooms and kitchens wheelchair accessible.

To check your understanding of this chapter, go to the companion website at www.prenhall.com/beirne-smith and select Chapter 8, and then choose the Self-Test module.

Summary

Characteristics of Severe Mental Retardation
- Definitions of severe mental retardation may focus on support needs, cognitive ability, or adaptive skills.
- Of the 1% to 3% of the population estimated to have mental retardation, only 15% have greater than mild disabilities.
- People with severe mental retardation often experience multiple disabilities.
- The extent of support a person requires is influenced by the environment.

Behavioral Characteristics
- The development of adaptive and challenging behaviors is influenced by training and environmental factors.
- The tools of behavior analysis have been successful in teaching a wide array of adaptive behaviors.
- The principles of reinforcement, environmental restructuring, and life enhancement are all useful in eliminating challenging behaviors.

Communication Characteristics
- Most persons with severe mental retardation have some form of speech/language disorder.
- Gesturing and manual signing are the most commonly used methods of nonverbal communication among persons with severe mental retardation.
- Naturalistic teaching methods have been shown to be the most effective approach for teaching communication skills.

Physical and Emotional Health Characteristics
- The need for extensive and pervasive supports for persons with severe mental retardation is in many cases directly related to physical or health-related concerns.

- In terms of physical and motor development, the group of persons with severe mental retardation is by no means homogenous. A wide array of functional abilities may be observed.
- Mental illness is suspected to occur at greater rates among persons with mental retardation than in the general population, but diagnosis is complicated by a lack of formalized assessment measures, barriers in communication, and atypical demonstration of symptoms.

Educational Concerns

- Historically, gross underestimates of the potential of persons with severe mental retardation resulted in prejudice, fear, and mistreatment.
- Persons with severe mental retardation do not follow a slowed version of normal cognitive development.
- Educational programming for persons with severe mental retardation should be functional, individualized, and age-appropriate.
- Instruction works best when it is community-referenced and delivered in the setting where the skill will be used.

Appropriate Outcomes

- Educational outcomes of interest include independence, productivity, and social integration.
- The construct of quality of life introduced such outcomes as happiness in interpersonal relationships and personal satisfaction.
- The process of person-centered planning delineates individualized outcomes that are developed by the person with mental retardation and his or her loved ones.

Supports

- Persons with severe mental retardation and their families can and should be consulted in the construction of educational and support plans.
- Extensive and pervasive supports differ from less intensive levels of support in frequency, duration, and urgency.
- Supplemental support services are particularly important for individuals with severe mental retardation because they are more likely than persons with mild mental retardation to continue to need supports over time.

References

Abery, B. H. (1994). A conceptual framework for enhancing self-determination. In M. F. Hayden & B. H. Abery (Eds.), *Challenges for a service system in transition.* Baltimore: Brookes.

Aman, M. (1986). *Aberrant behavior checklist.* East Aurora, NY: Slosson Educational Publications.

American Association on Mental Deficiency. (1974). *AAMD adaptive behavior scale—revised.* Washington, DC: Author.

American Association on Mental Retardation. (1992). *Mental retardation: Definitions, classification, and systems of support* (9th ed.). Washington, DC: Author.

American Psychiatric Association. (1994). *Diagnostic and statistical manual of mental disorders* (4th ed.). Washington, DC: Author.

Americans with Disabilities Act, 42 U.S.C.12101 (1990).

Baroff, G. S. (1991). *Developmental disabilities: Psychosocial aspects.* Austin, TX: PRO-ED.

Bellamy, G. T. (1990). Review of *Supported employment: Models, methods, and issues.* *Journal of the Association for Persons with Severe Handicaps, 15*(1), 261–265.

Bercovici, S. M. (1983). *Barriers to normalization: The restrictive management of retarded persons.* Baltimore: University Park Press.

Berkman, K. A., & Meyer, L. H. (1988). Alternative strategies and multiple outcomes in the remediation of severe self-injury: Going "all out" nonaversively. *Journal of the Association for Persons with Severe Handicaps, 13*(2), 76–86.

Blake, E. M., Prouty, R. W., & Lakin, K. C. (1995). *Reinventing quality.* Minneapolis: University of Minnesota, University Affiliated Program, Institute on Community Integration, Center on Residential Services and Community Living.

Blatt, B. (1987). *The conquest of mental retardation.* Austin, TX: PRO-ED.

Bleyer, K. (1992). The Americans with Disabilities Act: Enforcement mechanisms. *Mental and Physical Disabilities Law Reporter, 16*(3), 347–350.

Block, M. E., & Rizzo, T. L. (1995). Attitudes and attributes of physical educators associated with teaching individuals with severe and profound disabilities. *Journal of the Association for Persons with Severe Handicaps, 20*(1), 80–87.

Bondy, A. S., & Frost, L. A. (1994). The picture exchange communication system. *Focus on Autistic Behavior, 9*(3), 1–20.

Brown, L., Long, E., Udavari-Solner, A., Davis, L., Van Devon, P., Ahlgren, C., Johnson, F., Gruenewald, L., & Jorgensen, J. (1989). The home school: Why students with severe intellectual disabilities must attend the schools of their brothers, sisters, friends and neighbors. *Journal for the Association of Persons with Severe Handicaps, 14*(1), 1–7.

Bruininks, R. H., & McGrew, K. (1987). *Exploring the structure of adaptive behavior* (Report Number 87-1). Minneapolis: University of Minnesota, Department of Educational Psychology.

Bruininks, R. H., Woodcock, R. W., Weatherman, R. F., & Hill, B. K. (1996). *Scales of Independent Behavior—Revised (SIB-R).* Chicago: Riverside.

Campo, S. F., Sharpton, W. R., Thompson, B., & Sexton, D. (1997). Correlates of the quality of life of adults with severe or profound mental retardation. *Mental Retardation, 35*(5), 329–337.

Carr, E. G., & Durand, V. M. (1985). Reducing behavior problems through functional communication training. *Journal of Applied Behavior Analysis, 18*(2), 111–126.

Cronin, M. E., & Patton, J. R. (1993). *Life skills instruction for all students with special needs: A practical guide for integrating real-life content into the curriculum.* Austin: PRO-ED.

Dewey, J. (1966). *Democracy and education.* New York: Macmillan.

Dudley, J., Calhoun, M., Ahlgrim-Delzell, L., & Conroy, J. (1998). Measuring the consumer satisfaction of class members of a lawsuit. *International Journal of Disability Research, 42*(3), 199–207.

Egan, G. (1994). *The skilled helper: A problem-management approach to helping* (5th ed.). Pacific Grove, CA: Brooks/Cole.

Gaylord, V., Abery, B., & Schoeller, K. (Eds.). (1997). Feature issue on the social inclusion of adults with developmental disabilities. *Impact, 10*(3).

Gaylord-Ross, R., & Chadsey-Rusch, J. (1991). Measurement of work-related outcomes for students with severe disabilities. *Journal of Special Education, 25*(3), 291–304.

Goddard, H. H. (1920). *Feeble-mindedness: Its causes and consequences.* New York: Macmillan.

Gold, M.W. (1980). An alternative definition of mental retardation. In M.W. Gold (Ed.), *"Did I say that?" Articles and commentary on the Try Another Way System* (pp. 145–150). Champaign, IL: Research Press.

Grossman, H. J. (Ed.). (1983). *Manual on terminology and classification in mental retardation.* Washington, DC: American Association on Mental Deficiency.

Halle, J., Alpert, C. L., & Anderson, S. R. (1984). Natural environment language assessment and intervention with severely impaired preschoolers. *Topics in Early Childhood Special Education, 4*, 35–56.

Harris, L., & Associates, Inc. (1986). *International Center for the Disabled survey of disabled Americans: Bring disabled Americans into the mainstream.* New York: Author.

Hatton, C. (1998). Whose quality of life is it anyway? Some problems with the emerging quality of life consensus. *Mental Retardation, 36*(2), 104–115.

Heward, W. (1996). *Exceptional children: An introduction to special education* (5th ed.). Upper Saddle River, NJ: Merrill/Prentice Hall.

Heyne, L., Storley, C., Rone, C., Levine, B., & Denelle, D. (1996). Elders and preschoolers supporting each other: The JCC Intergenerational Program. *Impact, 9*(4), 10–11.

Hill, B. K., & Bruininks, R. H. (1984). Maladaptive behavior of mentally retarded people in residential facilities. *American Journal of Mental Deficiency, 88*(4), 380–387.

Hill, M. L., Wehman, P. H., Kregel, J., Banks, P. D., & Metzler, H. M. (1987). Employment outcomes for people with moderate and severe disabilities: An eight-year longitudinal analysis of supported competitive employment. *Journal of the Association of Severe Disabilities, 12*(3), 182-189.

Horner, R. D. (1980). The effects of an environmental "enrichment" program on the behavior of institutionalized profoundly retarded children. *Journal of Applied Behavior Analysis, 13*(3), 473–491.

Horner, R. H., & Carr, E. G. (1997). Behavioral support for students with severe disabilities: Functional assessment and comprehensive intervention. *Journal of Special Education, 31*(1), 84–109.

Individuals with Disabilities Education Act. 20 U.S.C. 1400 et seq. (1997).

Iwata, B. A., Dorsey, M. F., Slifer, K. J., Bauman, K. E., & Richman, G. S. (1994a). Toward a functional analysis of self-injury. *Journal of Applied Behavior Analysis, 27*(2), 197–209.

Iwata, B. A., Pace, G. M., Dorsey, M. F., Zarcone, J. R., Vollmer, T. R., Smith, R. G., Rodgers, T. A., Lerman, D. C., Shore, B. A., Mazalesli, J. L., Goh, H., Cowdery, G. E., Kalsher, M. J., McCosh, K. C., & Willis, K. D. (1994b). The functions of self-injurious behavior: An experimental-epidemiological analysis. *Journal of Applied Behavior Analysis, 27*(2), 215–240.

Johnson, D. R., & Lewis, D. R. (1994). Supported employment: Program models, strategies, and evaluation perspectives. In M. F. Hayden & B. H. Abery (Eds.), *Challenges for a service system in transition* (pp. 449–482). Baltimore: Brookes.

Kaiser, A. P. (1993a). Introduction: Enhancing children's social communication. In A. P. Kaiser & D. B. Gray (Eds.), *Enhancing children's communication: Research foundations for intervention* (Vol. 2, pp. 3–10). Baltimore: Brookes.

Kaiser, A. P. (1993b). Parent-implemented language intervention: An environmental system perspective. In A. P. Kaiser & D. B. Gray (Eds.), *Enhancing children's communication: Research foundations for intervention* (Vol. 2, pp. 63–84). Baltimore: Brookes.

Kaiser, A. P., Yoder, P. J., & Keetz, A. (1992). Evaluating milieu teaching. In S. F. Warren & J. Reichle (Eds.). *Causes and effects in communication and language intervention* (Vol. 1, pp. 9–47). Baltimore: Brookes.

Kaplan, O. L. (1943). Mental decline in older morons. *American Journal on Mental Deficiency, 47*(3), 277–285.

Kennedy, C. H., & Itkonen, T. (1994). Some effects of regular class participation on the social contacts and social networks of high school students with severe disabilities. *Journal of the Association for Persons with Severe Handicaps, 19*(1), 1–10.

King, B. H., DeAntonio, C., McCracken, J. T., & Forness, S. R. (1994). Psychiatric consultation in severe and profound mental retardation. *American Journal of Psychiatry 151*(12), 1802–1808.

Koegel, L. K., Koegel, R. L., & Dunlap, G. (Eds.). (1996). *Positive behavioral support: Including people with difficult behavior in the community*. Baltimore: Brookes.

Kubiszyn, T., & Borich, G. (1996*). Educational testing and measurement: Classroom application and practice* (5th ed.). New York: HarperCollins.

Larson, S. A. (1991). Quality of life for people with challenging behavior living in community settings. *Impact, 4*(1), 4–5.

Larson, S. A., & Lakin, K. C. (1989). Deinstitutionalization of persons with mental retardation: Behavioral outcomes. *Journal of the Association for Persons with Severe Handicaps, 14*(4), 324–332.

Lindley, L. (1990). Defining TASH: A mission statement. *TASH Newsletter, 16*(8), 1.

Luiselli, J. K., & Cameron, M. J. (Eds.). (1998). *Antecedent control: Positive approaches to behavioral support*. Baltimore: Brookes.

Mar, H. H., & Sall, N. (1999). Profiles of the expressive communication skills of children and adolescents with severe cognitive disabilities. *Education and Training in Mental Retardation and Developmental Disabilities, 34*(1), 77–89.

Matson, J. L. (1988). *The psychopathology inventory for mentally retarded adults*. Orland Park, IL: International Diagnostic Systems.

McDonnell, A., McDonnell, J., Hardman, M., & McCune, G. (1991). Educating students with severe disabilities in their neighborhood school: The Utah elementary integration model. *Remedial and Special Education, 12*(6), 34–45.

McDonnell, J., & Hardman, M. (1995). Planning the transition of severely handicapped youth from school to adult services: A framework for high school programs. *Education and Training of the Mentally Retarded, 20*(4), 275–286.

McLean, J., & Snyder-McLean, L. (1991). Communicative intent and its realizations among persons with severe intellectual deficits. In N. Krasnegor, D. Rumbaugh, R. Schiefelbusch, & M. Studdert-Kennedy (Eds.), *Biological and behavioral determinants of language development* (pp. 481–508). Hillsdale, NJ: Erlbaum.

McLean, L. K., Brady, N. C., McLean, J. E., & Behrens, G. A. (1999). Communication forms and functions of children and adults with severe mental retardation in community and institutional settings. *Journal of Speech, Language, and Hearing Research, 42*(1), 231–240.

Meins, W. (1995). Symptoms of major depression in mentally retarded adults. *Journal of Intellectual Disability Research, 39*(1), 41–45.

Meyer, L. H., Eichinger, J., & Park-Lee, S. (1987). A validation of program quality indicators in educational services for students with severe disabilities. *Journal of the Association for Persons with Severe Handicaps, 12*(4), 251–263.

Miller, L. K. (1997). *Principles of everyday behavior analysis* (3rd ed.). Pacific Grove, CA: Brooks/Cole.

National Institute of Neurological Disorders and Stroke. (1988). *Developmental speech and language disorders: Hope through research* (NIH Publications No. Pamphlet 88-2757). Bethesda, MD: Author.

Nirje, B. (1969). The normalization principle and its human management implications. In R. Kugel & W. Wolfensberger (Eds.), *Changing patterns in residential services for the mentally retarded* (pp. 231–240) Washington, DC: President's Committee on Mental Retardation.

O'Neill, R. E., Horner, R. H., Albin, R. W., Storey, K., & Sprague, J. R. (1990). *Functional analysis of problem behavior: A practical assessment guide*. Sycamore, IL: Sycamore.

Parsons, J. A., May, J. G., & Menolascino F. J. (1984). The nature and incidence of mental illness in mentally retarded individuals. In F. J. Menolascino & J. A. Stark (Eds.), *Handbook of mental illness in the mentally retarded* (pp. 3–44). New York: Plenum.

Paul-Brown, D., & Diggs, C. C. (1993). Recognizing and treating speech and language disabilities. *American Rehabilitation, 19*(4), 30–37.

Pearpoint, J., & Forest, M. (1998). Person-centered planning: MAPS and PATH. *Impact, 11*(2), 4–5, 26–27.

Reichle, J., & Light, C. (1992). *Positive approaches to managing challenging behavior among persons with developmental disabilities living in the community*. Minneapolis: University of Minnesota, University Affiliated Program, Institute on Community Integration, Research and Training Center on Community Living.

Reichle, J., & Wacker, D. P. (Eds.). (1993). *Communicative alternatives to challenging behavior: Integrating functional assessment and intervention strategies*. Baltimore: Brookes.

Reiss, S. P. (1987). *Reiss screen for maladaptive behavior*. Worthington, OH: International Diagnostic Systems.

Riordan, J., & Vasa, S. F. (1991). Accommodations for and participation of persons with disabilities in religious practice. *Education and Training in Mental Retardation, 26*(2), 151–155.

Romski, M. A., & Sevcik, R. A. (1993). Language learning through augmented means: The process and its products. In A. P. Kaiser & D. B. Gray (Eds.), *Enhancing children's communication: Research foundations for intervention* (Vol. 2, pp. 85–104). Baltimore: Brookes.

Rusch, F. R., Chadsey-Rusch, J., & Johnson, J. R. (1991). Supported employment: Emerging opportunities for employment integration. In L. H. Meyer, C. A. Peck, & L. Brown (Eds.), *Critical issues in the lives of people with severe disabilities* (pp. 145–170). Baltimore: Brookes.

Rusch, F. R., Enchelmaier, J. F., & Kohler, P. D. (1994). Employment outcomes and activities for youths in transition. *Career Development for Exceptional Individuals, 17*(1), 1–15.

Safford, P. L., & Safford, E. J. (1996). *A history of childhood and disability.* New York: Teachers College Press.

Salkind, N. J. (1994). *Child development* (7th ed.). Fort Worth, TX: Harcourt Brace.

Schalock, R. L. (1986). *Transition from school to work.* Washington, DC: National Association of Rehabilitation Facilities.

Schalock, R. L. (Ed.). (1996). *Quality of life. Volume I: Conceptualization and measurement.* Washington, DC: American Association on Mental Retardation.

Schalock, R. L. (1999). A personal odyssey Part II: The story continues. *Mental Retardation, 37*(4), 331-332.

Schalock, R. L., Keith, K. D., Hoffman, K., & Karan, O. C. (1989). Quality of life: Its measurement and use in human service programs. *Mental Retardation, 27,* 25–31.

Scheerenberger, R. C., & Felsenthal, D. (1977). Community settings for mentally retarded persons: Satisfaction and activities. *Mental Retardation, 15*(4), 3–7.

Schleien, S. J., Ray, M. T., & Green, F. P. (1996). *Community recreation and people with disabilities: Strategies for inclusion* (2nd ed.). Baltimore: Brookes.

Schoeller, K. (1997). Overcoming barriers to social inclusion. *Impact, 10*(3), 4–5.

Skinner, B. F. (1953). *Science and human behavior.* New York: Macmillan.

Smith, G. C., Majeski, R. A., & McClenny, B. (1996). Psychoeducational support groups for aging parents: Development and preliminary outcomes. *Mental Retardation, 34*(3), 172–181.

Snell, M. E. (1993). *Instruction of students with severe disabilities* (4th ed.). New York: Macmillan.

Soto, G., Belfiore, P. J., Schlosser, R. W., & Haynes, C. (1993). Teaching specific requests: A comparative analysis on skill acquisition and preference using two augmentative and alternative communication aids. *Education and Training in Mental Retardation, 28*(2), 169–178.

Sparrow, S. S., Balla, D. A., & Cicchetti, D. V. (1984a). *Vineland Adaptive Behavior Scales, interview edition, expanded form.* Circle Pines, MN: American Guidance Service.

Sparrow, S. S., Balla, D. A., & Cicchetti, D. V. (1984b). *Vineland Adaptive Behavior Scales, interview edition, survey form.* Circle Pines, MN: American Guidance Service.

Sparrow, S. S., Balla, D. A., & Cicchetti, D. A. (1985). *Vineland Adaptive Behavior Scales, classroom edition form.* Circle Pines, MN: American Guidance Service.

Spreat, S., Telles, J. L., Conroy, J. W., Feinstein, C., & Columbatto, J. J. (1987). Attitudes toward deinstitutionalization: National survey of families of institutionalized persons with mental retardation. *Mental Retardation, 25*(5), 267–274.

Stevens, H. A. (1964). Overview of Mental Retardation. In H. A. Stevens & R. Heber (Eds.), *Mental retardation* (pp. 3–15). Chicago: University of Chicago Press.

Strully, J. L., & Strully, C. F. (1989). Friendships as an educational goal. In S. Stainback, W. Stainback, & M. Forest (Eds.), *Educating all students in the mainstream of regular education* (pp. 59–68). Baltimore: Brookes.

Taylor, S. J. (1988). Caught in the continuum: A critical analysis of the principles of the least restrictive environment. *Journal of the Association for Persons with Severe Handicaps, 13*(1), 41–53.

Thorndike, R. L., Hagen, E. P., & Sattler, J. M. (1996). *Stanford-Binet Intelligence Scale: Fourth Edition.* Chicago: Riverside.

Van Houten, R., & Axelrod, S. (Eds.). (1993). *Behavior analysis and treatment.* New York: Plenum.

Vollmer, T. R., Iwata, B. A., Zarcone, J. R., Smith, R. G., & Mazaleski, J. L. (1993). The role of attention in the treatment of attention-maintained self-injurious behavior: Noncontingent reinforcement and differential reinforcement of other behavior. *Journal of Applied Behavior Analysis, 26*(1), 9–21.

Wechsler, D. (1991). *Wechsler Intelligence Scale for Children—Third Edition.* San Antonio, TX: Psychological Corporation.

Wehman, P., & Kregel, J. (1997). *Functional curriculum for elementary, middle, and secondary age students with special needs.* Austin, TX: PRO-ED.

Wehman, P., Kregel, J., & Seyfarth, J. (1985). Transition from school to work for individuals with severe handicaps: A follow-up study. *Journal of the Association for Persons with Severe Handicaps, 10*(3), 132–136.

Wehmeyer, M. (1993). Self-determination as an educational outcome. *Impact, 6*(4), 6–7.

Wilcox, B., & Bellamy, G. T. (1982). *Design of high school programs for severely handicapped students.* Baltimore: Brookes.

Wolfensberger, W. (1972). *The principle of normalization in human services.* Toronto: National Institute on Mental Retardation.

Zetlin, A. G., & Turner, J. L. (1985). Transition from adolescence to adulthood: Perspectives of mentally retarded individuals and their families. *American Journal of Mental Deficiency, 89*(6), 570–579.

Part Three

Programming and Issues across the Life Span

CHAPTER

9

Infancy and Early Childhood

OBJECTIVES

After reading this chapter, the student should be able to

- state the rationale for early childhood special education

- discuss the legislation and implementation affecting early childhood special education programs

- describe assessment procedures used with infants, toddlers, and young children who are disabled

- discuss considerations in programming for young children

 *To review the chapter objectives on-line, go to the companion website at http://www.prenhall.com/beirne-smith and select Chapter 9, and then choose the Objectives module.*

KEY TERMS

at risk

criterion-referenced testing (CRT)

curriculum

curriculum-based assessment (CBA)

early childhood special education

early intervention

family-directed assessment

individual family service plan (IFSP)

individualized education program (IEP)

informed clinical opinion

judgment-based assessment

mastery learning

norm-referenced testing

precision teaching

transition

RATIONALE FOR EARLY CHILDHOOD SPECIAL EDUCATION

Early childhood special education is a system of services for children from birth to 5 years of age who are disabled, developmentally delayed, or at risk of developing developmental delay. The system of services that are usually provided free of charge for these children and their families is known as early intervention.

For a complete on-line glossary of mental retardation terms, go to the companion website at http://www.prenhall.com/beirne-smith and select any chapter, and then choose the Glossary module.

Educational programs for infants and children with disabilities were virtually nonexistent 25 years ago. In recent years, due to legislation and effective early intervention techniques, early childhood special education has experienced phenomenal growth. Today, the focus is on early intervention and programming for children in the birth to 5-year age range who are disabled, developmentally delayed, or at risk of developing developmental delay.

Among the first to draw attention to the importance of the early years were Marie Montessori, Friedrich Froebel, and G. Stanley Hall. Other researchers have added their support. For example, Bloom (1964) found that children develop 50% of their total intellectual capacity by age 4 and 80% by age 8. White (1975) concluded that the period between 8 months and 3 years is of utmost importance in the development of intellectual and social skills. In addition, Hayden and Pious (1979), McDaniel (1977), Smith and Strain (1984), and Weissman and Littman (1996) have argued that for children with physical, social, emotional, or mental disabilities, educational programming should begin shortly after birth.

The rationale for early childhood special education has been built on research and scholarly writing that clearly demonstrates the importance of the early experiences of children to their later growth and development. Bricker and colleagues (Bricker & Cripe, 1992; Bricker, Pretti-Frontczak, & McComas, 1998; Bricker & Veltman, 1990) define the theoretical underpinnings of early intervention programs:

1. Children with developmental disabilities require more and/or different early experience than children without disabilities.
2. Formal programs with trained personnel are necessary to provide the required early experience to compensate for developmental difficulties.
3. Developmental progress is enhanced in children with disabilities who participate in early intervention programs. (Bricker & Cripe, 1992, p. 9)

Bailey and Wolery (1993) provide a knowledgeable argument for early childhood education. According to these authors, high-quality early intervention can successfully detect problems when they are distinct and remedial, change the behavior of children in different areas of development, prevent the secondary consequences of primary disability, reduce the cost of serving these children at a later age, and provide assistance and training to families in need. Similarly, in a review of early childhood programs for disadvantaged and high-risk children, Barnett (1997) concludes that high-quality early education programs positively affect children's intelligence quotient, school achievement, grade retention, placement in special education, and social competence. Guralnick (1998) concurs that comprehensive early childhood education reduces the decline in intellectual development that occurs without appropriate intervention.

Additionally, in a review of early intervention findings from the Abecedarian Project, Project CARE, and the Infant Health and Development Program, Ramey and Ramey (1992) found that the benefits of daily early educational intervention in the first 5 years of a child's life can improve a child's intellectual performance and academic achievement at least until early adolescence. Daily intervention activities considered essential to such outcomes are (a) to be encouraged to explore the environment; (b) to be guided toward basic thinking skills, such as sorting and sequencing; (c) to celebrate and reinforce accomplishments; (d) to practice the skills learned and to expand on these skills; (e) to avoid negative consequences during the trial-and-error process of learning; and (f) to provide a full verbal and written language experience for the child.

Families of children who are developmentally delayed or at risk for developmental delay form the other side of the rationale for early childhood special education (Baird, 1997; Raver, 1999; Thorp, 1997; Turnbull & Turnbull, 2000a, 2000b) with early intervention, families learn how to be better parents and thus are able to provide additional experiences on a continual basis for the young child in the home. Learning about their child's condition and how to help reduces the parenting stress level, which enables parents to make more positive contributions to their child's future.

LEGISLATION AFFECTING EARLY CHILDHOOD SPECIAL EDUCATION PROGRAMS

On October 8, 1986, Congress passed PL 99-457, the Education of the Handicapped Amendments, which extended to 3- through 5-year-old children who are disabled the rights and privileges that had been afforded individuals in the 6- to 21-year-old category. In July 1997, Congress amended the IDEA by PL 105-17 to extend the developmental delay state option for children aged 3 to 9 who have been determined to have a disability and who, by reason thereof, need special education. The purpose of the extension is to promote services that are not driven by a particular label. Under Part H of the IDEA, PL 99-457 also provided for the voluntary development of programs for children from birth through 2 years of age who had disabilities, were developmentally delayed, or were at risk for developing developmental delay and their families. The 1997 reauthorization of the IDEA moved the Part H legislation to Part C of the act.

To meet its objectives of serving the educational needs of preschool children with disabilities, PL 99-457 and its subsequent amendments were structured around two components. The preschool component was mandatory; it required that by the school year 1990–91 any state receiving funds under the law must have provided free appropriate preschool education with related services to all children with disabilities aged 3 through 5. The infant component of the law was voluntary; it provided individual states with incentive grants to assist in the development of an interagency council whose purpose was to ensure planned, coordinated services for children with disabilities aged birth through 2 years of age. A unique feature of the law was the recognition of the need for parental involvement in the education of their children. Under PL 99-457 and its amendments, parents must be assisted in determining the needs of their child and in obtaining services for their child.

While the purpose of PL 99-457 and its amendments was to extend the parameters of PL 94-142 to younger children with disabilities, the regulations for its implementation differed substantially from those of PL 94-142. In addition, regulations for implementing the law's preschool component differed from the requirements for the infant component.

Preschool Components

The preschool component of the law was mandatory. Regulations accompanying PL 99-457 and its amendments that differed from those of PL 94-142 follow:

1. Individual states serving 3- through 5 year-old children (now 3- to 9-year-old children) with disabilities were not required to report child count figures by existing disabilities categories.
2. Each Individualized Education Program (IEP) for children in the 3 through 5 age group (now 3 to 9 age group) had to include instructions for parents.
3. To allow local education agencies to use a variety of service delivery options (including full- or part-day, center-based, home-based, and combination programs), the length of the school day and school year can vary.

Services to children who are retarded are well-designed and systematically implemented.

4. Preschool education programs for children 3 through 5 years are administered through the state education agency; local education agencies (LEAs), however, can contract services from other programs (e.g., Head Start) or other agencies (e.g., Department of Social Services) to meet the requirement for provision of a full range of services.

5. Failure to comply with the new law resulted in the loss of federal funds generated by the Preschool Grant, funds generated under the larger PL 94-142 formula for children 3 through 5 years old, and federal grants and contracts for preschool education programs.

Infant Component (Part C, Formerly Part H)

Requirements accompanying the voluntary component of PL 99-457 and its amendments differ from those of PL 94-142 and from the mandatory component of PL 99-457 in the following ways:

1. Policymakers in states applying for grants to serve infants and toddlers with disabilities aged birth through 2 years had to establish an Interagency Coordinating Council to assist parents in determining needs and obtaining services. This council had to be composed of service providers and agencies that routinely served children in this age range.

2. Criteria for classification of infants and toddlers with disabilities aged birth through 2 years had to be established by the individual state. Eligible children included those who (a) were developmentally delayed, (b) had conditions that typically resulted in developmental delays, or (c) were considered at risk for substantial developmental delay (e.g., from poor prenatal care, low socioeconomic status, or other potential risk factors).

3. Every eligible child and family were assigned a service coordinator whose responsibility was to ensure that the child and family received appropriate services.

4. Except where federal or state law set a schedule of adjusted fees, services were free.

5. Services included (a) multidisciplinary assessment, (b) a design to address the child's developmental needs, and (c) a written **individual family service plan (IFSP)** developed by a multidisciplinary team with assistance from parents (see Table 9.1).

6. PL 105-17 required policies and procedures to ensure that, to the maximum extent possible, early intervention services were provided in natural environments. Also, the law required that the IFSP justify services provided outside natural environments.

PL 94-142 (1975) was reauthorized and amended in 1990 and 1997. In 1990, the law changed its name from the Education of All Handicapped Children Act to the Individuals with Disabilities Education Act (IDEA), PL 101-476. Both PL 101-476 and its 1997 amendment PL 105-17 reauthorized financial assistance to the states through state grants to address the needs of infants and toddlers with disabilities. All states ensured full implementation of the Part C program for infants and toddlers with disabilities by September 30, 1994.

TABLE 9.1

Components of the Individualized Family Services Plan: Part C of PL 105-17 (IDEA)

The IFSP must:
1. be based on a multidisciplinary assessment of the unique strengths and needs of the infant or toddler and identify the appropriate services to meet those needs [20 U.S.C. δ 1436 (a) (1)];
2. include a family-directed assessment of the resources, priorities, and concerns of the family and identify the supports and services necessary to enhance the family's capacity to meet the developmental needs of the infant or toddler [20 U.S.C. δ 1436 (a) (2)];
3. be developed in writing by a multidisciplinary team that includes the infant or toddler's parents [20 U.S.C. δ 1436 (a) (3)];

Further, the IFSP must include:
1. a statement of the child's present levels of physical, cognitive, communication, social or emotional, and adaptive development, based on objective criteria [20 U.S.C. δ 1436 (d) (1)];
2. a statement of the family's resources, priorities, and concerns relative to enhancing the development of the family's infant or toddler [20 U.S.C. δ 1436 (d) (2)];
3. a statement of the major outcomes expected to be achieved for the infant or toddler and the family, and the criteria, procedures, and timelines used to determine the extent to which progress toward achieving the outcomes is being made and whether modifications or revisions of the outcomes or services are necessary [20 U.S.C. δ 1436 (d) (3)];
4. a statement of the specific early intervention services necessary to meet the unique needs of the infant or toddler and the family, including the frequency, intensity, and method of delivering services [20 U.S.C. δ 1436 (d) (4)];
5. a statement of the natural environments in which early intervention services shall be provided appropriately, including justification of the extent, if any, to which services will not be provided in the natural environment [20 U.S.C. δ 1436 (d) (5)];
6. the projected dates for initiation of services and anticipated duration of services [20 U.S.C. δ 1436 (d) (6)];
7. identification of the service coordinator who will be responsible for implementating the plan and coordinating with other agencies and persons [20 U.S.C. δ 1436 (d) (7)];
8. the steps to be taken to support the toddler's transition to preschool or other appropriate services [20 U.S.C. δ 1436 (d) (8)];

Early childhood special education now provides services for children with disabilities from birth through 9 years of age and their families under Parts B and C of the IDEA. In accordance with other policies in the IDEA, the services are free of charge to the children and their families. The laws now support what educators, researchers, and scholars have long believed: Appropriate early intervention has a significant impact on a child's intellectual capacity and potential to learn and is cost-effective.

The IDEA (1997) established new priorities for meeting the needs of infants and toddlers with disabilities. Different from Part B, which provides free appropriate public education for school-aged children and only minimally addresses the role of parents in their child's education, Part C emphasizes the role of the family in the education of the infant or toddler who is disabled, developmentally delayed, or at risk (see Figure 9.1). Part C set five goals:

1. Develop the capacities of infants and toddlers and minimize their potential for developmental delay.
2. Reduce the cost of special education.
3. Minimize the likelihood that people with disabilities will be institutionalized.

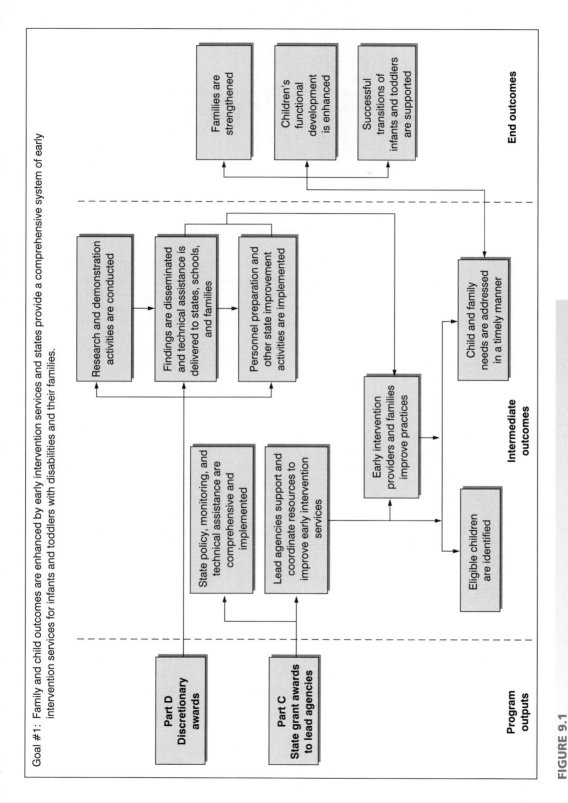

FIGURE 9.1

IDEA Programs for Infants and Toddlers with Disabilities

Source: U.S. Department of Education (1997).

TABLE 9.2
Types of Early Intervention Services

1. Family training, counseling, home visits
2. Special instruction
3. Speech-language pathology and audiology
4. Occupational therapy
5. Physical therapy
6. Psychological services
7. Service coordination services
8. Medical services for diagnostic and evaluation purposes
9. Early identification, screening, and assessment services
10. Health services necessary to help the infant or toddler to benefit from other intervention services
11. Social work services
12. Vision services
13. Assistive technology devices and assistive technology services
14. Transportation and related costs that are necessary for the infant, toddler, or infant or toddler's family to receive another service [20 U.S.C. δ 1432 (4) (E)].

4. Enhance families capacities for working with their children.
5. Enhance the capacities of state and local agencies and service providers to identify, evaluate, and meet the needs of historically underrepresented populations (20 USC 1431[a]).

Part C of the IDEA (1997) provides separate funding for infants and toddlers aged birth through 3 who qualify for early intervention services because they experience developmental delays or have diagnosed mental or physical conditions that have a high probability of resulting in developmental delays (20 USC 1432 [5]). Developmental delays must be in the areas of cognitive, physical, language and speech, psychosocial, or self-help. The states may otherwise define developmental delay, but the delay must be in the specified areas of development (20 USC 1432 [3]). Prior to the 1997 reauthorization of the IDEA, states could define and require LEAs to use the developmental delay category for children ages 3 to 9. The 1997 IDEA amendments allowed states to define developmental delay for children ages 3 to 9 or a subset of those ages (e.g., 3 through 5). Any state that uses the term *developmental delay* for children aged 3 to 9 also may use one or more of the disability categories for any child within that age range if it is determined through a proper assessment that the child has a disability that requires special education and related services. Furthermore, Part C allows LEAs to elect to use the developmental delay category. LEAs using the developmental delay category are obligated to use the state's definition of developmental delay and the age range specified by the state. Finally, each state and LEA has the option of serving infants and toddlers who are at risk of experiencing substantial developmental delays if they do not receive such early intervention services as those listed in Table 9.2.

One of the major dilemmas in implementing the "at-risk" early intervention programs lies in the definition of at risk. **At risk** "refers to children who, although not currently identified as having a disability, are considered to have a greater-than-

Maggie and Ida

Maggie Erickson, a preschool student, and Ida Singer, an 87-year-old elder who volunteers in the Intergenerational Inclusive Preschool Program, have become important parts of each others' lives. Just how important can be seen in the following excerpts from conversations with Cathy Erickson, who is Maggie's mother, and with Ida.

Maggie's mother says: My daughter, Maggie, attends the JCC preschool for two days each week. Ida comes in every morning that Maggie is at school to help her. During the evenings, Maggie and I talk about everyone at the JCC preschool and Maggie always speaks of Ida with fondness. Like any child, Maggie is sometimes slow about getting ready to go to school. When that happens, I remind her, "You will get to see Ida today!" and before I know it, she is out the door. Last year, Maggie had to have a cast put on her leg and she needed to stay home from school. She was thrilled when Ida made a special trip to visit her at our home.

Elders such as Ida provide love and acceptance to the children with disabilities and their classmates, and the children provide the same to the elders. Elders also contribute a wealth of life experience to the children and to the classroom curriculum. Too often, families who have children with disabilities tend to become isolated. It is nice to know that there is another adult in Maggie's life who can provide her with support and acceptance.

"Grandma" Ida says: I have always had a very wonderful feeling about grandparents. I never knew my own grandparents, but I've always thought they are very special—you can learn from them. I'm a different kind of grandma for the preschool children. Their grandmas are all young —busy and socializing. I'm the spoiling grandma.

When Maggie first came to the preschool, she used to play mostly by herself, with the dolls. At first she really needed me there. I tried not to hover over her or "smother" her with attention. I'm sure it is easy to do that, but I thought if I gave her too much attention, she couldn't grow. So I try to take a back seat. I keep an eye on what Maggie is doing, in case she needs my help, but also interact with all of the kids. Now Maggie is mixing well with the children. She is benefiting on her own because she is doing a lot on her own. She likes everybody.

I never realized that three-year-olds were so smart. You can carry on a conversation with a child and learn a lot from them. For instance, even though I have a disability—I walk with a cane—the children learn to handle it. They realize that I can't pick them up readily. They learn that people have limitations. Like with my glasses. They would ask, "Why do you have to war glasses, Ida?" They said, "Take them off!" I took them off and asked, "So how do I look?" "You still look like a grandma!" It keeps me young—keeps me younger—knowing that the children accept me for who I am.

I think it is important to get the different generations together. I think it is beneficial to the kids to have an overall picture of what people are—of what older people are, of what younger people are, of the different ways there are to live. If kids see an older person who can help themselves, it leaves an impression.

Working with the children makes a difference in how I feel about myself. I feel capable. It gives me a challenge, something to look forward to. If the children respond to something I do or say, then I feel good. I have a good feeling when I leave the classroom.

Source: From "Maggie and Ida" by L. A. Heyne, 1996, *Impact,* 9(4), p. 11. Copyright 1996 by Institute on Community Integration, University of Minnesota, Minneapolis. Reprinted by permission.

usual chance of developing a disability. The term is often applied to infants or children who, because of conditions surrounding their births or home environments, may be expected to experience developmental delays at a later time" (Heward, 2000, p. 4). Common examples of risk factors include the socioeconomic status of the family, the intellectual abilities of the parents (especially the mother), and the number of children in the family.

Zervigon-Hakes (1995) concludes that three types of children are at risk. This categorization highlights the point that there are important differences in the ways in which we should conceptualize at-risk children. The categories are as follows:

1. *Established risk:* Children in this category have known genetic and biomedical conditions that affect their lives. Chromosomal disorders and sensory loss are examples of established risk factors.
2. *Biological risk:* These children have developmental histories that suggest the presence of a biological problem, but the problem is not apparent. Low birth weight and premature birth are examples of biological risk factors.
3. *Economic and social risk:* Children who fit this group have no known medical or biological problem, but they do experience life situations that can give rise to problems. Persistent poverty, inadequate health care, and substance or child abuse are examples of economic and social risk factors.

When considering whether children are at risk, it is important not only to evaluate the children but also to investigate such external factors as their homes and life events. If efforts to identify and provide services to children who are at risk and their families are well designed and systematically implemented, then fewer children should fail at school, and consequently fewer will be identified as in need of special services.

It is important to compare the broad eligibility provisions of Part C (birth through age 2) with the more narrow eligibility provisions of Part B (ages 3 through 21). Under Part B of the IDEA, only children and youth beyond age 9 who need special education and related services and qualify by fitting within the definition of children with disabilities, which "means children with mental retardation; hearing impairments, including deafness; speech or language impairments; visual impairments, including blindness; serious emotional disturbance; orthopedic impairments; autism; traumatic brain injury; other health impairments; or specific learning disabilities" (34 CFR 300.7) are entitled to the benefits of the law. Part B

FIGURE 9.2

Number of Infants and Toddlers Served under the IDEA, Part C, 1994–1997[a, b]

Source: U.S. Department of Education, Office of Special Education Programs, Data Analysis System (DANS).

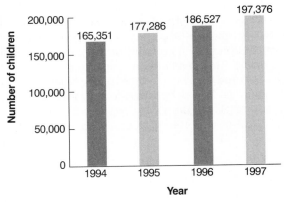

[a]Since states and outlying areas may update previously reported data as necessary, the data reported here may differ from those included in prior annual reports.

[b]Counts as of December 1, 1997.

FIGURE 9.3

Number of Children Ages 3 through 5 Served under the Preschool Grants Program, 1992–93 to 1997–98

Source: U.S. Department of Education, Office of Special Education Programs, Data Analysis System (DANS).

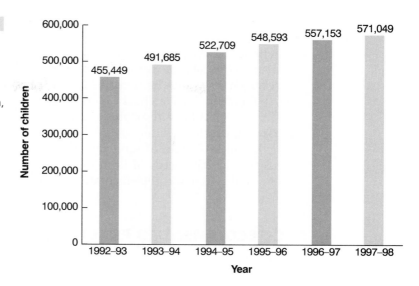

does not include 3- to 9-year-old children who are at risk for developing substantial development delays. Part B services are free and are provided by the LEAs. Furthermore, the children and their families have a due-process right in disputes between LEAs and themselves.

Children in the 3- through 5-year (now 6 to 9) range who qualify under Part B of the IDEA are served through the **individualized education program (IEP),** which is an individually written plan of instruction composed by a team specifying a child's present level of functioning, annual goals, short-term objectives, special education and related services required, extent of participation in the general education classroom, if appropriate, time line of initiation and duration of services, objective criteria, and evaluation procedures.

There are some notable differences between the IFSP used for children from birth through age 2 and the IEP used for children from 3 to 9 years. One of the main differences is the categorical approach used for the IEP. A statement of the family's strengths and needs as well as a service coordinator who is responsible for implementing the plan also are included in the IFSP; these are not included in the IEP.

As of December 1, 1997, 197,376 eligible infants and toddlers were served under the IDEA according to the U.S. Department of Education (1999) (see Figure 9.2). This represents a 19% increase from the 165,351 infants and toddlers reported served on December 1, 1994. The continued growth in the numbers of infants and toddlers served under the IDEA reflects continuing improvements in reporting procedures and more effective outreach efforts at the state level through child-find efforts.

Finally, the IDEA authorized grants to be awarded for developing and operating extended school-year demonstration programs for infants and toddlers with severe disabilities and for developing appropriate criteria to identify, evaluate, and serve infants and toddlers from minority backgrounds. In 1997-98, states and outlying areas reported that 571,049 children ages 3 through 5 were served under the Preschool Grants program. This number represents an overall increase of 25% from the number served in 1992–93 (see Figure 9.3). About two-thirds of the states (67%, or 37 states) reported no change in the number of 3- through 5-year-olds served under the Preschool Grants Program from 1995 to 1997. In general, the data indicated that while the percentage of 3- through 5-year-old children eligible for services under the IDEA has remained stable over the past 3 years, the number of children served by the Preschool Grants Program has continued to grow.

The system of birth through the age of 21 presently in place for children who are disabled, developmentally delayed, or at risk as presented in the IDEA represents a seamless system of service to these children and their parents. The law intends to meet the needs of both the child and the parents through individual planning and systematic implementation of the plan.

DEC-RECOMMENDED PRACTICES

To find resources related to early intervention, go to the companion website at www.prenhall.com/ beirne-smith and select Chapter 9, then choose the Web Destinations module.

In 1993, the Division of Early Childhood (DEC), a part of the Council for Exceptional Children (CEC), issued a set of recommended practices for infants and young children with disabilities and their families. Since no one practice is necessarily the best practice for all young children with disabilities, DEC addressed recommended practices across a broad spectrum. All practices fulfill the following obligations:

1. *Research or value based.* The practices are supported through research indicating a positive impact or through practices that are supported as deemed valuable by a consensus in the field of early childhood.
2. *Family centered.* The needs of the family as well as the child are considered as opposed to strictly child-centered approaches.
3. *Multicultural emphasis.* Benefits to the child and the child's family are viewed and adapted to support cultures and values that are different from the mainstream population of the United States.
4. *Cross-disciplinary participation.* Members of the various disciplines must work together as a team for the benefit of the child and the family and to share information and expertise.
5. *Developmentally/chronologically age-appropriate.* This is a match between what the child is capable of doing, the child's learning needs, and the environment that is most natural to the age of the child.

The components of these practices are to be observed throughout contact with the child or the child's parents. In the referral or evaluation phase of contact, for example, the instruments used should be multicultural in emphasis, developmentally and chronologically age-appropriate, and family centered with cross-disciplinary participation.

Referral

Under Part C of the IDEA, each state is required to have an early intervention system in place. The state will select a lead agency to implement Part C in the state, carry out the state plan, coordinate the work of the public and private agencies within the state, create a statewide comprehensive directory of services available, and create a statewide database containing numbers of children who have disabilities, are developmentally delayed, or are at risk. The states are responsible for creating a State Interagency Coordinating Council in the role of advisement to the lead agency.

The early intervention system within the state must also support child-find efforts to identify and locate families and their children who have disabilities, are developmentally delayed, or at risk. The system has further responsibility in arranging for evaluations for all referred children, preparing IFSPs and IEPs for all eligible children, and serving all eligible children and their families. Procedural safeguards are still in place for all children, and for children under Part C, referral for early intervention services may not be made without the parents' written consent.

Evaluation and Assessment

The terms *evaluation* and *assessment* are often used interchangeably, yet in Part C of the IDEA they are considered different. An *evaluation* is a formal process conducted by qualified, licensed personnel who administer standardized tests for initial placement and continued eligibility, whereas an *assessment* is an ongoing, often informal, process in which workers from many disciplines contribute information and participate in an ongoing process to determine specific strengths and weaknesses. The IDEA further emphasizes **informed clinical opinion,** which utilizes at least 50% of a clinician's expertise in addition to the formal testing results to aid in determining eligibility.

Testing of young children who are believed to have disabilities or delays or who are considered at risk requires prior parental consent. The IDEA (34 CFR 300.561) requires that parents or guardians receive prior written notice of any proposal to test a child in the parent's native language.

Based on DEC-recommended practices (DEC, 1993), assessments and evaluations should incorporate the following principles:

1. Use multiple sources and multiple measures gathered on multiple occasions in multiple settings.
2. Use approaches that are culturally and developmentally appropriate to determine the strengths and weaknesses of the child, capitalizing on the child's known interests and the family's sensitivities.
3. Use a collaborative decision-making process in conducting assessment and evaluation to determine the current status of the child and family, eligibility for services, and plan of action, should services be needed.

The quality of information obtained in psychoeducational evaluations depends, to a large extent, on the integrity of both the instruments and the methods used to obtain that information. Two basic approaches to the assessment of early childhood abilities have predominated in recent years, formal and informal methods. Although both dimensions are necessary for a comprehensive approach to service delivery, neither one alone can provide all the information necessary for effective intervention. While formal measures continue to serve as the standard means of assessment, teachers are increasingly turning to informal measure to assist with program planning and evaluation.

Evaluation

Formal assessment procedures are those with specific guidelines for administration, scoring, and interpretation (McLoughlin & Lewis, 1998). Formal assessment procedures generally include such norm-referenced tests as intelligence tests, achievement tests, and interest inventories. The term *standardized* refers as much to the rigors of administration and scoring as to the scores themselves. In standardized or **norm-referenced testing,** each child's test performance is compared to that of other children using a standardized score. The standardization sample serves as the basis for all comparisons in norm-referenced testing. While norm-referenced tests generally do not provide the classroom teacher with specific guidelines for instruction, they do allow a teacher to compare a child's test performance to that of other children of similar age and under similar conditions.

Neisworth and Bagnato (1988) identify three principal purposes for norm-based assessment: (a) to describe a child's level of development, (b) to place a child in a diagnostic category, and (c) to predict a child's future level of development. Well-designed tests with representative reference groups (age, race, sex, residence, geographic region, and socioeconomic status) allow educators to do more than just compare a child to other children on general measures of aptitude or ability; such tests also allow educators to estimate the child's unique skills and abilities.

Under the IDEA, Parts C and B, evaluation is to be comprehensive and multi-disciplinary. A multidisciplinary approach synthesizes the expertise of specialists in various areas and the expertise of parents and teachers who know the child well into a comprehensive plan for the child that includes intervention, preschool and elementary special education, and related services. Both Parts C and B are explicit against the use of any single test or procedure as the sole basis of placement.

The IDEA, Part C, requires that the evaluation be conducted in a timely manner. Based on the Department of Education's regulation, *timely* means "within 45 days after . . . referral" (34 CFR Regulations 303.321[e], 303.322[e]). The IDEA, Part B, further clarifies evaluation materials. The materials are provided and administered in the child's native language or preferred mode of communication.

Tests are to be appropriate by both validity and reliability for use with preschool populations. The validity and reliability of any tests rest on using the same kinds of children used to establish the original validity and reliability scores. In most instances, preschool children who are disabled, developmentally delayed, or at risk were not included in the original sampling of children. Limited meaning, therefore, can be gleaned from the results of standardized measures. Concurring, Fuchs, Fuchs, Benowitz, and Barringer (1987), in their evaluation of 27 widely used aptitude and achievement tests, and Bailey and Nabors (1996) report little support toward the appropriateness of such tests for the preschool population.

If describing a child's skills and abilities well enough to meet the qualifying criteria for placement is the letter of the law, then describing a child's strengths and weaknesses well enough to design effective interventions represents the spirit of the law. School-age children must have a diagnostic label before they can receive services, but preschoolers, infants, and toddlers need only be at risk for substantial delay to qualify. Early childhood educators are required to meet both the spirit and the letter of the law by designing interventions based more on needs of the child than on the stereotypical description of a label. Well-designed standardized tests can help educators assess the child's needs accurately.

Assessment

Informal assessment methods are similar to formal methods in that they are designed to elicit educationally relevant information, but they are also dissimilar in that they allow the examiner to obtain information under less stringent conditions. Because external criteria are absent, the teacher is free to design techniques and methods of assessment based on hypotheses about the particular preschool child's learning pattern. What these techniques lack in normative data they make up for in relevance to instruction. Using informal methods has several advantages: Test items may be designed and administered by the teacher; test items may coincide with instruction; the teacher can revise the items and the format as testing progresses; and the teacher can assess the child before, during, and after each lesson, depending on the type of information needed.

Although many different types of informal assessment exist (interviews, observations, task analyses, work samples), a frequently used in-class method is **criterion-referenced testing (CRT),** which is when the teacher attempts to measure the child's skills against preestablished levels of mastery (Salvia & Ysseldyke, 1995). CRT is based on the premise that a child's performance may be best understood in the context of what a child can do within a given content area, instead of simply how well a child performs relative to other children (Venn, 1994). A fundamental prerequisite to CRT is defining a content area well enough to represent it with prespecified questions. CRT is versatile enough to be appropriate for everything from school readiness to self-help skills.

Curriculum-based assessment (CBA) is one type of CRT in which test items are drawn directly from the teaching materials. This is a highly effective way of monitoring and modifying methods of instruction. Fuchs and Fuchs (1990) have identified two specific forms of CBA: precision teaching and mastery learning. In **precision teaching,** a lesson is broken down into a hierarchy of skills. Measurement procedures allow the teacher to analyze the child's performance at each step in the skills hierarchy. In **mastery learning,** the teacher tests a concept, gives feedback, and then tests the concept again until the child has completely mastered the task. Precision teaching and mastery learning share a number of elements in common: teacher-designed assessment tasks, assessment through short-term objectives, and measurement focus shift upon mastery.

Judgment-based assessment (JBA) provides a structured framework within which a teacher may include and quantify the opinions and impressions of primary caregivers (Neisworth & Bagnato, 1988). In JBA, the examiner constructs a scale or checklist designed to measure abilities not typically covered in standardized tests. The individual is the sole referent for each analysis. The principal advantage of JBA is that it provides a type of social validity (Wolf, 1978), a means of linking a child's traits and behaviors with results from other, more formalized tests.

Family-directed assessment is a special kind of assessment to study "the resources, priorities, and concerns of the family and the identification of the supports and services necessary to enhance the family's capacity to meet the developmental needs of their infant or toddler with a disability" (IDEA, section 677[a][2]). This assessment comes under Part C and not Part B of the IDEA. The inclusion of the family-directed assessment is especially critical for infants and toddlers, as they cannot be understood apart from their family. The assessment, however, is a voluntary component on the part of the family. The family has the right to determine whether and to what extent they will participate, knowing that the results of the family-directed assessment become part of the IFSP.

MEASURES OF EARLY CHILDHOOD DEVELOPMENT

Delays in and limitations in the domains of socioemotional, cognitive, speech and language, motor, and adaptive behavior development are important in early childhood education. Screening for educational and psychological delays, therefore, is a routine part of assessment at all levels of education. Cohn (1992) has suggested that a good preschool screening instrument is one that is easy to administer and score, allows for multidimensional assessment of different developmental areas, is valid and reliable across all ages for which it was designed, and is cost-effective given budgetary, time, and staff constraints.

Socioemotional Assessment

Delays in and limitations of social or emotional development in young children who are retarded are no less important than delays and limitations in young children who are not retarded. Benner (1992) defines the social and emotional domain as encompassing the development of individuation, attachment, and adaptive behaviors, including self-care skills and the emergence of emotions. During the early childhood years, early childhood professionals work more closely with the family than is possible during the elementary and secondary school years. This family focus gives professionals an opportunity to intervene to prevent, extinguish, or improve behaviors by the child.

Unfortunately, and because of the limited cognitive and verbal abilities of young children who are retarded, assessment and intervention are often extremely difficult. Assessment of socioemotional development requires that comparisons be made with reference to normal development (Martin, 1991). Generally, the decision regarding the socioemotional development is made based on one of two principal avenues: (a) assessment of personality through the use of projectives, drawing, dialogue, play therapy, or open-ended questions or (b) assessment of observable behavior in structured and unstructured settings. Aydlett (1993) expresses concern over the number of standardized tests available for use in the socioemotional development assessment of young children. Martin (1991) reports that as much as 90% of the information on socioemotional functioning in young children is derived from behavior-rating scales. The Personality Inventory for Children (Lachar, 1990), the Behavioral Evaluation Scale—II (McCarney & Leigh, 1990), the Child Behavior Checklist (CBCL; Achenbach, 1994), and the Test of Early Socio-Emotional Development (Hresko & Brown, 1984) are examples of frequently used measures of socioemotional development (see Table 9.3).

TABLE 9.3

Measures of Socioemotional Development

Instrument	Age Range	Domains/Areas	Scores Provided	Standardization Sample Size and Model	Median Scale Reliability Estimate
Behavior Evaluation Scale II (McCarney & Leigh, 1990)	K–12th grade	Learning problems Interpersonal difficulties Inappropriate behavior Unhappiness/depression Physical symptoms/fears	Behavior quotient scores ($M=100$, $SD=15$) Scaled scores ($M=10$, $SD=3$)	Not reported ($N=2,278$)	Not available
Burks' Behavioral Rating Scales: Preschool and Kindergarten Edition (Burks, 1977)	3.9–6.11	18 scales	Raw scores	Not reported ($N=464$)	Not reported
Child Behavior Checklist (CBCL) (Achenbach, 1994)	2.0–18.11	Parent rating scale Teacher rating scale Student rating scale Direct observation form Semistructured clinical interview		$N=1,100$ children nonreferred & 1,700 children referred $N=665$ teachers	0.89
Personality Inventory for Children (PIC); Revised Format (Lachar, 1990)	3.0–16.0	16 scales	Scaled scores ($M=50$, $SD=10$)	Not reported ($N=2,380$)	0.74
Test of Early Socioemotional Development (Hresko & Brown, 1984)	3.0–7.11	Parent rating scale Sociogram Student rating scale Teacher rating scale	Scaled scores ($M=10$, $SD=3$) Percentile ranks Deviation quotients ($M=100$, $S=15$)	1983 statistical abstract ($N=1,006$ children and teachers) ($N=1,773$ parents)	0.89*

*Asterisk denotes values calculated from standardization data for preschool ages only.

Abbreviations: *M*, mean; *SD*, standard deviation, *N*, sample size.

TABLE 9.4
Measures of Cognitive Development

Instrument	Age Range	Domains/Areas	Scores Provided	Standardization Sample Size and Model	Median Scale Reliability Estimate
Kaufman Assessment Battery for Children (Kaufman & Kaufman, 1983a)	2.6 to 12.6	Sequential processing Simultaneous processing Achievement Nonverbal	Standard scores ($M = 100$, $SD = 15$) Subtest scores ($M = 10$, $SD = 3$) Age equivalents Percentile ranks Stanines	1980 census ($N = 2,000$)	0.90[*]
Stanford–Binet Intelligence Scale: Fourth Edition (Thorndike, Hagen, & Sattler, 1986a)	2.0 to 23.11	Verbal reasoning Abstract/visual reasoning Quantitative reasoning Short-term memory	Standard scores ($M = 100$, $SD = 16$) Subtest scores ($M = 50$, $SD = 8$) Percentile ranks	1980 census ($N = 5,013$)	0.91[*]
Wechsler Preschool and Primary Scale of Intelligence— Revised (Wechsler, 1989a)	3.0 to 7.3	Verbal Performance	Standard scores ($M = 100$, $SD = 15$) Subtest scores ($M = 10$, $SD = 3$) Percentile ranks	1986 census ($N = 1,700$)	0.95[*]

*Asterisk denotes values calculated from standardization data for preschool ages only.

Cognitive Assessment

Understanding and explaining how young children obtain, modify, and use their cognitive abilities remains an extremely difficult task. Whether one conceptualizes a young child's intelligence as general ability or as a set of separate but related abilities, the capacity to solve problems for everyday living is paramount. Until recently, most definitions of intelligence were restricted to the quantity of one's knowledge rather than the quality of one's ability to process information. In an effort to keep pace with new developments in clinical, cognitive, and developmental psychology, however, researchers have proposed theories and tests that define intelligence in terms of one's ability to solve new and unfamiliar problems rather than simply in terms of how much a child has learned (Kaufman & Kaufman, 1983). Newly constructed or revised measures of intellectual functioning such as the Kaufman Assessment Battery for Children (Kaufman & Kaufman, 1983), the Stanford-Binet Intelligence Scale: Fourth Edition (Thorndike, Hagen, & Sattler, 1986), and the Wechsler Preschool and Primary Scale of Intelligence—Revised (Wechsler, 1989) continue to serve as the foundation for routine psychoeducational evaluations. (See Table 9.4 for a brief description of these instruments.)

Speech and Language Assessment

The ability to communicate is closely linked to other aspects of development in young children. Children vary in terms of the age at which they acquire spoken language and develop both receptive and expressive language. Many young children enter preschool unable to communicate effectively. Delayed speech and language in some children may be attributed falsely to mental retardation. Examiners with limited skills or experience may have difficulty distinguishing cause from effect because tests of intelligence frequently rely on verbal interactions between the examiner and the child. Thus, inexperienced or unskilled examiners may judge a young child with delayed speech or language to have developmental delays solely on the basis of a lack of communication skills (Cook, Tessier, & Klein, 2000).

Although the term *speech and language development* reflects the fact that speech and language are important components of communication, they are not synonymous with one another. *Speech* refers to the neuromuscular coordination of the lips, tongue, jaw, and vocal cord movement; *language* refers to the knowledge of rules allowing for the exchange of information between a speaker and listener (Seymour & Wyatt, 1992). Both are important parts of the communication process.

Well-designed assessment instruments are able to help identify the source of the difficulty and thereby guide the way for intervention. Standardized instruments commonly used by early childhood service providers are the Peabody Picture Vocabulary Test—Revised (Dunn & Dunn, 1981), Preschool Language Scales—3 (Zimmerman, Steiner, & Pond, 1992), the Receptive-Expressive Emergent Language Test (Bzoch & League, 1991), the Test of Early Language Development (Hresko, Reid, & Hammill, 1999), and the Utah Test of Language Development—III (Mecham, 1989). (See Table 9.5 for a brief description of these instruments.)

TABLE 9.5
Measures of Speech and Language Development

Instrument	Age Range	Domains/Areas	Scores Provided	Standardization Sample Size and Model	Median Scale Reliability Estimate
Peabody Picture Vocabulary Test—Revised (Dunn & Dunn, 1981)	2.0 to 17.0	Receptive language	Standard scores ($M = 100$, $SD = 15$) Age equivalents Percentile ranks Stanines	1970 census ($N = 4,200$)	0.76*
Preschool Language Scale—3 (Zimmerman, Steiner, & Pond, 1992)	Birth to 6.11	Auditory Comprehension Expressive Communication Total language	Standard scores ($M = 100$, $SD = 15$) Percentiles Age equivalents	1980 census ($N = 1,200$)	0.84
Receptive-Expressive Emergent Language Test (Bzoch & League, 1991)	Birth to 3.0	Expressive language Receptive language	Standard scores ($M = 100$)	Not available	0.96
Test of Early Language Development (2nd Ed.) (Hresko, Reid, & Hammill, 1991)	2.0 to 7.11	Expressive language Receptive language Syntax semantics	Language quotient ($M = 100$, $SD = 15$) Age equivalents Percentiles	1979 census ($N = 1,329$)	0.97
Utah Test of Language Development—3rd Ed. (Mecham, 1999)	3.0 to 9.11	Language comprehension Language expression	Percentiles Standard scores	1985 abstract ($N = 1,708$)	0.84

*Asterisk denotes values calculated from standardization data for preschool ages only.

TABLE 9.6
Measures of Self-Help Skills

Instrument	Age Range	Domains/Areas	Scores Provided	Standardization Sample Size and Model	Median Scale Reliability Estimate
AAMR Adaptive Behavior Scale—School (Lambert, Nihira, & Leland, 1993a)	3.0 to 16.0	Part One Independent functioning Economic activity Language development Numbers and time Prevocational/vocational activity Responsibility Self-direction Socialization Part two Violent and antisocial behavior Rebellious behavior Untrustworthy behavior Stereotyped and hyperactive behavior Eccentric behavior Withdrawal Disturbed behavior	Standard scores, quotients, percentiles	not available ($N = 1,000$) 1,000 students with no disabilities	0.80
Normative Adaptive Behavior Checklist (Adams, 1984)	Birth to 21.0	Self-help skills Home skills Independent living skills Social skills Sensory-motor skills Language concepts	Standard scores ($M = 100, SD = 15$) Age equivalents Percentile ranks Performance rankings	1980 census ($N = 6,014$)	0.94*
Vineland Adaptive Behavior Scales: Survey (Sparrow, Balla, & Cicchetti, 1984b)	Birth to 18.11	Communication Daily living skills Socialization Motor skills	Standard scores ($M = 100, SD = 15$) Age equivalents Adaptive level norms Composite and domains Percentile ranks Stanines	1980 census ($N = 3,000$)	0.89*
Scales of Independent Behavior—Revised (Bruininks, Woodcock, Weatherman, & Hill, 1996b)	0.3 to 29≤	Motor skills Social and communication skills Personal living skills Broad independence	Standard scores ($M = 100, SD = 15$) Age equivalents Functional performance level Instructional range Normal curve equivalents Percentile ranks Relative performance index Stanines	1980 census ($N = 1,764$)	0.90*

* Asterisk denotes values calculated from standardization data for preschool ages only.

333

Adaptive Behavior Assessment

"Adaptive behavior consists of changes in a child's behavior as a consequence of maturation, development, and learning to meet the increasing demands of multiple environments" (Division for Early Childhood Task Force, 1993, p. 89). Adaptive behavior skills assist individuals in meeting the social and cultural demands of their environments. Assessment for adaptive behavior evaluates activities that are both age- and situation-appropriate. Young children who fail to develop such basic adaptive skills as age-appropriate self-care, community self-sufficiency, personal-social responsibility, and social adjustment run the risk of developing maladaptive behaviors that decrease further the likelihood of adjustment to other environmental conditions. Tests designed to assist with diagnosis and intervention of adaptive behavior skills include the AAMR Adaptive Behavior Scale—School Edition (2nd ed.; Lambert, Nihira, & Leland, 1993), the Normative Adaptive Behavior Checklist (Adams, 1984), the Vineland Adaptive Behavior Scales (Sparrow, Balla, & Cicchetti, 1984a, 1984b, 1985), and the Scales of Independent Behavior-Revised (Bruininks, Woodcock, Weatherman, & Hill, 1996). (See Table 9.6 for a brief description of these instruments.)

Motor Assessment

Unlike for other, more elusive constructs such as cognitive and adaptive behavior, there appears to be relative agreement as to the general definition of motor development. Williams (1991) has defined *motor development* as the "gradual acquisition of control and/or use of the large and small muscle masses of the body" (p. 284). Although motor functioning and development are important at all ages, years 2 to 6 are considered to be the golden years of one's motor development (Williams, 1991). A child's level of development in all critical areas is dependent on success in the motor domain, as it is motor functioning that allows the young child to interact with and learn about the environment. Disabilities that negatively affect this interactive process increase the likelihood of delay in this and other areas of development affecting the child in both his or her daily life and assessment results.

Early childhood service providers have typically been interested in one of two types of motor development: fine-motor development and gross-motor development. Although most standardized tests intended for use at the early childhood level have fine- or gross-motor components, only a few standardized tests focus on motor development exclusively. Tests commonly used by early childhood service providers to provide information as to one's level of motor development are the Bruininks-Oseretsky Test of Motor Proficiency (Bruininks, 1978), the Peabody Developmental Motor Scales and Activity Cards (Folio & Fewell, 1983), and the Test of Gross Motor Development (Ulrich, 1985). (See Table 9.7 for a brief description of these instruments.)

ISSUES IN EARLY CHILDHOOD ASSESSMENT

The assessment and evaluation of young children with disabilities are crucial components to service delivery. School districts have policies and approaches that guide and assist service providers and that comply with the laws regulating special educa-

TABLE 9.7
Measures of Motor Development

Instrument	Age Range	Domains/Areas	Scores Provided	Standardization Sample Size and Model	Median Scale Reliability Estimate
Bruininks-Oseretsky Test of Motor Proficiency (Bruininks, 1978)	4.6 to 14.6	Fine motor Gross motor	Standard scores (*M* = 50, *SD* = 10) Battery composite Gross motor composite Fine motor composite Subtest scores (*M* = 15, *SD* = 5) Age equivalents Percentile ranks Stanines	1970 census (*N* = 765)	Not available
Peabody Developmental Motor Scales and Activity Cards (Folio & Fewel, 1983)	Birth to 6.11	Fine motor Gross motor	Standard scores (*M* = 100, *SD* = 15) Developmental motor quotient Gross motor composite Fine motor composite Age equivalents Percentile ranks	1976 census (*N* = 617)	Not available
Test of Gross Motor Development (Ulrich, 1985)	3.0 to 10.0	Gross motor	Composite quotient (*M* = 100, *SD* = 15) Subtest standard scores (*M* = 10, *SD* = 3) Percentile ranks	1980 census (*N* = 908)	0.86*

*Asterisk denotes values calculated from standardization data for preschool ages only.

335

tion. Yet this is an area of difficulty, since a wide range of acceptability appears within the developmental process. The process is further compounded by factors relating to personnel and procedures.

At the preassessment level, professionals and families should meet to share information and concerns regarding the assessment procedures. All questions regarding the choice of the assessment materials, procedures, and personnel should be fully explained. The assessment should be multidimensional with information gathered on multiple occasions. These informed participants can then design an individual assessment that conforms to the needs of the child and the family (Division for Early Childhood Task Force, 1993).

Personal

Each child is unique, regardless of disability or classifying condition. Factors such as age, place of residence, socioeconomic status, genetic factors, environmental factors, personality, cultural heritage, and gender all shape the developmental and educational status of the child and must be considered within the unique components of the child's development. Researchers have found that while some developmental patterns signal the possibility of difficulties later on, others do not, making early identification of certain disabilities extremely difficult. Logically, then, the occurrence of such a disability as mental retardation only serves to complicate a procedure that is already delicate and fragile. Early childhood service providers must assess these abilities using methods and instruments that fairly yet appropriately identify the disability and its related areas. Understanding how children grow and develop relative to their own unique conditions and abilities is essential to designing sound intervention strategies (Drew, Hardman & Logan, 1996).

Variables also exist in terms of time of day of alertness with each child, in particular with infants. Results can be affected if the child is not rested, fed, comfortable, and attentive. This means that only a few hours per day may be available for optimal testing.

The child's stage of development will also impact the test results. During particular developmental stages, children are strongly attached to the primary caregiver, which means that the primary caregiver must be present with the child for assessments to occur.

Children who are delayed in development may not comprehend the testing process and may need repeated prompts and encouragement as well as repeated explanations. This extra time required then impacts the physical and mental endurance of the child to attend to the task at hand, which, at times, requires extra sessions to complete the assessment.

Professional

Few components are as important to successful assessment, evaluation, and intervention as the training of early childhood service providers. Although recommendations for best practice vary from school to school and district to district, adequate preparation of professionals should be a constant. To increase the quality of services provided, examiners should have formal education in such areas as child development, assessment of mental and special abilities, and educational interventions, in addition to formal, supervised, field-based training experiences. Examiners may be required to modify test instructions and physically guide a child through the explanation process in order for the child to comprehend the requirements of the task. As this process demands a great deal of flexibility and understanding on the part of the examiner, he or she must be thoroughly familiar with the test materials and must have an organized plan or sequence of activities to facilitate comfortable interactions with the child (Bondurant-Utz & Luciano, 1994).

Equally important is the psychometric integrity of the respective instruments. Although the reliability and validity of preschool instruments have been criticized in recent years, their vulnerability appears to be diminishing as users have been demanding and test publishers have begun providing instruments with the same level of sophistication as those used with school-age populations (Fewell, 2000; McConnell, 2000). Standardized instruments with large, nationally representative normative samples, theoretically valid content areas, published validity information, and user qualification criteria are all hallmarks of a good instrument.

Procedural

Local educational agencies have little flexibility in the decision to provide service to 3- to 5-year-old children with disabilities. They do, however, have a great deal of flexibility in the process by which children with special needs are identified for service. For example, in some states, a delay of 25% or more is all that is required for service; in other states a delay of 25% in two or more areas is required; and, in still others, a 35% delay in a single area is necessary for qualification. As with other exceptionalities, state guidelines allow for such multiple criteria as standardized test scores, discrepancy formulas, or percentile ranks. For state and local agencies offering services to infants and toddlers, a service coordinator must be assigned to the child's family to coordinate educational services. The mechanics of evaluation also vary. For example, although most school districts require a multidisciplinary team approach to assessment, some bring the teams together only as referrals are made; therefore, some teams assist one child at a time. Other districts require that teams assemble on a routine basis to assess children in large numbers. Equally broad is the spectrum of settings used to offer such services (Thurlow, 1992). Understandably, school district personnel offering screening services to children individually after school in a quiet room will likely elicit very different results than will a team consisting of professionals and volunteers conducting a mass screening in a gymnasium on a Saturday morning with parents and peers watching. Professionals should make decisions based on the child's unique needs using sound logic and valid reasoning and not simply to meet the needs of the group making the decision or because it is the most cost-efficient and expedient route to take.

PROGRAMMING FOR YOUNG CHILDREN

An individual plan of action determines the framework for each young child. Such a plan becomes the group consensus on what is appropriate for each child. Programmatic issues addressed are "how to arrange environments, how teachers

To learn more about early intervention programming, go to the companion website at www.prenhall.com/ beirne-smith and select Chapter 9, then choose the Article Response module.

should interact, how programs should be monitored, and how data describing programs must be used to inform parents about their effectiveness in meeting children's needs" (Carta, Atwater, Schwartz, & McConnell, 1993, p. 243). Table 9.8 details the advantages and disadvantages of the various models.

Service Delivery Models

The educational needs of young children with disabilities differ from those of their school-age counterparts. To meet the diverse needs of younger children, greater flexibility and variety in service delivery options are needed in a coordinated plan.

TABLE 9.8
Advantages and Disadvantages of Programming Models

Model	Advantages	Disadvantages
Home-based	Rapport with family is more easily established.	Parents who may lack skills are responsible for implementing much of the intervention.
	Family routines are less likely to be disrupted.	Teachers spend potential planning and instructional time traveling from site to site.
	Children are more at ease, less frightened in familiar surroundings.	No opportunity exists for peer interaction and socialization.
	Materials can be designed to meet the needs of the natural setting.	
	Building and maintenance costs are unnecessary.	
Center-based	All primary and support services are housed in one location.	Cost of providing facilities and range of services is high.
	Teachers have more time for planning and instruction.	Center may need to provide transportation and bus aides, which increases cost.
	Situation promotes peer interaction and socialization.	Families may move and time may be lost in reorganizing bus routes or locating the family.
Combination	Greater flexibility in delivering services is possible.	Same as with home- and center-based models.
	Same as with home- and center-based models.	
Consultation	More efficient use of staff time.	Parents are responsible for implementation of the intervention.
		Imposes on parents to transport children.
		Limited amount of service can be provided to child or family.

Educators responsible for planning and implementing appropriate early intervention services must identify current resources, coordinate existing programs, and develop innovative service delivery models with the informed consent of the family. Figure 9.4 details the educational environments for preschoolers with disabilities. This information should be presented in the family's preferred language. Personnel within the programs should be schooled in the services, strategies, and interventions for children in the particular age group with whom they are working (Division for Early Childhood Task Force, 1993).

FIGURE 9.4
Educational Environments for Preschoolers with Disabilities

Source: OSEP Data Dictionary (Office of Special Education Programs, U.S. Department of Education, 1997).

Regular class includes children who receive services in programs designed primarily for nondisabled children, provided the children with disabilities are in a separate room for less than 21 percent of the time receiving services. This may include, but is not limited to, Head Start centers, public or private preschool and child care facilities, preschool classes offered to an age-eligible population by the public school system, kindergarten classes, and classes using co-teaching models (special education and general education staff coordinating activities in a general education setting).

Resource room includes children who receive services in programs designed primarily for nondisabled children, provided the children with disabilities are in a separate program for 21 to 60 percent of the time receiving services. This includes, but is not limited to, Head Start centers, public or private preschools or child care facilities, preschool classes offered to an age-eligible population by the public school system, and kindergarten classes.

Separate class includes children who receive services in a separate program for 61 to 100 percent of the time receiving services. It does not include children who receive education programs in public or private separate day or residential facilities.

Separate school (public and private) includes children who are served in publicly or privately operated programs, set up primarily to serve children with disabilities, that are NOT housed in a facility with programs for children without disabilities. Children must receive special education and related services in the public separate day school for greater than 50 percent of the time.

Residential facility (public and private) includes children who are served in publicly or privately operated programs in which children receive care for 24 hours a day. This could include placement in public nursing care facilities or public or private residential schools.

Homebound/hospital includes children who are served in either a home or hospital setting, including those receiving special education or related services in the home and provided by a professional or paraprofessional who visits the home on a regular basis (e.g., a child-development worker or speech services provided in the child's home). It also includes children 3–5 years old receiving special education and related services in a hospital setting on an inpatient or outpatient basis. However, children receiving services in a group program that is housed at a hospital should be reported in the separate school category. For children served in both a home/hospital setting and in a school/community setting, report the child in the placement that comprises the larger percentage of time receiving services.

Hospital-Based Services   Due to the emphasis on early detection among the medical and educational communities, newborns who are at high risk may be placed in neonatal intensive care units for specialized care. These units provide specialists in neonatology to care for the child and to provide education, guidance, and support for the parents. Referrals are made based on the individual children and their families (Division for Early Childhood Task Force, 1993).

Home-Based Services   The goal of home-based intervention, which is where the majority of infants and toddlers receive services, is to assist families in setting goals and acquiring the skills needed to meet them (U.S. Department of Education, 1999). Family training and cooperation are the keystones in service delivery. A teacher, consultant, or paraprofessional visits the home regularly, helping the family develop an appropriate home intervention program for the child who is retarded. Depending on the needs of the child and the family, visits may occur as often as several times weekly or as infrequently as once monthly. During visits, the teacher, consultant, or paraprofessional may assess the child and/or family situation, review the child's progress since the last visit, observe parent–child or family–child interactions and offer suggestions, demonstrate activities, or aid the parent in designing materials or developing activities.

Advantages to the home-based services are many. The home is the natural environment for the child. Parents, other family members, and friends become the first instructors for the child, and with the services of the professionals, these first lessons are designed for the individual child. This early intervention and training actively involve and educate the family so that they can participate at a higher level in planning later in the child's life when the learning environment shifts away from being primarily in the home. From a monetary viewpoint, home-based services are less expensive, as facilities do not need to be provided for education, and transportation costs are incurred only by the professionals.

With all the advantages of home-based service, the program is not without disadvantages. Not all families are willing or able to participate in services in their home. With the provision of a professional coming to the home, families are denied the services of the variety of professionals available in a center-based program; thus, the number of services provided is decreased. Finally, families and children are denied social interaction and support with others in similar circumstances.

Center-Based Services   Services in center-based programs take place in a single location outside the home. Professionals consider center-based programs most appropriate for preschool-age children who require services from a team of specialists, who need peer models or peer interaction, and whose parents are not always available to participate in their education. Some programs accommodate only children who are disabled, and others include children who are disabled with those who are not. Usually, the children attend the center for 3 to 5 hours per day, 4 to 5 days per week. Effective center-based programs have curricula that are unbiased and nondiscriminatory and are housed in buildings that are physically accessible to the children and their parents. Family participation in center-based programs varies and may include observation or classroom participation, scheduled meetings to review progress or to receive instruction for home implementation of center activities, and parent support groups.

The advantages of center-based programs include the availability of a wide variety of specialists, increased opportunity for contact with children who are developing at a normal rate, and a support group for parents. Disadvantages of such programs include the expense of transportation for each family, the cost and maintenance of the facility, and reduced individual contact for the family with a center professional.

Combined Home–Center Programs Combination service models offer various configurations of home- and center-based services. This allows the child and the family to receive the intensive help of the professionals in a center-based program along with the peer interaction and family support while maintaining the home atmosphere of attention and family interaction. Family training is conducted on multidimensional levels within the home and the center.

Consultation Services In the consultation service model, parents bring the child to the center, and professionals provide instruction for training. Unlike home-based parent training programs, however, consultation usually involves only one or two sessions. As with home-based programs, this method of service delivery relies on parents to implement the recommendations of professionals.

Curriculum

Curriculum is the planned sequence of content and methods of instruction for an individual student or groups of students to modify behavior. Most early childhood special education programs employ a variety of approaches in teaching infants and young children. Generally, the curriculum is derived from one of three theoretical perspectives on learning: developmental, behavioral, or functional.

Cognitive-Developmental Curriculum This curriculum is based largely on the work of the Swiss psychologist Jean Piaget. Piaget considered the child an active agent in the learning process of trial-and-error experiments. According to Piaget, skills develop hierarchically, and children pass through developmental stages in a highly predictable fashion. Development of higher-level skills is inextricably bound to development of lower-level skills. The teacher following the developmental curriculum matches tasks to normal developmental milestones, identifies deficits, and gears instruction to accelerating the rate of development of the child or infant who is disabled to the rate of peers who are not disabled. Cole, Mills, Dale, and Jenkins (1996) point out that the advantages of developmental curricula are that they use natural environments, follow the child's interests, promote generalization of skills, provide for distributed practice, and focus conversation on communication intent. The disadvantages, however, are that developmental tasks are based on normal development that presupposes all senses are intact and that children are to be guided through their current developmental level without instruction in higher developmental levels (Piaget & Inhelder, 1969). Berkeley and Ludlow (1989) also cite the limited sample of developmental indicators at each age, a lack of empirical support that children with disabilities follow the same course of development as children without disabilities, the possibility that curricular objectives may discourage individual program planning as children are moved through a standard curriculum at a slower rate, and the uncertainty that curricular objectives identify critical skills for present and projected future environments.

Behavioral Curriculum   Skinner (1953) gave us the approach of *operant conditioning*, in which behavior is related to consequences or reinforcements. Behaviors that have pleasant consequences or reinforcements tend to be repeated, whereas behaviors that have negative consequences or reinforcements tend to be avoided; consequences, therefore, shape behavior. This is the *principle of positive and negative reinforcement*. Contained within the principle of reinforcements is the concept of successive approximations in which the child is rewarded for steps toward the behavioral goal. Proponents of behavioral curricula believe that children learn best by experiencing repeated reinforcement for responses to environmental stimuli. Skills are taught in the behavioral curriculum according to the child's or infant's needs in the present or projected future environment. The model defines skills precisely in behavioral terms and states criteria for performance clearly and quantitatively. Supporters of this approach maintain that children who lack essential skills require a highly structured approach to learning and that the structure can be relaxed and skills integrated as learning progresses. Wolery, Bailey, and Sugai (1988) report that experimental evidence indicates that the behavioral curricula help children with disabilities but the method remains controversial. Fewell and Kelly (1983) point out that opponents of the behavioral approach argue that the use of such an approach inhibits the cognitive and emotional development of young children with disabilities by prohibiting interaction with the environment.

Functional Curriculum   The functional curriculum approach is a hybrid of the developmental and behavioral curricula, attempting to incorporate the best features of the two. In their emphasis on teaching interrelated classes of behavior and general-

Supporters of behavioral curriculum maintain that the structure can be relaxed and skills integrated as learning progresses.

ization within task classes, they are developmental; in their emphasis on teaching skills that the infant or child needs now or will need later, they are behavioral.

To date, no single curricular approach has been demonstrated to be superior to the others with all children. In practice, most early intervention programs combine approaches. When all is considered, professionals agree that the curriculum should be based on the individual needs of the child and the family.

To learn more about assessment and intervention, go to the companion website at www.prenhall.com/ beirne-smith and select Chapter 9, then choose the Web Destinations module.

Program Implementation

Programs for infants and preschoolers differ from programs for school-age children in the amount of time spent in school and in the goals and objectives for learning. Yet teachers of young children face similar challenges in arranging the classroom and scheduling the school day. Workable classroom arrangements and effective scheduling are crucial to the success of infant and preschool programs.

Classroom Accommodations and Adaptations

Organizing the physical space in the classroom is the first step in facilitating learning. Designing the optimal classroom, therefore, requires careful planning. Among the factors teachers must consider are the following:

1. *The space available*. State education agencies usually dictate the minimum allowable space for infant and preschool classrooms. But the shape of the room and the presence of such fixed features as windows, sinks, and toilets sometimes inhibit optimal classroom arrangements. Polloway and Patton (1997) suggest that teachers begin planning room arrangement by drawing a rough sketch of the room, then adding in such basic equipment as tables, desks, and chairs. In designing classroom space, materials should be placed to facilitate student learning and involvement. Teachers should be mindful of their schedule and create a traffic flowchart to and from activities in the classroom with discernible boundaries that separate areas of instruction.

2. *The physical needs of the students*. The physical needs of preschool children who are disabled often differ from those of their peers who are not disabled. Children in wheelchairs or walkers or on portable stretchers, for example, require carefully planned room arrangements. At the very least, the teacher must consider fixed barriers (e.g., doorways) and movable barriers (e.g., tables). For children who are not toilet trained or who are incontinent, the teacher must consider the need for privacy of changing tables. Finally, as with all children, the size of the furniture must match the size of the child. These types of physical accommodations should be reflected in the room arrangement and traffic pattern of the classroom to increase the comfort level of all children within the classroom.

3. *Group arrangements*. Infant and preschool programs use a variety of group arrangements during the school day. Individual work areas should be located together in a quiet area of the classroom to encourage attending to task. Group work areas should be away from the individual work area. The group area should be flexible and fluid to allow for configuration and recon-

figuration of small-, medium-, and large-group activities. The various areas should be plainly labeled to facilitate flow within the classroom, enable students to identify their assigned area, and promote student involvement.

4. *The purpose of instruction.* Lesson objectives frequently suggest the location and type of space needed. Activities that involve direct teacher instruction (e.g., language learning) require a more structured, quieter setting than activities that involve only teacher supervision (e.g., free play). Consideration must also be given as to how the students will interact socially. Peer interactions may involve individual activities, parallel activities, or cooperative activities. In an inclusive classroom, each child as well as the group must be considered in determining how instruction will be delivered.

5. *Material accessibility.* Searching for materials stored in out-of-the-way places can waste valuable teaching time, and materials that are not readily

---

Teacher: _____   Student: _____

Date: _____

SCHEDULING AND INSTRUCTIONAL ARRANGEMENTS

yes	no	1. Is the child positioned so that he or she can see and participate in the activity?
yes	no	2. Is the child positioned so that other children and teachers may easily interact with her or him (e.g., without an adult between the child and other children, not isolated from other children)?
yes	no	3. Is the child involved in the same activities as other children?
yes	no	4. Does the child engage in activities at the same time as other children?
yes	no	5. Is the child actively involved in activities (e.g., plays a role in group activities, asks/answers questions)?
yes	no	6. Is the child given assistance only as necessary?
yes	no	7. Does the child use the same or similar types of materials during activities as other children?
yes	no	8. Are the least intrusive, natural prompts and contingencies used, if needed, to help the child to participate in the activity?
yes	no	9. Are the materials appropriate for the chronological age of the child?
yes	no	10. Does the child participate in activities that are appropriate for his/her chronological age?

SOCIALIZATION AND COMMUNICATION

yes	no	1. Does the child have a way to communicate (e.g., signs, gestures, pictures, speech) with other children?
yes	no	2. Do the other children know how to communicate with the child (e.g., use gestures, understand simple signs, respond to pictures)?
yes	no	3. Does the child socialize with other children (e.g., playing at free time, using playground equipment)?
yes	no	4. Is the socialization/interaction with other children facilitated (e.g., children are prompted and reinforced for initiations and interactions)?
yes	no	5. Do teachers interact in the same way with the child as with other children (e.g., praise, hugs)?
yes	no	6. Is the child given opportunities to demonstrate competence (e.g., line leader, passing out snacks, helper of the day)?

FIGURE 9.5

Preschool Checklist: Integration of Children with Disabilities

available are less likely to be used. Also, because fostering independence is an important goal of early childhood special education programs, teachers should avoid making materials difficult for children to locate and secure on their own. Lund and Bos (1981) suggest placing instructional areas close to material storage places, keeping frequently used materials close together to facilitate accessibility, and labeling or color-coding storage areas.

ALTERNATIVE COMMUNICATION (If this section is not applicable to the child, please skip to the next section.)

yes   no   1. If the child uses an alternative communication system (e.g., signing, picture cards), do other children know how to use it?

yes   no   2. Do teachers know how to use the alternative communication system?

yes   no   3. Is the alternative communication system always available to the child?

APPEARANCE OF THE CHILD

yes   no   1. Does the child have accessories that are similar to those of other children (e.g., small backpack, hair clips)?

yes   no   2. Is the child's dress age appropriate?

yes   no   3. Is clothing for activities appropriate (e.g., paint shirts; napkins, not bibs)?

yes   no   4. Are personal belongings (e.g., change of clothing, diapers) carried discreetly?

yes   no   5. If the child has special equipment, is it kept clean?

yes   no   6. Is the child's hair combed and kept neat?

yes   no   7. Are the child's hands clean and dry?

yes   no   8. Is the child's clothing changed as necessary to maintain a neat appearance?

SUMMARY OF THE PRESCHOOL CHECKLIST

Scheduling and Instructional Arrangements: _____/10

Socialization and Communication: _____/6

   Alternative Communication: _____/3 (if applicable)

Appearance of the Child: _____/8

Total Score: _____/24 (or 27 if Alternative Communication is applicable)

GOAL AREAS

Please feel free to use this section to set goals for yourself and your assistant(s) on ways that you can more fully include the targeted student in preschool activities and routines.

Goal areas to lead to fuller inclusion:

_____

_____

FIGURE 9.5 (continued)

Preschool Checklist: Integration of Children with Disabilities

Source: From "The Preschool Checklist: Integration of Children with Severe Disabilities" by S. Drinkwater and M. Demchak, 1995, *Teaching Exceptional Children, 28*(1), pp. 4–8. Copyright 1995 by the Council for Exceptional Children. Reprinted by permission.

6. *Personal territory*. Like their school-age counterparts, children in preschool arrive with a variety of personal possessions. A safe and accessible space is needed in the classroom to store outerwear, storybooks, toys, and so on. Gray (1975) points out that personal space in the classroom contributes to the child's sense of belonging. Lund and Bos (1981) suggest using cubbies or lockers for children's personal belongings and picture cues to assist students in identifying their personal space.

In considering these six points, the teacher is viewing the individual child from various perspectives that will enable the teacher to determine not only what is best for the child but also to what extent the child can be included in a general education classroom for meaningful participation with children who are not disabled. One way to help teachers arrive at the proper balance for children with special needs is to use the preschool checklist presented in Figure 9.5 (Drinkwater & Demchak, 1995). The checklist covers the areas of scheduling and instructional arrangements, socialization and communication, alternative communication, and appearance of the child to aid teachers not only in including children with special needs in a general education classroom but also in creating goals to enable the inclusion to be successful. Benefits that can be gained from including students with special needs into the general education classroom are as follows: "(a) enhanced skill generalization, (b) increased self-initiations in social situations, (c) equivalent development gains to nondisabled peers, (d) preparation for dealing with the real world, (e) increased communication skills with peers and family members, and (f) increased number of nondisabled friends" (Drinkwater & Demchak, 1995, p. 7).

Scheduling

In arranging a schedule for a classroom, teachers should take into account the abilities, disabilities, personalities, mobility, and so on, of the various children enrolled in the class and the instructional objectives to be reached. Teachers may not know ahead of time the exact needs of each child, but they can still plan a schedule with all options included. Polloway and Patton (1997) point out that the first step is to determine how many hours the child is in school and how much of that time is available for instruction. Such events as snack or lunch, related services (e.g., physical therapy), sharing time, and so forth, must be scheduled in and deducted from instructional time. Once these factors are accounted for, the teacher should consider high- and low-probability activities. Low-probability activities require direct teacher instruction in a skill or concept (e.g., classifying words into categories like food, animals, transportation). The most difficult low-probability activities should be taught early in the day when children are most alert and, for variety, interspersed with such high-probability activities as story time or work centers designed to develop different skills. Next, the teacher must consider whether and how to schedule small group or one-on-one instruction. The schedule will direct the flow of the day, and each day, each child should find an area of joy in the schedule.

Many preschool programs provide for a half-day of direct instruction services. The teacher may spend the rest of the day in planning, conducting case management, consulting with other professionals, or meeting with parents. Other programs provide for a full day of services. Regardless of the length of the school day,

8:30–8:50	Interaction with children and parents, hang up coats, etc.
8:50–9:10	Circle time (days of the week, months, colors, etc.; varies with need).
9:10–9:20	Group 1 with teacher for direct instruction. Groups 2 and 3 with aide for activities.
9:20–9:30	Group 2 with teacher for direct instruction. Groups 1 and 3 with aide for activities.
9:30–9:40	Group 3 with teacher for direct instruction. Groups 1 and 2 with aide for activities.
9:40–10:10	Free play or outdoor play.
10:10–10:20	Transition, bathroom, etc.
10:20–10:40	Snack.
10:40–11:00	Circle time (language, cognitive development, etc.).
11:10–11:20	Story time.
11:20–11:30	Interact with children and parents, put on coats, etc.
11:30	Dismissal.

FIGURE 9.6
Half-Day Preschool Schedule with Direct Instruction

8:30–8:45	Interaction with children and parents, hang up coats, etc.
8:45–9:05	Circle time (days of the week, months, colors, etc.; varies with need).
9:05–9:35	Free play (activities designed to develop various areas—cognitive, motor, etc.).
9:35–9:50	Story time.
9:50–10:00	Transition, bathroom, etc.
10:00–10:20	Snack.
10:20–10:45	Outdoor play.
10:45–11:00	Circle time (language, cognitive development, etc.).
11:00–11:20	Free play (as above).
11:20–11:30	Interaction with children and parents, put on coats, etc.
11:30	Dismissal.

FIGURE 9.7
Half-Day Preschool Schedule without Direct Instruction

the daily schedule is an important ingredient in the effectiveness of the service and sets the tone for learning. Figures 9.6 to 9.9 provide examples of possible schedules for the preschool years.

FAMILY INVOLVEMENT

With the enactment of PL 99-457, families participate on the IFSP and IEP committees as collaborators. The law requires that family needs and resources be assessed and that parents be counseled about their child's needs and assisted in acquiring services for the child. Family members have the opportunity to participate in an active manner in the writing of the IFSP and IEP and in the child's instruction. The

8:00–8:30	Teacher planning.
8:30–9:00	Arrival, self-help (undressing).
9:00–11:00	Individual activities: physical management, gross motor, fine motor, cognition.
9:30–10:00	Language group 1 (augmentative).
10:00–10:30	Language group 2 (3–4 word utterances).
10:30–11:00	Language group 3 (imitation).
11:00–12:00	Lunch; self-help (eating, brushing teeth, toileting).
12:00–1:00	Nap.
	Arrival of nonhandicapped students.
1:00–1:30	Self-help (dressing), self-directed activities.
1:30–2:00	Individual language activities (groups 1, 2, 3).
	Language group 4 (integrated).
2:00–2:30	Snack and socialization groups (integrated).
2:30	Departure.
2:30–4:00	Teacher planning.

FIGURE 9.8
Full-Day Preschool Schedule

8:00–8:30	Teacher planning.[*]
8:30–9:00	Arrival and interaction with families.
9:00–11:00	Individual activities. [**]
	Physical management.
	Motor development.
	Language development.
	Cognition.
11:00–12:00	Lunch; oral motor skills, self-help (eating, brushing teeth, toileting).
12:00–1:00	Nap.
1:00–1:30	Self-help (dressing, toileting).
1:30–2:00	Sensory activities, individualized within group setting to enhance social skills.
2:00–2:30	Interaction with families.
2:30–4:00	Teacher planning; case management activities, home visits.

[*]The infant schedule must be flexible to take into consideration each child's schedule of eating and sleeping.
[**]These activities match the overlap between domains during infancy. Emphasis is placed on developing skills across domains to encourage the infant to interact with all facets of the environment.

FIGURE 9.9
Full-Day Infant Schedule

law does not explicitly define *family,* but the definition used in this chapter refers to "two or more people who regard themselves as a family and who perform some of the functions that families typically perform. These people may or may not be related by blood or marriage and may or may not usually live together" (Turnbull, Turnbull, Shank, & Leal, 1995, pp. 24–25).

When professionals gain information about the family in an individual and personal way, then the professional is in harmony with the family's strengths, weaknesses, desires, expectations, priorities, and needs. By using the Family Systems Conceptual Framework (Turnbull, Summers, & Brotherson, 1984), illustrated in Figure 9.10, the professional gains valuable facts about the interrelatedness of the family unit. This personalized knowledge aids the professional in the collaboration process by examining four components of the family unit: family characteristics, family interaction, family functions, and family life cycle. Turnbull and Turnbull (2000b) note that, historically, families and parents have been viewed as fulfilling eight major roles: (a) the source of the child's disability, (b) organization members, (c) service developers, (d) recipients of professionals' decisions, (e) teachers, (f) political advocates, (g) educational decision makers, and (h) collaborators.

Heward (2000) outlines seven roles that parents of children with special needs fulfill:

1. *Teaching.* Many children learn skills in an incidental fashion, but children with special needs must be directly instructed to learn many tasks. Since families are in day-to-day contact with these children, the family becomes the first teacher in early childhood. Some families must further learn to use special equipment and devices in order for their children to function in society.

2. *Counseling.* In addition to the normal counseling role that parents deal with in addressing emotions, feelings, and attitudes, the parents of the child with special needs must also deal with greater intensity of these areas due to the disability. The disability itself must be addressed with the child, siblings, and greater society. The parents must guide the child through the day-to-day life with a disability.

3. *Managing behavior.* This again is in addition to the normal role of parenting in training children toward the behavioral expectations of society. Many times these parents must first be taught how to handle behavior so that they in turn can teach the child and then society at large.

4. *Parenting siblings without disabilities.* No two children without disabilities are identical, but the difference is magnified when a disability is present. Parents must learn to parent both types of children so that all children reach their full potential. In the course of their parenting, parents must also teach siblings without a disability about the disability itself and how this disability impacts the sibling with the disability, the family, and the siblings without the disability.

5. *Maintaining the parent-to-parent relationship.* Having children decreases the time that parents have for themselves as a couple, but when a child with a disability is born, the time shrinks even further. To find time for themselves as a couple, the parent must leave the child with a disability in a competent care situation. This requires additional time for the parent in an already stressful situation, as the caretaker must be educated in the role of the parent. In addition to time is the factor of money. Many disabilities require additional funds to care for the child who is disabled, which decreases the funds available for parent time as a couple.

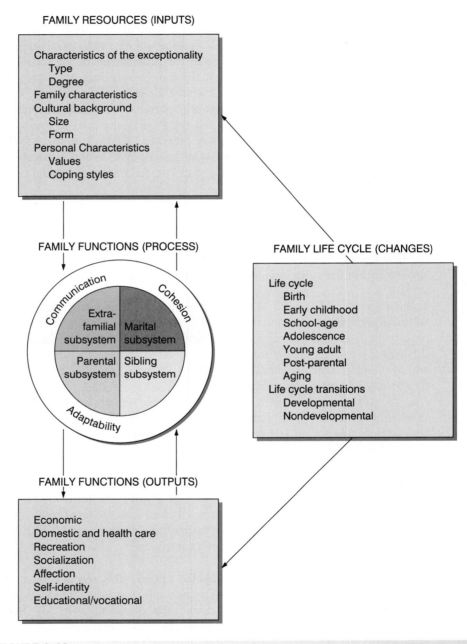

FIGURE 9.10

Family Systems Conceptual Framework

Source: From *Working with Families with Disabled Members: A Family Systems Approach* (p. 60) by A. P. Turnbull, J. A. Summers, and M. J. Brotherson, 1984. Lawrence: Kansas University Affiliated Facility. Copyright 1984 by the University of Kansas. Reprinted by permission.

6. *Educating significant others*. Just as parents must educate caretakers of their child with a disability, the parent must educate those in the family and the community who come in contact with their child. Children with disabilities require consistency in their lives, and this happens only when the family and the community as a whole can be educated and respond in a single-minded fashion toward the child with a disability.

7. *Relating to the school and community*. The parents' role is that of an advocate for their child. No one knows the child as intimately as the parent. The school and community, therefore, should seek to include the parents in an active collaboration role for the benefit of the child with a disability and for the benefit of the school and community. When all who work with the child are acting in a manner that is consistent, then the child with a disability benefits.

TRANSITION

In early childhood special education, **transition** is the passage or change from one stage or level to the next. Changes in programming needs may result in a number of transitions within the service delivery system for young children with disabilities and their families. Children often move from home-based to center-based programs or from programs sponsored by health care agencies to those sponsored by local education agencies. Families and children must adjust to new locations, to new teachers and staff, and to changes in program format, curriculum, and emphasis. The level of parental involvement, intensity of parental contact, or availability of services for parents changes in each location and at the various age levels of the child. The necessary changes as a child grows may affect adversely the child's ability to adjust to new settings or to acquire new skills. These transitions and the concerns of the family must be addressed in both the IFSPs and the IEPs.

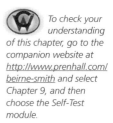

To check your understanding of this chapter, go to the companion website at http://www.prenhall.com/ beirne-smith and select Chapter 9, and then choose the Self-Test module.

Summary

Rationale for Early Childhood Special Education
- Research supports the importance of early childhood special education in growth and development of infants, toddlers, and young children with disabilities or who are at risk.
- The focus of early childhood special education is on early intervention and programming.

Legislation Affecting Early Childhood Special Education Programs
- Recently passed laws recognize the need for special education early intervention services for infants, toddlers, and young children with disabilities or at risk for disabilities and their families.
- Public Law 99-457 extended the rights and privileges of PL 94-142 to infants, toddlers, and preschoolers and their families.
- Public Law 101-476 established new priorities for meeting the needs of infants and toddlers with disabilities and their families.

DEC-Recommended Practices
- The DEC issued a set of broad-spectrum recommended practices for infants and young children with disabilities and their families.

Referral
- Each state is required to establish a lead agency for the implementation of the IDEA, Part C.
- Each state must have an early intervention system to identify and locate children who have disabilities, are developmentally delayed, or are at risk and their families.

Evaluation and Assessment
- *Evaluation* is a formal process conducted by qualified, licensed personnel who administer standardized tests for initial placement and continued eligibility, whereas *assessment* is an ongoing, often informal, process in which workers from many disciplines contribute information and participate in an ongoing process to determine specific strengths and weaknesses.
- Evaluation and assessment use multiple sources and multiple measures gathered on multiple occasions in multiple settings.

Measures of Early Childhood Development
- According to PL 99-457, assessment of preschool abilities must occur in each of five developmental areas: cognitive, socioemotional, motor, speech and language, and self-help skills.

Issues in Early Childhood Assessment
- Each child is unique regardless of disability or classifying condition.
- Professionals should be adequately prepared to perform evaluation and assessment, and the instrument used should possess a high degree of psychometric integrity.
- A multidisciplinary team approach should be used for evaluation, assessment, and placement.

Programming for Young Children
- Educators responsible for planning and implementing appropriate early intervention services must identify current resources, coordinate existing programs, and develop innovative service delivery models with the informed consent of the family.
- A variety of approaches should be used based on one of the following curricula: developmental, behavioral, or functional.
- Professionals must make classroom accommodations and adaptions based on space available, physical needs of the students, group arrangements needed, purpose of instruction, material accessibility, and personal territory.
- Scheduling should take into account the varied children enrolled and the instructional objectives to be reached.

Family Involvement

- With the enactment of PL 99-457, families participate on the IFSP and IEP committees as collaborators.
- Parents of children with special needs fulfill the following roles for their children: teaching, counseling, managing behavior, parenting siblings without disabilities, maintaining the parent-to-parent relationship, educating significant others, and relating to the school and community.

Transition

- As children with special needs and their families move through the various service options in special education, planned transition services are necessary.

References

Achenbach, T. M. (1994). *Child behavior checklist*. Burlington: University of Vermont, Department of Psychiatry.

Adams, G. L. (1984). *Normative adaptive behavior checklist*. San Antonio, TX: Psychological Corporation.

Aydlett, L. A. (1993). Assessing infant interaction skills in interaction-focused intervention. *Infant and Young Children, 5*(4), 1–7.

Bailey, D. B., & Nabors, L. A. (1996). Test and test development. In M. Bailey & M. Woolery (Eds.), *Assessing infants and preschoolers with special needs* (pp. 23–43). Upper Saddle River, NJ: Merrill/Prentice Hall.

Bailey, D., & Wolery, M. (1993). *Teaching infants and preschoolers with handicaps*. Upper Saddle River, NJ: Merrill/Prentice Hall.

Baird, S. (1997). Seeking a comfortable fit between family-centered philosophy and infant-parent interaction in early intervention: Time for a paradigm shift? *Topics in Early Childhood Special Education, 1,* 139–163.

Barnett, W. S. (1997). Long-term effects of early childhood programs on cognitive and school outcomes. [On-line]. Available: http://www.futureofchildren.org/lto/02.html.

Benner, S. M. (1992). *Assessing young children with special needs: An ecological perspective*. New York: Longman.

Berkeley, T. R. & Ludlow, B. L. (1989). Toward a reconceptualization of the developmental model. *Topics in Early Childhood Education, 9*(5), 51–66.

Bloom, B. S. (1964). *Stability and change in human characteristics*. New York: Wiley.

Bondurant-Utz, J. & Luciano, L. B. (1994). *A practical guide to infant and preschool assessment in special education*. Boston: Allyn & Bacon.

Bricker, D., Pretti-Frontczak, K. & McComas, N. (1998). *An activity-based approach to early intervention* (2nd ed.). Baltimore: Brookes.

Bricker, D., & Cripe, J. J. (1992). *An activity-based approach to early intervention*. Baltimore: Brookes.

Bricker, D., & Veltman, M. (1990). Early intervention programs: Child-focused approaches. In S. Meisels & J. Shonkoff (Eds.), *Handbook of early childhood intervention* (pp. 373–399). New York: Cambridge University Press.

Bruininks, R. H. (1978). *Bruininks-Oseretsky Test of Motor Proficiency*. Circle Pines, MN: American Guidance Service.

Bruininks, R. H., Woodcock, R. W., Weatherman, R. F., & Hill, B. K. (1985). *Scales of Independent Behavior*. Chicago: Riverside.

Bruininks, R.H., Woodcock, R.W., Weatherman, R.F., & Hill, B.K. (1996). *Scales of Independent Behavior—Revised (SIB-R): Comprehensive manual*. Chicago: Riverside.

Burks, H.F. (1977). *Burks Behavioral Rating Scales: Preschool and Kindergarten Edition*. Los Angeles: Western Psychological Services.

Bzoch, K., & League, R. (1991). *Receptive-Expressive Emergent Language Test*. Austin, TX: PRO-ED.

Carta, J. J., Atwater, J. B., Schwartz, I. S., & McConnell, S. R. (1993). Developmentally appropriate practices and early childhood special education: A reaction to Johnson and McChesney-Johnson. *Topics in Early Childhood Special Education, 13,* 243–254.

Cohn, M. (1992). Screening measures. In E. V. Nuttall, I. Romero, & J. Kalesnik (Eds.), *Assessing and screening preschoolers: Psychological and educational dimensions* (pp. 83–98). Boston: Allyn & Bacon.

Cole, K., Mills, P., Dale, P., & Jenkins, J. (1996). Preschool language facilitation methods and child characteristics. *Journal of Early Intervention, 20*(2), 113–131.

Cook, R. E., Tessier, A., & Klein, M. D. (2000). *Adapting early childhood curricula for children in inclusive settings* (5th ed.). Upper Saddle River, NJ: Merrill/Prentice Hall.

Division for Early Childhood Task Force. (1993). *DEC recommended practices: Indicators of quality in programs for infants and young children with special needs and their families.* Pittsburgh, PA: Council for Exceptional Children, Division for Early Childhood.

Drew, C. J., Hardman, M. L., & Logan, D. R. (1996). *Mental retardation: A lifecycle approach* (6th ed.). Upper Saddle River, NJ: Merrill/Prentice Hall.

Drinkwater, S., & Demchak, M. (1995). The Preschool Checklist: Integration of children with severe disabilities. *Teaching Exceptional Children, 28*(1), 4–8.

Dunn, L. M., & Dunn, L. M. (1981). *Peabody Picture Vocabulary Test—Revised.* Circle Pines, MN: American Guidance Service.

Fewell, R. R. (2000). Assessment of young children with special needs: Foundations for tomorrow. *Topics in Early Childhood Special Education, 20*(1), 38–42.

Fewell, R. R., & Kelly, J. F. (1983). Curriculum for young handicapped children. In S. G. Garwood (Ed.), *Educating handicapped children* (pp. 407-433). Rockville, MD: Aspen.

Folio, M. R., & Fewell, R. R. (1983). *Peabody Development Motor Scales and Activity Cards.* Chicago: Riverside.

Fuchs, D., Fuchs, L., Benowitz, S., & Barringer, K. (1987). Norm-referenced tests: Are they valid for use with handicapped students? *Exceptional Children, 54,* 263–272.

Fuchs, L. S., & Fuchs, D. (1990). Curriculum-based assessment. In C. R. Reynolds & R. W. Kamphaus (Eds.), *Handbook of psychological and educational assessment of children: Intelligence and achievement* (pp. 435–455). New York: Guilford.

Gray, G. (1975). Educational service delivery. In W. J. Cegelka (Chair), *Educating the 24-hour retarded child.* Symposium conducted at the National Training Meeting on Education of the Severely and Profoundly Retarded. Arlington, TX: National Association for Retarded Citizens.

Guralnick, M. J. (1998). Effectiveness of early intervention for vulnerable children: A developmental perspective. *American Journal on Mental Retardation, 102* (4), 319–345.

Hayden, A. H., & Pious, C. G. (1979). The case for early intervention. In R. York & E. Edgar (Eds.), *Teaching the severely handicapped* (Vol. 4). Seattle, WA: American Association for the Education of the Severely/Profoundly Handicapped.

Heward, W.L. (2000). *Exceptional children: An introduction to special education* (6th ed.). Upper Saddle River, NJ: Merrill/Prentice Hall.

Hresko, W. P., & Brown, L. (1984). *Test of early socioemotional development*. Austin, TX: PRO-ED.

Hresko, W. P., Reid, D. K., & Hammill, D. D. (1999). *Test of early language development*. Austin, TX: PRO-ED.

Kaufman, A. S., & Kaufman, N. L. (1983). *Kaufman Assessment Battery for Children: Interpretive manual*. Circle Pines, MN: American Guidance Services.

Lachar, D. (1990). *Personality Inventory for Children*. Los Angeles: Western Psychological Services.

Lambert, N., Nihira, K., & Leland, H. (1993). *AAMR Adaptive Behavior Scale—School* (2nd ed.). Austin, TX: PRO-ED.

Lund, K. A., & Bos, C. S. (1981). Orchestrating the preschool classroom: The early schedule. *Teaching Exceptional Children, 14,* 121–125.

Martin, R. P. (1991). Assessment of social and emotional behavior. In B. A. Bracken (Ed.), *The psychoeducational assessment of preschool chil*dren (2nd ed., pp. 450–464). Boston: Allyn & Bacon.

McCarney, S. B. & Leigh, J. (1990). *Behavioral Evaluation Scale—II (BES II)*. Columbia, MO: Hawthorne Educational Services.

McConnell, S. R. (2000). Assessment in early intervention and early childhood special education: Building on the past to project into our future. *Topics in Early Childhood Special Education, 20*(1), 43–48.

McDaniel, G. (1977). Successful programs for young handicapped children. *Educational Horizons, 56*(1), 26-27, 30–33.

McLoughlin, J. A., & Lewis, R. (1998). *Assessing special students* (5th ed.). Upper Saddle River, NJ: Merrill/Prentice Hall.

Mecham, M. J. (1989). *Utah Test of Language Development—3*. Salt Lake City, UT: Communication Research Associates.

Neisworth, J. T., & Bagnato, S. J. (1988). Developmental retardation. In V. B. Van Hasselt & M. Hersen (Eds.), *Psychological evaluation of the developmentally and physically disabled* (pp. 179-212). New York: Plenum.

Piaget, J., & Inhelder, B. (1969). *The psychology of the child*. New York: Basic Books.

Polloway, E. A., & Patton, J. R. (1997). *Strategies for teaching learners with special needs* (6th ed.). Upper Saddle River, NJ: Merrill/Prentice Hall.

Ramey, C. T., & Ramey, S. L. (1992). Effective early intervention. *Mental Retardation, 30,* 337–345.

Raver, S. A. (1999). *Intervention strategies for infants with special needs: A team approach*. Upper Saddle River, NJ: Merrill/Prentice Hall.

Salvia, J., & Ysseldyke, J. E. (1995). *Assessment* (6th ed.). Boston: Houghton Mifflin.

Seymour, H. N., & Wyatt, T. (1992). Speech and language assessment of preschool children. In E. V. Nuttall, I. Romero, & J. Kalesnik (Eds.), *Assessing and screening* preschoolers: Psychological and educational dimensions* (pp. 193–212). Boston: Allyn & Bacon.

Skinner, B. F. (1953) *Science and human behavior*. New York: Macmillan.

Smith, B. J., & Strain, P. S. (1984). *The argument for early intervention* (fact sheet). Reston, VA: Council for Exceptional Children.

Sparrow, S. S., Balla, D. A., & Cicchetti, D. V. (1984a). *Vineland Adaptive Behavior Scales: Interview edition, expanded form*. Circle Pines, MN: American Guidance Service.

Sparrow, S. S., Balla, D. A., & Cicchetti, D. V. (1984b). *Vineland Adaptive Behavior Scales: Interview edition, survey form*. Circle Pines, MN: American Guidance Service.

Sparrow, S. S., Balla, D. A., & Cicchetti, D. V. (1985). *Vineland Adaptive Behavior Scales: Classroom edition form*. Circle Pines, MN: American Guidance Service.

Thorndike, R. L., Hagen, E. P., & Sattler, J. M. (1986). *Stanford-Binet Intelligence Scale: Fourth Edition*. Chicago: Riverside.

Thorp, E. K. (1997). Increasing opportunities for partnerships with culturally and linguistically diverse families. *Intervention in School and Clinic, 32*(5), 261–269.

Thurlow, M. L. (1992). Issues in the screening of preschool children. In E. V. Nuttall, I. Romero, & J. Kalesnik (Eds.), *Assessing and screening preschoolers: Psychological and educational dimensions* (pp. 67–82). Boston: Allyn & Bacon.

Turnbull, A. P., Summers, J. A., & Brotherson, M. J. (1984). *Working with families with disabled members: A family systems approach.* Lawrence: University of Kansas, Kansas University, Affiliated Facility.

Turnbull, A. P., Turnbull, H. R., III, Shank, M., & Leal, D. (1995). *Exceptional lives: Special education in today's schools*. Upper Saddle River, NJ: Merrill/Prentice Hall.

Turnbull, H. R. III, & Turnbull, A. P. (2000a). *Families, Professionals, and exceptionalities: Collaborating for empowerment* (4th ed.) Upper Saddle River, NJ: Merrill/Prentice Hall.

Turnbull, H. R. III, & Turnbull, A. P. (2000b). *Free appropriate public education: The law and children with disabilities* (6th ed.). Denver: Love.

Ulrich, D. A. (1985). *Test of Gross Motor Development*. Austin, TX: PRO-ED.

U.S. Department of Education. (1997). *Nineteenth annual report to Congress on the implementation of the Individuals with Disabilities Education Act*. Washington, DC: Office of Special Education Programs, U.S. Department of Education.

U.S. Department of Education. (1999). *Twenty-first annual report to Congress on the implementation of the Individuals with Disabilities Education Act*. Washington, DC: Office of Special Education Programs, U.S. Department of Education.

Venn, J. (1994). *Assessment of students with special needs*. New York: Macmillan.

Wechsler, D. (1989). *Wechsler Preschool and Primary Scale of Intelligence—Revised.* San Antonio TX: Psychological Corporation.

Weissman, R. A. & Littman, D. C. (1996). Early intervention. In P. J. McLaughlin & P. Wehman (Eds.), *Mental retardation and developmental disabilities* (pp. 29–48). Austin, TX: PRO-ED.

White, B. L. (1975). *The first three years*. Upper Saddle River, NJ: Merrill/Prentice Hall.

Williams, H. G. (1991). Assessment of gross motor functioning. In B. A. Bracken (Ed.), *The psychoeducational assessment of preschool children* (2nd ed., pp. 284–316). Boston: Allyn & Bacon.

Wolery, M., Bailey, D., & Sugai, G. (1988). *Effective teaching: Principles and procedures of applied behavior analysis with exceptional students*. Boston: Allyn & Bacon.

Wolf, M. M. (1978). Social validity: The case for subjective measurement or how applied behavior analysis is finding its heart. *Journal of Applied Behavior Analysis, 11*(2) 203-214.

Zervigon-Hakes, (1995). Translating research findings into large-scale public programs and policies. *The Future of Children: Long-term Outcomes of Early Childhood Programs, 6*(3), 175-191.

Zimmerman, I. L., Steiner, B. G., & Pond, R. E. (1992). *Preschool Language Skills—3*. San Antonio, TX: Psychological Corporation.

10

School Years: Educational Programming

To review the chapter objectives on-line, go to the companion website at *http://www.prenhall.com/beirne-smith* and select Chapter 10, and then choose the Objectives module.

OBJECTIVES

After reading this chapter, the student should be able to

- discuss the key fundamental provisions of the Individuals with Disabilities Education Act (IDEA)

- explain the educational environment options available under the IDEA for students who are mentally retarded

- describe educational assessment and program planning procedures used with students who are mentally retarded

- discuss key elements or educational programming for school-age learners with mental retardation, with special attention to curricular and instructional issues

KEY TERMS

annual goals

behavioral objectives

benchmarks/short-term
objectives

categorical programs

collaborative consultation

collaborative teaming

cross-categorical programs

curriculum

IEP team

inclusion

individualized education
program (IEP)

mainstreaming

noncategorical programs

parity

reciprocity

Regular Education Initiative
(REI)

related services

We have already dealt with the causes, characteristics, and assessment of individuals who are mentally retarded. This chapter, using the information presented previously, focuses on the critical task of developing and implementing educational programs that give all individuals who are mentally retarded, regardless of their limitations, the opportunity to participate in the activities of their daily environment as much as possible.

In this chapter, we look at a number of key aspects in the process of educational programming for school-age learners. We begin our discussion with an overview of the fundamental components of the Individuals with Disabilities Education Act (IDEA). Next, we review the educational environment options and consider the appropriateness of these placement alternatives. In the subsequent section, we examine the basic elements of program planning, with an emphasis on the individualized education program (IEP). In the last section, we address programming for school-age learners by identifying various curricular orientations used in schools, discussing the curricular needs of students with mental retardation, and highlighting key instructional features.

INDIVIDUALS WITH DISABILITIES EDUCATION ACT (IDEA)

The main purpose of this section is to identify the major elements of the IDEA that have a direct effect on the educational programming of students with mental retardation. Twenty-five years have passed since the initial passage of the Education for All Handicapped Children Act (EHA, PL 94–142). In spite of various efforts to restrict its interpretation, its influence on the delivery of services to students with mental retardation has been profound, bolstered by significant amendments over the years that have strengthened and expanded various provisions of the law. The most recent amendments, enacted in 1997, continued this trend by enhancing certain existing facets of and adding new aspects to this legislation.

Key Components of the IDEA

Six key provisions form the essential components of the IDEA. For a detailed discussion of these principles, the reader may wish to consult a text on legal aspects such as Turnbull and Turnbull (1998).

Free, Appropriate Public Education   A free, appropriate public education implies that school districts provide special education and related services necessary to meet the needs of students with special learning requirements. These services are available to all students, regardless of severity of disability, and are provided at no cost to the family. If school programs cannot meet a student's specific needs, other agencies must provide necessary services at public expense.

The schools must also furnish any number of related services when deemed necessary to ensure an appropriate education. Many students with mental retardation will qualify for one or more related services. A listing of related services is provided in Figure 10.1.

The 1997 amendments underscored the original intent of the "appropriate education" provision of the IDEA and highlighted the importance of this concept to

FIGURE 10.1

Related Services Specified in the IDEA

Source: IDEA (1993), §300.24(b)(1–15).

Audiology
Counseling services
Early identification and assessment of disabilities in children
Medical services
Occupational therapy
Orientation and mobility services
Parent counseling and training
Physical therapy
Psychological services
Recreation
Rehabilitation counseling
School health services
Social work services
Speech-language pathology services
Transportation

students who are suspended, expelled, or in prison (if they are under 18 years of age). In addition, "orientation and mobility services"—available to any student with a disability—was added to the list of possible related services.

Appropriate Evaluation   The IDEA requires that, prior to a student with mental retardation receiving special education and related services for the first time, a "full and individual initial evaluation" be conducted. The law also requires the following safeguards: parental consent, implementation of nondiscriminatory evaluation practices, evaluation by a team, use of more than one procedure, testing in the student's native language, and reevaluations conducted when necessary.

Two noteworthy changes were incorporated into the 1997 amendments. First, the language of the law was very clear that a parent be part of the team that determines eligibility. Second, students with disabilities must participate in state- and districtwide assessments to the greatest extent possible. Allowances for accommodations and alternative versions of these tests were included in the regulations.

Individualized Education Program (IEP)   An **individualized education program** is a written document summarizing a student's learning program, and it is required for every student who qualifies as having a disability. The major purposes of an IEP are to establish learning goals for an individual child, to determine services the school district must provide to meet those learning goals, and to enhance communication among parents and other professionals about a student's program. Both the stated goals and the services to be delivered should depend on an analysis of a student's present levels of performance. The required elements of the IEP are discussed in more depth later in the chapter.

The IDEA emphasizes that attention must be given to "how a child's disability affects the child's involvement and progress in the general curriculum." Although consideration of a student's involvement in general education has been part of the IDEA over the years, the most recent amendments now require a statement explaining the extent, if any, to which the student will not participate with nondisabled students. Statements related to the student's participation, or lack of, in state- and districtwide assessments must also be included in the IEP. The 1997

For a complete on-line glossary of mental retardation terms, go to the companion website at http://www.prenhall.com/ beirne-smith and select any chapter, and then choose the Glossary module.

amendments also increase the role of the general education teacher in the development of the IEP.

The 1997 amendments to the IDEA retained the commitment to provide transition services to students. A statement of needed transition services is required beginning at age 16. Transition services are defined within the law as

> a coordinated set of activities for a student, designed within an outcome oriented process, which promotes movement from school to postschool activities including postsecondary education, vocational training, integrated employment (including supported employment), continuing and adult education, adult services, independent living, or community participation. The coordinated set of activities shall be based on the individual student's needs, taking into account the student's preferences and interests, and shall include instruction, community experiences, the development of employment and other postschool adult living objectives, and when appropriate, acquisition of daily living skills and functional vocational evaluation.

The amendments added two significant elements to the transition mandate. First, by age 14, and updated annually thereafter, a statement of transition service needs must be in place. Second, "beginning a least one year before the child reaches the age of majority under State law," a statement that the student has been informed of his or her rights that will transfer to the student on the age of reaching majority must be completed.

Least Restrictive Environment   Schools must educate children with mental retardation—to as great an extent as possible—in general education settings with their nondisabled peers. The least restrictive environment principle provides an opportunity for students with mental retardation to attend school in the most inclusive setting possible, which, most often, is defined as the general education (i.e., regular class) setting.

Parent and Student Participation in Decision Making   Parents have always been encouraged, at least legally, to participate in the special education process. Parental consent must accompany every decision affecting a child or youth who is disabled. Specifically, parents must consent to the evaluation of a student's educational abilities and needs, the determination of necessary services, and the actual placement of a child in any type of special program. In addition, parents have the right to obtain an independent educational evaluation (IEE) of their child. Lastly, parents have had the right to challenge or appeal any decision related to any aspect of the special education process.

The 1997 amendments make it clear that parents are primary members of the IEP team. The amendments also strengthen efforts to increase student involvement in the decision-making processes of their education, especially as this relates to transition planning.

Procedural Safeguards   A number of safeguards were included to protect the rights of both parents and their children. Parents are guaranteed the following rights: to obtain all educational records, to secure an IEE, to request a due process hearing, to appeal decisions, and to initiate civil action when appealing a final hearing decision. New disciplinary language and procedural safeguards, particularly in relation to change of placement due to violation of school rule or code of conduct, weapons, and illegal drugs were added to the 1997 amendments.

EDUCATIONAL ENVIRONMENT OPTIONS

The trend today toward providing beneficial, humanistic services to persons who are mentally retarded has led to changes in the structure of American schools, with a clear emphasis on providing appropriate education within inclusive settings whenever possible (Smith, Polloway, Patton, & Dowdy, 2001). The intent of this section is to provide a historical context for the evolution of services for children and youth with mental retardation and to discuss the various educational environments in which students with mental retardation are taught in schools today.

Evolution of Service Delivery

The free public school system in the New World was established in 1642 (Spring, 1986). Before that time, education was mostly limited to church-sponsored programs for which the provision of equal education for all children was not a concern. During the early part of the 19th century, states enacted laws that required communities to offer educational opportunities but did not make attendance mandatory. These efforts at mass education emphasized the importance of curricular content and not the needs of individual children. For the most part, children with mental and physical disabilities were excluded from school.

When students with mental retardation were provided an education, it was typically done so in segregated settings—often in separate schools. The "two-box" arrangement (Reynolds, 1989) (i.e., students with disabilities served in special education settings and students without disabilities served in general education settings) exists to this day. However, the incipient elements of a more inclusive system was woven into the Education for All Handicapped Children Act of 1975 (EHA, PL 94-142), with its stipulation that education should be provided in the least restrictive environment. Nevertheless, the original act (EHA) established, and all subsequent amendments/reauthorizations have maintained, the need for a continuum of educational alternatives.

As Reynolds (1989) has noted and Polloway, Smith, Patton, and Smith (1996) have documented, the history of special education is one of progressive inclusion. Over time, we have moved from exclusion to inclusion in school settings of students with disabilities. This trend, which includes phases when terms such as *integration* and *mainstreaming* were commonplace, has led to the current era of inclusive education. The conviction is to educate all students who are disabled, including those who are mentally retarded, in general education settings whenever possible.

The goal of the movement toward more inclusive education for students with mental retardation is to provide them with educational opportunities that will maximize their potential, give them access to the general education curriculum, and ultimately allow them to acquire the knowledge and skills to function fully in society. Interestingly, wholehearted agreement on how best to accomplish this goal is the subject of ongoing debate in the field of special education. Some special educators support full integration and the dissolution of the current special education system

TABLE 10.1
Percentage of Children Ages 6–21 Served in Different Educational Environments under the IDEA, Part B, during the 1997–98 School Year

State	Outside Regular Class			Separate Facility		Residential Facility		Home/Hospital Environments
	<21%	21–60%	>60%	Public	Private	Public	Private	
Alabama	6.90	50.03	40.40	2.23	0.07	0.08	0.11	0.19
Alaska	19.26	35.23	45.25	0.25	0.00	0.00	0.00	0.00
Arizona	7.26	21.56	66.63	2.90	1.30	0.05	0.06	0.25
Arkansas	10.48	51.44	35.05	0.08	1.78	0.00	0.72	0.45
California	5.66	13.17	72.10	5.52	1.93	0.00	0.19	1.44
Colorado	33.76	26.58	37.92	0.84	0.09	0.31	0.19	0.31
Connecticut	9.50	22.54	59.32	4.66	2.91	0.20	0.81	0.07
Delaware	4.93	54.56	25.37	13.26	0.00	0.37	1.31	0.21
District of Columbia	•	•	•	•	•	•	•	•
Florida	24.57	16.07	54.36	4.07	0.28	0.17	0.40	0.09
Georgia	5.40	26.05	66.69	0.66	0.00	0.91	0.08	0.22
Hawaii	15.42	39.31	44.28	0.32	0.04	•	0.24	0.40
Idaho	29.53	41.72	27.09	1.26	0.26	0.00	0.00	0.15
Illinois	6.53	4.93	72.25	10.56	4.95	0.19	0.49	0.12
Indiana	12.67	15.11	69.41	1.81	0.00	0.29	0.24	0.47
Iowa	30.29	38.43	28.33	2.41	•	0.31	0.15	0.08
Kansas	19.59	34.17	42.41	2.01	0.37	0.48	0.78	0.18
Kentucky	19.56	51.64	28.06	0.13	0.00	0.03	0.09	0.50
Louisiana	3.70	10.32	80.37	2.69	0.41	1.52	0.04	0.96
Maine	7.60	34.19	55.08	0.91	1.65	0.00	0.17	0.41
Maryland	8.00	14.79	58.05	15.95	2.43	0.06	0.44	0.27
Massachusetts	24.17	20.89	48.20	1.65	3.62	•	1.18	0.30
Michigan	23.89	17.99	44.98	12.82	•	0.09	0.06	0.17
Minnesota	20.27	40.64	31.18	6.97	0.12	0.17	0.30	0.35
Mississippi	3.07	28.79	65.15	1.06	0.00	1.03	0.07	0.83
Missouri	4.56	23.69	56.12	14.49	0.50	0.00	0.04	0.61

that maintains other placement options. Others maintain that a full range of placement alternatives is necessary to meet the special needs of students with disabilities.

From our perspective, professionals responsible for determining the initial educational environment for any student who is mentally retarded should always look first at the most inclusive setting. However, whichever setting is chosen, it should be considered as only a tentative commitment, with the option to make appropriate changes. Furthermore, the movement of students who are mentally retarded from more segregated to more inclusive settings should drive educational programming.

Setting Options

As mentioned previously, a continuum of options exists for providing an appropriate education to a student who is mentally retarded. The various educational envi-

TABLE 10.1 (continued)

Percentage of Children Ages 6–21 Served in Different Educational Environments under the IDEA, Part B, during the 1997–98 School Year

State	Outside Regular Class			Separate Facility		Residential Facility		Home/Hospital Environments
	<21%	21–60%	>60%	Public	Private	Public	Private	
Montana	8.25	42.78	47.85	0.26	0.26	0.00	0.09	0.52
Nebraska	22.30	49.30	23.72	1.40	0.43	0.47	0.93	1.45
Nevada	6.82	35.23	45.39	12.38	0.00	0.00	0.06	0.12
New Hampshire	21.87	27.16	39.78	3.87	3.46	0.20	2.54	1.12
New Jersey	1.82	15.34	48.77	17.33	14.13	1.34	0.15	1.13
New Mexico	11.42	13.01	74.64	0.09	0.00	0.28	0.05	0.51
New York	6.07	8.09	64.06	17.36	3.13	0.22	0.76	0.31
North Carolina	14.37	34.33	46.90	3.18	0.68	0.09	0.13	0.32
North Dakota	31.76	42.48	22.96	0.80	0.16	0.56	0.56	0.72
Ohio	24.37	63.13	11.28	0.40	0.00	0.56	0.00	0.25
Oklahoma	11.10	43.76	43.79	0.53	0.08	0.36	0.09	0.28
Oregon	29.35	25.04	40.84	2.15	0.50	0.28	1.31	0.53
Pennsylvania	6.27	29.71	57.62	5.25	0.49	0.18	0.15	0.32
Puerto Rico	1.49	36.81	50.52	8.23	1.14	0.15	0.22	1.46
Rhode Island	2.65	5.65	79.95	0.53	9.28	0.00	1.77	0.18
South Carolina	8.14	25.78	62.75	2.16	0.05	0.25	0.13	0.74
South Dakota	18.06	50.20	25.24	1.01	2.37	0.54	2.57	0.00
Tennessee	6.91	34.12	56.02	1.31	1.00	0.07	0.02	0.56
Texas	1.28	15.98	76.87	4.98	0.01	0.45	0.03	0.49
Utah	3.99	11.79	68.63	0.23	8.30	7.07	0.00	0.00
Vermont	71.53	11.82	13.28	0.80	0.73	0.00	0.73	1.09
Virginia	2.29	22.27	72.57	1.19	0.39	0.54	0.28	0.46
Washington	14.66	39.77	44.34	0.92	0.14	0.05	0.00	0.12
West Virginia	7.74	41.58	49.60	0.39	0.04	0.06	0.04	0.57
Wisconsin	7.57	31.21	57.41	2.92	0.05	0.45	0.02	0.37
Wyoming	8.76	42.86	45.62	0.92	0.15	•	0.46	1.23
American Samoa	0.00	20.00	80.00	•	•	•	•	0.00
Guam	7.84	29.41	58.82	2.94	0.00	0.00	0.98	0.00
Northern Marianas	•	•	•	•	•	•	•	•
Palau	0.00	0.00	100.0	0.00	0.00	0.00	0.00	0.00
Virgin Islands	•	•	•	•	•	•	•	•
Bur. of Indian Affairs	•	•	•	•	•	•	•	•
U.S. and outlying areas	12.55	29.58	51.66	4.26	0.94	0.33	0.24	0.44
50 states, D.C. and Puerto Rico	12.55	29.58	51.66	4.26	0.94	0.33	0.24	0.44

Source: U.S. Department of Education (2000, p. A-103).

ronments that are used by the U.S. Department of Education (DOE) are regular class, resource room, separate class, public separate facility, private separate facility, public residential facility, private residential facility, and home/hospital environment. Although some states use different terminology to describe placement options, we will use the U.S. DOE designations for organizational purposes.

The information on where students with mental retardation are served in schools can be found in *The Annual Reports to Congress* that the U.S. Department of Education publishes each year. Data for the 1997–98 school year (U.S. Department of Education, 2000), covering students whose ages are 6 to 21, are reported in Table 10.1.

What can be gleaned very quickly from this table is the fact that a large percentage of students with mental retardation remain in separate classes for the majority of their instructional day. The table also shows the interstate variation that exists as well. For instance, states such as Vermont and Texas report figures that are notably disproportionate—for different reasons—from the national averages.

Regular Class (General Education)

When placement decisions are made judiciously and reviewed routinely, the goal of providing the most beneficial services to students who are mentally retarded with minimal segregation from their peers is attainable. Many students who are mentally retarded can reach this goal in the general education classroom with only minor adaptations in instructional procedures or the learning environment. However, as can be seen from the 1996–97 data depicted in Table 10.1, only 12.6% of students identified under the category of mental retardation are in general education settings for more than 80% of their instructional day.

Instructing students who are mentally retarded in the general education classroom requires teachers who are highly skilled and sensitive to these learners' needs. Actually, successful inclusion is most likely to be achieved when five critical dimensions are in evidence. These dimensions are presented in Figure 10.2.

According to Keogh (1990), special education and general education teachers must be able to maintain a reasonable balance between the special needs of students who are disabled and other students in the classroom. In addition to creating settings, characterized by the attributes noted in Figure 10.2, general education teachers need to be skilled at judging the capacity of their students to learn and adjust instructions accordingly. They must also be able to predict and intervene,

FIGURE 10.2
Critical Dimensions of Inclusive Classrooms

Source: Adapted from Smith et al. (2001).

Sense of community and social acceptance

Appreciation of student diversity

Attention to curricular needs

Effective management and instruction
- Successful classroom management
- Effective instructional techniques
- Appropriate accommodative practices
- Instructional flexibility

Personnel support and collaboration

when problems arise among peers, and know how to handle the insecurities of students who are mentally retarded who cannot compete with their peers in all areas.

Instructional Supports In certain instances general education teachers are able to teach pupils who are mentally retarded in their classrooms with the help of some special education materials. The material may be a high-interest, low-vocabulary reading series, a programmed reader, a job-related mathematics book, or any material or hardware that allows the teacher to individualize instruction. This level of special education support requires a highly skilled general education teacher who is willing to adjust instruction to meet the needs of learners who are mentally retarded.

Personnel Supports In this arrangement, the special education teacher collaborates with the general education teacher in a variety of ways. For instance, the special education teacher may be involved in demonstrating materials or equipment, assessing the child's needs, developing teaching strategies, or providing instructional assistance. This level of support also requires that the general education teacher be willing to adapt instruction to meet the needs of learners who are mentally retarded.

The success of either of these two arrangements depends on a reasonable student/teacher ratio. When classrooms are overcrowded, teachers become frustrated; frustrated teachers are less likely to attempt to accommodate the special needs of students who are disabled. Mueller, Chase, and Walden (1988) recommend class sizes in the mid-20s and note that reasonable class sizes are particularly important in the earlier grades.

Itinerant Services Some school districts use itinerant services as a way of providing needed supports to the general education teacher. Itinerant teachers travel from school to school and provide consultative and instructional services as needed. These teachers visit each of their assigned schools periodically, usually working in individualized or small-group instruction with students who have special needs that hamper their scholastic progress. This option is especially useful for students who have vision or language disorders. Since these services are limited (visits are typically weekly or biweekly), responsibility for the student's education rests with the general education teacher.

The use of paraeducators (i.e., educational assistants, teacher's aides) has increased significantly as a way to provide support to students with mental retardation, especially those with more extensive needs, in general education settings. These support staff can fulfill many different roles in supporting students in general education settings. Pickett and Gerlach (1997) offer guidelines for supervising paraeducators in school settings.

Occasionally, school-based tutors can also be used in a support role. Student tutoring helps teachers individualize instruction; it is gaining popularity as a technique for assisting general education teachers with learners who are mentally retarded. Peer tutoring has also been successfully used to improve academic skills, foster self-esteem, help the shy youngster, help students who have difficulty with authority figures, improve race relations, and promote positive relationships and cooperation among peers (Beirne-Smith, 1991; Mercer & Mercer, 1997).

Resource Room (Services) The purpose of the resource room is to provide educational support to students who are mentally retarded and their teachers. The main difference from the previous educational arrangement is that the support provided occurs outside the general education classroom. In this arrangement, students who are mentally retarded remain in the general education classroom for the majority of the school day and receive supplemental instruction on a regularly scheduled basis in the resource room.

The role of the resource teacher is to instruct students and to consult or collaborate with the general education teacher, other service providers, and parents or guardians (see Figure 10.3). In a finely tuned resource program, there is consistency between what occurs in the resource room and what occurs in the general education classroom. Goals and objectives are similar, and methods of teaching and procedures for evaluating students and programs are coordinated and compatible. Such a program requires general and special education teachers who are attuned to the needs of the students and are highly skilled in both teaching technologies and collaborative consultation.

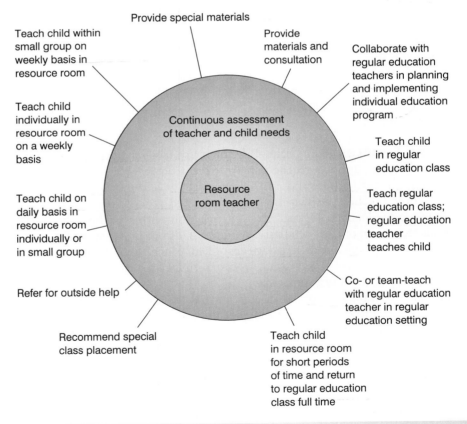

FIGURE 10.3
Service Alternatives for the Resource Room Teacher

Resource room programs vary substantially from school district to school district. Approximately 30% of students with mental retardation participate in some type of resource setting, based on interpretation of the most recent data. Regulatory requirements and preferences of school administrators usually dictate the way resource programs are organized. According to Wiederholt and Chamberlain (1989), resource programs are likely to be of one of three types: categorical, cross-categorical, or noncategorical.

- **Categorical programs** serve only students who are diagnosed with a specific disability (e.g., mental retardation). The purported advantage of categorical programs is that these programs are staffed with teachers certified in the disability area and thus presumably knowledgeable about the unique needs and characteristics of the particular group of students served by the program.
- **Cross-categorical programs** are also reserved for students who are officially placed in a special education program, but cross-categorical programs will serve students of varying disabilities (e.g., mental retardation, learning disabilities, emotional/behavior disorders). The purported advantage of the cross-categorical program is that students can be grouped according to their instructional needs rather than by disability.
- **Noncategorical programs** serve both students who are disabled and students who are not disabled but are in need of supplemental instruction. Noncategorical programs have the purported advantage of eliminating the need to label and place students in special education programs. This type of program often has a nondescript name such as "content mastery center" (which is used in Texas).

A variation of the resource model is the diagnostic-prescriptive teaching center. In this arrangement, students spend short periods of time at in-school centers staffed by a team of special educators and diagnosticians. The center's staff members assess the student's performance and develop an individualized educational strategy. The student returns to the general education class, but instruction is based on the program that the center's staff recommends.

Although the resource room is the most frequently used model for serving students with mild learning-related disabilities (U.S. Department of Education, 2000), its efficacy is presumed rather than documented. In their analysis of studies of resource rooms, Wiederholt and Chamberlain (1989) conclude that methodological problems so confounded the results that no firm conclusions about the efficacy of the models could be drawn. They state, "Given the complexities and difficulties inherent in the efficacy research, it is likely that this line of research will not provide an answer in the near future on the appropriateness of resource rooms as a viable service delivery system" (p. 22). Nonetheless, with the increased emphasis on serving students with disabilities in inclusive settings, the resource room, when designed correctly, provides a way of achieving a balance between providing intensive, specialized instruction and including students with mental retardation in general education settings.

Separate Class

Special class programs provide a self-contained instructional environment for students who are unable to profit fully from education in the general education classroom. Classes of this kind usually serve no more than 10 to 15 students and often have an aide to assist the teacher. The aide's duties may vary from preparing materials to instructing small groups under teacher supervision.

Self-contained special classes are designed for children who cannot keep up with the pace of instruction in a regular education classroom or for whom the nature of the curricular content is not appropriate. Generally, the special education class consists of a group of children identified as mentally retarded and in need of specialized intervention in terms of curriculum and instruction. Students typically receive all their academic instruction in the self-contained class; however, in some cases, they may divide their academic day between self-contained class instruction in some subjects and general education class instruction in others. Although special class students usually participate in general physical education, art, and music classes, they are largely segregated from the larger school environment. According to U.S. Department of Education (2000) statistics (see Table 10.1), over 51% of the students identified as mentally retarded receive their education in this type of setting.

Segregation in self-contained special classes is a significant concern, as such placement can be debilitating in its potential to stigmatize the student or discourage the development of social relationships with peers. Every effort must be made to determine the types and intensities of supports needed for the student to succeed in more inclusive environments. However, this need must be balanced by the assurance that the curricular needs of students are being met appropriately.

The placement of students in self-contained settings can only be justified after a thorough examination of student needs. Mercer (1991) offers the following criteria as a guide for determining when the special class is deemed appropriate:

- The special class teacher should be trained to teach the types of students in the class.
- The students should be selected on the basis of learning or social-emotional problems, not on the basis of socioeconomic status or race.
- Each child should receive intensive and systematic instruction tailored to his unique needs.
- A wide variety of teaching materials and resources should be available to the teacher.
- The class size should be considerably smaller than a regular class.
- A variety of teaching styles is needed to accommodate the different needs of the pupils.
- Each pupil's progress should be constantly monitored. Reintegration into the mainstream should be considered when it appears feasible.
- The class should have administrative support. (p. 185)

Separate Facilities

Historically, school districts placed the majority of their students who were mentally retarded in special schools. Under this arrangement, students were bused to a day school whose sole purpose was to serve students with disabilities. The separate facility option is still used today for approximately 5.2% of the school-age population of students with mental retardation (U.S. Department of Education, 2000). This figure includes both public and private settings.

In separate schools, it is possible to control for all the variables in the learning environment—scheduling, physical facilities, instructional climate, and so forth. Arguments favoring this arrangement suggest that such settings provide maximum benefit to certain students who have not faired well in their neighborhood schools.

The disadvantage of special schools is the absence of contact with peers who are not disabled. Thus, the educational experience presents an unrealistic picture of the world and eliminates the benefits that students, who are mentally retarded, gain through modeling and socialization with their peers. Such gains can be substantial, and as a result, few public school districts continue to have separate facilities for students whose academic and behavioral needs are not severe.

A student whose disability or combination of disabilities is so severe or unique as to prevent functioning in their neighborhood school may attend a special day school on either a part-time or a full-time basis. In systems combining general and special day schools, students with the most severe disabilities are bused to a central school for part of the day for essential educational services not provided in their home schools. In systems where services for students who are mentally retarded are not available in the general education school, they may receive their entire educational program in a special day school. In sparsely populated regions, it may be economically impractical to set up special classes in each local school, and district administrators may perceive that it is necessary to use a special school instead.

To read more about issues related to separate schools, go to the companion website at *www.prenhall.com/ beirne-smith* and choose Chapter 10, then choose the Article Response module.

Separate Residential Facilities

In cases in which a student who is mentally retarded has educational and social disabilities so pronounced (e.g., individuals with dual diagnosis) as to warrant round-the-clock attention, the student might attend a special residential school. Facilities of this kind have very low pupil/staff ratios, which benefit the students by allowing intensive instruction and support. Such facilities, however, deny pupils who are mentally retarded the opportunity to interact with peers who are not disabled.

It is important to note that a very small number (only 0.57% in the school year 1997–98) have needs so severe that they require the highly specialized treatment offered in residential facilities. Many of these individuals have behavioral disorders or physical conditions that demand close attention. The environment of a residential school may, then, for some individuals, be the least restrictive environment in which they can function effectively. Even then, according to the IDEA, constant monitoring is essential so movement back to other more inclusive educational placements can be considered.

Home/Hospital Environments

Homebound instruction and hospital tutelage represent the last two educational environments available for school-age children and youth with mental retardation.

Students who are retarded profit from being in an education environment that is as normal a setting as possible.

These options are usually considered more temporary settings for those students who are unable to participate in other settings, often due to illness or injury.

Homebound instruction is similar to hospital instruction in that it is provided for students who are temporarily unable to attend school. Itinerant or general education teachers usually furnish the instruction. Since it is costly, segregates the child from peers, and provides limited time for instruction, homebound instruction should be considered a last resort.

Hospital instruction is usually temporary and limited to students who are recovering from an illness or accident. For students confined to a hospital or convalescent home for serious, chronic afflictions, however, hospital instruction is a continuing process. Itinerant or general education teachers often teach such students, although some children's hospitals have fully developed educational programs. Such programs usually employ a multidisciplinary approach to the treatment of the individual's illness or injury and often include certified special education teachers who work with other team members in designing and implementing the educational component of the treatment plan.

Focus on Inclusion

As previously mentioned, researchers and educators have long questioned the efficacy of separate, special class placement for students with disabilities. Recently, the entire system of delivering services to students with disabilities has come under fire. In the mid-1980s, the Office of Special Education and Rehabilitation Services of the U.S. Department of Education advanced a proposal called the **Regular Education Initiative (REI)** (Will, 1984). In this proposal, Will recommended fundamental changes in the ways in which we educate students with disabilities, including those categorized as mentally retarded. The REI proposed a merger of special and general education services that would result in providing educational services to students with disabilities within the framework of the general education system.

As a result of the REI, professionals in special education began to make distinctions between the traditional special education practice of mainstreaming and the newer reform-based practice of inclusion. Generally, the term **mainstreaming** refers to the practice of placing students who are disabled in the general education classroom (physical integration) to the extent appropriate to their needs. Some mainstreamed students spent their entire school day in the general education classroom, but most utilized the resource room option. The special educator assumed primary responsibility for the education of students who were mainstreamed. The term **inclusion** implies more than simply physical integration. It is predicated on the idea that students with disabilities are welcomed and embraced as participating and contributing members of the general education milieu. The general educator assumes primary responsibility for the education of students who are included. However, as pointed out earlier in this section, inclusion will be successful if, and only if, the critical dimensions of inclusive classrooms are present.

Strong proponents of inclusion have viewed mainstreaming as an irresolute attempt to integrate students who are disabled in general education settings. In addition, some advocates of inclusion recommend the elimination of the full continuum of services for students who are disabled. Moreover, they argue that current special education practices, particularly identification, categorization, and separation of services, have proven ineffective in meeting the needs of large numbers of students with disabilities. One of the most powerful arguments against the placement of students in special education settings outside the general education classroom is that the instructional methodologies (i.e., what happens in special education) used by special educators are not that "special" and more like those of general educators (Lilly, 1986). Perhaps the most compelling argument for inclusion is that placement in a special education class is no more effective than placement in a general education class (Glass, 1983; Skrtic, 1991).

Staunch opponents of providing education to students with mental retardation in inclusive settings argue that diluting or eliminating hard-won services for students who had been poorly served in or excluded from general education programs without analysis of what will happen is dangerous (Keogh, 1988). Furthermore, many parents, students, and general and special education teachers are, for the most part, satisfied with the continuum of services (Guterman, 1995; Semmel, Abernathy, Butera, & Lesat, 1991). Concern has also been raised regarding the potential of the general education system to serve students with disabilities as untested and regarding the fact that resources to serve these students in general education settings are not now available (Baker & Zigmond, 1995; McKinney & Hocutt, 1988).

Those concerned about the demise of the availability of a continuum of services have also challenged the research questioning the effectiveness of special education. They point out that this research is less than substantial and methodologically flawed (Hallahan, Keller, McKinney, Lloyd, & Bryan, 1988; Kauffman, 1987; Schumaker & Deshler, 1988).

Efforts are currently under way to expand the role of and provide support for the general education teacher in educating students with special needs. Such innovations as teacher assistance teams (Chalfant & Pysh, 1989) and mainstream assistance teams (Fuchs, Fuchs, & Bahr, 1990) are designed to restructure referral procedures to include a prereferral component intended to limit the number of students referred to and subsequently placed in special education programs. Such approaches as collaborative consultation (Idol, Nevin, & Paolucci-Whitcomb, 1999), collaborative problem solving (Knackendofel, Robinson, Deshler, & Schumaker, 1992), peer collaboration (Pugach & Johnson, 1989), and peer coaching (Showers, 1985) are designed to deliver support to general education teachers in accommodating the needs of students with disabilities in their classrooms. Collaboration (discussed later in this chapter) is a common element in each of these innovative approaches.

The results of the research on attempts to meet the needs of students with disabilities in inclusive settings are equivocal (Salend & Duhaney, 1999). The long-term impact of inclusion practices on the delivery of services to students with disabilities is, as yet, unknown. Although educators have not reached a consensus, much is being written about the inclusion of students with disabilities in general education programs, and innovative programs are being implemented regularly.

We believe that inclusive settings are desirable and should always be considered when considering placement of students with mental retardation. However, we would quickly add that such consideration should be guided by the critical dimensions of successful inclusive settings that were highlighted at the beginning of this section. We also feel that it is important to be cognizant of the fact that a select group of students with mental retardation, particularly those whose needs are pervasive and not easily addressed by conventional interventions, will benefit from having available to them a range of educational options.

Final Thoughts on Placement

The characteristics of the individual, the philosophy and mission of the school, the parents, and the community influence the individual's assignment to an educational program. Child-related variables include the nature of the disability, motivation, academic skills, and behavioral characteristics. School variables include the nature of the general education class program, the availability of appropriate special education facilities, and the competence of educators. Parental and community factors include parental support, home environment, and community services.

Although these factors influence placement decisions, the strongest determinant in keeping with the prevailing trend toward inclusion should be the attempt to educate students who are disabled in as normal a setting as is feasible. The student should be integrated as much as possible within the school, the home, and the local community. In essence, programs that segregate students with disabilities from the normal environment are the least desirable placement alternative.

ASSESSMENT AND PROGRAM PLANNING

This section explores the important topics of assessment and the development of individualized education programs. The topic of assessment, particularly as it relates to eligibility determination, has been covered in Chapter 3. This chapter focuses on the use of assessment for the generation of information useful for program planning purposes.

Assessment

Comprehensive, accurate assessment is critical to the delivery of appropriate educational services to students with mental retardation. As one of the mandated components in the assessment process, educational assessment has three general purposes:

- To provide data that are usable by the interdisciplinary team in determining eligibility for special education services
- To determine the student's present level of performance and future instructional needs
- To evaluate the outcomes of educational programs

For students who are mentally retarded, educational assessment has two additional purposes:

- To identify the supports needed to further the learner's independence, productivity, and community integration
- To evaluate the effects of the supports (American Association on Mental Retardation [AAMR], 1992)

The first step in conducting a comprehensive educational assessment is to evaluate referral information and the accompanying documents (e.g., school records, work samples) to determine the areas for further assessment. Each technique that is selected should be multifaceted and tailored to the needs of the individual student. Furthermore, observations should be conducted across settings and over time. Once the initial test battery has been selected and administered, the resulting data should be analyzed to determine areas in need of further testing. The process of testing and analyzing data should continue until the tester is satisfied that all necessary information has been collected.

A comprehensive educational assessment should have several outcomes. First, it should give an overall picture of the student's present level of performance. Second, it should pinpoint the specific strengths and weaknesses in the student's behavioral repertoire. Third, it should clarify the logical next steps in the student's development—often the next steps on the assessment scale. Instead of coming up with a single score or label, the assessment process should yield many individual items of information and point to many different areas where instruction would be beneficial in moving the student toward more independent functioning.

Norm- and criterion-referenced assessments provide the assessor with different kinds of information. In *norm-referenced* assessment, a student's performance is compared to the performance of age- or grade-level peers. Norm-referenced measures provide a global picture of the student's level of functioning. Standardized achievement or intelligence tests are likely to be norm-referenced. Such measures are useful in obtaining information for placement decisions but are more limited in providing the type of information needed for program planning.

Criterion-referenced or *curriculum-referenced* assessments measure a student's mastery of specific, observable behavior and are more useful for program planning purposes. In criterion-referenced assessment, the student's performance is measured against a preset criterion (e.g., 80%) or the student's previous performance on a task, skill, or concept. Curriculum-referenced assessment is one type of criterion-referenced assessment. In curriculum-referenced assessment, the student is tested on what was taught. Both criterion- and curriculum-referenced assessments are useful in determining instructional objectives. Curriculum-referenced assessment, however, is more easily incorporated in daily lessons and thus provides the teacher with a clearer picture of the student's ongoing progress.

Hundreds of behavioral criterion-referenced assessment tools are available. They either include a range of skill areas or focus on one or two discrete areas (e.g., sight-word vocabulary, mathematical facts, or dressing behavior). Several disciplines (e.g., speech/language and physical therapy) have highly specialized but useful tools. Tools vary in their usefulness and objectivity, and prospective users must examine them carefully.

When selecting an assessment tool, the professional must take care to match its complexity and difficulty level with the student's functioning level. Special care, for instance, must be taken when selecting an assessment instrument for use with individuals whose cognitive functioning falls at the lower end of the scale. Testers must take care to select instruments that give credit to individuals who are lower functioning for rudimentary behaviors and that are sensitive to slight improvements in skill levels. For this reason, many teachers choose to develop their own assessment tools. Teacher-developed assessment tools often reflect what is being taught in the classroom and thus are useful in guiding the teacher in planning instruction and measuring student progress.

Whatever assessment tool is selected, teachers must ensure that the data collected are usable for the purposes of formulating goals and objectives for the IEP, planning instruction, or evaluating student learning. Finally, teachers must be aware that "testing conducted for the purposes of making a diagnosis and developing or evaluating educational programs measures an individual student's functioning level or ability at a given point in time, not the actual potential of that student" (AAMR, 1992, p. 113). In other words, assessment should be an ongoing process that is part of an ongoing educational program. Figure 10.4 lists the types of school assessment procedures that are relevant to students who are mentally retarded.

The IEP Team

The 1997 amendments of the IDEA stress the importance of the **IEP team**. This team essentially is charged with the task of developing a comprehensive and appropriate educational program for a student with a disability. As specified in the final regulations (§300.344[a]), the team should be composed of the following members:

- the parents of the student;
- at least one general education teacher of the student (if the student is participating in general education);
- at least one special education teacher of the student;
- a representative of the school system (public agency) who is (a) qualified to provide, or supervise the provision of, specially designed instruction to meet the unique needs of students; (b) knowledgeable about the general education curriculum; and (c) knowledgeable about the availability of resources of the school system;

Assessment function	Assessment method
1. To establish priority skill and students' activity needs for IEP in relevant skill domain	**Ecological inventory**: interview student, family, teachers, relevant community members, peers; observation in relevant home, school, work, leisure, and other community settings
Relevant to: Students of all ages *Frequency:* Roughly every 3 years unless student moves, then repeat following move	
2. To plan for school-to-work transition following graduation(ITP)[a]	**Transitional and vocational planning assessment**: interview and observation **Alternate methods**: work sampling, income and benefits, increased integrated activities, etc.
Relevant to: Students ages 14 to 16 through school completion *Frequency:* Update annually or as needed	
3. To evaluate IEP[b] objectives	**Observation in natural settings**: Probe and training data **Alternate methods**: family report, schedule changes, peer comments, self-assessment, etc.
Relevant to: All students *Frequency:* Roughly each week for performance data	
4. To evaluate behavioral problems	**Functional analyses**: interviews and program development observation **Direct observation**: mastery of replacement skills, reduction in excess behavior, increases in social interactions, etc. **Alternate methods**: interview and observation
Relevant to: Students whose behavior interferes with their health, with school and community acceptance, and/or with learning *Frequency:* Multiple times per day to less often	
5. To determine student and family satisfaction	**Satisfaction measures**: interview, questionnaire, observation **Alternate methods**: monthly pay, happiness self-report, emergency room visits and days of illness, number social activities, choices and peer contacts, etc.
Relevant to: All students *Frequency:* Annually or more often	

[a]Individualized Transitional Program   [b]Individualized Education Program

FIGURE 10.4

Types of School Assessment Relevant to Students with Mental Retardation

Source: From *Mental Retardation: Definition, Classification, and System of Supports* (9th ed., p. 118) by the American Association on Mental Retardation, 1992, Washington, DC: American Association on Mental Retardation. Copyright 1992 by the American Association on Mental Retardation.

- an individual who can interpret the instructional implications of the evaluation results;
- other individuals, at the discretion of the parent or the school system; and
- the student, if appropriate.

To meet the challenges and responsibilities of formulating the IEP and making a placement decision, IEP team members rely heavily on assessment data. Usable assessment data, therefore, are critical to the effective functioning of this team. The rationale behind the use of an IEP team is that students who are mentally retarded (as well as students with any disability) have a wide variety of needs that can best be met through input from individuals with a broad range of training, experience, skills, insights, and perspectives.

Each has an important contribution to make to the team effort. Typically, the size of the team increases proportionally to the degree or intensity of the student's needs. For instance, for some students who are mentally retarded and have extensive needs, the IEP team is likely to include a speech/language pathologist, a physical therapist, and an occupational therapist, to name a few. The team must make a coordinated effort to decide about such critical areas as instructional objectives, educational placement, instructional strategies, and evaluation. To maximize effects and avoid duplication of efforts, the team should meet regularly to plan and review programs and should carefully delineate each person's responsibilities.

The Individualized Education Program

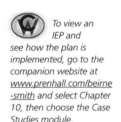

To view an IEP and see how the plan is implemented, go to the companion website at www.prenhall.com/beirne -smith and select Chapter 10, then choose the Case Studies module.

An **individualized education program (IEP)** is a written plan of action that specifies an individual's progress toward specific educational goals and objectives. The purpose of the IEP is to organize and integrate the total educational program to maximize instructional benefits for the learner. As previously emphasized, usable assessment data are necessary to fulfill this purpose. The IEP provides a measure of accountability for teachers and schools. The intent of the IDEA is that the IEP be used by teachers as a functional guide to confer with other service providers and parents about the educational program, to develop instructional plans, and to record student progress.

Historically, IEP committees have used levels of intellectual functioning to make placement decisions and design educational programs for students who were mentally retarded. Students who were more severely retarded, for example, were often placed in more restrictive, less inclusive settings and provided instruction in such basic areas as self-care, communication, and socialization. The supports-based definition of mental retardation (AAMR, 1992; see Chapter 1) recommends that the responsibilities of the IEP committee for students who are mentally retarded move beyond merely "matching" the student with a particular setting or set curriculum to an IEP committee that

- Collects and analyzes a broader set of assessment information (adaptive skills and limitations; physical, medical, and psychological characteristics and needs; and environmental strengths and limitations).

- Translates these assessment data into a profile of needed supports to compensate for, improve, or overcome the student's current performance in specific areas of weakness.
- Develops plans (i.e., IFSPs [individual family service plans], IEPs, ITPs [individual transition plans]) to address how the educational services and other needed supports will be delivered to the individual, involving agencies beyond the school when appropriate.
- Designs programs that include the student, to the greatest extent possible, in educational, social, and leisure activities with peers who do not have disabilities and supplies the educational supports to enable successful inclusion and prevent segregated programs.
- Evaluates the individual's progress under these plans and makes improvements on at least an annual basis considering assessment data, diagnosis, actual services and supports delivered, location of placement, the individual's progress, and the family's and student's degree of satisfaction. (AAMR, 1992, p. 116)

Components of the IEP

General Components The IDEA specifies the components but not the form of the IEP, so formats vary widely by locality. The final regulations of the 1997 amendments to the IDEA states that every IEP must have the following general components:

- *Statement of the student's present levels of educational performance.* This should include how the disability affects progress of the student in the general education curriculum.
- *Statement of measurable annual goals, including benchmarks or short-term objectives.* Annual goals and short-term objectives are derived from assessment data. **Annual goals** are statements of what the student can reasonably be expected to achieve in the course of one school year. **Benchmarks/short-term objectives** are behaviorally stated objectives, based on the annual goals, which provide a clear direction for instruction and ongoing evaluation of student progress. (Examples of behaviorally stated objectives are provided later in this chapter.) The 1997 amendments stress that annual goals should be tied to progress in the general education curriculum and drops the mandatory short-term objectives, making short-term objectives alternatively permissible with shorter, more usable benchmarks.
- *Statement of the special education and related services and supplemental aids and services and a statement of the program modifications or supports for school personnel that will be provided.* Each IEP must contain a statement of the type (e.g., resource) of special education services provided and who is responsible for providing those services. **Related services** refer to additional services (see Figure 10.1) needed to ensure that the program meets all of the student's educational needs. Related services may be delivered directly to the student, or they may take the form of family services (e.g., parent training).

The law also requires that all modifications and requisite supports for the student be documented. This requirement helps with advancement toward attaining the stated goals and continued progress in the general education curriculum as well as in extracurricular and other nonacademic activities.

- *Explanation of the extent, if any, to which the student will not participate with nondisabled students in the regular class.*   The extent of participation varies according to the individual's unique needs and is determined by the expected benefits on a case-by-case basis. Some students may benefit from full inclusion in the general education program, while the needs of others may prohibit participation in the general education program at the time in question.
- *Statement of any individual modifications in the administration of state- or districtwide assessments of student achievement.*   The 1997 amendments make it clear that students with mental retardation are expected to participate in high-stakes testing. If, however, participation, with or without accommodations, is not inappropriate for a student, an explanation must be provided, and an alternative plan for assessing the student must be offered.
- *Projected date for the beginning of the services and modifications and the anticipated frequency, location, and duration of those services and modifications.*   Each IEP must contain an indication of the date on which special education services will begin and their anticipated duration. Identification of the educational environment(s) in which services are to be delivered is also required.
- *Statement of how the student's progress will be measured and how the student's parents will be regularly informed.*   This statement provides more evidence of the increased attention to accountability promulgated in the 1997 amendments.

Transition Services   When students reach a certain age, additional pieces must be added to the IEP. In some states, these additional components will be in an individual transition plan (ITP). Two statements are needed:

- *Statement of transition service needs.*   This component is required for each student with a disability by age 14 (or younger). It serves to focus attention on a student's courses of study.
- *Statement of needed transition services.*   This statement is required for each student beginning at age 16 (or younger). Its intent is to ensure that a needed services are in place prior to the student leaving school.

Age of Majority   Beginning at least 1 year before the student reaches the age of majority, which varies from state-to-state, each IEP must contain a statement of information regarding rights transferred on reaching the age of majority.

Goals and Objectives

Determining goals and objectives is an important aspect of developing the IEP. IEP team members and teachers who write IEP goals and objectives must attend carefully to the results of assessment data. Teachers can draw on a number of sources to determine appropriate educational goals and objectives, remembering that a goal is relevant only to the degree to which it is functional for each individual and reasonably attainable during the school year. Goals and benchmarks/short-term objectives can be drawn from curriculum guides, assessment instruments that meaningful information on pertinent behaviors, or careful observation of a learner's needs in everyday settings.

As mentioned previously, goals refer to the broader, long-term outcomes. Examples of *functional* areas addressed by long-term goals are improving self-care skills, such as clothing selection; developing the skills associated with a specific occupation; or learning to make a weekly home budget. Examples of *academic* areas addressed by long-term goals are increasing mathematics skills in counting money, increasing sight vocabulary skills, or improving handwriting skills. Instructional or behavioral objectives are derived from long-term goals and refer to logically arranged sequences of specific, short-term steps toward meeting the annual goal. These objectives are important not only for planning purposes but also for monitoring the progress of a student.

Behavioral objectives are statements that specify an observable behavior, the conditions under which it will occur, and the acceptable standard for accuracy against which to measure performance. Listed here are examples of behavioral objectives that are appropriate for teaching academic and functional skills to students who are mentally retarded:

- Given 10 high-frequency sight vocabulary words, Robin will read each word within 5 seconds of presentation with 100% accuracy over three consecutive days.
- Given five coins of different denominations, Pedro will arrange the coins in order from most valuable to least valuable and state the value of each coin at least four of five times.
- Given a help-wanted newspaper ad, Chris Anne will say the meanings of four abbreviations with 100% accuracy.
- Given a toothbrush, toothpaste, and a cup of water, Mikala will brush her teeth, moving the brush along all surfaces and using a circular brushing pattern for at least 2 minutes.
- When his name is called, Curtis will maintain eye contact with the teacher for at least 2 seconds within 5 seconds of the cue.

Teachers of students who are mentally retarded too often concentrate instruction on discrete skill areas and fail to teach the student to generalize the use of the skill to other settings, with other people, or to similar tasks. Generalization is discussed in greater detail later in this chapter. For now, at the planning stage, it is important for teachers to remember that when they write a behavioral objective for teaching a skill in isolation, they must also write a corresponding objective for teaching the skill in context. For the first objective in our list, the teacher might write an objective that requires the student to use the skill on another task. For example:

- Given a five-sentence paragraph composed of known and recently introduced high-frequency sight vocabulary words, Robin will read the paragraph with 100% accuracy over three consecutive days.

Sometimes it is possible to include generalization of the skill in a single objective. For the last behavioral objective we listed, for example, the teacher might write an objective that requires the student to use the skill with various people. For example:

- When his name is called, Curtis will maintain eye contact with the teacher, the aide, or a peer for at least 2 seconds within 5 seconds of the cue.

Methods, Materials, and Activities

Most IEP formats, which are used in school districts, include space for the teacher to specify methods, materials, and activities that will be used to meet the annual goals and benchmarks/objectives. Specifying methods, materials, and activities at the planning stage assists teachers in thinking through how they will instruct the student in the classroom.

Methods   Instructional methods involve actively structuring the learning environment to promote learning of targeted objectives. Specifically, the teacher is concerned with choosing instructional methods that facilitate effective, efficient learning. These variables and corresponding instructional strategies and techniques are discussed later in this chapter.

Materials   Teachers should choose instructional materials that help promote active learning of targeted skills. Materials can run the gamut from textbooks and other print materials (e.g., handouts, workbooks), multimedia and software, audio- and videotapes, models/realia, and games and toys, to a range of assistive devices. Teachers should use materials that add interest to the lesson, are age-appropriate, closely match the student's ability level, and lead directly to skill acquisition. Materials geared for general education classrooms should be used, with or without adaptation, whenever possible.

Many checklists and scales are available to assist teachers in evaluating materials for use in their classrooms (see Figure 10.5 for an example of a materials evaluation checklist). Many teachers develop their own instructional materials, which are usually less expensive than commercially produced materials and often motivate their students more because they can be personalized.

Activities   Teachers also plan individual and small- and large-group activities that help in the acquisition of target behaviors. Activities can involve performing motor behaviors, talking, gesturing, writing, classifying, counting, role playing, participating in simulations, and so on. Activities should be varied to add interest to the curriculum and should provide many opportunities for learners to actively respond. When appropriate, they should take place in real-life settings (e.g., a store or laundry), so that the transition from the simulated to the real-life environment is easier.

Evaluation

According to the IDEA, the learners' progress toward targeted annual goals must be measured regularly and conveyed to parents periodically. Highly effective teachers

EDUCATIONAL MATERIALS EVALUATION CHECKLIST

Title: _____ Subject/Skill Area: _____

Publisher: _____ Brief Description: _____

Address: _____

Yes/No INSTRUCTIONAL SCOPE AND SEQUENCE

_____ 1. Are the scope and sequence of the material clearly specified?

_____ 2. Are behavioral objectives or learner outcomes specified?

_____ 3. Are student prerequisite skills specified in a hierarchical order?

_____ 4. Are skills, concepts, and facts ordered in a logical manner from simple to complex?

_____ 5. Does the instructional sequence proceed in small steps appropriate for difficult-to-reach students?

Comment: _____

CONTENT

_____ 6. Do the concepts and skills included adequately represent the content area?

_____ 7. Is the content consistent with the stated objectives?

_____ 8. Is the information presented in the material accurate?

_____ 9. Is the information presented in the material current?

_____ 10. Are various points of view concerning treatment of minorities, persons with handicapping conditions, ideologies, social values, sex roles, socioeconomic status, and so forth, objectively presented?

_____ 11. Are the content and topic of the material relevant to the needs of difficult-to-teach students as well as to other students in the general classroom?

_____ 12. Is the content appropriate to the

_____   a. chronological age of the targeted student(s)?

_____   b. mental age of the targeted student(s)?

Comment: _____

INITIAL ASSESSMENT/PLACEMENT

_____ 13. Does the material specify and provide a method for determining initial placement into the material?

_____ 14. Does the initial placement tool contain enough items to accurately assess and place the learner into the material?

Comment: _____

ONGOING ASSESSMENT/EVALUATIONS

_____ 15. Does the material specify and provide a method for determining ongoing progress in the material?

_____ 16. Are there sufficient evaluation items to accurately measure student progress?

_____ 17. Are procedures and/or materials for ongoing record-keeping provided that are useful to the student and teacher?

_____ 18. Is student progress monitoring possible by self-recording or charting?

Comment: _____

INSTRUCTION

_____ 19. Are instructional procedures for each lesson clearly specified?

_____ 20. Does the material provide for a maximum amount of direct teacher instruction on the skills/concepts presented?

_____ 21. Does the direct teacher instruction provide for active student involvement and response?

_____ 22. Are the direct instructional lessons adaptable to small-group/individual instruction?

_____ 23. Are a variety of cuing and prompting techniques used to elicit correct student responses?

_____ 24. When using verbal instruction, does the instruction proceed in a clear, logical manner?

_____ 25. Does the material provide for teacher modeling and demonstration when appropriate to the skills and concepts being taught?

_____ 26. Does the material specify correction and feedback procedures for use during instruction?

Comment: _____

PRACTICE

_____ 27. Does the material contain appropriate practice activities that contribute to mastery of the skills/concepts?

_____ 28. Are the practice activities directly related to the desired outcome skills/behaviors?

Comment: _____

REVIEW/MAINTENANCE

_____ 29. Are practice and review of content material provided?

_____ 30. Are review and maintenance activities systematically and appropriately spaced?

_____ 31. Are adequate review and maintenance activities provided for the difficult-to-teach student?

Comment: _____

FIGURE 10.5

Educational Materials Evaluation Checklist

MOTIVATION/INTEREST

___ 32. Are reinforcement procedures built in or suggested for use in the material?
___ 33. Are procedures specified for providing feedback to the student on his or her progress?
___ 34. Has the material been designed to motivate and appeal to students?

Comment: _____

ADAPTABILITY TO INDIVIDUAL DIFFERENCES

___ 35. Has the material been adequately field-tested with students with learning difficulties?
___ 36. Can the pace be adapted to variations in student rate of mastery?
___ 37. Can the method of response be adapted to the individual needs of the student?
___ 38. Can the method of instruction be adapted to the individual needs of the student?
___ 39. Can the student advance to subsequent tasks after demonstrating proficiency?
___ 40. Can the student be placed in the material at the learner's own level?
___ 41. Does the material offer alternative teaching strategies for students who are failing to master an objective?

Comment: _____

GENERAL USE CHARACTERISTICS OF THE MATERIAL

___ 42. Is a teacher's manual or set of teacher guidelines for use provided?
___ 43. Are teacher instructions clear, complete, and precise?
___ 44. Are teacher skills needed for appropriate use of the material with students specified?
___ 45. Is the amount of teacher preparation time for initial and daily use of the material specified?
___ 46. Is the estimated amount of daily or weekly time required of the student for effective use of the material specified?
___ 47. Are instructional grouping strategies provided for appropriate use of the material?
___ 48. Are the types of student responses needed for effective use of the material clearly specified for both instruction and practice situations?
___ 49. Is there a simple procedure for verifying correct responses and detecting errors in response?
___ 50. Are correction procedures specified when a student makes an error?
___ 51. Are other materials/media required for effective use of this material?

Comment: _____

PHYSICAL CHARACTERISTICS AND COSTS

___ 52. Is the initial cost per student reasonable?
___ 53. Is the replacement cost per student reasonable?

___ 54. Are there extra costs involved in effective use of the material (e.g., duplication, extra materials, equipment, etc.)?
___ 55. Is the material consumable?
___ 56. Is the material durable?
___ 57. Is the material warranted?
___ 58. Is the material safe?
___ 59. Can the materials be easily stored and organized for classroom use?
___ 60. Is the format of the material clear, attractive, and in a type size and style appropriate for targeted students?
___ 61. Are the directions and illustrations for use by the student clear?
___ 62. Are the auditory components of the material clear and adequate?

Comment: _____

EVALUATION SUMMARY

APPROPRIATE USE(S) WITH TARGETED STUDENT(S)   Comment: _____

___ Initial Assessment
___ Monitoring Progress/Mastery
___ Instruction
___ Practice
___ Reteach
___ Motivation
___ Not Appropriate

FIGURE 10.5 (continued)
Educational Materials Evaluation Checklist

Source: From *Effective Instruction of Difficult to Teach Students* (pp. 82–85) by L. Idol and J. F. West, 1993, Austin: TX: PRO-ED. Copyright 1993 by PRO-ED. Reprinted by permission. Adapted from *Teaching the Mildly Handicapped in the Regular Classroom* (2nd ed., pp. 125–127) by J. Q. Affleck, S. Lowenbraum, and A. Archer, 1980, Upper Saddle River, NJ: Merrill/Prentice Hall. Copyright 1980 by Merrill/Prentice Hall. Adapted by permission.

measure learner progress on a daily basis and use the results of the evaluation to make teaching decisions. These teachers test what is taught and use the results of the evaluation to determine what to teach next. Progress (or lack of progress) signals to the teacher as to when to move on to more complex objectives, when to repeat instruction, or when to change instructional objectives, methods, materials, and activities. Data on student performance, used to guide educators in the decision-making process, may be obtained in many different ways. Often, the simplest procedures (e.g., recording the number of correct and incorrect oral responses) provide the teacher with the most accurate indication of learner progress.

Final Thoughts on IEPs

Developing, writing, and monitoring IEPs is quite time-consuming, and some teachers report that the burden of the paperwork outweighs the usefulness of the document (Deno & Mirkin, 1980; Morgan & Rhode, 1983; Smith, 1990; Sugai, 1985). Computerized systems have proven useful as a time-saving device for developing and managing IEPs. Computers enable team members and teachers to collect and store student data efficiently, analyze these data rapidly, and produce multiple, legible copies of reports for educational planning (Smith & Wells, 1983; Nolley & Nolley, 1984). Some special educators have expressed concern that computer-generated IEPs foster a "cookbook mentality" and do not reflect a truly individualized program; Jenkins (1987), however, found that computer-generated IEPs were of higher quality than handwritten IEPs.

PROGRAMMING FOR SCHOOL-AGE LEARNERS

Educational programming for school-age learners who are mentally retarded involves a number of interrelated and mutually influencing components. Educational programs must be designed, implemented, and evaluated systematically so that educators make decisions that have an optimal effect on the development of each learner. Such programming requires that educators consider variables related to the student, the teacher, and the environment.

The programming process we describe next can work for all educational programs regardless of the learner's age, placement, or level of support needed. Based on the assessment process described earlier in the chapter, the first step is to determine the learner's current level of educational performance, followed by the identification of instructional needs. This particular sequence should result in the development of a comprehensive IEP. The next crucial step is the arrangement of the teaching/learning environment to facilitate the acquisition and maintenance of knowledge and skills deemed appropriate.

Providing effective instruction to any group of students is daunting due to the complexity of this process, when done correctly. Polloway, Pattton, and Serna (2001) have developed a model that depicts the many different dimensions of effective practice (see Figure 10.6). Without question, many of the instructional variables noted in the model are largely under the direct control of the teacher. However, many teachers are creating learning situations that strengthen the student's engagement in the learning process (e.g., student-directed learning).

Characteristics Revisited

Students who are mentally retarded often have characteristics that teachers must address to make learning profitable for the student. This topic was covered in great detail in Chapters 7 and 8; however, three particular characteristics are extremely important to the instruction and worth revisiting here.

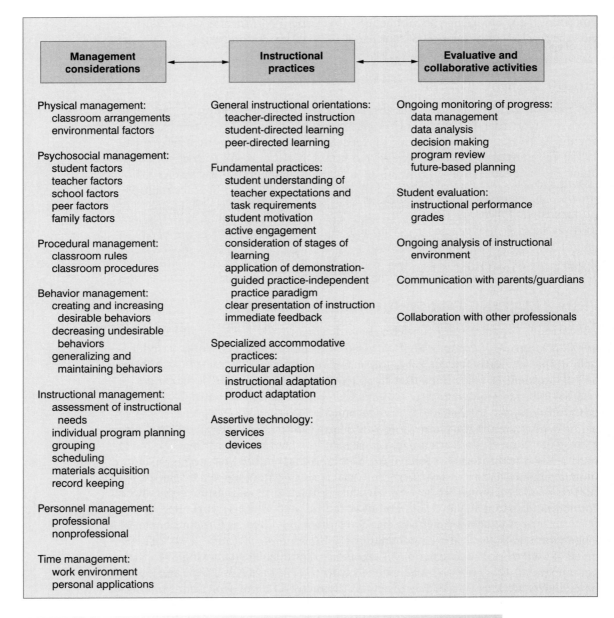

FIGURE 10.6

Dimensions of Effective Practice

Source: Polloway et al. (2001).

The first characteristic is the tendency to have an external locus of control; that is, individuals who are mentally retarded may think they have little control over the environment or the consequences of their actions. The teacher can use several strategies to help students become more internally oriented. First, students must acquire skills that are adaptive and functional, so that they actually achieve a measure of control over their environment. Second, instruction should teach the students to associate their actions with their consequences and then to anticipate probable consequences so that they can choose appropriate behaviors. An effective strategy for teaching this type of skill is role playing, which allows the student to practice repeatedly, in a nonthreatening situation, choosing and using suitable adaptive behaviors. Another strategy involves the use of a social learning contract that spells out, in writing or in pictures, the environmental factors linking various situation-specific behaviors and their possible positive, negative, and neutral results.

A second characteristic that teachers must address is the high expectancy for failure shown by many learners who are mentally retarded. This negative orientation is readily understandable, as many students who are mentally retarded have histories, sometimes extensive ones, of failing to learn new skills. Not only may these individuals anticipate failure when trying to learn new tasks; they may even refuse to attempt new tasks.

Teachers can counteract this commonly seen feature in several ways. First, they should look closely at the results of their assessments and set reasonable, achievable goals and objectives based on the student's demonstrated level of performance/functioning across skill areas. Second, they should structure the instructional program for success by breaking down objectives into small learning steps (via task analysis) and using a rich schedule of positive reinforcements. Third, they can reward effort and improvement along with reaching criterion. Fourth, they can teach students to use overt (i.e., spoken aloud) or covert (i.e., progressive whispers, inner talking, or thoughts) self-talk to monitor or reinforce their own behavior. These and similar strategies can help make students more willing to try new tasks and may lead to positive comments—"I can do it"—that indicate that they feel that they are likely to succeed, not fail. These types of techniques enhance the development of self-directed learning opportunities.

A third characteristic of learners who are mentally retarded is *outerdirectedness,* or a tendency to rely regularly on external cues or instructions for behavior. We all use external cues; however, many individuals with mental retardation may depend on them. For example, a student who needs help with work may always wait for the teacher to notice the problem and give advice and instructions. Teachers can reward more self-directed behaviors such as actively asking the teacher for help or independently identifying several possible solutions to the problem and then trying each one until the solution is reached. In every case, teachers must look beyond general characteristics to plan programs based on each individual's characteristics.

The Roles of the Teacher in a Collaborative World

The educator's primary goal in teaching is creating educational situations in which the student acquires knowledge, concepts, and skills that have been targeted. Meeting this goal involves making wise decisions about placement, assessment, the student, curriculum, instruction, and evaluation. Ultimately, the instructional envi-

Although children with disabilities have special instructional needs, they are, above all, children.

ronment must be arranged properly and effective practices instituted. Doing so ensures that the student who is mentally retarded (a) acquires a wide variety of academic, social, and functional skills; (b) learns when and where to use them; (c) generalizes learned skills to other new settings and situations; and (d) maintains the skills over time. The educator must keep these four objectives for the learner in mind. In this way, the tasks of teacher and learner will be complementary.

Acquiring a Wide Variety of Adaptive Behaviors Children and youth who are mentally retarded must function successfully in school, home, job, and community settings. To do so, they must acquire knowledge and develop skills in many areas, including many life-related skills (e.g., self-care), mobility, communication, social interactions, academics, health and safety, leisure, and vocational pursuits. While the teacher must target useful learning objectives in each of these areas, the degree to which each area is taught and the instructional procedures selected will vary, of course, according to the individual needs of the student.

Learning When and Where to Use the Skills Students who are mentally retarded must learn to observe and respond to environmental cues that signal that a particular behavior is warranted and appropriate in that setting. In other words, along with being able to perform a skill to a certain level of mastery, students must recognize the proper conditions for its performance. For example, when is it appropriate to approach, shake hands with, and introduce oneself to another person? At a party when a new person arrives, on the street to a complete stranger, or in a work setting while in the midst of completing a task? Or when is it appropriate to add numbers? When making a withdrawal from a checking account, when estimating the total cost of groceries to be purchased, or when determining the number of hours worked? Or when should one reach and grasp an object? When handed a soft toy, when given a bowl of hot cereal, or when within reach of another person's hair or eyeglasses? Discrimination tasks like these require learners who are mentally retarded to observe each setting to determine relevant cues and then quickly and reliably decide which behavior from their repertoire is appropriate. The teacher must structure educational programs so that students learn to attend to relevant cues, make adaptive responses, and receive positive reinforcement for their efforts.

Generalizing Adaptive Behaviors to Other Appropriate Settings

Generalizing behaviors is a corollary of learning skills. The person who is mentally retarded must be able to identify similar tasks for which a behavior is appropriate and respond correctly in those instances. For example, determining the amount of money owed when eating in a variety of fast-food restaurants, repotting several types of plants and flowers, and filling out job applications for different clerical jobs all require the use of learned skills to new settings.

Another important element is the person ability to generalize responses from the training situation to the real-life environment in which the behavior should occur. Whenever possible, skills developed in a classroom setting should also be trained in an authentic environment (i.e., community-based instruction). Teachers should not assume that teaching a student to count change in a classroom store, for example, will result in the student's being able to count change at a fast-food restaurant or a grocery store.

Maintaining the Performance of New Behaviors/Skills over Time

Many crucial behaviors/skills must continue in the person's repertoire past formal training into future environments and situations that occur throughout life. Here again, the quality of the instructional program (i.e., the extent that effective practices are incorporated) can either facilitate or hinder the generalization, maintenance, and adaptation of new behaviors.

Selecting Functional Behaviors
A key to successful educational outcomes for many students with mental retardation is the selection of functional behaviors as goals to be addressed by the IEP. A functional skill or behavior is one that is useful to students and that gives them some control over their environment in terms of obtaining positive and consistent results. A student will probably not maintain a nonfunctional behavior over time.

When selecting functional skills, teachers must ask whether the skill is likely to be useful in the student's present or projected future environments. Is it age-appropriate? Is the student likely to retain the skills over time? If the answer is no, then teachers should reconsider the nature of the individualized program that has been developed and identify more useful behaviors.

Regardless of the student's level of functioning, the educator should ask the following questions when selecting each target goal to be addressed in an individual's educational program:

- What skill clusters or activities does the person need to function in a variety of settings in the same way as do their (*sic*) same-age peers (e.g., in home, school, leisure, community, work)?
- What skill clusters of activities will the person need to learn in the near future to function like peers in these targeted environments (e.g., home, school, leisure, community, work)?
- What skill clusters or activities, either present or needed by the student, are highly preferred by the student?
- Which of these skill clusters are critical, essential, or of high priority to this student (or family) in terms of adult areas of functioning?
- Which of these skill clusters, if any, are critical to the student's health and safety?
- Which activities will promote increased independence and interdependence in inclusive community settings?
- Which activities will contribute to the student's happiness, acceptance by others, and personal life satisfaction?
- Which activities either cannot be taught or can only be taught with great difficulty (performed very infrequently, require great travel, necessitate simulation to teach)?
- Which activities (a) are or will be age inappropriate, or (b) are highly time-limited (not valuable beyond the student's near future), or (c) have questionable future value? (AAMR, 1992, pp. 130–131)

To learn more about teaching and learning, go to the companion website at www.prenhall.com/ beirne-smith and select Chapter 10, then choose the Web Destinations module.

Collaborative Efforts   The emerging nature of instructional practice in schools today is highlighted by increased collaboration among school-based personnel. Nowhere else is this more poignant than those situations in which students with disabilities are placed in inclusive settings. Recalling the critical dimensions of successful inclusion, depicted in Figure 10.2, one of the essential dimensions is "personnel support and collaboration."

Collaboration is referred to by a variety of terms (e.g., *peer collaboration, collaborative problem solving, collaborative consultation*). Each of these approaches differs in how the collaborative process is implemented. There are, however, some commonalities among the approaches. First, all approaches view collaboration as a process rather than as a service delivery model. Knackendofel, Robinson, Deshler, and Schumaker (1992), for example, define **collaborative teaming** as "an ongoing process whereby educators with different areas of expertise voluntarily work together to create solutions to problems that are impeding students' success, as well as to carefully monitor and refine these solutions" (p. 1). The definition of collaboration formulated by Idol, Nevin, and Paolucci-Whitcomb (1999) suggests that **collaborative consultation** is an interactive process that enables people with diverse expertise to generate creative solutions to mutually defined problems. Second, collaborative approaches are built on the principles of parity and reciprocity. Parity and reciprocity refer to the mutuality of the process. **Parity** means that all members are accorded equal status; no single individual is viewed as the expert, and all contributions are judged solely on their merit as a feasible solution to the problem. **Reciprocity,** as defined by West, Idol, and Cannon (1989) "means allowing all parties to have equal access to information and the opportunity to participate in problem identification, discussion, decision making and all final outcomes" (p. 1).

Approach	Nature of contact with student	Description
Collaboration-consultation	Indirect	General education teacher requests the services of the special education teacher (i.e., consultant) to help generate ideas for addressing an ongoing situation. The approach is interactive.
Peer support systems	Indirect	Two general education teachers work together to identify effective solutions to classroom situations. The approach emphasizes the balance of the relationship.
Teacher assistance teams	Indirect	Teams provide support to general education teachers. Made up of core members plus the teacher seeking assistance, it emphasizes analyzing the problem situation and developing potential solutions.
Co-teaching	Direct	General and special education teachers work together in providing direct service to students. Employing joint planning and teaching, the approach emphasizes the joint responsibilities of instruction.

FIGURE 10.7

Types of Collaborative Efforts

Source: From *Cooperative Teaching: Rebuilding the Schoolhouse for All Students* (p. 74) by J. Bauwens and J. J. Hourcade, 1995, Austin, TX: PRO-ED. Used by permission.

The most common collaborative approaches used in schools today include collaboration-consultation, peer support systems, teacher assistance teams, and coteaching. Figure 10.7 provides more detailed information on each of these approaches.

Curricular Considerations

So far in this chapter, we have discussed the fundamental provisions of the IDEA, the educational environment options available, and procedures that should guarantee access to an appropriate education for all school-age learners who are mentally retarded. Access alone, however, does not guarantee success. It is time now to turn our attention to areas concerned with the outcomes of the educational process. Decisions about what and how to teach are critical to the success of students who are mentally retarded. This point has been emphasized throughout the chapter. In this section, we discuss the curriculum and curricular alternatives for students who are retarded. In the next section, we focus on select variables that are important in designing an effective, efficient instructional program.

School-age learners who are mentally retarded have diverse learning needs, as heterogeneity certainly exists within this group. This diversity results from variations due to level of intellectual functioning, certain individual characteristics, age, present and projected future life situations, previous educational experiences, family factors, cultural and socioeconomic background, and a host of community variables (e.g., rural versus urban). To accommodate the diverse learning needs of these students, educators must first address what is taught in school. A primary concern in programming for students who are mentally retarded is the curriculum.

Curriculum has been defined in various ways. Hoover and Patton (1997) define **curriculum** as planned learning experiences that have intended educational outcomes. Armstrong (1990) defines it as a "master plan for selecting content and organizing learning experiences for the purpose of changing and developing learners' behavior and insights" (p. 4).

School-age learners who are mentally retarded have a wide range of skill levels and instructional needs. Therefore, curricula designed for this group of students must be individualized, functional, and comprehensive. Such curricula are built around the assessed needs of the student and based on a life span perspective, not just focusing on the typical school age period of five to eighteen years. Comprehensive curricula cover a wide range of content areas and levels of difficulty. Polloway et al. (2001) describe a comprehensive curriculum as one that

- Responds to the needs of the individual student at the current time.
- Accommodates the concurrent needs for maximum interaction with nondisabled peers, provides access to the general education curriculum, and gives attention to crucial curricular needs that are absent from the general education curriculum.
- Develops from a realistic appraisal of potential adult outcomes of individual students.
- Remains sensitive to graduation goals and specific diploma track requirements. (p. 165)

Figure 10.8 describes decision-making variables that should be considered when designing a comprehensive curriculum for learners who are mentally retarded.

Curricular Orientations

Polloway et al. (2001) have adapted a model of program orientations originally proposed by Bigge and Stump (1999) that identifies four general curricular orientations: general education curriculum without supports/accommodations; general education curriculum with supports/accommodations; special education curriculum with a focus on academic and social skill development or remediation; special education curriculum with a focus on adult outcomes.

General Education Curriculum without Supports/Accommodations
This orientation is based on the idea that students with mental retardation are in general education classrooms and therefore being exposed to the same exact curriculum as their classmates. The key feature here is that these students do not receive any assistance. This orientation will be the curricular option of choice when students exit special education.

A concern related to this approach includes the ability of students with mental retardation to deal successfully with the academic content presented. Another concern relates the functionality of the content to which students are exposed (i.e., are the student's long term curricular needs being met).

General Education Curriculum with Supports/Accommodations
Approaches that provide support to students placed in general education class-

1. Student Variables
   - cognitive-intellectual level
   - academic skills preparedness
   - academic achievement
   - grade placement
   - motivation and responsibility
   - social interactions with peers and adults
   - behavioral self-control

2. Parent Variables
   - short- and long-term parental expectations
   - degree of support provided (e.g., financial, emotional, academic)
   - parental values vis-á-vis education
   - cultural influence (e.g., language, life values)

3. Regular Class Variables
   - teacher and peer acceptance of diversity (classroom climate)
   - administrative support for integration
   - availability of curricular variance
   - accommodative capacity of the classroom
   - flexibility of daily class schedules and units earned toward graduation
   - options for vocational programs

4. Special Education Variables
   - size of caseload
   - availability of paraprofessionals or tutors
   - access to curricular materials (for specific curriculum models)
   - focus of teacher's training
   - consultative and materials support available
   - related services available to students

FIGURE 10.8
Decision-Making Variables

Source: From "Comprehensive Curriculum for Students with Mild Handicaps" by E. A. Polloway, J. R. Patton, M. H. Epstein, and T. E. C. Smith, 1989, *Focus on Exceptional Children, 21*(8), p. 8. Copyright 1989 by Love Publishing. Reprinted by permission.

rooms employ a variety of mechanisms for assisting students as well as the general education teacher.

Tutorial assistance provides additional instruction to the student on content covered in class. The advantages of tutorial instruction are that students, parents, and teachers tend to view this approach as less stigmatizing than remedial instruction, students may be motivated by instruction that corresponds to instruction in the general education classroom, and it allows the student to be maintained in the general education classroom. The disadvantage of this approach is that it is a short-term response that usually does not address the long-term needs of the student. That is, it may assist the student in succeeding in the class for which tutoring is provided, but it will not necessarily teach the student skills needed to succeed in subsequent classes.

A *learning strategies approach* focuses on teaching the student how to learn rather than what to learn. Such approaches emphasize the learner's role as an active participant in the learning process. The advantage of a learning strategies approach is that it clearly provides a student-focused system for dealing with the subject matter being presented in the general education classroom. It also emphasizes generalization of skills and concepts. Disadvantages of this approach are that many students who are mentally retarded lack the entry-level skills necessary to succeed with this approach, and it may be difficult to motivate students to learn a strategy that has long-term rather than short-term benefits.

Cooperative teaching is based on collaboration between the general education and the special education teacher and is designed to provide the support needed to maintain students with disabilities in the general education classroom. The advantages of cooperative teaching are that it draws on the combined expertise and knowledge base of the general education and special education teachers, and it provides a way to promote content learning and integration. The main disadvantage of cooperative teaching is that it requires a set of collaborative skills that few teachers have refined in their personal preparation programs.

Special Education Curriculum with a Focus on Academic and Social Skill Development and Remediation

This orientation has as a basic tenet the notion that some type of specialized instruction is implemented. Most of the time, as dictated by the directives of the 1997 amendments of the IDEA, the nature of what is taught is based on the goal of furthering the student's progress in the general education curriculum.

A *basic skills remedial approach* is most often used in elementary special education programs. In this approach, the student's skill deficits are identified and remedial instruction to address areas of academic need is provided. The advantage of the basic skills approach is that it directly addresses the identified needs of the student. Some disadvantages of this approach do exist. When a heavy emphasis on academic deficits is operative, teachers are apt to overlook the student's areas of strength. This approach may fail to program for generalization of skills learned. An overemphasis of this type of orientation may be inappropriate for secondary students who, at this point in their schooling, need instruction in a plethora of other adult outcome areas.

A *social skills remedial model* is characterized by its concentration on developing social competence in students with mental retardation. The advantage of this approach is that social competence is necessary to the student's success in general education settings and ultimately in most adult settings. Another important aspect of this orientation is that many students who have not developed appropriate social skills or who have developed inappropriate ones need direct instruction of social skills. The disadvantage of this approach is that few social skills curricula have demonstrated meaningful, observable change in students' behavior or generalization to other settings.

Special Education Curriculum with a Focus on Adult Outcomes

Adult outcomes curricula emphasize the acquisition of knowledge and development of skills that are directly related to the demands of adulthood and adult adjustment. Different taxonomies exist that provide schematas for organizing the various domains of adulthood in which some degree of competence will be needed. Figure

FIGURE 10.9

Adult Outcome Domains

Source: From *Major Areas of Transition* by the Hawaii Transition Project, 1987, Honolulu: Hawaii Transition Project. Copyright 1987 by the Hawaii Transition Project. Reprinted by permission.

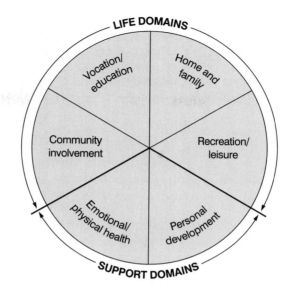

10.9 shows the general domains of one of these taxonomies. One advantage of this approach is that adolescents often have positive perceptions about curricula that they find more relevant to their lives and therefore may be motivated by such an approach. A potential disadvantage of this approach is that, without systematic attention to adult outcomes, the curriculum may provide limited long- or short-term benefits.

Instructional Considerations

The goal of instructional programming for students who are mentally retarded is to create a learning environment in which all learners reach their highest possible level of potential in a reasonable amount of time. Designing an instructional program that is both effective and efficient requires teachers to act as responsible, reflective decision makers and to exploit the knowledge that has been gained about practices that constitute effective teaching.

Over the past two decades, researchers in education have investigated the relationship between teaching and learning in an effort to identify instructional factors that influence academic outcomes for students who are disabled, including those who are mentally retarded. (Figure 10.6, which was introduced earlier in the chapter, organizes these important findings on effective practice.) Initially, this research focused on factors that were intrinsic to the learner. More recently, these studies have looked at a host of instruction-related variables that can have a profound effect on learning. A series of systematic studies now provides us with a knowledge base from which we can describe effective instruction for students with disabilities.

The results of this research confirm what we have long suspected: that teaching and learning are complex processes that involve both unique contributions from and interactions among the teacher, the learner, and the environment. Some

Technology Plan: Getting America's Students Ready for the 21st Century

In December 2000, Secretary of Education Richard Riley released a technology plan to guide the use of technology in elementary and secondary education. Five national education goals were introduced. Because these goals are intended to affect all students, it is important to analyze these goals in terms of their meaning and impact in students with mental retardation and their teachers.

- **Goal 1:** All students will have access to information technology in their classrooms, schools, communities, and homes.

- **Goal 2:** All teachers will use technology effectively to help students achieve high academic standards.
- **Goal 3:** All students will have technology and information literacy skills.
- **Goal 4:** Research and evaluation will improve the next generation of technology applications for teaching and learning.
- **Goal 5:** Digital content and networked applications will transform teaching and learning.

variables that affect learning (e.g., learner aptitude) are influenced by but are not under the direct control of the teacher. However, the teacher can manipulate other variables to make learning a more efficient and successful experience for learners who are retarded.

Christenson, Ysseldyke, and Thurlow (1989) identify 10 instructional factors that affect student achievement. These factors provide a useful set of ideas that teachers and administrators should consider in their efforts to provide appropriate educational programming to students with mental retardation.

1. *The degree to which classroom management is effective and efficient.* Effective classroom teachers are proactive in their management of time, class routines, and student behavior. They anticipate and plan for potential problems in the classroom. They make students aware of goals and expectations. They establish class rules and routines, routinely monitor student behavior and progress, and are fair and consistent in their application of rewards and punishment. Effective teachers protect instructional time. They secure administrative support to minimize interruptions in their classrooms and arrange the class schedule and activities to limit time lost during transition and instruction.

2. *The degree to which there is a sense of "positiveness" in the school environment.* Student achievement is higher in classrooms in which teachers foster positive attitudes toward learning. Effective teachers demonstrate their belief that all students can learn by setting high but realistic goals for student performance, actively monitoring and rewarding student progress, and stating explicitly that they expect all students to succeed.

3. *The degree to which there is an appropriate instructional match.* Effective teachers adapt instruction to meet the particular needs of each student. They use assessment data to determine each student's current level of performance, interests, motivation, use of strategies, processing skills, and persistence for learning and match these to the student's stage of learning and task difficulty. They also assess the appropriateness of environmental

conditions in the classroom to determine if the time allocated for instruction is sufficient to ensure learning.

4. *The degree to which teaching goals and teacher expectations for student performance and success are stated clearly and understood by the student.* Skilled teachers communicate goals effectively and frequently. They inform students of the quantity and quality of work needed for acceptable performance on a task. They preset criteria for mastery and provide students with task-specific feedback and correction. They provide equal opportunity for all students to respond and to participate in learning activities, and they reinforce or correct responses in a manner that facilitates student improvement on the task.

5. *The degree to which lessons are presented clearly and follow specific instructional procedures.* Effective teachers demonstrate concern for the quality of instruction in their classrooms. They encourage active student participation by using a demonstration–prompt–practice sequence and actively monitor student responses. They tie old knowledge to new learning by beginning each lesson with a review of previously learned material, and they include an overview of the lesson in their introduction. They use step-by-step presentation of instructional material to make explicit what skill is to be learned, why the skill is important, when the skill is useful, and how to apply it. They check student understanding of task demands frequently. They use positive reinforcement, spaced and repeated practice, and varied activities to gain and maintain student attention and to promote generalization.

6. *The degree to which instructional support is provided for the individual student.* Effective teachers use diagnosis, prescription, monitoring, interactive teaching, and record keeping to adjust instruction to meet the particular needs of individual students. They provide varied types and degrees of practice based on the student's ability or level of functioning. They adjust the amount of time devoted to learning certain tasks, skills, or concepts. They instruct the student in how to learn, in addition to what to learn.

7. *The degree to which sufficient time is allocated to academics, and instructional time is used efficiently.* Effective teachers recognize that time is a valuable teaching resource over which they exercise considerable control. These teachers work to increase student achievement by increasing the amount of time students are actively engaged in learning or by decreasing the amount of time students need to learn. They allocate sufficient time to instruction, use effective instructional procedures, and ensure that students are successfully engaged in academically relevant tasks.

8. *The degree to which the student's opportunity to learn is high.* Effective teachers provide frequent opportunities for students to respond. They interact frequently with students. They provide prompts or cues that lead the student to a correct response. They carefully sequence instruction to maintain high rates of accuracy. They use such teaching procedures as choral response, peer tutoring, and cooperative learning to increase students' opportunities to respond. Finally, they ensure that all students have an equal opportunity to participate.

To check your understanding of this chapter, go to the companion website at http://www.prenhall.com/beirne-smith and select Chapter 10, and then choose the Self-Test module.

9. *The degree to which the teacher actively monitors student progress and understanding.* Effective teachers use frequent and active monitoring of student progress. In addition to asking for a response to questions, they ask the students to demonstrate and describe how they perform the task. They scan the classroom frequently to monitor students' attention to task.

10. *The degree to which student performance is evaluated appropriately and frequently.* Effective teachers use frequent evaluation and ensure that the evaluation is congruent with what is taught. These teachers use data from their evaluations to make teaching decisions about the needs of individual students and what to teach next.

Summary

Individuals with Disabilities Act (IDEA)

- The IDEA has stressed, since its onset, that all students with disabilities are entitled to a free, appropriate education in the least restrictive environment.
- The most recent amendments to the law, which occurred in 1997, strengthened the fundamental provisions of the law.
- A major theme that evolved out of the recent amendments was the relationship of a student's program to the general education curriculum.

Educational Environment Options

- School-identified students with mental retardation are served in a variety of settings.
- The most common placement is in a special education setting outside the general education classroom.
- Relatively few students are in general education classrooms for the greater part of their instructional day.
- The number of students served in separate facilities remains low; however, this practice does still occur.
- The use of various placement options varies greatly from state to state.

Assessment and Program Planning

- Obtaining useful assessment information for the purpose of program planning is critically important.
- Comprehensive assessment is essential to the development and ultimate implementation of appropriate special education programs.
- Recent amendments to the IDEA clearly specify the membership of the IEP team.
- Required components have changed as a result of the recent amendments.

Programming for School-Age Learners

- Key elements of effective instruction should be characteristic of interventions.
- Educational programs for students who are mentally retarded involve a number of interrelated and mutually influencing factors.

- Curricular considerations in planning educational programs for students with mental retardation are very important.
- Ten instructional variables should be considered in designing effective programs.

References

American Association on Mental Retardation. (1992). *Mental retardation: Definition, classification, and systems of supports* (9th ed.). Washington, DC: Author.

Armstrong, D. G. (1990). *Developing and documenting the curriculum*. Boston: Allyn & Bacon.

Baker, J. M., & Zigmond, N. (1995). The meaning and practice of inclusion for students with learning disabilities: Themes and implications from the five cases. *Journal of Special Education, 29*(2), 163–180.

Beirne-Smith, M. (1991). Peer tutoring in arithmetic for children with learning disabilities. *Exceptional Children, 57,* 330–337.

Bigge, J. L., Stump, C. S., Spagna, M. E., & Silberman, R. K. (1999). *Curriculum, Assessment, and Instruction for Students with Disabilitiies*. Belmont, CA: Wadsworth.

Chalfant, J. C., & Pysh, M. V. (1989). Teacher assistance teams: Five descriptive studies of 96 teams. *Remedial and Special Education, 19*(6), 49–58.

Christenson, S. L., Ysseldyke, J. E., & Thurlow, M. L. (1989). Critical instructional factors for students with mild handicaps: An integrative review. *Remedial and Special Education, 10*(5), 21–31.

Deno, S. L., & Mirkin, P. K. (1980). Data based IEP development: An approach to substantive compliance. *Teaching Exceptional Children, 12,* 92–97.

Fuchs, D., Fuchs, L. S., & Bahr, M. W. (1990). Mainstream assistance teams: A scientific basis for the art of consultation. *Exceptional Children, 57,* 128–139.

Glass, G. V. (1983). Effectiveness of special education. *Policy Studies Review, 2* (Special No. 1), 65–78.

Guterman, B. R. (1995). The validity of categorical learning disabilities services: The consumer's view. *Exceptional Children, 62,* 112–124.

Hallahan, D. P., Keller, C. E., McKinney, J. D., Lloyd, J. W., & Bryan, T. (1988). Examining the research base of the regular education initiative: Efficacy studies and the adaptive learning environment model. *Journal of Learning Disabilities, 21,* 29–35.

Hoover, J. J., & Patton, J. R. (1997). *Curriculum adaptations for students with learning and behavior problems: Principles and practices*. Austin, TX: PRO-ED.

Idol, L., Nevin, A., & Paolucci-Whitcomb, P. (1999). *Models of curriculum-based assessment: A blueprint for learning* (3rd ed.). Austin: PRO-ED.

Jenkins, M. W. (1987). Effect of a computerized individual education program (IEP) writer on time savings and quality. *Journal of Special Education, 8*(3), 55–66.

Kauffman, J. M. (1987). Research in special education: A commentary. *Remedial and Special Education, 85*(6), 57–62.

Keogh, B. K. (1988). Improving services for problem learners. Rethinking and restructuring. *Journal of Learning Disabilities, 21,* 19–22.

Keogh, B. K. (1990). Narrowing the gap between policy and practice. *Exceptional Children, 57,* 186–190.

Knackendofel, E. A., Robinson, S. M., Deshler, D. D., & Schumaker, J. B. (1992). *Collaborative problem solving.* Lawrence, KS: Edge Enterprises.

Lilly, S. M. (1986). The relationship between good general and special education: A new face on an old issue. *Counterpoint, 10,* 1.

McKinney, J. D., & Hocutt, A. M. (1988). Policy issues in the evaluation of the Regular Education Initiative. *Learning Disabilities Focus, 4*(1), 15–23.

Mercer, C. D. (1991). *Students with learning disabilities* (4th ed.). Upper Saddle River, NJ: Merrill/Prentice Hall.

Mercer, C. D., & Mercer, A. P. (1997). *Teaching students with learning problems* (5th ed.). Upper Saddle, NJ: Merrill/Prentice-Hall.

Morgan, D. P., & Rhode, G. (1983). Teachers' attitudes toward IEPs: A two-year follow-up. *Exceptional Children, 50,* 64–67.

Mueller, D. J., Chase, C. I., & Walden, J. D. (1988). Effects of reduced class size in primary classes. *Educational Leadership, 45*(5), 48–50.

Nolley, D., & Nolley, B. (1984). Microcomputer data analysis at a clinical mental retardation site. *Mental Retardation, 22,* 85–89.

Pickett, A. L., & Gerlach, K. (Eds.). (1997). *Supervising paraeducators in school settings.* Austin, TX: PRO-ED.

Polloway, E. A., Patton, J. R., & Serna, L. (2001). *Strategies for teaching learners with special needs* (7th ed.). Upper Saddle River, NJ: Merrill/Prentice Hall.

Polloway, E. A., Smith, J. D., Patton, J. R., & Smith, T. E. C. (1996). Historical changes in mental retardation and developmental disabilities. *Education and Training in Mental Retardation and Developmental Disabilities, 31,* 3–12.

Pugach, M. C., & Johnson, L. J. (1989). Preferral interventions: Progress, problems, and challenges. *Exceptional Challenges, 56,* 217–226.

Reynolds, M. C. (1989). A historical perspective: The delivery of special education to mildly disabled and at-risk students. *Remedial and Special Education,* 19(6), 7–11.

Salend, S. J., & Duhaney, L. M. (1999). The impact of inclusion on students with and without disabilities and their educators. *Remedial and Special Education, 20,* 114–126.

Schumaker, J. B., & Deshler, D. D. (1988). Implementing the regular education initiative in secondary schools: A different ball game. *Journal of Learning Disabilities, 21,* 36–42.

Semmel, M. A., Abernathy, T. V., Butera, G., & Lesat, S. (1991). Teacher perceptions of the regular education initiatives. *Exceptional Children, 58,* 9–24.

Showers, B. (1985). Teachers coaching teachers. *Educational Leadership, 42*(7), 789–797.

Skrtic, T. M. (1991). The special education paradox: Equity as a way to excellence. *Harvard Educational Review, 61*(2), 148–206.

Smith, D. W., & Wells, M. W. (1983). Use of a microcomputer to assist staff in documenting resident progress. *Mental Retardation, 21,* 111–115.

Smith, S. W. (1990). Individualized Education Programs (IEPs) in special education—From intent to acquiescence. *Exceptional Children, 57,* 6–14.

Smith, T. E. C., Polloway, E. A., Patton, J. R., & Dowdy, C. (2001). *Teaching students with special needs in inclusive settings* (3rd ed.). Boston: Allyn & Bacon.

Spring, J. H. (1986). *The American School 1642–1985.* New York: Longman.

Sugai, G. (1985). Case study: Designing instruction from IEPs. *Teaching Exceptional Children, 17,* 239.

Turnbull, H. R., & Turnbull, A. P. (1998). *Free appropriate public education: The law and children with disabilities* (5th ed.). Denver: Love.

U.S. Department of Education. (2000). *Twenty-second annual report to Congress on the implementation of the Individuals with Disabilities Education Act.* Washington, DC: Author.

West, J. F., Idol, L., & Cannon, G. (1989). *Collaboration in the schools.* Austin, TX: PRO-ED.

Wiederholt, J. L., & Chamberlain, S. P. (1989). A critical analysis of resource programs. *Remedial and Special Education, 10*(6), 15–27.

Will, M. C. (1984). *OSERS programming for the transition of youth with disabilities: Bridges from school to working life.* Washington., DC: U.S. Department of Education, Office of Special Education and Rehabilitative Services.

11

Transitional Years: Preparing for Adulthood

 To review the chapter objectives on-line, go to the companion website at http://www.prenhall.com/beirne-smith and select Chapter 11, and then choose the Objectives module.

OBJECTIVES

After reading this chapter, the student should be able to

- list the goals of transitional planning
- compare and contrast career education and vocational education
- define transition services
- list the models of transition programs
- identify the types of vocational options available to students with disabilities

KEY TERMS

career development

job coach

life skills

natural supports

supported employment

transition education

transition services

vocational education

Human beings experience different types of transitions throughout life. These changes from one stage of life to another may involve education, work, and personal relationships (Ysseldyke, Algozzine, & Thurlow, 1992). In this chapter, we explore the concept of transition as related to the preparation for the multifaceted demands of adulthood. Some transitions are normative and predictable; others are time- or situation-specific and may not apply to everyone. Transitions typically involve a number of changes and require comprehensive planning.

BASIC CONCEPTS OF TRANSITION

To learn more about transition planning, go to the companion website at *www.prenhall.com/ beirne-smith* and select Chapter 11, then choose the Web Destinations module.

Comprehensive transition planning, which involves assessing needs, developing individual plans, carrying out the plans, and involving key personnel from the receiving environments, is necessary to best prepare individuals for the subsequent settings in which they will find themselves (Patton & Dunn, 1998). Transition planning and services are needed to help students with disabilities reach their fullest potential as adults. Halpern (1994), in a position paper approved by the Division on Career Development and Transition (DCDT) of the Council for Exceptional Children, refers to transition as

> a change in status from behaving primarily as a student to assuming emergent adult roles in the community. These roles include employment, participating in post-secondary education, maintaining a home, becoming appropriately involved in the community, and experiencing satisfactory personal and social relationships. The process of enhancing transition involves the participation and coordination of school programs, adult agency services, and natural supports within the community. The foundations for transition should be laid during the elementary and middle school years, guided by the broad concept of career development. Transition planning should begin no later than age 14, and students should be encouraged, to the full extent of their capabilities, to assume a minimum amount of responsibility for such planning. (p. 117)

A number of critical points are evident in this definitional perspective. First, individuals must be prepared for a number of different adult roles—of which employment is only one. Second, cooperation and communication are essential for this process to work. Third, transition efforts (instruction and planning) need to begin at an early age. The instructional aspect of this point, discussed in the previous chapter and addressed thoroughly by Clark, Carlson, Fisher, Cook, and D'Alonzo (1991), suggests that the precursors of transition planning and services should start at the elementary level. Furthermore, the comprehensive planning piece must begin many years before the student exits the school system. Fourth, a major effort needs to be made to empower students to become key players in their own transition-planning process.

The transition-planning process is, at its core, a shared responsibility of the school, the home, the student, and adult service providers. The process, if implemented appropriately, should lead to (a) the acquisition of important knowledge and skills and (b) the linkage to essential supports and services in the community—all of which contribute to assisting the individual to deal with the challenges and the demands of everyday life. Ultimately, if this outcome is achieved, the individual

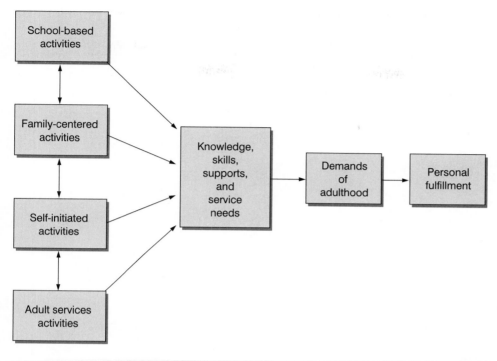

FIGURE 11.1
Adulthood Implications of the Transition Process

Source: From *Transition from School Young Adulthood: Basic Concepts and Recommended Practices* (p. 5), by J. R. Patton and C. Dunn, 1998, Austin, TX: PRO-ED. Reprinted by permission.

is likely to experience some sense of personal fulfillment. This process is graphically represented in Figure 11.1.

The concept of transition planning and services continues to evolve. Early transition initiatives, as promulgated by the Office of Special Education and Rehabilitative Services (OSERS) in Will's (1984) document, focused mainly on moving students from school to employment. Halpern (1985) brought professional attention to a more expanded notion of transition that included consideration of one's living environment and the adequacy of one's social and interpersonal networks. More recently, the critical areas of transition have broadened even further, as evidenced in the list of adult domains, on which transition planning should be based, presented in Figure 11.2.

The Federal Mandate for Transition

The 1990 Individual with Disabilities Act (IDEA, PL 101-476) mandated that a statement of transition services be included on a student's individualized education program (IEP) beginning no later than age 16. The IDEA defined **transition services** as

[a] coordinated set of activities for a student, designed within an outcome-oriented process, which promotes movement from school to post-school activities, including

Major domain	AL	AR	CA	CO	CT	FL	HI	IA	ID	IL	KS	KY	LA	MN	NJ	TX	UT
Adult services				*	*	*				*		*			*		
Advocacy/legal	*								*				*				
Assistive technology												*					
Career planning options									*								
Communication												*					*
Community participation	*			*	*	*	*		*	*	*	*	*	*	*		*
Daily living (including domestic areas)		*		*	*		*	*	*		*	*		*	*		*
Employment (including workplace readiness and specific job skills)	*	*	*					*	*	*	*	*	*		*	*	*
Financial/income/money management	*		*		*		*	*	*		*	*	*				
Functional academics															*		
Health (including medical services)	*			*	*		*	*	*		*	*	*		*		*
Independent living (including living arrangements)	*	*	*		*	*			*	*	*	*	*	*	*	*	*
Insurance									*		*						
Leisure/recreation		*	*	*	*		*	*	*		*	*	*	*	*	*	*
Lifelong learning								*									
Personal management	*																
Postsecondary education		*	*	*	*	*	*		*	*	*	*	*		*	*	*
Relationships/social skills			*	*	*				*	*	*	*	*		*		*
Self-determination/self-advocacy				*					*	*	*	*		*			*
Transportation/mobility	*	*		*	*		*	*	*		*	*	*	*	*		
Vocational evaluation	*																
Vocational training			*		*	*	*	*		*				*	*	*	*

FIGURE 11.2
Transition Planning Areas

Source: From *Transition Planning Inventory* by G. M. Clark and J. R. Patton, 1997, Austin, TX: PRO-ED, Inc. Copyright 1997 by PRO-ED, Inc. Reprinted by permission.

post-secondary education, vocational training, integrated employment (including supported employment), continuing and adult education, adult services, independent living, or community participation. The coordinated set of activities shall be based upon the individual student's needs, taking into account the student's preferences and interests, and shall include instruction, community experiences, the development of employment and other post-school adult living objectives, and, when appropriate, acquisition of daily living skills and functional vocational evaluation. (20 USC 1401 [a] [19])

The IDEA was reauthorized in 1997 by the 105th Congress (PL 105-17). While maintaining the basic tenets of the 1990 transition mandate, the law now requires inclusion of a statement of transition needs of the student under the applicable components of the student's IEP that focus on the student's courses of study. This statement must be in place by age 14 and updated annually, with the purpose of focusing attention on the student's educational needs. This statement precedes the statement of needed transition services, which must be in place by age 16.

Adult Outcome Data

Obvious reasons, as highlighted earlier, exist to support transition efforts. However, other compelling reasons have influenced the need for such activities. The following discussion focuses on the adult outcomes and functional competence of individuals with mental retardation who had been in special education for substantial periods of their school careers.

A significant factor, which drew much professional attention in the early days of the transition movement, was the data generated from various adult outcomes studies conducted in the late 1980s and early 1990s. These studies substantiated a rather bleak picture of unemployment, long-term underemployment for those individuals with jobs, minimal participation in postsecondary education—with even bleaker completion rates, few individuals living independent lives, limited social lives, and little community involvement (Hasazi, Gordon, & Roe, 1985; Mithaug, Horiuchi, Fanning, 1985). This picture of adult outcomes has been reinforced by later studies (Sitlington, Frank, & Carson, 1992; Wagner et al., 1991).

The curricular emphases of the educational programs of students with mental retardation provided another point of concern. Teachers have identified the need for functionally oriented curricula as an important way to improve instruction for students with disabilities at the secondary level (Halpern & Benz, 1987). The importance of functional curricula has also been recognized and championed by the Division on Career Development and Transition (Clark, Field, Patton, Brolin, & Sitlington, 1994).

Another way to examine how well curricular efforts are developing everyday living skills is the information provided by parents related to how they perceived the functional abilities of their sons and daughters. Wagner and colleagues (1993) collected data on this topic across disability areas; their findings are provided in Table 11.1. In looking at the data for individuals with mental retardation, it is startling to note that a substantial percentage of this group, as perceived by parents, do not demonstrate adequate functional abilities in the areas of self-care skills (67.4%), functional mental skills (32.8%), and community living skills (29.4%). It is important to understand the distinctions among the different types of skills being reported in this table, as described in the footnotes. Nevertheless, most professionals would agree that (a) these skills are important for dealing successfully with the demands of adulthood, (b) these skills should be taught in school, and (c) proficiency should be demonstrated prior to students exiting the system.

Sense of Perspective

From Edouard Seguin in the 1850s, to Richard Hungerford in the 1940s, to the present professional focus on transition to adulthood, practitioners in the field of

TABLE 11.1
Functional Abilities by Disability Category

Disability category	Percentage of youth with parents reporting		
	High self-care skills[a]	High functional mental skills[b]	High community-living skills[c]
All conditions	86.4	56.9	61.4
Learning disaabled	95.5	66.0	74.2
Emotionally disturbed	94.1	65.3	66.9
Speech impaired	91.8	68.9	67.3
Mentally retarded	67.4	32.8	29.4
Visually impaired	51.6	31.8	41.2
Deaf	83.4	44.3	43.4
Hard of hearing	92.3	60.7	45.8
Orthopedically impaired	42.3	50.5	32.5
Other health impaired	65.3	57.3	41.2
Multiply handicapped	34.5	12.8	21.3
Deaf/blind	21.0	6.8	13.2

[a]Skills include dressing oneself, feeding oneself, and getting around outside the home. Scale ranges from 3 to 12. High is 12.

[b]Skills include counting change, reading comon signs, telling time on an analog clock, and looking up telephone numbers and using the phone. Scale ranges from 4 to 16. High is 15 or 16.

[c]Skills include using public transportation, buying clothes, arranging a trip out of town, and using community resources, such as a swimming pool and/or library. Scale ranges from 4 to 16. High is 15 or 16.

Source: From *The Transition Experiences of Young People with Disabilities: A Summary of Findings from the National Longitudinal Study of Special Education Students,* by M. Wagner, J. Blackorby, R. Cameto, K. Hebbeler, and L. Newman, 1993, Menlo Park, CA: SRI International. Reprinted by permission.

mental retardation have recognized the need to prepare each student to be a contributing member of society. Seguin firmly stated that occupational preparation should have a place in educational programs. A century later, Hungerford outlined a comprehensive program of vocational education. His program, entitled "Occupational Education," was designed to build vocational and social competence skills. The program included occupational education, vocational training, and vocational placements (Hungerford, DeProspo, & Rosenzweig, 1948).

Professionals in special education, general education, and vocational education, whether optimistic or pessimistic about career programming for individuals who are mentally retarded, need to move forward in the development of stronger career preparation programs that prepare such individuals to be gainfully employed and to fit naturally into their communities. Today, many practitioners are seeking to provide more realistic vocational training for students who are mentally retarded, to integrate them into regular vocational education training programs, and to assist them in making a successful transition from school to work.

In this chapter, we focus on those transitional issues pertinent to the transition and vocational education of individuals with mental retardation. The next section examines the concept of transition education, including topics such as career education and life skills preparation. The subsequent section discusses specific aspects of the transition planning process, with primary emphasis on assessing transition needs and developing transition plans. Finally, we close by discussing various aspects of vocational preparation.

AAMR Policy Position on Self-Determination

The issue of "self-determination" is attracting much professional attention. Including persons with mental retardation in making important decisions about their lives is essential from a personal dignity perspective. The following policy position of the American Association on Mental Retardation underscores the importance of this topic.

Call for Action

The international, national, state, and local development and support of groups that provide opportunities for individuals with disabilities to advocate for themselves.

Background

In the mid-1970s, people with developmental disabilities began to advocate for recognition and acceptance of their ability to speak for themselves when making decisions affecting their lives. The self-advocacy movement is now an international movement.

The definition of self-advocacy is speaking for oneself, making decisions about one's life, participating on decision-making bodies, learning and exercising the full rights and responsibilities of citizenship, and participating in and contributing to the community.

Self-advocates continue to struggle with the low expectations of professionals, parents, and the public.

Principles

People with disabilities must be present and involved when decisions are being made about their lives.

Instrumental assistance may be needed before and during meetings.

Training and support in how the system works are needed for people who are not members of self-advocacy organizations.

Independent thinking must be encouraged.

Professionals must raise their expectations of people with disabilities.

Actions Proposed

- Publish information on effective efforts to support individual choice and decision making.
- Encourage individuals with disabilities to participate in presentations at conferences, including soliciting presentations from self-advocates.
- Plan to include and support the participation of people with disabilities in decision making bodies of the Association.
- Explore establishing an affordable membership fee for people with disabilities and reach out to self-advocacy organizations to facilitate membership recruitment.
- Encourage research concerning self-advocacy and self-determination.
- Explore the possibility of people with disabilities developing an oral history.
- Support developing self-advocacy groups that provide opportunities for individuals with disabilities to speak for themselves.
- Support forming a national network of self-advocacy organizations.

TRANSITION EDUCATION

The concept of **transition education** is used in this book as an umbrella term to describe all education-related activities, particularly in the areas of curriculum and instruction, which correspond with and prepare students for the demands of adulthood. Transition education includes knowledge acquisition and skill development across a number of important areas: academic skills, academic support skills (i.e., study skills), social/personal behaviors, life skills, self-determination, career development, and vocational preparation. All are important; however, some important topics are often not addressed. Patton, Cronin, and Jairrels (1997) point out this oversight: "consideration of specific content that must be taught to maximize stu-

For a complete on-line glossary of mental retardation terms, go to the companion website at http://www.prenhall.com/beirne-smith and select any chapter, and then choose the Glossary module.

dents' chances for successfully dealing with the demands of adulthood and methods for teaching this content have been largely overlooked" (p. 299).

Transition education is even more than the sum of these elements, because it is the unifying vehicle for ensuring that an individual has more than an even chance to become a contributing member of society. A number of models are available for describing the critical elements of what has been introduced as transition education (see Table 11.2). All models stress that transition education must include coverage of topics that prepares students for a range of adult roles and situations for which a host of competencies are needed. Two particular components of transition education, career development and life skills preparation, are discussed in more detail in the following sections.

Career Development

Career development for all students became a national priority in 1971, when U.S. Commissioner of Education Sidney P. Marland called attention to the insufficient preparation of our nation's youth for careers after completion of high school. Marland (1971) made three basic points:

TABLE 11.2
Career Education and Life Skills Education Models

Source	Major components
Life-Centered Career Education (LCCE) (Brolin, 1991)	Three major areas: • Daily living • Personal-social • Occupational guidance and preparation
School-Based Career Development and Transition Education Model (Clark & Kolstoe, 1990)	Four major areas: • Values, attitudes, and habits • Human relationships • Occupational information • Acquisition of job and daily living skills
Hawaii Transition Project (1987)	Four major areas: • Vocation/education • Home and family • Recreation/leisure • Community/citizenship
Community-Referenced Curriculum (Smith & Schloss, 1988)	Five major areas: • Work • Leisure and play • Consumer • Education and rehabilitation • Transportation
Community Living Skills Taxonomy (Dever, 1988)	Five major areas: • Personal maintenance and development • Homemaking and community life • Vocational • Leisure • Travel

1. All students need career education, whether they will work immediately after school ends or go to college.
2. Career education should occur throughout the individual's educational career, starting in kindergarten and continuing into adulthood.
3. Career education is meant to give the individual a start in making a living.

Nature of Career Development *Career development* and *vocational education* are not synonymous; career development has a broader meaning. According to the Division on Career Development and Transition of the Council for Exceptional Children, career development involves the preparation of the individual for the roles of student, worker, family member, and citizen. A multifaceted approach, which includes teaching, counseling, and community intervention, is used to facilitate career development. Career development and vocational education both accept the idea that schools are supposed to prepare students for participation in the larger society, but they differ in their interpretation of this idea.

TABLE 11.2 (continued)
Career Education and Life Skills Education Models

Source	Major components
Life Problems of Adulthood (Knowles, 1990)	Six major areas: • Vocation and career • Home and family living • Enjoyment of leisure • Community living • Health • Personal development
Domains of Adulthood (Cronin & Patton, 1993)	Six major areas: • Employment/education • Home and family • Leisure pursuits • Community involvement • Physical/emotional health • Personal responsibility and relationships
Post-School Outcomes Model (National Center on Educational Outcomes, 1993)	Seven major areas • Presence and participation • Physical health • Responsibility and independence • Contribution and citizenship • Academic and functional literacy • Personal and social adjustment • Satisfaction
Quality of Life Domains (Halpern, 1993)	Three major areas: • Physical and material well-being • Performance of adult roles • Personal fulfillment

Source: From "Transition to Living: The Neglected Components of Transition Programming for Individuals with Learning Disabilities" by P. L. Sitlington, 1996, *Journal of Learning Disabilities, 29,* p. 35. Reprinted by permission.

Vocational educators attempt to prepare students to enter the job market as competent, employable wage earners. To this end, vocational education focuses on the high school student who will soon be seeking full-time employment. Vocational educators perform such functions as assessing students' work potential, helping the workers-to-be explore different work possibilities in their community and arranging a number of trial work experiences through which to identify their preferences. Career educators, on the other hand, see preparing students for participation in adult life as their mission and emphasize that career development extends from the elementary grades through secondary school level.

Although most elementary pupils at some point discuss different kinds of jobs and the workers who do them, these discussions have typically been a matter of happenstance instead of a part of a predetermined curricular plan. Such discussions—at whatever school level—should become a required part of the curriculum. Thus, students can be continually exposed to different careers as they move up to higher grades. Career education also helps youngsters see how such basic subjects as reading and mathematics will enable them to succeed at certain jobs or functions in their communities.

Career Development for Students with Mental Retardation Since the goals of career development are appropriate for all students, career goals for students who are mentally retarded should be similar to goals for those who are not. However, the nature of these goals may vary as a function of each individual's general and specific characteristics. Individuals whose need for support is minor or nonexistent should be capable of independent living as adults. Those individuals who have greater needs for support in school and into adulthood may have more select options and may require various levels and types of support from others to achieve appropriate levels of success. However, the major goals remain operative.

Research on the community and postschool adjustment of individuals who are mentally retarded strongly supports the need for career development for these students. The information on the postschool adjustment discussed in a previous section indicates that persons with mental retardation have varying degrees of success in adjusting to life following school. Generally, though, most studies indicate that adults, even those who are transitioning from segregated institutional settings, can adapt to community life if given proper training supports and services.

Without question, adults who are mentally retarded are capable of being successful workers and making successful community adjustments. Being a successful worker and functioning successfully in the community are consequences of learned behaviors. We can analyze these learned behaviors in terms of the skills and knowledge needed for successful functioning and teach them as part of a comprehensive career education program.

Individuals who have extensive needs can likewise make successful adjustments to society and become contributing members of their communities. For example, workers with moderate and severe retardation have been successfully placed in competitive employment settings, performing such jobs as kitchen utility worker, porter, elevator operator, dishwasher, groundskeeper, janitor, and assembly-line worker.

The key to the success of competitive employment for individuals who need significant levels of support appears to be appropriate training and ongoing job assistance. Rusch (1983) recommends that training include a survey-train-place-train model. Using this model, the job counselor would "(a) survey potential employers to determine important skills that need to be trained, (b) train students to perform these skills, (c) place trained clients in nonsheltered settings, and (d) provide long-term follow-up training" (p. 503).

Although programs differ in the type of ongoing work support provided, Bellamy and Horner (1987) note that successful programs usually have four common elements: (a) use of systematic approaches to training and maintaining work behaviors; (b) focus on work opportunity over work preparation; (c) emphasis on social integration with coworkers, customers, and others in the workplace; and (d) definition of program success in terms of wages and work benefits. These authors also note that ongoing support in the form of retraining, contingency management (management based on behavior), and crisis intervention may be needed for some workers who are mentally retarded for as long as they are employed.

Life Skills Preparation

To prepare students for the challenges that will face them when they leave school, efforts must be focused on teaching them **life skills** that will facilitate their inclusion as contributing members of their communities and their successful adjustment to adulthood. The major functional domains of adulthood in which all of us must demonstrate some level of competence are represented in Figure 11.3.

Two important elements are crucial to providing life skills content to students: (a) identification of appropriate life skills that are locally referenced and culturally appropriate and (b) provisions for covering appropriate skills within existing curricular options. Cronin and Patton (1993) suggest a "top-down" strategy for identify-

FIGURE 11.3
Functional Demands of Adulthood

Source: From *Life Skills Instruction for Students with Special Needs: A Practical Guide for Integrating Real Life Content into the Curriculum* (p. 13), by M. E. Cronin and J. R. Patton, 1993, Austin, TX: PRO-ED. Copyright 1993 by PRO-ED. Reprinted by permission.

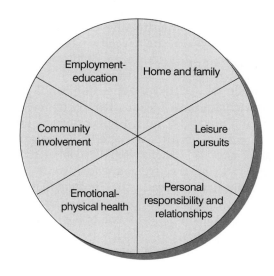

TABLE 11.3
Models of Adult Functioning

Model	Adult domain/ curriculum area	Subdomains/ competency areas
Domains of Adulthood (Cronin & Patton, 1993)	Employment/ education	General job skills General education/training considerations Employment setting Career refinement and re-evaluation
	Home and family	Home management Financial management Family life Childrearing
	Leisure pursuits	Indoor activities Outdoor activities Community/neighborhood activities Travel Entertainment
	Community involvement	Citizenship Community awareness Services/resources
	Physical/emotional health	Physical health Emotional health
	Personal responsibliity and relationships	Personal confidence/understanding Goal setting Self-improvement Relationships Personal expression

ing appropriate life skills. This system requires that the process of curriculum development begin by examining likely adult outcomes and then working down to specific life skills that are needed to deal successfully with these adult demands. Ultimately, these life skills must be addressed in the curriculum.

Demands of Adulthood A number of sources provide taxonomies of adulthood demands. One source for identifying major life demands is the Life-Centered Career Education (LCCE) model developed by Brolin (1997). The LCCE model identifies 22 major competencies and 97 accompanying subcompetencies, organized into three domains (daily living, personal or social, and occupational) that are necessary to function effectively in school, family, and community roles.

Another source is the Major Life Demands model developed by Cronin and Patton (1993). This model is organized according to six adult domains (see Figure 11.3), 23 subdomains, and 147 major life demands. Table 11.3 provides an overview of these two models.

The competencies and subcompetencies used by Brolin (1991), the list of major life demands developed by Cronin and Patton (1993), and the life skill topics that can be found in other sources tend to correlate with one another. One resource is

TABLE 11.3 (continued)
Models of Adult Functioning

Model	Adult domain/ curriculum area	Subdomains/ competency areas
Life Centered Career Education (Brolin, 1997)	Daily living skills	Managing personal finances
		Selecting and managing a household
		Caring for personal needs
		Raising children and meeting marriage responsibilities
		Buying, preparing, and consuming food
		Buying and caring for clothing
		Exhibiting responsible citizenship
		Utilizing recreational facilities and engaging in leisure
		Getting around the community
	Personal-social skills	Achieving self-awareness
		Acquiring self-confidence
		Achieving socially responsible behavior
		Maintaining good interpersonal skills
		Achieving independence
		Making adequate decisions
		Communicating with others
	Occupational guidance and preparation	Knowing and exploring occupational possibilities
		Selecting and planning occupational choices
		Exhibiting appropriate work habits and behavior
		Seeking, securing, and maintaining employment
		Exhibiting sufficient physical-manual skills
		Obtaining specific occupational skills

Source: From *Infusing Real-Life Topics into Existing Curricula at the Elementary, Middle, and High School Levels: Recommended Procedures and Instructional Examples* (p. 3), by J. R. Patton, M. E. Cronin, and S. Wood, 1999, Austin, TX: PRO-ED. Reprinted by permission.

not necessarily any better than another; they all represent valid efforts to assist practitioners in developing meaningful programs for students.

Instructional Considerations Life skills instruction can occur in any educational placement. The extent of content coverage can vary from the development of a set of life skills courses to infusion of life skills topics into the content covered in a general education course. Examples of how to integrate life skills into existing curricular content can be found elsewhere (Patton, Cronin, & Wood, 1999).

The relationship between the skills/competencies that are associated with effective schooling and the adult domains presented earlier is important to recognize. As can be seen in Table 11.4, these scholastic and social skills can relate closely to the demands of community living. For example, under the domain of emotional

TABLE 11.4
Secondary Matrix: Relationship of Scholastic/Social Skills to Adult Domains

	Employment education	Home and family	Leisure pursuits	Community involvement	Emotional–physical health	Personal responsibility relationships
Reading	Reading classified ads for jobs	Interpreting bills	Locating and understanding movie information in a newspaper	Following directions on tax forms	Comprehending directions on medication	Reading letters from friends
Writing	Writing a letter of application for a job	Writing checks	Writing for information on a city to visit	Filling in a voter registration form	Filling in your medical history on forms	Sending thank you notes
Listening	Understanding oral directions of a procedure change	Comprehending directions	Listening to a weather forecast to plan an outdoor activity	Understanding campaign ads	Attending lectures on stress	Taking turns in a conversation
Speaking	Asking your boss for a raise	Discussing morning routines with family	Inquiring about tickets for a concert	Stating your opinion at the school board meeting	Describing symptoms to a doctor	Giving feedback to a friend
Math applications	Understanding difference between net and gross pay	Computing the cost of doing laundry in a laundromat versus home	Calculating the cost of a dinner out versus eating at home	Obtaining information for a building permit	Using a thermometer	Planning the costs of a date
Problem-solving	Settling a dispute with a co-worker	Deciding how much to budget for rent	Role-playing appropriate behaviors for various places	Knowing what to do if you are the victim of fraud	Selecting a doctor	Deciding how to ask someone for a date
Survival skills	Using a prepared career-planning packet	Listing emergency phone numbers	Using a shopping-center directory	Marking a calendar for important dates (e.g., recycling, garbage collection)	Using a system to remember to take vitamins	Developing a system to remember birthdays
Personal-social	Applying appropriate interview skills	Helping a child with homework	Knowing the rules of a neighborhood pool	Locating self-improvement classes	Getting a yearly physical exam	Discussing how to negotiate a price at the flea market

Source: From *Life Skills Instruction for Students with Special Needs: A Practical Guide for Integrating Real Life Content into the Curriculum* (p. 33) by M. E. Cronin and J. R. Patton, 1993, Austin, TX: PRO-ED. Copyright 1993 by PRO-ED. Reprinted by permission.

and physical health, reading skills are needed to comprehend directions for taking medications. All the scholastic/social skill areas (reading, writing, listening, speaking, math applications, problem solving, survival skills, and personal-social skills) have practical applications and are fundamentally a part of life skills preparation.

TRANSITION PLANNING

Prior to the enactment of the IDEA, local educational agency personnel had begun to recognize the need to prepare students who were mentally retarded more comprehensively for life after high school. The literature had documented this need (Rusch & Phelps, 1987), and according to Will (1984), planning for the postschool adjustment of students with disabilities had already been targeted nationally as a top priority. It should be noted that in 1991 six national goals for education were published (see Figure 1.2). One of these goals is focused on such postschool outcomes as adult literacy and the ability of an individual to function successfully and to assume the responsibilities of citizenship.

The goal of transitional planning is to ensure that a plan for postschool adjustment exists that includes the teaching of requisite skills and establishing a support network before the student exits school. This process depends on the development of a separate individual transition plan or IEP that includes a transition plan, depending on the state in which a student resides.

As previously mentioned, the prospect of adjustment by adolescents who are mentally retarded to the world of work and community living depends greatly on how well various transition activities occur. The cooperative efforts of local education personnel, vocational rehabilitation counselors, postsecondary education staff, other adult service providers, and various community agencies that assist such young adults are vital to this transition process.

The IDEA requires that a statement of transition needs be developed by age 14 for all students in special education and a statement of transition services be in place by age 16. As expected, great variability is found across states in terms of the quality and comprehensiveness of assessing needs and generating transition goals.

The transition planning process involves a progression of activities (see Figure 11.4). The process begins with an explicit system of transition education, includes a mechanism for assessing a student's transition strengths and needs, and leads to the development of transition goals (instructional and linkage). Sometimes, a need for more in-depth information is needed that necessitates conducting further assessment, as noted in Figure 11.4.

Assessing Transition Needs

A variety of techniques yields information that can be useful for transition planning. Certain instruments, however, have been developed specifically for assessing transition-related areas. Some of these include the *Enderle-Severson Transition Rating Scales—Revised* (Enderle & Severson, 1997), *LCCE Knowledge Battery* (Brolin, 1992), *Life Skills Inventory* (Brigance, 1995), *Transition Behavior Scale* (2nd ed.; McCarney, 2000), and *Transition Planning Inventory* (Clark & Patton, 1997). For a more in-depth discussion of transition assessment, see Clark (1998) and Sitlington, Clark, and Kolstoe (2000).

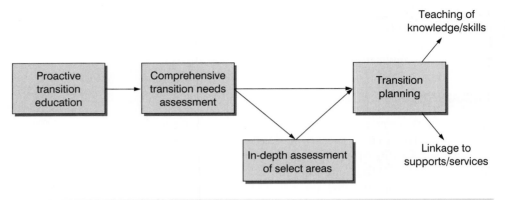

FIGURE 11.4

Transition-Planning Process

Source: Adapted from Patton and Dunn (1998).

Given that the transition process should be predicated on the student's preferences, interests, and needs, it is worthwhile soliciting information about the various transition domains from the student. For this reason, many of the transition instruments noted here request information from the student as well as from school-based personnel and the family. Information gathered through the implementation of a comprehensive transition needs assessment results in the acquisition of data on which postschool planning can be based.

Transition Planning

The actual document where transition plans are located depends on location. Some states (e.g., Texas) require a separate document called an individual transition plan (ITP); other states (e.g., Virginia) incorporate all transition goals within the IEP. The ideal ITP includes the following components: goal statements, present levels of performance, activities that need to be undertaken, time lines for accomplishing the goals, and the individuals who are responsible for carrying out the goal. An example of an ITP for a student with mental retardation appears in the appendix.

The IEP must include a transition needs statement for the student no later than age 14. This is extremely important so that sufficient time can be allocated to coordinate students' programs of studies for the remainder of the high school years so that they can move successfully from school to community living. It is equally important to consider all adult domains and not just the employment/education area.

The importance of empowering individuals with the necessary knowledge, attitude, and skills to make decisions about their current and future lives is being recognized by transition professionals across the country. Along with empowering students, families must also be intricately involved in this process (Wehmeyer, Morningstar, & Husted, 1999). A few notable curricular materials have been published in recent years that have been designed specifically to enable students to be the primary decision maker in their lives (see Field & Hoffman, 1996) and to become actively involved in the transition process (Halpern, Herr, Doren, & Wolf, 2001; Martin & Marshall, 1996).

VOCATIONAL PREPARATION

In this section, we discuss topics concerned with the relationship of career development and vocational preparation, the identification of job opportunities for students who are mentally retarded, traditional and emerging vocational training options, vocational assessment, vocational placement and follow-up, and various programming issues.

To read more about vocational issues, go to the companion website at www.prenhall.com/ beirne-smith, select Chapter 11, then choose the Article Response module.

Essential Elements of Vocational Preparation Programs

Regardless of the model one follows for developing a systematic view of how ultimately to prepare students who are mentally retarded for the world of work, the model chosen must contain several crucial elements. Among those elements are adequate program objectives, provision of counseling services, and a distinct stage for developing specific general job and vocational skills. These elements are not the only ones that can cause a vocational preparation program to succeed or fail, but if one or any combination of them is missing, then the program will be less than optimal. Without clear program objectives, vocational preparation efforts will lack direction. Without counseling services, program participants will not always make the best choices when confronted with career decisions. Lastly, unless students learn a host of general job skills along with some specific entry-level vocational skills, many participants will leave the program without skills that they can put to use.

Developing Program Objectives Analyses of comprehensive vocational preparation programs reveal that program objectives are delineated clearly. While not all programs will have the same objectives, because of differences in students' characteristics, jobs available in the community, and so on, certain objectives should be almost universal. The objective that should lead off any preparation program is the development of a continuing career profile of the student's skills and interests. Because students enter a program with different skill and interest levels, the program coordinator must assess these skills and interests to determine the appropriate beginning training level for each student. For example, if a student is interested in auto mechanics and has already been working in this area, she would probably be placed ahead of others just beginning an auto mechanics training program. As the student moves through the program, the instructor should gather and record additional information that reflects the trainee's changing or developing skills and interests. This information can then be used to motivate the student, as well as to convince employers that she is a desirable job candidate.

A second program objective should be to engage each student in actual or direct paid job experiences and activities. This objective is important because, as the ARC—U.S. has stated, many programs that attempt to train persons who are mentally retarded for different kinds of work have been too academically oriented. As discussed in the previous chapter, although academic skills are important, they should not be emphasized to the neglect of life skills (Polloway, Patton, & Serna, 2001). This oversight can be corrected by allowing the student on-the-job training opportunities, with support services and in any reasonably safe environment, whether it is a typical school or factory.

A third, related objective for all career development/vocational preparation programs is the development of entry-level vocational skills for every student. For this, students work on actual job sites both to learn how to adjust to the demands of the job and fellow workers and to begin building a repertoire of the requisite skills for employment in the particular area of work. For instance, the best way for aspiring cement masons to learn the latest mortaring techniques is to apprentice with a skilled craftsman under whose direction they can handle genuine masonry tools and do the actual cementing. Experiences of this kind are particularly beneficial for students who are mentally retarded.

The fourth important objective of all programs is to provide job placement and follow-up services for students who have completed or will complete the preparation program. Since many of the persons we are concerned with are likely to qualify for services from vocational rehabilitation or other employment-oriented agencies, personnel from those agencies can often provide placement and follow-up services. In other instances, schools may have their own vocational placement facilities. What is important here is to make placement and follow-up one of the goals of vocational preparation programs.

Providing Counseling Services Counseling is another essential ingredient in a vocational preparation program. Rehabilitation counseling is a related service that students with disabilities are entitled to receive under the IDEA. A rehabilitation counseling professional should be knowledgeable about career development, employment preparation, and methods to help the student achieve independence and integration in the community (56 Federal Register, 41, 266, 1991).

Developing Vocational Skills The culminating phase in the vocational training process involves the development of some specific vocational skills. We explore this topic more extensively in the next section, but we give here an overall view of what should take place at this time. First, job availability in the commu-

Career goals are appropriate for all students.

nity should be studied, and present and projected jobs should be analyzed to determine what skills are necessary to perform these jobs. Next, all students should have a thorough vocational evaluation completed to determine aptitudes and abilities. Once this is done, students should be trained on the basis of their present skill level, their interests, and projected job availability. Following training, students should be placed on permanent job sites. Worker and employer should receive follow-up services that identify potential problem areas and provide interventions to ameliorate or minimize the consequences of these problems. Finally, professionals should evaluate the program for how well it has prepared the student for employment and for how well community employment needs have been met.

Identifying Job Opportunities

The success of any vocational preparation program depends to a great extent on the accurate identification of available and appropriate jobs in the community. To meet the goal of job placement, personnel involved in preparing individuals who are retarded for employment should first conduct annual surveys of available community employment options. Information from this survey should then be used to conduct job analyses. A *job analysis* is "the process of analyzing the demands of working environments . . . in essence, it is a task analysis of the job and what it demands" (Sitlington, Clark, & Kolstoe, 2000, p. 119). Survey data should also be used to assess student skills and to develop goals and objectives for the vocational preparation program. Omitting this critical step may result in preparing students for jobs that are scarce or in mismatching students with jobs that are inappropriate for their skills or interests.

Traditional Vocational Training Options

The high school work-study program has been a frequently used model for teaching vocational and occupational skills to students who have few needs for support. In many cases, the high school work-study program usually ran over a 3-year period, encompassing grades 10 to 12. In the 1st year, lessons emphasize areas such as transportation, budgeting, peer relationships, personal hygiene, and measurement. Units were usually part of the academic portion of the program, which covered half of the school day. The student spent approximately half the day in the formal classroom setting and half in more practical instruction. In this part of the program, job analysis and job explorations, as well as specific assessment of the student's vocational skills and interests, began.

During the 2nd year of the program, students refined their skills by learning how to complete a job application and how to behave in a job interview. At this time, they developed some rudimentary skills in a number of areas, such as clerical work, food service, carpentry, or automobile repair.

During the 3rd year of the program, students began to concentrate on work skill refinement in one or two specific areas, spending part of the day on an actual job and the remaining time in school. As this year drew to a close, students spent more time on the job and less in school.

FIGURE 11.5
Contemporary Vocational Training Options

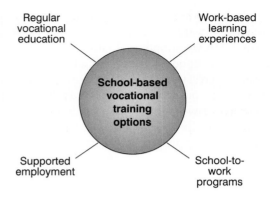

Because of requirements and constraints resulting from legislation passed over the last 20 years, work-study programs are not present in public schools to the extent that they were in the 1960s (Halpern, 1992). Elements of these programs, however, are found in various other vocational training models and transition programs.

Contemporary Vocational Training Options

Various school-based options are available for providing vocational training to students with disabilities. Figure 11.5 highlights the options that are most commonly found in schools today. Sitlington et al. (2000) provide a comprehensive discussion of these options.

Vocational Education **Vocational education** is an established discipline characterized by coursework found at the secondary level designed to prepare students for gainful employment as skilled or semiskilled workers. Courses are taught by professionals who are certified in the area of vocational education. Vocational education is composed of seven occupational areas: agriculture; business and office, health occupations, marketing; family and consumer sciences (i.e., home economics), trade and industry, and technology and technical education (i.e., industrial arts). Vocational education programs can be found either on the campuses of high schools or in separate vocational technical centers.

The typical problems associated with providing appropriate educational services to students with special needs in inclusive settings, which were highlighted in the previous chapter, apply to regular vocational education as well. For students with mental retardation to succeed in these settings, such programs will need to be capable of making certain curricular modifications. Furthermore, sufficient supports must be available to the vocational education staff.

Vocational education presents some major challenges (e.g., academic requirements) to students with mental retardation. However, as Sitlington et al. (2000) note, it possesses some very positive features for many students with mental retardation: "Vocational education tends to be tangible as well as goal and outcome oriented, and schooling is made relevant within the context of the world of work" (p. 156).

Work-Based Learning Experiences

Work-Based Learning Experiences A number of community-based opportunities may be available to students with mental retardation. These include cooperative education, student internship programs, youth apprenticeship programs, school-based enterprises, and job shadowing activities. In general, these programs allow students to gain valuable real-world job knowledge and/or experience.

School-to-Work Programs In 1994, Congress passed the School-to-Work Opportunities Act. This legislation was intended to prepare *all* students for work and further education. Students with mental retardation can be included in these school-to-work (STW) transition programs. The major thrust of this program was to provide a variety of school- and work-based learning opportunities, along with a coordinated set of connecting activities (e.g., partnerships) through the high school. Benz and Lindstrom (1997) offer a detailed description of the STW program.

Supported Employment **Supported employment** is paid employment for those with disabilities who need ongoing support on the job. Most professionals consider a supported employment model much more preferable to the longstanding sheltered employment model as a way to employ individuals with mental retardation (Wright, King, & National Conference of State Legislatures Task Force on Developmental Disabilities, 1991). As Wehman and colleagues (1998) stress, supported employment is based on a set of values (see Figure 11.6) that have been generally accepted by those within the field of mental retardation.

To learn more about supported employment, go to the companion website at www. prenhall.com/beirne-smith and select Chapter 11, then choose the Case Studies module.

McLaughlin and Wehman (1996) describe four types of supported employment programs:

FIGURE 11.6
Supported Employment Values

Source: From "Barriers to Competitive Employment for Persons with Disabilities," by P. Wehman, V. Brooke, M. West, P. Targett, H. Green, K. Inge, and J. Kregel, in P. Wehman (Ed.), *Developing Transition Plans,* 1998, Austin, TX: PRO-ED. Copyright 1998 by PRO-ED. Reprinted by permission.

Commensurate wages and benefits—People with disabilities should earn wages and benefits equal to that of coworkers performing the same or similar jobs.

Community—People need to be connected to the formal and informal networks of a community for acceptance, growth, and development.

Everyone can work—Everyone, regardless of the level or the type of disability, has the capability and right to a job.

Focus on abilities—People with disabilities should be viewed in terms of their abilities, strengths, and interests rather than their disabilities.

Ongoing supports—Customers of supported employment services will receive assistance in assembling the supports necessary to achieve their ambitions as long as they need supports.

Real jobs—Employment occurs within the local labor market in regular community businesses.

Right to the opportunity—Regardless of their disability, everyone has the right to an opportunity to work in the employment of his or her choice.

Self-determination—People have the right to make decisions for themselves.

Systems change—Traditional systems must be changed to ensure customer control, which is vital to the integrity of supported employment.

- *Individual Placement model.* A **job coach** or employment specialist provides on-the-job training to the individual. The job coach provides services and gradually decreases the time spent with an employee. At any point, however, the job coach can continue to provide services to the employee as needed. The job coach tries to make a successful match between the employee and the job.
- *Mobile Work Crew model.* Individuals with disabilities work in groups that travel from one work site to another. The supervisor is usually an employee of a supported employment agency. The work crew performs jobs such as custodial work on contracts negotiated by the supported employment agency with the business. One advantage, according to McLaughlin and Wehman (1996), is that individuals can have different job experiences by changing work crews.
- *Enclave model.* Employees with disabilities work in an integrated setting at a business or industry. They are allowed to compete for all job opportunities. Their supervisors are human service workers who remain on site permanently.
- *Entrepreneurial model.* Workers with and without disabilities work at a not-for-profit job site. Their supervisors are human service workers who serve permanently in those positions.

A key player in the supported employment model is the employment specialist or job coach. According to Winking, DeStefano, and Rusch (1988), the job coach helps make the match between the employee and the job and learns the job that will be taught to the individual with the disability. Winking et al. add that in a survey of program coordinators at supported employment agencies, program coordinators stated that the competencies needed by job coaches are flexibility, good oral and written communication skills, the ability to cope and manage stress, confidence, and the ability to take the initiative. Some of the duties of the job coach are to write task analyses, provide social skills training, maintain regular contact with parents, and provide job safety instruction. Winking et al. add that the work of a job coach can be quite varied, perhaps performing manual labor one moment, for example, and then attending an important meeting with a company representative the next.

Even though the job coach/employment specialist has traditionally played an important support role within the supported employment model, attention is being given to a broader notion of work supports, of which a job coach is only one. The importance of extending services through the use of **natural supports** has been underscored in recent times (Wehman, Bricout, & Kregel, 2000). A taxonomy of work supports that are available to persons with mental retardation in the workplace has been developed by Wehman and associates (2000). Four major categories comprise this taxonomy: agency-mediated supports, business-mediated supports, government-mediated supports, and family- and community-mediated supports. Figure 11.7 lists the four major categories of work supports along with their corresponding subcategories.

Individuals with mental retardation who are trained through a supported employment model may fare better in competitive employment than those who

Agency-mediated supports

Job coach assistance
- Specialized training
- Compensatory strategies

Compensatory strategies (e.g., memory aids)

Assistive technology

Counseling

Substance abuse services

Medical services

Specialized transportation

Vocational rehabilitation counselor

Business-mediated supports

Job restructuring

Workplace accommodations
- Environmental modifications
- Assistive technology
- Task modification
- Schedule modification

Co-worker mentoring
- Job task training and support
- Social support

Job creation

Employee Assistance Programs

Employment consultant (hired by business)

Government-mediated supports

Social Security work incentives
- Plan for achieving self-support
- Impairment-related work experience

Tax credits
- Work opportunity tax credit
- Disabled access credit
- Tax deduction to remove transportation and architectural barriers: Medicaid waiver

Family- and community-mediated supports

Personal care attendant
Peer mentors
Family members as job developers
Friends and neighbors
Social support networks

FIGURE 11.7
Taxonomy of Work Supports

Source: From "Supported Employment in 2000: Changing the Locus of Control from Agency to Consumer" (p. 130), by P. Wehman, J. Bricout, and J. Kregel, 2000, in M. L. Wehmeyer and J. R. Patton (Eds.), *Mental Retardation in the 21st Century,* Austin, TX: PRO-ED. Reprinted by permission.

have worked only in a sheltered workshop (Goldberg, McLean, LaVigne, Fratolilli, & Sullivan, 1990; Wehman et al., 1989). The benefits of supported employment for the employee with mental retardation may include competitive wages and desirable fringe benefits, long-term retention, and career ladder opportunities (Wehman et al., 2000). Benefits also exist for society in general, as more individuals with mental retardation become productive employees and contributing members of the community.

The supported employment option is faced with significant challenges today, as Wehman and his associates have noted (Wehman et al., 2000; Wehman & Kregel, 1995): "Many supported employment programs still yield employment outcomes that have fallen short of initial expectations. Lack of earnings and fringe benefits, integration in the workplace, employer attitudes, job retention, and job satisfaction remain issues of concern in supported employment program evaluation" (Wehman et al., 2000, p. 117). Nevertheless, supported employment remains an attractive option and one that is needed for some individuals with disabilities (Sitlington et al., 2000).

Vocational Assessment

Various methods can be used in vocational assessment, including personality tests, self-report devices, and rating devices (Sitlington et al., 2000). The most commonly used, and perhaps the most useful, are written tests, observation of work samples, and interviews. We can group written assessment devices into at least two categories: aptitude tests and interest inventories. Aptitude tests measure the abilities and traits of an individual in a certain area. For example, an aptitude test that measures word-processing abilities should indicate whether a person can word-process or learn how to word-process. Educators most often use results of these tests to predict an individual's chances for success in a stated field.

An example of an aptitude test is the *OASIS-2 Aptitude Survey* (Parker, 1991a). Interest inventories assess the student's feelings and preferences about types of occupations rather than measure potential proficiency. *The Harrington-O'Shea Career Decision-Making (CDM) System*, revised edition (Harrington & O'Shea, 1992), and the *OASIS-2 Interest Survey* (Parker, 1991b) are two such devices. The CDM-revised has two levels. Level 1 is written at a fourth-grade reading level and is designed for those with lower reading skills, including students in special education. Level 2 is designed for high school and college students. Both levels address abilities, job values, school subject preferences, and interests. The OASIS-2 Interest Schedule measures artistic, scientific, nature, protective, mechanical, industrial, business detail, selling, accommodating, humanitarian, leading–influencing, and physical performing interest factors.

Another way to assess work skills is through a work sample or job simulation. This procedure evaluates each individual's rate of production and general job-related behaviors. Brolin (1982) offers the following suggestions for making the most of this procedure: The job sample or work sample should be written up and organized with the requisite tasks in rank order from the least to the most demanding. The students should be allowed to practice each task and learn it completely before proceeding to the next one; in this way, they can master each task necessary for the production of a particular good or service.

One example of a job simulation device is *the Jewish Employment and Vocational Service Work Samples* (JEVS) package. Brolin (1982, 1986) has described these work samples as being composed of 28 tasks that measure worker skills in 14 general industrial categories. During the evaluation, which covers a 2-week period, the person being evaluated is required to perform work-related tasks that vary from simple (lettering signs) to complex (disassembling and rebuilding equipment).

Another procedure recommended for determining an individual's transition needs is curriculum-based vocational assessment. This type of assessment derives from an evaluation of a student's performance within the vocational curriculum (Ianacone & Leconte, 1986). The data collected can be used to guide efforts to improve curriculum and to assist program personnel in decision making (Porter & Stodden, 1986).

Interviewing can also be used as an effective method to obtain as much information as possible. A fundamental tenet of this approach is that the interviewee must understand the purpose of the interview. Some of the information obtained should include the interviewee's likes, interests, and future goals. The interviewer should attempt to verify the interviewee's statements through the use of follow-up and parent interviews, or rating scales, with special attention given to any discrepancies in the data from the various sources.

Although these instruments and procedures do yield valuable information about students' vocational capabilities, they have frequently been criticized for several reasons. First, the reading level for many of the paper-and-pencil tests is too high for many students who are mentally retarded (reading levels for these instruments are usually at or around a sixth-grade level). Second, few, if any, items relate directly to women. Third, socioeconomic differences are ignored (the preponderance of items reflects a middle-class orientation). Finally, racial and cultural diversity concerns are not taken into account. Work sample evaluations are criticized because they are expensive and time-consuming, often requiring extensive travel to and from the work site. The question of accuracy of the interview method is a problem. The information may be biased or limited in value as a result of misinformation or insufficient information. This is why the interviewer must attempt to verify statements made during the interview.

Vocational Placement and Follow-up

Once a student has acquired some vocational skills, either the school or some other agency or organization, such as vocational rehabilitation, seeks to place the student on a permanent job site. Smith and Payne (1980), Clark and Kolstoe (1995), and Wehman (1990) suggest a number of procedures to aid the placement specialist. The following list summarizes these procedures:

Well-designed employment models ensure that individuals receive follow-up services on a continuing basis to assess program effectiveness.

1. Make as many personal contacts with local employers as possible.
2. Use local clubs to advertise your program, as well as to secure information concerning placement sites.
3. Become more selective in the use of job sites as the program grows.
4. Consider employers an integral part of the program. Use them at different levels of the program—for example, the prevocational as well as the vocational level.
5. Obtain information from such resources as state job service centers, the state division of vocational rehabilitation, and the local Chamber of Commerce and job-training partnership program.
6. Program personnel should review the budget to ensure that job placement concerns are receiving the most favorable level of funding.

In the better-designed employment models, individuals receive follow-up services as needed, on a continuous basis (McLaughlin & Wehman, 1996). Information gained during the follow-up period can be used to assess program effectiveness. The relationship between follow-up and evaluation makes it possible for future as well as present program participants to benefit.

Programming Issues

Vocational preparation of students who are retarded has come a long way, but we do not have all the answers yet. Two problem areas still demand special attention.

The first, as mentioned previously, is the difficulty of the written material used in vocational programs with students who are mentally retarded. The reading level of much of this material is too high. Vocational and special educators have struggled with this problem for some time without being able to reach a workable solution.

The second problem relates to what to do when a person who is mentally retarded resigns or is fired from a job. A similar event causes some concern with a person who is not retarded, but it seems to occasion greater consternation on the part of family, friends, and professionals who work with people who have disabilities. Should a job termination be more of an issue for workers who are mentally retarded than for the rest of the labor force?

To check your understanding of this chapter, go to the companion website at http://www.prenhall.com/ beirne-smith and select Chapter 11, and then choose the Self-Test module.

We believe that an employee who is mentally retarded has as much right as the next person to like or dislike a job or coworkers and to leave an unpleasant or unproductive situation if necessary. To deny this is to deny equal rights (and responsibilities) to the adult who is mentally retarded. Furthermore, it runs wholly contrary to the idea of inclusion, self-determination, and empowerment.

Summary

Basic Concepts
- People experience many different transitions in their lives.
- Federal law mandates transition planning activities for only two transitions.
- Certain key elements should be present when transition planning is conducted.

- This process is a shared set of activities, with the student, family, school-based personnel, and adult service providers being the main players.

Transition Education

- Transition education refers to all activities of an instructional or curricular nature that relate to adult outcomes.
- *Career development* is a broad term that relates closely to the term *transition education,* indicating a program aimed at helping students prepare for life as well as for a job.
- Vocational education is an aspect of career education that focuses on employment.
- Life skills instruction is an important part of the preparation of all students.
- Various options exist for covering life skills topics, with infusion being the preferred for students who are in inclusive settings.

Transition Planning

- PL 101-476 mandated that, beginning no later than age 16, a student's IEP must include a statement of transition services.
- PL 105-17 now requires that a statement of transition needs to be in place by age 14.
- A comprehensive assessment of transition needs is essential for the development of quality transition plans.
- Transition plans should be based on a student's preferences, interests, and needs.
- The student should be as actively involved in his or her transition planning as is possible.

Vocational Preparation

- Vocational preparation programs should include specific program objectives, counseling services, and the development of specific vocational skills.
- A variety of traditional and contemporary vocational training options now exists in schools.
- Students with mental retardation should be included in various school-to-work activities that are offered to other students.
- Studies have shown that with systematic training and ongoing support, many individuals with more extensive needs can succeed in integrated, competitive work settings.

References

Bellamy, G. T., & Horner, R. H. (1987). Beyond high school: Residential and employment options after graduation. In M. E. Snell (Ed.), *Systematic instruction of persons with severe handicaps* (3rd ed., pp. 491–520). Upper Saddle River, NJ: Merrill/Prentice Hall.

Benz, M. R., & Lindstrom, L. E. (1997). *Building school-to-work programs: Strategies for youth with special needs.* Austin, TX: PRO-ED.

Brigance, A. H. (1995). *Life Skills Inventory*. North Billerica, MA: Curriculum Associates.

Brolin, D. E. (1982). *Vocational preparation of persons with handicaps* (2nd ed.) Upper Saddle River, NJ: Merrill/Prentice Hall.

Brolin, D. E. (1986). *Life-centered career education: A competency-based approach* (rev. ed.). Reston, VA: Council for Exceptional Children.

Brolin, D. E. (1991). *Life-centered career education: A competency-based approach* (3rd ed.). Reston, VA: Council for Exceptional Children.

Brolin, D. E. (1992). *Life-centered career education (LCCE) knowledge and performance batteries*. Reston, VA: Council for Exceptional Children.

Brolin, D. E. (1997). *Life-centered career education: A competency-based approach* (5th ed.). Reston, VA: Council for Exceptional Children.

Clark, G. M. (1998). *Assessment for transitional planning*. Austin, TX: PRO-ED.

Clark, G. M., & Patton, J. R. (1997). *Transition Planning Inventory*. Austin, TX: PRO-ED.

Clark, G. M., Carlson, B. C., Fisher, S., Cook, I. D., & D'Alonzo, B. J. (1991). Career development for students with disabilities in elementary schools: A position statement of the Division on Career Development. *Career Development for Exceptional Individuals, 14,* 109–120.

Clark, G. M., Field, S., Patton, J. R., Brolin, D. E., & Sitlington, P. L. (1994). Life skills instruction: A necessary component for all students with disabilities—a position statement of the Division on Career Development and Transition. *Career Development for Exceptional Individuals, 17,* 125–134.

Clark, G. M., & Kolstoe, O. P. (1990). *Career development and transition education for adolescents with disabilities*. Boston: Allyn & Bacon.

Cronin, M. E., & Patton, J. R. (1993). *Life skills instruction for all students with special needs: A practical guide for integrating real-life content into the curriculum*. Austin, TX: PRO-ED.

Enderle, J., & Severson, S. (1997). *Enderle-Severson Transition Rating Scale—Revised*. Moorehead, MN: Practical Press.

Field, S., & Hoffman, A. (1996). *Steps to self-determination*. Austin, TX: PRO-ED.

Goldberg, R. T., McLean, M. M., LaVigne, R., Fratolilli, J., & Sullivan, F. T. (1990). Transition of persons with developmental disabilities from extended sheltered employment to competitive employment. *Mental Retardation, 28,* 299–304.

Halpern, A. S. (1985). Transition: A look at the foundations. *Exceptional Children, 51,* 479–486.

Halpern, A. S. (1992). Transition: Old wine in new bottles. *Exceptional Children, 58,* 202–212.

Halpern, A. S. (1994). The transition of youth with disabilities to adult life: A position statement of the Division on Career Development and Transition, the Council for Exceptional Children. *Career Development for Exceptional Individuals, 17,* 115–124.

Halpern, A. S., & Benz, M. R. (1987). A statewide examination of secondary special education for students with mild disabilities: Implications for the high school curriculum. *Exceptional Children, 54,* 122–129.

Halpern, A. S., Herr, C. M., Doren, M., & Wolf, N. K. (2001). *Next S.T.E.P.: Student transition and evaluation planning* (2nd ed.). Austin, TX: PRO-ED.

Harrington, T. F., & O'Shea, A. J. (1992) *The Harrington-O'Shea Career Decision-Making System.* Circle Pines, MN: American Guidance Service.

Hasazi, S. B., Gordon, L. R., & Roe, C. A. (1985). Factors associated with employment status of handicapped youth exiting high school from 1979 to 1983. *Exceptional Children, 51,* 455–469.

Hungerford, R. H., DeProspo, C. J., & Rosenzweig, I. E. (1948). The non-academic pupil. In *Philosophy of occupational education.* New York: Association of New York City Teachers of Special Education.

Ianacone, R. N., & Leconte, P. J. (1986). Curriculum-based vocational assessment: A viable response to a school-based service delivery issue. *Career Development for Exceptional Individuals, 9,* 113–120.

Marland, S. P. (1971). Career education now. *Education Digest, 36,* 9–11.

Martin, J. E., & Huber Marshall, L. H. (1996). *Choicemaker self-determination transition assessment.* Longmont, CO: Sopris West.

McCarney, S. B. (2000). *Transition Behavior Scale* (2nd ed.). Columbia, MO: Hawthorne Educational Service.

McLaughlin, P. J., & Wehman, P. (1996). *Mental retardation and developmental disabilities* (2nd ed.). Austin, TX: PRO-ED.

Mithaug, D. E., Horiuchi, C. N., & Fanning, P. N. (1985). A report on the Colorado statewide follow-up survey of special education students. *Exceptional Children, 51,* 397–404.

Parker, R. (1991a). *OASIS-2 Aptitude Survey.* Austin, TX: PRO-ED.

Parker, R. (1991b). *OASIS-2 Interest Schedule.* Austin, TX: PRO-ED.

Patton, J. R., Cronin, M. E., & Jairrels, V. (1997). Curricular implications of transition: Life skills instruction as an integral part of transition education. *Remedial and Special Education, 18,* 294–306.

Patton, J. R., Cronin, M. E., & Wood, S. (1999). *Infusing real-life topics into existing curricula at the elementary, middle, and high school levels: Recommended procedures and instructional examples.* Austin, TX: PRO-ED.

Patton, J. R., & Dunn, C. (1998). *Transition from school to young adulthood: Basic components and recommended practices.* Austin, TX: PRO-ED.

Polloway, E. A., Patton, J. R., & Serna, L. (2001). *Strategies for teaching learners with special needs* (6th ed.). Upper Saddle River, NJ: Merrill/Prentice Hall.

Porter, M. E., & Stodden, R. A. (1986). A curriculum-based vocational assessment procedure: Addressing the school-to-work transition needs of secondary schools. *Career Development for Exceptional Individuals, 9,* 121–128.

Rusch, F. R. (1983). Competitive vocational training. In M. E. Snell (Ed.), *Systematic instruction of the moderately and severely handicapped* (2nd ed., pp. 503–525). Upper Saddle River, NJ: Merrill/Prentice Hall.

Rusch, F. R., & Phelps, L. A. (1987). Secondary special education and transition from school to work: A national priority. *Exceptional Children, 53,* 487–492.

Sitlington, P. L. (1996). Transition to living: The neglected components of transition programming for individuals with learning disabilities. *Journal of Learning Disabilities, 29,* 31–39, 52.

Sitlington, P. L., Clark, G. M., & Kolstoe, O. P. (2000). *Transition education and services for adolescents with disabilities* (3rd ed.). Boston: Allyn & Bacon.

Smith, J. E., & Payne, J. S. (1980). *Teaching exceptional adolescents*. Upper Saddle River, NJ: Merrill/Prentice Hall.

Wagner, M., Blackorby, J., Cameto, R. Hebbeler, K., & Newman, L. (1993). *The transition experiences of young people with disabilities: A summary of findings from the National Longitudinal Transition Study of special education students*. Menlo Park, CA: SRI International.

Wagner, M., Newman, L., D'Amico, R., Jay, E. D., Butler-Nalin, P., Marder, C., & Cox, R. (1991). *Youth with disabilities: How are they doing? The first comprehensive report from the National Longitudinal Transition Study of special education students*. Menlo Park, CA: SRI International.

Wehman, P. (1990). School-to-work: Elements of successful programs. *Teaching Exceptional Children, 23*(1), 40–43.

Wehman, P. (Ed.). (1998). *Developing transition plans*. Austin, TX: PRO-ED.

Wehman, P., Bricout, J., & Kregel, J. (2000). Supported employment in 2000: Changing the locus of control from agency to consumer. In M. L. Wehmeyer & J. R. Patton (Eds.), *Mental retardation in the 21st century*. Austin, TX: PRO-ED.

Wehman, P. & Kregel, J. (1995). At the crossroads: Supported employment a decade later. *Journal of the Association for Persons with Severe Handicaps, 20*, 286–299.

Wehman, P., Parent, W., Wood, W., Talbert, C. M., Jasper, C., Miller, S., Marchant, J., & Walker, R. (1989). From school to competitive employment for young adults with mental retardation: Transition in practice. *Career Development for Exceptional Individuals, 12*, 97–105.

Wehmeyer, M. L., Morningstar, M., & Husted, D. (1999). *Family involvement in transition planning and implementation*. Austin, TX: PRO-ED.

Will, M. (1984). *OSERS programming for the transition of youth with disabilities: Bridges from school to working life*. Washington, DC: Office of Special Education and Rehabilitative Services.

Winking, D. L., DeStefano, L., & Rusch, F. R. (1988). *Supported employment in Illinois: Job coach issues*. Champaign, IL: University of Illinois, Secondary Transition Intervention Effectiveness Institute. (ERIC Document Reproduction Service No. 295 407)

Wright, B., King, M. P., & National Conference of State Legislatures Task Force on Developmental Disabilities. (1991). *Americans with developmental disabilities*. Washington, DC: National Conference of State Legislatures Task Force on Developmental Disabilities.

Ysseldyke, J. E., Algozzine, B., & Thurlow, M. L. (1992). *Critical issues in special education*. Boston: Houghton Mifflin.

Chapter

12

Adult Years: Life in the Community

To review the chapter objectives on-line, go to the companion website at http:// www.prenhall.com/ beirne-smith and select Chapter 12, and then choose the Objectives module.

OBJECTIVES

After reading this chapter, the student should be able to

- identify and describe normative tasks associated with the three major developmental periods of adulthood

- discuss major changes that have occurred in the residential living patterns of adults with mental retardation

- identify and describe factors that contribute to a person's likelihood for success in community residential environments

- discuss key issues affecting the lives of adults with mental retardation today

KEY TERMS

community acceptance

community adjustment

economic integration

employment integration

need for support services

personal satisfaction

recreational/leisure integration

residential integration

social integration

Adulthood is a time of many changes. For some people, these changes are eagerly anticipated. For others, they may represent anything from an untimely predicament to an insurmountable crisis. Much is known about the development of children and adolescents, but we seem to know far less about the adult years, particularly for persons with mental retardation. Hence, professionals and laypersons remain divided as to the importance and appropriateness of different settings and services for adults with mental retardation. Some assert that institutional living offers the best, safest, and most cost-effective type of setting. Others believe that personal fulfillment is only possible through complete and unrestricted access to community services. Increasingly, adults and families of adults with mental retardation are favoring the latter—that is, life *in* the community as opposed to *near* the community. This chapter will highlight many of the key issues faced by adults with mental retardation as they strive to live, learn, and grow in the community of their choice.

ADULT DEVELOPMENT

Adulthood spans many decades of a person's life. As such, it encompasses everything from the end of adolescence up through and including old age. Because life experiences differ markedly from one person to the next, the developmental sequence of one person will naturally be quite different from that of another person. Despite obvious differences among people, there are several fairly consistent stages that virtually all people encounter as they journey through life. Following is a brief description of important components of three such periods.

Young Adulthood

To learn more about issues of young adulthood, go to the companion website at *www.prenhall.com/ beirne-smith* and select Chapter 12, then choose the Web Destinations module.

Young adults with mental retardation enter the adult world with many of the same expectations as young adults without mental retardation. Levinson and Levinson (1996) cite young adulthood as a very dramatic time of one's life. For many, it is a time of great vitality and fulfillment; it represents a time when life tasks and goals are outlined and pursued. Establishing and maintaining friendships, a career, and a residence are important tasks in the lives of most young adults, regardless of level of functioning.

Unfortunately, the transition for persons with mental retardation is generally much more difficult than for persons without mental retardation; often just the opportunity to strive for normative young adult milestones is what is appreciated. Very few adults have accomplishments that match their expectations, particularly young adults. For the young adult with restricted social opportunities, as is the case with many young adults with mental retardation, special occasions may take on an enhanced sense of importance. For example, promotions at work, major birthdays, and major family events (e.g., becoming a mother, father, aunt, or uncle) offer occasions of great personal significance that can help define one's role as an adult. Kail and Cavanaugh (1996) have suggested that cultural rituals signifying entrance into adulthood are often the most important rituals within a culture and very often have the greatest effect on the quality of one's early adult life.

Young adults with mental retardation share the same concerns about the adult world as do young adults without mental retardation.

Middle Adulthood

There is no formally agreed-on range that corresponds to middle adulthood, though many consider it to be roughly 40 to 60 years of age. Opinions differ, too, as to the nature of middle adulthood. Some consider it to be just another stage in one's life; others regard it as the prime of one's life when personal and professional achievements are at their maximum; still others believe it is a time of diminished demands and the beginning of a period of introspection. Erikson and Erikson (1998) describe this portion of the life span continuum as "generativity versus stagnation," the point at which the middle adult makes the decision to live for him- or herself or for others.

All middle adults must begin adjusting to the limits of the aging process. For many adults with mental retardation, this is a difficult task, especially for those who have already had to make many accommodations. Readjusting to a life without parents or to a life with aging parents, finding a niche in the local community that one can count on, and discovering new and enjoyable recreational/leisure activities are all hallmarks of the middle adult years (Rice, 1986).

Older Adulthood

Few trends characterize America more than the graying of its population. In 1900, older adults accounted for only 4% of the U.S. population. By 2030, it is expected that adults 65 years and older will account for approximately 20% of the population. More noteworthy perhaps is that people 85 years of age and older now constitute the fastest-growing segment of the older adult population, a group that is expected to double in size by the year 2030, with a fivefold increase expected by 2050 (U.S. Department of Commerce, 1996). While numbers alone do not make the aging process any easier, they do increase the likelihood that more services will be available for persons in need.

Older adulthood is often characterized by a profound reappraisal of one's life and often accompanied by turning inward and withdrawing from society. Establishing and accepting new roles in the family, adjusting to lowered social expectations, and adjusting to continued limitations of the aging process are all considered to be developmental tasks of older adulthood (Levinson, 1978; Levinson & Levinson, 1996).

To learn more about aging and other issues covered in Chapter 12, go to the companion website at www.prenhall.com/beirne-smith and select Chapter 12, then choose the Web Destinations module.

For the older adult with mental retardation, creating a new lifestyle pattern that allows one to deal with the onset of illness and the general sense of loss of one's abilities and youth are all factors that must be addressed to assure the highest quality of life possible. The developmental work of theorists such as Erikson and Levinson has much to offer persons who work with adults with mental retardation. Despite the increasing amount of information on normative life events for adults in general, a void of information persists on the development of adults with mental retardation. Some predict that life span issues pertaining to persons with mental retardation will become a paramount theme of the next few decades (Glidden & Zetlin, 1992).

PATTERNS OF RESIDENTIAL AND COMMUNITY LIVING

Dramatic changes have occurred in the lives of adults with mental retardation during the last several years. Yet, few have been as striking as the exodus of people from large public residential facilities to smaller community-based homes. *How* a person lives usually begins with *where* a person lives. For that reason, and because families of persons with mental retardation have historically selected between two different types of residential living options, public residential facilities and community residential settings, trends among the two most readily identifiable types of residential living options will be presented here.

Institutional Settings

Large public residential facilities are not unlike many other administratively complex organizations. *Public residential facilities* (PRFs) are state-supported facilities for persons with mental retardation and developmental disabilities designed to accommodate 16 or more live-in residents at any one time.

The types of services offered by PRFs vary from institution to institution. It is common for large congregate care settings to offer a wide range of services irrespective of the residential population. For example, boarding schools, colleges and universities, professional and military schools, and even large summer camps must offer a wide assortment of programs to meet the needs of their residents. The larger the program, the wider the range of services that must be offered. However, large, congregate care settings for people with disabilities must, out of necessity, offer a vast array of services in fairly large concentrations. Therefore, most PRFs offer a broad range of educational, social, recreational, medical, and health-related services. The range and depth of services is made even more challenging by the broad age range of residents, typically including everyone from birth through 90 or more years of age.

If services provided by institutions reflect the residents' needs, then it can safely be said that the PRFs of today are markedly different from the PRFs of 50 years ago. In the 1950s, the average institution had more than 1,500 residents, with some facilities housing as many as several thousand people at any one time. The decline in daily residency since the late 1960s has been both substantial and consistent (see Figure 12.1). For example, the average daily population of residents in large PRFs was 52,469 in 1998, down from an all-time high of 228,500 in 1967. This 76% drop in residency is best quantified by the following population-based ratios. While there were 116 people per 100,000 in the general population living in PRFs in 1967, there were only 19 people per 100,000 living in PRFs in 1997. During 1998 alone, 4,761 persons with mental retardation and developmental disabilities were released from institutions, constituting 9% of the year's average daily population of residents (Lakin, Prouty, & Bruininks, 1999). By June 30, 1998, six states and the District of Columbia had closed their last remaining facility (i.e., Alaska, New Hampshire, New Mexico, Vermont, Rhode Island, West Virginia), up from only three states 2 years before (Anderson, Clayton, Polister, Prouty, & Lakin, 1999). And, in the 7-year period from 1992 through 1998, a total of 80 large public residential facilities closed, representing a closure rate of 11.4 facilities per year.

Although all states are making progress in their efforts to depopulate state institutions, there remains great variability in the rates with which deinstitutionalization is occurring. For example, in the 1987–1997 period, 10 states had reduced their average daily populations by more than 75%, while 5 states had reduced their populations by no more than 10% (Anderson, Lakin, Mangan, & Prouty, 1998). Sadly, four states placed residents in PRFs at a rate of more than twice the national average as recently as 1998: Arkansas, Louisiana, Mississippi, and New Jersey (Clayton, Prouty, & Lakin, 1999).

FIGURE 12.1

Average Daily Population of Persons with Mental Retardation and Related Conditions Living in Large Public Residential Facilities, 1950–1998

Source: Data taken from Lakin, Prouty, and Bruininks (1999, p. 14).

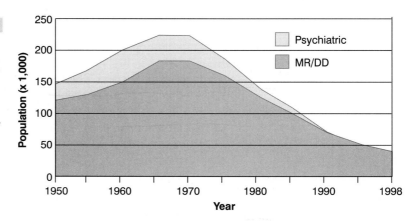

TABLE 12.1

Percentage of Residents of Large State-Operated Residential Facilities According to Age, Level of Mental Retardation, and Functional Limitations

Resident characteristics	Year				
	1977	1982	1987	1994	1998
Age					
0 to 21 years	35.8	22.0	12.7	6.1	4.8
22 to 39 years	41.3	50.2	54.1	47.1	38.1
40 to 62 years	19.2	22.9	27.3	39.7	48.9
63 ≤ years	3.7	5.0	6.0	7.1	8.2
Level of Mental Retardation					
Borderline/Mild	10.4	7.1	7.2	7.0	7.6
Moderate	16.4	12.5	9.8	9.0	9.5
Severe	27.6	24.2	20.0	18.5	18.3
Profound	45.6	56.2	63.0	65.5	64.6
Functional Limitations					
Cannot walk independently	23.3	25.5	29.5	33.4	38.9
Cannot talk independently	43.5	49.1	54.8	56.0	59.6
Not toilet-trained	34.1	38.0	53.4	55.3	59.5
Cannot eat independently	21.4	35.0	37.8	50.9	56.4
Cannot dress independently	55.8	60.9	60.5	65.6	69.9

Source: From "Characteristics and Movement of Residents of Large State Facilities" (p. 40), by L. Anderson, K. C. Lakin, R. W. Prouty, and B. Polister, in R. W. Prouty and K. C. Lakin (Eds.), *Residential Services for Persons with Developmental Disabilities: Status and Trends through 1998,* 1999, Minneapolis, MN: University of Minnesota, Institute on Community Integration. Reprinted by permission.

Not only have the facilities changed, but the characteristics of persons served in PRFs have changed as well. The nature of the disability is much more complex than it was 20 years ago, as 57% of the residents had two or more diagnosed disabilities in 1998 compared with 40% in the early 1980s. The data presented in Table 12.1 give some indication of the characteristics of residents inhabiting institutions over the past twenty years. For example, in a study of 272 large, state-operated facilities, Anderson, Lakin, Prouty, and Polister (1999) reported that 46% had epilepsy, 24% had cerebral palsy, 8% were deaf, and 41% had behavioral disorders. More telling, perhaps, is that administrators in 15 states have reported as many as 75% of their residents having multiple conditions. This increasingly complex pattern of disabilities is further highlighted by the advancing age of the residential population, a population that is aging faster than even that of the U.S. population. Table 12.1 illustrates the inverse relationship between the number of residents with borderline/mild mental retardation and those with profound mental retardation over time. In summary, residents today tend to be older, have greater levels of disability, and, as a result, have more extensive support needs.

Community Settings

A *community residential setting* (CRS) is typically much smaller in size and scope than a large public residential facility and, more important, is located in a traditional residential neighborhood. While CRSs by definition have 15 or fewer residents, many if not most are actually family homes and only resemble some of the smaller congregate care facilities on paper. Often, the distinctions are subtle and made based on the guidelines of the respective funding agencies. Just as no two public residential facilities are exactly alike, no two community residential settings are exactly alike, either.

At one end of the spectrum of community residential settings are *intermediate care facilities for persons with mental retardation* (ICF/MRs). These facilities serve as a residential hybrid between the large PRFs and the small family-type homes. While there are large ICF/MRs with room for 16 or more persons at a given time (namely, PRFs), the ICF/MRs in this case meet the definition of community residential settings in that they are likely to have 15 or fewer persons and reside in traditional residential neighborhoods. They are generally staffed by a number of paid educational, medical, and social service personnel who also provide services similar to those offered in the larger institutional settings. For some persons with mental retardation leaving the institutional setting, an ICF/MR is a first stop along the community residential setting continuum.

At the other end of the community setting continuum are *independent living settings* and *supervised apartments*. In an increasing number of cases, these dwellings are owned or leased by the resident who lives in the dwelling; that is, they hold the mortgage or lease on the residence. Although a paid, professional staff member may have responsibility for some or all of the formal operations of the setting, the assistance provided is one of support rather than overarching responsibility (e.g., payment of rent, connection of utilities, contact with maintenance personnel). The differences are certainly subtle, and much depends on the adjustment and adaptive capabilities of the people in these settings.

Not included in the aforementioned categories is the *family home*, a home that may or may not be owned or leased by a family member. These homes may or may not be licensed by the state for additional or reimbursable funds.

Presented in the preceding section was a fairly detailed account of the extent to which PRFs have decreased in size over the past three decades. Commensurate with the rather astounding decrease in the number of people living in PRFs has been an equally large increase in the number of people living in community residential settings. For example, from 1977 through 1998, the number of people living in CRSs increased from 40,400 to 256,200. As can be seen in Figure 12.2, the greatest portion of this increase has come from persons moving into settings with one to six residents, increasing from just over 20,000 persons in 1977 to well over 200,000 persons in 1998 (Polister, Prouty, Lakin, & Bruininks, 1999). Fortunately, state and federal funds allocated to community residential services have tended to follow suit, increasing from just under $1 billion in 1977 to well over $18 billion in 1998. Whereas 75% of all state and federal money spent on residential services in 1977 was allocated to PRFs, in 1998 approximately 72% of all state and federal monies allocated to the residential service system went to CRSs—the virtual opposite of 1977 (Braddock, Hemp, Parish, & Rizzolo, in press).

The residential service system is indeed a fluid one. One might imagine from the prior data that all movement for individuals as well as residential agencies is one-directional—that is, that individuals with mental retardation and developmental disabilities are moving to smaller facilities at the same time that state and

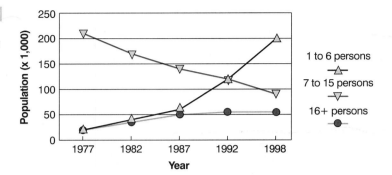

FIGURE 12.2

Trends in Residential Placements of Persons Residing in Community and Noncommunity Residential Settings, 1977–1998

Source: Data take from Polister et al. (1999, p. 8).

nonstate agencies are downsizing their entire residential service delivery system. Although these trends are correct and supported by the data, there remain people who must either move into a PRF for the first time or transition back into a PRF from a CRS. New admissions are down to a fraction of what they were 30 years ago (approximately 1,600 persons in 1998), but they do indeed still occur and tend to be youth and young adults more so than persons from any other age group. Furthermore, these new admissions tend to be less cognitively impaired than the general PRF population. The profile of persons requiring readmission to PRFs tends to mirror that of the new admissions. Interestingly, that means a higher percentage of persons with mild/no mental retardation and slightly older rather than younger residents (Anderson, Lakin, Prouty, & Polister, 1999). The fact that both new admissions and readmissions tend to have higher levels of cognitive functioning suggests two important phenomena. First, cognitive and adaptive functioning are not the only factors responsible for PRF placement; and, second, many of the community initiatives for persons with more extreme support needs seem to be working.

The United States has indeed moved from an institution-based model of residential living to one that is primarily community based. Whereas 25 years ago, 84% of people with mental retardation and developmental disabilities receiving residential services lived in large public residential facilities, today only about 26% do so. It must be kept in mind, however, that the figures reported thus far only represent people in the service delivery system and do not represent children, youth, and adults living in their natural, biological, or other homes outside the service delivery system, a group that accounts for approximately 85% of all persons with mental retardation and developmental disabilities (Larson et al., 2000).

ADJUSTING TO LIFE IN THE COMMUNITY

For a complete on-line glossary of mental retardation terms, go to the companion website at http://www.prenhall.com/ beirne-smith and select any chapter, and then choose the Glossary module.

The complexity of each person's life, variety of experiences, and opportunity to assume responsibility all depend on such things as the availability of community resources, community attitudes, and the characteristics of the people involved. Schalock and Kiernan (1990) have identified home, work, and recreational/leisure environments as the three major environments in which people operate, yet they contend that it is actually the community environment that unites all three.

The Importance of Direct Care Personnel

Heidi is an older woman of German background who works in a unit of very low functioning residents. Every day she wakes up her assigned group, attends to their immediate needs, cleans their beds, bathes, dresses, and feeds them. While she is doing the tasks most of us would find less than enjoyable, she is talking to these uncommunicative and mostly unresponsive persons, as if they were her best friends or close relatives, about all sorts of topics. The fact that none of them ever contributes to the conversation does not seem to affect her at all.

After witnessing these events on more than one occasion, I asked her why she carried on the way she did with people who probably don't understand a word she was saying. She looked at me strangely and said, "Got to be a person in there somewhere."

I left that particular unit very humbled but with a renewed respect for those who mean so much to those we actually know so little about. I was particularly struck by the idea that we don't know what is going on inside these individuals who perform so low on our existing measures of ability. Perhaps they hear and understand everything that is said to them but just can't communicate their feelings to us. (For a related example, read the book *Johnny Got His Gun,* by D. Trumbo [1959, Bantam Books].) On this particular day, I was also reminded of something that I tell students every time we visit such residential facilities: these individuals are much more like us than unlike us.

I also realized one other thing—to a small number of people, Heidi is more important than the president, the governor, Michael Jackson, Magic Johnson, or Roseanne Barr.

Source: From *Exceptional Children in Focus* (5th ed., pp. 71–72), by J. R. Patton, J. M. Kauffman, J. M. Blackbourn, and G. B. Brown, 1991, Upper Saddle River, NJ: Merrill/Prentice Hall. Copyright 1991 by Merrill/Prentice Hall. Reprinted by permission.

Community adjustment, then, implies more than simply one's physical location in a mainstream setting; rather, it is the "adjustment and integration of the whole person into community life" (Ittenbach, Larson, Spiegel, Abery, & Prouty, 1993, p. 19). Adulthood *is* complex; so, too, are the lives of persons with mental retardation.

Prior to the 1990s, results of research on the construct of community adjustment have not supported any one combination of variables that predicts successful adjustment. Though the literature base is modest to date, results of early studies appear promising. Researchers at the University of Minnesota's Institute on Community Integration and the University of Oregon's Rehabilitation and Training Center in Mental Retardation have sought to identify and measure outcomes of the community adjustment process (e.g., Halpern, Nave, Close, & Nelson, 1986; Ittenbach, Bruininks, Thurlow, & McGrew, 1993; McGrew, Bruininks, Thurlow, & Lewis, 1992; McGrew, Johnson, & Bruininks, 1994; Thompson, McGrew, Johnson, & Bruininks, 2000).

In a review of research on the dimensions of community adjustment, McGrew and Bruininks (1994) found as many as eight possible factors that characterize one's likelihood for success in community living (see Figure 12.3). Following is a brief description of research pertaining to the eight important areas of community adjustment: social integration, economic integration, employment integration, recreational/leisure integration, residential integration, personal satisfaction, community acceptance, and need for support services.

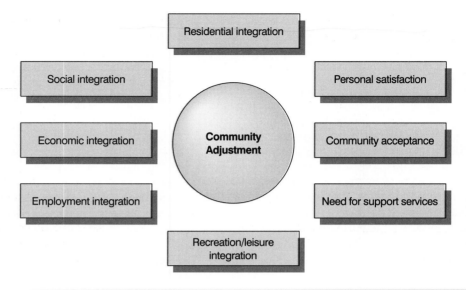

FIGURE 12.3
Life in the Community

Social Integration

Social relationships constitute the heart and soul of community integration (Kennedy, Horner, & Newton, 1989). Few will argue the importance of family, friends, and significant others to one's overall well-being. Fewer still will argue the importance of a strong and stable support network for persons experiencing difficulty with the community adjustment process. It seems ironic, then, that so little attention has been paid to the study of **social integration,** a person's general level of intra- and interpersonal involvement in community activities.

A major finding within social integration research is that persons with mental retardation tend to be accepted less often and rejected more often than persons without mental retardation, leading to less satisfaction with personal relations (Taylor, Asher, & Williams, 1987). Further, adolescents and young adults with mental retardation tend to report fewer friends, less intimacy, and less empathy among peers than that reported by adolescents and young adults without disabilities (Zetlin & Murtaugh, 1988). In a comprehensive review of the literature on social networks, Abery and Fahnestock (1994) found peers with disabilities, family members, and primary care providers to constitute the core of the social support system, much more so than for persons without mental retardation. Unfortunately, while many adults with mental retardation report a substantial number of friends, Kennedy et al. (1989) found a limited number of "companions who remained a part of a participant's social sphere for more than a few months" (p. 195).

Contributing to this lack of meaningful social relationships is a tendency toward a rather shy and reticent temperament, particularly in mainstreamed settings. Though researchers have contested the notion that people with mental retardation lack essential social skills, there appears to be agreement on the need for peers and confidants who can model effective social behaviors in community settings (Abery, Thurlow, Bruininks, & Johnson, 1990; Brinker, 1985). Peers without mental retardation offer opportunities for social involvement not always available to peers with mental retardation. For example, in a study involving 245 children, adolescents, and young adults from nine states, Brinker (1985) found that students without mental retardation extended more social bids to students with mental retardation than did peers with mental retardation. Equally important, students without mental retardation responded to more social bids from students with mental retardation than did peers with mental retardation.

Offsetting the difficulties inherent in the adjustment process is the finding that adults with mental retardation tend to make greater use of their rather limited social support networks than do adults without mental retardation (Rosen & Burchard, 1990). The many benefits to others of investing in social relationships with persons with mental retardation (such as an increased tolerance of others, a reduced fear of persons with disabilities, and added friendships) cannot be overlooked (Peck, Donaldson, & Pezzoli, 1990).

Economic Integration

Though many if not most adults with mental retardation benefit from entitlements that guarantee supports for their essential needs, there is more to community living than simply meeting basic financial obligations. **Economic integration**, for example, is the degree to which a person exercises the right to make decisions as to how his or her money is earned and spent.

Adults with mental retardation do not have the same income and financial independence as adults without mental retardation. As financial dependence increases, lack of access to other community-based programs increases. Lack of discretionary income affects more than just one's ability to purchase desired goods and services, it makes one less likely to participate in certain social, recreational, and vocational activities, missing out on many of the benefits of community living. At a time when other adults are assuming direct control over their financial lives, adults with mental retardation continue to be dependent on the wishes and preferences of others around them, their own income notwithstanding. Equally important is the fact that as consumers, their voices are not heard and they therefore miss the opportunity to influence manufacturers' habits.

As a way to provide regular income and health service coverage to persons with mental retardation, a number of federally funded programs are available. Following is a brief discussion of four programs as described in the U.S. Department of Health and Human Service's (1990) *Task II: Federal Programs for Persons with Disabilities* (see also Figure 12.4).

Social Security Disability Insurance Program   The Social Security Disability Insurance (SSDI) program offers monthly cash benefits to persons and the dependents of persons 65 years of age and younger who were previously insured and who have left the workforce because of a disability. Eligibility is based on two factors: (a) the presence of a disability according to Social Security Admin-

FIGURE 12.4

Matrix of Entitlement Programs

Source: From *How to Provide for Their Future* (p. 26), by the Association of Retarded Citizens of the United States, 1984, Arlington, TX: Association of Retarded Citizens of the United States. Copyright 1984 by the Association of Retarded Citizens of the United States. Reprinted by permission.

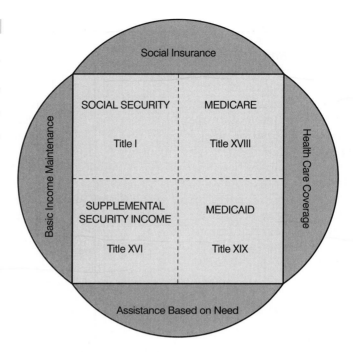

Matrix representing relationships among Social Security (SSDI, ADC). Medicare, Supplemental Security Income (SSI), and Medicaid for persons with disabilities. The criteria for eligibility based on disability are uniform for all programs in all states. The economic criteria differ. Social Security and Medicare are federally administered according to uniform rules in all states. SSI basic entitlements are federally administered according to uniform rules; most states provide state supplementation under state-specific criteria. Medicaid is a federally assisted, state-administered program. In most states, SSI-eligible persons are also eligible for Medicaid. In addition, some persons who meet the disability criteria may meet the economic criteria (means tests) for Medicaid even if ineligible for SSI. Children with disabilities may be eligible for SSI, Medicaid, or both.

istration guidelines and (b) insured status through prior employment. Although childhood benefits typically cease at 18 years of age, dependents who are disabled continue to qualify for SSDI benefits as long as the disability continues. Most adult dependents with disabilities receiving such services have a developmental disability such as mental retardation, autism, or cerebral palsy; cash benefits continue under this category as long as the person is a dependent.

Supplemental Social Security Income Program   The Supplemental Social Security Income (SSI) program offers monthly cash benefits to persons and dependents of persons who are aged or disabled and whose income falls below a certain level. The SSI program is a federally funded program supplemented by state funds to meet the basic living needs of its recipients. All but seven states provide funds to supplement federal benefits. The benefits are designed to reach those not previously employed and, thus, not covered by the SSDI program. As a group, SSI recipients are younger than SSDI recipients because of no requirement for prior insurance coverage and work history. Approximately 27% of all SSI recipients under the age of 65 have mental retardation; approximately 42% of the children with disabilities covered by these benefits have mental retardation. According to

Castellani (1987), SSI's importance is twofold: it directly assists individuals and is a source of funding to community-based services through its recipients.

Medicare   Medicare is a federally funded program that provides health insurance coverage (e.g., hospice, hospital, home health care) to persons with and without disabilities over the age of 65 and to persons who have left the workforce due to a disability prior to age 65. Disability criteria are identical to those in the previous two categories; eligibility requirements are closely aligned with SSDI requirements. Dependents of SSDI recipients are not covered until age 20. Of the nearly three million persons with disabilities receiving Medicare benefits in 1987, approximately 17% were adult dependents with disabilities.

Medicaid   Medicaid is a jointly operated federal and state health care program for people who cannot afford private insurance or medical services. Originally commissioned to serve the acute health care needs of persons with low incomes, "it has now become the nation's primary program for financing long term care services to elderly and disabled individuals" (U.S. Department of Health and Human Services, 1990, p. 102). Adults with mental retardation typically qualify for Medicaid. Though states are required to operate within federal guidelines, services vary widely from state to state. Disability criteria for the federal portion of the program are the same as for the other three previously mentioned programs; however, state eligibility criteria may vary. Under Medicaid, the federal government reimburses states for 50% to 77% of the costs incurred.

Work is just as significant for persons with mental retardation as it is for persons without mental retardation.

TABLE 12.2
Breakdown of Employment Options

Employment option	Dimension			
	Financial reimbursement	Employment supports	Community integration	Production of valued goods
Nonemployment	none	none	none	none
Unpaid	none	varies	likely	possible
Sheltered	below minimum	continual	none	unlikely
Supported	minimum+	continual/faded	yes	yes
Competitive	minimum+	varies	yes	yes

Source: From "New Directions and Strategies in Habilation Services: toward Meaningful Employment Outcome" (p. 201), by R. P. Schultz, 1988, in L. W. Heal, J. I. Haney, and A. R. Novek (Eds.), *Integration of Developmentally Disabled Individuals into the Community* (2nd ed.), Baltimore: Paul H. Brookes; and from "Establishing Community Employment Programs for Persons with Severe Disabilities: Systems Designs and Resolutions" (p. 131), by R. T. Vogelsburg and R. P. Schutz, 1988, in M. D. Powers (Ed.), *Expanding Systems of Service Delivery for Persons with Developmental Disabilities*, Baltimore: Paul H. Brookes. Adapted by permission.

Employment Integration

The routines, rhythms, and responsibilities of work are all part of **employment integration.** Defined simply as the extent to which a person is involved in normative, work-related activities, these activities are no less significant for the person with mental retardation than for the person without mental retardation. Changes in legislation, social policy, and public attitudes have allowed more people to share in the benefits of gainful employment than ever before. Whereas people with disabilities were once thought to possess little potential for gainful employment, even individuals with the most pervasive support needs are now considered by employers to be quite capable of performing complex vocational tasks (Chamberlain, 1988; Craig, & Boyd, 1990; Tilson, Luecking, & Donovan, 1994).

The ultimate goal of habilitation is placement in a regular, competitive job, yet some adults with mental retardation cannot meet this goal. Today a number of employment options are available for adults with mental retardation (see Table 12.2). Economic conditions, extent and adequacy of training, flexibility of employment sites, and individual characteristics all interact to determine which option is most appropriate for a specific person at a given time. Following are brief descriptions of three general categories of employment.

Nonemployment   This category is appropriate for three groups of people. The first group is composed of those whose need for supports is so pervasive or whose skills are so minimal that it is unlikely that vocational training can be undertaken and employment secured. The second group consists of those who are capable of working but who choose not to work. This group includes people who are influenced by disincentives that create compelling reasons for not seeking employment. The third group encompasses those who want to work but cannot find employment, including workers who have been temporarily laid off.

Unpaid Employment   Some adults with mental retardation may have opportunities to work but for whatever reason do not receive pay. In some instances, this situation is positive, as in the case of volunteer work, in which income is neither necessary nor expected. In other situations, this option may reflect unfair treatment, as when a person is not paid for work that usually generates income. Many have argued that persons with mental retardation, including persons with extensive support needs, should have access to the same vocational training and employment opportunities as persons without mental retardation. For some individuals, that means the right to forego paid employment in restrictive settings in favor of nonpaid employment in nonrestrictive settings (Brown et al., 1984).

Paid Employment   Few things are as important to employees as compensation. For most people that usually means a paycheck, but for others it often means payment through other types of goods or services. The range of paid employment options varies from highly protected to highly competitive settings. A brief breakdown of three types of settings follows:

- *Sheltered employment.*   Sheltered workshops consist of programs that provide daytime activities for persons who require continuous supervision. These workshops provide both long- and short-term placements, stress self-sufficiency over employability, and serve persons with intermittent to pervasive support needs. Most workshops provide basic rehabilitation services, including screening, evaluation, training, placement, and follow-up services.
- *Supported employment.*   For persons for whom competitive employment is not an option, supported employment is often used. Supported employment exemplifies the movement away from sheltered settings toward integrative ones. These programs allow for decreased supervision and segregation and increased autonomy and integration through structured support (job coaches), paid employment, and the opportunity to work in competitive settings.
- *Competitive employment.*   This category represents employment on the open market, usually alongside persons without mental retardation. More adults with mental retardation are obtaining placements in independent, competitive settings than ever before. Adults seeking this form of employment are as likely to obtain jobs through family, friends, or their own efforts as through organized vocational programs.

Forces still act against job attainment. Castellani (1987) has noted that employment is often at odds with certain community services, particularly income support and health care programs, which many adults with mental retardation receive. For example, Rabasca (1999) has reported that "as many as 70% of persons with severe cognitive and physical disabilities are unemployed even though three out of four say they would like to work" (p. 29). Factors such as loss of cash payments, loss of health insurance/benefits, and lack of guidance about relevant educational employment opportunities are all cited as potential impediments to full employment integration. Bowe (1993) offers this analysis on the 20th anniversary of the SSI program:

> [T]he disability employment figures from the Census Bureau loom large. They suggest, indirectly but provocatively, that the fall-off in employment by males with

disabilities since 1970 is at least in part a function of the attractiveness they find in the SSI program (and in the SSDI program, as well). . . . Women with disabilities, for their part, might have made more gains during the 1970–1990 period if they, too, did not have the options offered by SSDI and SSI. (p. 85)

Recreational/Leisure Integration

Like all people, adults with mental retardation need recreational and leisure activities to balance the rigors of daily living. Unfortunately, far too many individuals with mental retardation remain outside the mainstream of community life in these areas. According to the *National Consumer Survey* (Temple University Developmental Disabilities Center, 1990), one of every three persons with mental retardation in the United States has an expressed need for **recreational/leisure integration** but is unable to acquire it.

Though many persons with mental retardation have an interest in a wide range of leisure-time activities, the activities consist primarily of passive rather than active pastimes (e.g., watching TV, listening to the radio or CDs, reading magazines) (Aveno, 1987; Kregel, Wehman, Seyfarth, & Marshall, 1986). Recreational programs have been a part of institutional life for many years; however, there are no doubt times when the focus of such activities has been on keeping residents occupied and providing relief for staff than with developing lifetime skills. Schleien, Meyer, Heyne, and Brandt (1995) provide an extensive review of the literature related to leisure skills and leisure education for persons with mental retardation and conclude that the benefits of a high-quality leisure program are many. For example, skills learned during play extend across the curriculum (e.g., language, problem solving), increases in socially appropriate free-time activities decrease the likelihood of socially inappropriate free-time behaviors, and a well-developed repertoire of free-time activities increases the quality of the relationships with family and friends.

Advocates have begun demanding that community recreational opportunities available to persons without mental retardation be extended to persons with mental retardation. Such an approach is often referred to as *reverse-mainstreaming* (Schleien, Green, & Stone, 1999). The demands have been heard. Programs ranging from special skill-building programs to competitive international competition are now under way. While most human service providers are aware of the Special Olympics, less well known but potentially more important for encouraging community acceptance is the Special Olympics' Unified Sports program in which athletes with and without mental retardation participate in equal numbers on the same teams in local, regional, national, and international competitions. The growth of the Unified program remains unparalleled among organized athletic programs for persons with disabilities. According to Ms. Annette Lynch of Special Olympics International, 39,827 athletes in the United States participated in the program in 1996, representing a sixfold increase from the 6,636 participants who participated in 1990 (personal communication, December 18, 1996).

Park and recreation clubs, drama groups, day camps, craft guilds, jogging clubs, cooking groups, and other special organizations for combined involvement of persons with and without mental retardation are being formed with increasing frequency. The continued development of special equipment such as modified bowling balls and walkers for ice skating has broadened opportunities for participation in sports in ways not imagined even a few years ago. Instructions for home-centered hobbies such as card games, board games, stamp collecting, and other leisure projects are also being included in curriculum plans (e.g., Schleien, Ray, & Green, 1996).

If programs are so plentiful and efforts so numerous, why does one in three persons report an unmet need for recreational/leisure services? According to Ittenbach, Abery, Larson, Spiegel, and Prouty (1994), adults with mental retardation face three major barriers to recreational/leisure integration. First is the issue of lack of a friend or companion with whom to share the activity. No matter how enjoyable an activity is, it is more fun when it can be shared with someone else. Second is the general lack of guidelines for planning and implementing integrated programs available to recreational specialists. New guidelines have been developed in recent years, but more are needed. Third is a lack of skills necessary to take advantage of such programs. A willingness to try and pursue new activities is in part dependent on success in other, related areas.

Residential Integration

The actual location of a person's place of residence in a community, often referred to as **residential integration,** exerts a profound influence on that person's likelihood for acceptance in the broader community. That is, *where* people live determines to a great extent *how* they live. This seems obvious when one thinks of persons in institutions, but it is also true of those living in the community. For some people with mental retardation, that may mean an active life that includes interacting with neighbors, catching a bus to work, and planning for a party; for others, it may mean spending hours alone in a room, not knowing where to go or whom to visit.

The shift in placement patterns from residential to community settings over the past 20 years has been both profound and far-reaching. What began in the late 1960s as a modest but humanely justifiable initiative has, 40 years later, transformed into a national and increasingly international movement toward improved services for people with mental retardation and developmental disabilities (see Mansell & Ericsson, 1996).

Good homes are those in which individuals are allowed to balance an active community life with individually determined alone time. As indicated previously, residences that are placed in neighborhood communities are typically referred to as community residential settings. The orientation of these settings is usually a function of the characteristics and needs of their residents. Community residential settings vary in size, location, number of residents, staffing patterns, and degree of handicapping conditions of residents. The level of mental retardation does not determine the most appropriate residential setting. The match between an individual's needs and those of the setting defines the quality of the living arrangement. Areas in which community settings may differ include residents' role in facility policy, degree of residents' privacy, staff philosophy of community involvement, residents' responsibilities within the facility, and decor and furnishings.

Residential options represent a continuum of sorts; unfortunately, their availability in some locations, particularly rural settings, may be very limited, and quality may vary markedly from one setting to another. Following is a breakdown of the classes of residential facilities using the nine categories described by Amado, Lakin, and Menke (1990, p. 8).

Protected Settings   Certain community living arrangements afford adults with mental retardation protected settings with varying degrees of support and supervision. The most notable in this category are the foster homes and semi-independent living homes. The goal, in each case, is to allow individuals to live as completely and independently as possible in a family-oriented setting.

- *Generic foster homes*—a licensed foster care home providing services to persons with and without mental retardation.
- *Specialized foster care homes*—a licensed foster care home providing services to persons with mental retardation and other developmental disabilities, exclusively.
- *Semi-independent/supported living homes*—personal homes or apartments occupied by persons with mental retardation who require less than full-time supervision or support.

Group Homes   The group home is the most common community living arrangement available to adults with mental retardation and developmental disabilities. In these homes, a group of persons with mental retardation or other developmental disabilities lives within a residential neighborhood and receives support and supervision from live-in counselors. Some homes are transitional, others serve as long-term residences. Many evoke images of comfortable family settings with decorations and personal belongings of the residents to encourage a sense of ownership and responsibility among household members.

- *State-operated small group residences*—fully staffed, public residential facilities equipped to provide services to 15 or fewer people.
- *Nonstate-operated group residences*—fully staffed, privately (or local government) operated residential facilities equipped to provide services to 15 or fewer people.

Large Group Facilities   Although the number of people with disabilities living in large group facilities has dropped in recent decades, institutional living remains an option for many persons and families of persons with mental retardation. Following is a breakdown of three such types:

- *State-supported institutions*—fully staffed residential facilities equipped to provide services to 16 or more people at a time. There are two different categories of large, state-operated institutions: (a) those that provide services to persons with mental retardation and developmental disabilities exclusively and (b) those that offer services to persons with mental illness primarily but who also have mental retardation.
- *Nonstate-supported institutions*—fully staffed, privately (or local government) operated residential facilities to provide services to 16 or more people with mental retardation and developmental disabilities.
- *Nursing homes*—large group facilities offering medical, nursing, and personal care to persons with and without mental retardation.

Personal Satisfaction

Why do so many people without mental retardation try so desperately to distinguish themselves from others when persons with retardation try so hard to be like everyone else? This phenomenon has two different interpretations. In 1967, Edgerton used the phrase "cloak of competence" to describe the lives of 53 persons recently released from institutions who, he believed, attempted to cloak themselves in an air of normalcy. He was referring to their efforts to assume roles, behaviors, and life stories that essentially denied to themselves and others the reality of the label and previous years in an institution. In contrast to this is the more recent trend toward self-affirmation and self-determination in which adults with disabilities acknowledge their limitations but fail to let them stand in the way of optimum daily living.

At its most basic level, **personal satisfaction** is the level of contentment and fulfillment felt by a person with respect to his or her person-environment match. While some see personal satisfaction as synonymous with overall quality of life, others see the two constructs as somewhat different (e.g., Edgerton, 1990; Heal, Borthwick-Duffy, & Saunders, 1996; Stark & Goldsbury, 1990). A major point of difference in the positions is the amount of control people have over the parts of their lives that bring them satisfaction. Without getting caught up in the philosophical nature of the debate, adults with mental retardation are indeed entitled to a life that is both satisfying and of the highest quality possible. Whether or not one's life in the community meets these criteria is up to the individual. More difficult, perhaps, is their proficiency in keeping society's mores and standards from inappropriately affecting their own sense of self-worth and self-determination.

The terms used by members of society to define adulthood—*independence* and *productivity*—and the roles adults are expected to assume (worker, partner, parent, household manager, etc.) contrast sharply with the images often evoked by the term *mental retardation.* In fact, the expression "adults with mental retardation" often seems contradictory to many people who do not consider adults with mental retardation to be adults at all. Instead, they may view them as childlike, dependent, and unable to make the necessary decisions. They are not children; they are adults attempting to establish themselves in their own communities in the best way possible. If having a job, meaningful relationships, a home, and personal possessions are the hallmarks of normal adulthood, then many if not most adults with mental retardation living in the community have very likely achieved both. In the words of Leon, a former resident of an institution in Oklahoma since age 8 and who now lives in a community home as an adult: "When I was in the institution, I was shy. I like where I am now. I like myself. I'm better off now. I'm more happy now. I'm a regular person" (Hayden, 1997, p. 15).

Most adults with mental retardation want very much to be part of a system that is often hesitant to welcome them. Whether it is more accurate to see these adults resisting exposure for who they are or as simply not considering themselves mentally retarded, it is safe to say that the label of mental retardation is not a comfortable one. The development of a positive sense of self is a lifelong endeavor for adults without mental retardation; why should it be any different for adults with mental retardation? The answer is quite simple: For adults with mental retardation, the stakes are higher and the cards are often stacked against them.

✳ Independent Living

Timmy and Carol Savage presently live in an apartment, on their own and as independent as any couple could possibly be. Tim spent 37 years of his life in the state's institution for those who are mentally retarded, after which he lived in a group home. Tim now works full-time sanding picture frames for ACME Industries, while Carol performs routine maid services for the Best Western Inn. According to Tim, and, incidentally, confirmed by the landlord, "We pay on time, every time. We don't get behind."

Tom Houston, housing developer for the disabled with Mental Retardation Services, explains it has been a long process of educating landlords and neighbors alike that those who are mentally retarded are more similar to than different from those pegged as normal. "Many landlords have very legitimate concerns about disabled individuals, because if a tenant is impeded in his performance of his duties as a tenant, it could result in a loss to the landlord."

The Savages have access to a citizens advocacy program that matches a volunteer from the community with a "special friend," a process by which the program hopes to develop lasting friendships. The layperson acts as an advocate for the human and legal rights of the person with retardation. It is simply one more way that differences can be diminished; volunteers grow in their understanding of the disabled.

Houston feels compelled to assure a prospective landlord that when a tenant who is disabled has inadequacies, a professional or a layperson such as a citizen advocate will compensate. Some people like the Savages need little supervision. They have demonstrated a consistency of behavior that assures a landlord of their ability to handle most of their duties as tenants with little guidance from others.

When a client is deemed ready for independent living, Houston helps him work out an agreement for monthly rent payments, including utilities, which are not to exceed one-quarter of the individual's gross income.

Once an apartment is found to suit everyone's purposes, a 1-year lease is signed. The client is guaranteed that his rent subsidy will be renewed annually for the next 5 years.

"Some landlords are very responsive," says Houston. They call him up when they have a vacancy because they like the program and go out of their way to help the tenant. For the landlord, "It's just a cut-and-dried agreement, strictly business. He wants to know, 'Am I going to get my checks on time? Is my lease going to be violated?'"

Houston says over and over again that these tenants are turning out to be reliable. They like structure and adhere rather consistently to a routine once good habits are taught them. But Houston is quick to point out that "it's not a humanitarian thing. It's a good business deal.

"I wouldn't be on the phone to you," he tells a landlord, "if I didn't feel it was good business."

Community Acceptance

Few things are more important to the success of the community adjustment process than the goodwill, acceptance, and support of the public. Known simply as **community acceptance,** the public's knowledge and attitudes are key components in the psychological health and well-being of the environment in which persons with mental retardation live. Zoning laws, program proposals, and mandates of elected officials are essential and formal means of acceptance. Less formal but equally important are the subtle, day-to-day gestures of acceptance and support put forth by one's neighbors each day.

Although the public in general and communities in particular support the idea of community acceptance, there are substantial barriers yet to overcome. It is now coming to light that the public's understanding of mental retardation is deeply rooted in the structure of society. The roles and status people with mental retardation are allowed to achieve are tied firmly to the extent to which people in the community believe the new members are different from themselves (e.g., appearances, behaviors, values) (Calvez, 1993; Quinn, Sherman, Sheldon, Quinn, & Harchik, 1992). Simply stated, the more "normal" people appear, the more rights, privileges, and autonomy they are afforded in day-to-day living. Cnaan, Adler, and Ramot (1986) offer a New Jersey Department of Health study in which 50% of all planned community residential settings in that state were not opened due to community resistance. Specific fears have ranged from a decrease in property values to concerns for the health and well-being of neighborhood children (Lubin, Schwartz, Zigmond, & Janicki, 1982; Ryan & Coyne, 1985).

Fortunately, fears and reactions such as those just mentioned can generally be changed or averted altogether. Most people view those with mental retardation as unable to live independently and in need of close and constant supervision. These low expectations and the fears associated with them often dissipate when individuals get to know persons with mental retardation and recognize their abilities and potential. Seltzer (1984) found that efforts to educate the public about mental retardation and group homes correlated positively with community opposition and that "opposition is less likely when the community becomes aware either after the residence begins operations or more than six months before it opens" (p. 7). The implication of these findings is that it might be better to adopt a low-profile entry strategy rather than a high-profile one when establishing a community residential setting.

To facilitate acceptance of persons with mental retardation and their community residential facilities, professionals must address the need for public education. Efforts must be made to inform the public about the nature, causes, and implications of mental retardation and even how to respond to people with mental retardation. These educational efforts must provide opportunities for interaction that are both positive and progressive. The deinstitutionalization project of New York state serves as a model of comprehensive community education and involvement. Public media reports providing information on the needs and nature of mental retardation, task forces comprising community members who locate appropriate group home sites, and speakers' bureaus to address community concerns form the basis of this campaign to obtain community support. Not surprisingly, evidence in the literature suggests that positive outcomes are likely when planned and cooperative opportunities are created.

Need for Support Services

All adults require services for community living. Whether working, shopping, banking, or pursuing recreational pastimes, very few people are able to live successfully without the services and supports of others in the community. Some adults, like those with mental retardation, require more support services than others, services that are specific, costly, and critical to the community living status of a particular person. **Need for support services**, then, is the level of supports and services needed to live as fully and independently as possible in a normative community environment.

TABLE 12.3

Support Services Needed and Used by Persons with Mental Retardation

Types of Support	Supports Needed[a]	Supports Used in	
		Small Communities[b]	Public Institutions[c]
Financial			
Health Insurance	46		
Income Assistance	55		
Payment or Provision of Medical Equipment/Supplies	37		
Payment or Provision of Medication	52		
Medical			
Dentist	66	95	96
Medical Specialists		49	
Nurse	12	38	
Nutritional/Dietician		19	
Occupational Therapist	32	15	16
Physical Therapist	33	20	19
Physician	67	99	100
Psychologist		32	
Professional Counselor	24	10	15
Speech/Communication	40	33	17
Other			
Advocacy	34		5
Social/Recreational	55		35
Social Worker/Case Manager	60	62	
Transportation	50	62	16

Note. All values reported here are percentages. Small community facilities housed 1 to 6 persons with mental retardation. National Consumer Survey results include responses identified by 30% or more of the respondents. The absence of a value in any category means that the use of this type of support was not evaluated in the study. [a]N = 13,075, Temple University Developmental Disabilities Center, 1990; [b]N = 336, B. K. Hill et al. 1989; [c]N = 997, B. K. Hill, Lakin, Sigford, Hauber, & Bruininks, 1982.

Several studies have been conducted to determine the service needs of persons with mental retardation living in the community. In their review of research on supports required by residents of foster homes, group homes, and institutions, Ittenbach, Larson, et al. (1993) found medical services, social and recreational services, case management services, and income assistance to be the major support services needed for daily living (see Table 12.3). Of the 13,000 persons who participated in the *National Consumer Survey* (Temple University Developmental Disabilities Center, 1990), well over half reported needing recreational and leisure-time activities, and another 50% reported needing transportation to access these services. In the areas of economic and employment integration, 55% of all respondents reported a need in income assistance, and 28% required vocational and other employment-related services. Thirty-four percent reported needing a friend, companion, or advocate to assist with the adjustment process.

If full participation in community living is the goal of the community adjust-ment process, then full access to community supports should be a prerequisite to residential placement. The rationale is simple: Until people have the supports that are needed to actually participate in their activities of choice, they are powerless to act on their choices. In short, a lack of appropriate support services translates to a lack of autonomy and self-determination (Wehmeyer & Bolding, 1999). Not surpris-ingly, communities vary tremendously in the availability of services rendered. Com-plicating the situation further are the unique needs of the person, the family, and the community, all of which must be considered when attempting to match a per-son to a given environment and an environment to a person in need of supports.

To learn more about issues of adult life, go to the com-panion website at www.prenhall.com/ beirne-smith and select Chapter 12, then choose the Case Studies module.

ISSUES OF THE ADULT YEARS

Frustration, puzzlement, jubilation, and boredom are many of the feelings felt by adults with mental retardation as they venture out into community life. These feelings, and others like them, are a very typical part of everyday living for adults with and without mental retardation. Adequate resolution of these feelings and the predicaments that bring them about are the testing grounds for continued adult development. Following is a brief discussion of three issues affecting the lives of adults with mental retardation today: advocacy, lifelong learning, and sexuality.

Advocacy

Advocacy is the formal representation of one's interests in an effort to bring about changes in the broader social order. For persons with mental retardation, that means the elimination of barriers to full community living and inclusion. The true spirit of advocacy, however, extends well beyond simple legal rights to include the more basic rights of autonomy, independence, and self-determination. Further-more, it also includes such things as the freedom to live and move in the least restrictive environment, have gainful and productive employment, and marry and have a family (Schalock & Kiernan, 1990, p. 163). Over the past several decades, the advocacy movement has become a very popular and potent consumer force.

Despite the fact that most adults with mental retardation find mere survival sufficiently complex, many communities are still raising legal and social obstacles to the notion of full community living. Consequently, persons with mental retar-dation continue to be represented by many local, state, and national advocacy orga-nizations. The President's Committee on Mental Retardation, the Council for Exceptional Children, the Association for Persons with Severe Handicaps, and the ARC (formerly known as the Association for Retarded Citizens) are examples of such organizations. Additionally, legislation such as the Vocational Rehabilitation Act, the Developmental Disabilities and Bill of Rights Act, and the Americans with Disabilities Act have helped tremendously. But it is only through the patience and persistence of persons with mental retardation, their parents, professionals, and friends of persons with mental retardation that community initiatives and recent legislation have grown from simple ideas into participatory reality.

Adults with mental retardation are quite capable of expressing their opinions about issues that are important to them, but their concerns are sometimes very dif-

TABLE 12.4

Types of Advocacy

Type	Advocate	Purpose
Systems (corporate) advocacy	An independent collective of citizens	Represent the rights and interests of groups of people with similar needs Pursue human service system quality and progressive change
Legal advocacy	Attorneys-at-law	Represent individuals or groups of individuals in the litigation or legal negotiation process
Self-advocacy	Individuals whose rights are at risk of being violated or diminished	Represent one's own rights and interests; speak on one's own behalf
Citizen advocacy	A mature, competent, volunteer citizen	Represent, as if they were his or her own, the rights and interests of another citizen

ferent from those of their care providers and often must be elicited using focused or nontraditional means (Foxx, Faw, Taylor, Davis, & Fulia, 1993; Lohrmann-O'Rourke & Browder, 1998). Advocates can help make the wishes and preferences of persons with mental retardation known to others. At a less formal level, advocates can help by evaluating the availability and appropriateness of services at the local or community level and then serving as catalysts for change. Advocates can help people with mental retardation get jobs, stay in school, negotiate public transportation, and move about one's environment in a humane, respectful way. Advocates can also help by providing companionship to individuals who often have few friends. The role of advocates as models of acceptance cannot be underestimated and cannot be replaced by paid service delivery personnel.

Several types of advocacy now exist (see Table 12.4). Among the different types of advocacy is self-advocacy, a relatively new and highly effective movement that is increasing in popularity nationwide. One excellent example of an organized effort of self-advocacy is People First, a movement in which individuals with mental retardation have organized themselves at the local, state, and national levels to identify common needs and lobbying power. Systems advocacy is another type of advocacy in which a group of individuals with and without mental retardation forms to better serve the needs of persons with mental retardation. ARC is one such example. Though a relatively new social movement, advocacy has been heralded as a major force that can and will ensure success for persons with mental retardation in the coming years.

Lifelong Learning

Continuing education, whether formal or informal, is receiving growing emphasis as a means of achieving professional advancement, recreational outlets, and personal enrichment for persons with and without mental retardation. Institutions of higher learning (e.g., junior colleges, colleges, universities) have begun offering credit and noncredit courses to the general public to promote and further stimulate interest in continued educational development. Continued lifelong learning is essential for people to reach maximum levels of independence and to adapt to an ever-changing world. Consequently, lifelong learning is a logical endeavor for adults with mental retardation to undertake.

Instruction may occur in a number of different settings. Often, it takes place at the employment site or training center. The place of residence can also provide nontraditional educational opportunities; for example, educational programs are often part of the weekly schedules of many if not most group homes. Another setting sometimes used for continuing education for adults with mental retardation is the community college. McAfee and Sheeler (1987) found that one-third of the community colleges surveyed had students with mild mental retardation on their campuses. Some colleges and universities have established programs for adults with mental retardation, while others meet the needs of this group by providing counseling, remedial coursework, and other supplemental services. Adult education programs for students with mental retardation, specifically, have also been established. Many of them follow programs developed at the Metro College for Living in Denver, Colorado, and the Night College in Austin, Texas. Although most programs are still coordinated and funded by special services, the impetus for their adoption by regular continuing education facilities is rapidly growing.

In addition to the information provided, these colleges often furnish meaningful leisure-time activity for adults with mental retardation. Courses offered

TABLE 12.5
Course Offerings: Night College, Charlottesville, Virginia

I. Communication	IV. Community Education
Talk and Say a Lot	Riding the City Bus
Keep On Talking	How to Find and Keep a Job
Community Checklist	Know Your Community I
For Your Own Writing	Know Your Community II
Using the Telephone	Living on Your Own
The Communication Workshop	First Aid and Home Safety
II. Money and Money Management	Driver's Education
Money Skills Assessment	What's Cooking: The Basics in
Simple Money	Good Eating
Money I	**V. Leisure Time**
Money II	Fun in Your Free Time
Using Your Money	Bicycle Safety
Community Checklist	Swimming and Water Safety
Budgeting	Art and Nature
Opening a Checking Account	Photography
III. Sex Education, Hygiene, and Personal Adjustment	
Looking Good	
You and Others I	
You and Others II	
Understanding Yourself	

through the University of Virginia's Night College emphasize daily living skills and functional academics (see Table 12.5). They also provide opportunities for socialization not routinely found through other secondary and postsecondary training programs for adults with mental retardation. Programs such as the College for Living and Night College programs have broadened the opportunities for these adults to expand their behavioral repertoires and to participate in activities that foster dignity, responsibility, and contributions to others. They are a source of pride for the participants and also provide firsthand experiences for persons interested in pursuing careers in the human services field. Because they use regular college campuses and community resources, they also help educate those without mental retardation about the skills and abilities of those with mental retardation.

Sexuality

Sexual development and sexual activity may comprise the most controversial issues pertaining to adults with mental retardation. Although the sexual development of persons with mental retardation is, for the most part, no different from that of persons without mental retardation, many misconceptions remain. Parents, peers, and professionals continue to hold on to a number of misconceptions ranging from a lack of interest in sex on the part of the person with mental retardation to a fear that they will reproduce "their kind."

For many, the movement toward less restrictive living arrangements brings with it a number of opportunities not previously encountered in more restrictive settings. Many professionals argue that sexual development and sexual activity are a normal part of daily living and that the right to sexual expression should not be prohibited. Others disagree, citing a number of unfortunate and even life-threatening consequences of sexual activity as possible outcomes—for example, exploitation, unwanted pregnancy, sexual and physical abuse, and sexually transmitted diseases (Schwier & Hingsburger, 2000).

A number of factors make the right to socially appropriate sexual activity and sexual expression a bit more difficult. These include the heightened supervision and supports in comparison with individuals without mental retardation; lack of accurate information typically provided by service providers about sexual development and functioning; and fewer socialization opportunities in which to try out new behaviors, roles, and expectations. Something as simple as negotiating the boundaries between risk and opportunity for growth remains a paramount issue for adults with mental retardation (Schwier & Hingsburger, 2000). Increased independence and current patterns of social interaction now evidenced in the community necessitate, in practical terms, that the issue of sexuality no longer be ignored (Sundram & Stavis, 1994).

To check your understanding of this chapter, go to the companion website at http://www.prenhall.com/beirne-smith and select Chapter 12, and then choose the Self-Test module.

<hr>

Summary

Adult Development
- Young adults with mental retardation enter the adult world with many of the same expectations as young adults without mental retardation.

- Adjusting to a life with aging parents, finding a niche in the local community, and discovering new and enjoyable recreational/leisure activities are hallmarks of the middle adult years.
- Establishing and accepting new family roles, lowered social expectations, and adjusting to continued limitations of the aging process are characteristics of the later adult years.

Patterns of Residential and Community Living
- Residents of public residential facilities today tend to be older, have greater levels of disability, and, as a result, have more extensive support needs.
- Community residential settings constitute a wide range of living environments, from small, individually owned homes to 15-person ICF/MRs.

Adjusting to Life in the Community
- Adults with mental retardation generally have less extensive social networks than do adults without mental retardation.
- Economic integration depends on the degree to which adults with mental retardation experience the right to make decisions as to how their money is earned and spent.
- Nonemployment, unpaid employment, and paid employment are three general categories of employment options one must consider when evaluating a person's level of economic integration.
- More than one in three persons with mental retardation in the United States surveyed reported a need in the area of recreational/leisure integration activities.
- Residential living options for persons with mental retardation range from generic, small-group foster homes to public and private large-group institutions.
- Development of a positive sense of self-worth is a lifelong process; for adults with mental retardation, the stakes are often higher and the cards are usually stacked against them.
- For full community acceptance of persons with mental retardation, efforts must be made to inform communities about the nature, causes, and implications of mental retardation.
- Adults with mental retardation are similar to adults without mental retardation in that they require support services for daily living. The supports are generally specific, costly, and critical to the community living status of the person requesting the services.

Issues Related to Community Living
- Over the past several decades, the advocacy movement has become a popular and very potent consumer force.
- Formal educational opportunities beyond high school allow access to activities that foster dignity, responsibility, and contributions to others.
- Sexual development and sexual activity may comprise the most controversial issues pertaining to the lives of adults with mental retardation.

References

Abery, B. H., & Fahnestock, M. (1994). Enhancing the social inclusion of persons with developmental disabilities. In M. F. Hayden & B. H. Abery (Eds.), *Challenges for a service system in transition: Ensuring quality community experiences for persons with developmental disabilities* (pp. 83–119). Baltimore: Brookes.

Abery, B. H., Thurlow, M. L., Bruininks, R. H., & Johnson, D. R. (1990). *The social support networks of transition age young adults with mental retardation.* Paper presented at the annual meeting of the American Association on Mental Retardation, Atlanta, GA.

Amado, A. N., Lakin, K. C., & Menke, J. M. (1990). *1990 chartbook on services for people with developmental disabilities.* Minneapolis: University of Minnesota, Center for Residential and Community Services.

Anderson, L., Clayton, C., Polister, B., Prouty, R., & Lakin, K. C. (1999). Populations of state-operated residential settings in 1998. In R. W. Prouty & K. C. Lakin (Eds.), *Residential services for persons with developmental disabilities: Status and trends through 1998* (pp. 3–12). Minneapolis: University of Minnesota, Institute on Community Integration.

Anderson, L., Lakin, K. C., Mangan, T. W., & Prouty, R. W. (1998). State institutions: Thirty years of depopulation and closure. *Mental Retardation, 36*(6), 431–443.

Anderson, L., Lakin, K. C., Prouty, R. W., & Polister, B. (1999). Characteristics and movement of residents of large state facilities. In R. W. Prouty & K. C. Lakin (Eds.), *Residential services for persons with developmental disabilities: Status and trends through 1998* (pp. 40–57). Minneapolis: University of Minnesota, Institute on Community Integration.

Aveno, A. (1987). A survey of leisure activities engaged in by adults who are severely retarded living in different residence and community types. *Education and Training in Mental Retardation, 22,* 121–127.

Bowe, F. G. (1993). Statistics, politics, and employment of people with disabilities. *Journal of Disability Policy Studies, 4*(2), 83–91.

Braddock, D., Hemp, R., Parish, S., & Rizzolo, M. (in press). *The state of the states in developmental disabilities: Summary of the 1999 study update.* Chicago: University of Illinois at Chicago, Department of Disability and Human Development.

Brinker, R. P. (1985). Interactions between severely mentally retarded students and other students in integrated and segregated public school settings. *Journal of Mental Deficiency, 89,* 587–594.

Brown, L. F., Shiraga, B., York, J., Kessler, K., Strohm, B., Rogan, P., Sweet, M., Zanella, K., VanDeventer, P., & Loomis, R. (1984). Integrated work opportunities for adults with severe handicaps: The extended training option. *Journal of the Association for Persons with Severe Handicaps, 9*(4), 262–269.

Calvez, M. (1993). Social interactions in the neighborhood: A cultural approach to social integration of individuals with mental retardation. *Mental Retardation, 31*(6), 418–423.

Castellani, P. J. (1987). *The political economy of developmental disabilities.* Baltimore: Brookes.

Chamberlain, M. A. (1988). Employer's rankings of factors judged critical to job success for individuals with severe disabilities. *Career Development for Exceptional Individuals, 11*(2), 141–147.

Clayton, C., Prouty, R. W., & Lakin, K. C. (1999). Large state MR/DD residential facility closures, 1960–2000, and individual facility populations and per diem rates in fiscal year 1998. In R. W. Prouty & K. C. Lakin (Eds.), *Residential services for persons with developmental disabilities: Status and trends through 1998* (pp. 20–39). Minneapolis: University of Minnesota, Institute on Community Integration.

Cnaan, R. A., Adler, I., & Ramot, A. (1986). Public reaction to establishment of community residential facilities for mentally retarded persons in Israel. *American Journal of Mental Deficiency, 90*(6), 677–685.

Craig, D. E., & Boyd, W. E. (1990). Characteristics of employers of handicapped individuals. *American Journal on Mental Retardation, 95*(1), 40–43.

Edgerton, R. B. (1967). *The cloak of competence: Stigma in the lives of the mentally retarded.* Berkeley: University of California Press.

Edgerton, R. B. (1990). Quality of life from a longitudinal research perspective. In R. L. Schalock (Ed.), *Quality of life: Perspectives and issues* (pp. 149–160). Washington, DC: American Association on Mental Retardation.

Erikson, E. H., & Erikson, J. M. (1998). *The life cycle completed.* New York: Norton.

Foxx, R. M., Faw, G. D., Taylor, S. D., Davis, P. K., & Fulia, R. (1993). "Would I be able to . . . ?" Teaching clients to assess the availability of their living style preferences. *American Journal of Mental Retardation, 98*(2), 235–248.

Glidden, L. M., & Zetlin, A. G. (1992). Adolescence and community adjustment. In L. Rowitz (Ed.), *Mental retardation in the year 2000* (pp. 101–114). New York: Springer.

Halpern, A. S., Nave, G., Close, D. W., & Nelson, D. (1986). An empirical analysis of the dimensions of community adjustment for adults with mental retardation in semi-independent living programs. *Australia and New Zealand Journal of Developmental Disabilities, 12*(3), 147–157.

Hayden, M. F. (1997). *Living in the freedom world: Personal stories of living in the community by people who once lived in Oklahoma's institutions.* Minneapolis: University of Minnesota, Institute on Community Integration.

Heal, L. W., Borthwick-Duffy, S. A., & Saunders, R. R. (1996). In J. W. Jacobson & J. A. Mulick (Eds.), *Manual of diagnosis and professional practice in mental retardation* (pp. 199–209). Washington, DC: American Psychological Association.

Hill, B. K., Lakin, K. C., Bruininks, R. H., Amado, A. N., Anderson, D. J., & Copher, J. I. (1989). *Living in the community: A comparative study of foster homes and small group homes for people with mental retardation* (Report No. 28). Minneapolis: University of Minnesota, Center for Residential and Community Integration.

Hill, B. K., Lakin, K. C., Sigford, B. B., Hauber, F. A. & Bruininks, R. H. (1982). *Programs and services for mentally retarded people in residential facilities* (Report No. 16). Minneapolis: University of Minnesota, Institute on Community Integration.

Ittenbach, R. F., Abery, B. H., Larson, S. A., Spiegel, A. N., & Prouty, R. W. (1994). Community adjustment of young adults with mental retardation: Overcoming barriers to inclusion. *Palaestra, 10*(2), 32–42.

Ittenbach, R. F., Bruininks, R. H., Thurlow, M. L., & McGrew, K. S. (1993). Community adjustment of young adults with mental retardation: A multivariate analysis of adjustment. *Research in Developmental Disabilities, 14,* 275–290.

Ittenbach, R. F., Larson, S. A., Spiegel, A. N., Abery, B. H., & Prouty, R. W. (1993). Community adjustment of young adults with mental retardation: A developmental perspective. *Palaestra, 9*(4), 19–24.

Kail, R. V., & Cavanaugh, J. C. (1996). *Human development*. Pacific Grove, CA: Brooks/Cole.

Kennedy, C. H., Horner, R. H., & Newton, J. S. (1989). Social contacts of adults with severe disabilities living in the community: A descriptive analysis of relationship patterns. *Journal of the Association for Persons with Severe Handicaps, 14,* 190–196.

Kregel, J., Wehman, P., Seyfarth, J., & Marshall, K. (1986). Community integration of young adults with mental retardation: Transition from school to adulthood. *Education and Training of the Mentally Retarded, 21*(1), 35–42.

Lakin, K. C., Prouty, R. W., & Bruininks, R. H. (1999). Longitudinal trends in large state-operated residential facilities, 1950–1998. In R. W. Prouty & K. C. Lakin (Eds.), *Residential services for persons with developmental disabilities: Status and trends through 1998* (pp. 13–19). Minneapolis: University of Minnesota, Institute on Community Integration.

Larson, S. A., Lakin, K. C., Anderson, L., Kwak, N., Lee, J. H., & Anderson, D. (2000). *Final report: Center on emergent disability*. Minneapolis: University of Minnesota, Institute on Community Integration.

Levinson, D. J. (1978). *The seasons of a man's life*. New York: Knopf.

Levinson, D. J., & Levinson, J. L. (1996). *The seasons of a woman's life*. New York: Ballantine.

Lohrmann-O'Rourke, S., & Browder, D. M. (1998). Empirically based methods to assess the preferences of individuals with severe disabilities. *American Journal on Mental Retardation, 103*(92), 146–161.

Lubin, R. A., Schwartz, A. A., Zigmond, W. B., & Janicki, M. P. (1982). Community acceptance of residential programs for developmentally disabled persons. *Applied Research in Mental Retardation, 3,* 191–200.

Mansell, J., & Ericsson, K. (Eds.). (1996). *Deinstitutionalization and community living: Intellectual disability services in Britain, Scandinavia, and the USA*. London: Chapman & Hall.

McAfee, J. K., & Sheeler, M. C. (1987). Accommodation of adults who are mentally retarded in community colleges: A national study. *Education and Training in Mental Retardation, 22,* 262–267.

McGrew, K. S., & Bruininks, R. H. (1994). A multidimensional approach to the measurement of community adjustment. In M. F. Hayden & B. H. Abery (Eds.), *Challenges for a service system in transition: Ensuring quality community experiences for persons with developmental disabilities* (pp. 65–79). Baltimore: Brookes.

McGrew, K. S., Bruininks, R. H., Thurlow, M., & Lewis, D. (1992). An empirical analysis of multidimensional measures of community adjustment for young adults with mental retardation. *American Journal on Mental Retardation, 96,* 475–487.

McGrew, K. S., Johnson, D. R., & Bruininks, R. H. (1994). Factor analysis of community adjustment outcome measures for young adults with mild to severe disabilities. *Psychoeducational Assessment, 12*(1), 55–66.

Peck, C. A., Donaldson, J., & Pezzoli, M. (1990). Some benefits nonhandicapped adolescents perceive for themselves from their social relationships with peers who have severe handicaps. *Journal of the Association for Persons with Severe Handicaps, 15*(4), 241–249.

Polister, B., Prouty, R. W., Lakin, K. C., & Bruininks, R. H. (1999). Changing patterns in residential service systems: 1977–1998. In R. W. Prouty & K. C. Lakin

(Eds.), *Residential services for persons with developmental disabilities: Status and trends through 1998* (pp. 84–87). Minneapolis: University of Minnesota, Institute on Community Integration.

Quinn, J. M., Sherman, J. A., Sheldon, J. B., Quinn, L. M., & Harchik, A. E. (1992). Social validation of component behaviors of following instructions, accepting criticism, and negotiating. *Journal of Applied Behavior Analysis, 25*(2), 401–413.

Rabasca, L. (1999, November). Knocking down societal barriers for people with disabilities. *APA Monitor, 30*(10), pp. 1, 29.

Rice, F. P. (1986). *Adult development and aging.* Boston: Allyn & Bacon.

Rosen, J. W., & Burchard, S. N. (1990). Community activities and social support networks: A social comparison of adults with and adults without mental retardation. *Education and Training in Mental Retardation, 25,* 193–203.

Ryan, C. S., & Coyne, A. (1985). Effects of group homes on neighborhood property values. *Mental Retardation, 23,* 241–245.

Schalock, R. L., & Kiernan, W. E. (1990). *Habilitation planning for adults with developmental disabilities.* New York: Springer.

Schleien, S. J., Green, F. P., & Stone, C. (1999). Making friends within inclusive community recreation programs. *Journal of Leisurability, 26*(3), 33–43.

Schleien, S. J., Meyer, L. H., Heyne, L. A., & Brandt, B. B. (1995). *Lifelong leisure skills and lifestyles for persons with developmental disabilities.* Baltimore: Brookes.

Schleien, S. J., Ray, M. T., & Green, F. P. (1996). *Community recreation and people with disabilities: Strategies for inclusion* (2nd ed.). Baltimore: Brookes.

Schwier, K. M., & Hingsburger, D. (2000). *Sexuality: Your sons and daughters with mental disabilities.* Baltimore: Brookes.

Seltzer, M. M. (1984). Correlates of community opposition to community residences for mentally retarded persons. *American Journal of Mental Deficiency, 89*(1), 1–8.

Stark, J. A., & Goldsbury, T. (1990). Quality of life from childhood to adulthood. In R. L. Schalock (Ed.), *Quality of life: Perspectives and issues* (pp. 71–83). Washington, DC: American Association on Mental Retardation.

Sundram, C. J., & Stavis, P. F. (1994). Sexuality and mental retardation: Unmet challenges. *Mental Retardation, 32*(4), 255–264.

Taylor, A. R., Asher, S. R., & Williams, G. A. (1987). The social adaptation of mainstreamed mildly retarded children. *Child Development, 58,* 1321–1334.

Temple University Developmental Disabilities Center. (1990). *The final report on the 1990 National Consumer Survey of people with developmental disabilities and their families.* Philadelphia: Author.

Thompson, J. R., McGrew, K. S., Johnson, D. R., & Bruininks, R. H. (2000). Refining a multidimensional model of community adjustment through an analysis of postschool follow-up data. *Exceptionality, 8,* 73–99.

Tilson, G. P., Luecking, R. G., & Donovan, M. R. (1994). Involving employers in transition: The Bridges Model. *Career Development for Exceptional Individuals, 17*(1), 77–89.

U.S. Department of Commerce. (1996). *Current population reports: Population projections of the United States by age, sex, race, and Hispanic origin: 1995 to 2050* (pp. 25–1130). Washington, DC: Bureau of the Census, Economics and Statistics Administration.

U.S. Department of Health and Human Services. (1990). *Task II: Federal programs for persons with disabilities.* Washington, DC: U.S. Government Printing Office.

Wehmeyer, M. L., & Bolding, N. (1999). Self-determination across living and working environments: A matched-samples study of adults with mental retardation. *Mental Retardation, 37*(5), 353–363.

Zetlin, A. G., & Murtaugh, M. (1988). Friendship patterns of mildly learning handicapped and nonhandicapped high school students. *American Journal on Mental Retardation, 92*(5), 447–454.

Part Four

Future Issues

CHAPTERS

Chapter

13

Family Considerations

To review the chapter objectives on-line, go to the companion website at *http:// www.prenhall.com/ beirne-smith* and select Chapter 13, then choose the Objectives module.

OBJECTIVES

After reading this chapter, the student should be able to

- identify and describe several different models of family functioning
- discuss the major forces influencing family functioning
- discuss key issues faced by families during daily living

centrifugal forces

centripetal forces

empowerment

family

family personality

family support services

natural homes

wraparound services

E veryone is a member of a family, whether biological or social, organizational or spiritual, permanent or temporary; everyone has a family of one sort or another. For most people, however, the concept of **family** implies a combination of immediate and distant relatives who, through birth, adoption, or marriage, come to live together for extended periods of time. Goldenberg and Goldenberg (2000) state that these naturally occurring units have their own rules, roles, and methods of communication; they maintain their membership through good times and bad by such factors as affection, loyalty, and concern for one another. The family, then, represents the most basic and critical unit of a culture, the one with the strongest and most enduring influences.

For a complete on-line glossary of mental retardation terms, go to the companion website http://www.prenhall.com/ beirne-smith and select any chapter, then choose the Glossary module.

Several years ago, the traditional family unit consisted of a mother, father, and two or more children; however, the typical American family of the 1950s now represents more of an ideal than a reality. Despite a population that has increased by 18% over the past two decades, from 60 million families in 1980 to 71 million families in 1998, the size of the average family has remained relatively stable: 3.3 persons/family in 1980 as compared with 3.2 persons/family in 1998. Like families in other countries throughout the world, an increasing number of American children are growing up in single-parent households or no households at all. For example, the number of families headed by single men and single women has increased substantially over the past two decades, from 0.6 to 1.8 million families headed by men, and from 5.4 to 7.7 million families headed by women (Bureau of the Census, 1999; see Figure 13.1). Interestingly, the percentage of families in America headed by single women has increased by 43%, while the percentage of families headed by single men has increased by 200% during that same time period.

Although the demographics of families with a person with mental retardation are not always different from the demographics of families in the general population, they are different in some important ways. For example, in an analysis of household survey data conducted by the U.S. Census Bureau and focusing on peo-

FIGURE 13.1

Living Arrangements of Children under 18 Years by Marital Status (*N* = 68.4 million children)

Source: From The Congressional Information Service, Inc., 1999. *Marital Status and Living Arrangements: March 1998* (Update), Bethesda, MD: Author. Data taken from Current Population Reports Series P-20 (Report No. 514, Table 6), U.S. Department of Commerce, Bureau of the Census.

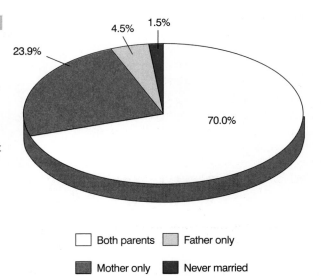

TABLE 13.1

Common Variations in Family Structure and Organization

Family type	Composition of family unit
Nuclear family	Husband, wife, children
Extended family	Nuclear family plus grandparents, uncles, aunts, and so on
Blended family	Husband, wife, plus children from previous marriage(s)
Common-law family	Man, woman, and possibly children living together as a family, although the former two have not gone through a formal legal marriage ceremony
Single-parent family	Household led by one parent (man or woman) possibly due to divorce, death, desertion, or never having married
Commune family	Men, women, and children living together, sharing rights and responsibilities, and collectively owning and/or using property, sometimes abandoning traditional monogamous marriages
Serial family	Man or woman has a succession of marriages, thus acquiring several spouses and different families over a lifetime, but one nuclear family at at time
Composite family	A form of polygamous marriage in which two or more nuclear families share a common husband (polygyny) or wife (polyandry), the former being more prevalent
Cohabitation	A more or less permanent relationship between two unmarried persons of the opposite sex who share a nonlegally binding living arrangement
Gay couples	Couples of the same gender who develop and maintain a homosexual relationship

Source: From *Family Therapy: An Overview* (2nd ed., p. 13), by I. Goldenberg and H. Goldenberg. Copyright © 1985 by Wadsworth, Inc. Reprinted with permission from Brooks/Cole Publishing Company, Pacific Grove, CA 93950.

ple with mental retardation/developmental disabilities, specifically, Larson et al. (2000) found that among those not living in large public residential facilities (institutions) in 1994 and 1995, 85% lived with relatives as compared with 41% of people in the general population. Furthermore, only about 7% of adults with mental retardation lived with their spouse as compared with 47% of all adults in the general population. Interestingly, while the married rates were very different from one another, the formerly married rates (i.e., divorced, separated, widowed) were about the same for both groups. With respect to children, youth, and young adults, 61% reported living with both parents, while 31% reported living with their mother only, 2% reported living with their father only, and 4% reported living with other relatives. When compared with the values in Figure 13.1, it is apparent that proportionately more children with mental retardation live in single-parent households than children in the general population.

While it may come as no surprise that children raised in a one-parent household receive less "parental attention, affection, and supervision than children raised in two-parent households," children raised in one-parent households have also been found to be at greater risk for accidents (20%–30%), grade retention (40%–75%), and expulsion from school (70%) (Family Research Council, 1992, p. 29). Based on data for the last three decades, there is no reason to expect these trends to change anytime soon. The range of children's living accommodations goes well beyond what it was only a few decades ago. Extended families, stepfamilies, common-law families, communal families, serial families, or some combination thereof may be the only reference point a child has (see Table 13.1). These new types of living arrangements often introduce their own unique sets of problems, everything from blatant discrimination to various social stigma (Edwards, 1995).

Understanding the factors that influence the development of persons with mental retardation requires that one understand the family environment, the dynamics of that environment, and the special needs of families of persons with mental retardation. Unlike other chapters in this book that focus on such matters as developmental periods, etiology, or legal issues, this chapter focuses on the family: the organization of families, the dynamics of family life, and the issues faced by families of persons with mental retardation. What follows is not a discussion of a storybook family, free from the stressors and problems of everyday living. Instead, the family is presented for what it is—a complex, dynamic, yet highly interdependent group of persons attempting to live, love, and work together.

ORGANIZATION OF THE FAMILY

Families may be organized along many different dimensions. This section offers a brief discussion of three such dimensions: family models, family development, and the family personality.

Family Models

The family represents the simplest yet oldest social unit of humankind. Whereas social scientists were once interested only in individuals, today they are interested in understanding people in general—large groups, small groups, and all groups in between. The family is one such example. Family psychology first began receiving prominence in the 1960s and, has, since then, been investigated with the same vigor as other, related subdisciplines of the behavioral sciences (Zigler, 1985). Consequently, and in light of the contributions of researchers from seemingly disparate disciplines, models have been developed that provide a framework for understanding the makeup of the family in much greater detail. The models that have been proposed borrow heavily from other disciplines and differ markedly from the ideal image of the American family of the 1950s. A brief discussion of three such models follows.

Family Paradigms Model   The family paradigms model of Reiss (1981) is based on a sociological framework focusing on the interactions of family members. This model classifies families into one of three different types based on their interpretation of and responses to events around them. *Environmentally sensitive families* comprise the first group and consist of people who see their life events as both knowable and orderly; all family members are expected to contribute to the sharing of ideas and efforts of orderly family functioning. *Interpersonally distant families* consist primarily of detached family members, loners, and those for whom independence is critically important. Consequently, these family members put very little emphasis on interactions with others in the family. *Consensus-sensitive families* constitute the third group and are those families whose need for conformance and family order is so strong as to isolate them from the rest of society. Dissension is not tolerated, especially when it comes from outside the family, as family members quickly surrender their own ideas for what they believe to be the good of the family.

Adaptability Model   Beavers and Hampson (1993) offer an adaptability model that includes concepts typically used in the physical sciences. For example, families and family functioning may be placed on a grid in which one continuum ranges from severely dysfunctional to optimal, and the other continuum from centripetal to centrifugal (see Figure 13.2). Those at the healthy end of the spectrum are more likely to be open, adaptable, and goal oriented, whereas the severely dysfunctional families are most likely to be rigid, have poor communication patterns, use ineffective coping strategies, and be inappropriately content with their existing family structure. Beavers and Hampson's connection with the physical sciences comes in the major tenet, entropy, or the degree to which families tend toward disorder. **Centripetal forces** are those that draw a family together, while **centrifugal forces** are those that push a family apart. The ability to balance out the attractive (centripetal) and repelling (centrifugal) forces is a major determinant of healthy family functioning. As Figure 13.2 illustrates, the healthy family is one in which choices are respected and members are allowed to move, within limits, into and out of the family unit as life events dictate.

Biologically Based Models   Biologically based models may take several different approaches. In the narrowest perspective, one may cite the continuation of the species as the sole reason for a family's existence. Within a broader perspective, people are considered to be biological systems that consist of and contribute to other, related biological systems. Those who take a still broader perspective may conceptualize families in terms of energy transformation and interactive elements, or they may define the family in terms of its evolutionary structure and view it as a specific subsystem moving toward equilibrium (balance) in light of internal and external forces. Miller and Sobelman (1985) contend that while some aspects of the family can indeed be reduced to chemical and biochemical components, a much broader definition is required to meet the needs of practicing professionals today.

Family Development

Families are referred to as "units" for lack of a better word. They are a collection of related, interdependent people with a shared sense of purpose, responsibility, and history. Their actions, behaviors, wishes, and intentions are often less a product of their own creation than of a desire to meet the needs of those around them. Their actions and interactions generally transcend any single member of the unit. For the individual family members to grow and develop, so must the family.

The notion that families develop along predictable lines is not a new one. In fact, some say that family psychology actually represents an elaboration of traditional developmental psychology—that is, the development of the individual.

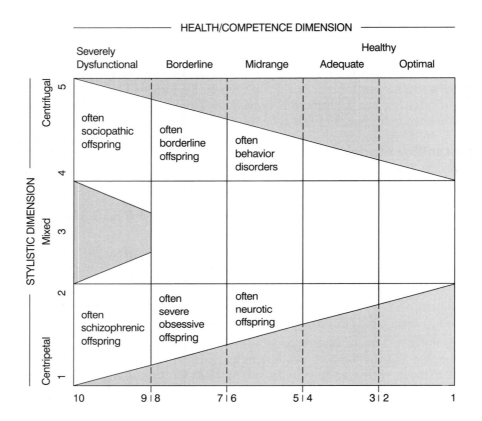

Health/Competence Dimensions

Severely Dysfunctional. Poor boundaries, confused communication, lack of shared attentional focus, stereotyped family process, despair, cynicism, [and/or] denial of ambivalence.

Borderline. Shifting from chaotic to tyrannical control efforts, boundaries fluctuate from poor to rigid, distancing depression, [and/or] outbursts of rage.

Midrange. Relatively clear communication, constant effort at control, "loving means controlling," distancing, anger, anxiety, or depression, [and/or] ambivalence handled by repression.

Adequate. Relatively clear boundaries, negotiating but with pain, ambivalence reluctantly recognized, some periods of warmth and sharing interspersed with control struggles.

Optimal. Capable negotiation, individual choice and ambivalence respected, warmth, intimacy, [and/or] humor.

FIGURE 13.2

Beavers and Hampson's Model of Family Functioning

Source: From "Measuring Family Competence," by W. R. Beavers and R. B. Hampson, in F. Walsh (Ed.), *Normal Family Processes* (2nd ed., p. 78), 1993, New York: Guilford. Copyright 1993 by Guilford Press. Adapted by permission.

Carter and McGoldrick (1999) have divided the family life cycle into six stages, beginning with single young adults who leave home to begin their lives in the community, and ending with families in later life. In between are the stages of newly joined families, families with young children, families with adolescents, and families who are transitioning their offspring into adulthood.

Goldenberg and Goldenberg (2000) have identified a number of tasks families are expected to meet in their cycle of development. Separation from their families of origin, new relationships and behavioral patterns, and the resolution of dependency issues at each of the respective stages are examples of stage-related tasks that must be addressed for all families. For Carter and McGoldrick (1999), the family system is an intergenerational unit with three to five primary cohorts that move through life together (e.g., children, adults, older adults). Much of Carter and McGoldrick's model is based on simple common sense, with the addition of the notion that the actions of people of each generation profoundly affect the actions of the other generations, thereby creating and changing the actual course of development of the people in each succeeding generation.

Just as most major theories of human development have failed to account adequately for nonnormative patterns of development for persons with disabilities, so, too, have most theories of family development. The literature is replete with studies addressing stressful life events, transition issues, and quality of life issues at various stages of normative family development; yet, the effect of persons with mental retardation on the family's growth and development is still far from certain. For example, whereas family care for a person with mental retardation terminated relatively early in life only a few decades ago, life expectancies are now commensurate with the population as a whole (Braddock, 1999; Eyman & Borthwick-Duffy, 1994), making planning for the later years a necessity for many. This added concern may well add stress to families in ways unforeseen just a few years ago.

The Family Personality

As a family continues its journey through life, its members experience many alternating periods of stability, change, and readjustment. For most families, that means growth, or movement toward a more flexible, integrated, adaptable family unit. Not surprisingly, a family's pattern of preferred responses to various events is considered to be both a cause and a consequence of its development (Swenson, 1985). That is, families that are actively trying to develop are likely to find many of the rewards necessary for continued and adaptive family functioning; those that are not actively trying to develop are likely to be frustrated by their efforts to adjust to the stressors of life and to resort to familiar but less successful approaches to functioning.

Because most children enter a family through birth or adoption and have little in the way of preestablished notions of family functioning, the parents generally set the tone for family functioning. As Hetherington and Blechman (1996) have suggested, there is no easy way of identifying which families are at greatest risk, how to reduce the risk of overwhelming stressors, or how to return to optimum levels of functioning once their development is hindered. What is considered healthy and adaptive in one environment may be considered dysfunctional and maladaptive in another. Adaptive behaviors are highly context-specific. For example, behaviors needed to survive in a war-torn country would be inappropriate in the American suburbs. Equally, an adolescent growing up in a serial family environment on "crack street" in urban America may have few positive family role models from which to learn. When daily promises from unrelenting others include alluring alternatives to a particular lifestyle, children and youth can hardly be blamed for adopting the prevailing mores of a particular neighborhood, however negative. For persons with mental retardation, the analogies are equally justified.

The ability to respond effectively to the challenges of everyday living depends to a large extent on the integrity of a family's personality. A family's ability to organize itself, solve problems, and grow and change in light of challenges faced, positive as well as negative, all depend on the family's level of health and well-being. At the heart of these tendencies are what many researchers refer to as *coping ability*, a family's collection of overt and covert strategies for responding to life's difficulties (Wills, Blechman, & McNamara, 1996). While all families tend to have their own unique sets of challenges and burdens, families of children with mental retardation can face some extraordinary challenges that profoundly effect day-to-day decisions. Leal (1999) outlines many of the special demands faced by families of children with mental retardation as they struggle with tasks of daily living (see Figure 13.3), demands that extend well beyond daily decisions to influence in a marked way the family's general level of adjustment and sense of well-being.

FAMILY FUNCTIONING

Hearing for the first time that a child has a disability is upsetting for the entire family. Finding out that the disability is mental retardation is even more difficult.

Financial

    Home modifications to accommodate child's physical needs

    Extra day-care or baby-sitting costs to meet child's special needs

    Job accommodations to meet special needs of child

Physical

    Extensive caregiving (i.e., inability to leave even older child or adult child alone)

    Sleep disruption because of child's physical or behavioral characteristics

    Meeting child's therapeutic needs

    Attending planning and team meetings

Medical

    Refusals or limits to health insurance or medical care

    Carry out daily medical treatments to meet child's physical needs

    Time devoted to medical appointments

Social/emotional

    Restricted time for leisure or social activities

    Explanations to siblings and other family members about child's condition

    Dealing with reactions from others

    Acceptance of child's mental retardation

    Scrutiny of privates lives by a variety of professionals

FIGURE 13.3

Demands Faced by Families of Children with Mental Retardation

Source: From *A Family Centered Approach to People with Mental Retardation* (p. 15), by L. Leal, 1999, Washington, DC: American Association on Mental Retardation. Reprinted by permission.

Families of children with mental retardation can vary greatly in their ability to cope with the extraordinary challenges that face them.

How a family actually responds to the subsequent challenges varies from family to family. Reaction to the news that a child has a disability, the long-term impact on family dynamics, and the presence of internal and external supports are three factors that are important to continued family development.

Family Reactions

The revelation that a person has a disability can occur anytime in one's life. Often it occurs at or near birth, as with many of the more prominent disabilities. Other times, it occurs later in childhood, as in the case of many mild learning disabilities. Some parents respond to the news with a sense of relief that their concerns about the child were well founded, that the disability has a name, a predictable course of development, and well-established treatments. More typically, parents of children with mental retardation respond with shock, disbelief, or an overwhelming sense of loss (Powers, 1992). Foster and Berger (1985) have reported that the news is initially so devastating that it strikes at the heart of a family's value system, disrupting its equilibrium and causing the family unit to freeze in its developmental cycle.

To conclude that there is a single, normative response to the news that a child has a disability is naive. Not only do families have their own unique ways of responding to the news, but it is quite common for a family's feelings and responses to the disability to vary throughout life. For some families, a mild disability is catastrophic; for others, a profound disability may be of little consequence. Because of the nature, prominence, and social stereotypes associated with mental retardation, however, there does tend to be a pattern to the types of responses that parents have when presented with the news that their child has mental retardation. Consequently, Batshaw, Perret, and Trachtenberg (1992) have outlined a num-

To learn more about family relations, go to the companion website at *www.prenhall.com/ beirne-smith* and select Chapter 13, then choose the Case Studies module.

ber of steps that they believe fairly represent the stages families of children with mental retardation go through in their acceptance of the disability. A brief discussion of each of the five stages follows.

Denial   It is quite common for parents and family members to resist the notion that their loved one is different from others. Refusal to accept the new information may be particularly acute when it pertains to a child who looks normal, is somewhat shy or reserved in temperament, and is an only or eldest child. The greater the severity, the earlier the diagnosis, the more arduous the denial. Parents (or grandparents) who lack experience with children of similar age to their own child, especially those without a disability, may be particularly resistant to the information.

Depression   Following an awareness that the threat of a disability is real and that the perceptions of qualified service providers (e.g., teachers, physicians, psychologists) have a basis in fact, family members often feel a weakening of their spirit, a sense of loss or even impending doom—and that the disability is greater than their resolve to overcome it. A general lack of interest in traditional social activities, routine health care, and normal daily activities are some of the many indicators of a brief depressive episode.

Anger and Guilt   Once the depression subsides and the family realizes that the disability is not likely to overwhelm them, their energy level starts to rise, and they begin to respond to the new and unfamiliar situation. Along with the increase in energy and unfamiliar feelings, however, comes a desire to fight back, to challenge the disability and challenge those they may consider to be responsible. Lack of knowledge about the disability and its causative factors often leads family members to strike out at unsuspecting others (e.g., self, friends, relatives, teachers, other professionals).

Bargaining   When parents realize that they, too, have a role to play in the course of the disability, they often set out in search of mitigating factors that will allow them to regain some control in their fight to overcome the disability. In an era of medical miracles, it is not uncommon for families to begin doctor shopping, to search endlessly for someone or something that can diminish or even cure the child of the disability. Concessionary statements and proposals to health professionals, other relatives, and perhaps even one's Creator are not unusual avenues of recourse for families in this stage of resolution.

Acceptance   Accepting the reality of a situation that is unwanted and unpleasant remains an extremely difficult task. Once the family has accepted the permanence of the disability and found that its values and structures have remained relatively intact, they are free to continue their family functioning, growing and developing as a new family unit, living, loving, and learning to the fullest extent possible.

Although the stages presented here offer a useful schema for service providers who routinely work with families of persons with mental retardation, the stages are only a framework for better understanding the *process* of acceptance. Several

✳ A Unique Parental Perspective

We who work with people with mental retardation are always inspired by parents who do things that make their child a significant part of the family. It is typical for proud parents to send out birth announcements of their new family member. Usually, these announcements are full of excitement and satisfaction. But how do you tell people that your newborn has mental retardation? Most of the time, this information is carefully disguised or withheld. To be sure, this is not an easy task or one that parents enjoy.

Sometimes interesting items come to our attention, and we do not know from where they came or who gave them to us; the following material falls into that category. It is a real birth announcement, but its authors are unknown. It demonstrates one of the most positive parental attitudes we have seen. We have omitted the child's name, date, and time of birth because it is not necessary; the important message is contained in the parents' words. This child who is retarded is lucky to be introduced into a family like this one.

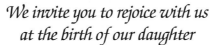

We invite you to rejoice with us
at the birth of our daughter

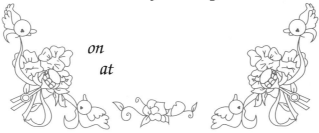

on

at

It is our belief as Latter-day Saints that we all lived a pre-earth life with our Heavenly Father. Certain valiant spirits were selected at that time for special missions during an earth life. One of these spirits has been chosen for our family. Our daughter is a child with Down Syndrome. We feel privileged to be entrusted with the care of this special child, who will return to her Heavenly Father at the end of her earth life and resume, for all eternity, her valiant status with her body and intellect completely restored.

caveats are in order. First, little empirical work has been done to verify the actual presence or invariant nature of these stages. Second, not all families proceed through the sequence at the same rate or with the same degree of success. Some families simply refuse to proceed through these stages while others do not need to—they may be quite comfortable with the disability and the adjustments that need to be made from the beginning. Although many parents do experience a sense of loss with respect to the *idealized child*, many if not most parents experience a sense of joy and appreciation for the new *realized child* that they now have. These notions are not, however, limited to children with disabilities. Virtually all parents must come to accept their children, their spouses, and themselves in light of who they are and not who they might have been.

Family Dynamics

Interpersonal relationships comprise the cornerstone of a family's existence. Inquiries into family relationships have generally taken one of two paths, parent–child attachments and child–other relationships. Both are embedded in larger social networks, and both have implications for persons with mental retardation. According to Collins and Gunnar (1990), secure attachments are the norm across cultures and subcultures. Yet, there are some cultures for which this is not the case. A number of interesting patterns in family dynamics have emerged in the literature pertaining to relationships involving children and families of children with mental retardation.

Many researchers have reported only the difficulties and negative reactions of families of children with mental retardation—although that trend is clearly changing (Helff & Glidden, 1998). Foster and Berger (1985) have reported that many of the experiences reported have been worst-case scenarios, and, even where demands are the greatest, many adults have modified their perspectives to "derive positive meaning from the experience of rearing a handicapped child" (p. 752). A commonly reported statistic among families of children with disabilities is the rate of marital breakups (e.g., Epstein, Cullinan, Quinn, & Cumblad, 1994; Hodapp & Krasner, 1995). Although the higher rate of single-parent families among families of children with mental retardation than among families of children without mental retardation is well documented here and elsewhere, the number of factors influencing such a finding are so complex and multiply determined that to attribute it to mental retardation exclusively is unrealistic (see Fujiura, 1998).

It should come as no surprise that the single greatest influence on the psychological health and well-being of a child is the psychological health and well-being of the parents. Said another way, the better the relationship between parents and the better integrated the family prior to the birth or adoption of a child with a disability, the better integrated the family is afterward. The adaptive capability of a family rests on two important factors: first, the general level of health and well-being prior to any adverse circumstances; and, second, the extent to which a family perceives the circumstances as adverse. Some families do not view disabilities as bad, they are simply viewed as individual differences. Hence, it adds little to their general level of stress. Furthermore, while there may indeed be increased levels of stress in many families of persons with mental retardation, increased levels of stress do not exist in all such families, and there is certainly no guarantee that the stress that is experienced leads to increased levels of maladjustment or psychopathology (Glidden & Johnson, 1999; Hannah & Midlarsky, 1999).

The relationship between a parent and child represents a special kind of relationship. Unlike work done in the 1960s in which the prevailing attitude about influence was primarily *of* the parents *on* the children, researchers now believe that there is a reciprocity of interactions between parents and their children (Powers, 1989; Reiss, 1981). Within the literature on families there remains a tendency to focus on mother–child interactions in general and mother–child interactions for very young children specifically. This focus is not without reason, given the differences in preferred methods of involvement between parents. For example, there seems to be little difference in the frequency of interactions between type of parent and child, but there do seem to be differences in the *types* of activities demonstrated by each parent. Mothers demonstrate more positive interactions in caretaking roles, while fathers demonstrate more positive interactions in play-related roles (Collins & Gunnar, 1990). Consequently, when parents of children with mental retardation do perceive the disability experience to be stressful, parents are likely to experience it in different ways, mothers through caregiving and fathers through more social, interactive means (Essex, Seltzer, & Krauss, 1999; Haldy & Hanzlik, 1990; Roach, Orsmond, & Barratt, 1999). However, just as not all studies have reported increased incidences of stress in families of children with disabilities, not all studies have reported differences in levels of stress or coping ability between groups of parents (e.g., Beckman, 1991; Bolger, 1992).

The physical and emotional contact of siblings throughout life represents the most critical and enduring set of relationships life has to offer. Whereas child–parent and parent–child relationships routinely span 40 to 60 years, sibling relationships may last 60 to 80 years or more and may share a number of intimate, developmentally important tasks (Cicirelli, 1994; Powell & Gallagher, 1993). The challenges experienced by the brothers and sisters of persons with mental retardation are particularly complex. At a time when young siblings are still learning about themselves and others, it is difficult to know how to interact with others considered by society to be substantially different. Foster and Berger (1985) have reported three rather prominent themes that have emerged in studies of child–sibling interactions:

- *Shaken sense of identity.* This level of awareness often raises questions such as "Am I disabled as well?" "Perhaps I am normal now, but can I also become disabled later on?" "If the disability is hereditary, will my children be disabled? Why my brother or sister and not me?"
- *Increased frustration.* Children who receive disproportionately less parental time and attention than a sibling with a disability often feel overlooked or taken for granted. Siblings without disabilities are often expected to assume responsibilities for tasks that their brother or sister cannot perform.
- *Adaptability and responsibility.* Children who are raised with a sibling with a disability often learn many of the benefits of shared responsibility. The very subtle pleasures and gratifications of helping others less capable as well

Nondisabled brothers and sisters often have special needs and concerns because of their sibling's disability.

as tendencies toward increased levels of maturation and compassion toward those who are different represent some of the many benefits of these relationships.

To learn more about siblings and other family issues, go to the companion website at www.prenhall.com/beirne-smith and select Chapter 13, then choose the Web Destinations module.

Although many researchers have focused on negative aspects of the sibling experience, others have found either no difference or positive experiences with respect to levels of adjustment (including pathology) between families with and without children with mental retardation (Glidden & Johnson, 1999; Hannah & Midlarsky, 1999). A comprehensive review of research by Powell and Gallagher (1993) further suggests that the published research of siblings with disabilities has resulted in fairly predictable conclusions. For example, siblings without disabilities typically take on more leadership roles within the family than would otherwise be the case, a finding that generalizes to younger as well as older siblings, with female siblings typically taking on a greater share of the caretaking role. Finally, difficulties in overall levels of adjustment that were observed for siblings without a disability tended to decrease as family size, socioeconomic status, and age differences in siblings increased. The negative aspects of growing up with a brother or sister with a disability should not be overlooked (e.g., anger, anxiety, isolation, sadness), but neither should the potential benefits. Children without disabilities who are the same sex and nearly the same age as the child with a disability stand to gain more from the relationship than others of opposite sex and a greater age difference, and both benefit more than children who do not have a sibling with a disability (Wilson, Blacher, & Baker, 1989).

Support Services

As indicated previously, families of persons with mental retardation face many demanding challenges. The challenges generally persist for the life of the person with mental retardation, affect virtually all life activity areas, and add a stressful dimension to life that most people would not, under other conditions, routinely accept. In short, families are committed to a lifestyle that is far different from that of most of their peers, thereby requiring a support system that is also far different from that of their peers. To do so means that they need **family support services,** services that will allow them to live as fully and as autonomously as possible in the community.

Prior to the 1980s, family support programs were largely child based and were often housed in child welfare agencies or organizations. The main purpose of these programs was to rescue children who had been hurt, abandoned, or neglected. Today, however, the purposes of most family support agencies is much broader in scope—to minimize out-of-home placements and prevent problems through appropriate and timely intervention services (Cole, 1995).

Foremost among the list of natural supports needed by families is a social support system that allows the family to feel that they and their problems are valued by others (Flynt, Wood, & Scott, 1992). Acquaintances, friends, and significant others offer the family a multitude of options that are essential to offsetting the stressors that pervade their lives. Covert (1992) reports that, despite the need for social supports, many families experience a sense of isolation in their own communities; they lack an extended family with whom to share some of the burden and are often unable to rely on many of the personal connections that others without disabilities often take for granted.

Financial resources are also a major area of needed support. The number of families actually served by state or federal MR/DD agencies has grown tremendously over the past 10 years, from just over 50,000 families in 1986 to more than 280,000 families in 1996, the last year for which data were available. Ironically, and somewhat sadly, the funding for these families comprised only 2% of the total $22.8 billion available for long-term care, leaving the remaining 98% for those requiring long-term, out-of-home care, such as those in institutions (Braddock, Hemp, Parish, Westrich, & Park, 1998). Especially noteworthy is the fact that approximately 90% of persons with mental retardation live in their **natural homes** (homes with other family members) and not within the state or federal service delivery system (Fujiura, 1998; Larson et al., 2000). Given the difficulties Americans without disabilities are having with spiraling medical costs, it is not surprising that sizeable percentages (15% to 40%) of persons with severe disabilities report medical and equipment costs that are both excessive and burdensome (Covert,

1992). Expenditures such as a motorized wheelchair, a new van with modifications, or a computer to assist with communication can be more than an average family's budget may allow.

A third but certainly not final area of needed supports is in the area of coordinated services. The ability to coordinate efforts effectively cannot be underestimated. The presence of duplicate, redundant, or competing services can be just as frustrating as the general lack of necessary services. Consequently, the notion of wraparound services has evolved. The term **wraparound services** describes an organized, integrated approach to service delivery that allows for a specially designed treatment plan at a specific point in time. Similar to individualized education plans used in the schools, wraparound services result from a meeting or meetings held by a service coordinator (or case manager), treatment team, and the family. According to Karp (1996), such services allow the "service coordinators to wrap the services around children and their families rather than forcing children into existing service programs" (p. 299). Ironically, in a recent survey of desired community activities, all that families really wanted was "assistance and support that would help them function as much like other families as possible" (Covert, 1992, p. 147); in other words, they wanted the opportunity to be like every other family.

Consultation with Professionals

Years ago, families of children with mental retardation were encouraged to transfer the care of their child with mental retardation to the trained professionals of a state institution rather than care for them at home. This is no longer true. Parents and other family members are accepting an increasing number of roles on behalf of their children with disabilities (e.g., teachers, political advocates, educational decision makers, and collaborators) (Turnbull & Turnbull, 1997). At a time when families of children without mental retardation appear to be abdicating the responsibilities of child rearing to organizations outside the home (e.g., boys/girls clubs, churches, schools), it seems ironic that families of children, adolescents, and adults with mental retardation are assuming a more prominent role in the service delivery process.

Understanding what families want in a helping relationship implies understanding what they do not want. They do not want to be told what is best for their child as much as they want options for care and action. Parents want to be seen as competent, capable, cooperative, and willing to pursue the right course of action once several paths have been identified. Parents want to be able to trust the professional relationship. Unfortunately, that relationship is often an awkward one, especially when the family does not agree with the professional's recommendation. The reason for the unbalanced nature of the relationship is fairly straightforward. Professionals often work with many families at a given time, whereas families may have a limited number of professionals to whom they can turn in a particular community at a given time. Hence, they do what the professional recommends or risk losing what care they have.

Families have known for years that professionals bring a special expertise to the disability at hand. Increasingly, professionals are coming to appreciate the special expertise that families bring to the therapeutic process. The term that we now

TABLE 13.2

A Model of Parent and Family Involvement

	NEEDS			
Information exchange	**Partnership and advocacy training**	**Home and community program implementation**	**Counseling and consultation**	**Parent/family-coordinated service programs**
Diagnostic testing and evaluation feedback	Training on parent rights and responsibilities, especially under the Education For All Handicapped Children Act	Behavior management training	Support groups	Parent advocacy group
Initial informational exchanges	Training sessions on participating in IEP, progress report, and other conferences	Home tutoring programs	Crisis intervention services	Parent advisory group
Initial and updated program descriptions	Advocacy training and methods for identifying and using appropriate community and school resources	Procedures for implementing specific education and training programs	Consultation for specific problems and issues	Parent and family classroom volunteers
Progress reports			Conflict resolution	Parent/family volunteer program
LEVELS OF PARTICIPATION				
Recognition and Awareness	Ongoing Communication	Advocacy and Representation	Skill Development and Application	Partnership

Source: From *Conferencing Parents of Exceptional Children* (3rd ed., p. 32), by R. L. Simpson, 1996, Austin, TX: PRO-ED. Copyright 1996 by PRO-ED. Reprinted by permission.

use to describe family-centered involvement and decision making is **empower-ment**. Without the family's help and input and, most important, the contribution of the family member in need of service, there would be no service delivery at all.

More children and families of children with mental retardation are accessing services than ever before. Yet, Simpson (1996) has reported that even special educators are often uncomfortable attempting to meet the special needs of parents and family members, a finding underscored by McGrew, Gilman, and Johnson's (1989) results in which 40% to 50% of the families in one school district indicated that specific priorities in their children's education were not being addressed by individualized educational plans. To help with this problem and to give all involved a template for better understanding parent–professional relationships, Simpson (1996) has offered a model with five principal components (information exchange, partnership and advocacy training, home and community program implementation, counseling and consultation, and parent-/family-coordinated service programs; see Table 13.2). Within each component are a host of needs that may be addressed in many different ways, each of which requires a broad-based, individualized program. Complementing the five components are five nonhierarchical levels of participation that allow for a range of options for family involvement.

Making the prescription for optimal service delivery so challenging is the realization that families of children with disabilities are not simply carbon copies of one another. While they may share much in common with other families, they have their own strengths and weakness, preferences and approaches, and, most important, attitudes about what is best for their loved one with mental retarda-

---

Do I respect the uniqueness of each family?

Do I value the expertise of family members?

Do I assume parents are competent or are capable of becoming competent?

Do I define and describe families in terms of their positive characteristics?

Do I consider how any one recommendation, support, service, or intervention might potentially affect all members of a family?

Have I identified immediate concerns and other unmet needs that might be consuming family members' time and energy?

Have I provided families with as much information as possible so they can make informed decisions?

Do I allow decision making to rest with the family, including the right to say no or refuse services?

Is my overall goal to build on family strengths?

Do I help families learn how to recognize their strengths and tap into information sources of support in order to reduce their need for formal support services?

FIGURE 13.4

Important Questions Service Providers Must Ask Themselves with Respect to Empowerment among Families

Source: From *A Family Centered Approach to People with Mental Retardation* (p. 22), by L. Leal, 1999, Washington, DC: American Association on Mental Retardation. Adapted by permission.

tion. Not surprisingly, the professionals with whom they work also have their own strengths and weaknesses, attitudes and preferences, and beliefs about what is right for the person in need of service. For the service delivery system to work as intended, the actions of both the service providers and the family members must be in concert with one another. Professionals and family members alike often need to be reminded of their unique but complementary roles in the service delivery relationship.

Building on the strengths of the family offers both parties a foundation for growth that might otherwise not be available. Leal (1999) identifies a number of possible sources of family strengths that professionals can use in their treatment plans. For example, professionals working with families with good, sound channels of communication can often use that communication to help facilitate treatment. Family members can be urged to talk about their plans and approaches on a daily, weekly, or biweekly basis. This approach may not be effective with families who have ineffective means of communicating with one another. In addition, cohesive, supportive families who enjoy spending time together may actually be energized from established home-based activities while other families may find home-based activities highly stressful. For the latter group, activities designed around community support groups (e.g., church programs, respite care programs, school programs) may be a better alternative. Professionals striving to empower the families with whom they work must know a great deal about the individual family and their own approach to service delivery. See Figure 13.4 for a brief listing of questions that service providers must ask themselves when providing such services.

Families need the assistance of capable professionals. Professionals exist to help meet the needs of persons and families of persons with disabilities. Together, the two groups form an alliance that must be strong, resilient, and broadly based if the service delivery system is to work to the benefit of those for whom it is designed.

To read more about services for families, go to the companion website at *www.prenhall.com/ beirne-smith* and select Chapter 13, then choose the Article Response module.

ISSUES IN FAMILY LIVING

Making life challenging for families of persons with mental retardation are several issues that families of persons without mental retardation respond to incidentally or without the same effort. This section focuses on such issues as personal safety, religion, and planning for the later years.

Personal Safety

Personal safety has become an increasingly important issue for all families, particularly those of persons with mental retardation. Susceptibility to crime, personal injury accidents, and an increased responsibility for oneself and others in times of emergencies are some examples of safety-related issues that arise. As the exodus from large public residential facilities continues, many will be leaving settings where 24-hour supervision was provided and opportunities for accidents were minimized. For persons with mental retardation, special care must be taken to reduce substantially the likelihood of injury from threats and misfortunes across a wide range of home-, school-, and work-related settings.

Would a young adult with mental retardation living away from home for the first time know what to do in the event of a fire, ruptured plumbing, or a gas leak? If the person is at school or work, someone will likely be there to whom the person can turn for help. But what about in the home? Are there others in the home who would know what to do if the young adult in question did not? Will there always be someone to consult when something just doesn't seem right? There should be. In addition, there should also be formal plans for contacting family members, support personnel, and even emergency personnel when necessary. What about if a passerby knocks on the door and asks to use the phone? Will the young adult know how to respond to the passerby's request? This simple dilemma puts many people without mental retardation in an awkward position and is certainly a part of living in a community.

Until just recently, school was considered to be a place of safety and support, even in the worst of locales. However, that does not seem to be the case anymore. A recent report by the Justice Policy Institute indicates that "nearly three-fourths of [all] Americans in a recent poll believe that a shooting could happen in their neighborhood school" (Bowler, 2000, p. 1). Not only are children and youth with disabilities more vulnerable to threats of injury and personal safety while at school; but, according to the same report, they are also more likely to be suspended due to higher anxiety levels and harsher discipline policies in schools nationwide. However, risks at school for children with mental retardation and other developmental disabilities extend well beyond those of illegal weapons. They include everything from accidents in and around bus stops to playground equipment to science labs. Parents may need to spend a day or two at school each year with their child to alert themselves to risks that might otherwise go unnoticed.

Integrated employment settings offer another opportunity for rich and fulfilling life experiences. Unfortunately, they also offer other opportunities for risk of personal injury. Fletcher and Abood (1988) have reported that even among those with mild mental retardation and a reading level of nearly fourth grade, 57% were unable to read important product warning labels because 42% of the words were

TABLE 13.3

Pecentage of Key Words on Product Warning Labels at Each Reading Level

Source: From "An Analysis of the Readability of Product Warning Labels: Implications for Curriculum Development for Persons with Moderate and Severe Mental Retardation" (p. 226), by D. Fletcher and D. Abood, 1988, *Education and Training in Mental Retardation, 23*(3). Copyright 1988 by the Council for Exceptional Children. Reprinted by permission.

Grade Level	Percent
1st	13
2nd	12
3rd	18
4th	12
5th	3
6th	24
7th	1
8th	4
9th	6
10th	2
*	5

at or above the sixth-grade level. Although words such as *eyes, milk,* and *avoid* can be found on many warning labels, so may such words as *inhale, flammable, discard, inaccessible,* and *chlorine,* words well beyond the reading ability of many persons with mental retardation (see Table 13.3). In addition, knowing whom to listen to and how to interact with others are important skills in most employment settings. As with home and school, extended visits to the job site or extended contacts with the employment supervisor may be critical to personal safety at work. Employers who have never had an employee with a disability may simply not know what risks to anticipate, risks that parents and family members can often spot quite quickly.

Religion

Involvement in civic and religious activities is another area of interest for many persons with mental retardation. While the Americans with Disabilities Act of 1990 has mandated access to more facilities and programs than ever before, the actual willingness of community leaders to embrace full community inclusion has been much slower to evolve. In contrast to the recent emphasis on physical integration over the past few decades, spiritual integration has received only passing attention. This deficit exists despite a well-accepted notion that parents frequently turn to religious organizations and clergy for assistance in times of difficulty. According to Fewell (1986), parents of persons with disabilities tend to look to religious leaders for support in several key areas:

- *Instrumental support.* Help with physical or financial supports of its members is a role that many religious communities willingly accept. Food, medical supplies, and money are often in short supply for the family of a person with a severe disability. Many churches and synagogues have access to people and resources that can circumvent some of the delays typically encountered in obtaining community resources.
- *Emotional/social support.* The very strong bonds of support felt among families who have worshiped together for many years cannot be underestimated. Many clergy, elders, and long-standing church members enjoy the privilege of being considered more a family member than an outsider, yet with special skills and abilities useful in times of spiritual need.
- *Educational support.* Help in understanding how a disability occurs, how to care for a person with mental retardation, and even how to explain certain religious concepts to persons with disabilities are questions that often arise. Sunday school programs and social activities provide outlets and opportunities for normalization that are open to persons with and without disabilities and, at the same time, offer an important avenue for involvement in church life.
- *Structural support.* Accommodations to major life changes (e.g., birth, marriage, death) are another responsibility of church leaders. Many of the rituals and routines of religious activities offer church members a source of strength in difficult times. Gaining access to important religious roles and responsibilities is no more important for persons without mental retardation than it is for persons with mental retardation.

❄ A Rite of Passage

Following is a brief story about one family's attempt to provide their daughter, Lesley, with a reception that marked her entry into adulthood. This particular reception, considered by her family and friends to be an important developmental milestone, parallels that of many other young adults without mental retardation. Most important, perhaps, is the realization that this reception occurred at a time when movement toward community involvement and full community inclusion was only just beginning. Irrespective of her disability, Lesley was entitled to all of the benefits and trimmings that most young women long for as they enter adulthood. For Lesley's family, the process of planning and preparing for this big occasion was as important as the event itself. Following are the words of Lesley's mother as she reflects on that big day more than 20 years ago.

On Lesley's 22nd birthday, we had a party for her at Eagle Creek State Park. The state park is not far from our home, is in the middle of a large nature preserve, and gives the appearance of being far from a large metropolitan area, which it is not. Though it was indeed a birthday party, it resembled a formal reception more than an actual birthday party. The reception was held on the grounds of the state park in a reception center, a large home formerly owned

by the Eli Lilly foundation, the service arm of a large pharmaceutical company in Indianapolis, and donated to Eagle Creek park for such activities.

Prior to Lesley's 22nd birthday, we decided that every girl needed and deserves to have a formal reception of her own, one that requires a lot of planning and preparation. As a part of our preparation, we were sure to include all of the formalities that seem so dear to a young woman's heart such as formal invitations, special napkins with her name and date of the reception on them, and a beautiful, many-layered cake. She needed to have the excitement of selecting the colors, planning the menu, planning the guest list, shopping for the cake, etc. It was to be a day for all to remember!

At the party itself we had a buffet, presents galore, and a guest book for people to sign as they entered the reception center. Similar to parties for other young adults without mental retardation, this guest list included immediate family members, friends, and other relatives. Parents of friends were not invited unless Lesley or the invited guest dearly wanted them. The guest list numbered about 40 people. Presents were listed according to guests so that thank-you notes could be written. In one guest's words, "Lesley had a beautiful gown on, the food was great, and the band made for a nice, festive

If people with mental retardation are to be self-determined in every sense of the word, then they will need to be free to make their own decisions about important aspects of their lives. Matters of spirituality offer an excellent example. People with mental retardation are indeed active in their church communities, yet researchers have demonstrated that neither their care providers nor their clergy have well-developed strategies in place for helping foster growth and development in this all-too important area of everyday life (Riordan & Vasa, 1991; Weisner, Beizer, & Stolze, 1991). Davie and Thornburgh (2000), through the National Organization on Disability, have produced a wonderful and well-received publication, *That All May Worship: An Interfaith Welcome to People with Disabilities*, that illustrates ways in which clergy, families, and religious communities can facilitate inclusion.

Hoeksema (1995) has suggested that common sense can be a most helpful ally in helping people meet their religious needs without infringing on the wishes and preferences of others, particularly within large nonsectarian, public residential facilities. Simple strategies such as trying to see life from another's point of view, avoiding coercion of uninvolved others, honoring the past practices of persons living in the home, and assisting with self-advocacy and conflict resolution skills are

atmosphere." Lesley is 44 now, and we have had several birthday parties for her since that summer afternoon in 1979. None, however, has matched the joy and splendor of her 22nd birthday.

Lesley no longer works at a sheltered workshop. She now works in the greenhouse of Dow Agro-Sciences. She is very dependable and has matured into a wonderful lady and very sociable person. Lesley has many happy and enthusiastic relationships at work and home. Most of her friendships away from work are with friends of the family and grew out of activities such as the Symphony Board, community opera, and People of Vision. Through these relationships and the interest others have taken in her, she has developed exceptionally well, verbally as well as socially. Dinner parties, bike rides, walks in the park, and lunch outings are some of the many opportunities that she is now able to take advantage of with her friends. Lesley also visits her sister, Clare, in Columbus, Ohio, at least once a year. They go shopping and do all the things sisters normally do.

At home, Lesley does almost all of the outside work, plus laundry and other errands for day-to-day life. Some of these errands include shopping for groceries at K-Mart and Kroger while I wait outside. Her contributions to the home are particularly valuable now because of my arthritis. When Lesley is not working, we enjoy walking and hiking along the trails of Eagle Creek State Park. Because we live on a small farm west of Indianapolis, we have many animals. Lesley takes care of her ducks, cats, dogs, goose, and pony as well as many inside pets.

Throughout Lesley's life, I have stressed the importance of her making her own decisions. I couldn't help but notice an almost universal feeling with respect to this among the other mothers of Lesley's contemporaries. Whether it is raining or snowing, hot or cold, it is up to Lesley to dress appropriately, which she does very well. In addition, she takes full responsibility for her personal hygiene such as bathing, shampooing, brushing teeth, changing clothes, etc., though I do help her change the linens on her bed. In other words, we have continued to treat her just as we would any of our other adult children.

This has not always been easy, however, as Lesley certainly understands that there are many privileges that she will never attain—and it hurts her. Our means of responding to her, her needs, and her hurts, when they arise, is simply to talk about them and remember that no one has a perfect life and that we will all have to be thankful for our blessings. We accept our disappointments and go on the best we can. Lesley has faith in God and in a life hereafter, which helps her immensely.

all as useful in matters of religion as they are in other areas of daily living. If persons without mental retardation value and require spiritual support from church leaders, shouldn't persons with mental retardation be able to do to the same? The trend toward community adjustment in spiritual areas of daily living is only just beginning.

Planning for the Later Years

The graying of the American population referred to in Chapter 12 takes on a new appearance when one reduces the trend to a single family. Older adults with mental retardation represent a unique challenge for an increasing number of families today. Persons who were once strong, energetic, and responsible for family decisions frequently become less willing or less able to make the necessary decisions over time. When decisions of aging caregivers affect the life of an adult with mental retardation, another important transitional phase must be addressed—planning for the later years.

Anderson and Kloos (1992) have reported that older persons (over the age of 65) with developmental disabilities represent the fastest-growing group of people with disabilities (approximately 12% of the total population of people over 65). Because of improvements in medicine, nutrition, education, and service delivery, persons with mental retardation, like those without mental retardation, are living longer than ever before. Not only is life expectancy for persons with mental retardation now similar to that of the general population, but, in most cases, that means living longer than their parents (Braddock, 1999; Eyman & Borthwick-Duffy, 1994). Embedded in this new trend are new roles and expectations for virtually all family members, the parents, the siblings, and the adult offspring with mental retardation.

Parents of adult offspring are often faced with the difficult decision of determining when they can no longer care for their loved one. Smith, Majeski, and McClenny (1996) suggest that the difficulties of this perpetual state of parenthood are further exacerbated by such things as age-related decrements in the offspring themselves, unavailability of resources for assisting with their care, and a chronic state of sorrow from the realization that the adult offspring had a less-than-typical life.

When parents are unable to care for the adult offspring and out-of-family placements are not desired, the shift in residence is often to the home of a brother or sister. In a study of 140 adult siblings of adults who resided in parental homes, Krauss, Seltzer, Gordon, and Friedman (1996) found that siblings maintained a connectedness with their brother or sister long after leaving home and that the siblings without mental retardation sustained "regular and personal contact, provided emotional support, and felt knowledgeable about the varied needs of their brother or sister with mental retardation" (p. 83). Approximately one-third of the siblings surveyed intended to live with their sibling upon moving him or her out of the parental home.

For families who have not planned for the time when siblings or other family members must take over for aging parents, the wait for services may be a long one. As recently as 1988, Seltzer found that 20% of persons with mental retardation who were elderly were on a waiting list for services—though only 5% of the people in Seltzer's sample required age-specific services. The fact that such a small percentage of people required age-related services is gratifying but offset by the realization that family and residential stability are generally tied to a family's and usually the parents' ability to cope—an ability that most often decreases with increasing age (Hogg & Moss, 1993).

Interestingly, Smith (1997) found that families with aging parents reported fewer unmet support needs than did families of younger parents. This occurred despite the presence of moderate levels of disability among the offspring and in spite of the presence of less involved siblings without mental retardation. Smith came to the conclusion that much depended on the perceived ability of the parents providing the care and the perceived level of stress in the family. Consistent with the information presented thus far, a family's ability to adapt to the presence of a disability seems to depend less on the disability itself or even on the severity of the disability than on the family's perceptions of the disability and their own abilities to care for the loved one.

Caring for a child with any type of disability can be demanding, no matter how able or stress-free the family may be. While support personnel do not want to interfere with the family's right to autonomy and self-determination, pragmatics dictate that as the family ages, different types of supports may indeed be needed. The supports may be in part directed at the disability, the age of the person with mental retardation, and/or the needs of the aging parents—whose own resources may be growing increasingly limited. In this case, it is not a matter of autonomy or self-determination but rather of vigilance in advocacy to see that the older adult's needs are met in a timely and respectful manner (Thorin, Yovanoff, & Irvin, 1996).

To check your understanding of this chapter, go to the companion website at http://www.prenhall.com/ beirne-smith and select Chapter 13, then choose the Self-Test module.

Summary

Organization of the Family

- Whereas social scientists were once interested only in individuals, they are now concerned with understanding people in general, individually and collectively.
- The actions, behaviors, wishes, and intentions of family members are often less a product of the family itself than of a desire to meet the needs of those around them.
- A family's patterns of responses are considered to be both a cause and a consequence of its development.

Family Functioning

- The news of a disability may be initially so devastating that it strikes at the heart of a family's value system.
- The major determinant of the psychological health and well-being of a child with mental retardation is the psychological health and well-being of the parents.
- Foremost among the list of supports needed by families is a social support system that allows families to feel that they and their problems are valued by others.

Issues in Family Living

- Susceptibility to crime, personal injury accidents, and an increased responsibility for oneself and others in times of emergencies are some examples of safety-related issues that arise.
- Gaining access to important religious roles and responsibilities is as important for persons with mental retardation as it is for persons without mental retardation.
- Older adults with mental retardation represent the fastest-growing age group of persons with mental retardation.

References

Anderson, D. J., & Kloos, E. T. (1992). Health issues and placement decisions for older persons with disabilities. *Impact: Feature Issue on Family and Empowerment, 5*(2), 17, 21.

Batshaw, M. L., Perret, Y., & Trachtenberg, S. W. (1992). Caring and coping: The family of a child with disabilities. In M. L. Batshaw & Y. Perret (Eds.), *Children with disabilities: A medical primer* (3rd ed., pp. 563–578). Baltimore: Brookes.

Beavers, W. R., & Hampson, R. B. (1993). Measuring family competence. In F. Walsh (Ed.), *Normal family processes* (2nd ed., pp. 73–103). New York: Guilford.

Beckman, P. J. (1991). Comparison of mothers' and fathers' perceptions of the effect of young children with and without disabilities. *American Journal on Mental Retardation, 95*(5), 585–595.

Bolger, M. (1992, May). *Stress, coping and psychological well-being in mothers and fathers of young children with a handicapping condition and typically developing children.* Paper presented at the annual meeting of the American Association on Mental Retardation, New Orleans.

Bowler, M. (2000, April 12). School violence less than thought. *Baltimore Sun,* pp. 1A, 11A.

Braddock, D. (1999). Aging and developmental disabilities: Demographic and policy issues affecting American families. *Mental Retardation, 37*(2), 155–161.

Braddock, D., Hemp, R., Parish, S., Westrich, J., & Park, H. (1998). The state of the states in developmental disabilities: An overview. In D. Braddock, R. Hemp, S. Parish, & J. Westrich (Eds.), *The state of the states in developmental disabilities* (5th ed., p. 41). Washington, DC: American Association on Mental Retardation.

Bureau of the Census. (1999). *Statistical abstract of the United States: 1998* (119th ed.). Washington, DC: U.S. Department of Commerce, Economics and Statistics Administration.

Carter, B., & McGoldrick, M. (1999). Overview: The expanded family life cycle: Individual, family, and social perspectives. In B. Carter & M. McGoldrick (Eds.), *The expanded family life cycle: Individual, family, and social perspectives* (3rd ed., pp. 1–26). Needham Heights, MA: Allyn & Bacon.

Cicirelli, V. G. (1994). The longest bond: The sibling life cycle. In L. L'Abate (Ed.), *Handbook of developmental family psychology and psychopathology* (pp. 44–59). New York: Wiley.

Cole, E. S. (1995). Becoming family centered: Child welfare's challenge. *Families in Society: The Journal of Contemporary Services, 76*(3), 163–172.

Collins, W. A., & Gunnar, M. R. (1990). Social and personality development. *Annual Review of Psychology, 41,* 387–416.

Covert, S. B. (1992). Supporting families. In J. Nisbet (Ed.), *Natural supports in school, at work, and in the community for people with severe disabilities* (pp. 121–163). Baltimore: Brookes.

Davie, A. R., & Thornburgh, G. (2000). *That all may worship: An interfaith welcome to people with disabilities.* Washington, DC: National Organization on Disability.

Edwards, R. (1995, September). Psychologists foster the new definition of family. *APA Monitor,* p. 38.

Epstein, M. H., Cullinan, D., Quinn, K. P., & Cumblad, C. (1994). Characteristics of children with emotional and behavioral disorders in community-based programs designed to prevent placement in residential facilities. *Journal of Emotional and Behavioral Disorders, 2*(1), 51–71.

Essex, L. E., Seltzer, M. M., & Krauss, M. W. (1999). Differences in coping effectiveness and well-being among aging mothers and fathers of adults with mental retardation. *American Journal on Mental Retardation, 104*(6), 545–563.

Eyman, R. K., & Borthwick-Duffy, S. A. (1994). Trends in mortality rates and predictors of mortality. In M. M. Seltzer, M. W. Krauss, & M. P. Janicki (Eds.), *Life *course perspectives on adulthood and old age* (pp. 93–105). Washington, DC: American Association on Mental Retardation.

Family Research Council. (1992). *Free to be family: Helping mothers and fathers meet the needs of the next generation of American children.* Washington, DC: Author.

Fewell, R. R. (1986). Supports from religious organizations and personal beliefs. In R. R. Fewell & P. F. Vadasy (Eds.), *Families of handicapped children: Needs and supports across the life span* (pp. 297–316). Austin, TX: PRO-ED.

Fletcher, D., & Abood, D. (1988). An analysis of the readability of product warning labels: Implications for curriculum development for persons with moderate and severe mental retardation. *Education and Training in Mental Retardation, 23*(3), 224–227.

Flynt, S. W., Wood, T. A., & Scott, R. L. (1992). Social support of mothers of children with mental retardation. *Mental Retardation, 30*(4), 233–236.

Foster, M., & Berger, M. (1985). Research with families with handicapped children: A multilevel systemic perspective. In L. L'Abate (Ed.), *The handbook of family psychology and therapy* (Vol. 2, pp. 741–780). Pacific Grove, CA: Brooks/Cole.

Fujiura, G. (1998). Demography of family households. *American Journal on Mental Retardation, 103*(3), 225–235.

Glidden, L. M., & Johnson, V. E. (1999). Twelve years later: Adjustment in families who adopted children with developmental disabilities. *Mental Retardation, 37*(1), 16–24.

Goldenberg, I., & Goldenberg, H. (2000). *Family therapy: An overview* (5th ed.). Pacific Grove, CA: Brooks/Cole.

Haldy, M. B., & Hanzlik, J. R. (1990). A comparison of perceived competence in child-rearing between mothers of children with Down syndrome and mothers of children without delays. *Education and Training in Mental Retardation, 25*(2), 132–141.

Hannah, M. E., & Midlarsky, E. (1999). Competence and adjustment of siblings of children with mental retardation. *American Journal on Mental Retardation, 104*(1), 22–37.

Helff, C. M., & Glidden, L. M. (1998). More positive or less negative? Trends in research on adjustment of families rearing children with developmental disabilities. *Mental Retardation, 36*(6), 457–464.

Hetherington, E. M., & Blechman, E. A. (Eds.). (1996). *Stress, coping, and resiliency in children and families.* Mahwah, NJ: Erlbaum.

Hodapp, R. M., & Krasner, D. V. (1995). Families of children with disabilities: Findings from a national sample of eighth-grade students. *Exceptionality, 5*(2), 71–81.

Hoeksema, T. B. (1995). Supporting the free exercise of religion in the group home context. *Mental Retardation, 33*(5), 289–294.

Hogg, J., & Moss, S. (1993). Characteristics of older people with intellectual disabilities in England. *International Review of Research in Mental Retardation, 19,* 71–96.

Karp, N. (1996). Individualized wrap-around services for children with emotional, behavior, and mental disorders. In E. H. Singer, L. E. Powers, & A. L. Olson (Eds.), *Redefining family support: Innovations in public–private partnerships* (pp. 291–310). Baltimore: Brookes.

Krauss, M., Seltzer, M. M., Gordon, R., & Friedman, D. H. (1996). Binding ties: The roles of adult siblings of persons with mental retardation. *Mental Retardation, 34*(2), 83–93.

Larson, S. A., Lakin, K. C., Anderson, L., Kwak, N., Lee, J. H., & Anderson, D. (2000). *Final report: Center on emergent disability*. Minneapolis: University of Minnesota, Institute on Community Integration.

Leal, L. (1999). *A family centered approach to people with mental retardation*. Washington, DC: American Association on Mental Retardation.

McGrew, K. S., Gilman, C. J., & Johnson, S. D. (1989). *Family needs survey results: Responses from parents of young children with disabilities*. Minneapolis: University of Minnesota, Institute on Community Integration.

Miller, D. R., & Sobelman, G. (1985). Models of the family: A critical review of alternatives. In L. L'Abate (Ed.), *The handbook of family psychology and therapy* (Vol. 1, pp. 3–37). Pacific Grove, CA: Brooks/Cole.

Powell, T. H., & Gallagher, P. A. (1993). *Brothers and sisters—A special part of exceptional families* (2nd ed.). Baltimore: Brookes.

Powers, L. E. (1992). Disability and grief: From tragedy to challenge. In G. H. Singer & L. E. Powers (Eds.), *Families, disability, and empowerment: Active coping skills and strategies for family interventions* (pp. 119–149). Baltimore: Brookes.

Powers, S. I. (1989). Family systems throughout the lifespan: Interactive consultations of development, meaning, and behavior. In K. Kreppner & R. M. Lerner (Eds.), *Family systems and lifespan development* (pp. 271–287). Mahwah, NJ: Erlbaum.

Reiss, D. (1981). *The family's construction of reality*. Cambridge, MA: Harvard University Press.

Riordan, J., & Vasa, S. F. (1991). Accommodations for and participation of persons with disabilities in religious practice. *Education and Training in Mental Retardation, 26*(2), 151–155.

Roach, M. A., Orsmond, G. I., & Barratt, M. S. (1999). Mothers and fathers of children with Down syndrome: Parental stress and involvement in childcare. *American Journal of Mental Retardation, 104*(5), 422–436.

Seltzer, M. M. (1988). Structure and patterns of service utilization by elderly persons with mental retardation. *Mental Retardation, 26*(4), 181–185.

Simpson, R. L. (1996). *Working with parents and families of exceptional children and youth: Techniques for successful conferencing and collaboration*. Austin, TX: PRO-ED.

Smith, G. C. (1997). Aging families of adults with mental retardation: Patterns and correlates of service use, need, and knowledge. *American Journal of Mental Retardation, 102*(1), 13–26.

Smith, G. C., Majeski, R. A., & McClenny, B. (1996). Psychoeducational support groups for aging parents: Development and preliminary outcomes. *Mental Retardation, 34*(3), 172–181.

Swenson, C. H. (1985). Personality development in the family. In L. L'Abate (Ed.), *The handbook of family psychology and therapy* (Vol. 1, pp. 73–101). Pacific Grove, CA: Brooks/Cole.

Thorin, E., Yovanoff, P., & Irvin, L. (1996). Dilemmas faced by families during their young adults' transitions to adulthood: A brief report. *Mental Retardation, 34*(2), 117–120.

Turnbull, A. P., & Turnbull, H. R. (1997). *Families, professionals, and exceptionality: A special partnership* (3rd ed.). Upper Saddle River, NJ: Merrill/Prentice Hall.

Weisner, T. S., Beizer, L., & Stolze, L. (1991). Religion and families of children with developmental delays. *American Journal on Mental Retardation, 95*(6), 647–662.

Wills, T. A., Blechman, E. A., & McNamara, G. (1996). Family support, coping and competence. In E. M. Hetherington & E. A. Blechman (Eds.), *Stress, coping, and resiliency in children and families* (pp. 107–134). Mahwah, NJ: Erlbaum.

Wilson, J., Blacher, J., & Baker, B. L. (1989). Siblings of children with severe handicaps. *American Journal on Mental Retardation, 27,* 167–173.

Zigler, E. (1985). Foreword. In L. L'Abate (Ed.), *The handbook of family psychology and therapy* (Vol. 1, p. v). Pacific Grove, CA: Brooks/Cole.

Chapter

14

Assistive Technology Applications

 To review the chapter objectives on-line, go to the companion website at http:// www.prenhall.com/ beirne-smith and select Chapter 14, then choose the Objectives module.

OBJECTIVES

After reading this chapter, the student should be able to

- discuss the concept of assistive technology and its relevance in the special education classroom
- list and discuss the various definitions of assistive technology
- identify the current trends and issues surrounding assistive technology
- discuss the benefits of assistive technology
- list and discuss the policies and legislation of assistive technology
- list competencies that teachers need to implement assistive technology
- explain assistive technology modifications that can be implemented in the classroom
- discuss strategies for overcoming barriers to assistive technology
- compare and contrast issues surrounding assistive technology at the preschool, school age, and postschool levels

KEY TERMS

aided systems

Americans with Disabilities Education Act

assistive technology

augmentative communication

communication boards

conversation aids

keyguards

speech input and recognition

Technology-Related Assistance for Individuals
with Disabilities Act

touch screens

unaided system

virtual reality

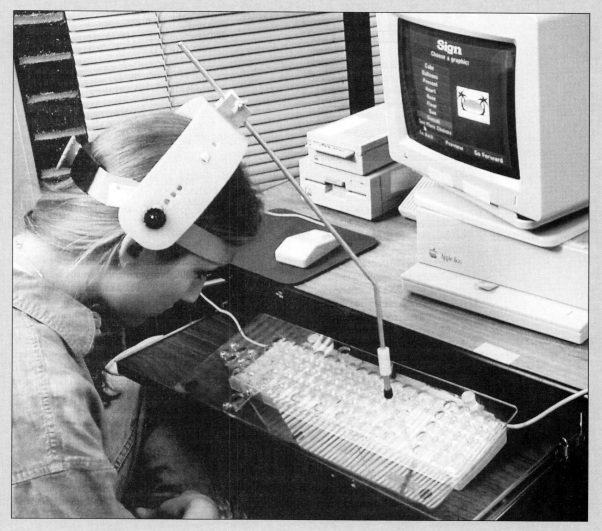

DEFINITION OF ASSISTIVE TECHNOLOGY

Students who have disabilities need a variety of adaptations to experience success in school as well as other facets of life. Over the years, various assistive technologies have been developed to help individuals with mental retardation cope with everyday chores or procedures that seem simple or natural for individuals without mental retardation (Bryant & Bryant, 1998a). Moreover, assistive technologies have the potential to reduce or prevent individuals from experiencing socioemotional and intellectual disabilities (Lesar, 1998). For this reason, educators have begun to explore technologies that have the potential to serve as solutions in helping students meet the demands of the classroom, the environmental demands of the workplace, and even the demands that can be found in the comfort of one's home (see Table 14.1).

Although **assistive technology** has been defined broadly it can be thought of as any device that has the ability to enhance the performance of persons with disabilities (Lewis, 1998). Hasselbring (1998) mentions that assistive technology allows persons with disabilities to become an integral part of school and the com-

For a complete on-line glossary of mental retardation terms, go to the companion website http://www.prenhall.com/ beirne-smith and select any chapter, then choose the Glossary module.

TABLE 14.1
Current Trends and Issues Shaping the Use of Technology in Education

Types of issues having impact on technology in education	Topics under each issue	Current issues having impact on technology in education	Implications for technology in education
Societal	Economic trends	Higher education costs	Distance learning emphasis to make education more cost effective
	Political trends	Politicians call for lower-cost, more effective education	More reliance on DL and other technologies to increase consistency of quality, stretch scarce resources
	Social trends	Recognition of need for technology literacy	Computers becoming a required student purchase
		Increased communications results in less privacy	Possible suspicion of technology-delivered education
		Growing popular distrust of technology	Possible suspicion of technology-delivered education
Cultural/equity	Economic/ethnic	Lower-income schools equals less access to computers	Low-income students must have equal access to technology
		More minority students in lower-income schools	Minority students must have equal access to technology
	Multicultural	"Computer culture" is pervasive in society	Students must use computers regardless of cultural bias
	Gender	Technology remains a male-dominated area	Females' use of computers in education must increase
	Special needs	Special devices and methods can allow special-needs students equal access to technology but are expensive to obtain and implement	Disabled students must receive equal access to technology regardless of high costs to educational system

munity. Congress did not want to limit the range of tools and equipment that might be made available to individuals with disabilities by committing to a specific definition. As a result, Congress developed a general definition to be reflected in the Individuals with Disabilities Education Act (IDEA). The IDEA defines assistive technology as the following: "Assistive technology device means any item, piece of equipment, or product system, whether acquired commercially off the shelf, modified, or customized, that is used to increase, maintain, or improve the functional capabilities of a child with a disability" (Section 300.5).

The Technology-Related Assistance for Individuals with Disabilities Act of 1998 (Tech Act) defines an assistive technology device as the following: "Any item, piece of equipment or product system, whether acquired commercially modified, or customized that is used to increase, maintain, or improve functional capabilities of individuals with disabilities" (p. 102, Stat. 1046). The Association for Retarded Citizens' (ARC) position on the use of assistive technology appears in Table 14.2.

Examples of commonly used assistive technology devices that illustrate the formal definitions include positioning equipment, mobility devices, computer applications, adaptive toys and games, adaptive environments, electronic inter-

To read the full text of the Tech Act and find assistive technology resources, go to the companion website at www.prenhall.com/ beirne-smith and select Chapter 14, then choose the Web Destinations module.

TABLE 14.1 (continued)
Current Trends and Issues Shaping the Use of Technology in Education

Types of issues having impact on technology in education	Topics under each issue	Current issues having impact on technology in education	Implications for technology in education
Educational	Directed vs. constructivist views	Directed uses of technology (drill, tutorial) are proven effective but often considered passé	Demonstrated effective technology uses may be discarded
		Constructivist uses are emphasized but little evidence exists on their effectiveness	More research needed on newer technology uses
	Single-subject vs. interdisciplinary	Past emphasis on teaching subjects in isolation	Continued emphasis on use of single skill software
		Current trend toward integrated curriculum or merging several subjects into one activity	Increasing use of multimedia and other technologies that support more complex, interdisciplinary activities
Technical	Rapid change	Technology changes too quickly for teachers to keep up	The latest technologies are in limited use in education
		Educators cannot afford most current technology	Schools usually have out-of-date equipment, materials
	Complexity	Teacher training is not keeping up with technology developments	Majority of teachers have insufficient training in technology materials and uses
		Schools lack the infrastructure to keep up with new technologies	Schools cannot take advantage of newest, most powerful technological developments

Source: From *Integrating Educational Technology into Teaching,* by M. D. Roblyer and J. E. Edwards, 2000, Upper Saddle River, NJ: Merrill/Prentice Hall. Reprinted by permission.

TABLE 14.2

Association for Retarded Citizens' Position on Assistive Technology

Source: From *Assistive Technology Position Statement,* by the Association for Retarded Citizens, 1997, Arlington, TX: ARC of the United States [On-line]. Available: http://www.TheArc.org/posits/astec.html.

People with mental retardation have the ability to use assistive technology and should be given the opportunity.
Assistive technology devices designed to meet individual needs must be available throughout the lifespans of children and adults with mental retardation and must be maintained and in working order, to be useful to support inclusion in the community.
Information on technology should be available to people with mental retardation, their families, friends, and support providers.
The principles of universal design[1] must incorporate the unique needs of people with mental retardation.
Technological innovators, designers, and manufacturers must be educated to the needs and preferences of individuals with mental retardation to ensure the production of useful products.
Individuals knowledgeable about people with mental retardation and current technology must be involved in assessing the needs of the person to ensure the selection of appropriate technology.
Effective use of assistive technology requires that (1) training must be provided to such groups as consumers, families, employers, educators, and other professionals and (2) effectiveness must be evaluated on an ongoing basis.
Decisions regarding assistive technology must include consumer preferences based on experience with the device and service.

[1]Universal design refers to designs that make all assistive technology products accessible to all people. Adherence to principles of universal design ensure that devices accommodate for individual preference and abilities; are easy to understand and are used regardless of the user's experience, language or cognitive skills; and minimize adverse consequences of accidental or unintended actions.

faces, homemade battery-powered toys, medical equipment, prostheses, and alternative and augmentative communication aids (Parette, Brotherson, Hourcade, & Bradley, 1996).

Lewis (1998) reports two purposes of assistive technology. First, technology can augment an individual's strengths by counterbalancing the effects of a disability. Second, it can provide alternative methods for performing a task so that disabilities can be compensated for or bypassed entirely. For example, an individual with difficulties in reading who possesses good listening skills can listen to books on tape rather than reading the print version. Persons with poor computational skills but good fine-motor skills may use a handheld calculator. Those with poor spelling ability but a measure of computer literacy may write with a word processor that offers assistance in spelling.

According to Blackhurst (1997), the assistive technology used for individuals with disabilities can range from high-technology solutions such as a speaking keyboard to low-technology solutions such a pencil grip. Included is the idea of a no-technology solution that involves the teaching or training of a device. The following list illustrates the continuum of technologies as described by Blackhurst:

- *High-tech* solutions involve the use of sophisticated devices, such as computers and interactive multimedia systems.
- *Medium-tech* solutions use less complicated electronic or mechanical devices, such as videocassette players and wheelchairs.

- *Low-tech* solutions are less sophisticated, such as adapted spoon handles, Velcro fasteners, or raised desks that can accommodate a wheelchair.
- *No-tech* solutions require no devices or equipment. These might involve the use of systematic teaching procedures or the services of related services personnel such as physical or occupational therapists. (p. 42.)

The expense of a device is often the determinant of how the device will fall into the low-tech to high-tech continuum. Often, the more expensive the device, the more high-tech in design (Parette & Murdick, 1998). Usually, the expense of a device is a result of the device having greater sophistication and better use in varying situations, and requiring more training for the teacher and the student to use effectively (Lewis, 1993). Low-tech devices are generally considered inexpensive and often require little training for their use.

To determine the type of technology or supports a particular student may need, it is a good practice to begin with no- or low-tech solutions and work up to more sophisticated levels of the continuum. However, it is critical to address the issues of individual needs and differences. Applying technology involves matching the individual's exhibited needs with the potential benefits possible through the use of the technology (Parette & Murdick, 1998). In addition, less emphasis should be placed on the categorization of the devices as being low or high-tech. Considering that students with disabilities possess individual interests, strengths, and weaknesses, we may conclude that a device appropriate for one person may be inappropriate for another. In a similar way, a device that may assist in one setting may be inappropriate in a different situation or environment (Bryant, Erin, Lock, Allan, & Resta, 1998). Once individual needs have

Any technology application must match the individual's needs with the potential benefits.

been targeted and appropriate technology has been applied, then the technology has the potential to provide a variety of needs for a person with a disability such as mental retardation.

BENEFITS OF ASSISTIVE TECHNOLOGY

Assistive technology provides a variety of benefits for individuals who are disabled (see Tables 14.3 and 14.4). Technology assists individuals with retardation in overcoming barriers toward independence by compensating for individuals' daily limitations. Additionally, technologies can decrease dependence on others by allowing individuals to become or remain integrated into their chosen communities (*Assistive Technology Messenger Newsletter,* 1998; Bieniewski, 1999). Specifically, the user may communicate with others, engage in social activities and recreation, and increase his or her daily living skills with the assistance of technology (ARC, 1997). In addition, technologies can be beneficial in assisting individuals daily in learning and working. Because benefits for using assistive technology are evident, individuals with mental retardation should be introduced to possible assistive technologies at an early age.

Assistive technology allows students with mental retardation to receive educational services in the same school and classroom as students who do not have individual education programs. Students can have additional access to instruction and other school activities and can learn from classroom activities at a faster rate. In addition, assistive technology allows students to make more progress in speech and language therapy, occupational therapy, physical therapy, mobility, orientation, and other related service programs.

In 1993, the National Council on Disability conducted a 19-month survey to explore the benefits of assistive technology devices and services. The following are some of its findings:

TABLE 14.3
General Benefits of Assistive Technology

Increases student independence
Advances academic standing
Increases participation in classroom activities
Improves time-management skills
Allows equal access to the school environment
Increases part-time job opportunities
Improves job search skills
Resolves transportation issues
Accomplishes activities of daily living
Advances considerations for continued training/education
Improves job opportunities
Enables performance of essential job functions

Source: From *Project Star,* by Mississippi State University, November 18, 1999 [On-line]. Available: www.msstate.edu/dept/tkmartin/.

TABLE 14.4

Academic Advantages of Assertive Technology as Reported by the U.S. Congress in 1988

Source: From *Power On! New Tools for Teaching and Learning,* U.S. Congress, Office of Technology Assessment, 1988, Washington, DC: U.S. Government Printing Office. Reprinted by permission.

Drill and practice to master basic skills
Development of writing skills
Problem solving
Understanding abstract mathematics and science concepts
Simulation in science, mathematics, and social studies
Manipulation of data
Acquisition of computer skills for general purposes and for business and vocational training
Access and communication for traditionally unserved population of students
Access and communication for teachers and students in remote locations
Individualized learning
Cooperative learning
Management of learning activities and record keeping

- Almost three-quarters of school age children with disabilities were able to remain in a regular classroom and 45% were able to reduce school-related services.
- Sixty-two percent of working age persons were able to reduce dependence on family members, 58% were able to reduce dependence on paid assistance, and 37% were able to increase earnings.
- Eighty percent of elderly persons studied were able to reduce dependence on others, half were able to reduce dependence on paid persons, and half were able to avoid entering a nursing home.
- Almost one-third of assistive technology users indicated that their family saved money, averaging around $11,110 per month, with assistive technology. At the same time, one-quarter of the users indicated that they experienced additional equipment related expenses that averaged around $287 per month.
- Of the 42 users of assistive technology who reported having paid jobs, 92% reported that the assistive technology enabled them to work faster or better, 83% indicated that they earned more money, 81% reported working more hours, 67% reported that the equipment had enabled them to obtain employment, and 15% indicated that the equipment enabled them to keep their jobs.
- When asked to estimate the impact of equipment on their quality of life, assistive technology users reported that without the equipment, their quality of life on a scale of 1 to 10 was about 3; as a result of the equipment, it jumped to approximately 8.4 points. (pp. 1–2)

POLICIES AND LEGALITIES SURROUNDING ASSISTIVE TECHNOLOGY

Individuals with Disabilities Education Act

The Individuals with Disabilities Education Act (IDEA; PL 94-142 and its amendments) guarantees the right of all children with disabilities to a free and appropriate education in the least restrictive environment. As a part of IEP/IFSP planning, parents, teachers and administrators are required to consider technologies that may help a child meet the IEP/IFSP goals and objectives. With the passage of the 1997 amendments to the IDEA (IDEA Amendments of 1997, PL 105-17), all teachers are expected to have knowledge and skill in various areas of special education. With this in mind, special and general education teachers should consider the appropriateness of assistive technology as a tool or an intervention for all students who have an IEP. Teachers who possess little knowledge about assistive technology may have difficulty fulfilling this new requirement without special training or assistance. Special educators currently working in the field may need to gain new competencies in the area of assistive technology. The 1997 IDEA amendments also suggested that general educators should receive professional development to help them better to teach individuals with disabilities in their classrooms.

Lahm and Nickels (1999) note that special educators must have an understanding of the legislation and regulations related to technology used in special education as well as develop a personal philosophy on the use of technology to guide them in the implementation of technology devices. Also, teachers need to know the terminology related to assistive technology to communicate accurately with others about its purpose. Furthermore, the IDEA specifies guidelines in assisting parents, professionals, and students in the selection, use, and acquisition of technologies. Assistive technology includes the following:

- The evaluation of the needs of a child with a disability, including a functional evaluation of the child in the child's customary environment;
- Purchasing, leasing, or otherwise providing for the acquisition of assistive technology devices by children with disabilities;
- Selecting, designing, fitting, customizing, adapting, applying, maintaining, repairing, or replacing assistive technology devices;
- Coordinating and using other therapies, interventions, or services with assistive technology devices, such as those associated with existing education and rehabilitation plans and programs;
- Training or technical assistance for professionals (including individuals providing education or rehabilitation services), employers, or other individuals who provide services to employ, or are otherwise substantially involved in the motor life function of that child. (IDEA Amendments of 1997, Section 602)

Individualized Education Program   The 1997 reauthorization of the IDEA requires IEP teams to consider assistive technology as a critical factor when developing a student's IEP. (A team may include the teacher, speech therapist, occupational therapist, physical therapist, and any other person who works with the student.) The IDEA requires schools to provide assistive technologies for a student with a disability if services and equipment are necessary to ensure a free and appropriate public education (IDEA, 1997, Section 300.308). One of the new requirements in the IEP section of the federal law is that for each student eligible for special education services, the IEP team must "consider whether the child needs assistive technology devices and services" (IDEA, Section 614[d][3][B][v]). A student's IEP should reflect necessary assistive technologies that have the potential to provide the child with an appropriate education. If assistive technology is represented in the IEP, then team members must take measures to provide technologies as stated in it. Discussions about assistive technology should be documented on the IEP and or in the meeting notes. Team decisions made and their rationale must be included in the IEP as well as determinations regarding assistive technology evaluations. If assistive technology and/or service are needed, then those also must be reflected in the IEP. When assistive technology is used to enable a student an appropriate education, the assistive technology must be provided at the school's expense.

Individualized Family Service Plan   Cooperation and participation of parents and siblings of an infant or toddler with a disability can enhance the use and practicality of assistive technology. Families of younger children with disabilities participate in the development of an individual family service plan (IFSP). The family's participation is reflected in the IFSP that is usually prepared when a child is first diagnosed with a disability. During these early years, emphasis is placed on providing services to the child and the child's entire family. The focus on family distinguishes early intervention programs from programs that are developed for school-aged children.

The IFSP is developed by a multidisciplinary team and contains statements about the family's resources and concerns with the intent to enhance the development of the special needs of the infant or toddler (Dunst, Trivette, & Deal, 1988). Consequently, family routines, values, and resources also must be considered when planning for technologies (Brinker, Seifer, & Sameroff, 1994). During the development of the IFSP, parents often target specific goals for their child with a disability (Butler, 1988; Parette et al., 1996). As parents come to see assistive technology raise their child's productivity, they increasingly request technologies and early intervention services to be documented and serviced through the child's IFSP (Parette et al., 1996). Indubitably, children in this category benefit from assistive technology as early as it can be provided.

Assistive technologies affect the entire family. Thus, the entire family should play an active role in all processes regarding assistive technologies (Dunst et al., 1988). Considering that family cultures differ greatly from those of the school system, when determining the use of technology, the IFSP team should address issues of independence, acceptance, and changes in the family routines (*CEC Today,* 1999). Consequently, assistive technology devices are of little value to a young child or their family without appropriate follow-up services. Problems can occur when families are not provided support services or training in methods of integrating the assistive device in the child's natural environment (Lesar, 1998). Support services ensure that the child and his or her family can adequately and readily use technologies on a regular basis. Assistive technology services may include such supports as purchasing and leasing devices and equipment; customizing and adapting devices, repairing devices; training the child and parents in the use of devices; and coordinating interventions, therapies, and services with assistive technology devices (RESNA Technical Assistance Project, 2000).

Technology-Related Assistance for Individuals with Disabilities Act

A result of a bipartisan effort in Congress, the **Technology-Related Assistance for Individuals with Disabilities Act** of 1998 (Tech Act) is one of the most influential and beneficial laws that supports the development of programs that ensure access to appropriate assistive technology devices and services for individuals and their families (Bryant et al., 1998a). It directly addresses the need for increased access to technology by individuals with disabilities and their families. The law provides flexibility to states in responding to the technology needs of their citizens with disabilities and builds on the accomplishments achieved by states over the past decade through assistive programs funded under the Tech Act.

The purpose of the Tech Act is to provide financial assistance to states to engage in activities that assist each state in maintaining and strengthening a permanent comprehensive statewide program of technology-related assistance. In addition, the act identifies federal policy that facilitates payment for technology devices and technology services, to identify those federal policies that prevent such payment and to eliminate inappropriate barriers to such payments. Specifically, the Tech Act mandates accommodations and accessibility for individuals with disabilities to promote full participation and integration into society. In summation, RESNA Technical Assistance Project (2000) reports three purposes of the Tech Act:

- Support States in sustaining and strengthening their capacity to address the assistive technology needs of individuals with disabilities.
- Support the investment in technology across federal agencies and departments that could benefit individuals with disabilities.
- Support micro-loan programs to individuals wishing to purchase assistive technology devices or services. (p. 1)

The Tech Act is intended to target individuals with disabilities of all ages and their family members, guardians, advocates, and authorized representatives. Also targeted are individuals who work for public or private entities that have contact with individuals with disabilities, educators and related services personnel, technology experts, health and allied health professionals, employers, and other appropriate individuals and entities.

Americans with Disabilities Act

The **Americans with Disabilities Education Act** (ADA) of 1990 (PL 101-336) is a civil rights bill intended to eliminate discrimination against individuals with disabilities (Lewis, 1993). The ADA similarly requires the delivery of auxiliary aids and services as needed to assure equal access to programs and services offered by the school. Equal access includes the provision of auxiliary aids and services that are needed for effective communication with individuals with disabilities. Although the ADA does not directly focus on technology, the law places requirements on public schools to provide access to the same services for individuals with and without special needs. In addition, technologies may be used to meet the law's requirements. As one requirement of the ADA, schools must be careful not to create barriers for any children.

Teacher Role

Teacher Training   Perhaps one of the most difficult issues schools will face in meeting the assistive technology needs of their students is developing sufficient staff expertise. The 1997 amendments to the IDEA mandated that any state receiving a State Program Improvement Grant is required to use no less than 75% of the funds to ensure that there are an adequate number of general education, special education, and related services personnel who have the skills and knowledge necessary to meet the needs of children with disabilities. Professional development for general educators, special educators, and related service personal should include training in selecting, implementing, and modifying assistive technologies (IDEA,

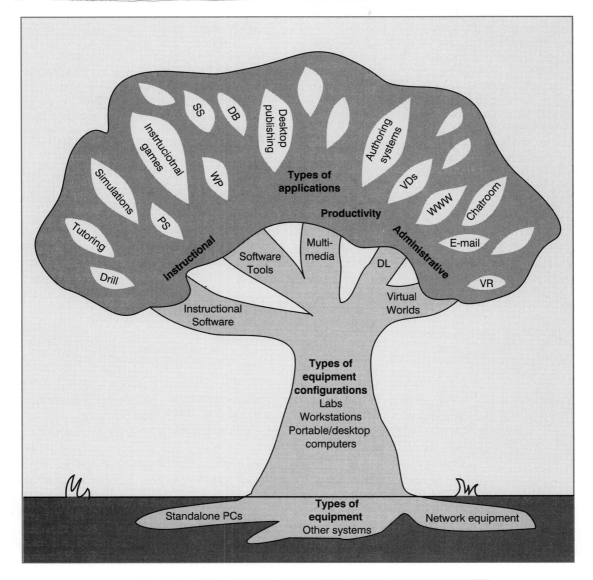

FIGURE 14.1

The Educational Technology Tree of Knowledge

Source: From *Integrating Educational Technology into Teaching,* by M. D. Roblyer and J. E. Edwards, 2000, Upper Saddle River, NJ: Merrill/Prentice Hall. Reprinted by permission.

ISTE Recommended Foundations in Technology for All Teachers

Standards Introduction

I. **Foundations**. The ISTE Foundation Standards reflect professional studies in education that provide fundamental concepts and skills for applying information technology in educational settings. All candidates seeking initial certification or endorsements in teacher preparation programs should have opportunities to meet the educational technology foundations standards.

A. **Basic Computer/Technology Operations and Concepts.** Candidates will use computer systems-run software; to access, generate and manipulate data; and to publish results. They will also evaluate performance of hardware and software components of computer systems and apply basic troubleshooting strategies as needed.

1. operate a multimedia computer system with related peripheral devices to successfully install and use a variety of software packages.

2. use terminology related to computers and technology appropriately in written and oral communications.

3. describe and implement basic troubleshooting techniques for multimedia computer systems with related peripheral devices.

4. use imaging devices such as scanners, digital cameras, and/or video cameras with computer systems and software.

5. demonstrate knowledge of uses of computers and technology in business, industry, and society.

B. **Personal and Professional Use of Technology.** Candidates will apply tools for enhancing their own professional growth and productivity. They will use technology in communicating, collaborating, conducting research, and solving problems. In addition, they will plan and participate in activities that encourage lifelong learning and will promote equitable, ethical, and legal use of computer/technology resources.

1. use productivity tools for word processing, database management, and spreadsheet applications.

2. apply productivity tools for creating multimedia presentations.

3. use computer-based technologies including telecommunications to access information and enhance personal and professional productivity.

4. use computers to support problem solving, data collection, information management, communications, presentations, and decision making.

1997). General and special educators must receive more professional development and training so that they can deliver appropriate instruction (Tech Act, 1998; Yell & Shriner, 1997). Figure 14.1 illustrates the types of technology knowledge that teachers should possess.

Bryant and colleagues (1998) reported three competencies that educators must possess to implement assistive technologies adequately. First, educators must have access to necessary assistive technology hardware and software. Second, educators should be comfortable with the use of the assistive technologies. Finally, educators should have access to adequate resources and training that assist with the implementation of assistive technologies. Furthermore, Roblyer and Erlanger (1998) summarize guidelines that make teacher-training programs more effective. These guidelines call for emphasizing hands-on integration; training over time; modeling, mentoring, and coaching; and posttraining access.

- *Hands-on integration emphasis.* Hands-on activities are necessary for teacher training. Skills needed to integrate technology cannot be effectively learned

5. demonstrate awareness of resources for adaptive assistive devices for student with special needs.
6. demonstrate knowledge of equity, ethics, legal, and human issues concerning use of computers and technology.
7. identify computer and related technology resources for facilitating lifelong learning and emerging roles of the learner and the educator.
8. observe demonstrations or uses of broadcast instruction, audio/video conferencing, and other distance learning applications.

C. **Applications of Technology in Instruction.** Candidates will apply computers and related technologies to support instruction in their grade level and subject areas. They must plan and deliver instructional units that integrate a variety of software, applications, and learning tools. Lessons developed must reflect effective grouping and assessment strategies for diverse populations.

1. explore, evaluate, and use computer/technology resources including applications, tools, educational software, and associated documentation.
2. describe current instructional principles, research, and appropriate assessment practices as related to the use of computers and technology resources in the curriculum.
3. design, deliver, and assess student learning activities that integrate computers/technology for a variety of student group strategies and for diverse student populations.
4. design student learning activities that foster equitable, ethical, and legal use of technology by students.
5. practice responsible, ethical and legal use of technology, information, and software resources.

Source: From *Standards* [On-line], by International Society for Technology in Education (ISTE). Available: www.iste.org/Standards/NCATE/found/html. Used by permission.

in a classroom watching demonstrations or listening to an instructor. Teachers in training must have an opportunity to navigate through a program and complete a set of steps of creating new products. However, the focus should be on how to use the technology in the classroom.

- *Training over time.* Professionals are discovering that traditional models of staff development, particularly those "one-shot" programs for the entire staff, are ineffective for teaching computer skills. Training in technology should be ongoing. Teachers need time to reflect, plan, and experiment on their successes and failures with computer technology. Teachers will need time to ask questions, get feedback, and explore new ideas. Successful staff development provides adequate examples and gives teachers opportunities to use technologies.

- *Modeling, mentoring, and coaching.* Instructors who model the use of technology in their own teaching have been acknowledged as the most effective teacher trainers. Research has indicated that one-to-one mentoring and coaching programs are effective for novice teachers. Most teachers seem to learn computer skills through colleague interaction, collaboration, and information sharing.

- *Posttraining access.*   Teachers need to have adequate access to technology for training to be successful. In addition, teachers need access to technology after training to practice what they have learned.

BARRIERS OF ASSISTIVE TECHNOLOGY

Although assistive technology adaptations are used to circumvent disability-related barriers, it is common to encounter barriers and complications when implementing such technologies. A recent national survey (Wehmeyer, 1998) indicated that in many cases, individuals with mental retardation and their families are unaware of the possible benefits that they could receive from assistive technology. Wehmeyer further reported that if they are aware of such benefits, they are not informed about the devices available, how to fund them, or where to obtain adequate assessment and training.

Bryant et al. (1998) report three basic barriers that prevent novice teachers from using technologies or cause teachers to abandon technologies altogether. The first barrier includes limited access to technology. Some individuals with mental retardation lack the information that may be needed to acquire assistive technology. More unfortunately, teachers may lack knowledge to assure that their students with physical or other disabilities receive necessary technologies. Similarly, colleges of education at universities often have limited equipment funding and are sometimes at the bottom of the university equipment funding priority list. These dilemmas can prevent or limit the appropriate education that individuals with mental retardation are entitled to receive.

Educators commonly receive limited technology training in their preservice training. The second barrier would include limited professional development opportunities. A challenge of integrating assistive technology in the classroom is the lack of faculty training and technical support within many colleges of education. Educators need time and training to explore new and progressive assistive technology devices and to implement those in their classrooms. As stated earlier in this chapter, the IDEA (Yell & Shriner, 1997) amendments mandated professional development for all educators who teach students with disabilities. Therefore, training will be essential for educators to be competent in integrating assistive technology.

The third barrier is a lack of incentives. This dilemma can be perceived within classrooms and at the university or college level. Unfortunately, educators often have little reason to make a major investment of their time in attempting to integrate assistive technology into coursework. Any encountered barriers to assistive technology can often leave an individual with mental retardation, their family, and professionals feeling frustrated that they have not acquired success in implementing technologies.

Clinton (1995) reports frustrations that may accompany the use of assistive technology. It is common for parents who provide support to have unrealistic expectations that technology will cure disabling conditions. Some special education teachers and students feel frustrated when technology requires initial training. For this reason, it can be easier when technologies offer plug-and-play solutions when possible so students can direct their efforts to learning. Although recent advances have been made in assistive technologies, disabilities for which present technology offers no solutions still exists. However, there is hope that advancements in the future will lessen these frustrations.

MODIFICATIONS

Bryant and Bryant (1998b) report that instructional modifications include changes to teaching procedures, curricula, management, materials and technology, and the physical environment to facilitate learning. Specifically, assistive technology may require simple, low-tech modifications. Off-the-shelf technologies can become adaptive when they are used to enhance the learning of a student who is retarded (Lewis, 1998). For example, an audiotape becomes assistive when it is used to compensate for an individual's memory or note-taking problems. In addition, low-tech modifications such as sticky notes, flags, and highlighters can enhance a student's organizational skills. Such modifications require minimal time and training to be implemented in the classroom.

Simple and uncomplicated modifications are sometimes all that are needed to allow a student to use a computer software program (Olson & Platt, 2000). Standard computer keyboards pose a number of problems for some students with mental retardation (Kincaid, 1999). Various modifications may need to be considered so that students with limited hand and finger mobility can access computer technology. Before a student can use computer technology for a given task, an appropriate method for inputting information must be available.

Word processing has the capability of helping individuals improve their writing skills (MacArthur, 1996). Students with retardation often possess limited conceptualization of editing and revising; thus, such students limit their revisions to minor errors that fail to strengthen a written document as a whole. Therefore, using a word processor may not only teach students who are retarded to edit their writing better but also can help these students to make frequent revisions without labored rewriting. MacArthur, Graham, and Schwartz (1991) report that word processing not only reduces resistance to revising as a whole but also eliminates errors due to transcription. They further note that word processing has the potential to facilitate other revision operations such as moving content and deleting material.

Today, word processors are accompanied with additional tools that can guide students with mental retardation as they learn to write. For example, most word processors are programmed with spell checkers that can prompt students as they transcribe. Spell checkers typically perform two functions: they identify misspelled words, and they suggest correct spellings (MacArthur, 1996). However, spell checking by use of a word processor may not promote greater spelling skills, especially for weak spellers. As MacArthur (1996) states, spell checkers sometimes fail to teach spelling skills since they simply compensate for poor spelling.

Over the past decade, technology has not only advanced but also become increasingly powerful. Some emerging technologies should be given merit based on their capability to enhance the learning of individuals with mental retardation. For example, virtual reality is one emergent technology that has notable potential for

To read more about the uses of computer technology, go to the companion website at www.prenhall.com/ beirne-smith and select Chapter 14, then choose the Article Response module.

individuals with mental retardation. **Virtual reality** involves the use of 3D graphics combined with direct manipulation and provides for the illusion of immersion into a virtual world (Olson & Platt, 2000). When applying virtual reality, the individual interacts with a computer-simulated environment in detail. One of the most unique characteristics of virtual reality is its potential contextualized instruction (Bottge & Hasselbring, 1993). Virtual reality simulates real-life experiences and can be used to construct conceptualized learning environments that promote generalization of skills (Lewis, 1998). Indeed, the concept of virtual reality portrays a promising future for individuals with mental retardation. The future of virtual reality has the potential to level the playing ground by providing unique modifications and accommodations for individuals with mental retardation.

Early Childhood

Young children learn from playing. Because play often involves social interaction, children have the opportunity to interact with and learn from others. Through this interaction, children develop their cognitive skills, learn new concepts, and enhance their motor and perceptual capabilities. However, some children with mental retardation lack the ability to interact socially due to their physical disabilities. Technology can make it possible for young children to interact at an early age so that they can have similar opportunities as those children without disabilities. The key to the success is to introduce the technology to children and their family as early as possible.

Modifications to standard computer keyboards might need to be considered for students with limited hand and finger mobility.

TABLE 14.5
Technologies for Young Children

> **Bump-and-go toys:** Examples are police cars and fire engines with flashing lights and sirens and a train with smoke, sound effects, and flashing lights.
>
> **Stuffed animals that move:** Examples are a dinosaur that walks on its hind legs, moving its head and front legs as its eye light up, and a pig that walks, wags its tail, says "oink" and wrinkles its nose.
>
> **Toys for dramatic play:** Include a toy sewing machine, blender, and mixer.
>
> **Musical toys:** Examples are a switch-operated drum, a musical top, and adapted versions of the Fisher-Price record player, music box radio, and music box TV.
>
> **Busy boxes activated by lightly touching built-in switches:** With the 5-Function Activity Center, the child touches an orange plate to turn on a light, a blue plate to play a radio, and a yellow plate to feel vibration. Pulling the string activates a music box, and moving the roller produces a buzzing sound.
>
> **Radios and tape recorders:** Include an adapted AM/FM radio with earphones.

Source: From *Special Education Technology: Classroom Applications,* by R. B. Lewis, 1993, Pacific Grove, CA: Brooks/Cole. Reprinted by permission.

Computers can help young children with mental retardation develop language. The goal of any language development program is to provide young children with the tools for independent communication. Some children will learn to speak, some will learn sign language, and others will need the assistance of augmentative communication. **Augmentative communication** refers to a set of approaches used to improve the communication skills of persons who do not speak or whose speech is not intelligible (Lewis, 1993; Olson & Platt, 2000). There are two basic types of augmentative communication: aided and unaided systems (Snell, 1993). **Aided systems** require the use of a picture or word board, a notebook, or a computerized aid. An **unaided system** requires the individual to use only hand or body motions to communicate (e.g., sign language). Augmentative communication options can range from high- to low-tech devices including such aids as symbol systems, manual communication boards, electronic communication devices, speech synthesizers, and communication enhancement software. Communication boards, a low-tech alternative to augmentative communication, assist young children in language expression. **Communication boards** are usually made of cardboard or another material used to display choices for children who cannot speak (Ysseldyke & Algozzine, 1990). For example, the young child can communicate by selecting from the options presented on the board. Table 14.5 briefly describes other assistive technologies for young children.

As mentioned earlier in this chapter, children benefit from receiving assistive technology at an early age. Under the 1997 regulations of the IDEA, assistive technology services for young children include a number of specific supports. Initially, a child must have an evaluation of his/her unique technology needs. This would include a functional evaluation in the child's customary environment. Furthermore, professionals should consider purchasing, leasing, or providing for the appropriate assistive technology device. Acquisition encompasses selecting, designing, customizing, fitting, adapting, applying, maintaining, repairing, or replacing assis-

To learn more about aided communication, go to the companion website at *www.prenhall.com/ beirne-smith* and select Chapter 14, then choose the Case Studies module.

tive technology devices. During this time it may be critical to coordinate therapies, interventions, or services associated with the child's IEP. Finally, service delivery systems are responsible for providing training and technical assistance to the child, their family, and the professionals who provide services to them (20 USC 1401, 26). Agencies who serve young children recognize the need for assistive technology and labor to meet challenges in a fashion that provides appropriate technology, trains professionals and families in the use of assistive technology, and demonstrates unique ways for families to access assistive technology (Lesar, 1998). As documented by professionals, it is critical for families to take an active part in implementing assistive technology (Brinker et al., 1994; Parette et al., 1996).

School Age

The task of providing school-age students with a free and appropriate public education is made more challenging with the 1997 reauthorization of the IDEA. As mentioned earlier, IEP teams are charged with the task of considering necessary assistive technologies for students with disabilities. In addition, general education teachers are required to attend and participate in IEP meetings. As schools grow increasingly inclusive, general educators' involvement in IEP development will grow accordingly. Similarly, special educators should remain current on the progression of assistive technologies. Also, as schools grow more inclusive, students with mental retardation may be challenged to participate in learning experiences that develop receptive and expressive literacy.

All too often technology is viewed as a stand-alone classroom element. Teachers may consider the computer as a place where students go to receive positive reinforcement when they've completed all their classwork, or where students work on drill and practice activities. Technology can be an even greater vehicle for instruction, curricular access, and accommodation, if that technology is incorporated into the curriculum and not viewed as an adjunct to teaching and learning activities (Rocklage & Lake, 1998). Technology should be viewed as a tool, much like a pencil or pad of paper. Also, students should be encouraged to use these technology tools across all learning and discovery activities within and outside the classroom.

Many classroom tasks involve expressing literacy in writing and computer software that assists the writing process can be useful in inclusive settings (Bryant & Bryant, 1998a; Lewis, 1998). Students with disabilities may struggle when trying to perform tasks that require them to communicate knowledge. For this reason, it can be helpful for school-age children to use technologies that level the playing field. Computers are increasingly being used to overcome visual, hearing, and physical disabilities. For students with extremely limited physical mobility, there are computers that can be operated just by moving the eyes. Computers are powerful teaching tools for all students.

Because students usually respond to instructional software programs by typing on the computer keyboard, they sometimes may need assistance. Various modifications can assist a student as they engage in such a task. Some students may benefit from the use of brightly colored stickers to illuminate keys that are frequently used with a software program. Keyguards can reduce the possibility of students hitting the wrong keys as they attempt to enter information. **Keyguards** are devices that fit over the regular computer keyboard and have holes cut out for an individual to access the keys on the keyboard with a stick, stylus, or finger (Olson & Platt, 2000). Another option that assists students with mental retardation in using computer technology is the touch-sensitive screen (Merbler, Hadadian, & Ulman, 1999). **Touch screens** overlay the computer's monitor with a touch-sensitive grid that is aligned with characters or graphics on the screen. A touch-sensitive screen allows students to use a stylus or finger to deliver input into a computer. The student enters information into the computer by simply pointing at the computer screen with a finger or pointing device. Once students are provided modifications to assist them in entering information into a computer, they can begin to learn skills that enhance their writing capabilities.

Recent advances in computer technology entail speech input and recognition (Merbler et al., 1999). **Speech input and recognition** programs are based on special software that permits students to input their ideas into the computer using their voices. Such systems can be beneficial for students who have limited hand and finger mobility. In contrast, students who have speech impairments may not find this method of inputting useful. Merbler et al. (1999) report that consistency of speech (e.g., pronunciation of words) is needed for these systems to work effectively. For this reason, as mentioned earlier, it is necessary to consider the appropriateness of computer programs based on each individual's needs.

Computers and word-processing software enable students to put ideas on paper without the barriers imposed by paper and pencil. Providing students with a word processor can be useful but should be accompanied with other training as well. MacArthur et al. (1991) state that students with retardation will not edit and revise papers unless they receive specific instructions in the editing process. Therefore, simply providing a student with a word processor may not be enough for students with mental retardation. Indeed, teaching the editing process is critical for these students.

Teachers can teach the editing capabilities of the word processor during the writing process. Computer editing can reduce or eliminate problems such as multiple erasures, torn papers, poor handwriting due to poor fine-motor skills, and the need to constantly rewrite text that needs only minor modifications. Moreover, spell checkers can improve the written expression products of students with disabilities. Although grammar checkers are becoming more efficient, these programs have not been found to be helpful for many students with writing problems (MacArthur, 1996).

A common reason for abandoning assistive technologies is due to an individual's, their family's, or their service provider's inability to maintain or adapt the device to meet the needs of the individual (Lesar, 1998). This dilemma can be bypassed or prevented entirely in the classroom if teachers are given necessary supports. Merbler et al. (1999) note some recommendations that can help teachers maximize assistive technology and student potential in their classroom:

- Use open-ended devices that permit customizing for the user and/or task are generally the most useful.
- Find the lowest technology solution that can provide a level of performance or function rather than a complex, high-technology device or system. Simply changing a student's angle of view of a computer monitor (e.g., placing the monitor at eye level

as opposed to hairline level or above) could reduce strain and improve performance. [See Figure 14.2.]

- Collaborate with other teachers. There are too many technologies developing too quickly for one teacher to monitor advancement in technology independently. Sharing expertise can help.
- Collaborate with parents to ensure that assistive technology devices that go home are properly used and maintained. Parents can also be an excellent source of evaluative information on how effectively a device or piece of software is working.
- Don't believe that you have to master a device or software application completely before you begin using it. Many times an application can be used successfully early in the learning curve, and learning by doing can promote eventual mastery.
- Assistive devices should match the age, gender, and preferences of the user to promote acceptance and use.
- The arrangement and separation of controls should be predictable and natural. Feedback to the user must be meaningful.
- Be sure that your school or school system has a comprehensive policy covering assistive technology, including the protection of student and teacher privacy, the repair and maintenance of equipment, and the home use of the school purchased equipment. Be sure also that the policy states who the assistive technology resource for IEP teams is.
- Simply purchasing assistive technology equipment will not ensure its use. Funds must also be allocated to ensure that teachers and other potential assistive technology services providers receive training in the use of the equipment.
- Do not be afraid to experiment. Assistive technology is a very young field, and everybody is learning. (para. 23)

Although assistive technologies are necessary for some children, some parents are unaware of how to request technologies. California Assistive Technology Sys-

FIGURE 14.2

Attributes and Examples in the Continuum of Low- and High-Tech Assistive Technology Devices

Source: From "Assistive Technology and IEPs for Young Children with Disabilities," by H. P. Parette and N. L. Murdick, 1998, *Early Childhood Education Journal, 25*(3), 193–197. Reprinted by permission.

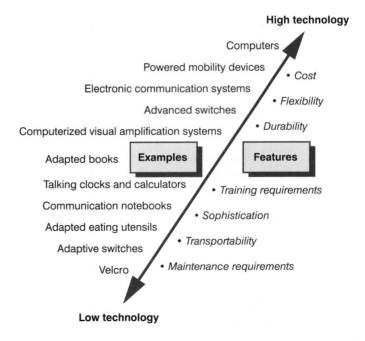

tems (2000) recommends the following steps for parents to request technology for their child:

> A written request should be made to the school asking for the assistive technology that the student needs or stating the student's need if you don't know exactly what is needed. Once your request is made, the local education agency has 15 days to give you a proposed assessment plan. Parents have 15 days to consent to the proposed assessments. Once the local education agency receives the parent's consent, it has 50 days to complete the assessment and develop the IEP. (p. 1)

Postschool Years

The adult years of individuals with mental retardation can be fulfilled with meaningful occupations, socialization, communication, and recreation. In fact, the development of technological devices has contributed greatly to the integration of the individuals with mental retardation (Morris & Blatt, 1986). However, some persons cannot experience successful adulthood without the assistance of technology. For the adult population, assistive technology should target means and methods for allowing them to experience a comfortable, possibly independent, and productive life.

Technology training for adults with mental retardation should be emphasized during transition programming. More specifically the technology training should focus on an individual's support needs in the community, at home, and with employment (Hallahan & Kauffman, 1997). Generally, students with mental retardation need technological supports as they prepare for their adult roles as workers, consumers, and participants in a community (Lewis, 1993). Individuals may need technical assistance in managing money, preparing meals, grooming, maintaining a clean house, and keeping one's clothing clean. For example, adults with mental retardation may use switches for chores such as brushing their teeth or making tea. In addition, those on the vocational track may need supported technology to help them accomplish their job with a degree of success.

The use of computer technology has considerable promise for adults with mental retardation. Today, these individuals are accommodated for cognitive impairments that are impediments to independence and self-determination. Those who might not be able to balance a checkbook due to a lack of prerequisite skills can use a computer to overcome that barrier. However, few software programs are designed for adults with mental retardation (Wehmeyer, 1998). Present software programs are often too difficult, and when they are not, they are usually age-inappropriate. Even when software may be obtainable, existing operating systems create a barrier for individuals with mental retardation.

One key to an adult's ability to live in a community successfully is the ability to socialize and recreate. Conversation aids can be designed to enable an adult with mental retardation to engage in social activities (Snell, 1993). **Conversation aids** are books or tablets organized by topic according to home and community environments used by individuals with mental retardation to enhance their ability to communicate and/or socialize. The adult can select photos, pictures, or illustrations for places, people, or objects. The photos are placed into the tablet and attached to the student. With the proper training, the student can learn to use the conversation aid to converse with family or peers.

TABLE 14.6
Useful Resources and Web Sites

Association for Retarded Citizens P.O. Box 6109 Arlington, TX 76005 817-640-0204	CSUN: Technology and Persons with Disabilities Center on Disabilities 18111 Nordhoff Street Northridge, CA 91330-8340 818-677-2578 www.csun.edu/cod/center.html
Inclusive Technologies Temper Complex 37 Miriam Drive Matawan, NJ 07747 732-441-0831 www.inclusive.com	The Association for the Severely Handicapped 7010 Roosevelt Way, NE Seattle, WA 98115 206-283-5055 www.tash.org/
RESNA 1700 N. Moore Street, Suite 1540 Arlington, VA 22209-1903 703-524-6686 www.resna.org/	ABLEDATA Newington Children's Hospital 181 Cedar Street Newington, CT 06111 203-667-5200 www.abledata.com
Assistive Technology Research Center National Rehabilitation Hospital 102 Irving Street, NW Washington, DC 20010-2949 202-877-1000 www.nrhatrc.org	Trace Research and Development Center S-151 Waisman Center 1500 Highland Avenue Madison, WI 53705-2280 608-262-6966 www.trace.wise.edu/
Closing the Gap P.O. Box 68, 526 Main Street Henderson, MN 56044 507-248-3294 www.closing the gap.com	United Cerebral Palsy Association 1660 L Street, NW, Suite 700 Washington, DC 20036 www.ucpa.org
The Council for Exceptional Children 1920 Association Drive Reston, VA 20191-1589 703-620-3660 www.cec.spec.org www.ucc.uconn.edu/~tam/	California Assistive Technology Systems 660 J Street, Suite 270 Sacramento, CA 95814-2413 916-325-1690 www.catsca.org
National Easter Seal Society 2023 West Ogden Avenue Chicago, IL 60612 312-243-8400 www.easter.seals.org/	

To check your understanding of this chapter, go to the companion website at *http://www.prenhall.com/ beirne-smith* and select Chapter 14, then choose the Self-Test module.

Table 14.6 presents the contact information for a variety of organizations that can provide further information on selecting and using appropriate assistive technology for persons with mental retardation.

Summary

Definition of Assistive Technology

- The IDEA defines assistive technology as "any item, piece of equipment, or product system, whether acquired commercially off the shelf, modified, or customized, that is used to increase, maintain, or improve the functional capabilities of a child with a disability."
- Assistive technology can range from high-tech solutions, sophisticated devices, to no-tech solutions that require no devices or equipment.

Benefits of Assistive Technology

- Assistive technology assists individuals with mental retardation in overcoming barriers toward independence by compensation for their daily limitations.
- Technologies can decrease dependence on others by allowing individuals to become or remain integrated into their chosen communities.
- Assistive technology allows individuals with mental retardation to receive similar educational services as students without disabilities.

Policies and Legalities Surrounding Assistive Technology

- In accordance with the IDEA, special and general education teachers should consider the appropriateness of assistive technology as a tool or an intervention for all students who have individual education programs.
- The Tech Act provides flexibility to states in addressing the need for increased access to technology by individuals with disabilities and their families.
- The ADA requires the delivery of auxiliary aids and services as needed to assure equal access to programs and services.

Teacher Training

- Teachers must have access to necessary hardware and software, should be comfortable with the use of technology, and should have adequate training to implement assistive technologies effectively.

Modifications

- Technologies for young children should provide opportunities for interaction and play at an early age.
- IEP teams are charged with the task of considering necessary assistive technologies for school-age children with mental retardation.
- Keyguards, touch-sensitive screens, and speech input and recognition systems provide assistance for individuals with mental retardation as they use computers.
- Technology training for adults with mental retardation should be emphasized during transition programming.
- Technologies for adults should address an individual's support needs in the community, at home, and with employment.

━━━━━ **References** ━━━━━

Assistive Technology Messenger Newsletter. (1999). Study points to unmet technology needs among those with mental retardation. Retrieved September 27, 1999, from the World Wide Web: www.asel.udel.edu/dati/Atmessenger/julaugsep98/study.html

Association for Retarded Citizens. (1993). *Assistive technology position statement.* Arlington, TX: ARC of the United States [On-line]. Available: www.TheArc.org/posits/astec.html

Bieniewski, M. (1999). *Assistive technology* [On-line]. Available: http://members.tripod.com/mwb626/scripts/techb.html

Blackhurst, A. E. (1997). Perspectives on technology in special education. *Teaching Exceptional Children, 29*(5), 41–48.

Bottge, B. A., & Hasselbring, T. S. (1993). A comparison of two approaches for teaching complex, authentic mathematics problems to adolescents in remedial math classes. *Exceptional Children, 59,* 556–566.

Brinker, R. P., Seifer, R., & Sameroff, A. J. (1994). Relations among maternal stress, cognitive development and early intervention in middle- and low-SES infants with developmental disabilities. *American Journal on Mental Retardation, 98,* 463–480.

Bryant, D. P., & Bryant B. R. (1998a). Using assistive technology adaptations to include students with learning disabilities in cooperative learning activities. *Journal of Learning Disabilities, 31,* 41–54.

Bryant, D. P., & Bryant, B. R. (1998b). Using assistive technology to enhance the skills of students with learning disabilities. *Intervention in School & Clinic, 34*(1), 53.

Bryant, D. P., Erin, J., Lock, R., Allan, J. M., & Resta P. E. (1998). Infusing a teacher preparation program in learning disabilities with assistive technology. *Journal of Learning Disabilities, 31,* 55–66.

Butler, C. (1988). High tech tots: Technology for mobility, manipulation, communication, and learning in early childhood. *Infants and Young Children, 1,* 66–73.

California Assistive Technology Systems. (1999). *At network* [On-line]. Available: www.catsca.org/

CEC Today. (1999). Technology in school and at home [On-line]. Available: www.cec.sped.org/bk/cectoday/hometech.html

Clinton, J. (1995). *Taming the technology.* Materials distributed at the Florida Assistive Technology Impact Conference, Orlando, FL.

Dunst, C., Trivette, C., & Deal, A. (1988). *Enabling and empowering families.* Cambridge, MA: Brook.

Hallahan, D. P., & Kauffman, J. M. (1997). *Exceptional learners.* Boston: Allyn & Bacon.

Hasselbring, T. S., & Peabody College of Vanderbilt University (1998). *The future of special education and the role of technology* [Online]. Available: http://peabody.vanderbilt.edu/ltc/hasselbringt/futute.html

Kincaid, C. (1999). Alternative keyboards. *Exceptional Parent, 29*(2), 34–37.

Lahm, E. A., & Nickels, B. L. (1999). Assistive technology competencies for special educators. *Teaching Exceptional Children, 32*(1), 56–63.

Lesar, S. (1998). Use of assistive technology with young children with disabilities: Current status and training needs. *Journal of Early Intervention, 21*(2), 146–159.

Lewis, R. B. (1993). *Special education technology: Classroom applications.* Pacific Grove, CA: Brooks/Cole.

Lewis, R. B. (1998). Assistive technology and learning disabilities: Today's realities and tomorrow's promises. *Journal of Learning Disabilities, 31*(1), 16–26.

MacArthur, C. A. (1996). Using technology to enhance the writing processes of students with learning disabilities. *Journal of Learning Disabilities, 29*(4), 344–354.

MacArthur, C. A., Graham, S., & Schwartz, S. (1991). Knowledge of revision and revising behavior among students with learning disabilities. *Learning Disability Quarterly, 14,* 61-73.

Male, M. (1994). *Technology for inclusion* (2nd ed.). Boston: Allyn & Bacon.

Merbler, J. B., Hadadian, A., & Ulman, J. (1999). Using assistive technology in the inclusive classroom. *Preventing School Failure, 43*(3), 113–118. (From Academic search elite on-line: EBSCO Publishing [Producer and Distributor].) Retrieved February 14, 2000, from the World Wide Web: www.epnet.com/ehost/login.html

Mississippi State University. (November 18, 1999). *Project Star* [On-line]. Available: www.msstate.edu/dept/tkmartin/

Morris, R. J., & Blatt, B. (1986). *Special education: Research and trends.* New York: Pergamon.

National Council on Disability. (1993). *Study on the financing of assistive technology devices and services for individuals with disabilities: A report to the president and the Congress of the United States.* Washington, DC: Author.

Olson, J. L., & Platt, J. M. (2000). *Teaching children and adolescents with special needs.* Upper Saddle River: Merrill/Prentice Hall.

Parette, H. P. Brotherson, M. J., Hourcade, J. J., & Bradley, R. H. (1996). Family-centered assistive technology assessment. *Intervention in School & Clinic, 32,* 104–112.

Parette, H. P., & Murdick, N. L. (1998). Assistive technology and IEPs for young children with disabilities. *Early Childhood Education Journal, 25*(3), 193–197.

RESNA Technical Assistance Project. (2000). *Tools for 2000: Assistive technology.* Arlington, VA: Author.

Roblyer, M. D., & Edwards, J. E. (2000). *Integrating educational technology into teaching.* Upper Saddle River, NJ: Merrill/Prentice Hall.

Roblyer, M. D., & Erlanger, W. (1998). Preparing Internet ready teachers. *Learning and Leading with Technology, 26*(4), 58–61.

Rocklage, L. A., & Lake, M. E. (1998). Inclusion through infusion: A technology/curriculum partnership for all children. *Closing the Gap* [On-line]. Available: www.closingthegap.com/cgi-bin/lib/libDsply.pl?a=1049&b=3

Snell, M. E. (1993). *Instruction of students with severe disabilities.* Upper Saddle River, NJ: Merrill/Prentice Hall.

U.S. Congress, Office of Technology Assessment. (1988). *Power on! New tools for teaching and learning.* OTA-SET-379. Washington, DC: U.S. Government Printing Office.

Wehmeyer, M. L. (1998). National survey of the use of assistive technology by adults with mental retardation. *Mental Retardation, 36*(1), 44–51.

Yell M. L., & Shriner, J. G. (1997). The IDEA amendments of 1997: Implications for special and general education teachers, administrators, and teacher trainers. *Focus on Exceptional Children, 30,* 1–20.

Ysseldyke, J. E., & Algozzine, B. (1990). *Introduction to special education.* Boston: Houghton Mifflin.

An Example of an Individual Transition Plan

Student Profile

Garland is a 21-year-old student with mental retardation. He is verbal and ambulatory. Garland can read approximately 30 sight words and complete simple written math problems with a calculator. He knows coin values but cannot count change. Garland can print his name and copy other words. He is strong and frequently engages in unorganized sports with classmates and family. Garland lives with his parents and younger brother and sister in a low-middle income suburb.

Individual Transition Plan

Student's Name ___Garland_____
                First   M.I.   Last

Birthdate _____   School ___Turner High_____

Student's ID No. _____   ITP Conference Date _____

Participants

Name	Position
Garland	student
Sam and Susan	parents
Mary	teacher
Miller	case manager
Laurence	vocational rehabilitation (VR) counselor

An Example of an Individual Transition Plan (continued)

I. Career and Economic Self-Sufficiency

1. Employment Goal	Garland will work full time in the deli department of a local grocery store with supported employment.
Level of present performance	Garland has been employed by school enclaves at two sites and has taken a vocational food preparation course at school.
Steps needed to accomplish goal	(1) Assist Garland with applying for jobs at local groceries; (2) arrange for transportation by carpool; and (3) provide job training assistance and support as needed.
Date of completion	6/98
Person(s) responsible for implementation	VR counselor
2. Vocational Education/Training Goal	Garland will work part time with supported employment prior to graduation
Level of present performance	Garland has received vocational situational assessment at two grocery stores and has been assigned a Department of Rehabilitative Services (DRS) counselor.
Steps needed to accomplish goal	(1) Meet with DRS counselor and assist in job application as needed; (2) arrange Garland's school schedule to accommodate work schedule; (3) provide staff for job-site training; (4) provide transportation; and (5) share information and responsibilities with DRS counselor.

An Example of an Individual Transition Plan (continued)

Date of completion	12/97
Person(s) responsible for implementation	teacher
3. *Postsecondary Education Goal*	Garland will attend classes of interest offered by Parks and Recreation
Level of present performance	Garland can follow modeled instructions and is interested in working on cars, with wood, and other manual activities
Steps needed to accomplish goal	(1) Seasonally obtain brochures of classes; (2) budget for classes; (3) complete applications; and (4) arrange for transportation
Date of completion	3/98
Person(s) responsible for implementation	case manager
4. *Financial/Income Needs Goal*	Garland will be independent of his parents for basic financial needs.
Level of present performance	Garland receives a paycheck and SSI. He has a savings account. His parents provide basic needs and make deposits for him.
Steps needed to accomplish goal	(1) Assist Garland in planning budget for basic needs; (2) initiate payment of rent to parents until alternative residence is secured; and (3) assist Garland in budgeting for and purchasing food and clothing.
Date of completion	5/98
Person(s) responsible for implementation	parents

An Example of an Individual Transition Plan (continued)

II. Community Integration and Participation

5. *Independent Living Goal*	Garland will live in a supervised apartment with one to two roommates close to his parents.
Level of present performance	Garland is close to his family but wants to be independent. Garland is independent in personal hygiene and basic household chores.
Steps needed to accomplish goal	(1) Apply for residential services; and (2) provide instruction in responding to emergencies.
Date of completion	8/98
Person(s) responsible for implementation	case manager, Garland, and parents
6. *Transportation/Mobility Goal*	Garland will use a taxi to travel to destinations nearby but not within walking distance.
Level of present performance	Buses are not available in Garland's area. He can ride a bike, use a telephone (given a written number), and cross streets safely.
Steps needed to accomplish goal	(1) Teach Garland to access taxi service by phone; (2) teach Garland to identify list of usual destinations by name and street; and (3) teach Garland to use "Dollar-move" strategy to pay for taxi.
Date of completion	3/98
Person(s) responsible for implementation	VR counselor and teacher
7. *Social Relationships Goal*	Garland will enjoy safe social/sexual relationships with female peers.

An Example of an Individual Transition Plan (continued)

Level of present performance	Garland likes the company of girls and has several "girlfriends" among his disabled peers.
Steps needed to accomplish goal	(1) Provide family life instruction; and (2) access appropriate co-ed recreational group activities.
Date of completion	12/97
Person(s) responsible for implementation	teacher and parents
8. *Recreation/Leisure Goal*	Garland will join a Saturday bowling league.
Level of present performance	Garland's parents have been on bowling teams. Garland is a good bowler but cannot keep score.
Steps needed to accomplish goal	(1) Assist Garland in joining a team; (2) obtain a teammate mentor for Garland; and (3) assist Garland in budgeting for leagues and obtaining transportation.
Date of completion	3/98
Person(s) responsible for implementation	parents

III. Personal Competence

9. *Health/Safety Goal*	Garland will maintain control over seizures.
Level of present performance	Garland had infrequent grand mal seizures as a young child. He has remained seizure-free since age 15 but still takes low doses of Dilantin.

An Example of an Individual Transition Plan (continued)

Steps needed to accomplish goal	(1) Assist Garland in taking daily medications as recommended; and (2) continue regular checkups with family physician.
Date of completion	12/97
Person(s) responsible for implementation	family
10. Self-Advocacy/Future Planning	Garland will benefit from family estate planning. He will assume his own guardianship and his siblings will act as future trustees.
Level of present performance	Garland's parents are his guardians. His siblings are 2 and 4 years younger than Garland. Garland stands to share the inheritance of property.
Steps needed to accomplish goal	Obtain legal counsel to advise and prepare plan
Date of completion	6/98
Person(s) responsible for implementation	parents

Student Career Perference

Working at a grocery store

Student's Major Transition Needs

1. Employment

2. Residential Services

3. Transportation

An Example of an Individual Transition Plan (continued)

4. *Financial Management* _____

5. *Social Relationships* _____

6. _____

7. _____

8. _____

9. _____

Additional Notes

_____

_____

_____

_____

_____

_____

_____

_____

_____

_____

_____

_____

_____

_____

_____

_____

_____

Adaptive behavior "Degree and efficiency with which the individual meets the standards of personal independence and social responsibility expected of his age and cultural group" (Grossman, 1983, p. 1; see Chapter 2).

Aided systems Augmentative communication systems that require the use of a picture or word board, a notebook, or a computerized aid.

American Association on Mental Retardation (AAMR) The nation's leading professional association of and for persons who are mentally retarded.

Amniocentesis Analysis of amniotic fluid during the second trimester of pregnancy to allow for biochemical analysis of fetal cells; can indicate presence of genetic and chromosomal disorders and indicate sex of fetus.

Annual goals Statements of what the student with disabilities can reasonably be expected to achieve in the course of one calendar year.

Anoxia Oxygen deprivation severe enough to cause permanent brain damage and retardation.

Assessment Collecting information through observation, testing, and task analysis to determine strengths and weaknesses for the purpose of making decisions.

Assistive technology Devices used to enhance the performance of persons with disabilities.

At risk Describes a child who is in danger of substantial developmental delay because of medical, biological, or environmental factors if early intervention services are not provided.

Augmentative communication Methods used to improve the communication skills of persons who do not speak or whose speech is not intelligible.

Autosomes Twenty-two matched pairs of chromosomes (44 of normally present 46). See *Sex chromosomes*.

Behavior analysis The study of environmental events that change behavior.

Behavioral objectives Statements that specify an observable behavior, the conditions under which it will occur, and the acceptable standard for accuracy against which to measure performance.

Behavioral risk factors The repetitive, willful actions that contribute to the development of related or secondary conditions.

Benchmarks See *Short-term objectives*.

Career development Curricula designed to give the individual a start in making a living.

Categorical program Educational programs serving only students who are diagnosed with a specific disability and who are officially placed in a special education program.

Centrifugal forces Experiences or interactions among family members that push them apart.

Centripetal forces Experiences or interactions among family members that draw them together.

Cerebral palsy Any neuromuscular disability resulting from damage to the brain at birth or during the first 4 years of life.

Chromosomes Threadlike bodies containing genes (hereditary factors) occupying specific loci.

Collaborative consultation Process through which people with diverse expertise determine solutions to mutually defined problems.

Collaborative teaming Process through which educators with different areas of expertise voluntarily work together to create, monitor, and refine solutions to problems that impede students' success.

Communication board Devices that employ icons or pictures to assist persons with communication.

Community acceptance The extent to which a person who is mentally retarded is accepted and supported in the community environment.

Community adjustment An individual's ability to adjust to the multiple demands of life in the community.

Community-based instruction Teaching a skill to a student in the actual environment as opposed to teaching the skill in a classroom with the expectation of transference, generalization, and application of knowledge when skill use is required.

Community-referenced instruction Educational programs that are directly related to actual incidents that occur naturally in the environment.

Conversation aids Books or tablets organized by topic according to home or community environments used by individuals with mental retardation to enhance their ability to communicate and/or socialize.

Criterion-referenced testing (CRT) Measure of a child's skill in terms of a preestablished level of mastery in a given content area.

Cross-categorical program A program reserved for students who

531

are officially placed in a special education program but may serve students from more than one disability area. Students can be grouped according to their instructional needs rather than by disability.

Curriculum The sequence and content of what is taught on school.

Curriculum-based assessment A criterion-referenced type of test with test items drawn directly from the instructor's teaching materials, considered to be a highly effective measure of student performance.

Deletion In genetics, a process where a portion of original genetic material is absent from a specific chromosomal pair.

Deviation IQ In contrast to ratio IQ, assumes IQ is normally distributed with 100 as average and a standard deviation that is the same for every age level.

Disablism (formerly *handicapism*) Practices and beliefs that promote differential treatment of individuals because of apparent or assumed physical, mental, or behavioral differences.

Dominant inheritance Inheritance in which an individual gene has control or can mask the other gene in the pair.

Dual diagnosis Describes people with mental retardation who also have a psychiatric disorder.

Due process A constitutional guarantee that prohibits any state from depriving any person of life, liberty, or property, without due process of law.

Early childhood special education A system of services for children from birth to 5 years of age who are disabled, developmentally delayed, or at risk of developmental delay, and their families.

Early intervention System of services that are usually provided free of charge for children who are disabled, developmentally delayed, or at risk of developmental delay and their families.

Ecological model Instructional methodology designed to enhance the ability of persons with mental retardation to participate fully in the community. Includes the belief that people with disabilities have a right to participate in educational, economic, and social aspects of the community. Individualized programs of instruction are developed for each student, and skills are taught in the settings where they are to be used.

Economic integration The extent to which a person is able to obtain and disburse income as it relates to life in the community.

Educability The ability of an individual to learn from experience and to apply learning in various settings.

Educable mental retardation (EMR) Term used to refer to students whose abilities are adequate to become self-sufficient and learn academic skills through the upper elementary grades. The individual's score on an individual test of intelligence is approximately 55 to 70.

Employment integration An individual's adjustment to the routines, rhythms, and responsibilities of work.

Empowerment Family-centered involvement and decision making.

Equal protection The principle of the 14th Amendment, which allows the same rights and benefits to all citizens according to government practice unless there is a compelling reason to withhold these rights.

Eugenics movement The science movement that manipulates breeding to improve the quality of the human race.

Extensive supports Resources utilized by persons with disabilities to promote independence, productivity, and community integration. Extensive supports are provided regularly, in at least some environments, and on a long-term basis.

Family (1) A group of individuals consisting of immediate and distant relatives who are related through birth, adoption, or marriage; (2) a group of people who love and care for each other.

Family-directed assessment Assessment to study the resources, priorities, and concerns of the family and the identification of the supports and services necessary to enhance the family's capacity to meet the developmental needs of their infant or toddler with a disability.

Family personality The alternating periods of stability, change, and readjustment that families experience over time.

Family support services Services beyond basic residential and vocational/habilitative services that people with mental retardation require for normal community living.

Feebleminded An obsolete British term for intelligence that coincides with the educational classification of educable mentally retarded or the American Association of Mental Retardation's classification of mild mental retardation.

Functional assessment Examination of the content in which a behavior occurs and the function the behavior serves.

Gene therapy A process of cloning a gene to perform the appropriate metabolic task (e.g., the conversion of phenylalanine to tyrosine in the case of phenylketonuria).

Genetics The study of heredity and variation.

Grand mal seizure The most severe type of epileptic seizure, in which the individual has violent convulsions, loses consciousness, and becomes rigid.

Grouping Clustering material based on sameness prior to presentation.

Habilitation The acquisition and use of skills to allow for successful functioning in independent living and employment.

Handicapism   See *Disabilism*.

Heritability   The proportion of total trait variance that is directly due to genetic, measurable factors.

Heterozygous   Having to do with pairs of genes carrying different traits.

Homme sauvage   Human savage.

Homozygous   Having to do with pairs of genes carrying the same trait.

Human Genome Project   A concerted, multinational effort to identify the location and function of all parts of the genetic code of humans.

Hydrocephalus   A disorder resulting from blockage of cerebrospinal fluid in the cranial cavity that causes an enlarged head and undue pressure on the brain.

Incidence   The number of new cases of a condition identified within a population over a specific period of time.

Inclusion   Placing students who are disabled, regardless of the type or degree of disability, in general education classrooms in their home-school. The general education teacher assumes primary responsibility for students who are included.

Inclusive environments   The placement of students with special learning needs in settings with peers who have no special learning needs.

Individual family service plan (IFSP)   A document prepared as part of the voluntary component of PL 99-457, developed by a multidisciplinary team with the assistance of the child's parents or guardians, and detailing the year's plan for the child with disabilities aged birth to two and the child's family.

Individualized education program (IEP)   Individually written plan of yearly instruction by a committee required by the Individuals with Disabilities Education Act for every child or youth who is disabled.

Informed clinical opinion   An opinion formed by using at least 50%

of a clinician's expertise in addition to the formal testing results to aid in determining eligibility for special education services.

Innate   Inherent; use of abnormal chromosome arrangements present from conception but most often not the product of hereditary exchange.

Job coach   A person who provides on-the-job training to individuals with disabilities.

Judgment-based assessment   An appraisal according to a scale or checklist usually developed by a classroom teacher to measure abilities not typically identified by standardized instruments.

Karyotypes   Graphic chromosomal pictures in descending order based on size.

Keyguards   Devices that fit over the regular computer keyboard and have holes for an individual to access the keys of the keyboard with a stick, stylus, or finger.

Learned helplessness   A pattern of submissiveness that develops in individuals when they believe that their actions are of no consequence and that outcomes are beyond their control.

Life skills   Abilities necessary to function as an independent individual within the community.

Locus of control   The hypothetical construct that people attempt to reach a goal within their own power (internal locus of control) or through events controlled by others (external locus of control).

Long-term memory   The ability to retrieve information from storage after a few days or several years.

Mainstreaming   The practice of placing students who are disabled in the general education classroom to the extent appropriate to their needs.

Maintenance   The ability needed to retain skills or knowledge over time.

Mastery learning   The teacher tests a concept, gives feedback, and then tests the concept again until the child has completely mastered the task.

Mediation   (1) A memory strategy in which an individual connects a verbal label and information to be learned; (2) the process parents and school systems may use to agree upon identification, placement, and evaluation of a student with special needs.

Meiosis   The division and pairing of gametes to form the genetic foundation for an embryo.

Mental retardation   "Significantly subaverage general intellectual functioning resulting in or associated with concurrent impairments in adaptive behavior and manifested during the developmental period" (Grossman, 1983, p. 11; see Chapter 2).

Mental test   An obsolete name for an intelligence test.

Metabolic disturbance   See *Phenylketonuria*.

Mildly retarded   A slight deviation below the normal range of intelligence and adaptive behavior. Individuals who are mildly retarded can usually benefit from academic instruction and are often referred to as educable mentally retarded.

Mosaicism   (1) Uneven division of cells in mitosis, resulting in unequal or extra chromosomes; (2) a form of Down syndrome in which not all cells have unusual chromosome composition.

Myelomeningocele   A condition characterized by a saclike mass on the spinal cord containing membrane tissue of the central nervous system and cerebrospinal fluid but no spinal nerves on the spinal cord.

Need for support services   The level of supports and services needed to live as fully and independently as possible in a normative community environment.

Natural home A place of residence where one lives with biological or adoptive family members.

Natural supports The resources accessed by persons with disabilities that promote independence, productivity, and community integration. Natural supports are selected from resources preexisting in the person's environment and are provided without the aid of technology or services agencies.

Nature–nurture controversy The debate as to whether intelligence is either innate or acquired.

Noncategorical program An educational program designed to serve both students who are disabled and students who are not disabled but who need supplemental instruction.

Nondisjunction The failure of one pair of chromosomes to split correctly at meiosis resulting in a trisomy. Produces such conditions as Down syndrome (trisomy 21).

Normalization The process of providing for and, to the maximum extent possible, treating an individual with special needs in the mainstream of society as if the individual has no special needs.

Norm-referenced test A test that has been given to a large number of subjects and for which standard procedures for administration, scoring, and interpretation are published; standard procedures must be followed for results to be valid.

Observational learning Learning from watching demonstrations.

Ombudsman One whose role is to protect the rights of individuals seeking services from government agencies.

Outerdirectedness Looking to others for guidance or cues in developing appropriate responses in demanding situations.

Parenting style The ways in which parents or guardians meet the social and emotional challenges of caring for a family member with mental retardation.

Parity Equal status of all members involved in the collaborative consultation process; no single individual is viewed as the expert, and all contributions are judged solely on their merit as a feasible solution to the problem.

Pedigree studies Examination and research on a particular topic through generations.

Person-centered planning Involving the person who is retarded and other significant people in that person's life in the planning process.

Personal satisfaction The extent to which an individual's life has satisfaction and optimum quality.

Pervasive supports Resources provided on a constant basis and across all environments to promote the independence, productivity, and community integration of persons with mental retardation. Pervasive supports are of a potentially life-sustaining nature.

Phenylketonuria (PKU) An inherited metabolic disease resulting from the absence of an enzyme for digestion that causes a toxic buildup of substances in the blood and urine; if undiagnosed at birth, it causes mental retardation.

Polygenetic inheritance Inheritance in which more than one gene pair affects the appearance of a particular trait.

Precision teaching The teacher breaks a lesson into a hierarchy of skills.

Prevalence The total number of cases of a disorder existing within a population at a particular place or at a particular time.

Procedural due process Guaranteed by the Fifth Amendment, the right to fairness in regard to property or liberty. In PL 94-142, it refers to the individual's right to a hearing, to be

notified of a hearing, to be represented by counsel at a hearing, to be able to question and cross-examine witnesses, and to present witnesses.

Psychopharmacology The use of medications to treat psychiatric disorders.

Quasi-suspect class A group for whom there will be an intermediate or heightened analysis of alleged equal protection statutory violations.

Recessive inheritance Inherited traits that do not express themselves when paired with dominant genes and are influential only when matched with another identical recessive gene.

Reciprocity Providing equal access to information and the opportunity to participate in problem identification, discussion, decision making and outcomes to all persons involved in the collaborative process.

Recreational/leisure integration The extent to which an individual harmonizes home and out-of-home free-time activities.

Related services Supportive services (e.g., special transportation, speech or language therapy, occupational or physical therapy) needed to ensure that the special education program meets all of the student's educational needs.

Residential facility Twenty-four-hour-a-day housing.

Residential integration Placing the residence of an individual with disabilities in a community.

Right to education Correct, free, and appropriate public school education for all children regardless of ability, age, race, religion, or gender.

Short-term objectives Behaviorally stated objectives based on annual goals that provide a clear direction for instruction and ongoing evaluation of the progress of students with disabilities.

Six-hour retarded child A child who is considered mentally retarded at school but appears to function normally with family and peers outside of school.

Social integration An individual's general level of intra- and interpersonal functioning, particularly as it relates to persons who are mentally retarded.

Sociopolitical forces Societal and civic strength.

Speech input and recognition Permits students to input their ideas into the computer using their voices.

Standard deviation The unit used to measure the amount by which a particular score varies from the mean with respect to all the scores in a norm sample.

Stanford-Binet IV The Stanford-Binet Intelligence Scale: Fourth Edition. The most recent version of the original Binet-Simon Scale used in the United States after the turn of the century.

Sterilization The process of rendering an individual unable to produce offspring.

Substantive due process A constitutional guarantee that provides for protection against unreasonable governmental action.

Supported employment The placement of individuals with special needs into competitive employment positions with a job coach who does on-the-job training and supervision to facilitate employment and enhance job retention.

Technology-Related Assistance for Individuals with Disabilities The Tech Act of the 1998 law that supports the development of programs that ensure access to appropriate assistive technology devices and services for individuals with disabilities and their families

Teratogens Substances that can negatively affect prenatal development and result in a severely deformed fetus.

Touch screens Overlay the computer's monitor with a touch sensitive grid that is aligned with characters or graphics on the screen.

Trainable mental retardation (TMR) An educational term used for individuals functioning in the lower range of mental retardation who will not benefit from general education training but who require training in basic functional skills (e.g., self-help skills). Their score on an individual test of intelligence is usually 35 to 55.

Transition (1) A carefully planned educational process bridging the gap between school and employment; (2) the passage or change from one stage or level to the next (e.g., third to fourth grade, preoperational stage to concrete operations).

Transition education The unifying vehicle for ensuring that an individual has a more than even chance to become a contributing member of society.

Transition programs Programs designed to identify appropriate intervention and to provide training to facilitate the transition from level to level within school and from school to life after school.

Transition services Those services, such as vocational rehabilitation or postsecondary vocational training, provided to individuals with disabilities and leading to employment.

Transition shock A condition that is analogous to the adjustment problems of people who have recently gotten divorced, returned from war, been released from prison, or relocated to new countries.

Translocation Exchange of a fragment of chromosomal material within the same chromosome or to another chromosome. Can result in Down syndrome.

Unaided systems Augmentative communication systems that use only hand and body motions to communicate.

Virtual reality The use of 3D graphics combined with direct manipulation that provides the illusion of immersion into a virtual world.

Vocational education A program aimed at preparing an individual for a specific occupation or upgrading of existing skills.

Wechsler scales The Wechsler Intelligence Scales used for identification and classification of countless preschool children, school-age children, adolescents, and adults for nearly half a century.

Wraparound services A name given to an organized, integrated approach to service delivery that allows for a specially designed treatment plan at a specific point in time.

evaluation and, 325, 361, 362
family-directed assessment, 327–328
family interventions, 220–223
functioning of, 476–487
historical perspective of, 6
individualized education program team and, 28, 316, 323, 362, 376, 380, 486
individual rights and, 23
issues in family living, 487–493
language and, 256
living arrangements and, 211, 212, 213
middle adulthood and, 438
milder forms of mental retardation and, 242
models of, 472–473, 474
older adulthood and, 438
organization of, 472–476
Parent Information Centers, 301
parenting style and, 210
personality of, 475–476
physical therapy and, 227
prematurity and, 177
psychosocial functioning and, 207–211
reactions of, 477–480
siblings without disabilities, 349, 481–483, 492
single-parent families, 209, 210, 242, 470, 471–472, 480
social integration and, 444
summary, 493
support needs and, 299, 301, 483–484, 489–490, 492–493
supports-based orientation and, 28
transition and, 418, 475
Family home, 441
Family paradigms model, 472–473
Family support services, 483–484, 486–487
Family Systems Conceptual Framework, 349, 350
FAPE (free appropriate public education), 127–130, 143, 360–361, 506
FAS (fetal alcohol syndrome), 172, 174–175
Federal constitutional arguments, 116–118
Federal statutes and regulations, 118–119, 128
Feeblemindedness, 5, 8, 12, 13, 43, 44, 103
Fetal alcohol effects (FAE), 174
Fetal alcohol syndrome (FAS), 172, 174–175
Fetal biopsy, 183
Fetoscopy, 183
Fluid-analytic abilities, 86
Folic acid, 172
Fragile X syndrome, 163–164
Free appropriate public education (FAPE), 127–130, 143, 360–361, 506
Functional analyses, 377
Functional assessment, 224, 283–284
Functional behaviors, 389–390
Functional curriculum, 342–343, 407
Functional mental skills, 407, 408

Galatosemia, 158, 159

Gender
chromosomes and, 69, 156
fragile X syndrome and, 163, 164
milder forms of mental retardation and, 241
observational learning and, 256
prevalence and, 69, 208
sex-linked inheritance and, 162–164
General education. *See also* Inclusion
appropriate placement and, 128–129
assistive technology and, 505, 506
at-risk children and, 24
classroom accommodations/adaptations, 346
curriculum without supports, 392
curriculum with supports, 392–394
early intervention programs and, 339
educational environment and, 366–369
historical perspective of, 19, 26
inclusion and, 372–374
individualized education program and, 323, 362, 516
least restrictive environment and, 362
milder forms of mental retardation and, 263, 264, 265
social skills training and, 248
Generalization of skills, 219, 381–382, 389, 394, 514
Generalized seizures, 204, 205
General learning disabilities, 44
Gene replacement therapy, 30
Generic foster homes, 452
Genes, 156–157
Genetics
at-risk children and, 322
ethics and, 187–189
etiology and, 152, 153, 156–165, 190
eugenics movement and, 12–13
genetic screening, 158, 180–181, 183, 185, 187
nature-nurture controversy, 20, 25, 82–83, 92
supports-based orientation and, 30
technology and, 143
Group homes, 452, 459
Grouping, 254
Group therapy, 225
Guggenbühl, Johann, 8–9

Habilitation, 131, 133–134, 448
Halderman v. Pennhurst (1977), 131, 133–135
Handicapped Children's Protection Act of 1986 (PL 99–372), 119
Harrington-O'Shea Career Decision-Making (CDM) System, 426
Hawaii Transition Project, 410
HCBS (Home and Community Based Services), 23
Head injuries, 178
Head Start, 22, 317
Health and Human Services, U.S. Department of, 301, 302
Health issues. *See also* Physical health characteristics; Preventive health measures
ethics and, 188, 189
health care access, 30–31
illness, 262, 287, 438

About the Authors

Mary Beirne-Smith

Mary Beirne-Smith is associate professor in the Programs in Special Education at The University of Alabama. Her previous experience includes general and special education classroom teaching and public school administration. Her research interests center around academic interventions for students with mild learning disorders who are included in general education classrooms. She is currently involved in implementing a collaborative consultation project with several local education agencies. Mary received her M.Ed. and Ed.D. from the University of Virginia.

Richard F. Ittenbach

Richard F. Ittenbach is a biostatistician in the Division of Biostatistics and Epidemiology at the Children's Hospital of Philadelphia. He has written numerous articles on the adjustment of persons with mental retardation, young adult development, and issues pertaining to the measurement of mental and special abilities. He received his Ph.D. in Education/School Psychology from the University of Alabama in 1989.

James R. Patton

James R. Patton is the executive editor at Pro-Ed and adjunct associate professor at the University of Texas at Austin. He has experience teaching students with special needs at the elementary, secondary, and post-secondary levels. His research interests include curriculum development, life-long learning, instructional methodology, and teaching science. Currently he is developing integrated curricula and life skills programs. Jim earned his B.S. from the University of Notre Dame and his M.Ed. and Ed.D. from the University of Virginia.

Veda Jairrels

Veda Jairrels is an associate professor of Exceptional Student Education at Clark Atlanta University in Atlanta, Georgia. She was a special education teacher in New York City Public Schools for several years where she taught students with learning disabilities and behavioral disorders. Veda is interested in the issue of cultural diversity and how it affects the teacher preparation process and curriculum. She received her A.B. and law degrees from Indiana University, and her M.A. and Ph.D. degrees from Columbia University and The University of Alabama, respectively. She is a member of the Pennsylvania Bar.

Edward A. Polloway

Edward A. Polloway is Vice President for College and Community Advancement at Lynchburg College, where he also serves as Professor of Special Education. Prior to coming to Lynchburg College, his previous experience included teaching elementary and special education public school classes. He has published ten special education textbooks and a number of journal articles focused on mental retardation and learning disabilities. He is the former president of the division on mental retardation and developmental disabilities of the Council for Exceptional Children, having served two terms in this position. He received his B.A. from Dickinson College and his M.Ed. and Ed.D. from the University of Virginia.

J. David Smith

J. David Smith is Dean of the School of Education and Human Services at Longwood College. He previously served as chair of the Department of Educational Psychology at the University of South Carolina. His career has also included tenure as a faculty member at Lynchburg College, work as a special education teacher, counselor, and Peace Corps Volunteer. He has written numerous books and articles. Social policy and the rights of individuals with disabilities has been a theme of his work. He received his B.S. and M.S. from Virginia Commonwealth University, and his M.Ed. and Ed.D. from Columbia University.

Shannon H. Kim

Shannon H. Kim is currently employed by the Mississippi Bureau of Mental Retardation. She supervises psychological services for persons with mental retardation residing in community homes throughout Northern Mississippi. Shannon has published in the areas of assessment, deinstitutionalization, and service provision. She received her M.Ed. and Ph.D. from the University of Mississippi.

Mitylene Arnold

Mit Arnold is Associate Professor of Special Education at the University of Mississippi, where she teaches classes related to individuals with severe mental retardation. Dr. Arnold, the author of textbooks and numerous articles, directs states and federally funded projects to improve the quality of life for individuals with severe disabilities. She is affiliated with various professional organizations and serves on the editorial board of journals such as *Autism and Developmental Disabilities* and *Career Development for Exceptional Individuals*. She holds a B.A. from Baylor University and has been a classroom teacher in Austin, Texas, and Madison, Georgia. She completed the Master's and Doctoral degrees at the University of Georgia, where she served as project director at the University Affiliated Program for Developmental Disabilities.

Charlotte Sonnier-York

Charlotte Sonnier-York is an assistant professor in Programs in Special Education at William Carey College in Hattiesburg, Mississippi. She was a special education teacher in Petal, Mississippi, for several years, where she taught students with learning disabilities and behavior disorders and worked in inclusive settings. Charlotte received her B.S. and M.Ed. of special education from the University of Southern Mississippi, and her Ph.D. from The University of Alabama. Her research interests include the least restrictive environment, portfolio assessment, and computer technology.